Communication and Mental Illness

Communication and Mental Illness

Theoretical and Practical Approaches

Edited by Jenny France and Sarah Kramer

Jessica Kingsley Publishers
London and Philadelphia

First published in the United Kingdom in 2001 by
Jessica Kingsley Publishers Ltd,
116 Pentonville Road, London
N1 9JB, England
and
325 Chestnut Street,
Philadelphia PA 19106, USA.

www.jkp.com

© Copyright 2001 Jessica Kingsley Publishers

Library of Congress Cataloging in Publication Data
Communication and mental illness : theoretical and practical approaches / edited by Jenny France and Sarah Kramer.
 p. cm.
 Includes bibliographical references and index.
 ISBN 1-85302-732-4 (pb : alk. paper)
 1. Mentally ill--Language. 2. Language disorders--Psychological aspects. 3. Speech disorders--Psychological aspects. I. France, Jenny. II. Kramer, Sarah, 1969-
 [DNLM: 1. Mental Disorders--rehabilitation. 2. Communication Disorders--therapy. 3. Rehabilitation of Speech and Language Disorders--methods. WM 307.M5 C734 1999]
 RC455.4.P78 C65 1999
 616.85'5'0019 21--dc21   99-042860

British Library Cataloguing in Publication Data
Communication and mental illness : theoretical and practical approaches. – New edition
 1. Mental illness 2. Communicative disorders 3. Speech therapy
 4. Mentally ill – Language
 I. France, Jenny II. Kramer, Sarah III. Muir, Niki
 IV. Communication and the mentally ill patient
 616.8'9

ISBN 1 85302 732 4

Printed and Bound in Great Britain by
Athenaeum Press, Gateshead, Tyne and Wear

Contents

ACKNOWLEDGEMENTS   9

FOREWORD   11
John Cox, Royal College of Psychiatrists

Part I: Background

1   Disorders of communication and mental illness   15
Jenny France

2   Anxiety disorders: neurotic, stress-related and somatoform disorders   26
Jenny France

3   Schizophrenia and other psychotic disorders   42
Sarah Kramer, University College, London and Jenny France

4   Depression and other mood disorders   65
Jenny France

5   Personality disorders   81
Jenny France

6   Communication, language and mental illness   101
Trevor Walt, Broadmoor Hospital, Sarah Kramer, University College, London and Jenny France

7   Assessment of speech and language in mental health   110
Karen Bryan, University College, London and Jan Roach, St. Andrews Hospital, Northampton

8   Neuropsychiatry and language   123
Karen Bryan, University College, London

9   Neuropsychology in psychiatric practice   136
Mary Hill, Broadmoor Hospital

Part II: Management of Mental Health Services

10 Introduction to management and patient care 147
Niki Muir, Speech and Language Therapist

11 Functioning of the multidisciplinary team
and the speech and language therapist 154
Margaret Orr, Broadmoor Hospital

12 The speech and language therapist as a member of the mental health
multidisciplinary team 158
Yvette Crompton, Broadmoor Hospital

13 Setting up a speech and language therapy network in mental health 167
Kathleen Gilmour, Speech and Language Therapist

14 Developing a speech and language therapy service in mental health 172
Elaine Hodkinson, Speech and Language Therapist

15 General psychiatry 181
Andy Hamilton, New Malden Community Mental Health Team

16 Services for older people in mental health settings 192
*Jane Maxim, University College, London and Cathy Timothy, Bath and
West NHS Trust*

17 Child psychiatry 208
Alison Wintgens, St. Georges Hospital, London

18 Mental health, offenders and the criminal justice system 221
*Karen Bryan, University College, London and Nicci Forshaw, North
Warwickshire NHS Trust*

19 Forensic psychiatry 231
Jenny France and Sarah Kramer, University College, London

20 People with borderline-mild learning disability 236
*Karen Elliott, Rampton Hospital and Nicci Forshaw,
North Warwickshire NHS Trust*

21 What can we learn from the deaf patient? 251
Alice Thacker, St. Georges Hospital Medical School, London

22 Communication and mental health in people
with autism and Asperger's Syndrome 262
Jane Shields, National Autistic Society and Dougal Hare, Clinical Psychologist

23 Gender identity disorders   267
    Judith Chaloner, Speech and Language Therapist and Lesley Cavalli,
    University College, London

24 Milieu therapy   280
    Tim Brett, Clinical Nurse Specialist and Eric Wilkinson, Psychiatric
    Nurse, Broadmoor Hospital

25 Personal construct psychology   284
    Carmel Hayes, Camden and Islingington Community Health Services
    NHS Trust and Louise Collins, Camden and Islington Community
    Health Services NHS Trust and Haringey Healthcare NHS Trust

26 Neurolinguistic programming in mental health   297
    Laurie Macdonald, Independent registered neurolinguistic
    psychotherapist, London

27 A multidisciplinary therapeutic alliance:
    group work developed through cognitive behavioural principles   303
    Marie Quayle, Broadmoor Hospital

28 Interpersonal skills as part of social skill training for
    schizophrenic patients   312
    Rachael Henton, Ruth Sinclair, Surrey Oaklands NHS Trust
    and Vasiliki Sideras, West Park Hospital

Part III: The Way Forward

29 Human communication, language and mental health:
    some general challenges for research in this field   325
    Pamela J. Taylor, Broadmoor Hospital and the Institute of Psychiatry, London

30 Communication and formal thought disorder in schizophrenia   335
    David Newby, High Royds Hospital, Leeds Community and Mental Health
    (Teaching) Trust

31 Language and communication in schizophrenia:
    a communication processing model   351
    Irene P. Walsh, Trinity College, Dublin

32 Linguistic deviance in schizophrenia: preliminary report   371
    William Sledge, Yale School of Medicine, Ralph Hoffman, Yale School of
    Medicine, Keith Hawkins, Yale School of Medicine, Nancy Docherty, Kent
    State University, Donald Quinlan, Yale School of Medicine and Jaak Rakfeldt,
    Southern Connecticut State University

33 Discourse analysis in psychiatry   393
    Ian Thompson, Charles Sturt University, Australia

34　What is different about the language of persons with mental illness?　407
Sarah Kramer, University College, London

35　Language difficulties or emotional difficulties –
what comes first?　433
Sarah Kramer, University College, London

36　Communication and mental health: the way forward　439
Sarah Kramer, University College, London

APPENDIX　444

THE CONTRIBUTORS　447

INDEX

Acknowledgements

First, we would like to thank the staff at the Patrick MacGrath Library, Broadmoor Hospital, without whose constant helpful support the book would never have been completed. We similarly thank Simon Morgan, whose assistance was invaluable in the 'early days' of the book. Thanks are also due to the Special Interest Group in Mental Health for their financial contribution to the book.

We would also like to thank Thomas France, whose tolerant expertise with modern communication techniques saved time and prevented disasters; Diana France, for her timely and generous professional support and Richard France, for his loyal forbearance and holding the fort throughout the preparation of this book.

Thanks are also due to my husband, Jeremy Waller, for his unquestioning adoption of many new roles, Raphael and Abigail Waller for their welcome and regular distractions, reminding us of true priorities in life (like playing Monopoly).

We cannot fail to mention that this book would not have been possible without my parents, Mr Abraham and Mrs Micheline Kramer, re-living the joys of parenthood, and my parents-in-law, Mr Gerald and Mrs Lydia Waller, who have been unfailing in their interest throughout the long 'incubation' period.

These acknowledgements would also be incomplete without mentioning Nechama Baker. She was our constant backstop, even without being asked.

Sarah Kramer

Foreword

This scholarly book builds a strong bridge between speech and language therapists and mental health professionals – as well as with those who suffer from mental disorders. The book is indeed about 'mental illness' and the way in which it can distort communication; it is also about mental health and how this can be achieved in the presence of mental illness. It makes a cogent case for speech and language therapists becoming integral members of mental health teams. It is clearly born out of familiarity with the impact of severe mental illness, the inherent importance of its knowledge base and the need to evaluate treatment outcomes.

At a time when all health professionals are relocating their own profession specific skills and recognising those skills which are generic, Jenny France and Sarah Kramer have clarified the specific roles of speech and language therapists within the mental illness field. In so doing they have helped to clarify the roles and responsibilities of others.

They make a cogent case for the 'added value' provided by speech and language therapists which is self-evident to practitioners in the field. The academic training of speech and language therapists is apparent in this comprehensive and well referenced text.

Indeed it is the communication difficulties associated with cognitive impairment as well as mood disorder which can make the management of patients with mental disorder daunting even for the experienced clinician, and difficult for students. To understand more fully the neurophysiology of speech disorders and to appreciate what treatments are available can help overcome these problems.

Practitioners in this field, including psychiatrists, will welcome this book so evidently derived from firsthand knowledge of the devastating effect of mental illness on communication, and yet of the prospect for improvement and, at times, cure.

It is much to be hoped that this text will unlock the research funding which will allow greater evaluation and audit of this evidence-based discipline. Because of the scarcity of resource the more precise targeting of these specialist skills may then emerge. It is characteristic of their profession that the editors do not beat about the bush with regard to the nature of mental disorder and the need for a diagnostic assessment approach. It is here that speech and language therapists have such concise skills that must surely lead to improved management.

John Cox,
President,
Royal College of Psychiatrists

PART I

Background

Disorders of Communication and Mental Illness

Jenny France

Speech, language and/or hearing can be impaired in individuals with a diagnosis of mental illness. Difficulties in these areas can result in the reduced intelligibility of messages, or in deficient listening skills. This imposes limitations on the communication of thoughts and feelings. It frequently also engenders messages of intolerance, ridicule and rejection by society. This can encourage feelings of isolation, hostility and anger in those affected, which are frequently accompanied by feelings of low self-esteem, a lack of self-confidence, and worthlessness and uselessness (France 1996).

This book has been planned to fulfil a dual purpose. One, that of providing information to those multidisciplinary professionals who work in mental health and have little awareness and/or appreciation of the prevalence of various forms of communication breakdown in people with mental illness and therefore the place that speech and language therapy might play in helping to alleviate these problems. Two, to provide a text to support qualified clinical speech and language therapists, undergraduate and postgraduate speech and language therapy (SLT) students in gaining an understanding of aspects of mental health, mental illness and related communication disorders and difficulties. This would seem particularly important due to the frequently limited awareness by those involved in mental health services of the role of SLT. The contribution to the multidisciplinary team and to the services for mentally ill patients made by occupational therapists, psychologists, and art and music therapists, for example, would appear to be more widely known. Perhaps this is in part the result of the limited provision of SLT services within the mental health setting both historically and geographically.

Until the late 1960s, most SLTs working in psychiatry were extremely isolated, working in different locations and with varied client groups, whilst also working only part-time. Broadmoor Hospital was one of the first authorities to take the step of appointing a full-time SLT. Prior to that time patients were referred for therapy only if they developed specific communication disorders independent of their diagnosis as mentally ill, for example for hysterical aphonia, or as a result of a cerebro-vascular accident.

The exploration of the speech and language of people with a diagnosis of mental illness began to develop alongside the advent of major developments in the study of linguistics. The SLT's knowledge and skills in areas including psychology, neurology, linguistics and speech and language pathology suggest the appropriateness of SLT in monitoring the effects of new forms of pharmaceutical treatment, in improving prognoses and offering a wider range of treatments.

SLTs would endorse Hume and Pullen's (1994) view that no one profession has all the skills necessary for the assessment, treatment and rehabilitation of mentally ill people, just as no one treatment has been found to be fully effective in all cases. It would seem important to draw attention to the contribution of SLT as many professionals working in mental health areas are unaware of, and lack knowledge of, such services, specialisms and skills.

The national special interest group (SIG) was founded in the early 1980s, and this brought together many therapists around the country for purposes of support and training, helping the development of the specialism and encouraging the setting up of new services, whilst acting in an advisory capacity and maintaining links with the Royal College of Speech and Language Therapists (RCSLT) and other bodies such as the Royal College of Psychiatrists (RCP). Thus, the SIG is active in supporting SLT services which are already established and those which are just being set up.

Where services are already in place, demonstrating, describing, teaching and convincing other professionals of the value of a SLT service, there will only be the usual working problems. The difficulties of setting up a new service in areas where little if anything is known of the advantages of the service are fraught with problems, not only those of achieving funding for a post but in order to gain a hearing to present the idea of this service (see Chapters 4 and 5). Many SLTs in the past have carried out surveys of the needs of mentally ill patients, in both hospital and community settings, and have described the extent of the communication problems, the type of service that might be best suited to the patients, and how this service could be delivered. Commonly this has resulted in a consensus that the patients' needs were not being fully met – however, frequently funds have not been available to develop further services. Thus, attempts to continue to develop and expand services presents daunting and exhausting difficulties, with the communication breakdown experienced by so many mentally sick people still often misunderstood, misinterpreted and mismanaged. Hence the need to create opportunities to share knowledge and information about SLT not only with psychiatrists, but also with other mental health professionals.

The particular SLT service for people with a diagnosis of mental illness will vary according to the particular patient population and the setting in which the service is delivered. Wherever possible it is viewed within the context of a multidisciplinary approach where it aims to assist patients in leading as full and valued lives as possible. The service provided must be sufficiently flexible to meet individual needs, and be delivered across a range of mental health settings for all, or some, of the major mental illness diagnostic groups, the service being prioritised according to need (France and Muir 1997). Of course, its role within the treatment package being offered must be appreciated by members of the multidisciplinary team.

At the Winter Meeting of the Royal College of Psychiatrists in 1997, Dr John Cox, Dean of the College, took a great interest in a symposium presented by a small group of speech and language therapists on the place of SLT in Mental Health. Dr Cox initiated discussion as to how best to educate psychiatrists on the role of SLT to ensure that the service was better understood, valued and used. It was suggested that during the psychiatrists' early training would assist in their recognition of SLT and so aid support for developing services. Also when the SLT is working in co-operation with other members of the multidisciplinary team opportunities can be created to extend information either through specifically designed staff training sessions or as an example in treatment, whether individually or in co-operation with other members of the team.

The prime concern of SLT services in mental health settings is the communication skills of the individual patient, whilst recognising the relationship of these skills with other aspects of the individual and his/her environment. France and Muir (1997) suggest that SLT treatment should begin at the point of communication breakdown (Cox's quote). The provision of SLT assessment and therapy is within the context of the multidisciplinary team and it is recognised that many other team members have contributions to make in evaluating and treating environmental, attentional and perceptual needs and deficits. However, in skills related to speech and language function, it is the SLT whose training provides specialist knowledge and skills relating to their neuropathology and psychopathology. This improves the adequacy of descriptions of the disorder, assisting in the achievement of a differential diagnosis. Chapter 9 on Neuropsychology will develop this topic further.

Another major contribution by the SLT to the team is that of describing, assessing and managing specific features of functional communication, including specific treatment programmes. In Chapter 19 on communication and social skills training, Henton and Sideras elaborate in some detail on the methods and techniques. These include structured programmes in which various aspects of communication are experienced and practised, with elaboration of different details relating to the pragmatic aspects of communication.

The specialised training of SLTs also enables them to have developed the listening and reflective skills required for many aspects of work in mental health. This is frequently followed by further training in areas such as counselling, personal construct psychotherapy and neurolinguistic programming, so that these additional skills are applied to the management of communication disorders, as seen in Chapters 25 and 26. Work initially includes a focus on re-establishing and developing the individual patient's communication and linguistic skills with a common aim for the patient to progress sufficiently to benefit from other verbally mediated treatments. After the development of a successful working relationship with the high level of understanding regarding the person's communication that has been achieved, continued direct/indirect involvement of the SLT in the provision of other treatment modules is generally beneficial. The emphasis is on helping the person to maintain and/or restore his/her communication skills as far as possible, whilst also improving the individual's sense of personhood and self-worth (Dalton 1994).

The SLT has an additional role as an intermediary. This is twofold. Frequently, patients have great difficulty understanding the language used by mental health professionals, which includes jargon. They often misunderstand what we perceive as a clear message, and how often do we check we have been understood? It is quite likely to be the SLT's responsibility to translate and/or clarify information shared with the patient by other professionals. Additionally, breakdowns in communication are not always patient-orientated! It would appear that the SLT is particularly adept at identifying when confusion or apparent misunderstandings occur and this provides the opportunity to interject to ensure that the message has been given, received and understood by all.

Sharing information with fellow professionals and with relatives and carers, who might well benefit from having clearly written and verbal explanations of the complexities of communication, is a skill which should not be underestimated. It can help avoid misunderstandings and avert intensification of relationship breakdown between the family, the patient and the therapist and ensure that all have the same information and the same understanding of that information.

Chapters 2–5 aim to help fill in the background information on mental disorders and their related speech, language and communication problems, and therefore will be of use to students and those new to the idea of SLT in mental health.

Mental disorder

The problem raised by the term 'mental disorder' has, according to the *Diagnostic and Statistical Manual of Mental Disorders – Fourth Edition* (DSM-IV 1994), been much clearer than its solution, and, unfortunately, the term persists in the present volume as no appropriate substitute has been found. No definition adequately specifies precise boundaries for the concept of mental disorder, and like many other concepts in medical science, this lacks a consistent operational definition that covers all situations. Each of the mental disorders have been conceptualised as a clinically significant behavioural or psychological syndrome or pattern that occurs in an individual and that is associated with present distress or disability or with a significantly increased risk of suffering death, pain, disability or an important loss of freedom.

In the *Pocket Guide to the Classification of Mental and Behavioural Disorders* (Cooper 1994), the Foreword begins by informing us that mental and behavioural disorders are frequent, can be grave in their consequences and cause suffering to hundreds of millions of people, worldwide. The care these people receive – or should receive – depends on better education of health workers and the general public and on commitments of governments to the development of services to the mentally ill and their communities.

Both the DSM-IV and the ICD-10 are systems which are thought to be complementary, and to be more similar with each revision. The DSM-IV is widely used in the USA whilst the ICD-10 is widely used in the UK. However, both systems are familiar to those in the field, and easy to understand, remember and use by members of the multidisciplinary team.

Also relevant to definitions of mental disorder is the Mental Health Act of 1983. This defines mental disorder as 'mental illness, arrested or incomplete development of the mind, psychopathic disorder and any other disorder or disability of the mind'. The Act has four categories, of which mental illness is by far the largest. The second group is psychopathic disorder, which is defined as a persistent disorder or disability of the mind which results in abnormally aggressive or seriously irresponsible misconduct and is therefore viewed solely in terms of its being antisocial behaviour (see Chapters 5 and 12). The inclusion of this in mental health legislation still raises much controversy. The third and fourth categories are mental impairment and severe mental impairment discussed in Chapter 20.

Mental illness

To understand the causes of mental illness, and even to define mental illness satisfactorily, is far from easy and within medicine it is considered an elusive concept. Definition, diagnosis and measurement lack the precision of somatic illnesses, yet it is recognised that mental illness is prevalent (Gravell and France 1991). Ineichen (1979) reported that there is a predominance of women, one in eight, and one in twelve men in Great Britain who will be assessed or treated in hospital for a mental illness during their lifetime. These statistics represent about 5–10 per cent of the total psychiatric morbidity in a community. General practitioners manage 90–95 per cent of identified psychiatric problems, and only seek the help of the psychiatric services with 5–10 per cent of cases (Pullen 1993). Rates of psychiatric morbidity are about 15 per cent in women and 10 per cent in men.

The fact that women do appear to be more likely to suffer from psychiatric illness than men, in all levels of society, suggests that social factors play an important part in the aetiology of mental illness. This is supported further by evidence that people lower on the social scale are also more vulnerable to mental illness, and the search for the causes of mental illness has thus led into examination of relationships within families, local communities and places of work.

In fact, there has been debate as to whether there is such an entity as mental illness. Szasz (1960) states that, in his opinion, the concept of mental illness does not exist as illness can only be defined in terms of physical pathology and most mental disorders have no such demonstrable pathology. He goes on to say that mental disorders are therefore not the province of doctors. Variously people have proposed that these 'patients' are not ill but showing the effects of the problems of living or that some people are responsible and others not. Trower, Bryant and Argyle (1978) suggest that some forms of mental disorders are caused or exacerbated by lack of social competence and that this can be cured or alleviated therefore by means of social skills training.

However, according to Roth and Kroll (1986), mental illnesses definitely exist, and are usually divided into two major groups – the psychoses and the neuroses, although at times there can be difficulties distinguishing between the two. They refer to neurotics as living in our world partly or wholly whilst they note that in contrast the psychotic is not only out of his mind, but also out of our world. Psychoses are considered the major mental illnesses and involve distorted perception of reality whereas the neurotic conditions do not involve such a distortion. Psychotic conditions are relatively few and are considered more serious, the most severe of them being schizophrenia. Neurotic conditions are often milder in relative terms as well as more common. The latter include such feelings as tension and anxiety, unreasonable fears and phobias, hysteria and obsessional behaviour. Unless severe these are less likely to be treated by a psychiatrist than psychotic disorders and patients are rarely admitted to hospital.

Mental health problems are in fact one of the leading causes of morbidity, bringing distress to individuals and families and constituting a substantial and costly public health burden (Effective Health Care 1997). The causes of mental health problems are contested but are often understood as resulting from the interaction between social and biological predisposing factors whilst also influenced by adverse events. Psychological variables, such as low self-esteem, can put individuals at risk of developing mental health problems; others, such as emotional resilience, protect them from the consequences of adverse events. It is thought that intervention for the promotion of mental health problems can be applied at three levels: at general population level; by targeting people who are at high risk of experiencing mental health problems; or by early detection and treatment of people with existing mental health problems.

Epidemiological studies highlight the role of social environment and life experience in the development of mental health problems. They identify the presence of an adverse social environment as a contributory factor. Specifically, poverty, lack of supportive relationships and severe life events such as the early loss of a parent have been shown to be associated with the common forms of mental ill health (Newton 1988; Murray 1995).

Some of those at high risk are children who are living in poverty, exhibiting behavioural difficulties, experiencing parental separation or divorce and living within families experiencing bereavement. Adults at high risk are those undergoing divorce or separation, unemployed, at risk of depression in pregnancy and experiencing bereavement; and long-term carers of people who are highly dependent (Paykel 1978; Brown and Harris 1978; Graham 1994).

A generation ago, it was very rare for children to have a psychiatric illness or disorder diagnosed. Severe anxiety, agitation, depression and suicidal tendencies were confined to adolescence and adulthood. Children were thought to be immune. *The Times* correspondent Sue Corrigan (1997) goes on to inform us that this is now no longer so; over the past twenty years psychiatric, emotional and serious behavioural disorders have begun to invade childhood, causing suffering and distress to children as young as eight. Corrigan goes on to report that a child psychiatrist, Peter Wilson, director of the charity Young Minds, states there is clear evidence that rates of criminal behaviour, violence, suicide, drug abuse and anorexia are increasing among children and adolescents under 16. Dr Wilson suggests that the fundamental cause is the rapid rate of technological change in society over the past 30 to 40 years, affecting all aspects of the way we live – employment patterns, educational pressures and family structures are all being greatly altered, which makes growing up harder and confusing.

An important fact, increasingly brought to our attention through the media, is that once admitted to a hospital, psychiatric patients are generally left on hospital wards with little to do. According to the Mental Health Commission, patients have limited opportunities to talk to the staff and the distribution of medication can frequently form the main focus of the day. Once admitted to hospital, patients are likely to find staff preoccupied with those who are at risk or need special observation. If this is so, communication skills have little chance to flourish, and opportunities to establish, build and maintain relationships, a fundamental need for those suffering from mental illness, is severely limited.

Diagnosis

As is seen in the recent revisions of DSM-IV (1994) and ICD-10 (1992), the move from diagnostic categories towards the use of descriptions is taking place. Psychiatry, as in any other profession, has its own language/terminology, but many of these terms are used generally by the public in everyday speech. Terms like paranoid, deluded and psychotic are used quite freely, and sometimes quite different and misleading meanings are attached to these terms, compared with those intended when used in psychiatry, thus perpetuating confusion. The psychiatrist relies predominantly on a specialised language to assist towards diagnosis, ensuring that some form of terminology will be always be needed.

Psychiatric diagnoses are further hampered by the fact that some patients may be given different diagnoses by different psychiatrists. Kendell (1993) identifies the shortcomings of diagnosis as fourfold. First, it conveys relatively little information about aetiology, symptomatology, treatment and prognosis. Second, few patients fit neatly into textbook categories and as a result reliability of diagnosis is low. Third, the diagnosis often influences other people's behaviour towards the patient and their own attitude towards themselves in unhelpful ways. Finally, labelling creates a spurious impression of understanding and this encourages naive assumptions about disease entities. Those who would abolish diagnoses commonly argue that each person is unique and their individual problems should be formulated in detail and treated on their own merits.

Kendell (1993) discusses in detail the question of diagnosis and classification, speaking of features each patient shares with all other patients, those the patient shares with some but not all, and those which are unique to himself or herself. In the first case classification is unnecessary as apart from superficial differences all patients will require the same treatment. In the case of unique features being dominant, classification is impossible and nothing useful can be learnt from textbooks, colleagues or the accumulated wisdom of previous workers in the field. Indeed, even personal experience would have no value if there were no significant similarities between patients. Attention must therefore focus on the features shared by some, in order to recognise, identify and distinguish the important aspects – which is the process of diagnosis. If more than one type of treatment is available and to be desired, it is essential to distinguish between types of patients. Thus Kendell argues that some classification is inevitable, but stresses that it is impossible not to lose sight of the fact that all diseases and diagnostic categories are simple concepts. Certainly it is true that while diagnoses may exclude issues that might otherwise have arisen, they do allow better communication between and within disciplines. It is widely agreed that classifications of disorders should, whenever possible, be based on aetiology of the illness.

Classifications

The DSM-IV (1994) is a multiaxial system involving assessments on several axes, each of which refers to a different domain of information that may help the clinician plan treatment and predict outcome. There are five axes included in the DSM-IV: Axis I, Clinical Disorders; Axis II, Personality Disorders and Mental Retardation; Axis III, General Medical Conditions; Axis IV, Psychosocial and Environmental Problems; and Axis V, Global Assessment of Functioning.

The tenth revision of ICD-10 (1992), developed by WHO, was prepared in close co-ordination with those who prepared DSM-IV and led to much mutual influence. This resulted in a great reduction in meaningless differences in wording between the two systems. The ICD-10 consists of an official coding system and other related clinical and research documents and instruments.

Legal aspects in mental health

The Mental Health Act of 1983 established the Mental Health Commission, which gives patients the opportunity to challenge their present placement and treatment. The Act has put in place increased safeguards for detained patients, allows opportunity to appeal against detention and new laws which relate to consent to treatment for detained patients, stricter conditions for compulsory admission and detention and new measures for admitting offender patients to hospital.

There are three main groups of compulsory order for assessment and intervention, where a person's illness puts him/herself and/or others at risk. Admission and assessment sections are 2, 4, 5, 135 and 136; treatment section 3; and, for admission and transfer of patients concerned with clinical proceedings, sections 37, 41, 47 and 49. Each relevant section of the Act specifies strict procedural restrictions and allows certain time-spans over which the orders are valid.

Communication

Successful communication is concerned with the ability to set up and maintain the full interaction of utterance and response which achieves a mutually acceptable outcome. It is a social process, used for the flow of information, the circulation of knowledge and ideas and to achieve shared meanings. Language is the most important tool of communication as it permits people to exchange a tremendous range of attitudes and information, biases and truths. It allows people to communicate via a mutually accepted pattern of rules and conventions, be they verbal or non-verbal, and is a continuing process, a constantly changing dynamic function. Speaking well (that is, the use of verbal language) is usually associated with effective living, allowing people to make links with others and to effect mutual change, by solving problems and influencing each other. Burgoon and Ruffner (1978) state that when a person is isolated they may become prey to delusions and fantasies about themselves in relation to the rest of the world, but that through interaction with others they can be made aware of reality.

Human communication is a complex phenomenon and one that most people take for granted, but satisfactory social relationships go hand in hand with effective communication, a complex process.

Psychiatry and communication

Diamond (1981) states that psychiatrists are interested in the speech content and the linguistic aspects of the patient's communication, which are most important in establishing the psychiatric diagnosis. They rely on what their patients tell them of their history, feelings, complaints, present thoughts, hopes and fears. These are the verbal communications that predominate among the diagnostic criteria, but non-verbal communications are also of importance. Body language, gestures, mannerisms, unusual or odd behaviour and activities, facial expression and signs of emotion in expression or tone of voice all communicate to experienced diagnosticians information about the patient's psyche, whether used intentionally as communicative devices or not. Similarly, appearance and such behaviours as how close a person stands to the person with whom they are communicating are relevant. Psychiatrists are trained to recognise such signs and to interpret their significance as evidence of psycho-pathology or of normal mental processes.

People generally are becoming more aware of and interested in communication, which has become a major topic of conversation and is thought to be at the root of many problems. However, there is still a lack of consensus regarding the nature of competence in communicating or the best way to identify the ability to communicate well. Communicative competence is the yardstick for measuring the quality of interpersonal relationships and is necessary to fulfil the general need of all people to exert control over their environment. Effective environmental control requires a successful interface with other people who are an integral part of that environment. Today's communicative environment presents many challenges that make this competence an important and highly relevant concern, although many seem to believe that they need no training or education in an activity they are performing adequately every day. A variety of indicators suggest that some people's communicative needs are not always necessarily being met. It has been suggested that 7 per cent of the 'normal' adult population have fairly serious difficulties with social behaviour and therefore skill in communicating is not something that should be taken for granted (Argyle 1981).

Sullivan (1950) was among the first to elaborate an entire psychiatric theory of human development in which the interpersonal system was the primary unit of analysis and in which competence in interpersonal skills was a central notion. He identified stages of psychosocial development (infancy, childhood, juvenile, pre-adolescence, late adolescence and maturity) in which relations with others provided the basis for developing competence as a mature adult. If an individual is prevented from fully developing in any stage, later stages are impaired, resulting in mental disturbances such as anxiety and incompetence. Sullivan presented evidence that socially competent people were less likely to manifest certain psychopathological symptoms, were less likely to be institutionalised and where this was the case it was for shorter periods of time, and were less likely to be reinstitutionalised as compared with socially incompetent people. He therefore felt that the concept of mental health is strongly grounded in the way people interact in social contexts. Obviously this is one theory and others have taken other approaches. These range from the purely biological to the psychoanalytical; however, social behaviour – and this necessarily implicates communicative ability – does seem to be crucial at some level of involvement with the mentally ill, whether or not it is seen as a causative factor.

Interaction with others has been considered as one of a great number of human activities that cannot usually be avoided. It is by talking to others that personality is conveyed and there is no way a person can avoid being evaluated on the way he or she speaks. Sullivan (1950) suggests that personality is nothing more than the regular interpersonal contacts that a person carries on by talking. With all the communicative devices available, it is almost impossible not to communicate; even trying not to communicate itself communicates something!

Psychiatrists are interested not only in interpersonal communication but equally importantly in intrapersonal communication, otherwise referred to as the 'inner voice'. Ultimately all communicative responses take place within a person as they react to various communicative cues. Intrapersonal communication can take place without communication in other areas, but communication in those other areas cannot take place without intrapersonal communication.

This is explained clearly by Reusch (1987). He states that the majority of phenomena traditionally described as psychopathology are in fact communication difficulties and that such disturbances are in part defined by the culture in which they occur'. He suggests that as a result of this psychiatric theories are in reality theories of communication, thus psychiatric therapy aims at improving the communicative system of the patient. Restoration of a broken-down system of interpersonal communication on a semantic or interactional level is achieved either by reducing the number of incoming messages and preventing 'jamming', or by increasing the number of messages in transition and preventing isolation and starvation. It is thought that once the communication of the patient with others is improved, correction and self-correction of information will provide the foundations for a change in the conduct of the patient. Therapies all take place in a social context and all use communication as a method of influencing the patient. Reusch goes on to state that the psychiatrist's work is aimed at helping the patient to acquire a communication system which is similar to that of the core group and to prevent disturbances of communication which in turn are responsible for disturbed behaviour.

Speech and language therapy in psychiatry

Speech and language therapists who work with the mentally ill are aware of subtle changes in communication and these changes may be among the first signs of the onset of mental illness. It is through the way in which people begin to communicate differently that it becomes apparent that all is not well (France 1985). Speech and language therapists are interested in the quality, quantity, content and use of language and the identification, diagnosis, observation and treatment of all speech and language pathology. Towards this latter aim they have highly trained listening skills. Over recent years they have moved away from the earlier limited view of speech/language to consider 'communication' – that is, the overall skills, disorders, dys-functions and inadequacies of communication, recognising that non-verbal skills are as much part of human communication as verbal.

Finally, the aim of the SLT service in mental health is to maximise communication potential within a patient's and carer's environment. The linguistic and communicative breakdown is central to mental illness, in terms of both diagnosis and pathology. Mental illness states are vastly complex and the whole microcosm of speech and language disorders can be found in mental health settings, suggesting that a SLT service has a part to play in contributing towards diagnosis and management, both with patients and carers.

All professionals who work in mental health have a responsibility to improve comm-unication, but the processes are often incompletely understood and seldom directly taught. Training is not only essential for students but should be accessible for members of other clinical specialisms and carers.

References

Argyle, M. (1981) The contribution of social interaction research to social skills training. In J. Wine and M. Smye (eds) *Social Competence*. New York: Guildford Press. p.264.

Brown, G.W. and Harris, T.O. (1978) *Social Origins of Depression*. London: Tavistock.

Burgoon, M. and Ruffner M. (1978) *Human Communication*. New York: Holt, Rinehart and Winston.

Cooper, J.E. (1994) *Pocket Book Guide to the ICD-10 Classification of Mental and Behavioural Disorders.* Edinburgh: Churchill Livingstone.

Corrigan, S. (1997) Anxious, depressed, suicidal – and still only a child. *The Times.* 19 August 1997.

Dalton, P. (1994) *Counselling People with Communication Problems.* London: Sage Publications.

Diagnostic and Statistical Manual of Mental Disorders (DSM-IV) (1994) Washington, DC: American Psychiatric Association.

Diamond, B. (1981) The relevance of voice in forensic psychiatric evaluations. In J.K. Darby (ed) *Speech Evaluation in Psychiatry.* New York: Grune and Stratton.

Effective Health Care (June 1997) *Financial Times: Healthcare 3,* 3.

France, J. (1985) Broadmoor: a venture into the unknown. *Speech Therapy in Practice 1,* 2, 4–5.

France, J. (1996) Communication, speech and language. In C. Cordess and M. Cox (eds) *Forensic Psychotherapy: Crime, Psychodynamics and the Offender Patient.* London: Jessica Kingsley Publishers.

France, J. and Miur, N.J. (eds) (1997) *Communication and the Mentally Ill Patient: Developmental and Linguistic Approaches to Schizophrenia.* London: Jessica Kingsley Publishers.

Graham, P. (1994) Prevention. In M. Rutter, E. Taylor and L. Hersov (eds) *Child and Adolescent Psychiatry: Modern Approaches.* Oxford: Blackwell Scientific Publications.

Gravell, R. and France, J. (1991) Mental disorders and speech therapy: an introduction. In R. Gravell and J. France (eds) *Speech and Communication Problems in Psychiatry.* London: Chapman and Hall.

Hume, C. and Pullen, I. (1994) *Rehabilitation for Mental Health Problems: An Introductory Handbook* (second edition). Edinburgh: Churchill Livingstone.

Ineichen, B. (1979) *Mental Illness.* London: Longman.

ICD-10 (1992) *Classification of Mental and Behavioural Disorders.* Geneva: World Health Organization.

Kendell, R.E. (1993) Diagnosis and classification. In R.E. Kendell and A.K. Zealley (eds) *Companion Guide to Psychiatric Studies* (fifth edition). Edinburgh: Churchill Livingstone. pp.277–294.

Mental Health Act (1959) London: HMSO.

Mental Health Act (1983) London: HMSO.

Murray, J. (1995) *Prevention of Anxiety and Depression in Vulnerable Groups. A Review of the Theoretical, Epidemiological, and Applied Research Literature.* London: Gaskell.

Newton, J. (1988) *Preventing Mental Illness.* London: Routledge and Kegan Paul.

Paykel, E.S. (1978) Contribution of life events to causation of psychiatric illness. *Psychological Medicine 8,* 245–253.

Roth, M. and Kroll, J. (1986) *The Reality of Mental Illness.* Cambridge: Cambridge University Press.

Reusch, J. (1987) Values, communication and culture. In J. Reusch and O. Bateson (eds) *Communication in the Social Matrix of Psychiatry* (third edition). London: Norton. pp.3–20.

Sullivan, H.S. (1950) Tensions interpersonal and international: a psychiatrist's view. In H. Cantrill (ed) *Tensions That Cause Wars.* Champaign: University of Illinois Press.

Szasz, T. (1960) The myth of mental illness. *American Psychologist 15,* 11–18.

Trower, P., Bryant, B. and Argyll, M. (1978) *Social Skills and Mental Health.* London: Methuen.

CHAPTER 2

Anxiety Disorders

Neurotic, Stress-Related and Somatoform Disorders

Jenny France

Hibbert (1994), who uses the term 'neuroses', defines these disorders as those without demonstrable organic basis, where the patient does not lose touch with reality or experience psychotic symptoms, and in which anxiety states are the most common. The term 'neurotic' will therefore be used in this chapter as it occurs in many of the references and is still a term commonly used. It is also important to note that individual neurotic symptoms, such as anxiety or obsessional thoughts, frequently occur in other psychiatric disorders, particularly in depression.

The term neurotic is not currently included in the DSM-IV (1994) classification of mental disorders. Instead, the whole group of disorders comes under the heading of Anxiety Disorders. They include: Panic Attack, Agoraphobia, Panic Disorder Without Agoraphobia, Compulsive Disorder, Post-traumatic Stress Disorder, Acute Stress Disorder, Generalised Anxiety Disorder, Anxiety Disorder Due to a Medical Condition, Substance-Induced Anxiety Disorder and Anxiety Disorder Not Otherwise Specified.

ICD-10 (1992) still retains the concept of neurosis, although it has not been used as a major principle of classification. The neurotic, stress-related and somatoform disorders have been brought together in one large group because of their historical association with the concept of neurosis and the association of a substantial proportion of these disorders with psychological causation. Under this heading there are the Phobic anxiety disorders, Other anxiety disorders, Obsessive-compulsive disorder, Reaction to severe stress, and adjustment disorders, Dissociative (conversion) disorder, Somatoform disorders and Other neurotic disorders.

These two classification systems are summarised in Tables 2.1 and 2.2.

'Neurotic disorders' was a term used to cover all minor psychiatric conditions such as anxiety, depression, obsessional and phobic disorders. They are conditions without an apparent organic basis and where the patient does not lose touch with reality. Neurotic disorder was initially used to define disorders of sense and motion caused by a 'general affliction of the nervous system', covering a wide range of conditions such as hysteria, hypochondriasis, melancholia, palpitations, epilepsy, mania, chorea, astheima and diabetes. The concept of neurosis was later to mean psychiatric disorders which did not include either mania or psychotic states.

Table 2.1 Anxiety disorders (DSM-IV 1994)

Panic Attack

Agoraphobia

Panic Disorder Without Agoraphobia

Agoraphobia Without History of Panic Disorder

Specific Phobia

Social Phobia

Obsessive-Compulsive Disorder

Post-traumatic Stress Disorder

Adjustment Disorders

Generalised Anxiety Disorder

Anxiety Disorder Due to a Medical Condition

Substance-Induced Anxiety Disorder

Anxiety Disorder Not Otherwise Specified

Dissociative (conversion) disorders

Table 2.2 Neurotic, Stress-related and Somatoform disorders (ICD-10 1992)

Panic disorder

Phobic anxiety disorders

Agoraphobia

Social phobias

Specific (isolated) phobias

Obsessive-compulsive disorder

Reaction to severe stress, and acute stress disorders

Post-traumatic stress disorder

Adjustment disorders

Other reactions to severe stress

Reaction to severe stress, unspecified

Generalised anxiety disorder

Mixed anxiety and depressive disorder

Other mixed anxiety disorders

Somatoform disorders

Other neurotic disorders

Freeman (1993) states that Freud introduced the term psychoneurosis, which he used to mean three specific syndromes: anxiety-hysteria (phobic anxiety); obsessive-compulsive neurosis; and hysteria proper. He saw the actual neuroses as being predominantly physical and chemical in nature and not due to underlying conflict, and the psychoneuroses as all forms of non-psychotic and non-organic disorders. The move to abandon the term neurosis has been accomplished by the DSM-IV; ICD-10, as previously stated, retains the term 'neurosis' but only to cover a whole group of syndromes, and the individual syndromes are referred to as disorders. DSM-IV states that features of this group of disorders are symptoms of anxiety and avoidance behaviour, and include Panic Disorder, Phobic Disorders and Obsessive-Compulsive Disorder.

Anxiety and stress-related disorders

Anxiety disorder is not synonymous with anxiousness, which is a symptom rather than a syndrome. Anxiety symptoms and attacks can occur as part of any psychiatric illness. It is only when they occur in the absence of other significant psychiatric symptoms that a diagnosis of anxiety disorder should be made (Freeman 1993).

Rutter's (1972) research informs us that most 'neurotic' children become normal adults and most 'neurotic' adults develop their 'neurotic' disorder only in adult life; that women are the more likely sufferers, whereas in the case of children boys are more likely to suffer and the ratio of predominance changes from boys to girls during adolescence. Research into childhood behaviours and personality traits may help the understanding of any links with adult 'neurotic' disorders.

Anxiety disorders are minor psychiatric disorders and only the most severe are referred to a psychiatrist. These patients are usually seen by their general practitioner and many are then referred on to psychologists, and those with obvious voice or speech pathology to a speech and language therapist. A minority of these disorders are severe and disabling and some of these show poor response to treatment.

About 7 per cent of people suffering with anxiety disorders are seen in psychiatric practice according to Goldberg and Huxley (1992), and of the 67 per cent of all psychiatric cases seen in general practice the most frequent symptoms are anxiety, depression, irritability, insomnia and fatigue (Hibbert 1994). Women are the largest percentage of patients treated (Shepherd *et al.* 1966), and a study of those patients treated by their general practitioner, carried out by Mann, Jenkins and Belsey (1981), found that 24 per cent improved, 52 per cent showed a variable course through the year and 25 per cent showed a chronic course. A positive outcome was associated primarily with the patient having a stable supportive family life, being young and male and without a physical illness and not receiving psychotropic medication. A chronic course is associated with the patient being older, having more psychological disturbances at onset, concomitant physical illness and recurring medication (Freeman 1993). It is still thought that social measures and severity of illness rather than type of disorder or personality assessment are the most useful means of predicting outcome. Huxley *et al.* (1979) showed that the initial severity of neurotic illness rather than any particular diagnosis was the best predictor of the eventual outcome of the neurosis.

Anxiety and stress-related disorders can be considered at three levels:

1. Individual symptoms which may be experienced by normal people from time to time and are common in the general public.

2. The undifferentiated 'neurotic syndrome' (sometimes called minor emotional disorder), which is when a variety of 'neurotic' symptoms occur together without any one predominating – these people are usually seen in general practice and show a wide variation.

3. Specific 'neurotic syndromes' when one type of symptom predominates.

There are acute and chronic anxiety states. The acute states have a sudden onset and can occur as a reaction to severe external stress; they tend to run a short course, have a good prognosis and resolve completely. In contrast the chronic states run a prolonged course and are not necessarily associated with stressful events – these people are known to worry and have high anxiety traits. (Traits are habitual tendencies towards certain behaviours, for example worrying.) The sufferers are older, having more psychiatric disturbance at onset, having concomitant physical illness and receiving psychotropic medication (Freeman 1993).

Anxiety disorders present with a number of symptoms which are centred around anxiety, such as attacks of anxiety or panic which can last for minutes, hours or days, or become chronic. Other symptoms may be physical bodily tension and a dry mouth, sleep disturbance, apprehension, poor concentration, fear of losing control, and fears of impending disaster or disease. Irritability, depersonalisation, dizziness, faintness, sweating, tremors, chest pain, palpitations and respiratory distress might also be present (Lader and Marks 1971) with the addition of worrying thoughts of maladaptive cognitions.

Anxiety symptoms occur in all psychiatric illnesses and in some cases there might be difficulty in diagnosis; for example, anxiety is a common symptom of depressive illness (Gelder et al. 1996). Also, those suffering anxiety often experience depressive symptoms. In fact, some of the less severe forms of depressive disorders have features that meet the criteria for neurotic disorders, as they include prominent anxiety symptoms.

Anxiety disorders in children and adolescents

Anxiety disorders in children and adolescents are recognised as one of the most common types of emotional disorder. Their physical and psychological components are similar to those in adult anxiety. They may represent the persistence and exaggeration of normal developmental fears and range in severity from an acute panic attack to a chronic anxiety state over several months (Hoare 1993). Like adults, children use defence mechanisms to protect themselves.

Aetiology of anxiety

GENETICS

Studies continue to confirm that the tendency of anxiety disorders to run in families applies in cases diagnosed specifically as generalised anxiety disorder. These studies demonstrate that this is largely due to genetic factors rather than shared family environment (Gelder et al. 1996).

PSYCHOANALYTIC THEORIES

Gelder *et al.* (1996) state that in generalised anxiety disorder, anxiety is experienced directly unmodified by the defence mechanisms that in other people might cause phobias to develop. This supports theories that anxiety is experienced when the 'ego' is overwhelmed by excitation (Freud 1894).

LEARNING THEORY

Learning theory suggests that where a person becomes frightened by an experience or sensation, or experiences frightening sensations in particular circumstances, anxiety may be subsequently provoked repeatedly by these physical symptoms or in these circumstances. Patients with severe anxiety give an account of such learning experiences, while those with milder forms do not (Hibbert 1994).

Panic attack, panic disorder (DSM-IV 1994; ICD-10 1992)

The ICD-10 definition of panic disorder states that the essential features are recurrent attacks of severe anxiety (panic) which are not restricted to any particular situation or set of circumstances, and which are therefore unpredictable. As in other anxiety disorders, the dominant symptoms vary from person to person, but sudden onset of palpitations, chest pain, choking sensations, dizziness, and feelings of unreality are common. There is also a secondary fear of dying, losing control, or going mad. Individual attacks usually last for a few minutes only, although sometimes longer; their course and frequency are variable.

Panic disorder must be distinguished from panic attacks occurring as part of established phobic disorders. They may be secondary to depressive disorders, particularly in men.

DSM-IV describes panic attacks as occurring in the context of several different anxiety disorders. The essential feature of a panic attack is a discrete period of intense fear accompanied by at least 4 of 13 somatic or cognitive symptoms, as previously identified in ICD-10. The attack has a sudden onset and builds up to a peak. The DSM-IV and ICD-10 descriptions are very similar.

The essential feature of panic disorder (DSM-IV) is the presence of recurrent, unexpected panic attacks followed by at least one month of persistent concern about having another panic attack, worry about the implications or consequences of the panic attacks, or a significant behavioural change related to the attacks.

Prevalence

Epidemiological studies throughout the world consistently indicate the lifetime prevalence of panic disorder (with or without agoraphobia) to be between 1.5 per cent and 3.5 per cent. Approximately one-third to one-half of individuals diagnosed with panic disorder in the community samples also have agoraphobia.

Agoraphobia (DSM-IV 1994; ICD-10 1992)

DSM-IV places Agoraphobia with Panic Disorder with Agoraphobia and Agoraphobia Without History of Panic Disorder. The essential feature of agoraphobia is anxiety about being in places or situations from which escape might be difficult, or in which help may not be available in the event of having a panic attack or panic-like symptoms. The anxiety leads to a pervasive avoidance of a variety of situations that may include being alone outside the home or being at home alone; being in a crowd of people; travelling in cars, buses or planes; or being in a lift or on a bridge.

The ICD description is similar to that found in DSM-IV and in the diagnostic guidelines states that anxiety must be restricted to at least two of the following situations: crowds, public places, travelling away from home, and travelling alone; and avoidance of the phobic situation must be, or have been, a prominent feature.

Specific phobia, phobia anxiety disorders (DSM-IV 1994; ICD-10 1992)

DSM-IV states that the essential feature of Specific Phobia is marked and persistent fear of clearly discernible, circumscribed objects or situations. Exposure to the phobic stimulus almost invariably provokes an immediate anxiety response and the response may take the form of a situationally bound predisposed panic attack. Anxiety is almost invariably felt immediately on confronting the phobic stimulus, and the level of anxiety or fear usually varies as a function of both the degree of proximity to the phobic stimulus and the degree to which escape from the phobic stimulus is limited. Adults with this disorder recognise that the phobia is excessive or unreasonable.

The subtypes of Specific Phobia are Animal Type, Natural Environment Type, Blood-Injection-Injury Type, Situational Type and Other Type which might include children's fears of loud sounds or costumed characters (DSM-IV).

The ICD-10 reports that specific (isolated) phobias are related to highly specific situations such as proximity to particular animals, heights, thunder, darkness, flying, closed spaces, eating certain foods, dentistry, the sight of blood, or injury and the fear of exposure to specific diseases. These phobias usually arise in childhood or early adulthood and can persist for decades if untreated.

Social phobia (DSM-IV 1994); Social phobias (ICD-10 1992)

The ICD-10 informs us that social phobias often start in adolescence and are centred around a fear of scrutiny by other people in comparatively small groups, leading to avoidance of social situations. Unlike most other phobias, social phobias are equally common in men and women and at their worst can result in almost complete isolation.

The DSM-IV description of Social Phobia is: a marked and persistent fear of social or performance situations in which embarrassment may occur, and exposure to these situations provokes an immediate anxiety response.

Prevalence

Community-based studies report a lifetime prevalence ranging from 3 per cent to 13 per cent; this may vary depending on the threshold used to determine distress or impairment and the number of types of social situations specifically surveyed.

Generalised anxiety disorder (DSM-IV 1994; ICD-10 1992)

The essential feature of a generalised anxiety disorder is that the anxiety is generalised and persistent but not restricted to, or even strongly predominating in, any particular environmental circumstances (ICD-10). The dominant symptoms are highly variable, but complaints of continuous nervousness, trembling, muscular tension, sweating, lightheadedness, palpitations, dizziness and epigastric discomfort are common, and these can be accompanied by a variety of worries and forebodings. The disorder is more common in women and is often related to chronic environmental stress (ICD-10).

The DSM-IV states that the essential feature of generalised anxiety disorder is excessive anxiety and worry, occurring more days than not for a period of at least six months, about a number of events or activities. The anxiety and worry are accompanied by at least three additional symptoms from a list that includes restlessness, being easily fatigued, irritability, muscle tension and disturbed sleep.

Prevalence

In a community sample, the one-year prevalence rate for generalised anxiety disorder was approximately 3 per cent, and the lifetime prevalence rate was 5 per cent. In anxiety disorder clinics, approximately 12 per cent of the individuals present with generalised anxiety disorder (DSM-IV).

Anxiety disorder due to a general medical condition (DSM-1994)

The essential feature of this condition is clinically significant anxiety that is judged to be due to the direct physiological effects of a general medical condition (only in DSM-IV).

Substance-induced anxiety disorder (DSM-IV 1994)

In this disorder(s) are prominent anxiety symptoms which are judged to be due to the direct physiological effects of a substance (i.e. drug abuse, a medication or toxin exposure) (DSM-IV).

Obsessive-compulsive disorder (DSM-IV 1994); Obsessive-compulsive disorder (ICD-10 1992)

DSM-IV identifies the essential features of obsessive-compulsive disorder as recurrent obsessions or compulsions that are severe enough to be time-consuming or cause marked distress or significant impairment. At some point during the course of the disorder, the person has recognised that the obsessions or compulsions are excessive or unreasonable.

Obsessions are persistent ideas, thoughts, impulses or images that are experienced as intrusive and inappropriate and that cause marked anxiety or distress. The individual has the sense that the content of the obsession is alien, not within his or her own control, and not the kind of thought that he or she would expect to have. The most common obsessions are repeated thoughts about contamination, repeated doubts, a need to have things in a particular order, aggressive or horrific impulses and sexual imagery. A person with obsessions usually attempts to ignore or suppress such thoughts or impulses, or to neutralise them with some other thought or action.

Compulsions are repetitive behaviours or mental acts, the goal of which is to prevent or reduce anxiety or distress. In most cases the person is driven to perform the compulsion to reduce the distress that accompanies an obsession or to prevent some dreaded event or situation. Adults with obsessive-compulsive disorder have at some time recognised that the obsessions or compulsions are excessive or unreasonable. In the course of the disorder, after repeated failure to resist the obsessions or compulsions, the individual may give in to them and/or no longer experience a desire to resist them, and may perhaps incorporate the compulsions into his/her daily routines.

The obsessions or compulsions must cause marked distress, be time-consuming, i.e. take more than one hour per day, or interfere with the individual's normal routine, occupational functioning or usual social activities or relationships with others.

ICD-10 reports that obsessive-compulsive disorder is equally common in men and women, and there are often anankastic features (that of being compelled or forced) in the underlying personality.

Prevalence

Although obsessive-compulsive disorder was previously thought to be relatively rare in the general population, recent community studies have estimated a lifetime prevalence of 2.5 per cent and one-year prevalence of 1.5 per cent – 2.1 per cent.

Reaction to severe stress, and adjustment disorders (DSM-IV 1994; ICD-10 1992)

In the ICD-10 this category differs from others in that it includes disorders identifiable not only on grounds of symptomatology and course but also on the basis of one other of two causative influences – an exceptionally stressful life event producing an acute stress reaction, or a significant life change leading to continued unpleasant circumstances that result in an adjustment disorder. Under this heading is acute stress reaction, post-traumatic stress disorder and adjustment disorders. The DSM-IV lists post-traumatic stress disorder and acute stress disorder under separate headings.

Post-traumatic stress disorder (DSM-IV 1994); Post-traumatic stress disorder (ICD-10 1992)

This arises as a delayed and/or protracted response to a stressful event or situation (either short or long-lasting) of an exceptionally threatening or catastrophic nature, which is likely to cause pervasive distress in almost anyone, for example natural or man-made disaster, combat, serious accident, witnessing the violent death of others, or being a victim of torture, terrorism, rape or other crimes (ICD-10). Typical symptoms include episodes of reliving of the trauma in intrusive memories ('flashbacks') or dreams, or occurring against a background of a sense of 'numbness' and emotional blunting, detachment from other people, unresponsiveness to surroundings and avoidance of activities and situations reminiscent of the trauma.

Prevalence

DSM-IV reports that community-based studies reveal a lifetime prevalence for victims of post-traumatic stress disorder ranging from 1 per cent to 14 per cent, with the variability related to methods of ascertainment and population sampled. Studies of at-risk individuals (e.g. combat veterans, victims of volcanic eruptions or criminal violence) have yielded prevalence rates ranging from 3 per cent to 58 per cent.

Acute stress disorder (DSM-IV 1994); Acute stress reaction (ICD-10 1992)

This is a transient disorder of significant severity which develops in an individual without any other apparent mental disorder in response to exceptional physical and/or mental stress and which subsides within hours or days (ICD-10) and consists of the development of anxiety, dissociative and other symptoms that occur within one month after exposure to the traumatic stressor. The DSM-IV adds that there should be three or more accompanying dissociative symptoms, such as: a sense of numbing detachment, or absence of emotional responsiveness; a reduction in awareness of his or her surroundings; derealisation; depersonalisation and dissociative amnesia.

Dissociative (conversion) disorders (DSM-IV 1994; ICD-10 1992)

The common theme shared by dissociative (or conversion) disorders is a partial or complete loss of the normal integration between memories and the past, awareness of identity and immediate sensations, and control of bodily movements. There is normally a degree of control over the memories and sensations that can be selected for immediate attention, and the movements that are to be carried out. These disorders include conversion hysteria, conversion reaction, hysteria and hysterical psychosis, but exclude malingering (ICD-10).

These disorders have previously been classified as various types of 'conversion hysteria', but now it is thought best to avoid the term 'hysteria' due to its many varied meanings. They have been thought to be 'psychogenic' in origin, being associated closely in time with traumatic events, insoluble and intolerable problems, or disturbed relationships. The term 'conversion' implies that unpleasant affect, engendered by the problems and conflicts that the individual cannot solve, is somehow transformed into the symptoms (ICD-10). DSM-IV includes Conversion Disorder within the group of Somatoform Disorders, not with Anxiety Disorders, and says that the symptoms are related to voluntary motor or sensory functioning and are thus referred to as 'pseudoneurological'. Motor symptoms or deficits include impaired co-ordination of balance, paralysis or localised weakness, aphonia and difficulty swallowing, for example. Sensory symptoms or deficits include loss of touch or pain sensation, double vision, blindness, deafness and hallucinations.

DSM-IV has a separate grouping for Dissociative Disorders apart from Anxiety Disorders and this includes Dissociative Amnesia, Dissociative Fugue, Dissociative Identity Disorder, Depersonalisation Disorder and Dissociative Disorder Not Otherwise Specified.

Hysteria

The concept of hysteria

Apparently one of the few things that is certain in psychiatry is that no two psychiatrists can agree on what the terms hysteria and hysterical convey. The term hysteria is currently used in a number of different senses; the links between some of the uses are obvious, but the only thing that others appear to have in common is the term hysteria or hysterical itself (Freeman 1993). It is a term that doctors cannot do without – it will not disappear, but will continue to reflect change in the ideas of acceptable illness held by doctors and patients alike (Lewis and Wessely 1997).

The variety of symptoms is enormous and patients suffering from hysteria often show less than the expected amount of distress. Hysteria can be accompanied by motor symptoms but no signs of genuine physical illness such as no changes in reflexes, or muscle, and there is a reduction in symptoms with distraction and an increase with attention.

Stemple *et al.* (1995) are of the opinion that at times environmental stress may become so severe that avoidance behaviours may be developed to counteract stressful situations. It is known that avoidance behaviours become an unconscious substitution of a somatic symptom, involving the sensory or motor nervous systems, for the unpleasant or intolerable emotional event or conflict. Sensory and motor symptoms may also be present. Stemple (1984) reported that hysterical or conversion aphonia manifested by whispering, muteness or unusual dysphonias permits people to avoid awareness of stress or emotional conflict.

Somatoform disorders (DSM-IV 1994; ICD-10 1992)

In ICD-10 these disorders are included within the neurotic and stress-related groupings (F40–F48). They include Somatoform disorder, Undifferentiated somatoform disorder, Hypochondriacal disorder (which includes body dysmorphobia), Somatoform autonomic dysfunction, Persistent somatoform pain disorder, Other somatoform disorders and Somatoform disorder, unspecified.

DSM-IV has a separate grouping for Somatoform Disorders apart from the Anxiety Disorders and lists Somatisation Disorder, Undifferentiated Somatoform Disorder, Conversion Disorder, Pain Disorder, Hypochondriasis, Body Dysmorphobic Disorder and Somatoform Disorder Not Otherwise Specified.

Other neurotic disorders (ICD-10 1992)

The ICD-10 concludes the group of neurotic and stress-related somatoform disorders and other neurotic disorders with neurasthenia, depersonalisation-derealisation syndrome and other specified and unspecified neurotic disorders.

Aetiology of anxiety disorders/neurotic, stress-related and somatoform disorders

Major happenings in a person's life, especially stressful events and losses, will predispose them to neurotic illness (Freeman 1993). Studies show that there is a definite association between low social class and psychological disturbance. Brown and Harris's (1978) work on depressed women states that three factors operate: vulnerability factors, long-term difficulties and provoking agents.

Social relationships

It may not be the lack of social relationships that is aetiologically important so much as the way they are perceived by the individual. Those who view their relationships as inadequate have an increased risk of developing neurotic symptoms under conditions of adversity. Neurotic symptoms then emerge in individuals who consider themselves deficient in care, support or concern from those around them. In this sense neurotic symptoms can be seen as care-eliciting behaviour (Freeman 1993).

The predisposition to neurotic disorders arises partly from inheritance and partly from upbringing, and the patient's capacity to withstand stress and its converse. There is a fair degree of agreement that the most important period is *not* limited to early childhood and that relatives outside the family are as influential as those within the family.

Marriage and family

Freeman (1993) observes that the prevalence of psychiatric disorders in both husband and wife is greater than would be expected by chance, and that most of this morbidity is neurotic illness and/or personality disorders.

Male patients have sick wives more often than female patients have sick husbands. It appears that neurotic couples spend more time alone together, are less socially integrated and have more conflict over roles than non-neurotic couples. All these factors are thought to contribute to the onset of neurosis in the spouse.

Physical illness and organic pathology

Somatisation is a very common process by which patients present with their psychological disorders to their doctors (Lewis and Wessely 1997) and about 20 per cent of new attenders in general practice are somatisers in contrast to the 5 per cent who present solely with psychological symptoms (Goldberg and Bridges 1988).

Employment factors

Freeman (1993) reports that there is a confirmed relationship between unemployment and psychiatric status which applies for both men and women.

Sociological aspects

Pilowsky (1978) identified the need to look beyond behaviour, symptoms or underlying pathology in order to examine psychological gains and advantages that the patient accrues from their prolongation.

Associated communication and speech problems

The speech and language therapist is in an unusually fortunate position in being able to help recognise, offer support and recommend other agencies for further assistance, through the way in which the speech and language therapy service is delivered. Patients and their families can be offered regular weekly sessions, particularly if treatment is necessary, which might carry on for some weeks, months or, in some cases, years. Sessions can last up to an hour each and the support allows, if possible, for post-therapy communication, during which time relationships with other carers, such as parents, sons and daughters, grandparents, friends, neighbours and employers, provide much useful information and confidences, thus helping to identify problem areas. During discussion, identification of stresses, anxieties and other invaluable information often comes to light, allowing the opportunity to adapt the present treatment, to refer on to other healthcare professionals, or to offer joint support to both patients and carers.

Communication and speech problems associated with anxiety and other stress-related disorders encompass every aspect of speech, language and communication. There are those speech disorders which accompany anxiety disorders and those which result from them, and there are the communication problems that result from social inadequacy and perhaps exacerbate an anxiety disorder. The dividing line between these three categories is difficult to define (France 1991), and research continues into whether social incompetence produces failure, avoidance, anxiety and phobias, or whether anxiety results in incompetent social functioning and inadequate communication. Stemple (1984) is of the opinion that by the time patients are referred to a speech therapist or pathologist they are truly seeking relief from the disorder and are subconsciously ready for a change. He goes on to state that some patients may continue to receive secondary gains from the disorder and resist therapeutic modifications, but the majority will respond quickly to direct therapy, e.g. for voice pathology. It is always essential to establish that there is no organic pathology before proceeding with therapy. Few stutterers are socially at ease; the majority suffer from anxiety, particularly in speech situations, and in their negative attitudes produce avoidance strategies in relation to communication (Dalton 1983).

It is known that some people develop phobias to specific social situations (Trower, Bryant and Argyle 1978), e.g. the fear of being the centre of attention, or misinterpreting the reactions of others; this might result in problems with non-verbal communication and poor verbal competence, and such people do not understand the possibility of pleasure from human interaction (Phillips 1984). Chronic anxiety can also be a source of voice disorder.

According to Brody (1943), the voice is considered to be a 'sensitive reflector of emotional states and that speech is not always used solely for the communication of meanings but may also constitute the expression of feelings'. Moses (1954) believed that neurotic patterns can be discovered through the voice and that content and meaning of speech are useful differentiations between neurotic disorders and schizophrenia and personality disorders. Moses was able to differentiate between the neurotic and schizophrenic patient by their vocal expression! This demonstrates the need to listen as broadly as possible and attribute vocal styles to voice pathology, emotional states and mental disorders as well as making use of language as a major indicator of pathology (France 1991).

Green (1975) states that the recovery of the voice is not the sole aim of treatment of voice disorders and that therapy must aim at removing or alleviating the causes and obtaining better adjustment to the difficulties by gaining some insight into the connection between the vocal symptoms and the precipitating factors. Voice disorders also occur in obsessional states and compulsive idiosyncratic speech mannerisms might also be evident. Green and Mathieson's (1989) chapter on Psychogenic Voice Disorders is helpful in expanding this subject further.

Prescribed medication can affect speech and articulation in particular, although the associated dysarthrias and other side-effects are considerably less than in the cases of more severe mental illnesses.

Assessments

It is of paramount importance to establish that there is no organic pathology, such as disease, affective disorder, schizophrenia and dementia, before proceeding with any speech and language intervention. Close multiprofessional liaison is desirable and is likely to assist in the patient's future management. (See Chapters 7 and 8 for further information.)

General management

Management should, wherever possible, come from within a multidisciplinary team as interventions may involve more than one professional; this in turn aids good team communication and is a source of support and feedback for therapists and patients alike.

Sources of referral

In a community clinic the general practitioner or clinical psychologists might be the referring agencies; in the out-patient clinic or in a ward setting, it may be the psychiatrist. The psychiatrist is usually pleased to supervise treatment, and help with future referral to other agencies. It is also possible that other members of the clinical team make the first referral approach, and in some cases the patient will self-refer.

Treatment of anxiety disorders

Drugs are avoided where possible unless other methods of treatment fail. Although in severe cases drugs relieve symptoms, they might encourage dependence. Hibbert (1994) is of the opinion that if support, discussion and reassurance is sufficient, then a clear plan of treatment will be welcomed.

Drugs for anxiety disorders

Drugs used in the treatment of anxiety disorders may be divided into two groups: those which act on the central nervous system and those which block peripheral autonomic receptors (Silverstone and Turner 1995):

- The Benzodiazepines are often prescribed for severe anxiety disorders. They are centrally and long-acting drugs and considered more suitable than hypnotic agents. They act on the brain stem and can therefore produce drowsiness, increase the seizure threshold and thus act as an anticonvulsant. As they depress activity in the limbic system recent memory may be impaired. Another negative aspect is that they are known to create dependency. The toxic effects of diazepines may increase anxiety and produce hostility and confusion in elderly people. Other occasional side-effects are confusion and dry mouth. Benzodiazepines depress spinal reflexes but do not produce dysarthria except in toxic dosage and when abused with other drugs (Maguire 1986).

- Buspirone, which is a 5–HT agonist, is a possible alternative to the Benzodiazepines, particularly when rapid relief of symptoms is not an urgent clinical problem (Silverstone and Turner 1995).

Behaviour and cognitive therapy

Anxiety management training is a name given to a package of techniques for tackling anxiety. Patients may be encouraged to use some or all of these depending on the analysis and requirements of their particular disorder and the patients may be treated individually or in groups. The content of the package consists of three groups of elements (France and Robson 1997):

1. Explanation of the nature of anxiety and the rationale of treatment to the patient.

2. Control of symptoms using relaxation, distraction, exercise, restructuring of thoughts, panic management, etc.

3. Reducing Avoidance by graded exposure and confidence building.

It is thought that relaxation training may be helpful and, if practised regularly, the effects can equal those of anxiolytic drugs (Gelder *et al.* 1996).

Treatment of phobias and obsessive-compulsive and conversion disorders

Anxiolytic drugs will give symptom relief and help any accompanying depression, but should not be relied upon in the long term. Behaviour therapy is known to help some of these patients, particularly for treating obsessive thoughts. Other forms of psychotherapy are thought to be less helpful.

Gelder *et al.* (1996) suggest that the exposure form of behaviour therapy can be beneficial. Although it is unusual for the phobia to be lost completely, Benzodiazepines reduce symptoms of social phobia more than does placebo treatment (Gelernter *et al.* 1991) but there is a risk of dependency if their use is prolonged.

Behaviour therapy has a limited value for hysteria and medication is thought to have no part to play, according to Gelder *et al.* (1996). Most of these patients, they report, do well with simple treatment, unless there is a strong motivation to remain ill, and all patients should be followed carefully for long enough to exclude organic disease, particularly neurological disease, as a cause of their problems.

The identification, recognition and support of anxiety problems, particularly when they occur with other mental disorders, and the understanding of the way in which they affect the functioning and well-being of the patient and his or her family, are essential prerequisites to treatment. Service provision should include: training programmes for staff and other carers about social and communication inadequacy in mental illness; organisation of treatment and its delivery, together with support for these packages for patients; and assessment and management of specific voice, speech and language pathology, most commonly voice disorders. Treatment for some specialised speech performance such as public speaking in various social settings can be included in a social skills package.

References

Brody, M.W. (1943) Neurotic manifestations of the voice. *Psychoanalytic Quarterly 12*, 371–380.

Brown, G. and Harris, T. (1978) *Social Origins of Depression.* London: Tavistock Publications.

Dalton, P. (1983) Psychological approaches to the treatment of stuttering. In P. Dalton (ed) *Approaches to the Treatment of Stuttering.* London: Croom Helm.

DSM-IV (1994) *Diagnostic and Statistical Manual of Mental Disorders* (fourth edition). Washington, DC: American Psychiatric Association.

France, J. (1991) Neurotic disorders. In R. Gravell and J. France (eds) *Speech and Communication Problems in Psychiatry.* London: Chapman and Hall.

France, R. and Robson, M. (1997) *Cognitive Behavioural Therapy in Primary Care: A Practical Guide.* London: Jessica Kingsley Publishers.

Freeman, C.P.L. (1993) Neurotic disorders. In R.E. Kendell and A.K. Zeally (eds) *Companion Guide to Psychiatric Studies* (fifth edition). Edinburgh: Churchill Livingstone.

Freud, S. (1894) *On the Grounds for Detaching a Particular Syndrome from Neurasthenia under the Description Anxiety Neurosis* (standard edition). London: Hogarth Press, 1992. Vol. 3.

Gelder, M., Gath, D., Mayou, R. and Cowen, P. (1996) *Oxford Textbook of Psychiatry* (third edition). Oxford: Oxford University Press.

Gelernter, C.S., Uhde, T.W., Cimbolic, P. *et al.* (1991) Cognitive-behavioural and pharmacological treatments of social phobia – a controlled study. *Archives of General Psychiatry 49*, 938.

Goldberg, D. and Bridges, K. (1988) Somatic presentation of psychiatric illness in primary care settings. *J. Psychsom. Res. 32*, 137–144.

Goldberg, D. and Huxley, P. (1992) *Common Mental Disorders. A Bio-Social Model.* London: Routledge.

Green, M.C.L. (1975) *The Voice and its Disorders.* London: Pitman Medical.

Green, M.C.L. and Matheson, L. (1989) *The Voice and its Disorders* (fifth edition). London: Whurr.

Hibbert, G.A. (1994) The neuroses. In N. Rose (ed) *Essential Psychiatry* (second edition). Oxford: Blackwell Scientific Publications. pp.74–83.

Hoare, P. (1993) Psychiatric disorders of childhood. In R.E. Kendell and A.K. Zeally (eds) *Companion to Psychiatric Studies* (fifth edition). Edinburgh: Churchill Livingstone. pp.649–679.

Huxley, P.J., Goldberg, D.P., Maguire, P. and Kincey, V. (1979) The prediction of the course of minor psychiatric disorders. *British Journal of Psychiatry, 135*, 535–543.

ICD-10 (1992) *Classification of Mental and Behavioural Disorders.* Geneva: World Health Organization.

Lader, M.H. and Marks, I.M. (1971) *Clinical Anxiety.* London: Heinemann.

Lewis, G. and Wessely, S. (1997) Neurosis and personality disorders. In R. Murray, P. Hill and P. McGuffin (eds) *The Essentials of Postgraduate Psychiatry* (third edition). Cambridge: Cambridge University Press. pp.145–191.

Maguire, T. (1986) Pharmacological Effects in Speech and Language. Paper presented at Speech Therapy Special Interest Group, Broadmoor Hospital, Crowthorne, Berks.

Mann, A.H., Jenkins, R. and Belsey, E. (1981) A twelve month outcome of patients with neurotic illness in general practice. *Psychological Medicine 11*, 3, 535–550.

Moses, P. (1954) *The Voice of Neurosis.* New York: Grune and Stratton.

Phillips, G. (1984) A perspective on social withdrawal. In J.A. Daly and J.C. McCroskey (eds) *Avoiding Communication: Shyness, Reticence and Communication Apprehension.* Beverley Hills: Sage Publications. pp.51–66.

Pilowsky, I. (1978) A general classification of abnormal illness behaviours. *British Journal of Medical Psychology 51*, 131–137.

Rutter, M.L. (1972) Relationships between child and adult psychiatric disorders. *Acta Psychiatrica Scandinavica 48*, 3–21.

Shepherd, M., Cooper, B., Brown, H.C. and Kalton, C.W. (1966) *Psychiatric Illness in General Practice*. Oxford: Oxford University Press.

Silverstone, T. and Turner, P. (1995) *Drug Treatment in Psychiatry*. London: Routledge.

Stemple, J.C. (1984) *Clinical Voice Pathology Theory and Management*. Oxford: Charles E. Merrill.

Stemple, J.C., Glaze, L.E. and Gerdeman, B.K. (1995) *Clinical Voice Pathology: Theory and Management*. San Diego, California: Singular Publishing Group Inc.

Trower, P., Bryant, B. and Argyle, M. (1978) *Social Skills and Mental Health*. London: Methuen.

CHAPTER 3

Schizophrenia and Other Psychotic Disorders

Sarah Kramer and Jenny France

The pychoses are considered to be the major mental illnesses. Individuals with these diagnoses demonstrate varied signs and symptoms; these include incoherent speech, bizarre and idiosyncratic beliefs and purposeless or unpredictable or violent behaviour with apparent absence of concern for one's own safety and comfort (Roth and Kroll 1986). Psychotic illnesses encompass organic psychoses, drug psychoses, the major affective (mood) disorders (see Chapter 4), schizophrenia and paranoid states.

DSM-IV (1994) classifies these disorders into Schizophrenia and Other Psychotic Disorders; Substance-Related Disorders are more recently classified within a separate group, ICD-10 (1992), where there are also two separate groups. F20–F29, the first group, headed schizophrenia, schizotypal and delusional disorders; and the second group, F10–F19 includes mental and behavioural disorders due to psychoactive substance abuse.

In both classification systems the substance-related disorders are included here as they feature the misuse of substance such as alcohol, opioids, cannabinoids, sedatives or hypnotics, cocaine, hallucinogens, tobacco, volatile solvents, and multiple drug use of other psychoactive substances. DSM-IV includes a subheading of Substance-Induced Psychotic Disorder within the group that includes Schizophrenia and Other Psychotic Disorders as the symptoms are in excess of those usually associated with substance intoxication and they are considered severe enough to warrant independent clinical attention. The ICD-10 subdivides these disorders under the subheadings of acute intoxication, harmful use, dependence syndrome, withdrawal state, withdrawal state with delirium, psychotic disorder, amnesic syndrome, residual and late-onset psychotic disorder, other mental and behavioural disorders, and unspecified mental and behavioural disorder. Substance abusers can develop long-term mental disorders, and patients with diagnosed mental illnesses are commonly known to supplement their medication with other drugs which they abuse, giving rise to an exacerbation of symptoms of their mental illness, occasionally with catastrophic results.

Organic psychoses feature cognitive impairments of memory, orientation, comprehension, calculation, learning capacity and judgement, together with alterations of mood, disturbance of behaviour and personality and impairment of volition. Acute disorders with a short course are referred to as delirium while dementia runs a chronic course. Organic psychoses include both senile and pre-senile conditions, while alcoholic psychoses include delirium tremens, Korsakov's psychosis, other alcoholic dementia and/or hallucinations and alcoholic jealousy.

However, the schizophrenic disorders are the most prevalent of the psychoses. The affective mood disorders including bipolar affective disorder (ICD-10 1992), Major Depressive Disorder (DSM-IV 1994), and other non-organic psychoses are less frequent with schizophrenic illness when, at their most severe, patients' behaviour is far from everyday life; they live in a world of their own and fantasy may seem fact to them. Glimpses of their world show that they answer voices that others cannot hear or suffer torment and punishments that are not understood by others. They have severe problems relating to their environment and other people, their contact with reality is poor and they lack insight. It is the patients' disorganisation of the mind that is involved in the illness, and many patients refuse to believe they suffer from this illness. If eventually they develop insight into their predicament the resulting horror, in some cases, can be overwhelming.

The size of the problem that psychotic illnesses present to the health services is represented by the number of admissions and readmissions to hospital. In 1986 schizophrenia and paranoid illness took up 29,419 beds, the affective psychoses 24,633, senile and pre-senile dementias 20,858, alcoholic psychoses 775, other psychoses including drug-induced psychoses 17,992, with a final total of 93,677 (DHSS 1986).

Throughout this chapter when referring to psychotic symptoms certain terms will be used, and so before discussing specific disorders in more detail, this terminology will be explained briefly.

Description of psychotic symptoms

Perceptions of imagery

Perceptions can alter in intensity and quality. In mania perceptions often seem very intense whereas in depression sounds and colours may seem less intense. In schizophrenia, changes in quality occur and sensations sometimes appear distorted and unpleasant.

The abnormality of perception most frequently treated in mental health settings is hallucinations, which are perceptions occurring in the absence of a stimulus and which the patient takes to be real. Hallucinations come in many forms – auditory, visual, gustatory, tactile or somatic – and they may be simple or complex. For example, simple auditory hallucinations would include indistinct sounds or mutterings whereas those that are complex might be voices speaking clearly and sometimes a recognisable voice of a relative or friend. These voices may appear to speak words, phrases or sentences and some voices even anticipate what the patient thinks, or speak the patient's own thoughts as he thinks them.

Pseudo-hallucinations are similar to true hallucinations but lack the full qualities of true perceptions. A patient might hear a voice in his or her head; this would be a pseudo-hallucination. Illusions are deceptions of the sense where the sufferer misperceives things he sees or hears.

Hallucinations may occur in all kinds of psychoses but are not necessarily an aid to diagnosis as healthy people experience hallucinations too. However, the form and content of auditory hallucinations can help diagnosis; for instance, voices heard talking to or about the patient and voices which appear to be talking to each other and referring to the patient in the third person are called third-person hallucinations and are frequently associated with schizophrenia. Voices with derogatory content are commonly associated with depressive psychosis, especially when the patient accepts that these are unjustified. In contrast a schizophrenic patient is more likely to resent justified content. Visual hallucinations experienced are not as indicative of particular diagnosis. Hallucinations of taste and smell, which are less frequent, may occur in schizophrenia or severe depressive disorders. Tactile and somatic hallucinations also occasionally occur in schizophrenia.

Disorders of thinking

The main way of recognising disorders of thinking is through the patient's speech and writing. Thought disorder can be classified in four categories: stream, connection, possession and content of thought.

The stream of thought is how fast one thought follows another, and can be slowed as in depression or accelerated as in hypomania. The stream of thought might take the form of pressure of thought, in which the thoughts follow the same topic, or flight of ideas where the topic changes rapidly.

Disorders of connections between thoughts are seen in schizophrenia, hypomania and organic disorders. Thought blocking is the stopping of a line of thought and occurs in an extreme form in schizophrenia. Schizophrenic thought disorder may also include, for example, 'knight's move' – where talk moves from one thought to another without any logical sequence. There may be a loosening of the associations between thoughts in schizophrenia and this may be combined with interpenetration of themes, where there are two or more subjects woven randomly into the patient's speech. Overinclusiveness, which sometimes occurs, is a tendency to excessive generalisation. Concrete thinking is also apparent at times. This is an acquired inability to think in abstract terms. Schizophrenic patients sometimes produce neologisms (new words) and metonyms (approximately correct use of real words and phrases). The overall effect of a combination of these features of disordered thought is likely to bemuse the listener. At its worst, schizophrenic speech may become completely unintelligible – this is called word 'salad' or verbigeration. Some of the features of speech described here occur in hypomania, eg neurologisms and metonyms but in hypomania, the flight of ideas has some logical connection between thoughts. Organically impaired patients show a related difficulty, perseveration. This is a repetitive activity in which there is an inability to stop one thing and move on to the next.

Disorders of possession of thought occur in schizophrenia and include thought insertion. The patient experiences the thoughts in his head as those of some other person or agency or thoughts put there by somebody else. Thought withdrawal is the experience of one's thoughts being taken out of one's head. Thought broadcasting is an extension of thought withdrawal in which the patient experiences his thoughts travelling out of their head and other people having access to these thoughts.

Delusions are abnormal beliefs and constitute one type of abnormality of thought content. They are false beliefs which are firmly held and are not susceptible to the ordinary processes of reasoning and appeal to evidence, and are culturally atypical or out of step with the beliefs conventionally held among people of the same culture and ethnic background as the patient (Fulford 1994). The most common delusions are persecutory or paranoid delusions and these reflect a distorted relationship between patient and the world about them; they as persecutory, self-referential and grandiose. Other delusions include hypochondriacal delusions, which are concerned with illness; religious delusions; jealousy, which is more common among men; guilt and worthlessness, which are usually found in depressive illnesses; and nihilism, which includes pessimistic ideas about death or impending doom and is usually associated with degrees of depressive mood change. Delusions of grandeur occur in mania and schizophrenia and are beliefs of exaggerated self-importance. Delusions of reference are ideas that events or people have a personal significance for the patient. Delusions of control are delusions where the patient believes that their actions, impulses or thoughts are controlled by an outside agency.

Disorders of emotion

Changes of emotion are found in all kinds of psychiatric disorders, particularly in the affective disorders (depression and elation) and anxiety states. They are also common in organic psychoses and schizophrenia.

Depersonalisation and derealisation are feelings of unreality which are difficult to describe and are said to be unpleasant. These feelings are often accompanied by morbid experiences and include changes in the experience of time and body image (such as a feeling that a limb has altered and is deformed), and feelings of being outside one's own body and observing one's activities from above. There are various theories about the causes of depersonalisation and derealisation but no satisfactory explanation has been found.

Motor symptoms

These include abnormalities of social behaviour, facial expression and posture, and are common in all mental illnesses. Motor symptoms are obscure among schizophrenic patients and include mannerisms such as making the sign of the cross as a greeting. Stereotypes are repeated movements such as rocking, posturing, adopting and maintaining unusual body postures and echopraxia (the imitation of movements of others).

Disorders of body image

Abnormalities of body image occur and little is known about the cause. They arise in neurological as well as psychiatric disorders and they might include, for example, continuous awareness of parts of the body that have been lost or feelings that a limb is enlarging, becoming smaller or distorted.

Disorders of memory

Disorders of memory might include amnesia (the failure of memory) or short, medium and long-term memory disorders, where registration, retention, recall and recognition may be impaired. Other forms of memory impairment include *déjà vu*, when a patient describes a situation or event as having been encountered before, and *jamais vu*, the reverse situation, when the patient fails to recognise a situation or event encountered before (Gelder, Gath and Mayou 1986).

Disorders of consciousness

Consciousness is awareness of one's environment. In acute organic disorders confusion, partial impairment of consciousness, illusions, hallucinations, delusion and mood change may be experienced.

Insight

Insight is described as being the awareness of one's own mental condition. It is thought that loss of insight distinguishes psychoses from neuroses and that neurotic patients retain insight while psychotic patients lose it. Most patients do not accept that their experiences result from illness, but usually ascribe them to the malevolent actions of other people. This lack of insight is often accompanied by unwillingness to accept treatment (Gelder *et al.* 1996).

Defence mechanisms

Mechanisms of defence are processes that may help to explain certain kinds of experience or behaviour; they are automatic and unconscious and are said to have been used to account for the psychopathology of everyday life and to explain the aetiology of mental disorders (Freud 1936).

Bateman (1996) identifies five functions of defence phenomena: as a way of deflecting and adapting to internal feelings and fantasies; as a part of stable defence style; as defensive interactions with the environment; in the context of attachment patterns; and as primitive or mature developmental phenomena. Defence mechanisms include repression, which is the exclusion from awareness of impulses, emotions and memories that would distress if allowed to enter the conscious; denial, when a person behaves as though unaware of something which they may reasonably be expected to know; and projection, the unconscious attribution to another person of thoughts or feelings, so rendering them more acceptable. Regression is the adoption of behaviour appropriate to an earlier stage of development; for example dependence on others. If regression persists it can be maladaptive because it reduces the patient's ability to take responsibility for himself (Gelder *et al.* 1996).

Schizophrenia

According to Kendell (1993) schizophrenia is the heartland of psychiatry and the core of its clinical practice. It is a relatively common condition which often cripples people in adolescence or early adult life, and probably causes more suffering and distress that most other illnesses. About 10 per cent of all hospital beds are occupied by schizophrenic patients (Kendell 1993) and so this condition places an enormous burden on the health services. Blakemore (1988) talked of 1 per cent of the world's population suffering from schizophrenia, and stated that it is a disease of the brain and mind, it causes global impairment and disrupts personality. Blakemore added that one-third of the people who suffer one or two episodes recover, another third respond to therapy and the last third become chronically sick.

Schizophrenia is a term that can be defined broadly or narrowly and means different things to different people – some even doubting the existence of the condition. Those arguing against the use of this term at times refer to schizophrenia as medical fiction. This may be related to the negative impact of receiving a diagnosis of schizophrenia. Once a person is diagnosed as schizophrenic this can considerably alter the individual's relationships with others. Murray (1997) comments on the possibility that a failure to discover the aetiology of schizophrenia will continue to lead to confusion as to the existence of schizophrenia. However other researchers, such as Tidmarsh (1990) are insistant that schizophrenia is a disease and that the medical model is appropriate and useful. Murray notes that varied definitions are the result of attempts to define schizophrenia in different ways e.g. on the basis of symptoms, involved in the climatic course, or by its consideration as a syndrome. Tidmarsh (1990) notes that in 1973 the World Health Organization initiated a pilot study of schizophrenia and it demonstrated conclusively that psychiatrists in different countries do agree about what they observe, even though they do not all make the same deductions from their observations. When a standard method was used to arrive at a diagnosis, then both the incidence of schizophrenia and its symptoms were remarkably similar in all of the nine countries taking part in the study. This is consistent with diagnosis of other medical conditions.

Freeman (1988) explains that schizophrenia is a condition that seems to be associated with a fundamental biological fault. A fault involved in processing stimuli from the outside world reduces the person's ability to cope with stress or with intense and complex relationships.

Definition of schizophrenia

The DSM-IV definition of schizophrenia states that the essential features of this disorder are the presence of characteristic psychotic symptoms during the active phase of the illness and a functioning below the highest level previously achieved. Also both children and adults fail to achieve the expected level of social development. The difficulties persist for at least six months although this period may induce the person experiencing prodromal or residual symptoms rather than manifest psychosis. As an example, prior to the manifest onset of the psychosis, as well as during many stages of its course, many patients present a disturbance of attention. In quite a large number of patients there is inability to keep attention fixed for any length of time and they may hear what is said to them, but they do not register the meaning of the words (Arieti 1974).

At some phase of the illness schizophrenia always involves delusions, hallucinations or certain characteristic disturbances in affect and the form of thought. A diagnosis of schizophrenia is made when it cannot be established that an organic factor initiated and maintained the disturbances. Delusions and hallucinations involving the five senses are apparent, the patient's affect is disturbed and their global behaviour is affected. The patient withdraws from social contact and loses interest in other people, his or her actions may appear bizarre or inexplicable and the patient may display behavioural abnormalities of catatonia, muteness or stupour. In the chronic stage the delusions and hallucinations may disappear; this may involve a temporary or a complete recovery, but the more acute episodes the patient experiences, the more likely there is to be residual damage. The patient may become apathetic, and lose determination and interest in others. This will mean the patient talking less so that an ability to form long-lasting relationships is reduced in schizophrenia.

It is the apathy and emotional blunting which makes schizophrenia the terrible illness it is, according to Kendell (1993), and it is the permanent changes in the personality which handicap the subject in every sphere – the ability to get and keep a job, to be an effective husband, wife or parent, or to achieve or fully enjoy anything. The symptoms can be described as solitariness, impaired empathy and emotional detachment, increased sensitivity, suspiciousness and unusual or odd styles of communicating (Wolff and Cull 1986). Most of these patients will have recurrent psychotic episodes and suffer depression. Infact, some 10 per cent of schizophrenic patients die by suicide, usually in the early years of their illness (Miles 1977). Individuals with schizophrenia also frequently have difficulties with 'thought content' and 'thought form'.

Patients

Disturbances of thought content involve delusions that are often multiple, fragmented or bizarre. More detail of delusions has already been given under the subheading 'Disorders of thinking' earlier in this chapter.

If there is disturbance in the form of thought it is called 'formal thought disorder'. An example is loosening of associations, in which ideas shift from one subject to another, completely unrelated or only obliquely related to the subject. Statements that lack a meaningful relationship may be juxtaposed, or the person may shift idiosyncratically from one frame of reference to another. When loosening of association is severe, a person may become incoherent; that is, his or her speech may become incomprehensible due to consecutive utterances being only loosely related to each other. There might also be poverty in content of speech, in which although the speech is adequate in amount it conveys little information because it is vague, abstract, concrete, repetitive or stereotyped. Less common disturbances include neologisms, perseveration, clanging and blocking.

Classification of schizophrenia

Symptoms listed by DMS-IV are divided into two categories, positive and negative. The positive symptoms are those where they reflect an excess or distortion of normal functions, whereas the negative symptoms are those behaviours that reflect a diminution or loss of normal functions. The positive symptoms include distortions or exaggerations of inferential thinking (delusions), perception (hallucinations), language and communication (disorganised speech), and behavioural monitoring (grossly disorganised or catatonic behaviour). Negative symptoms include restrictions in intensity of emotional expression (affective flattening), in fluency and productivity of thought and speech (alogia), and the initiation of goal-directed behaviour (avolition).

ICD-10 states that the schizophrenic disorders are characterised in general by fundamental and characteristic distortions of thinking and perception, and by inappropriate or blunted affect.

As a group, psychoses include disorders in which there is a fundamental disturbance of personality, characteristic distortion of thinking, often a sense of being controlled by alien forces, delusions which may be bizarre, disturbed perception, abnormal affect out of keeping with the real situation, and autism. Nevertheless, clear consciousness and intellectual capacity are usually maintained. The disturbance of personality involves its most basic functions those that give the normal person their feeling of individuality, uniqueness and self-direction. The most intimate thoughts, feelings and acts that are often felt to be shared by others and explanatory delusions may develop. Perception is frequently disturbed, as is thinking, which becomes vague, elliptical and obscure, and its expression in speech sometimes incomprehensible. Breaks and interpolations in the flow of consecutive thought are frequent and the patient may think that his thoughts are being withdrawn by some outside agency. Mood may be shallow, capricious and incongruous and catatonia may be present, diagnosis of 'schizophrenia' is not made unless there is, or has been evident during the same illness, characteristic disturbance of thought, perception, mood, conduct or personality – see table below.

Table 3.1 DSM-IV (1994)
Schizophrenia
Schizophreniform Disorder
Schizoaffective Disorder
Delusional Disorder
Brief Psychotic Disorder
Shared Psychotic Disorder
Psychotic Disorder Due to a General Medical Condition
Substance-Induced Psychotic Disorder
Psychotic Disorder Not Otherwise Specified

Table 3.2 ICD-10 (1992) F20–F29
Schizophrenia
Schizotypal disorder
Persistent delusional disorder
Acute and transient psychotic disorders
Induced delusional disorder
Schizoaffective disorders
Other nonorganic psychotic disorders
Unspecified nonorganic psychosis

Incidence of schizophrenia

In most industrial countries in which population surveys have been carried out the lifetime risk of schizophrenia is about 1 per cent and the incidence in the order of 15 new cases per 100,000 population per annum (Kendell 1993). DSM-IV states that the lifetime prevalence of schizophrenia is usually estimated to be between 0.5 per cent and 1 per cent, but because schizophrenia tends to be chronic, incidence rates are lower than prevalence rates and are estimated to be approximately 1 per 10,000 per year.

Kaplan and Saddock (1988) report that rates for the age group 15 years and over range from 0.3 to 1.20 per 1000 population, and that pooled studies show an incidence of approximately 1 per 1000 population. Approximately 200,000 new cases are diagnosed each year in the USA, with about 2 million worldwide. There is a lifetime prevalence of about 1 per cent; that is about 2 million Americans suffer from schizophrenia, approximately 0.025 per cent to 0.05 per cent of the total population is treated for schizophrenia in any one year; two-thirds of these patients require hospitalisation.

Studies have found that statistics showed higher expectations of schizophrenia among four peoples – the Tamils of southern India and Sri Lanka, the people of northwest Croatia, Roman Catholics in Canada, and the southern Irish – but reasons for these findings are uncertain. Studies also suggest that people who migrate are more susceptible to schizophrenia (Murphy 1968). There are differences in the symptomatology across cultures, although apparently not enough to make schizophrenic illness unrecognisable. Paranoid illnesses are seen more frequently in urban populations; religious delusions in Christian populations, and less frequently in Buddhists or Hindi populations; catatonic symptoms less frequently in Euro-American; and delusions of grandeur are most frequent in rural populations and in the Japanese. This information is based on anecdotal and impressionistic studies from the work of 40 psychiatrists in 27 countries (Murphy et al. 1963).

The onset of schizophrenia can occur in people from 7 to 70 years old, but the most usual onset time is early adolescence or early adult life and it can develop gradually over months or years or the onset can be acute. Before the age of 35 years, males are affected more than females; after this age the reverse is true and, due to the late onset of the condition, women are more likely to be married at their initial hospitalisation (Murray 1986).

Aetiology of schizophrenia

The aetiology of schizophrenia is not known, but schizophrenia is thought to be a heterogeneous disorder (Kaplan and Sadock 1988).

Genetic inheritance is considered a convincing predisposing factor associated with the risk of developing schizophrenia. Genetic studies have found that the lifetime expectancy of developing schizophrenia in relatives of schizophrenics is 8–16 per cent, that genetic factors do influence the risk of developing schizophrenia and that if environmental factors have a part to play it is in those patients who are already generally at risk (Rose 1994).

First degree biological relatives with schizophrenia have a risk for schizophrenia that is about 10 times greater than that of the general population (DSM-IV).

Stressful life events are thought possibly to precipitate schizophrenia in those already predisposed to the condition, and social and family circumstances may maintain an illness by maintaining stress or depriving a patient of opportunities for help. Other studies identify stressors including family conflicts, physical illness and major loss or change (Rose 1994). Studies have established the fact that many schizophrenic individuals come from disturbed families, and a patient who lives with a family with high levels of tension is more likely to relapse than a patient whose family is more tolerant. Systematic studies have demonstrated that the underprivileged social status of schizophrenics is due to the gravitation down the social scale. This may follow the onset of symptoms or it may be a result of the personality disorder already present in many of those who will develop a schizophrenic illness (Roth and Kroll 1986).

Biochemical approaches to schizophrenia have been given consideration, one theory being that schizophrenia results from an imbalance of central neurotransmitters in the brain, which may be caused by a variety of influences. This theory is supported by the observation that dopamine receptors are blocked by drugs which control schizophrenic symptoms, but as yet there is no evidence that this is the underlying malfunction in schizophrenia (Rose 1994). It is known that there are no consistent neurological abnormalities in this condition although some schizophrenic patients have enlarged cerebral ventricles, some have abnormal EEGs and others have abnormal sensory neurological signs.

Course and prognosis of schizophrenia

The onset of schizophrenia is usually in adolescence and there may be an identified precipitating factor. The course is of exacerbations and relative remissions, with deterioration commonly progressing for about five years, after which most patients then reach a plateau (Kaplan and Saddock 1988).

The prognosis of schizophrenia varies according to the style of onset. The more acute the onset, the better the prognosis for recovery. If a life event has triggered true breakdown the chances are more favourable towards recovery. The younger the patient is at the onset the worse his prognosis; patients who break down in childhood or early puberty seldom recover completely. Married schizophrenics have better prognosis than single, divorced or widowed patients. Those patients who relate well to people in their environments and who are capable of emotional warmth and natural reactions have a good chance for reintegration (Kaplan and Saddock 1985).

Delusional disorder (DSM-IV 1994), persistent delusional disorders (ICD-10 1992)

The psychopathology in delusional disorders is different from schizophrenia in that delusions are present in the absence (or near absence) of hallucinations and thought disorder.

Delusional (paranoid) disorders are otherwise referred to as paranoid states; the term paranoid refers to a morbid distortion of beliefs or attitudes concerning relationships between one's self and others and there should be an absence of schizophrenic mood.

Social, marital or work problems can result from the delusional beliefs and ideas of reference (e.g. that random events are of special significance) that are common in people with this disorder (DSM-IV).

Classification of delusional disorders

DSM-IV classifies delusional disorders into seven subtypes and ICD-10 has three subgroups under the heading of persistent delusional disorders (Tables 3.3 and 3.4).

Table 3.3 DSM-IV (1994)
Erotomania Type
Grandiose Type
Jealous Type
Persecutory Type
Somatic Type
Mixed Type
Unspecified Type

Table 3.4 ICD-10 (1992) F22.0, F22.8 and F22.9
Delusional disorder
Other persistent delusional disorders
Persistent delusional disorder, unspecified

ICD-10 refers to delusional disorders as a variety of disorders in which longstanding delusions constitute the only, or the most conspicuous, clinical characteristic and which cannot be classified as organic, schizophrenic or affective. They are thought to be heterogeneous, and have an uncertain relationship with schizophrenia.

DSM-IV describes delusional disorder as having the presence of one or more non-bizarre (i.e. plausible, for example situations that can conceivably occur in real life) delusions that persist for at least one month.

Assessment towards diagnosis may be difficult; in some cases the delusions are obvious while in others the symptoms may be difficult to elicit. If the patient is suspicious or angry they may offer little speech, or if more at ease might talk fluently and convincingly about other things or may even deny delusional beliefs and ideas (Gelder *et al.* 1986). The major issue in treatment is whether the patient is likely to behave dangerously as a result of their delusions, which necessitates careful study of the patient's personality, delusions and associated hallucinations.

Incidence of delusional disorder (paranoid states)

Delusional disorder or paranoid states are considered to be relatively uncommon. It is estimated that within a population the prevalence of the disorder is around 0.03 per cent which, due to the late onset of this disorder, suggests a lifetime morbidity risk of between 0.05 per cent and 0.1 per cent (DMS-IV 1994). Additionally it must considered that there may be an under-reporting of delusional disorders since these patients rarely seek help unless forced to do so by their family or the courts. Kaplan and Sadock (1988) go on to report that the mean age of onset is about 40 years, but the age range is from 25 to the 90s and that slightly more women than men are sufferers. David (1997) reports that, as a group, the patients are more often male (70%) and have a relatively late onset.

Aetiology of delusional disorders (paranoia)

Once again the cause for this disorder is not known. There is apparently no conclusive evidence to indicate that either hereditary factors or neuropathological abnormalities cause paranoid disorders, but it is thought that psychological factors are important in the development of this disorder. Predisposing factors towards paranoid disorders are immigration and emigration, deafness, other severe stresses and low socio-economic status.

The psychoses in childhood

Mental disorders and schizophrenia are rare in children, but by the age of 17 these conditions are more frequently encountered (Hill 1997). In his chapter 'Psychiatric Disorders in Childhood', Hoare (1998) explains that the general term 'childhood psychosis' was previously a combined heading which has now been divided into childhood autism (pervasive developmental disorder), schizophrenia and related syndromes. As autistic children do not experience hallucinations or delusions, or other characteristics of psychosis, and have had the abnormality from early infancy it was thought advisable to separate these disorders from other psychotic conditions. Hoare states that schizophrenia in childhood is rare and that there is good evidence of a genetic component; where this does occur, approximately 10 per cent of relatives have the disease.

Psychoses in childhood include the disintegrative psychoses and a group of poorly understood conditions that are also known as childhood psychoses. Schizophrenia and manic-depressive disorders are occasionally seen in older children.

The most common form of 'childhood psychosis' is infantile autism, and even this is a rare disorder. Wing and Gould (1979) state that the approximate ratio of boys to girls is 3 to 1 with approximately 70 per cent to 80 per cent of these also suffering from general mental retardation.

Prognosis is poor; only one in six children have a reasonably satisfactory work and social adjustment in adolescence and over 50 per cent may, in adult life, need long-term residential care. DSM-III-R (1987) stated that the prevalence of developmental disorder (autistic disorder and pervasive developmental disorder not otherwise specified) has been estimated at 1–15 children in every 10,000.

The ICD-9 (1975) definition of psychoses with origin specific to childhood states that this category should only be used for psychoses which begin before puberty and that adult-type psychoses such as schizophrenia and manic-depressive psychoses when occurring in childhood should be coded elsewhere under the appropriate heading.

There are thought to be a wide range of pre-, peri- and post-natal conditions causing brain dysfunction and pervasive developmental disorders.

Childhood disintegrative disorder is a disorder related to conditions where there have been two years of normal early development followed by a marked regression with loss of language, social and other skills with the qualitatively abnormal functioning resembling autism.

Adult-type schizophrenia, like manic-depressive psychosis, can start around puberty and occurs very rarely in younger children. The overall picture, cause and outcome for children are similar to that of adult psychosis.

Schizoid disorder of childhood is classified as a pervasive disorder in ICD-10 as it resembles those features of autism. Schizoid children usually come to medical attention during their school years due to educational failure and poor social relationships with others. They are withdrawn, aloof, solitary and unable to make normal emotional contact with others, and their lack of interest, motivation and competitiveness leads to school failure in often highly intelligent children. Some of these children are quiet, secretive and silent at school. Others are superficially communicative but express themselves oddly and metaphorically (Wolff 1988).

Definition of childhood psychoses

Autism

Recent work and literature suggests that early infantile autism is in a sense a man-made syndrome, that it is a useful shorthand communication of a clinical picture between mental health professionals or educationalists but not a syndrome having a unitary cause or even a unitary symptomatology (Tanguay 1984). Autism is a descriptive rather than an aetiological diagnosis (Rutter and Lord 1987) marked by social withdrawal, a desire for sameness and communicative impairment. This latter is evident in both verbal and non-verbal development. Although in the past these children have been described as uncommunicative there is an increasing body of literature supporting the theory that they use what appear to be abnormal or bizarre behaviours in a communicative way (e.g. Wetherby 1986; Prizant and Rydell 1984). In the DSM-III-R (1987) 'pervasive developmental difficulties', symptoms range from classically autistic to less and less 'autistic' until arriving at mentally handicapped with no autistic features or those children who have serious disorders of communication and little disturbance relating to others. The DSM-III-R definition of pervasive development disorders is 'the impairment in the development of reciprocal social interaction, in the development of verbal and non-verbal communication skills and in imaginative activity. Often there is a restricted repertoire of activities and interests, which are frequently stereotyped and repetitive.' It is the language/ communication behaviours seen in autistic children that most often first lead to referral. Intellectual skills, comprehension of meaning of language and the production of speech, posture and movements, patterns of eating, drinking or sleeping and responses to sensory input are likely to be affected. Impairment in communication includes verbal and non-verbal skills; language may be absent, immature, delayed or echolalic or idiosyncratic. The melody of speech may be abnormal, monotonous or with inappropriate inflexions, particularly at the ends of phrases.

Childhood schizophrenia

Tanguay (1984) states that 'childhood schizophrenia' does exist, not only in the 'late-onset childhood psychosis' but in the three symptoms described by Cantor (1984): the 'disorganised type'; the 'undifferentiated type' which is the most common type; and finally the 'paranoid type', in which there are delusions of either persecutory or grandiose types or both. In this last type, by the time the child reaches the seventh or eighth year, although the child has previously been verbal and asked questions, they will typically no longer value others enough to ask questions and will invent their own answers based on faulty information and this, according to Cantor, is the beginning of true paranoia.

Cantor (1984) is of the opinion that all schizophrenic disorders are thought disorders and the normal 3-year-old child is aware of 'what goes with what', whereas the schizophrenic child appears to be completely unable to note context; in other words, all incoming information is learned and stored but is devoid of context. The children will learn but the pace at which they learn is modified by their tendency to perseverate, fragment, ignore context and be oppositional. Of course thought disorder will be reflected in disordered language, and Cantor goes on to suggest that there are two extremes in communication styles: children with impoverished speech may talk very little sense, and children with marked pressure of speech find themselves talking a lot with little understood by the listener. Their speech styles include neologisms and word approximations; that is, making up new words and articulating near approximations to the real word. Word salad, echolalia and unintelligible speech, including whilst talking to him or herself, are common. Finally, the schizophrenic child often speaks so softly that they are difficult to hear but are still able on occasions to produce a good and powerful voice.

Assessments of psychoses

Assessing acute schizophrenia poses two particular problems, according to Rose (1994). First, it is often associated with total lack of insight on the part of the sufferer leading to a reluctance to seek help and a frequent lack of subsequent co-operation; second, it can be associated with alarming and sometimes life-threatening consequences including gross self neglect, suicide, assault and self-mutilation, making assessment very difficult.

Assessment of chronic schizophrenia includes a detailed history of the symptoms, the family, personal and past medical history, past psychiatric history and personality.

Psychological tests can be used to indicate, confirm or rule out a diagnosis of schizophrenia. A diagnosis is supported if tests reflect unusual or bizarre perceptual and conceptual processes. Tests that might be used, for example, are the Rorschach (1942), Thematic Apperception Tests (TAT) (Murray 1943) and the Wechsler Adult Intelligence Scale (WAIS) (Wechsler 1981). Self-report inventories such as the Minnesota Multiphasic Personality Inventory (MMPI)

(Hathaway and McKinley 1970) can also be helpful. (These tests are discussed in Chapters 7, 8 and 9) Some psychiatrists are of the opinion that such tests seldom add anything towards diagnosis. The Rorschach and the TAT are used to examine thought processes, and the Grid Test of Schizophrenic Thought Disorder (GTSTD) is a diagnostic instrument designed to test whether a patient is thought disordered or not (Bannister and Fransella 1966, 1967) and also add some useful information. Careful neuropsychological testing reveals many cognitive deficits (Tamlyn *et al.* 1992), although these abnormalities have to take into account factors such as poor motivation and the effects of antipsychotic drug treatment (Gelder *et al.* 1996). Psychometric assessments may add little to the diagnosis but quantitative assessments of specific abnormalities of behaviour are useful for planning and evaluating social relationships (Gelder *et al.* 1986)

Recently a number of imaging techniques have become available which allow visualisation of the intact human brain, and an assessment of both its structure and its functional activities. These include:

1. Magnetic resonance imaging (MRI)

2. Positron emission tomography (PET)

3. Single photon emission computed tomography (SPECT)

and electrocephalographic mapping. The MRI has confirmed earlier CT scan data revealing increase in size of the cerebral ventricles of some schizophrenics. PET scan findings show a reduction in the metabolic activity of the limbic system in some schizophrenic patients and measurement of blood flow. PET can measure three types of abnormality, which appears to correspond to different forms of the illness (Silverstone and Turner 1995).

Communication speech and language disorders associated with the psychoses

It is accepted that all aspects of communication and speech can be affected in those suffering from psychotic disorders. Changes in speech behaviour can have a profound influence on some or all aspects of communication, both verbal and non-verbal. The changes can be varied, with mutism as one extreme, whereas the other extreme involves the overproductive, excitable speech of the manic patient. Additionally, incongruency between verbal and non-verbal channels has been noted in clinical descriptions of schizophrenia.

Furthermore, the quantity and quality of personal interaction can suffer, perhaps due in part to the perceptual changes commonly caused by the illness. These can reduce and distort visual and listening skills.

Communication and speech difficulties can be divided artificially into three possible areas for consideration: first, the communication and speech pathology evident prior to the onset of the illness and possibly maintained and exacerbated by the psychosis; second, communication and language disruptions caused predominantly by the psychosis; and finally additional problems resulting from drug and physical treatments and organic conditions.

Communication and speech problems that developed prior to the onset of the psychotic illness can be present for any number of reasons: for instance, as a result of residual developmental speech problems when they may be represented by expressive language problems; vocal disorders or vocal misuse (including faulty phonation); language and articulation disorders caused by organic conditions which are not associated with psychosis; sensory impairment such as deafness; dysfluency/stuttering; and psychogenic communication and speech difficulties. If the onset of the psychosis was in adolescence, the development of the symptoms might well influence communication breakdown by gradual social withdrawal and isolation, caused by the developing psychosis, even before the realisation and eventual diagnosis of the psychosis. These factors play an important part in inhibiting the continuing development of adult language. Restricted life experiences will restrict language use; if, for instance, a person is damaged enough to be unable to live a full adult life it is possible that adult language is unlikely to continue to develop normally.

Those patients whose primary problem is that of speech and communication difficulties may well have contact with a speech and language therapist within a number of different types of therapeutic encounter – on an individual basis to work predominantly on the speech and language pathology, and in group work to concentrate on communication difficulties. The need or motivation to communicate is of primary importance and so often individual speech therapy may wait until patient and therapist have established a good communication relationship through group work or individual sessions, when little emphasis will be put on clarity of speech. As happens in many therapeutic settings, the very fact that a speech and language therapist is present tends to produce spontaneously heightened effort to be understood.

Arieti (1974) states that language and its relations with thought processes are so characteristic in schizophrenia as to lead in typical cases to a prompt diagnosis, and in the most pronounced cases schizophrenic language appears obscure or utterly incomprehensible. In mild cases of schizophrenia, patients may show very little, if any, change in the form of their speech, whereas the very ill may show every variety of speech and language abnormality.

Voice may demonstrate changes in pitch, volume and quality, and vocalisation can be influenced by bizarre behaviour, such as vocalising on inspiration rather than expiration, production of nasalised speech, and sub-vocal speech (inducing voice and superimposing appropriate inflections on the voice without articulation or normal vocal resonance). This latter condition is fairly rare and there are a number of theories as to its provenance. One such theory is that the patient is sub-vocalising their auditory hallucinations and/or their replies. Breathiness and tension, irregular volume and uncontrolled pitch may also be features. Abnormal language content and style are very much a part of psychoses and may present as rigid, stilted or unusual. Language articulation may be affected by sub-vocalisation and by tardive dyskinesia. The rhythm, delivery and fluency of speech, and its speed, smoothness and musical quality, may also be abnormal.

Thought disorder

It is probably appropriate here to consider thought disorder in more detail as this is the term that is used to describe abnormality of the form rather than the content of speech and is particularly relevant in schizophrenia.

Thought disorder is a characteristic feature of schizophrenia, but Kendell (1993) believes the term to be unsatisfactory, as traditionally it had been applied to a variety of ill-defined abnormalities of the subject's speech and writing which are assumed to be secondary to a more fundamental disturbance of thinking. Kendell goes on to draw attention to the fact that it is sometimes erroneously thought that the semantic content rather than the syntactic structure of speech remains intact until a late stage. However, some detailed linguistic analysis suggests that the syntactic structure of schizophrenics' speech differs from that of both manics and normal controls (Morice and Ingram 1982). Kendell (1993) debates the possible benefits of modern linguistic analysis, but he suggests that future research is more likely to illuminate the fundamental nature of thought disorder if it is based on linguistic concepts like cohesion, lexical density and dysfluency rather than on ancient clinical metaphors like derailment. It has been suggested that the cause of the listener's difficulty in understanding the schizophrenic's speech is brought about by the patient's failure to provide normal cohesive links between one sentence and the next. The problem is often compounded by the patient's preoccupation with abstruse themes and their failure to appreciate their listener's difficulties. The recognition of these factors is music to the speech and language the therapist's ears.

Schizophrenic speech

The exact nature of "Schizophrenic speech" is difficult to define. There are differences reflecting different phases of the illness. Schizophrenic speech may be more difficult to understand in the acutely ill patient as the patient is often excited and preoccupied with odd themes and delusional ideas. Speech is considered more normal in the chronic stage but overall the total quantity of speech is reduced. Terms are used in different ways in the literature. Andreason (1979) attempted to define thought disorder by suggesting that it should be re-titled 'disorders of thought, language and communication' as it includes all of these difficulties. Harrow and Quinlan (1985) draw attention to the fact that their observations lead them to believe that bizarre idiosyncratic verbalisations and thinking are not exclusive to schizophrenia and that it is also common in acute manic patients and occasionally in other acute psychotic patients too, so that it is difficult to refer to 'schzophrenic speech'.

Management and treatment of the psychoses

Autism

The speech and language therapist may see pre-school autistic children, but diagnosis is often delayed or referral for specialist language therapy not made. Frequently it is the therapists working within special units or schools who see these children. Differential diagnosis is difficult and should be a team decision; suggestions have been made that empirical measures of communicative behaviour may be of value in the diagnostic process (Wetherby 1986). Rutter and Lord (1987) suggest that 'precise categorisation is less important than careful assessment of a child's strengths and weakness and the identification of factors most likely to enhance learning and development.'

Treatment may be medical, educational and/or family based, to help parents understand and develop realistic expectations. Speech and language therapy provision should be considered for each child. In the past, most intervention has been largely based on operant conditioning theory, providing structure via the use of reinforcement, with varying degrees of success (Baltaxe and Simmons 1981), and Rutter (1985) offers an excellent introduction to the use of behavioural and educational approaches. Recently there has been a move towards alternative approaches, partly due to an increased interest in psycholinguistics, which has resulted in attempts to use signing and symbols (e.g. Kiernan 1983), computer programs and non-verbal linguistic systems (e.g. Lovaas 1968).

Research into the pragmatic aspects of communicative failure in autism has led to suggestions of language intervention programmes that base on communicative intentions and that deviate from the normal developmental models on the basis of evidence that there is a pattern of autistic development. Such programmes stress the need to consider the social context and to use pragmatic rewards if operant methods are followed (Wetherby 1986).

Other psychoses

Generally, aetiological factors need to be taken into consideration when planning treatment and thinking in terms of future prevention of the illness. Treatment methods might also differ according to whether the illness is acute or chronic; if acute, the aims are to treat the illness as rapidly as possible and to provide support and counselling to the patient and their relations. Hospital admission is usually indicated, particularly if behaviour is severely disturbed. If behaviour is less disturbed, the patient may be managed at home, provided conditions there are satisfactory for support and rehabilitation.

Rose (1994) suggests that there should be two aims of management: first, to return the patient to the best level of functioning; and second, to prevent the recurrence of the acute illness. Management of acute schizophrenia aims to effectively treat the illness as safely as possible, taking account of any risk factors present as well as the needs of the relatives. Treatment is usually by a combination of intensive care and support together with medication.

Therefore management of both acute and chronic patients needs to be considered. The possibility of the recurrence of the illness needs to be taken into account as well as considering the best way to rehabilitate the patient to the best level of functioning. The aims of rehabilitation will vary according to individual needs and will usually need to be on a long-term basis. Rehabilitation will aim to cover both social and psychological aspects of the patient's disabilities but will also include maintenance treatment for medication if necessary. There is still some controversy as to whether all schizophrenic patients should receive maintenance therapy. Studies find that patients with a poor prognosis should receive maintenance therapy as they tend to relapse despite receiving drugs, whilst those with a good prognosis tend not to relapse even without drugs.

Treatment with drugs

The anti-psychotic drugs that are effective in the treatment of schizophrenia are grouped in three ways: according to their chemical configuration; by their pharmacological specificity; and by their spectrum of clinical actions. The neuroleptic drugs, otherwise known as antipsychotic agents or the major tranquillisers, are used in both schizophrenia and mania. All neuroleptic drugs block dopamine receptors in the brain; this is responsible for their tendency to produce extrapyramidal movement disorders as side-effects. There are three groups of antipsychotic drugs: phenothiazines, thioxanthenes and butyrophenones. Chlorpromazine, one of the phenothiazines, is popular and may be prescribed initially during the acute phase of the illness. It acts as a sedative within hours, although its effect on the psychotic symptoms usually takes about three weeks and has a full effect in about six to twelve weeks. These drugs produce sedation, and reduce anxiety; suppress spontaneous movement and complex behaviour; but preserve intellectual functioning so that incoherent thinking and thought disorder tend to clear, leading to more intelligible language production, but less spontaneity and more circumscription in speech (Silverstone and Turner 1995). The introduction of long-acting depot preparations given by intramuscular injection at intervals of 1–4 weeks helps these difficulties. Only a proportion of patients respond to treatment with standard anti-psychotic drugs; thus there is no answer as to how long to go on treating acute episodes of schizophrenia, but if, following the first attack, the patient relapses after medication has been stopped, then it is likely that he/she is suffering from a chronic form of the condition and will require continuous medication for years or for life.

Silverstone and Turner also inform us that no one drug stands out from the rest in terms of efficacy providing the drug is taken. If the patient stops taking medication because they feel well or dislike the side-effects, the introduction of a long-acting depot preparation given by intramuscular injection at intervals of 1–4 weeks can be appropriate.

Deconate (Modocate), flupenthixol deconate (Depixol) and haloperidol deconate (Halodol deconate) are preparations used and those patients who fail on these drugs might well be prescribed clozapine (Silverstone and Turner 1995).

Side-effects from the neuroleptics are of three types of extrapyramidal symptoms – Parkinsonism, dystonia and akathisia – and these symptoms can all usually be relieved by anti-Parkinsonian agents. The effects of Parkinsonism on speech are that it produces jerky, dysrhythmic phonation, poor articulation, monotonous intonation, and a soft voice. Other side-effects may also be distressing, including blurring of vision, producing difficulty in reading, and decreased salivation which leads to a dry mouth and difficulty in articulation, but it is important to note that not all patients on neuroleptic drugs develop side-effects.

Tardive dyskinesia is produced by a prolonged high-dosage neuroleptic medication and is characterised by slow, irregular movements in the region of the mouth, such as grimacing, smacking of lips and protrusion of the tongue. It also results in poor articulation of speech, but produces loud phonation and hyperkinetic dysarthria. Dysarthria has been reported as being similar to a stutter but is really of basal ganglion origin and scanning speech has been noted in some patients recovering from toxic doses of drugs. Stopping the medication does not necessarily lead to the disappearance of the dyskinesia and may sometimes make it worse.

Psychological treatments

There is a divergence of psychiatric opinion as to whether psychotherapy in any or all of its many forms actually offers effective treatment to this group of patients. It is even considered by some psychiatrists as being harmful, the pressure of treatment creating enough stress to cause remission of the illness. Others think that with careful monitoring and sensitive handling benefits result and progress can be achieved, even if at a slow and limited pace. In other cases considerable progress can be made and patients themselves appreciate the opportunity to join in and be accepted in the therapeutic milieu.

Most patients benefit from the combined use of antipsychotic medication and psychosocial treatment. Individual psychotherapy can provide a positive treatment relationship and thera-peutic alliance. Supportive psychotherapy is the type most often used; establishing the therapeutic relationship is often very difficult as the schizophrenic patient is desperately lonely, yet defends against closeness (Kaplan and Saddock 1988). Group therapy can work well focusing on real-life plans, problems, and relationships, and the groups can be behaviourally orientated, psychodynamically or insight orientated, or supportive. Overall group therapy helps to reduce social isolation, increasing a sense of cohesiveness, and improving reality testing (Kaplan and Saddock 1988).

MILIEU THERAPY

Milieu therapy, although regarded as inconclusively researched as to its effectiveness, together with the use of modern psychotropic drugs can often deepen insight, or provide new social patterns, particularly for the patient in hospital care. Milieu therapy (the therapeutic effects from the environment in which the patient is living) may be added to by group meetings aiming to increase self-reliance, to share responsibility for treatment, and to help other patients. This can include a wide range of rehabilitation programmes to help domestic and social skills towards living a more independent life (see Chapter 24).

PSYCHOANALYTIC (DYNAMIC) THERAPY

Psychoanalytic (dynamic) therapy is aimed at effecting a change in personality structure or character and so does more than just reduce symptoms. Psychotherapy is thought by an increasing number of psychiatrists to be beneficial, although it has been questioned in cases of active psychoses. The therapeutic relationship needs to be flexible, direct, sincere and respecting of privacy. The aim is to convey a need to understand the patient, however disturbed, hostile or bizarre in behaviour. Group therapy combined with drug treatment has been found to produce better results than drug treatment alone. Positive results are more likely when treatment focuses on real-life plans, problems and relationships, on social and work roles and interaction, or when in co-operation with drug therapy and discussion of its side-effects and on recreational or work activities (Kaplan and Sadock 1988). This type of therapy encompasses rehabilitation, communication, support, problem solving and sharing and is an ideal setting for a speech and language therapist to share skills with nursing staff and/or with other professional staff such as psychologists, social workers and psychiatrists.

BEHAVIOUR THERAPY

Behaviour therapy is also successful as a method of reducing frequency of bizarre, disturbing and deviant behaviour by increasing adaptive and normal behaviour; direct work on reinforcing appropriate behaviour and training in social skills can offer remedial support. It is known that individuals with a diagnosis of schizophrenia are deficient in a number of components of social skills. Their social behaviours exhibit greater levels of anxiety and less skill than non-sufferers and they are less efficient in decoding non-verbal cues and in their judgement of appropriateness of social behaviour, but they appear to be aware of their deficient social behaviour (Monti and Fingeret 1987). Trower, Bryant and Argyle (1978) base the need for treatment on the patient's social inadequacy as this tends to show a particular style of behaviour. The patient will probably appear rather cold, unassertive and unrewarding to others, will show little expressive variation in face, voice and posture, will look rather infrequently at the other person, will make little effort to produce a spontaneous and interesting flow of speech, and will take little part in the management of conversations. Once again a speech and language therapist has skills and expertise to offer here, particularly if in co-operation with a psychologist, as it appears that the problem is as much of communication as overall social deficiencies.

FAMILY THERAPY

Family therapy can play an important role as the patient's illness is usually accompanied by serious family problems. This treatment can be extended from the hospital and into the community.

PERSONAL CONSTRUCT PSYCHOTHERAPY

The personal construct approach to treatment, as already explained, can be particularly useful for assessing patients with schizophrenia as well as offering an increasingly useful means of treatment. Van den Bergh, De Boeck and Claeys (1986) give details of work and research in this area and are also optimistic that personal construct psychotherapy with schizophrenic patients will continue to develop and become more widely used. Bannister and Fransella (1966) found that schizophrenic patients differed from normal people in that they have low correlations between different constructs, and Bannister (1962) theorised that, as a result of being repeatedly invalidated in their attempts to develop a meaningful personal construct system, schizophrenic individuals may end up with a very loose construct system. If true, this theory would provide a mechanism whereby abnormal family interaction such as 'double-bind' communication might, by weakening a child's construct system, eventually lead to thought disorder (Murray 1986). It is known that schizophrenic patients respond to personal construct psychotherapy (Button 1986).

Communication and language disruption or disorders that are predominantly caused by the psychoses have been discussed throughout this chapter, and experience proves that with an understanding and sensitive approach improvements can be made. The speech and language therapist's appreciation and reinforcement of co-operation, effort and motivation help to maintain progress and can, in some cases, be enough alone to produce improvement. Certainly the therapist's expectation of clear, intelligible speech will be necessary and might even be part of the contract for treatment. Further details on treatment techniques are discussed more fully in Chapter 27.

References

Andreason, N.C. (1979) Thought, language and communication disorders. *Archives of General Psychiatry 36*, 1315–1325.

Arieti, S. (1974) *Interpretation of Schizophrenia* (second edition). London: Crosby Lockwood Staple.

Baltaxe, C.A.M. and Simmons, J.Q. (1981) Disorders of language in childhood psychoses: current concepts and approaches. In J.K. Darby (ed) *Speech Evaluation in Psychiatry.* New York: Grune and Stratton. pp.285–328.

Bannister, D. (1962) The nature and management of thought disorder. *Journal of Mental Science 108,* 825–842.

Bannister, D. and Fransella, F. (1966) A grid test of schizophrenic thought disorder. *British Journal of Social Clinical Psychology 5,* 95–102.

Bannister, D. and Fransella, F. (1967) *A Grid Test of Schizophrenic Thought Disorder. A Standard Clinical Test.* Barnstaple, Devon: Psychological Test Publications.

Bateman, A. (1996) Defence Mechanisms. In C. Cordess and M. Cox (eds) *Forensic Psychotherapy: Crime, Psychodynamics and the Offender Patient.* London: Jessica Kingsley Publishers. pp.41–51.

Blakemore, C. (1988) *Madness* (Programme 6), The Mind Machine, BBC2, UK, 18 October.

Button, E. (1986) *Personal Construct Theory and Mental Health.* London: Croom Helm.

Cantor, S. (1984) *The Schizophrenic Child.* Milton Keynes: Open University Press.

David, A.S. (1997) Atypical psychosis. In R. Murray, P. Hill and P. McGuffin (eds) *Essentials in Postgraduate Psychiatry* (third edition). Cambridge: Cambridge University Press. pp.352–361.

DHSS Mental Health Statistics for England (1986) *Mental Illness Hospitals and Units in England: Diagnostic Data. Booklet 12.* A Publication of the Government's Statistical Service.

DSM-III-R (1987) *Diagnostic and Statistical Manual of Mental Disorders* (third edition, revised). Washington DC: American Psychiatric Association.

DSM-IV (1994) *Diagnostic and Statistical Manual of Mental Disorders* (fourth edition). Washington DC: American Psychiatric Association.

Freeman, H. (1988) The long term treatment of schizophrenia with neuroleptic drugs. In P. Hall and P. Stonier (eds) *Perspectives in Psychiatry.* Chichester: Wiley. pp.167–176.

Freud, A. (1936) *The Ego and the Mechanisms of Defence.* London: Hogarth Press. (1958) Adolescence 1: adolescence in the psychoanalytic theory. In A. Freud (ed) *The Psychoanalytic Study of the Child.* New York: International University Press.

Fulford, K.W.M. (1994) Diagnosis classification and phenomenology of mental illness. In N. Rose (ed) *Essential Psychiatry* (second edition). Oxford: Blackwell Scientific Publications. pp.3–16.

Gelder, M., Gath, D. and Mayou, R. (1986) *Oxford Textbook of Psychiatry.* Oxford: Oxford University Press.

Gelder, M., Gath, D., Mayou, and Cowen, P. (1996) *Oxford Textbook of Psychiatry* (third edition). Oxford: Oxford University Press.

Harrow, M. and Quinlan, D.M. (1985) *Disordered Thinking and Schizophrenic Psychopathology.* USA: Gardener Press.

Hathaway, S. and McKinley, J. (1970) *Minnesota Multiphasic Personality Inventory.* Windsor: NFER-Nelson.

Hill, P. (1997) Child psychiatry. In R. Murray, P. Hill and P. McGuffin (eds) *Essentials of Postgraduate Psychiatry* (third edition). New York: Grune and Stratton. pp.97–144.

Hoare, P. (1998) Psychiatric disorders in childhood. In E. Johnstone, C.A.L. Freeman and A.K. Zealley (eds) *Companion to Psychiatric Studies* (sixth edition). Edinburgh: Churchill Livingstone.

ICD-9 (1975) *Manual of the International Statistical Classification of Diseases, Injuries and Causes of Death,* Vol. 1. Geneva: World Health Organization.

ICD-10 (1992) *Classification of Mental and Behavioural Disorders.* Geneva: World Health Organization.

Kaplan, H. and Sadock, B. (1985) *Modern Synopsis and Comprehensive Textbook of Psychiatry* (fourth edition). Baltimore: Williams and Wilkin.

Kaplan, H. and Saddock, B. (1988) *Synopsis of Psychiatry: Behavioral Sciences Clinical Psychiatry.* Baltimore: Williams and Wilkins.

Kendell, R.E. (1993) Schizophrenia. In R.E. Kendell and A.K. Zealley (eds) *Companion Guide to Psychiatric Studies* (fifth edition). Edinburgh: Churchill Livingstone.

Kiernan, C. (1983) The use of non-vocal communication techniques with autistic individuals. *Journal of Child Psychology and Psychiatry 24,* 339–375.

Lovaas, I. (1968) A programme for the establishment of speech in psychotic children. In H.N. Sloan and B.D. MacAulay (eds) *Operant Procedures in Remedial Speech and Language Training.* Boston: Houghton Mifflin.

Miles, C.P. (1977) Conditions predisposing suicide. *Review Journal of Nervous and Mental Disease, 164,* 4, 231–246

Monti, P.M. and Fingeret, A.L. (1987) Social perceptions and communication skills among schizophrenics and non-schizophrenics. *Journal of Clinical Psychology 43*, 2, 197–204.

Morice, R.D. and Ingram, J.C.L. (1982) Language analysis in schizophrenia: diagnostic implications. *Australian and New Zealand Journal of Psychiatry 16*, 11.

Murphy, H.B.M. (1968) Cultural factors in the genesis of schizophrenia. In D. Rosenthal and S. Kety (eds) *The Transmission of Schizophrenia*. Oxford: Pergamon Press.

Murphy, H.B.M., Wittower, F.D., Fried, J. and Ellenberger, H. (1963) A cross-cultural survey of schizophrenic symptomatology. *International Journal of Social Psychiatry 9*, 237–247.

Murray, H.A. (1943) *Thematic Apperception Test TAT*. Cambridge, Massachusetts: Harvard University Press.

Murray, R. (1986) Schizophrenia. In P. Hill, R. Murray and A. Thorley (eds) *Essentials of Postgraduate Psychiatry* (second edition). New York: Grune and Stratton.

Murray, R. (1997) Schizophrenia. In R. Murray, P. Hill and P. McGuffin (eds) *Essentials of Postgraduate Psychiatry* (third edition). New York: Grune and Stratton. pp.339–379.

Prizant, B.M. and Rydell, P.J. (1984) Analysis of functions of delayed echolalia in autistic children. *Journal of Speech and Hearing Research 27*, 18–92.

Rorschach, H. (1942) *Rorschach Inkblot Test Psychodiagnostics*. Berne: Hans Huber.

Rose, N. (1994) Schizophrenia. In N. Rose (ed) *Essential Psychiatry* (second edition). Oxford: Blackwell Scientific Publications. pp.55–70.

Roth, M. and Kroll, J. (1986) *The Reality of Mental Illness*. Cambridge: Cambridge University Press.

Rutter, D. (1985) Language in schizophrenia: the structure of monologues and conversations. *British Journal of Psychiatry 146*, 399–404.

Rutter, M. and Lord, C. (1987) Language disorders associated with psychiatric disturbance. In W. Yule and M. Rutter (eds) *Language Development and Disorders*. London: MacKeith Press. pp.206–233.

Silverstone, T. and Turner, P. (1995) *Drug Treatment in Psychiatry* (fifth edition). London: Routledge.

Tamlyn, D., McKenna, P.J., Mortimer, A.M., *et al.* (1992). Memory impairment in schizophrenia: its extent, affiliations, neuropsychological character. *Psychological Medicine 22*, 105–115.

Tanguay, P. (1984) Preface. In S. Cantor (ed) *The Schizophrenic Child*. Milton Keynes: Open University Press.

Tidmarsh, D. (1990) Schizophrenia and crime. In R. Bluglass and P. Bowden (eds) *Principles and Practice of Forensic Psychiatry*. Edinburgh: Churchill Livingstone.

Trower, D., Bryant, B. and Argyle, M. (1978) *Social Skills and Mental Health*. London: Methuen.

Van den Bergh, O., De Boeck, P. and Claeys, W. (1986) Schizophrenia: what is loose in schizophrenic construing. In E. Button (ed) *Personal Construct Theory and Mental Health*. London: Croom Helm. pp.59–81.

Wechsler, D. (1981) *The Wechsler Adult Intelligence Scale*. Sidcup, Kent: Psychological Corporation.

Wetherby, A.M. (1986) Ontogeny of communicative functions in autism. *Journal of Autism and Developmental Disorders 16*, 3, 136–295.

Wing, L. and Gould, J. (1979) Severe impairments of social interaction and associated abnormalities in children: epidemiology and classification. *Journal of Autism and Developmental Disorders 9*, 11–29.

Wolff, S. (1988) Psychiatric disorders of childhood. In R.E. Kendell and A.K. Zealley (eds) *Companion Guide to Psychiatric Studies* (fifth edition). Edinburgh: Churchill Livingstone.

Wolff, S. and Cull, A. (1986) Schizoid personality and anti-social conduct: a retrospective case note study. *Psychological Medicine 16*, 677–687.

CHAPTER 4

Depression and Other Mood Disorders

Jenny France

Depression and mania come under the heading of affective mood disorders, which are so called because the main feature is an abnormality of mood. Both depression and mania can occur as separate illnesses or in combination as classified under the bipolar disorders. They include a wide range of disorders from mild to severe states.

Depression

Approximately 3 per cent of the world's population, that is about 100 million people, suffer from depressive states at a given time, according to the World Health Organization (Kelly 1987a). It has been established that there will be 34 per cent of men and 74 per cent of women in the community suffering from a depressive illness at any one time. It is thought that one of the reasons for the discrepancy between the figures for men and women suffering from depression is due to the fact that more women will admit to depressive symptoms than men and that some men will abuse alcohol, thus confusing the diagnosis of depression. In one study depression accounted for 12 per cent of the problems presented to the family practitioner for the first time (Pennell and Creed 1987).

The causes of depression can be divided into three categories: predisposing factors, precipitating factors and maintaining factors.

Kelly (1987a) suggests that there is a greater awareness of depressive disorders. This is due to recent progress on the diagnosis of depression and the fact that more people are now seeking help for this condition, although the true extent of the disorders is difficult to define due to the differing diagnostic definitions. Certain facts are that depressive symptoms are common and are more frequent among women than in men, particularly in women of the lower socio-economic groups. Symptoms vary with age, the highest rate being in those between 35 and 45 years old whereas the rate of depression in men increases with age. Surveys suggest that many cases of depression go unrecognised and untreated even though depressives are the most treatable of all psychiatric patients.

Severe depression, or psychotic depression, includes features such as delusions and hallucinations and is accompanied by feelings of worthlessness and guilt, the results of which may even be life-threatening. These severe depressions are included in this chapter rather than in the chapter on other psychotic illnesses due to the reclassification in DSM-IV (1994) and

ICD-10 (1992). Some of the mildest forms may be self-limiting but the more severe forms, which are less common, need early recognition by health professionals due to the possible risk of the person committing suicide and in order that the person receives the present effective treatments as soon as possible. Pennell and Creed (1987) state that approximately 25 per cent of people with depressive illness who attend the family practitioner make a rapid recovery, 50 per cent show a fluctuating course over one year, and 25 per cent show chronic illness.

Depression is known as the common cold of psychopathology and has touched the lives of everyone. When depressed, a person is characterised by depressed mood, pessimistic thinking, lack of enjoyment, reduced energy and slowness. The mood may occur infrequently and be of short duration for some people and yet for others the mood is recurrent, pervasive, and at times of lethal intensity. Seligman (1975) goes on to inform us that to be depressed is to endure terrible isolation and that one out of every 200 persons affected by depressive illness will die a suicidal death; this estimate is thought to be probably on the low side.

Kelly (1987b) notes that in addition to these people presenting with the complaint of depression, there are others who can be classified as having a masked depression. He comments that this is a condition which doctors often fail to diagnose as the person does not necessarily complain of feeling depressed. In the course of various clinical encounters, these people may present with a condition unrelated to depression, but nevertheless vigilant diagnostic skills detect depressive symptoms requiring clinical intervention.

It is not surprising that psychiatrists find it difficult to agree on the classification of these conditions, or indeed on the classification of affective disorders. A wide variety of terms are used which can result in considerable confusion. Kendell (1993) notes that the classification of these illnesses is unsatisfactory and controversial, and has been so since the 1920s. Mood disorder, as in the major classifications, is applied to a large group of related conditions in which a disturbance of mood – either depression or elation – is prominent, and believed to be fundamental. Illnesses in which the prevailing affect is depression are much commoner than those based on an elevation of mood, and people who suffer from manic illness usually suffer from depression as well at some stage. This makes it difficult when attempting to classify depressions because the concept of depressive illness embraces a wide variety of disorders differing in severity, symptomology, course and prognosis. Storr (1983) states emphatically that depression is not an illness, but a psychobiological reaction which can be provoked in anyone. Storr thinks that use of terms such as depressive illness or affective disorder and their underlying assumptions have prevented the understanding of depression. Furthermore, depressive symptoms span the historical distinction between neurosis and psychosis and, finally, the prevailing mood of sadness, helplessness and hopelessness tends to provide a common core, a unifying theme, to all depressions.

Description of depression

Psychological and behavioural symptoms of depression include loss of ability to enjoy life, feelings of sadness, grief and regret, accompanied by crying, and possibly suicidal ideas when the mood is at its lowest. There is a loss of mental energy, indecision, slowness of thinking and memory disturbance. Feelings of guilt and pessimism, a reduced desire and interest in life, self-isolation and avoidance of people, and carelessness in appearance all add to the picture. Some of the associated symptoms present as anxiety, tension and headaches, phobias, panic attacks or obsessional symptoms. Worrying may give rise to somatic symptoms such as insomnia, weight loss or gain associated with appetite loss or gain, loss of libido, menstrual disorders and other psychosomatic disturbances. Alcoholism may also be an added problem.

Depression in children may present as a normal mood change of sadness in response to difficulties or it may occur as an illness with an identifiable aetiology and outcome, with one of the symptoms being depressive thinking.

As the patient's moods vary, the mental state at interview may appear normal; it is therefore difficult to diagnose and at times may well be mistaken for an anxiety state. The mood changes may last a few days or long enough for the practitioner to experience difficulty distinguishing between depression and personality disorder. Occasionally antisocial and/or aggressive behaviour which is out of character may signal the onset of depression. Depressions are variable in symptomatology, severity and duration and are extremely common, as previously stated.

Classification of depression and other mood disorders

DSM-IV (1994) classifies all depressive illnesses under the heading of Mood Disorders, while the ICD-10 (1992) classification heading is mood (affective) disorder.

The DSM-IV classification refers to disorders that have a disturbance in mood as the predominating feature as one category which then divides them into three parts. The first includes Mood Episodes (Major Depressive Episode, Manic Episode, Mixed Episode, and Hypomanic Episode), the second group includes the Mood Disorders (e.g. Major Depressive Disorder, Dysthymic Disorder, Bipolar Disorder), whilst the third includes the specifiers that describe either the most recent mood-episode or the course of recurrent episodes.

DSM-IV further divides the Mood Disorders into Depressive Disorders ('unipolar depression'), the Bipolar Disorders, and two disorders based on aetiology – Mood Disorder Due to a Medical Condition and Substance-Induced Mood Disorder.

ICD-10 classifies mood (affective) disorders included under seven headings F30–F39, and states that distinguishing between grades of severity remains a problem. It notes that there are three grades, mild, moderate, and severe, which have been specified for those clinicians who wish to have them available. The terms 'mania' and 'severe depression' are used in the ICD-10 classification to denote the opposite ends of the affective spectrum; whilst 'hypomania' is used to denote an intermediate state without delusions, hallucinations or complete disruption of normal activities, a state which is often seen as patients develop or recover from mania.

The more serious disorders of major depressive disorder, the bipolar disorders and mania have complex classifications and for the purpose of this book general descriptions only will be given. For further information see DSM-IV (1994) and ICD-10 (1992).

Major Depressive Disorder DSM-IV (1994);
Depressive episode (ICD-10 1992, F32)

The diagnostic feature of this disorder is a clinical course that is characterised by one or more major depressive episodes without a history of manic, mixed, or hypomanic episodes (DSM-IV). An associated feature of this disorder is that there is a high mortality rate, with about 15 per cent of individuals dying by suicide. The disorder may be preceded by dysthymic disorder, and other mental disorders may co-occur such as substance-related disorders, panic disorder, obsessive-compulsive disorder, bulimia nervosa, and borderline personality disorder. Major depressive disorder is also associated with chronic general medical conditions, such as diabetes, carcinomas and strokes, and is twice as common in adolescent and adult females as in adolescent and adult males.

ICD-10 has a heading of depressive episode (F32) and divides the depressive states into three groups: mild, moderate and severe depressive episodes. That which is considered a mild depressive episode commonly includes depressed mood, loss of interest and enjoyment and increased fatiguability. The patient will be distressed by the symptoms and experience difficulty continuing with work and social activities; there may be some somatic symptoms.

Moderate depressive episode will produce more symptoms, several of which are likely to be present to a marked degree, and the individual will usually have considerable difficulty in continuing with social, work or domestic activities.

In cases of severe depressive episode without psychotic symptoms, the sufferer will usually show considerable distress or agitation, loss of self-esteem or feelings of uselessness or guilt, and some of the somatic syndrome will almost always be present. The sufferer is unlikely to be able to continue with work, social or domestic activities, except in the most limited of ways. In those with severe depressive episode with psychotic symptoms, delusions, hallucinations or depressive stupor are present. The delusions usually involve ideas of sin, poverty or imminent disasters, for which the patient might assume responsibility. Auditory or olfactory hallucinations are usually of defamatory or accusatory voices or of rotting filth or decomposing flesh.

Abnormalities of speech and thought are demonstrated by slow, monotonous speech, brief utterances and a limited range of expression, increased pauses before answering and an increased poverty of speech, marked poverty of thought content and little spontaneous speech. The latter characteristic is called retardation and is accompanied by slowed body movements and reduced facial expression and restricted gestures accompanying speech. In this condition the voice becomes quieter, dull and monotonous. The changes can be slight or so marked that the patient is mute and motionless for hours on end, which understandably results in impaired attention and concentration.

People with these symptoms have thoughts that match the low mood and are pessimistic and distressive in content, they view themselves negatively, develop low self-esteem and view the past as worthless and the future as hopeless. Suicidal ideas are common. Patients also complain of difficulty thinking and express problems when attempting to concentrate. Their beliefs are often of delusional intensity, hence the past association with psychotic depression. Delusions of guilt, poverty and persecution occur, and the patient will accept blame unnecessarily. Perceptual abnormalities are often present and can be severe enough to present as hallucinations. The overall picture is one of avoidance of social interaction, impaired work performance, self-neglect, not meeting responsibilities and possibly suicide attempts.

Bipolar Disorders (DSM-IV 1994); Mania (ICD-10 1992)

The bipolar disorders are divided into two groups in DSM-IV, and are classified as Manic Episodes or More than One Depressive Episode. In some cases manic episodes occur immediately before or after a major depressive episode, and most individuals return to a fully functional life between episodes.

ICD-10 introduces manic episode separately from bipolar affective disorder. This category includes cases confined to a single manic episode, and is included after a description of the various degrees of severity of elevated mood. Symptoms can include increase in the quantity and speed of physical and mental activity. If previous or subsequent affective episodes occur, then the illness comes under the bipolar heading of hypomania. This is the persistent mild elevation of mood, lasting for about several days, with increased energy and activity, and usually with marked feelings of well-being, increased sociability, talkativeness, overfamiliarity, increased sexual energy and a decreased need for sleep. Concentration and attention may be impaired but this may not prevent the appearing of interests in new ventures and activities, or mild overspending.

Mania without psychotic symptoms should last for at least a week, be severe enough to disrupt work and social activities, perhaps completely, and be accompanied by pressure of speech, decreased need for sleep, grandiosity and excessive optimism.

Mania is the elevation of mood, with the possibility of a wide range of accompanying abnormalities. Episodes of mania appear between bouts of normal behaviour and sometimes manic bouts are interrupted by brief episodes of depression. Abnormality of mood presents in feelings of well-being and expansiveness, and is possibly not in keeping with the circumstances. This mood can last for some time and in some patients there might be a tendency towards irritability and anger and even at times aggressive responses towards others.

Abnormalities of speech and thought present as garrulousness or pressure of speech, flights of ideas, distractability, and grandiose and persecutory delusions. Speech is likely to be too rapid, too much (pressure of speech), unnecessarily loud and not taking into account the present social setting; it is, in addition, difficult to interpret and full of jokes, puns, plays on words and amusing irrelevancies. It may become theatrical and full of dramatic mannerisms and singing. Sounds rather than meaningful conceptual relationships may govern word choice (clanging).

Frequently there is a flight of ideas, which is a nearly continuous flow of accelerated speech, with abrupt changes from topic to topic, usually based on understandable associations, distracting stimuli, or play on words. When the flight of ideas is severe, speech may be disorganised and incoherent. However, loosening of association and incoherence may occur even when there is no flight of ideas, particularly if the person is on medication. Ideas are expansive, extravagant, reckless and often accompanied by grandiose and other delusions. Delusions usually disappear within days. Insight is usually also impaired, the patient seldom thinks they are ill and so sees no need to receive treatment.

Biological symptoms lead to disturbed sleep; after a brief period of sleep the patient wakes full of energy and ideas and does not display exhaustion. Appetite is increased and in the case of hyperactive patients, in spite of the increased food intake, there might even be a weight loss. Sexual activity increases and with grandiose ideas may lead to sexually disinhibited behaviour that can lead to unlawful acts.

Perceptual abnormalities include illusions, misinterpretations and hallucinations, which are usually consistent with mood, taking the form of voices talking to the patient about his or her special powers or, occasionally, of visions with a religious content (Gelder *et al.* 1996). Abnormal behaviour is presented as overactivity which may lead to exhaustion. Patients may start many activities and leave them unfinished as new ones take their fancy.

In the foreword of David Wigoder's book *Images of Destruction* (1987), Anthony Storr quoted the author's summary of his own life: 'By the time I was forty I had destroyed two successful careers, served a prison sentence, been made legally bankrupt, lost a treasured professional qualification, attempted to kill two people, and isolated myself from most of my family and friends.' Storr went on to write that 'any psychiatrist reading these words would guess that the man who wrote them was suffering from a major form of psychiatric disorder which afflicts at least one in a hundred individuals in our society – that is, mania.'

Incidence, aetiology and predisposing factors of major depressive disorders and mania

The lifetime risk of major depressive disorder in community samples has varied from 10 per cent to 25 per cent for women and from 5 per cent to 12 per cent for men, and appears to be unrelated to ethnicity, education, income or marital status (DSM-IV 1994).

The cause of depressive disorder is suggested through family studies which have shown that major depression is 1.5–3 times more common among first-degree biological relations with this disorder than among the general population.

A lifetime prevalence of bipolar disorders, those disorders that include both severe depression and mania, suggest a figure of approximately 0.4 per cent to 1.6 per cent in community samples (DSM-IV 1994).

Genetic and biological factors

In the study of the aetiology of bipolar disorders there is some evidence for genetic differences between bipolar disorders and unipolar disorders. Patients with bipolar illness are likely to have relations with the same form of disorder, while those with unipolar disorders have relations both with unipolar and bipolar conditions (Catalan 1994). Catalan also states that there is still no evidence for the existence of predisposing biological features apart from the general influence of genetic factors – it might be that individuals likely to become depressed may be different in terms of the action and metabolism of the neurotransmitters involved in the regulation of mood.

There is strong evidence for a genetic contribution to the major depressive and manic disorders, and patients are likely to have a history of affective disorder (Catalan 1994). Genetic studies report a morbidity rate of 10–15 per cent for a first-degree relative of a patient with depression. This risk is increased in female relations and in the relations of patients who have become depressed before the age of 40. Twin studies and adoption studies provide convincing evidence that there is a genetic aetiology of depression (Checkley 1986).

Psychosocial factors

Psychosocial factors include life events and environmental stress. Research has proved that there is a relationship between life events and depression. It is thought that some personality traits predispose towards affective disorders. Personality and psychodynamic factors suggest that people prone to depression suffer low self-esteem and there are features in the personality which predispose towards depression. Psychodynamic theory believes that mania is a defence against depression, but Gelder *et al.* (1996) do not find this explanation convincing.

There appears to be a slightly higher incidence among upper socio-economic classes than among other classes and it has been found that bipolar disorders may be more common amongst divorced persons than others. The age of onset is from late adolescence and usually before the age of 30. There is no conclusive evidence to prove that there is any difference between black and white races with affective disorders.

Psychoanalysts have suggested that deprivation of maternal affection through separation or loss predisposes to depressive disorder in adult life (Gelder *et al.* 1996). Current literature on the relationship between depression and parental loss is large, conflicting and inconclusive and suggests that it is unlikely that death or loss of a parent in childhood does predispose to depression in later life. In fact Brown and Harris (1978) in their studies concluded the opposite. It has been found that when attempting to assess a depressed patient's poor family relationships the patient's memories may well be distorted (due to the present depression) and so memories of negative events and relationships are more likely to be quoted than positive ones and so give an unbalanced bias to the past relationships with parents and siblings.

Psychoanalytic factors

Psychoanalytic factors include pre-morbid factors such as introversion, dependency, narcissism and insecurity which are thought to lead to feelings of guilt. Manic patients tend to have more normal pre-morbid personalities than depressed patients. Finally, learned helplessness is mentioned as a possible factor in the cause of bipolar disorders (Kaplan and Saddock 1988).

Childhood and adolescence

Manic-depressive disorders can occur in childhood and adolescence and are generally associated with a family history of functional psychosis, and if they occur before puberty are likely to recur later in life. The clinical manifestations and treatment are similar to those for adult patients.

Personality factors

Personality factors are not thought to be relevant in cases of unipolar depressive disorders, but features of obsessional traits and anxiety may be as they influence the way people respond to stressful life events.

Social factors

Social factors predispose towards depression as it is thought more likely to occur where there is a chronic long-standing stress or illness in the family, unresolved conflicts in family relationships and excessive alcohol consumption. Brown and Harris (1978) show that mothers are at special risk from depression if they lost their own mother before adolescence, have three or more children under the age of 14, have marital difficulties, and do not have a job outside the home. These 'at risk' women cannot easily cope with adverse life events or continuing difficulties. Adverse events with a long-term threat, such as a spouse threatening to leave or who becomes unemployed, if there is family bereavement, and caring for a physically or mentally handicapped child or adult may provoke a depressive episode in an 'at-risk' mother. Depression may also be provoked by financial, housing or other difficulties and it is known that poor housing conditions prevent a woman recovering from depression, and women from low-income families are at much greater risk from depression because they have more 'at-risk' factors, and more persistent difficulties (France 1988).

Precipitating factors

Precipitating factors include stressful life events such as threat and loss, and death or separation are thought to be of particular relevance. The maintaining factors of depression may include many of the factors that predispose towards and precipitate depression (Catalan 1994), and it has been estimated that the depressed patient experiences three times as many life events in the preceding six months as normal controls.

Organic factors

Organic factors such as cerebral diseases including senile dementia, arteriosclerosis, brain tumour, epilepsy and post-traumatic disorders are thought to cause depression (Kielholz 1987, Thursfield 1987).

Physical factors

Physical factors, for example the after-effects of a viral infection such as influenza or glandular fever, following intoxication, an operation, or of sleep deprivation, anaemia, and endocrine disorders such as diabetes, can also cause depression (Kielholz 1987).

Drug and alcohol abuse

Drug and alcohol abuse are known to induce depression. Selected drugs, particularly the steroids, amphetamines, barbiturates and central nervous system depressants, are known to produce depression after periods of heavy use. A chronic depression secondary to heroin use or long-term methadone use has also been described. Kaplan and Saddock (1985) suggest that drugs of various kinds have often been blamed for causing depression. The contraceptive pill and neuroleptic drugs, particularly intramuscular Depo preparations, are also thought to cause depression. Kaplan and Saddock also draw attention to the high percentage of chronic alcoholics who develop secondary depression, the rates ranging from 25 per cent to 50 per cent.

Social factors

Social factors can cause depression in childhood. A child whose mother is depressed may well become apathetic and depressed due to lack of maternal comforting and warmth, maternal anger and inconsistent discipline. Conflict within the parental relationship commonly causes depression. Parental standards set above the child's abilities, producing failure and low self-esteem in some children are more likely to develop depressive disorders (Thursfield 1987).

Psychological theories

These theories are concerned with the psychological mechanisms by which recent and past life experiences can lead to depression (Gelder *et al.* 1996).

Psychoanalysis

The psychoanalytic theory was developed by Freud in 1917 and published in an essay called *Mourning and Melancholia*. Freud suggested that mourning results from loss by death, while melancholia results from loss of other kinds. The role in depression of the super-ego (a structure in the unconscious built up by early experiences), of ambivalence and of narcissistic identification (extreme self-love), were ideas developed by Melanie Klein and others who described the depressive position to which patients are thought to regress (Klein 1934).

Klein suggests that the infant must acquire confidence that when his or her mother leaves them she will return, even when she has been angry, and this stage is called the 'depressive position'. If this stage is not passed through successfully, the child will be more likely to develop depression in later life.

Behavioural therapy

Many of the behavioural formulations are based on Skinner's ideas (1953). He proposed that depression could be understood as an extinction of normal behaviour due to lack of positive reinforcement from the social environment. Depression is also seen to be due to a low rate of positive rewards and a high rate of negative rewards based on arousive interactions with the environment producing distress, for example negative sexual and marital experiences and experience of incompetence in any field.

Cognitive theory

Beck (1967) states that mood is determined by a central cognitive process (scheme) which filters all incoming stimuli from the environment and determines the way in which they are interpreted. He has proposed that three particular thinking patterns are common. First, depressed people have a negative concept of self; second, they interpret their experiences in a negative way; and third, they take a negative view of the future. Depression is therefore primarily a disorder of thinking and secondarily of mood.

Assessments of depression and affective mood disorders

Emphasis is placed upon the patient's case history and behaviour prior to the onset of the illness with an examination of both physical and mental states. Investigators need to establish that there is no organic disease present and that the patient has not previously received drugs in other treatments that would be likely to induce depression. The diagnosis is further confounded by the fact that many psychiatric patients with schizophrenia, borderline personality disorders, organic brain syndromes, paranoid disorders and other various physical illnesses may also suffer varying degrees of depression. Storr (1983) comments that learned helplessness is also a feature of the apathetic variety of chronic depression which accompanies institutionalisation and which, if prolonged, makes the individual incapable of living an ordinary life. Psychoanalytic thinking has emphasised the role of self-esteem in depression. Self-esteem may be lost if someone important withdraws their attention or concern; similarly, self-esteem may also suffer if a person loses status or position. Many depressed people do, of course, view themselves as ordinary people who are suffering from a severe impairment in their capacity to sleep, eat, concentrate and function normally.

Detecting depression is obviously important as it may not be directly presented to the doctor and so non-verbal cues such as poor eye contact and moist eyes, excessive anxiety and choking or pausing during sentences may be indicators of existing depression (Pennell and Creed 1987).

Kupfer et al. (1987) suggest that there are four methods of assessing depression. The first is through the patient's body movement, which may provide cues that would help improve reliability and validity towards assessing diagnosis in affective disorders. Dittman (1987) calls for a series of research studies to refine and enhance our knowledge base in this area. The second is facial expression: indeed, it seems logical to measure the face in studies of affective disorder because the face is one of the main emotion signal systems, and Ekman and Fridlund (1987) state that it is surprising that there have been so few studies on this topic. Third, vocal assessments of affective disorders are seen as being increasingly important. Scherer (1987) points out that clinicians are trained to be sensitive to the sound and enunciation of speech and are aware that the tempo of speech and the non-linguistic elements of communication and other aspects of vocalisation can play an important part in the diagnosis of affective disorders. Finally, the tempo or pacing of speech in depressed individuals is important as observations of tempo could serve as objective markers for major affective disorders and it is suggested that depression is possibly associated with high pause times and slow speech rates (Siegman 1987).

The Beck Depression Inventory (BDI)

The Beck Depression Inventory (Beck et al. 1979) can be used for measuring depression and might usefully be part of the initial assessment prior to treatment as well as being used on occasions during the course of treatment. The inventory is an extremely useful monitor of the patient's present condition as it is designed to measure the behavioural manifestations of depression. It is a quantitative inventory which assesses the intensity of depression and can reflect changes of depression after an interval of time, but it is important to point out that this inventory does not set out to distinguish among standard diagnostic categories. The inventory can be used frequently at varying intervals; it takes a modest amount of time to complete and analyse. Furthermore it provides information that can usefully form part of the treatment plan or perhaps direct the course of treatment.

Grids

The personal repertory grid is a further useful means of assessing the patient's present state, monitoring progress and in particular identifying objectives and determining where change is needed (Fransella and Bannister 1977). For further information regarding this topic see Chapter 25.

Communication and speech problems associated with depression and other mood disorders

Psychiatrists have noted that depressed patients have difficulty communicating within their social environment. Speech and language therapists view it as important to consider the overall communication problems of the patient in association specifically to speech and language. The patient's reluctance to talk of their distress, problems, hopes and fears, and their denial of difficulties, is often seen to be the easiest and simplest way out. To admit to problems is thought, by the patient, to be a sign of weakness and it may also promote unwanted change and produce further difficulties, thereby adding to the patient's feelings of hopelessness. Patients may talk about other symptoms as these are perceived to be respectable, such as physical symptoms of feeling tired or ill, but they are unlikely to discuss the major problem, that of the depression. Feelings of low self-esteem and the risk of being rebuffed prevent disclosure.

Depression of mood can be manifested by sadness, tearfulness, hopelessness and gloominess, together with feelings of despair, conflict and alienation thus creating social changes and difficulties. The depressed person is more likely to avoid social intercourse, is therefore less likely to seek help and through reduced non-verbal communication will signal 'keep your distance' and thereby limit social approaches and resulting interactions.

Non-verbal communication

The patient's non-verbal communication will emphasise how he or she feels. Changes in posture, gesture and facial expression may give the appearance of dejection by displaying slow and restricted body movements such as a stooped or hunched posture with the head held low thus minimising eye contact. Facial expression may be 'mask-like' and immobile and therefore displaying little expression or with obvious expressions of sorrow. There might be accompanying tensions demonstrated by rigidity of posture and movement and a set facial expression. In some patients agitation may be common, accompanied by restlessness and pacing up and down and nervous fidgeting movements of the hands.

Speech and language

The speech style of agitated patients is often demonstrated by their asking the same question repeatedly, which hints at poor concentration, and talking in short staccato-like phrases. The less active depressed person uses a slow speech tempo with frequent pauses and hesitations and so the overall effect is a 'dead', 'listless' voice with reduced volume, stress and rhythm. Pitch changes of the voice might be narrower due to lessened emotional expressions and resulting speech sounds dull and lifeless, and resonance will sometimes be abnormally nasal or pharyngeal. Language tends to be limited to convey the minimum of information and the response is short or non-verbal and little speech is initiated. Those suffering from 'chronic states of gloom', are said to show a different speech pattern from those with other depressions. Rather like the masked depression, articulation can be clear and normal and vocal pitch described as relatively lively, tempo normal and pauses infrequent. These people often look normal, smile and even seem happy but it is known that this is deceptive behaviour as demonstrated through their reduced use of language and avoidance of communication situations. Depressed or low mood restricts language and renders it colourless and limited. During the course of treatment it will be observed that there is a reduction in the negative content of the patient's speech. Language will become more descriptive and expressive, vocal volume will increase and become more normal, with increased flexibility of pitch, stress and rhythm and more obvious appropriate accompanying non-verbal gestures.

Breznitz and Sherman (1987) found that speech of depressed patients is often punctuated by long pauses, due possibly to the interjection of depressed thoughts that interfere with the patient's speaking rather than being reflective of overall motor retardation. It has been hypothesised by Breznitz and Shermon that such slowing down would be apparent in the interaction of depressed women and their children in that the depressed women would respond more slowly than normal mothers to the cessation of speech of their children. They go on to state that children adapt to their unwelcoming mothers and the negative effects on the child's continued social, emotional and cognitive development may be profound. Research is needed to discover the effects on the speech behaviour of the young child as a result of living with a depressed mother.

Speech changes in depression have been described in a number of studies and one of the approaches to measuring psychomotor function in depression is to assess the voice functions of depressed people, as the intricate neuromuscular system of the larynx is likely to be affected by changes in neural motor function, due to depression. Acoustic properties of the voice can be analysed instrumentally to show voice changes associated with depression.

Nilsonne (1988) draws attention to areas of research of the effects of medication on speech, variable voice changes, and word finding difficulties, and further elucidation of the complex relationship between speech and depression which would be of theoretical and clinical value. It is also thought that the acoustic study of voice may contribute to the differentiating of emotions and moods as well as various other psychopathological states.

Management and treatment of depression and other mood affective disorders

As the patient's lifestyle is usually severely impaired by the effects or results of the illness, a special programme of rehabilitation is required in conjunction with medical care in order that full function, health and happiness can be restored. The aims of the programme will be to change faulty habits, restore self-esteem, reduce social isolation by joining self-help groups, restore family relationships and achieve a return to work by structuring the day and thereby changing the negative to positive and achieving goals very gradually. Therapy providing support and empathy assist in gaining good results. The emphasis is on restoring self-esteem and avoiding isolation, which is disruptive (Kelly 1987c).

Drugs and other medical treatments

The biological treatments of depression with antidepressant drugs can restore a normal sleep pattern, reduce tearfulness, lighten the patient's pathological mood and improve coping behaviour. Depressive and manic illnesses are associated with biochemical changes in the brain and other parts of the body. These changes involve the brain amines (neurotransmitters), the electrolytes sodium and potassium, and certain hormones, particularly thyroid and adreno-corticosteroid hormones (Silverstone and Turner 1995). It has been suggested that there is a biochemical basis for the affective disorders and that depression is due to an absolute or relative decrease in the monoamines, or receptor sensitivity at certain sites in the brain, whereas mania is due to an absolute or relative excess of monoamines, or an increase in receptor sensitivity, at these sites (Silverstone and Turner 1995).

Antidepressant drugs not only have therapeutic effects on depressive illness but also have mood-stimulating effects. Most patients respond to one of the monoamine reuptake inhibitor group of antidepressants. These are the two main groups of drugs, the tricyclic antidepressants and the monoamine oxidase inhibitors (MAOIs) although the effects of MAOIs are questioned. Of considerable interest are the more recently introduced selective 5–hydroxytryptamine reuptake inhibitors which are less likely to cause impairment in psychomotor function and also less prone to cause cognitive problems, particularly in the elderly. In psychotic depression the addition of an antipsychotic drug to the antidepressant treatment is often required (Silverstone and Turner 1995).

Tricyclic antidepressant drugs remain the cornerstone for treatment of depressive illness. Amitriptyline has marked side-effects as well as working as an antidepressant and so is helpful if the depressive illness is accompanied by anxiety or agitation, as it has a sedating quality and is thought to be one of the best drugs for most patients. These drugs are rapidly absorbed and have a long action and need to be given only once a day. Dosage will be adjusted to individual clinical response and to the side-effects of the drug. The side-effects may include a dry mouth and disturbance of visual accommodation and these can affect communicative ability if severe. Tiredness and drowsiness may affect concentration and motivation; memory impairment has also been noted in some cases. Speech blockage (difficulty in word retrieval) has been reported. Dysarthria has also been reported of a kind that is similar to a stutter but really of basal ganglion origin. Speech scanning has been noted in patients recovering from toxic doses (Maguire 1986). Once a therapeutic effect has been achieved the drug is continued for at least six weeks; it is then reduced for a further six months, all being well.

MAOIs are drugs thought to have anxiolytic properties and possibly a weak antidepressant action too, and are likely to be prescribed for the less severe depressive disorders. The therapeutic effects in depression are therefore considered to be modest. The side-effects include a dry mouth and this again can be a handicap to speech clarity and fluency.

In the severely manic patient it is usually necessary to start treatment with an antipsychotic drug at first, such as haloperidol, as other drugs such as lithium take longer to act. Lithium has a definite therapeutic effect in mania, but this effect takes about a week to appear; it has fewer side-effects than other drugs and produces only little sedation (Silverstone and Turner 1995).

Electroconvulsive therapy (ECT)

The use of ECT in psychiatry has always been associated with a degree of controversy (Cowan 1994). The induction of bilateral seizures appears to act by increasing dopomine function; the treatment is given twice weekly and the number of treatments given is about 6–8.

ECT remains a valuable treatment for severe affective disorder and some treatment-resistant psychoses. It is considered an effective treatment for severe depressive illness, particularly if associated with life-threatening complications, or if the patient is suffering from delusional (psychotic) depression. When drug treatment for mania fails ECT can prove an effective alternative.

Psychological therapies

Psychological therapies for depression include clinical management, supportive psychotherapy, dynamic psychotherapy, marital therapy, interpersonal psychotherapy and cognitive therapy (Gelder et al. 1996). Interpersonal psychotherapy is a treatment approach aimed at assisting in relationship and life problems.

Speech and language therapists are unlikely to be referred a clinical case with depression as the major problem; it is much more likely that depression is discovered as one of the presenting clinical problems associated with speech pathology that might have resulted from either cerebral trauma, organic illness (which might result in major surgery such as a laryngectomy), physical or mental handicap, degenerative illness or a long-standing speech disability such as a severe stutter.

In a formal psychiatric setting where communication problems rather than speech pathology are associated with depression, the speech and language therapist could be involved in either individual or group work as part of the treatment plan. Group work is generally favoured as the support offered by the group is possibly the most important aspect of the treatment in the early stages. Few demands need to be made of the patient except to attend and survive the session with the knowledge that they are safe, wanted and valued as a group member and when ready to participate in group activities will be encouraged and rewarded. The group is a place where treatment can focus on current rather than past problems and the patient is helped to cope with everyday living. When adjusted to the group, the patient can explore past problems and share feelings openly. The group is somewhere to cry, laugh and grieve, talk about anger, frustration, loving, hating, failure and success, past and present relationships and eventually hopes and plans for the future.

Recognition of depression during the course of treatment of speech pathology is important as conventional speech and language therapy methods can be developed to encompass both problems. Without doubt the depression is the most important of the two problems and, if unrecognised or ignored, little progress is likely to result. During the course of therapy it might be possible to help the patient to assess beliefs objectively and reject those thinking patterns that make them depressed, working towards changing negative patterns of thinking to positive ones.

References

Beck, A.T. (1967) *Depression: Clinical, Experimental and Theoretical Aspects.* New York: Harper and Row.

Beck, A.T., Rush, A.J., Shaw, B.F. and Emery, G. (1979) *Cognitive Therapy of Depression.* Chichester: Wiley.

Breznitz, Z. and Sherman, T. (1987) Speech pattern of normal discourse of well and depressed mothers and their young children. *Child Development 58,* 395–400.

Brown, G. and Harris, T. (1978) *The Social Origins of Depression.* London: Tavistock Publications.

Catalan, J. (1994) Affective disorders. In N. Rose (ed) *Essential Psychiatry* (second edition). Oxford: Blackwell Scientific Publications. pp.71–83.

Checkley, S. (1986) Affective disorder: depression. In P. Hill, R. Murray and A. Thorley (eds) *Essentials of Postgraduate Psychiatry* (second edition). London: Grune and Stratton. pp.381–403.

Cowan, P.J. (1994) The physical treatments. In N. Rose (ed) *Essential Psychiatry* (second edition). Oxford: Blackwell Scientific Publications. pp.209–223.

DSM-IV (1994) *Diagnostic and Statistical Manual of Mental Disorders* (fourth edition). Washington DC: American Psychiatric Association.

Dittman, A.T. (1987) Body movements as diagnostic cues in affective disorders. In J.D. Maser (ed) *Depression and Expressive Behaviour.* London: Lawrence Erlbaum Associates. pp.1–36.

Ekman, P. and Fridlund, A.J. (1987) Assessment of facial behaviour in affective disorders. In J.D. Maser (ed) *Depression and Expressive Behaviour.* London: Lawrence Erlbaum Associates. pp.37–56.

France, R. (1988) *Symposium on Depression for Speech Therapists.* Speech Therapy Special Interest Group in Psychiatry, Broadmoor Hospital, Crowthorne, Berks.

Fransella, F. and Bannister, D. (1977) *A Manual for Repertory Grid Technique.* London: Academic Press.

Freud, S. (1917) *Mourning and Melancholia: Standard Edition,* Vol. 14. London: Hogarth Press. pp.243–258.

Gelder, M., Gath, D., Mayou, R. and Cowen, P. (1996) *Oxford Textbook of Psychiatry* (third edition). Oxford: Oxford University Press.

ICD-10 (1992) *Classification of Mental and Behavioural Disorders.* Geneva: World Health Organization.

Kaplan, H.I. and Saddock, B.J. (1985) *Modern Synopsis of Comprehensive Textbook of Psychiatry* (fourth edition). Baltimore: Williams and Wilkins.

Kaplan, H.I. and Saddock, B.J. (1988) *Synopsis of Psychiatry: Behavioral Sciences Clinical Psychiatry.* Baltimore: Williams and Wilkins.

Kelly. D. (1987a) Introduction. In D. Kelly and R. France (eds) *A Practical Handbook for the Treatment of Depression.* Lancs: Parthenon Publishing Group. pp.1–16.

Kelly, D. (1987b) Diagnosis of masked depression. In D. Kelly and R. France (eds) *A Practical Handbook for the Treatment of Depression.* Lancs: Parthenon Publishing Group. pp.25–27.

Kelly, D. (1987c) Overcoming depression. In D. Kelly and R. France (eds) *A Practical Handbook for the Treatment of Depression.* Lancs: Parthenon Publishing Group. pp.57–64.

Kendell, R.E. (1993) Mood (affective) disorders. In R.E. Kendell and A.K. Zeally (eds) *Companion to Psychiatric Studies* (fifth edition). Edinburgh: Livingstone.

Kielholz, P. (1987) The classification of depression. In D. Kelly and R. France (eds) *A Practical Handbook for the Treatment of Depression.* Lancs: Parthenon Publishing Group. pp.41–43.

Klein, M. (1934) A contribution to the psychogenesis of manic-depressive states. Reprinted in *Psychiatry,* 13–282. Contributions to psycho-analyses 1921–5, *Developments in Child and Adolescent.* London: Hogarth Press.

Kupfer, J., Maser, J.D., Blehar, M.C. and Miller, R. (1987) Behaviour assessments in depression. In J.D Maser (ed) *Depression and Expressive Behaviour.* London: Lawrence Erlbaum Associates. pp.1–15.

Maguire, T. (1986) Pharmacological Effects in Speech and Language. Paper presented at Speech Therapy Special Interest Group Seminar, Broadmoor Hospital, Crowthorne, Berks.

Nilsonne, A. (1988) Speech characteristics as indicators of depressive illness. *Acta Psychologica Scandinavica 77,* 253–263.

Pennell, I. and Creed, F. (1987) Depressive illness. *Medicine International*, August 1987.

Scherer, K.R. (1987) Vocal assessments of affective disorders. In J.D. Maser (ed) *Depression and Expressive Behaviour*. London: Lawrence Erlbaum Associates. pp.59–82.

Seligman, M.E.P. (1975) *Helplessness: On Depression, Development and Death*. San Francisco: Freeman.

Siegman, A.W. (1987) The pacing of speech in depression. In J.D. Maser (ed) *Depression and Expressive Behaviour*. London: Lawrence Erlbaum Associates. pp.83–102.

Silverstone, T. and Turner, P. (1995) *Drug Treatment in Psychiatry* (fifth edition). London: Routledge.

Skinner, B.F. (1953) *Science and Human Behaviour*. New York: Free Press.

Storr. A. (1983) A psychotherapist looks at depression. *British Journal of Psychiatry 143*, 413–415.

Storr, A. (1987) Foreword. In D. Wigoder *Images of Destruction*. London: Routledge and Kegan Paul.

Thursfield, D. (1987) Childhood depression. In D. Kelly and R. France (eds) *A Practical Handbook for the Treatment of Depression*. Lancs: Parthenon Publishing Group. pp.12–26.

Wigoder, D. (1987) *Images of Destruction*. London: Routledge and Kegan Paul.

CHAPTER 5

Personality Disorders

Jenny France

There is more controversy over personality disorder than almost any other area of psychiatric practice. It is a confusing area, and an important one that Lewis and Wessely (1997) consider we know little about.

The concept of personality disorder can be understood as a medical model of severe social maladjustment and this maladjustment, or deviance, does not equate with disease or illness unless it is a consequence of, for example, brain damage (Hibbert 1994). Nevertheless, Hibbert goes on to state that psychiatrists often attempt to treat people with personality disorders even though there is no evidence of only partial function; this may be due to the demand for medical intervention by patients, relatives and society. Tyrer and Stein (1993) suggest that personality disorder is a redundant term, describing either a moral judgement or an untreatable condition, or that such a label is a technique used by psychiatrists to dispose of patients they do not wish to treat. Whatever the outcome, patients with personality disorders are important consumers of health services, particularly in the emergency and forensic settings.

Gelder *et al.* (1996) report that in abnormal personality unusual behaviour occurs even in the absence of stressful events and at times these anomalies of behaviour may be so great that it is difficult to decide whether they are due to personality or neurotic illness. Extreme cases of abnormal behaviour are obvious as, for example, in cases of violence and repeated behaviour of harming others and showing no remorse. Abnormality of personality causes problems to both the patient and others due, in the severest cases, to the unacceptable, antisocial behaviour exhibited by the patient which may lead to dislike of that person and the possibility of rejection. These people may profoundly affect others, often in subtle and unconscious ways. There have always been people who have suffered with personality disorder and those who work with these people need to consider the positive qualities as opposed to the negative ones when considering management and treatment. It needs to be stressed that a diagnosis of personality disorder in some cases will occur with affective disorders, organic states or schizophrenia and it is frequently found in association with neurotic disorders.

The antisocial or sociopathic personality disorder was until recently the most familiar and commonly studied section of personality disorder and therefore those patients with whom the psychiatrists and psychologists were likely to have most contact. Many of the less serious personality disorders might never seek help and therefore the cause of their conditions and alleviation of their problems are seldom faced either by psychiatrists or other authorities unless problems escalate to such a degree where help is sought. Those with antisocial/sociopathic personality disorder are on occasions most likely to cause social disruption and in some cases come into contact with the law; they may even receive considerable publicity and at times their behaviour will result in tragic consequences.

There is confusion of the terms psychopath or psychopathic personality and antisocial or sociopathic personality disorder, as often the term psychopath has been used when describing all personality disorders rather than referring to the severest of the personality disorders. This confusion is possibly associated with the evolution of the terminology and redefining of the classification of personality disorder with particular emphasis on psychopathy. There is also confusion about whether psychopathy refers to all those with personality disorder or only those who are classified as suffering from antisocial sociopathic personality disorder.

The term sociopathic disorder is referred to in the Mental Health Act 1983, which also still uses the term psychopathic disorder. Equally the Act divides mental disorders into four groups, the second of which is psychopathic disorder, and in the Act is defined as a persistent disorder or disability of the mind which results in abnormally aggressive or seriously irresponsible misconduct and is therefore viewed solely in terms of being antisocial behaviour. Therefore, psychopathic disorder is a legal definition and not a diagnosis, although the term 'psychopath' is still used widely today to represent the more severe personality disorders. This dates back to the earlier difficulties of finding an appropriate term for those people with marked abnormalities of behaviour in mental illness. Sir David Henderson (1939), who wrote *Psychopathic States*, defined psychopaths as 'people who, although not mentally abnormal, throughout their lives or from a comparatively early age, have exhibited disorders of conduct of an antisocial or social nature, usually of a recurrent or episodic type which in many instances have proved difficult to influence by methods of a social, penal and medical care or for whom we have no adequate provision of a preventative or curative nature.' He defined three groups of psychopaths: predominantly aggressive; predominantly passive or inadequate; and creative.

Normal personality

The type of personality disorder is likely to be described not in the diagnosis but in descriptive accounts of the patient's problems as based on the classifications from ICD-10 (1992) and DSM-IV (1994), and so in order to understand personality disorders a description of normal personality will be attempted. Normal personality will include personal features that have been apparent since adolescence, have been stable despite mood changes, observable in different environments and recognisable to others known to the person. Personality is that which makes one person different from another and this will include characteristic patterns of behaviour and thinking that include intellectual functioning, attitudes, beliefs, moral values, emotional reactivity and motives acquired in the process of growing up (Freeman 1993). Most definitions of normal personality include some or all of the following features: present since adolescence; stable over time despite fluctuations in mood; manifested in different environments; and recognisable to friends and acquaintances.

Trethowan and Sims (1983) consider personality subjectively – in other words what the patient believes and describes about himself or herself as an individual – and objectively, in terms of what an observer notices about the patient's more consistent patterns of behaviour. Personality is a unique quality and is the characteristic behaviour that allows others to predict how a person will act in a particular circumstance. It is emphasised that personality, which includes prevailing attitudes and opinions, is manifested in social relationships and must be assessed by observing what people actually do in a social context. It has been found that people behave in a certain way because of the situation they find themselves in, but many qualities do remain constant, for example physical appearance, gestures and way of speaking. (Freeman 1993).

Abnormal personality

Freeman (1993) suggests that personality disorder or abnormal behaviour imply a judgement that certain traits or features of the personality are 'good' or 'bad'.

Those with abnormal personality and/or personality disorder are said to display no apparent guilt, tend to be impulsive, manipulate others, are often aggressive and accused of being unloving. Nevertheless it is important to recognise that even those with abnormal personalities will have positive traits as well as negative ones and these positive traits need recording and taking into account when planning treatment. Therefore as part of collecting a full history a complete description of an individual's personality might include factors such as intellectual ability, attitudes, beliefs, moral values, emotional reactivity and motives acquired in the process of growing up – hence the importance of gaining a full medical and social history and the desirability of interviews with others who know or have known the patient previously.

Doren (1987) reports that psychiatrists in Canada filled in a questionnaire that ranked the most significant characteristics of personality disorder as being: does not learn from experience; lacks a sense of responsibility; unable to form meaningful relationships; lacks control over impulses; lacks a moral sense; chronologically or recurrently antisocial; punishment does not alter behaviour; emotionally immature; unable to experience guilt; and being self-centred. Other observations listed by workers include: having superficial charm and good intelligence; poor judgement; untruthfulness and insincerity; making suicide threats; failure to follow any plan; unable to show empathy or genuine concern for others; lack of feeling or affection; and lack of shame accompanied by aggressiveness.

Classification of personality disorders (DSM-IV 1994; ICD-10 1992)

The DSM-IV states that there are ten specific personality disorders (Table 5.1), and that these disorders can be defined as being enduring patterns of inner experience and behaviour that deviate markedly from the expectations of the individual's culture, they are pervasive and inflexible, have an onset in adolescence or early adulthood, are stable over time, and lead to distress or impairment. There is a brief description with each heading, followed by an in-depth description of each disorder, which includes diagnostic features, recording procedures, features such as culture, age and gender, course, and differential diagnosis.

ICD-10 divides personality disorders into nine groups which are then subdivided giving descriptions under the main heading (Table 5.2). Under the main heading of disorders of adult personality and behaviour, ICD-10 adds that it is unlikely that the diagnosis of personality disorder will be appropriate before the age of 16 or 17 years.

Table 5.1 Personality disorders DSM-IV (1994)

Paranoid Personality Disorder

Schizoid Personality Disorder

Schizotypal Personality Disorder

Antisocial Personality Disorder

Borderline Personality Disorder

Histrionic Personality Disorder

Narcissistic Personality Disorder

Avoidant Personality Disorder

Dependent Personality Disorder

Obsessive-Compulsive Personality Disorder

Personality Disorder Not Otherwise Specified

Table 5.2 Disorders of adult personality and behaviour (ICD-10 1992)

Specific personality disorders

Mixed and other personality disorders

Enduring personality changes, not attributable to brain damage and disease

Habit and impulse disorders

Gender identity disorders

Disorders of sexual preference

Psychological and behavioural disorders associated with sexual development and orientation

Other disorders of adult personality and behaviour

Unspecified disorders of adult personality and behaviour

DSM-IV divides the personality disorders into three groups. The first group, cluster A, includes the Paranoid, Schizoid and Schizotypal Personality Disorders where the individuals often appear odd or eccentric. The second group, cluster B, includes Antisocial, Borderline, Histrionic and Narcissistic Personality Disorders; people with these disorders often appear dramatic, emotional, or erratic. Finally, the third group, cluster C, includes Avoidant, Dependent, and Obsessive-Compulsive Disorders; people with these disorders often appear anxious or fearful. Individuals often present with co-occurring personality disorders from different clusters.

ICD-10 (F60–F69) divides specific personality disorder into ten subgroups: paranoid, Schizoid, Dissocial, Emotionally unstable (Impulsive type and Borderline type), Histrionic, Anankastic, Anxious (avoidant), Dependent, Other specific, and Personality disorder, unspecified. Specific personality disorder and Mixed and other personality disorders (F60 and F61) are described as those types of condition comprising deeply ingrained and enduring behaviour patterns, manifesting themselves as inflexible responses to a broad range of personal and social situations. They represent either extreme or significant deviations from the way the average individual in a given culture perceives, thinks, feels, and particularly relates to others.

The enduring personality changes not attributable to brain damage and disease (group 3, F62) include personality changes after catastrophic experience, after psychiatric illness, and other enduring personality changes, specified and unspecified.

F63, Habit and impulse disorders, include pathological gambling, fire-setting, and stealing as well as sexual relationship disorder, and other psychosexual development disorders together with gender identity disorders, specified and unspecified. F65, Disorders of sexual preference, list fetishism, fetishistic transvestism, exhibitionism, paedophilia, sadomasochism, and multiple disorders of sexual preference. F66, Psychological and behavioural disorders associated with sexual development and orientation, includes in the list sexual relationship disorder and other psychosexual development disorders, for example.

F68 and 69, Other disorders of adult personality and behaviour include the elaboration of physical symptoms for psychological reasons, intentional feigning of symptoms or disabilities, either physical or psychological, and other disorders of adult personality and behaviour, specified and F69, unspecified.

Antisocial personality

As antisocial personality disorder is most likely of all the personality disorders to come into contact with the health care services, further description of this disorder appears appropriate here.

Diagnosis of Personality Disorders (DSM-IV 1994) requires an evaluation of the individual's long-term patterns of functioning, and particular personality features must be evident by early childhood. The personality traits (which are enduring patterns of perceiving, relating to, and thinking about the environment and oneself that are exhibited in a wide range of social and personal contexts) that define these disorders must also be distinguished from characteristics that emerge in response to specific situational stressors or more transient mental states (e.g. Mood or Anxiety Disorders, Substance Intoxication).

Judgement about personality functioning must take into account the individual's ethnic, cultural and social background. There are also differences between the sexes, with certain disorders diagnosed more frequently in men, for example Antisocial Personality Disorders, and others, for example Borderline, Histrionic and Dependent Disorders, diagnosed more frequently in women (DSM-IV 1994).

By far the most detailed information results from the particular interest paid to the antisocial (psychopathic) personality disorder. More articles and books are written about this personality disorder than any other and it is thought that the reason for this is the profound effect these people have on society, due possibly to their criminal propensities. McCord (1982) quotes results of studies which estimated that approximately 20 per cent of incarcerated criminals could be labelled 'psycho-pathic' and English psychiatrists thought that their prisons contained 18 per cent of 'psychopaths' (Hyland 1942). In the 1980 survey McCord found that institutions for juvenile delinquents held approximately 30 per cent of psychopaths and it has been suggested therefore that about 10 per cent of all criminals are, on a cross-cultural basis, psychopathic (McCord 1982). It is likely that most of these individuals treated, particularly in secure units or secure hospital settings, are psychopaths, or suffering from the severest forms of personality disorders, and this may in some cases be associated with other forms of mental illness. McCord (1982) agrees that there has been an attempt to change the term 'psychopath' to 'sociopath', and then to 'antisocial personality'; he argues that the psychopath is not 'antisocial' but 'asocial' and to use the term antisocial is likely to 'lump' all criminals, drunkards and many other deviants together.

DSM-IV (1994) states that the essential feature of this disorder is a pervasive pattern of disregard for, and violation of, the rights of others that begins in childhood or early adolescence and continues into adulthood. It is often referred to as psychopathy, sociopathy, or dyssocial personality disorder, of which deceit and manipulation are central features. The antisocial behaviour must not occur exclusively during the course of schizophrenia or manic episode.

For the diagnosis to be given, an individual must be at least 18 years old with some symptoms of conduct disorder before the age of 15 years. The specific behaviours characteristic of conduct disorder fall into one of four categories: aggression to people and animals; destruction of property; deceitfulness or theft; or serious violation of rules. DSM-IV (1994) also reports that these people frequently lack empathy and tend to be callous, cynical and contemptuous of the feelings, rights and sufferings of others; have an inflated and arrogant self-appraisal; and are excessively opinionated, self-assured or cocky.

Prevalence in community samples is about 3 per cent in males and about 1 per cent in females. Prevalence estimates within clinical settings have varied from 3 per cent to 30 per cent, and higher rates when associated with substance abuse treatment settings and prison or forensic settings (DSM-IV 1994).

ICD-10 (1992) states that assessment should be based on as many sources of information as possible, that it is sometimes possible to evaluate a personality condition in a single interview with a patient, but it is often necessary to have more than one interview and to collect history and data from informants.

McCord (1982) defines a 'psychopath' as an asocial, emotionally and psychologically insensitive person, who feels no guilt and is unable to form emotionally affectionate relationships with people. McCord goes on to state that the core 'psychopath' exhibits all of these characteristics, but he or she is very rare, resting at one end of a continuum which stretches from 'normal', displaying all of these traits, to an extreme degree and in such a manner that they constantly direct or inform his or her life.

Personality disorders in children and adolescents include disorders of childhood or adolescence such as conduct disorder, avoidant disorder of childhood or adolescence, identity disorder and personality disorders, antisocial personality disorder, avoidant personality disorder and borderline personality disorder. The diagnosis of conduct disorder, rather than antisocial personality disorder, is made if the person is under 18 years of age.

Gelder *et al.* (1996) see the necessity to classify abnormal personalities for the purpose of collecting statistics. They are of the opinion that it is better to give a description of the main features of personality such as being anxious or dependent. It is also stated that clinicians should be careful not to be misled into thinking that they understand any more about the patient just because they have assigned a personality to one of the classification categories.

Incidence of personality disorder

Study of the epidemiology of personality disorders has included statistics across the range of personality disorders rather than isolating each disorder accordingly. Problems of obtaining true statistics are due to the difficulties of diagnosis of personality disorders as well as their distribution; that is, for example, whether the population studied is from the mental hospitals or the community. Worldwide epidemiological studies of personality disorder may vary due to inconsistency of the statistics, as in some studies a wider diagnostic range of disorders has been used and some figures include admissions and readmissions to hospital, thus accounting for the large discrepancy of prevalence of personality disorder. The problem of studying personality disorder in populations is compounded by alcohol and substance abuse as these occur frequently in antisocial people as well as those who are diagnosed as having an antisocial personality disorder (Cadoret 1986). Cadoret goes on to give details of recent population studies in several major American cities, including some rural areas in one survey; these studies showed that there was a male predominance of the diagnosis of personality disorder with male to female ratios varying from 4: 1 to 7 or 8: 1. There is little reliable difference between races (that is, between blacks and non-blacks), with a lower prevalence of antisocials among college graduates, as many antisocials drop out of formal schooling early. The highest prevalence of personality disorders is said to be in central city populations, rather less in inner suburbs and less still in smaller towns, but the reasons for this distribution are not clear.

Norton and Hinshelwood (1996) report Casey's (1988) findings that severe personality disorder occurs in approximately 4 per cent of the adult population.

We are also reliably informed that conduct disorder is the commonest childhood psychiatric condition affecting 9 per cent of the urban population and 4 per cent of the rural population and it is reported that three times more boys than girls show typical symptoms of temper tantrums. As they get older these children bully, fight, carry and use knives, mistreat animals, mug, play truant, run away from home and commit arson. A third are known to be dyslexic and most have a lower IQ than their peers.

It is known that 40 per cent of seven- and eight-year-olds with conduct disorder become recidivist delinquents as teenagers; and over 90 per cent of the recidivist juvenile delinquents had conduct disorder as children. It is further reported that by the time they become adults they are fixed in a pattern of violence, dishonesty, drink-driving and unemployment.

All or some of these aspects are in the histories of those with personality disorder and case histories and therapy highlight their presence and the influential part they played in the development of the personality disorder.

Aetiology of personality disorders

It is widely thought that if personality disorders were better understood perhaps the concomitant behaviours could be brought under control, but since little is known about the factors accounting for normal variations in personality it is not surprising that difficulties are encountered when studying abnormal personality. Gelder *et al.* (1996) stress that two departures from the normal pattern of upbringing have been thought to contribute to the development of antisocial personality disorders: separation from parents, and disordered behaviour in the parents.

It is thought that certain aspects of personality disorder are evident in childhood; these might, in some part, be attributed to the effects of the people around the child. Most patients with severe personality disorder have histories of serious physical and/or sexual abuse or neglect in their formative years and in relation to their parents or substitute carers (Norton and Hinshelwood 1996).

Genetic causes

Generally there is not conclusive evidence to suggest that there is a genetic contribution to personality disorders, but DSM-IV (1994) reports that adoption studies indicate that both genetic and environmental factors contribute to the risk of this group of disorders.

Biological/neurological influences

People with antisocial personality seem so different from normal people, and so similar in their behaviour to some patients with brain injuries, that organic causes have been suggested for the personality disorder. There is no convincing evidence linking antisocial personality in adult life with brain injury in childhood, although it has been suggested that antisocial behaviour in childhood can be caused by minor degrees of damage to the brain ('minimal brain dysfunction') (Gelder *et al.* 1996). It has been quoted that 'almost all of the clinical features of the psychopath can be produced by physical disorders of the brain' (Elliott 1978). There is a possibility that personality disorder might result from delay in the development of the brain, and electroencephalographic abnormalities consistent with maturational delays have been reported in people with antisocial personalities. A previous study by Hare (1970) confirmed that antisocial personalities have atypical wave patterns and EEG research shows that there is widespread slow wave activity. This led earlier workers to suggest that psychopathy was caused by cortical immaturity, and that these people supposedly have the brain of a child and therefore exhibit the behaviour of a child. However 15 per cent of the population apparently have similar brain waves to the antisocial personality and they are normal. It is thought by some that 'psychopaths' suffer from a dysfunction in the underlying temporal and limbic mechanisms (Hare 1970). The limbic system has inhibitory effects on behaviour, particularly that related to fear, hence lesions in the limbic mechanisms could well interfere with learning to inhibit a punished response and so a person suffering from a dysfunction in the limbic system would tend to respond with the same behaviour, even if it had previously been inhibited because of punishment (McCord 1982).

Freeman (1993) writes that it has been found that these people have a slower rate of cortical recovery as measured by cortical-evoked potentials and the slower recovery would indicate lowered cortical arousal. It is thought therefore that these people are chronically under-aroused and that much of their behaviour is attention-seeking and motivated by a desire to increase arousal.

Personality disorder and upbringing

Considerable attention has been given to disturbances in parent–child relationships, particularly maternal deprivation, as factors influencing personality development. Psychological causes have been suggested for most types of personality disorder, but there is no scientific evidence on which to judge their importance. Gelder *et al.* (1996) emphasises that very little is known about the psychological causes of abnormalities of personality. However, theorists highlight the life-long process in personality disorder so that changes occurring later in life will have an influence on personality development. There have been many modifications and reappraisals of the psychoanalytic approaches to personality, and it has been stressed that the unconscious and the id (which is the primitive pre-formed psychic force in the unconscious – the source of the instinctive energy necessary for self-preservation and propagation) are less powerful than Freud had thought, and that personality is shaped more by the individual's life experiences than by instincts (Freeman 1993). Rogers' (1951) 'self-theory' is based on the individual's view of himself or herself – their self-concept – and this determines their view of the world and his/her behaviour. The self consists of all the cognitions and perceptions related to the 'I' or 'me' and the individual evaluates every experience in relation to this self-concept.

Social and environmental influences on personality development

There is no evidence to prove that disturbances in parent–child relationships, and in particular maternal deprivation, have any influence on personality disorders other than in the antisocial personality. But it is known that if personality traits are inherited the parents and families of people with personality disorders are likely to be abnormal too, leading to disturbing early experiences to complicate the life of the individual with the personality disorder (Hibbert 1994).

In an article published in *The Times* in January 1998, under the heading 'Criminal tendencies evident in childhood', Ian Murray reported from a survey that many future delinquents can be identified by the time they are seven by their aggressive behaviour and the ineffective way their parents are bringing them up.

The antisocial personality disorder is considered to begin during childhood as findings demonstrate that it is more frequent in childhood than adult life and becomes less so during adolescence. Rather less than half of all conduct disorders in childhood go on to become antisocial personality disorders in adult life, but children who had conduct disorders have deficits in a number of areas of social functioning in adulthood (Hill 1997). One of the major problems is how to tell which conduct disorders in childhood will go on to become antisocial personality disorder in adult life (Rutter and Garmezy 1983; Rutter and Giller 1983).

During the course of working with personality disordered patients it has been found that many of these patients might previously have attended a child guidance clinic, exhibited difficult behaviour, might have had a father with a criminal record or was an alcoholic, or have been taken into care and/or repeatedly moved during childhood. Research into psychopathology has been limited predominantly to the study of aggressive criminal or delinquent 'psychopaths', due possibly to psychopathy in its more violent forms presenting a threat to human life. The non-criminal 'psychopath' is difficult to distinguish from the rest of society.

In the Young Persons Unit at Broadmoor Hospital (an all-male ward), many patients were found to have come from disturbed family backgrounds: absent parents in childhood; criminal parents; violent parents; parents with a history of substance abuse; and parents who had been psychiatric in-patients (Reiss, Grubin and Meux 1996).

Assessments

Hibbert (1994) believes that rather than assigning a category to the personality, it is more useful to describe the main features of the person's behaviour in the descriptive terms used by ICD-10 (1992) or DSM-IV (1994). The description should include an assessment of strengths and weaknesses, and attention should be paid to identifying circumstances that provoke undesirable behaviour.

Initial assessments rely upon careful interviewing of the patient and members of their families, as it is not possible to judge the personality of these patients in the same way as judging other forms of mental illness. Those with personality disorder seldom complain of any difficulties and so the diagnosis can rarely be made just by listening to the patient. Personality therefore can only be judged by reliable accounts of the person's behaviour. As usual, accurate historical information is essential, all available records should be checked, and if the patient is unable to give a good account of their behaviour, assessment may rely on information obtained from other informants, such as relatives, partners or employers, and from social workers and public officers (Hibbert 1994). It is commonly thought that reliable information of personal history and past behaviour can be obtained from other informants and it is necessary to obtain a detailed account of the patient's behaviour in the past and under a wide range of circumstances. Hibbert tells us that observations of behaviour in a hospital setting may not be an accurate guide to a patient's normal behaviour.

The patient's self-given history cannot always be relied upon due to their propensity for lying or denying, but the diagnosis might well be aided by the therapist's feeling of frustration and helplessness brought about by the verbal battle and 'push' on the emotions during interactions (Doren 1987). The presence of the personality disorder will become increasingly apparent with continued contact with the patient (Hibbert 1994).

During this process several consultations may be necessary. Strengths and weaknesses need to be ascertained and investigation and detailed observation of undesirable behaviour, over a period of several weeks, might be necessary. Problems that are not apparent, but perhaps suspected and reported by others, can add useful information and aid in treatment planning.

Deciding upon the presence or absence of another psychiatric disorder can be difficult, particularly distinguishing episodes of depression from temporary crises provoked by a life event (Lewis and Wessely 1997).

Medical and case histories

A full medical history is necessary together with investigation of possible physical illnesses and organic brain disease (with access to CAT scan and EEG), and an intellectual assessment. Psychosis, neurotic disorders and knowledge of alcohol and substance abuse also need investigation.

A social history is also important as knowledge of the family, the accommodation and living conditions, educational and occupational history may also make a useful guide for management decisions. A legal history will immediately suggest the seriousness of the problem to the current forensic status. This will include recent offences, prison and institutional experience and delinquent behaviour and trouble with the police.

Personality

The identification of triggers that provoke dangerous behaviour, outbursts or other disturbing behaviour is important (Hibbert 1994). Therefore a number of investigations need to be implemented to discover whether there is evidence of empathy and ability to form a rapport: is the patient able to tell the truth and degrees of truth; does the patient lose their temper, fight or become violent, or is the patient excessively shy; and what are the general relationship problems?

Personality testing

Personality and intellectual functioning assessments may well give a lead towards detecting abnormal traits in personality. Traits are considered to be universal to differing degrees in people as they influence behaviour in the same ways in different situations and at different times, so that trait measures can be used predictively. The trait approach is popular in psychology as a number of apparently valid objective personality tests have been derived from it (Freeman 1993), such as the 16 Personality Factor (16PF) questionnaire. In the 16PF, 12 factors were obtained from factor analysis of ratings of one person by another and four from self-ratings. These were combined to form the 16PF, which is a hundred-question yes/no test, and by plotting the scores a personality profile results (Cattell and Butcher 1968).

The Eysenck personality system is made up of four dimensions: extraversion–introversion; neuroticism–stability; psychoticism–stability; and intelligence (Eysenck and Eysenck 1963). These measures apply not just to normal and abnormal personality but to mental illness, criminals and those suffering from antisocial personality disorder (Freeman 1993). From this personality system a succession of personality inventories have been produced to measure such traits: the Eysenck Personality Inventory (EPI) and, more recently, the Eysenck Personality Questionnaire (EPQ) (Eysenck and Eysenck 1975), which also contains items for measuring psychoticism and has a lie scale.

The Minnesota Multiphasic Personality Inventory (MMPI) (Hathaway and McKinley 1970) measures traits such as depression, hypochondriasis, hysteria, psychopathic deviation, masculinity, femininity, paranoia, psychasthenia, schizophrenia, hypomania and finally social introversion. The inventory has 550 statements about attitudes, emotional reactions, physical and psychological symptoms and past experiences to which the subject answers 'true', 'false', or 'cannot say'. Items on the scale differentiate between eight clinical groups, and other scales test for the reliability and consistency of the responses which are subject to deliberate false reporting. The final score is plotted on a profile and any score that is two standard deviations above the mean is considered potentially pathological. The test was designed to identify people with serious personality disorders but it is also widely used in studying normal populations (Hathaway and McKinley 1970).

The Rorschach (1942) is a test in which a standard set of ten inkblots serve as a stimulus for associations. The series of inkblots is administered in order and they are reproduced on cards which are numbered one to ten. A verbatim record is kept of the patient's responses with reaction times and total time spent on each card (Kaplan and Saddock 1988). This test is a particularly useful diagnostic tool as the thinking and associational patterns of the patient are highlighted or brought more clearly into focus, largely because the ambiguity of the stimulus provides relatively few areas for what may be conventional or standard responses. The Rorschach also elicits data that can aid in differential diagnosis, particularly in evaluating whether or not thought disorder exists. For example, patients with schizotypal or borderline personalities are characterised by idiosyncratic thought, peculiarities of language and unconventional thinking.

Tyrer and Alexander (1979) developed a structured interview, the Personality Assessment Schedule (PAS) for rating of personality disorder, and this is conducted with a relative or close friend. These assessments are aimed at helping to highlight strengths as well as weaknesses as treatment is based on attempting to build favourite features as well as modifying unfavourable ones (Gelder et al. 1996).

Once a diagnosis is arrived at, the usual battery of pre-treatment assessments might also be completed. These will be carried out by those who will be involved in the treatment and they will vary according to the overall treatment plan. They might include behavioural and cognitive assessments, investigation into the suitability for dynamic psychotherapy – either in groups or for individual treatment – educational assessment and assessment of overall communicative ability, with particular emphasis on language.

Communication problems associated with personality disorders

There is no specific communication problem associated with personality disorders, but a general difficulty which is likely to be identified during the course of assessment and treatment. Details of the patient's history, acquired from their family, may include observations such as a lack of maternal/infant bonding, or rearing a placid, quiet, unresponsive or rejecting baby; the child who develops temper tantrums and frustrations that later lead to the inability to discuss, negotiate or share feelings and information is found to be a regular pattern of the background to personality disorder. This all adds further useful information in discovering the origins of some of the problems and also helps towards deciding upon areas of treatment. Parents often tell of difficulty communicating with their child stemming from early childhood and the problems associated with this, particularly when other children in the family do not present in the same ways. Patients themselves report similar difficulties when talking about the past – 'I couldn't talk with my family'; 'I felt like an outsider'; 'I was a loner for as long as I can remember' – are the sort of comments regularly heard. During the course of talking about these details in treatment the patient discovers that the family isolation was often engineered by the patient themselves. It is interesting to note how in many cases there is a 'close' relationship built between the patient and a member of the extended family (such as an aunt, grandmother or close family friend) which has produced friction within the family and has provided a certain 'power' for the patient. Reference to these people features regularly during the course of therapy.

Few personality disordered people excel academically, although intellectually they are often capable of achieving successful educational standards. Educational interest and competence decline during adolescence when truanting (a regular addition to the history), delinquency, alcohol and substance abuse take the place of formal education. The result is poor literacy and numeracy skills, linked with equally poor language skills. Many patients have reported experiencing difficulty concentrating at school, their minds always being on other things, suggesting an active fantasy life. Maturing verbal skills are also handicapped as formal peer group and teacher-organised groups will be shunned. This seldom leads to social and educational accomplishments and so the communication problems increase. If perhaps there should be a period of enforced detention resulting from criminal behaviour, the patient will have lived in close contact with others whose histories are similar to his or her own. The patient will have been exposed to the tough 'macho' communication style of prison life where the use of prison jargon, swearing and obscene language is normal and social refinements are scorned and ridiculed.

Patients may give the impression of being verbally capable. For example, one young man said, 'I've always been good with words. I had a better vocabulary than most, it was how I used those words that was wrong; all the words were negative and I used them to intimidate.' Another young man stated that he could not talk about his feelings as all he ever felt was anger; this was demonstrated by his inability to use or find words related to his anger. Yet another young man said that he 'hadn't got anything to say', and some time later was to remember that statement with incredulity. Some patients unable to express anger verbally may state their difficulties with silence, a mute refusal, and in some extreme moments of tension self-expulsion from the therapeutic situation. When this occurs this patient usually returns for the next session and explains their dilemma, which might be a chain of negative thoughts or panic and eventual helplessness compounded by a paucity of adequate accompanying expressive language.

A limited vocabulary might be accompanied by non-verbal communication abnormalities with a seeking of greater body distance than is usual, a reluctance to be touched, with gestures which are minimal or when accompanied by anger are exaggerated or intimidating. Facial expressions tend to be more limited than normal, and in cases of antisocial personality disorder thunderous looks accompanied by tension and aggressive postures with harsh, loud and perhaps abusive speech are used to keep others at bay.

Cleckley (1976) speculates that antisocial personalities suffer from a deep-rooted semantic disorder in which the normal connections between semantic and affective components of language are missing or dysfunctional. There is also an assertion that the left hemisphere of 'psychopaths' (and schizophrenics) are damaged or dysfunctional and that there is something 'odd' about the way in which psychopaths use language. Their behaviour is often strikingly inconsistent with their verbalised thoughts, feelings and tensions, and there may be something pathological about the structure and dynamics of this person's language processes. Recent research suggests that there may be subtle deficits or anomalies in the interhemispheric organisation of the 'psychopath's' language processes (Hare 1986). Louth *et al.* (1998) state that a key feature of psychopathy is the ability to deceive, manipulate, and con the unwary, while seeming to be sincere. They questioned whether sincerity is achieved solely through body gestures and facial expression, or whether there is something different about the voice quality of psychopaths. The results of a study carried out by Louth *et al.* (1998) indicate that psychopaths are insensitive to the emotional connotations of language, and that their vocal characteristics may be part of a self-presentation mode designed to manipulate and control interpersonal interactions.

Particular problem areas

Speech problems may more likely be to do with lack of experience through restricted exposure to the usual variety of speech situations. In some cases these difficulties are accompanied by speech pathology, such as a severe stutter, voice disorders and continuing articulatory disorders inherited from childhood, all of which help to complicate the general impoverished language pattern. From case histories it is found that many patients have received formal speech and language therapy either before or during the early years at school, or during attendance at a special school or unit, and in some cases these patients may still demonstrate an inadequate use of both expressive and receptive language. It would appear that even with early treatment and support, full resolution of the speech and communication problems was not achieved, as during the course of development difficulties maintaining and developing adequate adolescent and adult use of language continued. The patient's preoccupation with their own position and problems might well reduce their listening skills which may, as a result, become overselective and handicapping. Poor concentration and language development and maturation are unlikely to improve, unless these problems are addressed early in treatment.

In some cases working in groups with these patients can be difficult as there are those patients who attempt and succeed, through inappropriate laughing, and voicing unpleasant and derogatory comments, in making others feel uncomfortable. This behaviour can prove both destructive towards other group members and exhausting for the therapists. In individual sessions silence might also be used to control, confront and demonstrate hostility or to bring about some response such as anger in the therapist.

Management and treatment

There is a difference of opinion about the usefulness of treating personality-disordered patients. Many say that this work is unrewarding but it is known that a substantial number of patients improve with time and the intervention of treatment. But we are reliably informed that patients within the category of severe personality disorder make extensive use of the health services, social services, and other agencies (Norton and Hinshelwood 1996). Reiss *et al.* (1996) assure us that young patients with personality disorder can be successfully treated.

Taylor (1996) reports that the delivery of treatment to those diagnosed as having personality disorders depends on choice – the choice of the prospective patient, but also choice of the prospective treater. Some of the discrepancy between treatment needs and provision may be accounted for by lack of patient motivation, perhaps especially within prison where there can be no compulsion into treatment. Taylor continues by highlighting some of the further problems associated with treatment, in particular that personality disorder can induce counter-reactions from others, which are so similar in quality to their own pathology that they not only impair immediate clinical judgements but probably in part explain the dearth of effort to define and treat the problems of these people effectively.

Pines' (1978) description of working in therapy with these patients sums up the treatment conflicts: 'Those attending personality disordered patients feel impelled to conform to a pattern imposed by the patient, so that we begin to feel provoked, hostile, persecuted and to (have) to behave exactly as the patients need us to, becoming rejecting and hostile!'

It is thought that to gain benefits, treatment needs to start early (Murray 1998). A survey relating to children with conduct disorders and developing delinquency showed that it is important to establish strong home backgrounds, help teachers acquire techniques to reduce disruptive behaviour and teach parents the importance of praising their children. These aspects should be taken into consideration when treatment is planned, where past deficits and abnormal circumstances and behaviours need to be understood, their histories traced, and to be able to look towards a positive and productive future.

Freeman (1993) reminds us that a number of principles should be kept in mind when thinking about management and specific aspects of treatment. First, recognise that progress will be slow. Think about the situation as well as the person – management might be easier if aimed at changing life circumstances rather than changing personality. Second, ensure that treatment expectations can be met, and that the change is geared towards the real world and not just towards the therapeutic environment.

It is not surprising that in many cases it is thought that medical help is often denied these patients due to the ingrained nature of their personality features and their apparent non-compliance with medical treatment and direction.

On the whole the management offered to these patients will depend on where and when they are seen. Patients are found in certain settings and are unlikely to be found in others; for instance, they rarely refer themselves for treatment and so are unlikely to be treated in the community, and if referred by others will resist help as in some cases they perceive that the problems are not theirs. A patient can spend a great deal of time attempting to change the environment rather than himself or herself; and is reluctant to discuss their problems with a stranger and yet equally resists prolonging a relationship in order to develop a satisfactory environment for discussion. A substantial number of these people will be seen in a locked or controlled environment, either prison or special (forensic) hospitals, regional secure units or other specialised units. Once in such an environment the patient's options for affecting their environment are substantially decreased.

Resistance to treatment

Boredom is a major problem and, added to the initial reluctance to accept a treatment regime, the resistance to conform might well be channelled into seeking stimulation the patient enjoys, so creating frustration and difficulties for others. Eventually, once it is found that the system cannot be 'beaten' and that the patient can be partly responsible for himself or herself, the carers are given opportunity to offer and provide help. This realisation will vary in time from patient to patient and in some cases resistance to treatment will be maintained indefinitely, whereupon treatment will eventually be terminated. Even so, offers to help the patient will be tested by the patient, and so the therapist also needs to test by setting tasks and assignments to complete between treatment sessions. The excuses for not completing these tasks are legion but without doubt their completion is a rewarding sign of positive motivation and acceptance of treatment.

It is known, to this author, that these patients when seen in speech and language therapy out-patient clinics pose extra problems; they see their rights to receive treatment yet are often poor attenders. Some manipulate numerous appointments within the local services, not always presenting with the same speech symptoms, and they allow little chance for the therapists to establish a diagnosis, let alone collect all the relevant medical and psychiatric notes. In the case of one young man it was not until he was admitted to a special hospital that the size of the problem and the energy he expended seeking his idea of the ideal treatment came to light. Five different speech and language therapy appointments for assessment in five different centres were manipulated, whilst intermittently attending a psychiatric out-patient clinic and occasional short- stay in-patient treatment. The result presented confusion for the professional carers as well as the patient and could well have continued, but for admission, at which point care was organised by a clinical team. There was no opportunity to manipulate treatment or the therapists, and no choice of therapy, and so with compliance the therapeutic results were eventually rewarding, including satisfactory remediation of the speech pathology.

Treatment

Few therapists will agree that they enjoy working with personality-disordered patients. This is probably due to the results of treatment being less observable than with other patients and the additional frustration of observing the patient persistently performing self-destructive and self-defeating behaviour (Doren 1987). The patient–therapist relationship is also less rewarding as responsiveness is frequently negative, but this can also be a guide to progress when emotional responsiveness improves and becomes more normal. Lion (1981) states that treatment and rehabilitation of personality disorder, when carried out with realistic optimism, empathy and enthusiasm, leads to slow but significant change and improvement. Drugs have little part to play in personality disorder; the aim is to build up a trusting relationship so that the patient can talk openly. Treatment is not aimed at altering personality but altering the behaviour or unacceptable symptoms resulting from the personality and associated with the abnormality. The treatment is not hopeless – just difficult. Many therapists persist in this work as they find it so interesting and this interest leads to reward and satisfaction.

Drug treatment

It is thought there is little place for medication, although there is some evidence of a reduction of the difficulties in those with severe impulsive disorders of a borderline type using low doses of major tranquillizers (Hibbert 1994).

Other therapies

Treatment might involve various types of psychotherapy as angry and antisocial people often value a contract that allows access to staff or a place where they can discharge their anger safely or verbally ventilate their feelings. Individual and group psychotherapy might be appropriate; cognitive and behavioural approaches are particularly helpful in cases where patients experience social anxiety and fear and for those with low self-esteem. The passive dependent personalities are often helped by assertiveness training and almost all patients may benefit from some degree of social skills training (Argyle, Trower and Bryant 1974). It is thought that in some cases patients will benefit from a total therapeutic environment such as in a special unit or hospital where treatment can be organised towards gradual changes and where the aims should be modest. It should also be recognised that there are some patients, as already mentioned, who due to their resistance will not benefit from treatment, however sensitive and skilful the therapist, and therefore sessions should not continue. The prerequisites to treatment are that the patient 'needs' to be there proving that they are motivated and that they see the advantage of developing this particular interpersonal relationship. The therapist should be able to exploit the patient's positive qualities, to help put them to use, and must not fear the treatment and so should be able to confront the patient in order not to be manipulated.

The multidisciplinary team possibly offers the greatest scope for treatment and has the advantage of supporting individual team members constantly throughout their endeavours. This support is vital for the continuation of therapeutic energy and inspiration, as well as monitoring 'across the board' progress and may possibly be the only way, in some cases, to receive rewards in this work. The therapeutic team has a great deal to offer. No one person will make a decision and this helps to reinforce and support any therapeutic decision made on behalf of the patient. This also endorses an eclectic approach to treatment and gives the patient every opportunity to make progress. A highly co-ordinated team approach is needed for successful treatment.

The younger the patients the more likely they are to respond to treatment. This is thought to be due to the more recent onset of symptoms than, for instance, in the cases of hardened antisocial criminal adults where a 'cure' is unlikely but treatment towards a more adaptive functioning for daily living might be achieved. There is a need to stress that most of the treatment programmes assume, at the least, a modest linguistic skill as without this ability the more sophisticated psychodynamic treatments present problems for the patient. The behavioural treatments, and in particular cognitive therapy and speech and language therapy, may help to address these linguistic difficulties as they may introduce and develop a vocabulary that can be extended for daily use as well as in various group therapy settings. An area of great difficulty for many patients concerns feelings where the paucity of vocabulary limits the patient's ability to participate fully in treatment. A variety of treatments can be organised to take place side by side if necessary.

Psychotherapy

Verbal skills in group psychodynamic therapy need to be adequate to allow for personal development and progress for both the patient and the group, and linguistic imbalance in a group is not only a handicap to the patient but to the group as a whole. Although many people progress and develop language skills in this kind of group it is a slow process and supplementary treatment to assist the development of language competence is desirable in some cases. Individual psychotherapy offers the chance to continue development of language use and incorporate the more conventional psychodynamic approach. The personality-disordered patient demonstrates a pronounced reluctance to commit thoughts to paper, but if prepared to do so a diary is a means of setting and maintaining a regular task demonstrating an investment in treatment. Both patient and therapist share the contents and this helps to develop an important level of trust. It is another way of monitoring the developing use of language, gives permission for therapeutic direction and ultimately is a clear way of demonstrating to the patient a number of fundamental points of importance and interest. The diary may become spontaneously more elaborate and emphasis develop from self to others. Attitudes change with mellowing of opinions; expansion, flexibility and creativity of language is ongoing; and feelings rather than actions prevail. There might be an occasional bonus of sharing a dream, joke, sad or happy event and occasionally there might be a written reward or compliment for the therapist's persistence.

Supportive psychotherapy

Supportive psychotherapy might be the gentle way towards initiation into more formal psychotherapy and offers the chance to experiment with talking in a group and getting the 'feel' of group dynamics, learning that a group *can* be supportive, like a family, and that it can also produce a few pressures aiding personal growth.

Personal construct psychotherapy

Personal construct psychotherapy (which is covered in more detail in Chapter 25) offers the choice of where to begin in therapy as a result of viewing where the patient is on their personal construct grid. It is a way of monitoring change and development, reducing suspicion and developing trust, and is often seen by the personality-disordered patient as being a safe method of treatment. It is a particularly useful means of working on language development and the development is demonstrated on subsequent grids.

Cognitive therapy

Cognitive therapy focuses on cognitive processes as mediators of behaviour and emotion and suggests that disordered behaviour and emotion are largely consequences of various cognitive deficiencies. It relies chiefly on speech as the vehicle for identifying and remediating these deficiencies (Barley 1986). During their recent cognitive work with personality-disordered patients, Beck and Podesky (1989) focused on the person's main beliefs and strategies such as the avoidant personality's belief that it is terrible to be rejected, that people don't really know them and that they cannot tolerate unpleasant feelings, for example. Or the antisocial personality patient who believes they are entitled to break the rules, sees that other people are weak and are capable of being exploited, and so their main strategy is to attack, rob, deceive and manipulate.

Behaviour therapy

Cognitive and behavioural therapy may be introduced in a group setting and might include social and communication skills, assertiveness training, anger management and work on interpersonal skills. Quayle and Moore (1998) evaluate the impact of such structured group work in a high security hospital and their findings suggest that a range of factors, including group work, generate a statistically significant and clinically important difference in the patient's presentation and behaviour.

Formal educational programmes and specialised programmes such as sex education, family therapy, groups for alcohol and substance abuse problems, community skills programmes and domestic and social rehabilitation might be some of the appropriate therapies offered. Not all of the patients will need all of these treatments; some might well be involved in a number of complementary groups or individual sessions. The speech and language therapist's skills can be used in many of these treatment areas as well as to help augment programmes by providing formal treatment for any speech pathology, either as a separate treatment or within a structured group.

Speech and language therapy

The speech and language therapist is more likely to provide a service for this particular group of patients in either a special hospital, a regional secure unit, or within the penal services, in particular working with young offenders.

Service delivery should be from within the multidisciplinary team. It is essential that treatment is multifaceted so that vital support and supervision can be given by other professionals to those involved in the assessment and therapy programmes.

References

Argyle, M., Trower, P. and Bryant, B. (1974) Explorations in the treatment of personality disorder and neurosis by social skills training. *British Journal of Medical Psychology* 47, 63–72.

Barley, W.D. (1986) Behavioural and cognitive treatment of criminal and delinquent behaviour. In W.H. Reid, D. Don, J.I. Walker and J. Bonner (eds) *Unmasking the Psychopath*. New York: Norton. pp.159–190.

Beck, A. and Podesky, C. (1989) *Cognitive Therapy of Personality Disorders*, World Congress of Cognitive Therapy, Oxford, June 1989.

Cadoret, R. (1986) Epidemiology of antisocial personality. In W.H. Reid, D. Dorr, J.I. Walker and J. Bonner (eds) *Unmasking the Psychopath*. New York: Norton. pp.28–44.

Cattell, R.B. and Butcher, H.S. (1968) *The Prediction of Achievement and Creativity*. London: Bobbs-Merrill.

Cleckley, H. (1976) *The Mask of Sanity* (fifth edition). St Louis: Mosby.

DSM-IV (1994) *Diagnostic and Statistical Manual of Mental Disorders* (fourth edition). Washington, DC: American Psychiatric Association.

Doren, D.M. (1987) *Understanding and Treating the Psychopath*. Chichester: Wiley.

Elliott, F.A. (1978) Neurological aspects of antisocial behaviour. In W.H. Reid (ed) *The Psychopath*. New York: Brunner/Mazel. p.146.

Eysenck, H.S. and Eysenck, S.B.G. (1963) *Eysenck Personality Inventory.* Windsor: NFER-Nelson.

Eysenck, H.S. and Eysenck, S.B.G. (1975) *Manual of the Eysenck Personality Questionnaire (Junior & Adult).* Sevenoaks: Hodder and Stoughton.

Freeman, C.P. (1993) Personality disorder. In R.E. Kendell and A.K. Zeally (eds) *Companion to Psychiatric Studies* (fifth edition). Edinburgh: Churchill Livingstone. pp.407–432.

Gelder, M., Gath, D., Mayou, R. and Cowen, P. (1996) *Oxford Textbook of Psychiatry* (third edition). Oxford: Oxford University Press.

Hare, R.D. (1970) *Psychopathy: Theory and Research.* Chichester: Wiley.

Hare, R.D. (1986) Twenty years of experience with the Cleckley psychopath. In W.H. Reid, D. Dorr, J.I. Walker and S. Bonner (eds) *Unmasking the Psychopath.* New York: Norton. pp.3–27.

Hathaway, S. and McKinley, S. (1970) *The Minnesota Multiphasic Personality Inventory.* Windsor: University of Minnesota/NFER-Nelson.

Henderson, D. (1939) *Psychopathic States.* New York: Norton.

Hibbert, G.A. (1994) The personality disorders. In N. Rose (ed) *Essential Psychiatry* (second edition). Oxford: Blackwell Scientific Publications. pp.107–113.

Hill, P. (1997) Child psychiatry. In R. Murray, P. Hill and P. McGuffin (eds) *Essentials of Postgraduate Psychiatry* (third edition). London: Grune and Stratton. pp.97–144.

Hyland, H.H. (1942) Psychoneuroses in the Canadian Army Overseas. *Canadian Association Journal 47*, 432–440.

ICD-10 (1992) *Classification of Mental and Behavioural Disorders.* Geneva: World Health Organisation.

Kaplan, H.I. and Saddock, B.J. (1988) *Synopsis of Psychiatry: Behavioral Sciences Clinical Psychiatry* (fifth edition). Baltimore: Williams and Wilkins.

Lewis, G. and Wessely, S. (1997) Neurosis and personality disorder. In R. Murray, P. Hill and P. McGuffin (eds) *Essentials of Postgraduate Psychiatry* (third edition). Cambridge: Cambridge University Press. pp.145–191.

Lion, J.R. (1981) A comparison between DSM-III and DSM-II personality disorders. In J.R. Tonin (ed) *Personality Disorders: Diagnosis and Management* (second edition). Baltimore: Williams and Wilkins.

Louth, S.M., Williamson S., Alpert, M., Pouget, E.R. and Hare, R.D. (1998) Acoustic distinctions in the speech of male psychopaths. *Journal of Psychlinguistic Research 27*, 3, 375–384.

McCord, M.W. (1982) *The Psychopath and Milieu Therapy: A Longitudinal Study.* New York: Academic Press.

Murray, I. (1998) Criminal tendencies evident in childhood. *The Times.* 16 January.

Norton, K. and Hinshelwood, R.D. (1996) Severe personality disorder: Treatment issues and selection for in-patient psychotherapy. *British Journal of Psychiatry 168*, 723–731.

Pines, M. (1978) Group analytic psychotherapy with borderline personality disorder. *Group Analysis 11*, 115–126.

Quayle, M. and Moore, E. (1998) Evaluating the impact of structured groupwork with men in a high security hospital. *Criminal Behaviour and Mental Health 8*, 77–92.

Reiss, D., Grubin, D. and Meux, C. (1996) Young 'psychopaths' in special hospital: treatment and outcome. *British Journal of Psychiatry 168*, 99–104.

Rogers, C. (1951) *Client Centred Therapy.* Boston: Houghton Mifflin.

Rorschach, H. (1942) *Rorschach Inkblot Test Psychodiagnostics.* Berne: Hans Huber.

Rutter, M. and Garmezy, A. (1983) Developmental psychopathology. In E.M. Heatherington (ed) *Socialisation, Personality and Social Development*, Vol.4 (fourth edition). New York: Wiley. pp.775–911.

Rutter, M. and Giller, H. (1983) *Juvenile Delinquency: Trends and Perspectives.* Harmondsworth: Penguin.

Taylor, P.J. (1997) Forensic psychiatry. In R. Murray, P. Hill and P. McGuffin (eds) *Essentials of Postgraduate Psychiatry* (third edition). Cambridge: Cambridge University Press.

Trethowan, W. and Sims, A.C.P. (1983) *Psychiatry* (fifth edition). London: Bailliere Tindall.

Tyrer, P. and Stein, G. (1993) *Personality Disorder Reviewed.* London: Gaskell, Royal College of Psychiatrists.

Tyrer, P. and Alexander, J. (1979) Classification of Personality Disorder. *British Journal of Psychiatry 135*, 163–167.

CHAPTER 6

Communication, Language and Mental Illness

Trevor Walt, Sarah Kramer and Jenny France

It is becoming increasingly apparent that mental disorders are thought to have their origins in early adolescence and research is beginning to show that perhaps influences in early childhood also play a significant part. It has been reported in the media that profound effects occur in those who live with sufferers of mental illness, as their odd and unusual behaviour and communication subject others to bewilderment, misery and fear. This can lead to social isolation of patients and their families through misunderstandings, usually perpetuated by a lack of information and knowledge of the patient's predicament and equally by a lack of knowledge generally about mental illness. This is thought, in part, to be due to attempts by sufferers and their families to disguise the illness and the accompanying problems, thus preventing appropriate treatment for the sufferer and support for other family members and in particular the children, whose own development may be affected by exposure to the effects of mental illness in the family.

Speech and language therapy research leads us to believe that parental mistreatment, and this might including living in an abnormal environment, as already mentioned, may lead to children having difficulty developing normal language, and this in turn can lead to communication problems. The required skills, in particular verbal skills, are known to deteriorate under stress and children with learning difficulties, in particular, have difficulty in interpreting social situations. This information is regarded as being highly relevant in mental illness and also in mentally disordered offender patients.

The creativity, fluidity, and spontaneity of utterance can be affected by developmental delay which in turn may cause speech pathology and many forms of mental illness. As communication is a two-way process, to be effective there must be a transmitter of information and a receiver, both of whom must have a common language and be able to interpret the non-verbal skills accompanying spoken language. In some cases this is particularly important, as in communication with people who are deaf. It is accepted that non-verbal performance of those suffering from mental illnesses is affected and this contributes to differential diagnosis within psychiatry. It is also the unusual and bizarre non-verbal behaviours that affect relationships with others and negatively influence communication.

Speech is the major component of effective communication from which people may develop satisfactory social relationships (France 1996). The pragmatic criterion for communication competence is the appropriateness of speech used in context and this requires co-operation and emphasises the usefulness and effectiveness of form and the accountability procedures practised by speakers in negotiating their different scenes. The analytical criteria for evaluating linguistic competence can be based on a sentence's grammatical structure (syntax), its semantic content and the pragmatics or appropriateness of speech in context (Dore 1986). Therefore non-verbal aspects of communication are important alongside the verbal aspects; these consist of postures, gestures, facial expression and body space, for example. Other elements such as vocal volume, stress/emphasis, intonation and rhythm of speech also affect the message conveyed. Should any of these aspects of speech be absent or faulty the effect on the overall communication style is obvious and highlights a difficulty or problem, of the sort that is often associated with mental disorders, and it is likely to further disrupt the acquisition of language, will affect educational opportunities and social interaction and thus limit exposure to all aspects of good communication.

Language is the most important tool of communication (Foss and Hakes 1978). We do not think much about language, we just use it. A native speaker of a language knows a great deal about the language that they are never taught, implying that learning the words of, for example, English script requires knowledge about the structure of words and that this is acquired through exposure (France 1996). According to Bolinger (1975), acquiring a language calls for three things: a predisposition, a pre-existing language system and a competence. Its attainment is life-long, and so learning never ceases, is never completely learned, and is very complex. The rate of learning a language diminishes rapidly so that well before adolescence it seems to come to a stop. Adding to the known creativeness of language and to the multifaceted human life experiences, then we are aware that language is always changing and needs to be flexible in order to adapt from one situation to another.

Environment

Having worked in a special hospital, where the patients live without access to the community and where their stay is 'without limit of time', we have been able to use these benefits. The patients' disadvantage, as they see it, is our advantage; this 'time' allows us to be involved in the clinical care and observation of patients, and to establish long-term therapeutic relationships over months and years rather than a few irregular sessions or number of weeks. During the patient's passage through the hospital, we can witness, and be part of, their developing mental health, and in particular their improving linguistic skills, at many varied levels and in an assortment of situations. It is regularly reported at case conferences that a patient's comm-unication changes, sometimes quite dramatically, from one hospital area to another. The patient might be reticent and difficult to engage in conversation on the ward for example, but be voluble, outgoing and easily approachable in another setting, such as in occupational therapy, an educational class, the chapel, or during visits or other social occasions. The opposite can also apply, when patients who are at ease, socially well skilled and good communicators in a ward setting, are unable to take these skills to other locations. This information is a useful pointer for the patient's future management, not only in a hospital setting but in other treatment centres and perhaps in his or her own home.

Identity

As hospital chaplain for some years, and previously a psychiatric nurse at the same hospital, one of the authors, Trevor Walt, has been conscious of the varying levels of communicative needs of the patients in a special hospital. To meet these needs a number of different therapeutic hats have been worn, and interchanged, sometimes at speed, to suit the ever-changing therapeutic temperature, i.e. from chaplain to nurse; to Walt himself, as a psychotherapist, friend, or 'just' another member of staff. All or any combination of these identities might be called upon during the same session or in any situation; for example, in a formal therapeutic session, before or after a service in the chapel, a specially arranged pastoral ward visit, during passage about the hospital, at a social function or another more formal one. This calls for swift, sensitive and intuitive adaption of role, sensitive observation and well practised listening skills.

It is interesting to note that in the early days of psychiatric in-patient care (1863 in Broadmoor Hospital) medical autocracy reigned, and after the Medical Superintendent, the second most important person was the chaplain as the only other professional in the hospital! He could not give Holy Communion to a patient without the express permission of the Medical Superintendent, but his did mean that the chaplain and doctor talked to one another about the mental state and fitness of the patient to interact in this way. Are we moving in that desirable direction again by including hospital chaplains in clinical teams?

The speech and language therapist's place in any mental health setting is still a mystery to many members of the clinical team, hospital managers and the patients too. Broadmoor, Rampton and Ashworth Special Hospitals have all employed a speech and language therapist for many years, and Broadmoor saw the need to develop a service well over twenty years ago, so the idea of speech and language therapy and the specialist skills this service can provide is accepted and used, often in an imaginative and extended way. Thus, a speech and language therapist, with perhaps the addition of supplementary training, can offer a number of skills associated with communications, speech and language therapy, with the emphasis on both using highly trained listening skills and training staff and patients as to their importance and use.

Listening skills

Before exploring further the fascinating subject of spoken and written language, we should pay some attention to the listener's skills and the effect mental illness has upon both the speaker and the listener.

What is it the listener 'hears'? How is what is 'heard' interpreted by the listener? What affects the listener that might influence the interpretation? How do we know that what the listener hears is the exact message the speaker intended? Do different clinicians and other health-care professionals hear the same message from the patient? What other individual aspects in the listener, either personal or professional, influence their ability to fully understand the patient? For example, will the psychiatrist, psychotherapist, nurse, speech and language therapist, chaplain, social worker and other therapists and teachers hear a message and interpret it similarly, and if not how do they come to realise any discrepancy and share their experiences?

Few health care professionals are actually trained to listen and therefore rely on their own skills and interest in the patient to achieve an understanding. It does not occur to many that special skills are needed, we hear what we hear – all of us hear the same utterance in the same way and so the assumption can be that we all understand the message similarly. This is, of course, not so. There are many reasons why we all might interpret one message differently; the reason is not solely to do with the speaker, but as much to do with the receptive skills of the listener. These skills can be taught and are increasingly being introduced into training programmes for professionals and other carers. This is bound to add positively to the quality of clinical skills and resulting patient management.

This chapter is written by people who had the opportunity to be formally taught about the advantages and complexities of listening during their professional training, and agree that listening cannot be taken for granted. Emphasis throughout training was placed on interpretation of speech, in particular, as well as communication in its broadest sense. We also believe that there is an innate curiosity in some listeners that makes these exchanges not only fascinating but important, stimulating, supportive and rewarding for both participants. This assists in the processes of building trust, developing relationships and helping to increase the patient's feelings of self-esteem and self-worth.

In the past, when working with groups of schizophrenic and personality-disordered patients, whatever the group is designed to attempt, we have begun, after the formal assessments, with explanations, video proof and other examples of how listening skills have suffered as a result of years of mental illness and/or social deprivation. Viewing video recordings of a group's assessment has been wonderfully illuminating to the patients, many of whom have been quite shocked at their appearance and their disregard for the spoken rights of other group members. They have subsequently enjoyed the fun and co-operation and sharing of acquiring new skills, brushing-up and using old ones, finding out that they are not alone with their problems and that a group can be an unthreatening and enjoyable place to be.

Individual therapy places different strains on the patient, one of which is sitting alone in a room with a stranger who has been introduced to them as the speech and language therapist. They might never have been aware of how their communication problems have affected their lives, or in fact even admitted to, or agreed with, ever having these problems. Consequently some unusual responses to these sessions have been recorded: 'It's no good you coming to see me – I can't talk'; 'I've got nothing to say'; 'Who says I can't talk, everyone understands me'; 'I've got nothing wrong with me, but I don't mind if you want to talk to me.' A senior nurse expressed amazement when learning of a particular patient's inclusion in a communication skills group; his opinion was that the patient could 'talk the hind-leg off a donkey'. Another nurse present during this discussion remarked that it was a pity the patient never listened to anyone but himself! This patient was a difficult man to help, but his arrogance did not stop other patients in the group telling him to 'shut up' at regular intervals; this was then supported at ward level, gradually assisting him in his development of insight into his social problems and those of other patients with whom he lived and regularly bored to frustration.

Encouraging some patients to stay for any time and talk about their daily lives is a problem, whilst with others, bringing to an end the huge outpouring of amazing and detailed personal information about their lives is another. What is surprising is how often we are warmly thanked for our time and other sessions requested. It becomes apparent that few of the patients have ever had the 'luxury' of 'telling their story' to anyone, and they certainly appreciate the comfort of empathic listening and understanding. Patients come to respect these sessions as special; not all have access to the same treatment opportunities and therefore patients feel special consideration is given to them, thus improving their status on the ward.

Expressive and receptive language

Language that conveys meaning can be expressed in a number of ways and we need to be sensitive to the patient's route to self-expression. One of the reasons he or she needs particular support, other than with the comprehension of language, is because of difficulties with self-expression: 'I haven't got the words'; 'I get tongue-tied, I'm all teeth.' Equally, we must monitor our own use of language to ensure that what we say is clearly understood, perhaps avoiding the use of medical jargon when with patients. Many times we have assumed that patients have understood us, and upon checking, find out that only some, or none, of the exchange was understood. We are aware that if patients have specific expectations on important matters they are likely to mishear/misinterpret the message. For example, the consultant might say, 'Next year we will consider a move to…', which is regularly heard as, 'Next year we will move you…'! Quite a different statement, accompanied by great disappointment after a translation, and much repair work needed. The patient might be unable to confront the clinical team as her or she is anxious, unassertive and unable to access appropriate language, or if too distressed the wrong response is given and so is the wrong impression. This is another guide to future management needs.

If use of language is a problem the therapists might need to adopt other approaches in order to achieve a beginning. Various ways have been successful, but these need to be dictated by the patient and can take both time, effort and sensitivity to identify and establish. Discovering the patient's interests and skills is often helpful; although many find the spoken word a challenge, the written word can unexpectedly be fluent and graphic, thereby providing an alternative way into treatment.

We should highlight literacy problems here. Many people with mental health disorders have poor or no literacy skills; it is therefore important to check on their abilities before embarrassing or angering the patient.

Access to these skills can be gained in a number of ways.

Examples

Example 1

A self-isolated 35-year-old schizophrenic man began his individual therapy, following on from a social skills course, by listing his symptoms on his computer and bringing a print-out to each session. He went on later to rate the intensity of the symptoms against each other, later again dividing the day/night into four parts which provided a sequence of changes from hour to hour. When reading the diary each week we were able to see a distinct pattern of his illness and how it was changing, with particular reference to changes around the time of his depot injection. During this exercise, lasting for many months, it was noted that his self-distinct style was becoming evident, not only in the sessions, but in other locations. He confessed to having begun to write short stories again and brought them spontaneously to the sessions (they were very good). At about that time his computing diary stopped and the sessions became more lively and a two-way dialogue then moved on to being patient-dominated, with jokes, anecdotes, gossip and eventually that patient being able to share his agonised past. He was then able to move on to consider the future.

Example 2

A young man with a personality disorder, resistant to help and very angry, eventually agreed to individual sessions in an attempt to develop a more sociable and fluent conversational style. No emphasis was placed on discussing his past history. These tortuous sessions began with the patient determining the room layout in order that he could sit as far away from the therapist as possible. There was a minimum of eye contact and his facial expression was a constant reminder of his anger and a message for his need and to keep control. The first session began with his question, 'What are *you* going to talk about?' After a short presentation about social skills, communication in particular, and the need to build relationships, the session struggled to a close. At the parting he asked if he could write something for next time as this would help him during the session. He arrived the following week with a handful of A4 sheets, covered with neat legible writing (no margins), pages numbered and the promise of more to follow. Then a stilted conversation about his daily routine and football concluded his time. On parting he stated that the therapist could keep the papers and he did not want them returned. The content of his writing, over the following months, was a detailed account of his life, his views and justifications for his offending history. He was never able to talk about his past with any fluency, but he did develop a superficial working relationship with the therapist; the space between them closed, eye contact increased, he was more relaxed, smiled occasionally and even appeared to enjoy some sessions. He refused the return of his 'life-story', which by its completion was an enormous box full of 20+ years of abuse, loneliness, bullying, violence, failed relationships and two terms in prison. Quite a gift!

Example 3

Another young schizophrenic man, whose acute illness made it difficult for him to participate in regular weekly sessions, but who valued those times he was well enough to attend, spent time talking repetitiously about his illness. He arrived for a session with some scraps of paper, apologised for the 'bad spelling and handwriting' and asked the therapist's opinion of the poems written on every surface. There were unexpectedly clear, moving, sad, amusing and profound. He was hoping some of them would be chosen for publication in the hospital patients' magazine. In this he was successful and was delighted; this was a great boost to his self-esteem. The poetry section of the magazine is always well subscribed to and competition for selection is severe.

Poetry is a surprisingly popular means of self-expression for many people with mental illnesses. For patients from all walks of life, educational backgrounds and differing states of mental health, it would appear to be a spontaneous avenue for the passage of emotions, reflection on past history, ideas, fantasies and reality; the medium is their choice and is one over which they have full control.

Example 4

A very disturbed woman with a personality disorder and intermittent symptoms of mental illness was prescribed individual therapy as she wanted help in order to talk about her past. Her educational standard was low and her language skills were poor.

After weeks of sitting in near silence, that patient stated that she did not know how to begin. She went on to explain that she had experienced therapy failures in the past and really wanted to succeed this time. She asked permission to bring some drawings to a session, as she thought these might help 'get started'. The drawings arrived for the next week and were a series of crudely sketched cartoons (5/6-year-old level), which she proceeded to describe, with the help of questions from the therapist. The drawings clearly showed aspects of her dreadful past and helped stimulate further memories and more drawings. With passing time the drawings became less frequent as access to words, loss of fear and the development of trust took their place. She eventually realised that she was managing on her own and was impressed with her progress, seeing it as all her own work. It was important that she dictated the pace and timing of progress, enabling her to experience control and the direction of her disclosures.

Example 5

A newly admitted 20-year-old young woman with an acute psychotic illness was diagnosed as being severely deaf. Learning to adapt to her hearing disability was greatly aided by her willingness to attend the patients' education centre where she was assisted with her literacy skills, including learning to use a computer, and encouraged to develop her artistic abilities. As a result she initiated the plan to design, write and illustrate a pamphlet about deafness. The finished product was professional enough to be distributed hospital-wide and the pride in her achievement went a long way to help boost her self-esteem. The diversion caused by the concentration and effort in completing the pamphlet also helped to distract her from the symptoms of her psychotic illness and greatly advanced her progress.

During therapy with individuals, couples and groups the quality, quantity and creativity of expressive language can be monitored, giving an indication of the patient's well-being, the return of symptoms of illness, sharing success or progress, or underlying problems, and the recognition of developing trust, through changing styles of communication and increasing linguistic competence and complexity.

Content of language

One of the many mysteries about mental illness is the effect it has upon thought and language, about which there is now considerable research in progress. The state and severity of the patient's illness will be reflected through their speech, ranging from clear comprehensible conversation to unintelligible utterances and, in rare cases, mutism. All of these speech patterns can occur from the same patient, and over a very short period of time. We know that many mentally ill people incorporate their religious beliefs into their delusions and these affect their lives and, in particular, their communication with others.

Religious language is particularly distinct and it is quite common to hear evidence of religiosity during the chaplain's first meeting with a newly admitted patient. The chaplain has designed a spiritual care assessment tool which includes provision for recording this evidence, including a simple listing of the patient's religious activity and exposure to spiritual influence. This may add a further dimension to the clinical assessment process and assist with the patient's diagnosis and treatment planning. It also brings the chaplain into closer contact with the clinical team and appropriately extends his role.

The chaplain may meet a new patient who believes he is God or that God in some way is controlling his behaviour. It is not uncommon to encounter patients who have committed very serious offences under such influence. The chaplain, by carefully listening to the patient's language and interpreting its meaning, may be able to offer valuable insight into the interface between disordered perception and religious experience. Equally, the chaplain has learned from experience that he can be spiritually and theologically enriched himself by tuning in to a patient's perception of God behind the views of mental disorder. Sometimes, what on the surface may be regarded as a disordered view of God may in fact be an insight that is otherwise difficult to perceive.

Psychotic patients who have evidence of religiosity within speech are often attracted to the more mystical and poetic forms of religious writing. When reading the Bible, for example, such patients are much more likely to be drawn to books which have been written in complex literary styles rather than those which are simply descriptive. For example, when reading the New Testament, patients are often magnetically attracted to the Book of Revelation rather than the Acts of the Apostles. Revelation is full of mystical poetic, apocalyptic language with powerful and often alarming imagery. The Acts of the Apostles is a narrative and literal description of life and times. This raises the question of why some forms of language are more attractive in this way. Also the issue of whether or not the writer of Revelation was himself disordered has been referred to in the past by many Bible commentators.

It is clear that as chaplains, like speech and language therapists and other professionals attached to clinical teams become more clinically orientated, it is more likely that care teams will be able to assess patient needs holistically and accept the importance of placing spiritual and religious needs alongside those which are purely physical or psychological. The assessment of not just the choice of words themselves but also the possible psychiatric insights behind the words is a valid part of this process.

Thoughts for interpretation and research

We, the writers, wonder if it would be helpful to 'listen-in' to two deeply psychotic men or women talking. Would it give us any clues, would it make sense to us, does it make sense to them?

When working in a group where a man 'knew' he was Jesus Christ, and also knew that other group members did not believe this, both that patient and the other group members were able to function at two levels. The man who 'knew' he was Jesus Christ was able to talk with the group at 'our level', as he was safe in his belief and able to accept us and our disbelief. He was also able to listen and accept us at our level, providing we did not attempt to 'convert' him.

In another group setting, a man 'knew' he was God; he was confronted by a group member who knew he had 'been' God, and explained to the man that, once his illness had been treated, he then realised that he was not God. The first patient was not convinced, but neither was he unsettled by the exchange. The lesson here is that when a patient is totally deluded, we need to deal with it as we would any other delusion, that is, we should accept the reality for the patient. When, or if, they begin to question things, then opinions of others are more likely to be considered.

What then is the relationship between the disordered mind and the use of different language? What is the attraction of any particular mentally ill person to certain forms of words? Is the Bible, especially in its older translation, attractive because of its poetry or powerful imagery or simply because the words do not change, can be accessed on demand and bring comfort to an individual, disturbed mind searching for answers? What is certain is that as therapists we must continue to listen carefully to the words our patients use as they so often indicate both the level of disorder and the level of insight into disorder that the patient is experiencing. For example, one clinically psychotic man when speaking with the chaplain after a service of Holy Communion said, 'He must have been a bloody big bloke.' When asked to whom he was referring, he replied, 'Jesus, because we keep eating him!' – the concrete language of schizophrenic disorder making what could be interpreted as a wonderful, theological insight about the greatness of God.

A concluding example demonstrates that although suffering from disorder, the author of this poem (published in the Broadmoor Hospital Chronicle patient magazine) captures so well in a few powerful words the paradox of the comedy and tragedy of mental illness:

I always mope
I can't cope
I never use soap
I think I'm the Pope
Is there any hope?
If not, bring me a rope.

References

Bolinger, D. (1975) Aspects of Language. New York: Harcourt Brace.

Dore, J. (1986) The development of conversational competence. In R.L. Schiefelbusch (ed) Language Competence: Assessment and Intervention. London: Taylor and Francis.

Foss, D.J. and Hakes, D.T. (1978) Psycholinguistics – Introduction to the Psychology of Language. Englewood Cliffs, N.J.: Prentice Hall.

France, J. (1996) Communication speech and language. In C. Cordess and M. Cox (eds) Forensic Psychotherapy: Crime, Psychodynamics and the Offender Patient. London: Jessica Kingsley Publishers.

CHAPTER 7

Assessment of Speech and Language in Mental Health

Karen Bryan and Jan Roach

Speech and language assessment in psychiatry may have the following functions:

- contributing information to assist psychiatric diagnosis
- highlighting specific communication problems
- providing diagnosis of any speech pathology
- assisting in differential diagnosis, for example dementia and dysphasia, dementia and depression, schizophrenia and dysphasia, paranoia and hearing impairment, language disorder and intellectual impairment
- providing a baseline for therapy
- evaluation of ongoing treatment
- providing additional information for the patient's overall care plan; all aspects of care and treatment are likely to be more effective with appropriate language input, related to the patient's comprehension ability
- helping the multidisciplinary team to understand the patient's communication difficulties, so that the patient's frustration may be reduced
- giving the more able patient insight into an important aspect of his or her illness; in turn, understanding may bring some relief and perhaps increase motivation to work on communication skills.

Assessments may be client-centred, e.g. evaluating the strengths and weaknesses of a particular client; or disorder-centred, concentrating on the common features of a particular disorder. Procedures vary from inventories or checklists to comprehensive test batteries and may be asset-based or deficit-based. Wirz (1993) states that the therapist must determine from a matrix of possibilities which type of assessment is applicable. There are no specific tests as yet for mental health so the speech and language therapist must rely on his or her knowledge of language pathology and processes to guide in selecting tests or parts of tests developed in other speech and language therapy disciplines.

Even without formal assessments, speech and language therapists can gain valuable assessment information through detailed observation of their clients as they communicate with various people such as carers, peers, family members and unfamiliar people. Different stress levels may affect speech and language functioning in clients with mental health problems.

France (1993) advocates a holistic approach to assessment and treatment of speech, language and communication problems in patients with mental illness, with consideration of communication in different settings and with different people.

There are few studies of the incidence and prevalence of speech and language problems in mental health populations. However, Emerson and Enderby (1996) conducted an extensive survey to investigate the prevalence of speech and language problems in people receiving care from the mental health unit of a district health authority. A screening assessment was devised using modified standardised tests: the Boston Naming Test (Goodglass, Kaplan and Weintraub 1983); the cookie theft picture description from the Boston Diagnostic Aphasia Examination (Goodglass and Kaplan 1983); and the Auditory Comprehension Test for Sentences (Shewan 1979). Subjective four-point ratings for spontaneous conversational speech, voice, articulation and fluency were also used. The results showed that two-thirds of the people assessed (138 in all) had moderate or severe problems in at least one aspect of speech and language. The most common problems occurred in comprehension and naming: a quarter had problems with spontaneous speech and problems with voice, articulation and fluency were less common. In relation to mental health diagnosis, 56 per cent of people with schizophrenia and 52 per cent of those with depression had speech and language problems. These incidence figures represent substantially higher numbers than those prevalent in the normal population (Enderby and Phillipp 1986; Enderby and Davies 1989; Bryan, Maxim, MacIntosh *et al.* 1991). Brewin *et al.* (1987) drew a distinction between competence and performance and discussed the need to establish whether a skill is not performed due to lack of ability or because of lack of opportunity, motivation or interest. As Emerson and Enderby (1996) point out, this distinction is crucial but is in practice extremely difficult to make.

The survey yields valuable quantitative and qualitative information on the prevalence of speech and language problems in a mentally ill population. It also illustrates some of the difficulties of arriving at a definitive population estimate. The study included all those having contact with a district health authority service, but probably did not include people treated entirely by their GPs or people detained for treatment. Neither does the study address causes of the speech and language problems, as the authors point out. However, the survey does show that even a relatively short speech and language assessment can identify people with speech and language difficulties that are likely to affect interpersonal communication. Emerson and Enderby (1996) state that:

> a speech and language therapy assessment should be offered as part of a detailed
> medical assessment to offer the possibility of more appropriate care and management in
> the light of increased knowledge of speech and language abilities. (p.234)

Evidence of speech and language difficulties in different mental health conditions will be reviewed in detail in some of the following chapters of this book. We will now review a small number of studies in which speech and language is assessed in some detail.

Kaczmarek (1993) used discourse analysis (particularly examining deviations) to show that discourse profiles vary in violent and non-violent schizophrenics. Fine *et al.* (1991) suggest that detailed analysis of features such as intonation is important in detecting changes in language usage.

Landre, Taylor and Kearns (1992) examined language functioning in groups of speech-disordered schizophrenic and aphasic patients who did not differ significantly on measures of education. The tests used were repetition from the BDAE (Goodglass and Kaplan 1983), the Boston Naming Test (Goodglass, Kaplan and Weintraub 1983), the shortened version of the Token Test (De Renzi and Faglioni 1978), the spontaneous speech subtest of the Western Aphasia Battery (Kertesz 1982) and the Raven's Coloured Progressive Matrices (Raven 1962) as a test of general intellectual functioning. The results indicated that the two groups did not differ on any of the measures, and therefore support the hypothesis that speech-disordered schizophrenics exhibit disturbances in language functioning that are similar to those of fluent aphasics. The authors suggest the results indicate that rather than being secondary to thought disorder, language difficulties in schizophrenia may be part of a more generalised cognitive deficit. The results may also be interpreted as indicating that detailed language testing is required to make such a distinction in language pathology. Muir, Tanner and France (1991) reported that both psychiatrists and neurologists have difficulty in differentiating schizo-phrenic from dysphasic speech, whereas speech and language therapy assessment is known to be more reliable.

However, there are alternative theories to that of language difficulty being a part of a more general cognitive problem. Thomas (1995) applied linguistic analysis to the speech of people with schizophrenia and proposed that a communication disorder may underlie thought disorder. Similarly, recent research on auditory-visual hallucinations is examining the theory that hallucinations may best be understood within a model of language production, reception and monitoring (David and Busatto 1998). Thomas and Fraser (1994) discuss the application of linguistic science to psychiatry, indicating that there is some recent recognition of the value of detailed language assessment beyond speech and language therapy itself.

Cutting (1985) reviewed investigations into language in schizophrenia and suggested that these patients have particular difficulties with pragmatics and prosody, suggesting that right hemisphere dysfunction may be implicated.

There is controversy as to whether children who later develop schizophrenia have differences in their speech and language as children. Done *et al.* (1994) suggest that social aspects of communication may be different in children who later develop schizophrenia, but a study by Done *et al.* (1998) suggests that their speech is not syntactically less complex. Although the results of these studies remain contentious, there is a clear need to consider whether an adult client has completed language development or whether pervasive develop-mental language difficulties are still evident. An example is a study of young offenders (Pryor 1998) which showed that 8/11 subjects, aged between 17 and 20 years, had difficulties on the CELF–R (Semel, Wiig and Secord 1987) with a mean age equivalence of 12 years, 4 months and on the BPVS with a mean age equivalence of 11 years, 1 month. In addition, seven of the subjects had significantly lower expressive language skills compared with their receptive language skills. These were not specifically subjects with documented mental health problems although it is widely accepted that significant numbers of people entering penal establishments are mentally ill (Gunn, Maden and Swinton 1991). Also, systematic assessment of patients entering a high security hospital for people with mental illness showed that of the sixteen people assessed, twelve had speech, language and communication problems that would affect interpersonal functioning and which would need to be considered in verbally mediated interventions (Bryan 1998). The incidence of literacy problems was also high.

The value of assessment and remediation of speech and language difficulties is discussed in relation to the prison population (Bryan, France and Kramer 1996). A number of the issues raised are shared with mental health populations. Being an able communicator is an essential component of family, social and work-related activities both within an institution such as a hospital and in the community. In addition, there are important management and resource implications in providing interventions for people with difficulties or limitations in their speech and language functioning. Information on an individual's speech and language functioning is essential to the multidisciplinary team in relation to other interventions which are primarily verbally mediated such as courses on drug usage and some forms of psychotherapy. The value of detailed speech and language assessment can be seen in a small body of literature on drug usage (referring to the use of illicit drugs such as cannabis). A study by Block *et al.* (1990) showed that even with relatively short periods of usage significant effects were evident on a language measure among young people using marijuana. In particular, a decrease in verbal expressive skills without a decrease in vocabulary or reading comprehension was evident. A study by Tarter *et al.* (1995) investigated female adolescents who used a range of drugs and found significant effects using the Wiig and Secord (1989) Test of Language Competence. All measures except listening comprehension were significant. The most significant problems occurred in comprehension of ambiguous sentences and expressing intents. These results lend support to the assertion of Block *et al.* (1990) that language usage rather than underlying language skills *per se* is most vulnerable to the effects of drugs. These studies illustrate the value of speech and language assessment in both detecting and monitoring even subtle changes in language performance.

Brief consideration of the main types of mental health disorders and their associated speech and language pathology gives an indication of the diversity of communication problems that may be evident.

Psychotic disorders such as schizophrenia may be associated with three types of pathology:

- speech and language disorders which may have been evident prior to the onset of the psychosis
- speech and language disorders which are directly caused by the psychosis
- additional problems resulting from treatments such as psychotropic drugs and organic conditions such as dysarthria.

Changes in speech and language can vary from mutism to the excitable, overproductive speech of the manic patient. Content of speech may also reflect other pathological behaviours such as thought disorder.

Affective disorders such as depression are abnormalities of mood. Depressed patients are often reluctant to talk, avoid social contact where possible, eye contact, facial expression and intonation may be reduced and response latencies may be increased. Responses tend to be short, but patients with depression may perform better on structured tasks such as picture description (Maxim 1991). It is important that depression is differentiated from dementia and there is some evidence that language assessment can be useful. Emery (1989) reported that depressed elderly people performed significantly better than Alzheimer patients on the Western Aphasia Battery, and only scored lower than the control subjects on measures that involved errors on the most complex items.

Personality disorders are not particularly associated with communication problems. However, where patients have a disrupted social and/or educational history, language and literacy skills may be limited. These limitations may contribute to difficulties in expressing needs and opinions and may contribute to over-reliance on behaviours such as hitting out when explanation is not within the person's language capability. Pervasive developmental disorders such as a stammer or articulatory difficulties may be evident. Restricted social experience and lack of exposure to a variety of speech situations may result in communication difficulties.

Neurotic disorders such as obsessional and phobic conditions can be associated with a variety of speech, language and communication problems. For example, muscle tension can affect breathing and voice, anxiety can result in dysfluency, behaviours such as continuous checking can disrupt conversation, avoidance of conversation and interpersonal contact can contribute to social skills difficulties. Therefore functional assessment and consideration of communication and social skills is essential.

Although mental health diagnoses may suggest specific areas of difficulty (as indicated above) it is important to approach speech and language assessment in an open manner with investigation of speech, language and communication as the central aim of the assessment. For example, a depressed patient may on enquiry have reading difficulties from childhood or a poor memory as a result of an earlier head injury.

We will now turn our attention to how the process of speech and language assessment can be achieved. This raises a number of important issues:

- There are few tests specifically designed to assess speech and language in people with mental illness. Typically developmental tests or tests primarily devised for the assessment of acquired aphasia are applied to this population.

- There are no standardised tests for the mental health population.

- Norms are a problematic area. Many people with mental illness (but not necessarily all) have other associated difficulties. These may range from drug side-effects to subtle brain damage, pervading learning difficulties, lack of opportunities for social interaction, institutionalisation and a whole host of other potential difficulties. These problems may affect a person's response to assessment and may mask or exacerbate any speech and language problems that may exist.

- The application of existing norms for language tests, where these exist, may also be questionable.

- The language and pictorial material used in tests may be of little relevance or may even be inappropriate for people who may have led impoverished, street or institutionalised lifestyles. For example the composite picture in the Whurr test (Whurr 1996) is helpful as it should elicit both factual and inferred information but clients are frequently noted to comment that 'happy families and holidays' are not within their experience.

- Fluctuation in performance is a feature of many mental health disorders, raising issues of when to test and the need to monitor performance over time.

- Drug effects may increase fluctuation and any change in drug regimes may alter the client's speech and language profile (although this may be a useful indicator of the positive effects of drug treatment).

It is therefore important when using speech and language therapy assessments to consider:

- what the test assesses
- the purpose of the test
- who the test was designed for and the assumptions entailed
- how the particular language function is assessed
- the level of detail provided
- how the particular test performs in a mental health population.

We will now review speech and language therapy assessments that can be useful in mental health.

The interview may be seen as vital to speech and language therapy assessment. Case history information particularly relating to education, language usage and any previously noted speech and language difficulties is important in guiding further investigation. During the interview, video and auditory tape recordings may be made. Video recording is particularly valuable for later analysis of aspects of language such as conversation skills, as well as providing a record for later comparison. Discussion with more able patients may also reveal important information about their insight, motivation, co-operation and approach to testing which may be of use to the multidisciplinary team. Initial enquiries need to target areas for further assessment. The following skills may need to be assessed.

HEARING

There appears to be a higher incidence of hearing problems within the mentally ill population although there are a number of methodological difficulties associated with the studies in this field (see Denmark 1995 for a detailed review of this subject). Observation of a patient may indicate that he or she is relying heavily on lip-reading, a lack of attention may suggest a hearing problem or sometimes patients tend to turn slightly towards the speaker to use their 'better' ear. Patients report continuous or buzzing noises suggestive of tinnitus. In other cases patients may be adept at hiding a problem, particularly if they are concerned about the stigma of deafness. Freefield testing and screening audiometry may be useful in identifying patients who require more detailed investigation. Where a hearing problem is suspected or apparent, patients should undergo aural examination in order to eliminate build-up of wax secretions as a cause of hearing problems.

AUDITORY DISCRIMINATION

The sound discrimination test of the Aston Index (Newton and Thomson 1976) can be given to any patient who understands the concept of same and different, and helps to identify or eliminate auditory discrimination problems. Mentally ill patients with learning difficulties may require a simpler test such as the Auditory Discrimination and Attention Test (Morgan Barry 1989).

AUDITORY SEQUENTIAL MEMORY

The sentence recall and oral directions tests from the Clinical Evaluation of Language Fundamentals – Revised (CELF–R (UK)) (Semel *et al.* 1987) may be useful in differentiating memory difficulties from comprehension problems. The Aston Index Auditory Sequential Memory Test gives a measure of forward and reverse digit span. For patients functioning at a higher level the oral commands subtest from the Fullerton Language Test for Adolescents (Thorum 1986) may be useful.

AUDITORY MEMORY

The listening to paragraphs subtest of the CELF–R (Semel *et al.* 1987) may be useful, although the content is aimed at schoolchildren. The paragraphs are graded for difficulty and give an indication of equivalent developmental age based on the patient's performance. The CELF–R oral directions subtest indicates the level at which comprehension of commands breaks down, and this information can be valuable in explaining to carers the need to simplify sentence structures. The Rivermead Behavioural Memory Test (Wilson, Cockburn and Baddeley 1991) may be useful in giving an indication of the functional effects of memory impairment.

With language-based memory tests, the testing process may yield important information on motivation. Some patients are noted to give up very quickly, others proceed to their limit but some will continue to the end of a test despite experiencing difficulty.

PHONOLOGY

Adults with mental health problems may present with pervasive developmental disorders. A rapid phonological screening test such as the South Tyneside Assessment of Phonology (Armstrong and Ainley 1988) may be helpful in confirming whether or not the phonological system is fully developed. The Photo Articulation Test (Prendegast *et al.* 1984) uses pictures that may be more apt for adult patients.

VERBAL COMPREHENSION

The Test for the Reception of Grammar (TROG) (Bishop 1989) assesses the understanding of grammatical structures. The picture choice format of the test is accessible to most patients and patients' awareness or lack of awareness of errors can be revealing. The test gives a profile of the structures that a patient does not understand. Norms for children and some adult norms are given in the manual. Where patients have difficulties, an estimate of their comprehension age can be very helpful in conveying to other members of the multidisciplinary team the level at which the patient is functioning. Similarly, carers can often relate well to being given information about age equivalence of comprehension, e.g. that the patient's comprehension is approximately that of a seven-year-old. It is, however, important to note that an adolescent or an adult's life experience will usually be in advance of their comprehension level.

RECEPTIVE VOCABULARY

The British Picture Vocabulary Scale (BPVS) (Dunn *et al.* 1997) is designed to measure the patient's receptive vocabulary for Standard English. Age equivalent scores are computed. In mental health the cause of such problems needs to be carefully considered. Issues such as lack of educational opportunities may be relevant. It may also be useful to compare BPVS and TROG age scores. A deficit in either test can be a useful indicator for further investigation.

NAMING

The Graded Naming Test (McKenna and Warrington 1983) tests the patient's naming ability. The test can detect subtle problems in naming. The test score correlates with other widely used intelligence measures and therefore gives an estimate of the subject's pre-morbid IQ. Where naming problems are less subtle, the Test of Adolescent and Adult Word Finding (German 1990), the Test of Word Finding (German 1986), the Test of Word Finding in Discourse (German 1991) and the Boston Naming Test may be more useful in determining whether word retrieval is the major difficulty in naming problems.

EXPRESSIVE LANGUAGE

The CELF–R formulated sentences tests the subject's syntactic abilities in language output. The Fullerton test battery contains a test of morphological competency. The Mount Wilja High Level Language Battery (which is unfortunately unpublished although it exists in many clinics) contains a number of useful subtests such as sentence construction and verbal reasoning.

Description of a complex picture, description of picture sequences and production of procedural discourse such as 'how to make a sandwich' are also useful, but findings need to be interpreted with care.

Despite the pictures, the Renfrew Action Picture Test (Renfrew 1988) can be helpful in giving an indication of the patient's sentence structures without making too many demands upon a severely mentally ill patient.

LANGUAGE

Speech and language therapists working in mental health frequently use tests originally designed for acquired aphasia such as the Boston Diagnostic Aphasia Examination (Goodglass and Kaplan 1983), and the Aphasia Screening Test (Whurr 1996). These tests explore comprehension, production, reading and writing.

Where deficits are identified, a more detailed neuropsychological examination using tests such as the Psycholinguistic Assessments of Language Processing in Aphasia (PALPA) (Kay, Lesser and Coltheart 1992) and the Pyramids and Palm Trees Test (Howard and Patterson 1993) may be necessary to pinpoint the deficits and to guide intervention.

RIGHT HEMISPHERE LANGUAGE

The Right Hemisphere Language Battery (Bryan 1995) assesses areas of language competence where the right hemisphere is known to have a contribution to language such as in understanding metaphor and in the production of prosody. Burns, Halper and Mogil (1985) include non-verbal tests of right hemisphere functioning in their test battery.

PRAGMATIC/FUNCTIONAL COMMUNICATION

The Test of Language Competence – Expanded Edition (Wiig and Secord 1989) can be useful in exploring whether patients can utilise language skills which are evident on testing but which may not be so evident in functional situations.

The Lets Talk Inventory for Adolescents (Wiig 1982) asks patients to suggest what the patient portrayed in a picture would be likely to say. Disordered emotional/interpersonal perception may be relevant to performance on a test such as this and may invalidate the norms given but may in itself be revealing in assessment.

Profiles such as the Personal Communication Plan (PCP) (Hitchings and Spence 1991) assess functional communication. The PCP was designed for clients with learning difficulties and considers factors such as environmental opportunities for communication, making it highly applicable for people with mental illness who also have learning difficulties and for whom environmental opportunities may be restricted. The Communication Assessment Profile for Adults with a Mental Handicap (CASP) (Van der Gaag 1988) may also be helpful for clients who have learning difficulties.

Pragmatic profiles such as those by Penn (1985), Prutting and Kirchner (1987) and Dewart and Summers (1996) are useful in qualitative assessment of language and communication.

LITERACY

Many of the tests mentioned above include assessment of literacy. The therapist needs to select assessments that are geared to the patient's level of functioning. The Boder Test of Reading and Spelling Patterns (Boder and Jarrico 1982) can be useful in differentiating specific reading difficulties from reading difficulties which are associated with physical, mental or educational impairment. Case history information on literacy skills, educational background and educational achievement will be important when interpreting test results.

COGNITIVE FUNCTIONING

Where a differential diagnosis includes dementia, tests such as the Arizona Battery for Communication Disorders in Dementia (Bayles and Tomoeda 1993) may be useful (see Armstrong 1996 and Chapter 16 for further information on language assessment in dementia).

The National Adult Reading Test (Nelson 1982) provides a means of estimating the pre-morbid intelligence levels of adult clients suspected of having an intellectual deterioration.

STAMMERING

The S24 Scale (Andrews and Cutler 1974) is a single-page questionnaire designed to measure the stutterer's attitude to interpersonal communication and is a useful and rapid screening instrument.

MOTOR SPEECH DISORDERS

Specific assessments for dysarthria such as the Frenchay Dysarthria Test (Enderby 1983) and the Robertson Dysarthria Profile (Robertson 1982) may be required.

For dyspraxia the Apraxia Battery for Adults (Dabul 1979) or the Nuffield Centre Dyspraxia Programme (Nuffield Speech and Hearing Centre 1982) could be used.

DYSPHAGIA

Fioretti, Glaccotto and Melega (1997) state that choking while eating or drinking has long been known and studied within psychiatric populations. They cite risk factors as psychiatric medications, movement disorders, seizures, neurological impairments, poor dentition and bad eating habits. Dysphagia assessment such as that described by Logemann (1997) and Groher (1992) may be indicated.

DEPRESSION

The Beck Inventory (Beck 1967) and the Hospital Anxiety and Depression Scale (HAS) (Zigmond and Snaith 1983) can be used to measure depression and to monitor the depression over time.

More details on speech and language therapy assessments and specific descriptions of some of the assessment procedures cited above can be found in Beech, Harding and Hilton-Jones (1993) and Kersner (1992).

In this chapter we have advocated and have attempted to justify the need for detailed assessment of speech and language in clients with mental health disorders. Such disorders are complex and we have illustrated above the diversity and complexity of speech and language assessment. We need detailed assessment in order to find out about what is going wrong in speech and language processing and to promote the understanding of the impact of communication difficulties for other members of the multidisciplinary team. Just as we use tests from other branches of speech and language assessment, so we can learn from theoretical developments in other areas. The application of cognitive neuropsychological modelling to the study of aphasia has greatly increased our knowledge of how language breaks down after focal brain damage. Similarly the application of conversation analysis to the study of functional communication in aphasia has enhanced our understanding of language usage in aphasia and is leading to specifically targeted therapies. We have a long way to go in mental health but there are grounds for optimism. The potential value of the application of linguistic analysis to assessment in psychiatry is now recognised (Thomas 1997; Kramer 1997) and developmental models are being used to examine possible language antecedents of mental illness (for example: Benaish, Curtiss and Tallal 1993; Giddan, Milling and Campbell 1996; Done *et al.* 1998).

On the negative side there is often pressure on therapists to assess patients quickly as a mistaken indicator of clinical efficiency. This pressure needs to be avoided, hopefully supported by future studies illustrating the value of detailed and precise assessment.

References

Andrews, G. and Cutler, J. (1974) Stuttering therapy: the relationship between changes in symptom level and attitudes. *Journal of Speech and Hearing Disorders 39*, 313–319.

Armstrong, L. (1996) Language, cognition and communication assessment of older people with psychiatric disorders. In K. Bryan and J. Maxim (eds) *Communication Disability and the Psychiatry of Old Age*. London: Whurr.

Armstrong, S. and Ainley, M. (1988) *South Tyneside Assessment of Phonology*. Bicester: Winslow Press.

Bayles, K.A. and Tomoeda, C. (1993) *The Arizona Battery for Communication Disorders in Dementia*. Bicester: Winslow Press.

Beck, A.T. (1967) Measurement of depression: the depression inventory. In A.T. Beck (ed) *Depression: Clinical, Experimental and Theoretical Aspects*. London: Harper and Row. pp.186–207.

Beech, J.R., Harding, L. and Hilton-Jones, D. (1993) *Assessment in Speech and Language Therapy*. London: Routledge.

Benaish, A.A., Curtiss, S. and Tallal, P. (1993) Language, learning and behavioural disturbances in childhood: a longitudinal perspective. *Journal of the American Academy of Child and Adolescent Psychiatry 32*, 585–594.

Bishop, D.V.M. (1989) *Test For Reception of Grammar* (second edition). Available from the author at MRC Applied Psychology Unit, 15 Chaucer Road, Cambridge CB2 3EF.

Block, R.I., Farnham, S., Braverman, K., Noyes, R. and Ghoneim, M.M. (1990) National Institute on Drug Abuse Research Monograph Series. *Research Monograph 101*, 96–111.

Boder, E. and Jarrico, S. (1982) *The Boder Test of Reading and Spelling Patterns – A Diagnostic Screening Test for Sub-types of Reading Disability*. London: Grune and Stratton.

Brewin, C.R., Wing, J.K., Mangen, S.P., Brugha, T.S. and MacCarthy, B. (1987) Principles and practice of measuring needs in the long term mentally ill: the MRC needs for care assessment. *Psychological Medicine 17*, 971–981.

Bryan, K. (1995) *The Right Hemisphere Language Battery* (second edition). London: Whurr.

Bryan, K. (1998) Speech and language therapy admission assessments. January–June 1998. Internal Report. Broadmoor Hospital.

Bryan, K., France, J. and Kramer, S. (1996) Communication therapy for the prison population. In N. Squires and J. Strobel (eds) *Healthy Prisons: A Vision For The Future*. Liverpool: Liverpool University.

Bryan, K., Maxim, J., MacIntosh, J., McClelland, A., Wirz, S., Edmundson, A. and Snowling, M. (1991) The facts behind the figures: a reply to Enderby and Davies (1989). *British Journal of Disorders of Communication 26*, 253–261.

Burns, M.S., Halper, A.S. and Mogil, S.I. (1985) *Clinical Management of Right Hemisphere Dysfunction*. Maryland: Aspen Systems Corporation.

Cutting, J. (1985) *The Psychology of Schizophrenia*. Edinburgh: Churchill Livingstone.

Dabul, B.L. (1979) *Apraxia Battery for Adults*. Bicester: Winslow Press.

David, A.S. and Busatto, G. (1998) The hallucination: a disorder of brain and mind. In M.A. Ron and A.S. David (eds) *Disorders of Brain and Mind*. Cambridge: Cambridge University Press.

Denmark, J.C. (1995) *Deafness and Mental Health*. London: Jessica Kingsley Publishers.

De Renzi, E. and Faglioni, P. (1978) Normative data and screening power of a shortened version of the token test. *Cortex 14*, 41–49.

Dewart, H. and Summers, S. (1996) *The Pragmatics Profile of Everyday Communication Skills*. Windsor: NFER-Nelson.

Done, D.J., Crow, T.J., Johnstone, E.C. and Sacker, A. (1994) Childhood antecedents of schizophrenia and affective illness: social adjustment at ages 7 and 11. *British Medical Journal 302*, 1576–1580.

Done, D.J., Leionen, E., Crow, T.J. and Sacker, A. (1998) Linguistic performance in children who develop schizophrenia in adult life. *British Journal of Psychiatry 172*, 130–135.

Dunn, L.M., Dunn, L.M., Whetton, C. and Burley, E. (1997) *British Picture Vocabulary Scale*. Windsor: NFER-Nelson.

Emerson, J. and Enderby, P. (1996) Prevalence of speech and language disorders in a mental health unit. *European Journal of Disorders of Communication 31*, 221–236.

Emery, O.B. (1989) Language deficits in depression: comparisons with SDAT and normal aging. *Journal of Gerontology 44*, M85–M92.

Enderby, P. (1983) *Frenchay Dysarthria Assessment*. Windsor: NFER-Nelson.

Enderby, P. and Davies, P. (1989) Communication disorders: planning a service to meet the needs. *British Journal of Disorders of Communication 24*, 301–331.

Enderby, P. and Phillipp, R. (1986) Speech and language handicap: towards knowing the size of the problem. *British Journal of Disorders of Communication 21*, 151–165.

Fine, J., Bartollucci, G., Ginsberg, G. and Szatmari, P. (1991) The use of intonation to communicate in pervasive developmental disorders. *Journal of Child Language and Psychiatry 32*, 771–782.

Fioretti, A., Glaccotto, L. and Melega, V. (1997) Choking incidents among psychiatric patients: retrospective analysis of thirty-one cases from the west Bologna psychiatric wards. *Canadian Journal of Psychiatry 42*, 515–520.

France, J. (1993) Assessment in psychiatry. In J.R. Beech, L. Harding and D. Hilton-Jones (eds) *Assessments of Speech Therapy*. London: Routledge, NFER Assessment Library.

France, J. and Muir, N. (eds) (1997) *Communication and the Mentally Ill Patient*. London: Jessica Kingsley Publishers.

German, D.J. (1986) *Test of Word Finding*. Leicester: Taskmaster.

German, D.J. (1990) *Test of Adolescent and Adult Word-Finding*. Leicester: Taskmaster.

German, D.J. (1991) *Test of Word Finding in Discourse*. Leicester: Taskmaster.

Giddan, J.J., Milling, L. and Campbell, N.B. (1996) Unrecognised language and speech deficits in preadolescent psychiatric inpatients. *American Orthopsychiatry 66*, 85–92.

Goodglass, H. and Kaplan, E. (1983) *The Boston Diagnostic Aphasia Examination*. Philadelphia: Lea and Febiger.

Goodglass, H., Kaplan, E. and Weintraub, S. (1983) *The Boston Naming Test*. Philadelphia: Lea and Febiger.

Groher, M.E. (1992) *Dysphagia: Diagnosis and Management*. London: Butterworth-Heinemann.

Gunn, J., Maden, A. and Swinton, J. (1991) Treatment needs of prisoners with psychiatric disorders. *BMJ 303*, 338–341.

Hitchings, A. and Spence, R. (1991) *Personal Communication Plan*. Windsor: NFER-Nelson.

Howard, D. and Patterson, K. (1993) *The Pyramids and Palm Trees Test*. Bury St Edmunds: Thames Valley Test Company.

Kaczmarek, B.L.J. (1993) Neurolinguistic aspects of crime-related frontal lobe deficits. In H.V. Hall and R.J. Sbordone (eds) *Disorders of Executive Functions: Civil and Criminal Law Applications*. Florida: DMD Publishers Group Inc.

Kaplan, E., Goodglass, H. and Weintraub, S. (1983) *The Boston Naming Test*. Philadelphia: Lea and Febiger.

Kay, J., Lesser, R. and Coltheart, M. (1992) *Psycholinguistic Assessments of Language Processing in Aphasia*. Hove: Erlbaum.

Kersner, M. (1992) *Tests of Voice Speech and Language*. London: Whurr.

Kertesz, A. (1982) *The Western Aphasia Battery*. Orlando: Grune and Stratton.

Kramer, S. (1997) The language disorder and auditory hallucinations in schizophrenic patients: background to the research study. In J. France and N. Muir *Communication and the Mentally Ill Patient – Developmental and Linguistic Approaches to Schizophrenia*. London: Jessica Kingsley Publishers.

Landre, N.A., Taylor, M.A. and Kearns, K.P. (1992) Language functioning in schizophrenic and aphasic patients. *Neuropsychiatry, Neuropsychology and Behavioural Neurology 5*, 7–14.

Logemann, J. (1997) Evaluation and Treatment of Swallowing Disorders (second edition). Texas: Pro-Ed.

Maxim, J. (1991) Can elicited language be used to diagnose dementia? *Work in Progress 1*, 13–21. London: National Hospitals College of Speech Sciences.

McKenna, P. and Warrington, E. (1983) *The Graded Naming Test*. Windsor: NFER-Nelson.

Morgan Barry, R. (1989) *Auditory Discrimination and Attention Test*. Windsor: NFER-Nelson.

Muir, N., Tanner, P. and France, J. (1991) Management and treatment techniques: a practical approach. In R. Gravell and J. France (eds) *Speech and Communication Problems in Psychiatry*. London: Chapman and Hall.

Nelson, H.E. (1982) *The National Adult Reading Test*. Windsor: NFER-Nelson.

Newton, M. and Thomson, M. (1976) *The Aston Index*. Wisbech: LDA.

Penn, C. (1985) The profile of communicative appropriateness: a clinical tool for the assessment of pragmatics. *The South African Journal of Communication Disorders 32*, 18–24.

Nuffield Centre for Dyspraxia Programme (1992) London: Nuffield Speech and Hearing Centre.

Prendegast, K., Dickey, S., Selmar, J. and Soder, A. (1984) *The Photo Articulation Test*. Texas: Pro-Ed.

Prutting, C.A. and Kirchner, D.M. (1987) A clinical appraisal of the pragmatic aspects of language. *Journal of Speech and Hearing Disorders 52*, 105–119.

Pryor, A. (1998) A systematic assessment of the prevalence of communication difficulties within a small group of young offenders. Unpublished thesis, University of Reading.

Raven, J.C. (1962) *Coloured Progressive Matrices*. London: H.K. Lewis.

Renfrew, C.E. (1988) *The Action Picture Test*. Bicester: Winslow Press.

Robertson, S.J. (1982) *Robertson Dysarthria Profile*. Bicester: Winslow Press.

Semel, E., Wiig, E.H. and Secord, W. (1987) *Clinical Evaluation of Language Fundamentals – Revised*. Sidcup: Psychological Corporation.

Shewan, C.M. (1979) *Auditory Comprehension for Sentences*. Chicago: Biolinguistics Clinical Institute.

Tarter, R.E., Mezzich, A.C., Hsieh, Y-C. and Parks, S. (1995) Cognitive capacity in female adolescent substance abusers. *Drug and Alcohol Dependence 39*, 15–21.

Thomas, P. (1995) Thought disorder or communication disorder: linguistic science provides a new approach. *British Journal of Psychiatry 166*, 287–290.

Thomas, P. (1997) What can linguistics tell us about thought disorder? In J. France and N. Muir (eds) *Communication and the Mentally Ill Patient*. London: Jessica Kingsley Publishers.

Thomas, P. and Fraser, W.I. (1994) Linguistics, human communication and psychiatry. *British Journal of Psychiatry 165*, 585–592.

Thorum, A.R. (1986) *Fullerton Language Test For Adults*. Oxford: Oxford Psychologists Press.

Van der Gaag, A. (1988) *The Communication Assessment Profile for Adults with a Mental Handicap*. Bicester: Winslow Press.

Whurr, R. (1996) *Aphasia Screening Test*. London: Whurr.

Wiig, E. (1982) *Let's Talk – Inventory for Adolescents*. Sidcup: Psychological Corporation.

Wiig, E. and Secord, W. (1989) *Test of Language Competence* (extended edition). New York: Harcourt Brace Jovanovitch.

Wilson, B., Cockburn, J. and Baddeley, A. (1991) *The Rivermead Behavioural Memory Test*. Bury St Edmunds: Thames Valley Test Company.

Wirz, S.L. (1993) Historical considerations in assessment. In J.R. Beech, L. Harding and D. Hilton-Jones (eds) *Assessments of Speech Therapy*. London: Routledge, NFER Assessment Library.

Zigmond, A. and Snaith, P. (1983) The hospital anxiety and depression scale. *Acta Psychiatrica Scandinavica 67*, 361–370.

CHAPTER 8

Neuropsychiatry and Language

Karen Bryan

Benson (1998) states that:

> A number of fundamentally different components make up the current setting of neuro-psychiatry. These include basic biological, chemical, pharmacological and anatomical investigations, the field of genetics and clinical studies (both neurological and psychiatric). Brain imaging and quantitative brain mapping provide vast reservoirs of information for the new neuropsychiatry. Neuropsychiatry has become a diverse, burgeoning field commanding armies of dedicated workers. (p.5)

Starr and Sporty (1994) suggest that the disciplines of neurology and psychiatry appear to investigate similar disorders viewed from different perspectives. This is a useful view for clinicians, as, in practice, many individuals will present with psychological as well as organic impairments. Similarly the presence of 'organic' components to diseases such as schizophrenia are now recognised in work on neurotransmitter deficits and imbalances. However, Ron and David (1998) state that until recently the study of the brain and the study of the mind have remained apart. Neuropsychiatry is the bridging discipline between these two fields. Neuro-psychiatry has benefited from technological developments such as functional imaging and neurobiological and neuropsychological models of behaviour. Information on neurochemical processes underlying normal and abnormal behaviour is also becoming available.

Having described neuropsychiatry as a bridging discipline, it is less easy to define its parameters. There have been important historical contributions to the discipline. Wernicke (a nineteenth-century neurologist) described localisation of brain functions – language in particular – at about the same time as Kraepelin (a psychiatrist) developed a phenomen-ologically based classification of mental illness. The ideas of these scientists remain influential today. Trimble (1993) discusses the influence of Hughlings Jackson who developed a hierarchical model of mental activities with high-level cognitive functions (including lang-uage) superimposed over more primitive behaviours. This model implied that mental dys-function represented a dysfunction at a higher level than other neurological problems.

The extent to which the gap between psychiatry and neurology can be bridged remains a question (Marshall and Halligan 1996). Shallice, Burgess and Frith (1991) suggest that study of the signs and symptoms shown by individual patients may be beneficial to neuropsychiatry just as a similar emphasis has led to advances in neuropsychology in the last decade. In mental illness much emphasis is laid on the description of symptoms, for example to achieve DSM classification. Marshall and Halligan (1996) suggest that a further level of analysis in relation to models of normal performance is necessary in order to understand the form and organisation of mental functions. For example, Ellis and Leafhead (1996) detail the language, cognitive and social deficits evident in an adult who has Asperger's syndrome. The authors suggest that the profile of difficulties seen can be explained by a central neurodevelopmental disorder (proposed by Rourke 1987) arising from destruction or dysfunction in white matter. This has a consequent impact especially on right hemisphere functioning where intermodal integration of information is required. Explicit information processing models have been used to explain psychiatric symptoms, such as thought echo (David 1994). Study of schizophrenia in relation to cognitive neuropsychological modelling has proved beneficial (Bentall 1990; Frith 1992). Much work has been done on cognitive neuropsychological modelling in some of the more precisely defined (albeit more rare) psychiatric conditions such as Capgras syndrome (see Halligan and Marshall 1996). In the future, there may also be possibilities for the application of cognitive processing models in other areas such as depression (Peterson, Maier and Seligman 1993) and personality disorder (Blair 1995).

Pharmacological intervention

Pharmacological intervention is also important in the development of neuropsychiatry as a discipline. Lishman (1989) discusses the fact that beneficial pharmacological intervention in conditions such as schizophrenia allowed scientific study of changes in neurophysiological functions brought about by drugs.

Neuropsychiatry and brain damage

This chapter will now attempt to examine how damage to the brain produces changes in behaviour and mood that might be termed as 'psychiatric' disorders. The possible effects of frontal lobe damage on mood and behaviour are considered in detail. Then, as it is not possible in one chapter to review all possible neuropsychiatric disorders, the remainder of the chapter will consider neurological disorders where speech and language disorders as well as changes in behaviour, mood and personality are likely to occur.

Frontal lobe damage

Study of frontal lobe functioning suggests that damage to the frontal lobes or to its connections to subcortical structures is important in the development of a number of behavioural and mood disturbances in neurological disorders. Patients with frontal lobe dysfunction exhibit impaired attention and concentration, reduced verbal fluency, poor ability to plan and carry out goal-directed behaviour and motor disturbances. Memory deficits can result from an inability to organise the information to be recalled, an inability to shift recall from one memory trace to another or deficits in selective attention. Similarly, visuospatial deficits in patients with frontal lobe damage reflect an inability to generate and implement an adequate constructional strategy (McPherson and Cummings 1998).

Deficits on frontal lobe tests must be interpreted carefully; for example, patients with dysphasia produce poor word-list generation, but may perform within normal limits on non-verbal frontal lobe tests. Also sorting tasks are sensitive to frontal lobe dysfunction, but patients with generalised damage such as dementia also have difficulties with these tasks (Robinson, Heaton and Lehman 1980).

Fronto-subcortical connections

The cognitive and behavioural complexes described with frontal dysfunction have also been observed in patients with damage to the basal ganglia and the thalamus. Five fronto-subcortical circuits have been described (Alexander and Crutchner 1990) and they provide a framework for understanding why similar behaviours emerge with lesions in different parts of the frontal-subcortical system.

Three of the circuits originate in the prefrontal cortex and each of these connects with the basal ganglia and the thalamus and damage anywhere in these circuits produces the same behavioural effects as prefrontal damage.

Caudate nucleus/striatal damage is associated with impaired executive functions, but two possible circuits can be differentially disrupted. If the dorso-lateral prefrontal circuit is implicated, disinhibition and inappropriate behaviour may result, e.g. in Huntington's disease. Damage to this circuit may also produce depression. If the ventral caudate nucleus is damaged, apathy and lack of initiative may result, for example due to tumours in the region of the third ventricle. Damage in this area has also been associated with akinetic mutism (Klee 1961; Messert, Henke and Langheim 1966).

If the anterior cingulate circuit is damaged symptoms include profound apathy, lack of spontaneous speech, lack of emotion even in the presence of pain and indifference to the impairments (Fesenmeer, Kuzniecky and Garcia 1990). When bilateral lesions are present, akinetic mutism is likely.

Thalamic lesions affect all of the three circuits affected above and are associated with dysphoria, irritability, disinhibition, apathy and distractibility (Bogousslavsky, Ferrazzini and Regli 1988). Lesions of both the left and right thalamus are associated with decreased word fluency, memory impairment, difficulty with executive functions and apathy (Pepin and Pepin 1993).

While more research is needed into fronto-subcortical connections, we can begin to see the emergence of an understanding of neural networks and connections which provides insights into why patients with damage in several areas can have the same behavioural consequences, and also why small differences in lesion site or lesion extension can result in characteristically different behavioural patterns as a disease progresses.

Unilateral stroke

Starkstein, Robinson and Price (1987) suggest that left anterior lesions, especially those involving the caudate nucleus, will be associated with depression in 90 per cent of cases. However, there are methodological problems with the studies associated with narrow patient selection. Evidence from the Perth study of stroke (Burvill *et al.* 1995) suggests that genetic and

environmental influences are much more significant than lesion localisation in the development of depression after stroke.

Emotional changes after stroke

Pathological crying and laughing has a reported prevalence of 20 per cent after stroke and
emotionalism 57 per cent after stroke, this being commoner with left fronto-temporal lesions.
Cummings (1997) produced a seminal review of neuropsychiatric manifestations of right
hemisphere damage. Secondary mania, mania occurring after a brain injury, is associated with
right hemisphere dysfunction and has been reported in association with stroke, multiple
sclerosis, brain tumour and head injury. Mania occurring after brain damage is very rare,
although it is more common after trauma (Jorge, Robinson and Starkstein 1993). Mania is
associated with brain injuries involving right frontal-limbic structures. Starkstein *et al.* (1990)
reported on eight patients with mania following focal brain injury. Seven had right hemisphere
damage and one had bilateral damage. The lesions involved the orbito-frontal cortex,
baso-temporal region, thalamus or caudate nucleus. Starkstein *et al.* (1991) reported that right
infero-frontal and baso-temporal lesions gave rise to pure mania whereas right caudate and
thalamic lesions produced bipolar disorders with recurrent periods of mania and depression.

Depression after stroke

Studies of depression remain equivocal as to the relationship of depression to lateralised
hemispheric lesions, suggesting that lesion localisation may not be a major determinant of
post-stroke depression. Starkstein *et al.* (1989) suggest that right brain lesions and inherited
vulnerability to mood disorder (family history of psychiatric disorder) may interact to produce
depression.

Pychosis after stroke

Psychosis following focal brain injury is rare and lesions of either hemisphere are equally likely
to cause it (Feinstein and Ron 1990). However, the content of the delusional beliefs may be
influenced by the laterality of the lesion. Studies of a particular psychosis – the Capgras
syndrome, where the delusional belief is that someone has been replaced by an impostor who
appears identical – suggest that it is not exclusively associated with right hemisphere damage,
but that any damage which disrupts the connections between frontal, parietal and temporal
multimodal cortical association areas with one another and with limbic structures may be
responsible for producing psychosis with different types of symptoms occurring depending
upon the exact locus of the damage within the neural pathways (Weinstein 1996).

Anosagnosia

Anosagnosia (lack of recognition or denial of deficits that may be total or partial) and
somatophrenia (denial of limb ownership) are delusional disorders, which only occur after
brain damage. Furthermore, the abnormal beliefs are different to the content of delusions
encountered in idiopathic psychiatric disorders and reflect the role of the right hemisphere in
mediating the mental representation of the body (Cutting 1990). Anosagnosia may be

associated with depression but the relationship (if any) between these two conditions remains unclear (Cummings 1997).

Effects of right hemisphere damage

Right hemisphere lesions have been associated with certain patterns of alterations in personality. Alexithymia is associated with difficulty in recognising and verbalising emotions, sparse fantasy life and concrete thought patterns. This behavioural style has been observed in patients with right hemisphere damage (Horton 1976).

Van Lancker (1991) reviews the evidence for the right hemisphere's role in the processing of emotion, which is reflected in comprehension, and production of emotional prosody and emotional facial expression. Disruption of these functions has profound consequences for interpersonal behaviour. There is also evidence to suggest that the right hemisphere has a role in the comprehension and production of propositional (non-emotional) aspects of emotion (Bryan 1989; Bryan and Kent submitted). Difficulty in comprehending prosodic information may disrupt interpersonal communication. It is important that right hemisphere functioning is investigated in patients who exhibit difficulties in interpersonal activities in order to identify any possible organic dysfunction.

Anxiety has been associated with right hemisphere dysfunction although more recent MRI studies have yielded more equivocal results. This suggests that straightforward left versus right comparisons are too simplistic and no longer valid. What is needed is understanding of the neural networks and pathways that can be hypothesised to be vulnerable to damage anywhere along their course. It is possible that intra- and interhemispheric asymmetries in, for example, neurotransmitters may provide neurophysiological explanations of particular vulnerabilities in due course. (Cummings 1997). However, what is also evident is that other factors contribute to the vulnerability to neuropsychiatric disorders after brain injury. Cummings (1997) cites factors such as previous brain dysfunction, hereditary effects and psychosocial influences.

Head injury

Trauma to the head is a relatively common injury. In the UK there are 9 deaths from head injury per 100,000 of population per year. Outcome surveys indicate that for every 100 head injury survivors, up to 15 remain in a vegetative state, up to 15 are still severely disabled six months after the injury, 20 have minor psychiatric or psychological problems and 60 make a good recovery (Roberts, Leigh and Weinberger 1993). Neurological consequences of head injury depend upon the nature, location and extent of the damage:

- Lesions of cranial nerves lead to disorders such as anosmia and visual field defects. The nerves most vulnerable to damage are nerves I (olfactory), II (optic), VII (facial) and VIII (auditory).

- Motor disorders such as dysarthria and hemiplegia can occur due to lesions of the cortex or brain stem.

- Lesions from intracranial bleeding and penetrating head injuries give rise to focal neurological damage related to the area of brain damaged.

Psychiatric consequences resulting from head injury are many and varied and clearly arise due to a combination of factors such as:

1.   Pre-morbid personality.

2.   Extent and location of brain damage.

3.   Emotional consequences of the injury and response to impairments.

4.   Development of secondary consequences such as epilepsy.

5.   Environmental factors.

6.   Legal issues (compensation and litigation).

The type of problems which occur include:

- anxiety states
- depression
- phobias
- neurotic disorders
- psychosis (although this is extremely rare).

These problems may be highly significant, particularly if the patient has made a good physical recovery, as they can interfere with interpersonal and social interaction, and the prospects for independent living and employment.

The incidence of schizophrenia after head injury is above that of the general population and is estimated at 2–4 per cent. However, there is no consensus as to whether this reflects direct effects of the head injury or whether the head injury acts as a trigger in people with a relevant psychiatric history (McMillan and Greenwood 1993).

Psychiatric problems need to be differentiated from transient acute confusion, agitation and disorientation that can arise due to post-traumatic amnesia.

In children, behavioural disturbances are common after head injury. Behavioural disturbances can occur in the absence of obvious cognitive or neurological deficits and may give rise to difficulties in learning and difficulties in social adjustment or antisocial behaviour (Roberts *et al.* 1993). Clinicians need to be alert to possible early head injury when taking a case history.

The epilepsies

The majority of people with epilepsy have well-controlled seizures with no significant cognitive changes (Thompson and Shorvon 1993). A minority have more problematic epilepsy and are likely to have brain dysfunction of some sort which is evident between seizures. Fish (1989) states that poor seizure control almost always indicates brain dysfunction. Frequent seizures also place the individual at risk of repeated minor head injuries from falls and the side-effects of medication may also impair cognitive functioning. Comprehensive and systematic assessment of neuropsychological functioning is necessary, as deficits will reflect the locus and extent of the damage to the brain.

A study by Davey and Thompson (1992) examined the language abilities of 60 consecutive admissions to an epilepsy assessment centre. More than a third of the subjects showed difficulties with language, particularly comprehension. It is important that comprehension deficits – even subtle ones – are recognised, as receptive language disorders can be a factor in behaviour often labelled as unco-operative.

Psychological and psychiatric disturbance in epilepsy

Psychological and psychiatric disturbance may present in association with epilepsy, particularly temporal lobe epilepsy. Anxiety may be linked to the unpredictability of attacks and may lead to isolation from social contact. Anxiety and stress are also associated with triggering seizures and psychological interventions aimed at reducing anxiety can reduce seizure frequency (Gillham 1990).

Depression occurs more frequently in people with epilepsy (Robertson 1986). With adult-onset epilepsy, the patient may experience a feeling of loss of control of their life and behaviour with restrictions being imposed, such as no longer being able to drive a car, so that depression is not infrequent.

Aggression and difficult behaviour are often the result of maladaptive coping strategies (Thompson 1988). Aggressive acts may take place during the seizure as a result of 'automatisms' but these are extremely rare.

Epilepsy may be associated with psychosis that can be confined to the ictal period or may be more enduring. Psychosis may develop years after the onset of epilepsy and was thought to be associated with seizures originating in the temporal lobe, although some studies fail to demonstrate such a relationship (Ramani and Gumnit 1982). A syndrome of medial temporal lobe epilepsy has been described. Here the connection of the medial part of the temporal lobe to the limbic system is disrupted, often by damage to the limbic system. In this form of epilepsy, complex partial seizures that are difficult to control are associated with behaviour disorder, personality change, affective symptoms and occasionally psychosis (Trimble 1998).

Parkinson's disease

Personality, mood and cognitive functioning may be changed in Parkinson's disease, although such changes are by no means universal and controversy exists as to the frequency of such disorders (Pentland 1993). Depression is common and affects about half of all cases and correlates with severity of illness and degree of functional disability (Cummings 1992). Depression in Parkinson's disease is characterised by pessimism, hopelessness, reduced drive and motivation and increased concern with health (Gotham, Brown and Marsden 1986).

Dementia and Parkinson's disease

There is considerable debate over the incidence of dementia and cognitive impairments in Parkinson's disease with reported frequencies varying from 10–80 per cent. The presence of depression and the effects of medication may account for some of the variability seen. Similarly the features of Parkinsonian dysarthria may convey an impression of slowness of thought and cognitive dysfunction which is not necessarily confirmed on testing (Maxim and Bryan 1996).

The dementia associated with Parkinson's disease is often described as subcortical dementia, but there is some evidence for language deficit due to reduced cortical functioning (Kuhl, Metter and Reige 1984). There is some evidence that PD patients have difficulty in monitoring their language due to frontal system dysfunction (McNamara *et al.* 1992). Knight (1992) reviews evidence for PD patients being significantly worse than normals on word fluency tasks. Sentence comprehension problems have also been noted (Grossman *et al.* 1992).

Progressive supranuclear palsy (PSP)

PSP is one of the Parkinson-plus syndromes. Extrapyramidal signs are prominent, but PSP typically includes a gaze palsy, pseudobulbar palsy, dysarthria dysphagia and dystonic rigidity of the neck and upper trunk. As the disease progresses a subcortical dementia becomes apparent. Maher, Smith and Lees (1985) described the main dysarthria features as slow mentation, forgetfulness, emotional or personality changes and impaired ability to manipulate acquired knowledge in the absence of dysphasia, agnosia and perceptual abnormalities. Language disturbances are not a feature of the disease although dysarthria and motor initiation problems can produce a disturbance in communication (Lebrun, Devreux and Rousseau 1986). Palilalia (reiterative productions associated with initiation difficulty) may be present and is associated with disturbances of the articulatory buffer (Garratt, Bryan and Maxim submitted).

Multiple sclerosis

Impairment in cognition is common in multiple sclerosis and makes an important contribution to disability and handicap (Barnes 1993). Fatigue is a frequent symptom and is relevant to testing of mental functions. Problems with information processing speed, anterograde learning and memory are described as a commonly occurring pattern (Rao 1990). Beatty and Goodkin (1990) suggest that the Mini Mental State examination (Folstein, Folstein and McHugh 1975) is a useful predictor of cognitive impairment, particularly in relapsing remitting patients.

Depression and anxiety are reported in multiple sclerosis and are more frequent in older and in more disabled patients (Berrios and Quemada 1990). Euphoria and pathological crying are also reported but appear to be relatively rare (Herndon 1990).

Alzheimer's disease

Alzheimer's disease is primarily a disease of old age and is the most common form of dementia seen in the UK. However, there is no definitive test for AD and diagnosis is by exclusion criteria and examination of behavioural, cognitive and language data. In addition there may be different forms of the disease such as familial, early onset, late onset. Or, AD may represent a single pathological entity that presents in different forms (Hardy 1992). Language functioning in AD is extensively reviewed in Maxim and Bryan (1996).

Psychiatric disturbances are not a key feature of Alzheimer's disease, in fact one of the DSM-II-R (American Psychiatric Association 1987) criteria for diagnosis is exclusion of non-organic psychiatric disorders. However, symptoms such as depression, anxiety and avoidance strategies may be apparent in the early stages of the disease process. In the middle stages, apathy and sleep disturbance may occur and in the late stages inappropriate social behaviour may be apparent.

Diffuse lewy body disease (DLBD)

DLBD, sometimes also called senile dementia of lewy body type, is now thought to be the second most common form of dementia after Parkinson's disease (Burns *et al.* 1990). This form of dementia is characterised by interneuronal inclusions called lewy bodies found in the cortex and the subcortical nuclei.

The clinical features are described by Byrne (1992) as early fluctuation in cognitive state with periods of acute confusion, cognitive impairment is less than would be expected in Alzheimer's disease, and extrapyramidal deficits of rigidity and tremor are present. Although the progress of the disease is variable, all patients develop dementia and have at least one extrapyramidal deficit and psychiatric symptoms. Visual hallucinations are particularly common.

Fearnley *et al.* described a patient with hyperkinetic dysarthria and nominal dysphasia. Ballard *et al.* (1996) found that verbal fluency declined faster in DLBD than in Alzheimer's disease and vascular dementia.

Huntington's disease

Psychiatric disorders are almost universal in Huntington's disease and may be the presenting problem (Morris 1991). Cognitive and behavioural symptoms are associated with damage to the caudate nucleus and its connections to the dorsolateral prefrontal region. Insidious changes in personality and behaviour often predate the first physical symptoms and then become increasingly obvious (Ward, Dennis and McMillan 1993). The common pattern is one of irritability, culminating in outbursts of verbal and physical aggression. A variety of sexual dysfunctions have also been described. Major depressive illness is common with an increased risk of suicide in younger patients (Schoenfield *et al.* 1984). Euphoria, and manic episodes have been reported and there is an increased incidence of schizophrenia-like psychosis (Morris 1991). Insight may be preserved but denial is common and can interfere with management strategies (Martindale 1987).

Cognitive dysfunction also occurs associated with cortical and basal ganglia degeneration. But this is variable and does not necessarily correlate with severity of the disease. Unlike Alzheimer's disease, Huntington's disease has relatively little impact on language (Butters *et al.* 1978). However, spontaneous speech is often sparse with hyperkinetic dysarthria, changes in prosody, decreased phrase length and lack of initiation as key features (Ross, Cummings and Benson 1990). Reduced word finding and verbal fluency have been described (Podoll *et al.* 1988). Impairment in understanding the emotional content of speech has also been reported (Speedie *et al.* 1990). As HD advances, the amount of functional communication decreases to the point, in the late stages, where the patient is mute and the extent of cognitive impairment is difficult to judge.

Cognitive assessments show a pattern of difficulty with planning, with shifting mental set and with flexibility (Brandt and Butters 1986). Difficulties with visuospatial tasks and with memory recall (rather than encoding) are also evident (Butters *et al.* 1978).

Pick's disease

Pick's disease can present with a specific language impairment and relatively spared cognitive functioning (Hodges 1994). Cummings and Benson (1992) describe three stages of the disease. Initially patients present with personality changes such as lack of spontaneity and inactivity and emotional changes such as inappropriate laughter. Language abnormalities are among the earliest intellectual deficits, but impaired insight and judgement are also a feature. As the disease progresses, language impairment increases, often with relative sparing of cognitive functions such as mathematical skills, memory and visuospatial skills. In the final stages of the disease, patients develop extrapyramidal disorders, intellectual decline in all areas and mutism. Holland *et al.* (1985) described a patient who was mute by the middle stages of the disease although at that stage he had relative sparing of written language skills. Pick's disease is a rare form of dementia but should be considered if there are initial personality and/or specific language changes.

AIDS dementia

Two forms of dementia associated with AIDS have been described: one being steadily progressive with periods of accelerated deterioration and the other (occurring in 20% of cases) having a slower and more protracted course (Navia, Jordan and Price 1986). It might be envisaged that improvements in drug therapy for AIDS patients would increase the proportion of AIDS patients with the slow form of the disease in the future.

Subcortical functions are thought to be more affected than cortical functions (Van Gorp *et al.* (1989). In the early stages there may be a dysarthria, and motor problems with speech and writing. Word-finding difficulties may be apparent and language may reflect slowness of thought and mood changes. As the dementia progresses, verbal responses become slower and less complex with mutism in the final stages of the disease (Cummings and Benson 1992).

Conclusion

Ron (1998) states that a wide range of psychiatric symptoms similar to those observed in primary psychiatric illness may be present in patients with brain disease. Likewise, the possibility of organic brain damage as an underlying cause or as a contributory factor needs to be considered in patients presenting to mental health services. The link between psychiatric symptoms and brain disease may be difficult to establish and the influence of environmental and genetic factors which predispose an individual to psychiatric disturbance may be as important as brain damage *per se* in leading to abnormalities of behaviour and mood. It is important that neurological and psychiatric factors in any disease process are recognised so that appropriate diagnosis, prognosis and rehabilitation can be provided.

References

Alexander, G.E. and Crutcher, M.D. (1990) Functional architecture of basal ganglia circuits: neural substrates of parallel processing. *Trends in the Neurosciences 13*, 226–271.

American Psychiatric Association (1987) *Diagnostic and Statistical Manual of Mental Disorders* (third edition). Washington: American Psychiatric Association.

Ballard, C., Patel, A., Oyebode, F. and Wilcock, G. (1996) Cognitive decline in patients with Alzheimer's disease, vascular dementia and senile dementia of lewy body type. *Age and Ageing 25*, 209–213.

Barnes, M.P. (1993) Multiple Sclerosis. In R.J. Greenwood, M.P. Barnes, T.M. McMillan and C.D. Ward (eds) *Neurological Rehabilitation.* Edinburgh: Churchill Livingstone.

Beatty, W.W. and Goodkin, D.E. (1990) Screening for cognitive impairment in multiple sclerosis: an evaluation of the Mini Mental State examination. *Archives of Neurology 47*, 297–301.

Benson, D.F. (1998) Introduction. In M.A. Ron and A.S. David (eds) *Disorders of Brain and Mind.* Cambridge: Cambridge University Press.

Bentall, R.P. (1990) *Reconstructing Schizophrenia.* London: Routledge.

Berrios, G.E. and Quemada, J.I. (1990) Depressive illness in multiple sclerosis. Clinical and theoretical aspects of the association. *British Journal of Psychiatry 156*, 10–16.

Blair, R.J.R. (1995) A cognitive developmental approach to morality: investigating the psychopath. *Cognition 57*, 1–29.

Bogousslavsky, J., Ferrazzini, M., Regali, F., Assal, G., Tanabe, H. and Delaloye-Bishop, A. (1988) Manic delirium and frontal lobe syndrome with paramedian infarction of the right thalamus. *Journal of Neurology, Neurosurgery and Psychiatry 51*, 116–119.

Bogousslavsky, J. and Regli, F. (1990) Anterior cerebral artery territory infarction in the Lausanne Stroke Registry. *Archives of Neurology 47*, 144–150.

Brandt, J. and Butters, N. (1986) The neuropsychology of Huntington's disease. *Trends in Neurosciences 93*, 118–120.

Bryan, K. (1989) Language prosody and the right hemisphere. *Aphasiology 3*, 285–299.

Bryan, K. and Kent, L. (submitted) Language difficulties after right hemisphere damage: a single case study of a bilingual patient.

Burns, A., Luthert, P., Levy, R., Jacoby, R. and Lantos, P. (1990) Accuracy of clinical diagnosis of Alzheimer's disease. *British Medical Journal 301*, 1026.

Burvill, P.W., Johnson, G.A., Jamrozik, K.D. *et al.* (1995) Prevalence of depression after stroke: The Perth community stroke study. *British Journal of Psychiatry 166*, 320–327.

Butters, N., Sax, D., Montgomery, K. and Tarlow, S. (1978) Comparison of the neuropsychological deficits associated with early and advanced Huntington's disease. *Archives of Neurology 35*, 585–589.

Byrne, E.J. (1992) Diffuse lewy body disease. In T. Arie (ed) *Recent Advances in Psychogeriatrics.* Edinburgh: Churchill Livingstone.

Cummings, J.L. (1992) Depression and Parkinson's disease: a review. *American Journal of Psychiatry 149*, 443–454.

Cummings, J.L. (1997) Neuropsychiatric manifestations of right hemisphere lesions. *Brain and Language 57*, 22–37.

Cummings, J.L. and Benson, D.F. (1992) *Dementia: A Clinical Approach.* Boston: Butterworths.

Cutting, J. (1990) *The Right Cerebral Hemisphere and Psychiatric Disorders.* Oxford: Oxford University press.

Davey, D. and Thompson, P.J. (1992) Language and epilepsy. *Journal of Neurolinguistics 6*, 381–399.

David, A.S. (1994) Thought echo reflects the activity of the phonological loop. *British Journal of Clinical Psychology 33*, 81–83.

Ellis, H.D. and Leafhead, K.M. (1996) Raymond: a study of an adult with Asperger's Syndrome. In P.W. Halligan and J.C. Marshall (eds) *Method in Madness: Case Studies in Neuropsychiatry.* Hove: Psychology Press.

Fearnley, J.M., Revesz, D.J., Franckowiak, R.S.J. and Lees, A.J. (1991) Diffuse lewy body disease presenting with supranuclear gaze palsy. *Journal of Neurology, Neurosurgery and Psychiatry 54*, 159–161.

Feinstein, A. and Ron, M.A. (1990) Psychosis associated with demonstrable brain disease. *Psychological Medicine 20*, 793–803.

Fesenmeier, J.T., Kuzniecky, R. and Garcia, J.H. (1990) Akinetic mutism caused by bilateral anterior cerebral tuberculous obliterative arteritis. *Neurology 30*, 1005–1006.

Fish, D. (1989) CT and PET in drug-resistant epilepsy. In M.R. Trimble (ed) *Chronic Epilepsy, Its Prognosis and Management.* Chichester: John Wiley.

Folstein, M.F., Folstein, F.E. and McHugh, P.R. (1975) Mini Mental State: a practical method of grading the cognitive state of patients for the clinician. *Journal of Psychiatric Research 12*, 189–198.

Frith, C.D. (1992) *The Cognitive Neuropsychology of Schizophrenia.* Hove: Erlbaum.

Gallagher, J.P. (1989) Pathological laughter and crying in ALS: a search for their origin. *Acta Neurologica Scandinavica 80*, 114–117.

Garratt, H., Bryan, K. and Maxim, J. (submitted) Palilalia in progressive supranuclear palsy: failure of the articulatory buffer and subcortical inhibitory systems.

Gillham, R.A. (1990) Refractory epilepsy: an evaluation of psychological methods in outpatient management. *Epilepsia* *32*, 427–432.

Gotham, A-M., Brown, R.G. and Marsden, C.D. (1986) Depression in Parkinson's disease: a quantitative and qualitative analysis. *Journal of Neurology, Neurosurgery and Psychiatry 51*, 767–772.

Grossman, M., Carvell, S., Gollomp, S. and Hurtig, H.I. (1992) Sentence comprehension in Parkinson's disease: the role of attention and memory. *Brain and Language 42*, 347–384.

Halligan, P.W. and Marshall, J.C. (eds) *Method in Madness: Case Studies in Neuropsychiatry.* Hove: Psychology Press.

Hardy, J. (1992) Alzheimer's disease: many aetiologies; one pathogenesis. In F. Florette, Z. Khachaturian, M. Poncet and Y. Christen (eds) *Heterogeneity of Alzheimer's Disease.* Berlin: Springer-Verlag.

Herndon, R.M. (1990) Cognitive deficits and emotional dysfunction in multiple sclerosis. *Archives of Neurology 47*, 1, 18.

Hodges, J.R. (1994) Pick's Disease. In A. Burns and R. Levy (eds) *Dementia.* London: Chapman and Hall.

Holland, A.L., McBurney, D.H., Moossy, J. and Rernmirth, O.M. (1985) The dissolution of language in Pick's disease with neurofibrillary tangles: a case study. *Brain and Language 24*, 36–38.

Horton, P.C. (1976) Personality disorder and parietal lobe dysfunction. *American Journal of Psychiatry 133*, 782–785.

Jorge, R.E., Robinson, R.G., Starkstein, S.E., Arndt, S.V., Forrester, A.W. and Geisler, F.H. (1993) Secondary mania following traumatic brain injury. *American Journal of Psychiatry 150*, 916–921.

Klee, A. (1961) Akinetic mutism: review of the literature and report of a case. *Journal of Nervous and Mental Diseases 133*, 536–553.

Knight, R.G. (1992) *The neuropsychology of degenerative brain diseases.* London: Erlbaum.

Kuhl, D.E., Metter, E.J. and Reige, W.H. (1984) Patterns of local glucose utilisation determined in Parkinson's disease with [F18] flurodeoxyglucose method. *Annals of Neurology 15*, 419–424.

LeBrun, Y., Devreux, F. and Rousseau, J.J. (1986) Language and speech in a patient with a clinical diagnosis of progressive supranuclear palsy. *Brain and Language 27*, 247–256.

Lishman, W.A. (1989) Neurologists and psychiatrists. In E.H. Reynolds and M.R. Trimble (eds) *The Bridge Between Neurology and Psychiatry.* Edinburgh: Churchill Livingstone.

Maher, E.R., Smith, E.M. and Lees, A.J. (1985) Cognitive deficits in Steele–Richardson–Olszewski syndrome. *Journal of Neurology, Neurosurgery and Psychiatry 48*, 1234–1239.

Marshall, J.C. and Halligan, P.W. (1996) Towards a cognitive psychiatry. In P.W. Halligan and J.C. Marshall (eds) *Method in Madness: Case Studies in Neuropsychiatry.* Hove: Psychology Press.

Martindale, B. (1987) Huntington's Chorea: some psychodynamics seen in those at risk and in the response of the helping professions. *British Journal of Psychiatry 150*, 319–323.

Maxim, J. and Bryan, K. (1996) Language, cognition and communication in older mentally ill people. In K. Bryan and J. Maxim (eds) *Communication Disability and the Psychiatry of Old Age.* London: Whurr.

McMillan, T.M. and Greenwood, R.J. (1993) Head injury rehabilitation. In R.J. Greenwood, M.P. Barnes, T.M. McMillan, and C.D. Ward (eds) *Neurological Rehabilitation.* Edinburgh: Churchill Livingstone.

McNamara, P., Obler, L.K., Au, R., Durso, R. and Albert, M.L. (1992) Speech monitoring skills in Alzheimer's disease, Parkinson's disease and normal aging. *Brain and Language 42*, 38–51.

McPherson, S.E. and Cummings, J.L. (1998) The neuropsychology of the frontal lobes. In M.A. Ron and A.S. David (eds) *Disorders of Brain and Mind.* Cambridge: Cambridge University Press.

Messert, B., Henke, T.K. and Langheim, W. (1966) Syndrome of akinetic mutism associated with obstructive hydrocephalus. *Neurology 16*, 635–649.

Morris, M. (1991) Psychiatric aspects of Huntington's disease. In P.S. Harper (ed) *Huntington's Disease.* London: W.B. Saunders.

Navia, B.A., Jordan, B.D. and Price, R.W. (1986) The AIDS dementia complex, I: clinical features. *Annals of Neurology 19*, 517–524.

Pentland, B. (1993) Parkinsonism and dystonia. In R.J. Greenwood, M.P. Barnes, T.M. McMillan and C.D. Ward (eds) *Neurological Rehabilitation.* Edinburgh: Churchill Livingstone.

Pepin, E.P. and Pepin, A.P. (1993) Selective dorsolateral frontal lobe dysfunction associated with diencephalic amnesia. *Neurology 43*, 733–741.

Peterson, C., Maier, S.F. and Seligman, M.E.P. (1993) *Learned Helplessness.* Oxford: Oxford University Press.

Podoll, K., Caspari, P., Lange, H.W. and Noth, J. (1988) Language functions in Huntington's disease. *Brain 3,* 1475–1472.

Ramani, V. and Gumnit, R.S. (1982) Intensive monitoring of interictal psychosis in epilepsy. *Annals of Neurology 11,* 613–622.

Rao, S.M. (1990) *Neurobehavioural Aspects of Multiple Sclerosis.* Oxford: Oxford University Press.

Roberts, G.W., Leigh, P.N. and Weinberger, D.R. (1993) *Neuropsychiatric Disorders.* London: Woolf.

Robertson, M. (1986) Depressive illness in epilepsy. In M.R. Trimble and T.G. Bolwig (eds) *Aspects of Epilepsy and Psychiatry.* Chichester: John Wiley. pp.213–234.

Robinson, A.L., Heaton, R.K. and Lehman, R.A.W. (1980) The utility of the Wisconsin Card Sorting Test in detecting and localizing frontal lobe lesions. *Journal of Consulting and Clinical Psychology 48,* 605–614.

Ron, M.A. (1998) Psychiatric manifestations of brain disease. In M.A. Ron and A.S. David (eds) *Disorders of Brain and Mind.* Cambridge: Cambridge University Press.

Ron, M.A. and David, A.S. (1998) *Disorders of Brain and Mind.* Cambridge: Cambridge University Press.

Ross, G.W., Cummings, J.L. and Benson, D.F. (1990) Speech and language alterations in dementia syndromes: characteristics and treatment. *Aphasiology 4,* 339–352.

Rourke, B.P. (1987) Syndrome of non-verbal learning difficulties: the final common pathway of white-matter disease/dysfunction? *Clinical Neuropsychologist 1,* 209–234.

Schoenfield, M., Myers, R.M., Cupples, A. *et al.* (1984) Increased rate of suicide among patients with Huntington's disease. *Journal of Neurology, Neurosurgery and Psychiatry 47,* 1283–1287.

Shallice, T., Burgess, P.W. and Frith, C. (1991) Can the neuropsychological case-study approach be applied to schizophrenia? *Psychological Medicine 21,* 661–673.

Speedie, L.J., Brake, N., Folstein, S.E., Bowers, D. and Heilman, K.M. (1990) Comprehension of prosody in Huntington's disease. *Journal of Neurology, Neurosurgery and Psychiatry 53,* 607–610.

Starkstein, S.E., Federoff, P., Berthier, M.L. and Robinson, R.G. (1991) Manic-depressive and pure manic states after brain lesions. *Biology and Psychiatry 29,* 149–158.

Starkstein, S.E., Mayberg, H.S., Berthier, M.L., Federaff, P., Price, T.R., Dannals, R.F., Wagner, H.N., Leiguarda, R. and Robinson, R.G. (1990) Mania after brain injury: neuroradiological and metabolic findings. *Annals of Neurology 27,* 652–659.

Starkstein, S.E., Robinson, R.G., Honig, M.A., Rarikh, R.M., Joselyn, J. and Price, T.R. (1989) Mood changes after right hemisphere lesions. *British Journal of Psychiatry 155,* 79–85.

Starkstein, S.E., Robinson, R.G. and Price, T.R. (1987) Comparison of cortical and subcortical lesions in the production of post-stroke mood disorders. *Brain 110,* 1045–1059.

Starr, A. and Sporty, L.D. (1994) Similar disorders viewed with different perspectives: a challenge for neurology and psychiatry. *Archives of Neurology 51,* 977–980.

Thompson, P.J. (1988) Methods and problems in the assessment of behaviour disorder in epileptic patients. In M.R. Trimble and E.H. Reynolds (eds) *Epilepsy Behaviour and Cognitive Function.* Chichester: John Wiley. pp.27–40.

Thompson, P.J. and Shorvon, S.D. (1993) The epilepsies. In R.J. Greenwood, M.P. Barnes, T.M. McMillan and C.D. Ward (eds) *Neurological Rehabilitation.* Edinburgh: Churchill Livingstone.

Trimble, M.R. (1993) Neuropsychiatry or behavioural neurology. In M.A. Ron and A.S. David (eds) *Disorders of Brain and Mind.* Cambridge: Cambridge University Press.

Trimble, M.R. (1998) A neurobiological perspective of the behaviour disorders of epilepsy. *Neuropsychiatry, Neuropsychology and Behavioural Neurology 6,* 60–69.

Van Gorp, W.G., Mitrushina, M., Cummings, J.L., Satz, P. and Modesitt, J. (1989) Normal aging and the subcortical encephalopathy of AIDS. *Neuropsychiatry, Neuropsychology and Behavioural Neurology 2,* 5–20.

Van Lancker, D. (1991) Personal relevance and the human right hemisphere. *Brain and Cognition 17,* 64–92.

Ward, C.D., Dennis, N.R. and McMillan, T.M. (1993) Huntington's disease. In R.J. Greenwood, M.P. Barnes, T.M. McMillan, and C.D. Ward (eds) *Neurological Rehabilitation.* Edinburgh: Churchill Livingstone.

Weinstein, E.A. (1996) Reduplicative misidentification syndromes. In P.W. Halligan and J.C. Marshall (eds) *Method in Madness: Case Studies in Neuropsychiatry.* Hove: Psychology Press.

CHAPTER 9

Neuropsychology in Psychiatric Practice

Mary Hill

Introduction

The importance of cognitive impairment in major mental illness has long been recognised, and was described and embodied by Kraeplin (1919) in his initial designation of schizophrenia as 'dementia praecox', with more detailed clinical and experimental analyses of thought processes characteristic of the disorder following in the work of authors such as White (1928) and Cameron (1938). Throughout a similar period, further understanding of the relationships between cognitive deficit, psychological reactions and underlying brain pathology also came in the research of authors such as Goldstein (1936) and Brickner (1936), and by the 1950s cognitive assessment had become a widespread adjunct to psychiatric practice. The initial emphasis was often upon the evaluation of a general level of intellectual functioning using measures such as those developed by Wechsler, but the introduction of 'diagnostic methods' also became prominent as a means of detecting potential brain lesions underlying psychiatric presentations. These tasks have norms comparing performance in neurological patients and those with psychiatric disorders, and many involve the measurement of memory functions, and particularly the retention and reproduction of complex geometrical designs such as the Memory for Designs Test (Graham and Kendall 1960), or the Visual Retention Test (Benton 1974). A comprehensive review of 94 studies in this area was compiled by Heaton, Baade and Johnson (1978). It was found that despite methodological variations, in most cases patients with organic disorder performed less well on such tasks than those with psychiatric diagnoses, other than schizophrenics. The probability of an accurate discrimination between schizophrenia and organic brain pathology appeared little more than chance, and in discussion the authors considered the accruing evidence that in many schizophrenics observed test abnormalities might be the reflection of a genuinely high rate of underlying neuropathology, a point of view which has been endorsed in ensuring years. From the late 1970s, there has been a more widespread adoption of the term 'neuropsychology' in clinical practice in the UK, and with this a rapidly increasing awareness of the potential of cognitive assessment in a wide range of psychiatric patients. Increasingly complex theoretical models based upon experimental cognitive neuropsychology have been applied to the understanding of psychiatric symptoms, and there have been more ambitious attempts to relate test results to the real 'everyday' difficulties experienced by patients and to use this in the planning of treatment strategies.

Methods of assessment

Methods of cognitive and neuropsychological assessment may be classified in a number of ways, but clinically the most important distinctions consider the attributes and skills which are measured. Only the briefest summary of the most common interventions is attempted here: general texts include Lezak (1995) and Crawford, Parker and McKinlay (1992).

General intellectual functioning

Much of the origin of psychometric testing lies in the measurement of general ability or 'IQ', and in many assessments the concept of a general level of functioning remains an important benchmark against which more specific functions (e.g. memory or reading) may be measured. In this field the Wechsler Intelligence Scales remain the most commonly applied and versatile measure of IQ. There are scales for children from the age of 3 years and in its latest revision the Wechsler Adult Intelligence Scale (WAIS III R, Wechsler 1997) can be used for the adult population from 16 to 80 years. All Wechsler scales are designed such that the mean population IQ is 100, with half the population obtaining an IQ within the 'average' range of 90 to 110, and the age-corrections which are embodied in these scales mean that an IQ estimate measured early in life should remain constant throughout the life span. If the measured IQ changes significantly at any stage, it suggests that there may have been an intervening event which has interrupted the normal pattern of aging – e.g. a stroke or the onset of dementia – and this concept is often useful in clinical diagnosis.

Traditionally, the WAIS Full Scale IQ has been based upon a compilation of 11 different tasks or 'subtests', six of which are considered to have a 'Verbal' bias, and five of which are more concerned with non-verbal or 'Performance' skills. It has provided two main subscale IQs, Verbal and Performance, also with a mean of 100. In the recently introduced WAIS III R, three new subtests have been added, increasing the range of skills sampled and the kind of analyses which can be made. In addition to the two main subscales, subtests can be regrouped into 4 'indices' which have been defined by factor analysis, and labelled Verbal Comprehension, Perceptual Organisation, Working Memory and Processing Speed. The majority of those who have an uninterrupted 'normal' cognitive development will show a broad consistency in their pattern of WAIS attainment, and if statistical variations become large, this can suggest that there are atypical underlying reasons – e.g. brain pathology. The kind of errors which people make, and the way in which they approach tasks, may also provide additional information and reinforce inferences of this kind. All of the Wechsler intelligence scales have undergone a number of revisions since their initial introduction, and all supply 'supplements' in different languages to facilitate an international application (e.g. the British supplement).

The clinical use of Wechsler is ubiquitous and eclipses a range of other less widely applied intellectual measures, but some short estimates of IQ remain of value. Raven's Matrices (Raven 1952) provide a good brief indication of 'performance' IQ, and may be used in combination with a measure of vocabulary to provide an estimate of verbal skills.

Literacy

Literacy is important both in developmental neuropsychology and in the acquired dyslexias of adulthood. Developmentally, a lag in the rate of acquisition of literacy may imply either an environmental or educational disadvantage, or a primary specific skills deficit, and indications of the latter may come from both general intellectual testing and a range of more specific diagnostic instruments. Neurological disorders in adults can give rise to a range of different kinds of dyslexia which are related to the site of the lesion, and there are also specialist techniques for the analysis of these syndromes (Seymour 1992).

With a normal developmental history, the acquisition of reading and the eventual level reached has been shown to have a good correlation with IQ, and this finding together with a relative retention of the recognition of previously learnt words in later life has been used in the development of the National Adult Reading Test (NART, Nelson 1982). The NART is a very widely adopted technique which provides an estimate of pre-morbid ability based upon current reading level, and can provide an inference of possible intellectual decline if present IQ based upon the WAIS appears substantially lower than the pre-morbid estimate.

Memory and attention

Deficits in the capacity to remember existing information, or to acquire new information, provide both very frequent symptoms of all forms of brain pathology and are amongst the most common category of presenting complaints of cognitive failure, and the importance of memory in neuropsychology is reflected in a very wide range of measurement techniques. These vary between 'batteries' of tasks which recognise the heterogeneity of memorisation processes, and single measures which are intended to look at particular problems.

Traditionally, the Wechsler Memory Scale (WMS, Wechsler 1997) has been amongst the most widely used approaches in the UK, offering a battery of tasks which consider orientation in time and place, and attentional and control processes, in addition to the acquisition of new verbal and visual materials. In the latest version, the WMS III R (1997), 11 subtests can be grouped into 3 main indices based upon the kind of memory involved. Refinements in the relationship between the WAIS III R and WMS III R also facilitate comparisons between general intellectual ability and memory functioning. The revised version of the WMS remains an important method of appraisal, but to it have been added the British Adult Memory and Information Processing Battery (Coughlan and Hollows 1985) which considers a range of attentional, memory and information processing functions, together with tasks which replicate problems more often encountered in 'everyday life' and are thus thought to have a greater 'ecological validity'. These include the Rivermead Behavioural Memory Test (Wilson, Cockburn and Baddeley 1985), the Test of Everyday Attention (Robertson et al. 1994). The Autobiographical Memory Inventory (Kopelman, Wilson and Baddeley 1990) structures long-standing information about events which have occurred throughout life.

Specific skill impairments

Discrete lesions, and particularly those which have a recent neurological origin, may give rise to a range of specific neuropsychological impairments which can be loosely divided into 'verbal' deficits which usually arise from major pathology to the left cerebral hemisphere, and visuospatial and non-verbal problems which are usually more pronounced with pathology to the right hemisphere. Specific skill impairments occur in agnosia (a deficit in integrating and construing information arising from one of the senses), the dyspraxias (difficulties in the integration of movement and constructional abilities), or dysphasias of different kinds. Indications of a need to screen for such specific symptoms can come from either the specification of the referral and the known history of the patient, or could arise within the course of more general assessment – e.g. from the response to certain WAIS items. More comprehensive neuropsychological texts offer a full discussion of specialised assessment techniques.

'Executive function' deficits

'Executive functions' are concerned with the overall planning and integration of skilled and 'intelligent' behaviour, and deficits are associated with lesions and dysfunction in the anterior neocortex. Shallice (1988) has described a 'Supervisory Attentional System' which is located in this part of the brain and is seen as having a modulatory role, co-ordinating functions in other parts of the brain. Clinically, there are two main kinds of executive function deficits. There are symptoms which impinge upon abstract thought processes and are expressed in difficulties in the derivation and manipulation of abstract constructs, and which can be measured by 'sorting tasks', such as the Modified Wisconsin Card Sorting Tasks (Nelson 1976), or by tasks which look at more complex abstraction processes in the use of existing knowledge, e.g. Cognitive Estimation (Shallice and Evans 1978). However, some patients may also demonstrate impulsive behaviours or deficits in the suppression of irrelevant and competing ideas, and these are symptoms which may emerge in a lack of the response inhibition required by tasks such as the Stroop, or sometimes classical maze problems. Newer approaches to executive functioning have also sought a greater ecological validity, for example the Behavioural Assessment of the Executive Syndrome (Wilson *et al.* 1996) or in the Multiple Errands Test (Shallice and Burgess 1991).

Clinical presentations

Patients with a primary complaint of cognitive failure

There is a large group of patients in whom the primary symptom is a complaint of recent cognitive deterioration or associated behavioural change. Clinically, the task is one of evaluating the presenting symptom and its possible origin, using both a personal history and an appropriate psychometric approach. Usually this will involve a comparison between a present estimate of general functioning based upon an administration of all or part of the WAIS-R and an estimate of pre-morbid ability based upon educational and vocational history or current reading level (NART-R), together with an assessment of reported specific areas of weakness; where discrepancies are found, the most likely diagnosis will be one of dementia.

Statistical analyses of the psychometric results of large numbers of patients in the intermediate stages of Alzheimer's disease have also suggested that it may be possible to differentiate three basic varieties of the condition on the basis of the relative deterioration observed in verbal and non-verbal domains (Fisher *et al.* 1996).

However, a series of studies have illustrated the importance of self-esteem and depression in the self-perception of ability (e.g. Khan *et al.* 1975; Broadbent *et al.* 1982), and particularly in the earlier stages of deterioration it is important to distinguish between the reactive stress which may result from an encroaching difficulty, and the role of pre-existing stress in creating or emphasising the presenting complaint. Patients who function normally on psychometric tests may experience cognitive failures in everyday life of psychogenic origin. In a mixed neurological/psychiatric out-patient clinic, patients presenting with organic and psychogenic aetiologies could be shown to occur in roughly equal numbers (Hill 1984), and an appreciation of the circumstances in which cognitive failure has occurred can be crucial in the interpretation of results. In a proportion of patients, apparent test deficits can be shown to have a more long-standing origin (e.g. remote head injury), but may present for the first time only when particular demands are made, and with appropriate counselling these patients may have a relatively favourable prognosis. In patients with a progressive dementia, it may be necessary to make a series of appraisals of possible rate of decline, and to offer advice on remediation strategies and ways of minimising the impact of the disorder. There are more specific techniques available for assessment in elderly groups at more advanced stages of deterioration, e.g. Middlesex Elderly Assessment of Mental State (Golding 1989) and the Severe Impairment Battery (Saxton *et al.* 1993).

Patients presenting in other psychiatric groupings

There are many other patients referred for assessment with a different primary psychiatric diagnosis, but in whom it is recognised that cognitive failure is a risk factor which may be making a variable contribution in presenting symptomatology.

(A) COGNITIVE FUNCTIONING IN MAJOR MENTAL ILLNESS

Early observations of intellectual dysfunction in schizophrenia have been succeeded by progressively more complex findings of a range of serious cognitive impairments in the disorder. These have emphasised both a deterioration in general intellectual functioning (McKenna 1995) and a range of more specific deficits such as a poor capacity to store and retain new information (Tamlyn *et al.* 1992), decline in speed of responding and information processing (Nelson *et al.* 1990; Hemsley 1994) and particular difficulties in executive functioning, such as the ability to manipulate complex constructs and plan problem solving strategies (Shallice, Burgess and Frith 1991). Recent reviews of cognitive functioning in psychosis have been provided by O'Carroll (1992) and Rossell and David (1997). Questions raised include the extent to which it may be of value to seek specific patterns of functioning associated with different schizophrenic presentations or 'syndromes' (Liddle 1987; Norman *et al.* 1997), and sometimes to go beyond this and to recognise the heterogeneity of the disorder in the analysis of the cognitive functioning of the single case (Shallice *et al.* 1991) or the analysis of specific symptoms (David 1994; Bentall 1994). There have also been trends a greater understanding of the relationship between formal cognitive test results and the implications of such deficits in everyday skills (Green 1996), and in the development of cognitive models to guide the remediation of deficits.

Fewer reports consider less common psychotic presentations and bipolar affective disorder, but cognitive impairment has been observed in these conditions also. Christodolou (1991) reported frequent neuropsychological impairment and neurological abnormality in delusional 'misidentification' syndromes, and also suggested a right cerebral hemisphere bias in many patients. Morice (1990) compared schizophrenics and patients with bipolar disorder on a range of psychometric tests and found the latter group to be generally less impaired, but to share deficits on tasks requiring abstract thinking, such as card sorting.

(B) COGNITIVE FUNCTIONING IN CONDUCT DISORDER AND FORENSIC POPULATIONS

Golden *et al.* (1996) have reviewed a large literature considering the neuropsychological correlates of violence and aggression. It has long been recognised that those who commit offences or present with a more general behavioural disorder are likely to show a cognitive disadvantage, and that children who present with conduct disorder and adolescent psychopaths are likely to show both slightly below average general functioning and poorer verbal skills on conventional IQ scales (Wechsler 1944). In an important longitudinal study in New Zealand, Moffitt (1988) traced around 1000 children from birth, and demonstrated the development of this cognitive pattern in boys who later reported delinquency in their teens, and a pattern of more pervasive mild impairment in delinquent girls. Adult prison populations have also been found to provide slightly below-average estimates of IQ (Robertson, Taylor and Gunn 1987), and poor verbal skills and impairments in executive functioning have been reported amongst sexual and violent offenders (Galski, Thornton and Shumski 1990; Miller 1987). Not surprisingly, populations of violent offenders who are also recognised as psychiatrically ill provide very high rates of neuropsychological disturbance. Martell (1992) found a substantial majority of American maximum security forensic psychiatric patients to exhibit some form of brain pathology, and Lumsden, Chesterman and Hill (1998) have reported clear cognitive disturbance in about 60 per cent of a series of male admissions to an English Special Hospital.

(C) NEUROPSYCHOLOGICAL SEQUELAE OF ALCOHOL ABUSE

The effects of prolonged alcohol abuse in producing both brain pathology and accompanying neuropsychological deficit were first described in the late nineteenth century in the classical Wernicke–Korsakoff syndrome. In its acute phase, the periventricular lesions of Wernicke's encephalopathy were reported to incur a symptomatology of confusion, delirium, a staggering ataxic gait, and oculomotor disturbances. With resolution, although many patients were thought to return to an apparently adequate level of general intellectual functioning, they were reported to be left with a pronounced memory deficit – described by Korsakoff as an 'Amnesic Syndrome'. Subsequent research has validated much of these initial findings, but more complete studies of neuropsychological functioning have also demonstrated a wider spectrum, and often a more pervasive pattern of deficits associated with prolonged alcohol abuse. In a series of 1100 patients assessed at an alcoholic treatment unit Horvath (1975) reported that around 10 per cent suffered serious permanent impairment, but that only about one-fifth of these presented as a classical amnesia. Age has emerged as the most important correlation with intellectual impairment, with consumption variables having much less importance (Grant, Adams and Reed 1984). Few cases of serious permanent deficit are reported below the age of 40 years.

Many patients presenting with alcoholism will have an associated psychiatric disorder or emotional disturbance, and the sequelae of alcohol and substance abuse are a frequent complication amongst offender populations. Many violent offences occur in conditions of 'alcohol provocation', in itself a state of temporary neuropsychological dysfunction.

Methodological issues

Choice of methodology/testing approach

The most important factor which will influence the approach adopted is the reason for referral. Psychological testing is essentially a matter of hypothesis testing (Heilbrun 1992), and the purpose of testing will define the nature and length of the assessment. Clinically, the best strategy is usually the minimal strategy, using the most concise and least demanding techniques which are available to consider a particular difficulty, and much skill may be needed with disturbed and poorly motivated patients to maintain attention. Where there are several tests which could be used to assess a problem, the level of statistical and conceptual sophistication of a technique and the associated literature may be important considerations. Occasionally, a need for information about population characteristics may suggest a 'standard battery' of tasks, but more usually the procedure will be flexible and designed for an individual.

Factors influencing results

When well standardised psychometric methods are used, the aim is to obtain a valid estimate of current attainment on the task which is representative of underlying ability – or deficit. However, attainment may be constrained by a number of other factors. There are those which are directly associated with the psychiatric condition itself, such as mental state, distractions from hallucinations and delusional ideas, and in many psychiatric patients these may interact with variable motivation, fatigue and possible side-effects from essential medication and other drugs. Specific sensory or physical handicaps may need to be taken into consideration, and the pre-morbid educational experiences and representation of other skills will also enter into present achievement. Such observations are made within the process of interviewing and test administration, and are an important foundation upon which more formal analyses of statistical variabilities in test scores and qualitative features in task approach can be evaluated.

References

Bentall, R.P. (1994) Cognitive biases and abnormal beliefs: towards a model of persecutory delusions. In A.S. David and J.C. Cutting (eds) *The Neuropsychology of schizophrenia.* Hove: Lawrence Erlbaum Associates.

Benton, A.L. (1974) *The Revised Benton Visual Retention Test* (fourth edition). New York: Psychological Corporation.

Brickner, R.M. (1936) *The Intellectual Functions of the Frontal Lobes.* New York: MacMillan.

Broadbent, D.E., Cooper. P.F., Fitzgerald, P. and Parkes, R.R. (1982) The Cognitive Failures Questionnaire and its correlates. *British Journal of Clinical Psychology 21*, 1–16.

Cameron, N. (1938) Reasoning, regression and communication in schizophrenics. *Psychological Monographs 1 50*, 1–34.

Christodolou, G.N. (1991) The delusional misidentification syndromes. *British Journal of Psychiatry 159*, (supp. 14). 65–69.

Coughlan, A.K. and Hollows, S.E. (1985) *The Adult Memory and Information Processing Battery.* Leeds: St. James University Hospital.

Crawford, J.R., Parker, D.M. and McKinlay, W.W. (1992) *A Handbook of Neuropsychological Assessment.* Hove: Lawrence Erlbaum Associates.

David, A.S. (1994) The neuropsychological origin of auditory hallucinations. In A.S. David and J.C. Cutting (eds) *The Neuropsychology of Scizophrenia.* Hove: Lawrence Erlbaum Associates.

Fisher, N.J., Rourke, B.P., Bieliauskas, L.A., Giordani, B., Berent, S. and Foster, N. (1986) Neuropsychological subgroups of patients with Alzheimer's disease. *Journal of Clinical and Experimental Neuropsychology 19*, 713–754.

Galski, T., Thornton, K.E. and Shumsky, D. (1990) Brain dysfunction in sex offenders. *Journal of Offender Rehabilitation 16*, 1, 65–80.

Golden, C.J., Jackson, M.L., Peterson-Rohne, A. and Gontkovsky, S.T. (1996) Neuropsychological correlates of violence and aggression: a review of the clinical literature. *Aggression and Violent Behaviour 1*, 1, 3–25.

Golding, E. (1989) *The Middlesex Elderly Assessment of Mental State.* Bury St. Edmunds: Thames Valley Test Company.

Goldstein, K. (1936) The significance of the frontal lobes for mental performance. *Journal of Neurology and Psychopathology 17*, 27–40.

Graham, F.K. and Kendall, B.S. (1960) Memory-for-Designs Test: revised general manual. *Perceptual and Motor Skills 11*, 147–188.

Grant, I., Adams, K.M. and Reed, R. (1984) Aging, abstinence and medical risk factors in the prediction of neuropsychological deficit amongst long-term alcoholics. *Archives of General Psychiatry 41*, 710–718.

Green, M.F. (1996) What are the functional consequences of neurocognitive deficits in schizophrenia? *American Journal of Psychiatry 153*, 3, 321–330.

Heaton, R.K., Baade, L.E. and Johnson, K.L. (1978) Neuropsychological test results associated with psychiatric disorders in adults. *Psychological Bulletin 85*, 1, 141–162.

Heilbrun, K. (1992) The role of psychological testing in forensic assessment. *Law and Human Behaviour 16*, 257–272.

Hemsley, D.R. (1994) Perceptual and cognitive abnormalities as bases for schizophrenic symptoms. In A.S. David and J.C. Cutting (eds) *The Neuropsychology of Schizophrenia.* Hove: Lawrence Erlbaum Associates.

Hill, G.M. (1984) *Dimensions of self appraisal of cognitive functions in patients referred to a neuropsychological practice.* University of London: Unpublished PhD thesis.

Horvath (1975) Clinical spectrum and epidemiological features of alcoholic dementia. In J.G. Rankin (ed) *Alcohol, Drugs and Brain Damage.* Toronto: Addiction Research Foundation.

Khan, R.L., Zarit, S.H., Hilbert, N.M. and Niederehe, G. (1975) Memory complaint and impairment in the aged. *Archives of General Psychiatry 32*, 1569–1573.

Kopelman, M., Wilson, B.A. and Baddeley, A. (1990) *The Autobiographical Memory Inventory.* Bury St. Edmunds: Thames Valley Test Company.

Kraeplin, E. (1919) *Dementia Praecox.* New York: E&S Livingstone.

Lezak, M.D. (1995) *Neuropsychological Assessment.* New York: Oxford University Press.

Liddle, P.F. (1987) Schizophrenic syndromes, cognitive performance and neurological dysfunction. *Psychological Medicine 17*, 49–57.

Lumsden, J., Chesterman, L.P. and Hill, G.M. (1998) Neuropsychiatric indices in a maximum secure psychiatric admission sample I: estimating the prevalence. *Criminal Behaviour and Mental Health 8*, 285–310.

McKenna, P. (1995) General intellectual function in psychosis. *Schizophrenia Monitor 5*, 4, 1–5.

Martell, D.A. (1992) Estimating the prevalence of neuropsychiatric disturbance in maximum security forensic psychiatric patients. *Journal of Forensic Science 37*, 3, 878–893.

Miller, L. (1987) Neuropsychology of the aggressive psychopath: an integrative review. *Aggressive Behaviour 13*, 119–140.

Moffitt (1988) Neuropsychology and self-reported early delinquency in an unselected birth cohort. In T.E. Moffitt and S.A. Mednick (eds) *Biological Contributions to Crime Causation.* New York: Martinuus Nijhoff.

Morice, R. (1990) Cognitive inflexibility and prefrontal dysfunction in schizophrenia and mania. *British Journal of Psychiatry 157*, 50–54.

Nelson, H.E. (1982) *National Adult Reading Test (NART)*. Windsor: NFER-Nelson.

Nelson, H.E. (1976) A modified card sorting test sensitive to frontal lobe defects. *Cortex 12*, 313–324.

Nelson, H.E., Pantelis, C., Carruthers, K., Speller, J., Baxendale, S. and Barnes, T.R.E. (1990) Cognitive functioning and symptomatology in chronic schizophrenia. *Psychological Medicine 20*, 357–365.

Norman, R.M.G., Malla, A.K., Morrison-Stewart, S.L., Helmes, E., Williamson, P.C., Thomas, J. and Cortese, L. (1997) Neuropsychological correlates of syndromes in schizophrenia. *British Journal of Psychiatry 170*, 134–139.

O'Carroll, R. (1992) Neuropsychology of psychosis. *Current Opinion in Psychiatry 5*, 38–44.

Raven, J.C. (1958) *Standard Progressive Matrices*. London: H.K. Lewis.

Robertson, G., Taylor, P.J. and Gunn, J. (1987) Does violence have cognitive correlates? *British Journal of Psychiatry 151*, 63–68.

Robertson, I.H., Ward, T., Ridgeway, V. and Nimmo-Smith, I. (1994) *The Test of Everyday Attention*. Bury St. Edmunds: Thames Valley Test Company.

Rossell, S. and David, A.S. (1997) The neuropsychology of schizophrenia: recent trends. *Current Opinion in Psychiatry 10*, 26–29.

Saxton, J., McGonigle, K.L., Swilhart, A.A. and Boller, F. (1993) *Severe Impairment battery*. Bury St. Edmunds: Thames Valley Test Company.

Seymour, P.H.K. (1992) The assessment of reading disorders. In *A Handbook of Neuropsychological Assessment*. Hove: Lawrence Erlbaum Associates.

Shallice, T. (1988) *From Neuropsychology to Mental Structure*. Cambridge: Cambridge University Press.

Shallice, T. and Burgess, P.W. (1991) Deficits in strategy application following frontal lobe damage in man. *Brain 114*, 727–741.

Shallice, T., Burgess, P.W. and Frith, C.D. (1991) Can the neuropsychological case study approach be applied to schizophrenia? *Psychological Medicine 21*, 661–673.

Shallice, T. and Evans, M.E. (1978) The involvement of the frontal lobes in cognitive estimation. *Cortex 14*, 294–303.

Tamlyn, D., McKenna, P.J., Mortimer, A.M., Lund, C.E., Hammond, S. and Baddeley, A.D. (1992) Memory impairment in schizophrenia: its extent, affiliations and neuropsychological character. *Psychological Medicine 22*, 101–115.

Wechsler, D. (1944) *The Measurement of Adult Intelligence* (third edition). Baltimore: Williams and Wilkins.

Wechsler, D. (1986) *Wechsler Adult Intelligence Scale – Revised (WAIS-R)*. Sidcup: Psychological Corporation.

Wechsler, D. (1987) *Wechsler Memory Scale – Revised*. Sidcup: Psychological Corporation.

Wechsler, D. (1997) *Technical Manual: WAIS III and WMS III*. Sidcup: Psychological Corporation.

White, W. (1928) The language of schizophrenia. In *Schizophrenia: An investigation of the most recent advances, as reported by the Association for Research in Nervous and Mental Disease*. New York: Association for Research in Nervous and Mental Disease.

Wilson, B.A., Cockburn, J. and Baddeley, A. (1985) *The Rivermead Behavioural Memory Test*. Bury St. Edmunds: Thames Valley Test Company.

Wilson, B.A., Alderman, N., Burgess, P., Emslie, H. and Evans, J.J. (1996) *Behavioural Assessment of the Dysexecutive Syndrome*. Bury St. Edmunds: Thames Valley Test Company.

PART II

Management of Mental Health Services

CHAPTER 10

Introduction to Management and Patient Care

Niki Muir

Key Words: role, service provision, models of care, differential diagnosis.

Speech and language therapy is a small profession which only reached its golden jubilee year in 1995. In the last few years the greatest developments have been in the area of cognitive neuropsychological and functional (pragmatic) models for the assessment and management of language and communication. Use of the skills of speech and language therapists can enhance assessment, differential diagnosis and therapeutic management. Speech and language therapists are likely to prove flexible and valuable members of the multidisciplinary team, with the ability to contribute a further dimension to care planning – that of specific clinical input to the wide range of language, speech and communication impairments associated with the major mental illnesses.

Diagnostic judgements are made on behaviours of language, speech and functional communication and many of the classifications of DSM-IV (1994) and other psychiatric diagnostic tools contain descriptions of linguistic breakdown and use speech and language pathology terms. However, once diagnosis of mental state has been reached therapeutic intervention tends, still, to be mainly pharmacological and activity-based. The place of speech and language therapy is to enhance and bring specificity to these models of care.

Care in the Community means that many more people with a history of mental illness are going to be receiving their health care in general settings, thus requiring adequate levels of social and communication skills and placing demands on the speech and language therapy profession to make local responses to meeting needs. Flexible models of care are required, which can allow psychiatric teams access to a level of service whilst making the best use of a small specialist network.

The profession

The following are examples of real referrals received by a speech and language therapy department in a large psychiatric hospital between 1992 and 1995:

'Please see – this man keeps swearing in the corridors.'

'Please see – mute.'

'Please see – never stops talking.'

'Please see – expressive dysphagia.'

'Please see – feeding problems, doesn't eat peas.'

'Please see – everyone else has.'

These referrals come about through understandable misconceptions regarding the precise nature of speech and language therapy. In the psychiatric professions it may be found that people make the response that they feel they must watch WHAT they say. For speech and language therapists the comment is often along the lines of needing to watch HOW they say it.

It comes as a surprise to many to be apprised of the level and standard of the honours degree course undertaken by speech and language Therapists. The profession is still linked in the minds of many with the elocution teachers from whom it had its genesis fifty years ago. The profession was the first of the 'therapies allied to medicine' to introduce the degree course and in many universities now this is spread over four years, in order to satisfactorily encompass all that is required by the syllabus. Central to the course and running in parallel with core learning on speech and language pathology and therapeutics are the studies, in some considerable depth, of psychology, neurology and linguistics. It could be argued that this combination creates an ideal platform for work in psychiatry.

It is indisputably true that, amongst other behaviours, judgements as to mental state are made on those behaviours of language, speech and functional communication. Yet, as previously stated, therapeutic intervention is seldom directly managed. It could be said with some veracity that language is the most significant of the cognitive skills, involving as it does aspects of thought, memory, planning, perception and sensation. Language is central in diagnosis but often peripheral in treatment. All aspects of speech and language pathology are likely to be present across the range of mental illness states, but still it is unlikely to be a formal part of care planning. Research into localisation theory has taken us in to the linguistic functions of the right hemisphere as in Cutting (1991) and in much recent research and publication by speech and language therapists (Bryan 1996), thus further expanding our horizons. Since differential diagnoses, based on the proven principles of cognitive neuro-psychological models, are now possible between distinct types of disorder within the continuum of aphasia (Kay, Lesser and Coltheart 1992), it could be contended that expanded analysis and description of linguistic and communicative behaviours might contribute to a broader understanding of all mental illness states and even add significant depth to differential diagnoses. Weight may also be added to the neurodevelopmental implications currently under discussion, which are supporting the theory that early behavioural disturbances, many of which could be seen to be linked to specific delay in language acquisition or in the pragmatic elements of communication, are of high significance among the predisposing factors for psychotic and affective disorders in later life, as reference the studies by Done *et al.* (1994) and Jones *et al.* (1994).

The role

Figure 10.1 is a model of how speech and language therapists might view language and communication and therefore it could suggest the specific areas in which a dedicated service, or at the least some access to a level of consultancy input, might contribute to the team. It shows language at the heart of the model with communication surrounding the whole. It also pinpoints the discrete skills which would be assessed and managed as part of the overall multidisciplinary care plan.

Specifically in relation to mental health disorders looking, for example, at **schizophrenia**, theories as varied as cognitive, psychoanalytic and existentialist converge in their claims that a deficit of language or discourse is central to the disorder and yet the locus of the problem and the postulated causality vary and targeted language and communication therapy is, as yet, not

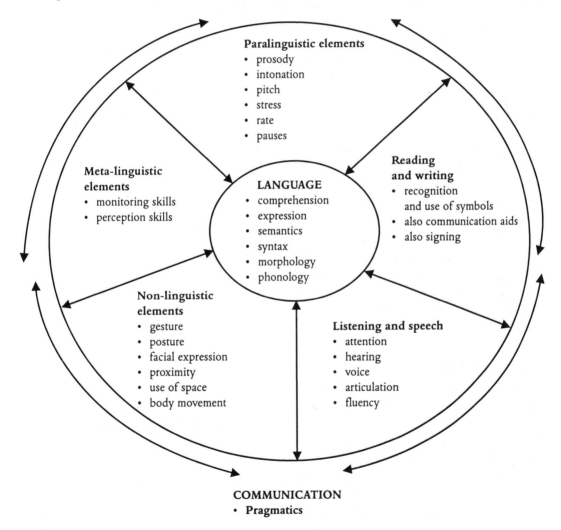

Figure 10.1 A linguistic model – as used by speech and language therapists

prevalent even though cognitive neuropsychological models for schizophrenia, in particular, are to the fore in current thinking (Frith 1992). A 1993 study by Hoffman and Satel explored the value of direct language therapy with schizophrenic clients suffering auditory hall-ucinations and reported good results. Yet this kind of approach is seldom undertaken. The need to assess, differentially diagnose and manage the receptive language, expressive lang-uage, speech and functional communication aspects of pervasive mental health disorders is self-evident.

In the **dementias** the multiple lesions throughout the cortex will cause manifest disturb-ances of memory and language functioning as well as of sensory abilities and functional communication skills. There may also be high levels of need to manage feeding and swallowing disorder where there is complex neurological deterioration. In **personality disorders** there may well be underlying evidence of delayed or deviant language development and/or immaturities of speech. There may also be significant developmental delay or acquired degradation of interpersonal (pragmatic) behaviours. In the **eating disorders** there may be an acquired organic voice disorder and speech, fluency, voice and functional communication can all be found to be affected in **depressive illnesses** as well as in **obsessive compulsive disorders.** Symptoms perhaps and not underlying causation, but valuable to treat nonetheless. Speech disorder resultant from **drug regimes** may also require treatment and it should not be forgotten that diagnosis and management of language, speech and communication delay resulting from a co-existing **learning disability** will also provide an aspect of the speech and language therapist's role.

Speech and language therapists are trained listeners and learn to become adept at decoding and reconstructing degraded speech and disordered language. The findings of the paper by Faber, Abrams and Taylor in 1983 in relation to the efficacy of speech and language therapists in reconstructing the language of schizophrenia, as well as in aphasia, have been borne out in other studies, most recently Fraser *et al.* (1997). Part of speech and language therapy training will be focused at enabling therapists to learn the arts of reflecting back, judging correct level of input and eliciting and maximising output. These elements would surely be central to the cognitive behavioural models of therapeutic management, the efficacy of which for clients with a mental illness is now well reported.

Service provision

Speech and language therapy is a small profession, so access to a service will be a very real problem. Looking flexibly at how to gain even a part-time service is very relevant, given that in all but the most ideal of situations currently a speech and language therapist could perhaps only be a very part-time member of a team or even teams. It is understood that the role of that therapist will need to be undertaken as part of a team and that most members of that team will be much more full-time, much longer established and will have their own contributions to make in evaluating and treating environmental, attentional and perceptual needs and deficits. However, in all skills related to speech and language function, it is the speech and language therapist who will have significant grasp of the specific neuropathology and psychopathology which can raise the level of description of the disorder and be of value in differential diagnosis.

We are all aware that there are many barriers to effective team work and in this instance, with justification, most team members will claim to work with 'communication' and may feel threatened by what may only be very infrequent input from yet another therapist and one who moreover has no real 'history' in psychiatry. But consider the enhancement and the specificity that the speech and language therapist could bring, not just through assessment and management approaches but through *education*, in the broadest sense of the word, and the fostering of *information sharing* between team members. Erber (1994) suggests that team members will gain greater satisfaction from encounters if they feel their own communication skills have been maximised and are therefore more adequate to the task. This seems to be particularly true for the subjective communication acts of demonstrating active listening and activating conversational repair strategies. It is interesting to note that, before the advent of the Project 2000 nurse training, nurses on the Registered Mental Nursing training course received little or no grounding in neurology and to date most psychiatrists receive no instruction on linguistics. Indeed, until recently the medical profession as a whole had little direct work on their own communication skills. Now the importance of 'bedside manner' is being more fully acknowledged and both medical students and qualified doctors are beginning to have access to communication skills workshops and evaluation sessions.

In the UK, speech and language therapy in psychiatry has been developing over the past 20 years. Each of the special hospitals has a full-time therapist and many of the past and present large psychiatric hospitals have a provision of speech and language therapy services, which continues into the community bases. In total there are about 40 speech and language therapists working in various branches of general psychiatry. The profession itself is small and has had to make significant changes to encompass the demands of its increased knowledge of the range and depth of speech and language pathology. Small specialisms within the profession have therefore had to find ways both to expand and to offer mutual support and the Royal College of Speech and Language Therapists registers Special Interest Groups on either a local, regional or national basis.

The National Mental Health Special Interest Group was set up in the early 1980s in order to foster peer group supervision and to provide elements of specialist training and broader education to its members and to interested others. This group has now begun the task of widening its remit and attracting others to the value of the specialism. This is being done by taking every opportunity for publication, by undertaking research as part of masters' or doctoral theses, by doing teaching sessions on many of the speech and language therapy degree courses and by undertaking talks and seminars for other professional groups to establish firmer links and look at ways forward. There is great difficulty in being a small profession with a very wide remit and there is a great need to look at flexible methods of service delivery which will make the best use of resources, particularly given that within the national group members are offering service provision to child and adolescent psychiatry, forensic psychiatry, acute and rehabilitation services and the psychiatry of old age.

For services without any access to speech and language therapists, requesting training sessions or information packs on all or any of these areas may be a way of acquiring some level of input. Most speech and language therapists working in the NHS are usually willing to undertake training sessions on the nature of speech, language and communication and members of the Mental Health Special Interest Group offer specific training packages on all aspects of communication and mental health. This is seen as having potential for developing the specialism and as an effective way for unprovided units to use limited resources. A further way of flexible working in the current financial climate might be the instigation of short-term contracts, enabling speech and language therapists to be seconded to undertake needs surveys, prioritisation ratings and efficacy measures, which could lead to informed discussions as to providing a level of dedicated service. Rotational services could be considered between various localities, determined on the unique profile of priorities that the unit yields, both in regard to client and staff need.

The aim of speech and language therapy is to maximise each person's communication potential within their own environment. Linguistic and communicative breakdown is central to mental illness, both in terms of diagnosis and pathology. For carers it is often the difficulties in communication and interaction which sadden them the most. In mental illness states the whole microcosm of speech and language disorder can be found and it therefore seems logical that the speech and language therapist has a part to play in contributing to diagnosis and management, both with the clients and with the carers. However, it is scarcely an ideal world and much still remains to be done by the small specialist group of speech and language therapists working in psychiatry in terms of even more publication and of seeking every opportunity for research. It will also be important to look at establishing a forum for postgraduate training of speech and language therapists, so that more will feel able to address the communication needs of clients with a mental health problem in generalist, community settings. It takes a great deal of time to make change for these clients and also to change public perception. Therefore, it follows that it takes a great deal of time to make professional and service developments; however, the currently small voice of speech and language therapists in psychiatry is now becoming heard and validated. The Royal College of Speech and Language Therapist's groundbreaking handbook *Communicating Quality 2* (1996) demonstrates the profession's willingness to work flexibly in a variety of ways, to undertake audit procedures and to provide quality and outcome measures. It is hoped that further service developments and increased opportunities for speech and language therapists to be involved in research at the cutting edge may be possible as awareness is raised and interest is generated, both within the profession and within mental health generally.

References

Bryan, K. (1996) *The Right Hemisphere Language Battery, 2nd edition.* London: Whurr.

Cutting, J. (1991) *The Right Cerebral Hemisphere and Psychiatric Diagnosis.* Oxford: University Press.

DSM-IV (1994) *Diagnostic and Statistical Manual of Mental Disorders* (fourth edition). Washington DC: American Psychiatric Association.

Done, D.J., Crow, T.J., Johnstone, E.C. and Sacker, A. (1994) Childhood antecedents of schizophrenia and affective illness: social adjustments at ages 7 and 11. *British Medical Journal 309*, 699–703.

Erber, N.P. (1994) Conversation as therapy for older adults in residential care: the case for intervention. *European Journal of Disorders of Communication 29*, 269–278.

Faber, R., Abrams, R. and Taylor, M. (1983) Comparison of schizophrenic patients with formal thought disorder and neurologically impaired patients with aphasia. *American Journal of Psychiatry 139*, 1348–1351.

Fraser, W., Thomas, P., Joyce, J. and Duckworth, M. (1997) 'By our frames are we hung': clinicians' descriptions of interviews. In J. France and N. Muir (eds) *Communication and the Mentally Ill Patient: Developmental and Linguistic Approaches to Schizophrenia.* London: Jessica Kingsley Publishers.

Frith, C.D. (1992) *The Cognitive Neuropsychology of Schizophrenia.* Hove: Lawrence Erlbaum Associates.

Hoffman, R.E. and Satel, S. (1993) Language therapy for schizophrenic patients with persistent 'voices'. *British Journal of Psychiatry 162,* 755–758.

Jones, P., Rodgers, B., Murray, R. and Marmot, M. (1994) Child developmental risk factors for adult schizophrenia in the British 1946 cohort. *Lancet 344,* 1398–1402.

Kay, J. Lesser, R. and Coltheart. M. (1992) *Psycholinguistics Assessments of Language Processing in Aphasia.* Hove: Lawrence Erlbaum Associates.

Royal College of Speech and Language Therapists (1996) *Communicating Quality 2.* London: RCSLT.

CHAPTER 11

Functioning of the Multidisciplinary Team and the Speech and Language Therapist

Margaret Orr

Much interest has been shown in developing multidisciplinary teams working in psychiatric treatment facilities and this was a priority for the Special Hospital Services Authority (SHSA) who managed the three Special Hospitals for England and Wales (Ashworth in Liverpool, Rampton in Nottinghamshire and Broadmoor in Berkshire) from 1989 until 1996. It was important to retain the positive elements of the long-standing medical leadership model which had operated since the beginning of these hospitals in the mid-nineteenth century but to lessen the autocracy. Thus organised treatment plans, times of meetings, recording of information and the legal aspects of administration of medicines and detention were maintained and developed. However, through team-building days funded directly by the SHSA and attended by as many disciplines as possible (psychiatrists, nurses, psychologists, psychotherapists, creative therapists, S&L therapists, personal assistants, educational lecturers, occupational therapists and chaplains), it was hoped to foster individual members' sense of value to the team. It was a time of change when people defined their roles and gained respect for others and knowledge of fellow professionals' skills. When these days were approached with a true desire to learn and adapt there were marked changes in team cohesion and improved communication. The role and functions of the multidisciplinary team are nicely covered by a chapter in Gravell and France (1991). The development of multidisciplinary working in such institutions as special hospitals must inevitably be slow but the changed atmosphere over a few years has been remarkable.

For the first six years of my work as a consultant forensic psychiatrist at Broadmoor Hospital I had the benefit of a speech and language therapist as a member of the multidisciplinary care team. She attended weekly team meetings to discuss the 25 patients, worked individually with several of the patients and ran a weekly psychotherapy group along with a team of nurses acting as co-conductors. In addition we jointly facilitated workshops relating to the attendance of the Royal Shakespeare Company and the National Theatre who played several times at the hospital between 1989 and 1996. We also worked together with a visiting drama therapist running two courses at weekends over 12–week periods, exploring the use of mask and mime to improve self-image and self-understanding related to the patients' offending behaviour. The hospital has two main tasks: to safely contain and treat those who suffer from a mental disorder and who have proved too violent, dangerous or criminal to help in lesser security; and to prepare and rehabilitate for discharge or transfer as many patients as possible by increasing their knowledge of their behaviour and illness and improving their self-esteem, confidence and responsibility. These tasks demand a combination of skills and disciplines working together. The speech and language therapist can play a vital role in communication for the patient and the team itself.

The overall success of the team has proved difficult to measure as any improvement is likely to be slow and benefits only seen many years after the patient leaves the hospital with a dependence on after-care: supervision, social circumstances and life events (Bailey and MacCulloch 1992) all affecting the outcomes in terms of reoffending and recurrence of illness. Yet I have witnessed dramatic change in behaviour in the short term and improvements in understanding of illness and contributing factors as a result of the multidisciplinary aspect of therapy. The speech and language therapist has skills which directly contribute to this change and it is the nature of the therapist's professional competence which encourages greater cohesion, empathetic understanding and communication within a team (and this can be of inestimable value).

Over the last four years two part-time speech and language therapists have joined the hospital. Their attendance at team meetings is less regular than previous post-holders as they are not directly attached to one or two teams but work more widely across the hospital. Their attendance at case conferences and at team meetings for discussion on individual patients is nevertheless important.

However, where a professional attends a team meeting irregularly it is of paramount importance that the leader acknowledges this 'visitor's' contribution, ensures they are treated as an equal to others at the meeting and that they receive minutes regularly and are involved in decision-making for the patient and in the team's activities. This is a complicated task where the leader needs to have a knowledge of team dynamics, an understanding of potential conflicts and insights into their own strengths and weaknesses. Genuine support, praise and constructive suggestions are the order of the day with exclusion of gossip and innuendo. There are inevitable overlaps between professionals. The nurse and psychiatrist will use cognitive techniques which overlap with the psychologist who has undergone advanced training in this field. The psychologist will use psychodynamic skills gained from experience which tread into the field of the psychotherapist who in turn intrudes into the speech and language therapist's territory. The patient must remain the focus and the team members must balance their contribution with that of others.

In this chapter I would like to describe the three ways in which I have personally found the speech and language therapist's role to be of unique and particular importance.

First, there is the traditional and most easily recognised role in assessment of speech and language development: the identification of specific problem areas or deficits, the measurement of skills and the assessment of hearing. However, it is in the relay back to the clinical team with interdisciplinary debate that the true benefit of the assessment bears fruit for the patient.

I am reminded of some of the elderly women who came to Broadmoor many years ago when infanticide was the major reason for women's admission. (Nowadays the major reason is arson.) They have stayed so long that many of their families have died out or forgotten them. It has been a pleasure to see how the work of the speech and language therapist has identified the problem areas – be they deafness, articulation, speed and volume of speech or poor comprehension – and by careful one-to-one work with games, diagrams and exercises the therapist has improved communication such that it is not by aberrant behaviour (throwing objects, removing clothes or wetting hair with water from the WC) but by speech that these women can now communicate their distress. Previously nursing staff had built up knowledge of how the patient was feeling from observation of behaviour and the nurses were the sole communicators of this, restricting families and other disciplines from playing a useful role. Now there is the possibility for these women to move on by liaison with external agencies. This means a loss of power for nurses and needs to be explored within the team in a sensitive and supportive way. The nurses care very deeply for their patients and it is difficult to trust a 'new' professional input, but when they see the enthusiasm of the greeting by their patients for the speech and language therapist the delight is shared by all members of the team.

During the admission/assessment period the role of the speech and language therapist is at times crucial. By identifying deficits or delays in development, areas for therapeutic intervention may be elucidated. This may link with factors from the social history. Many of our patients, both male and female, have been subjected to physical, sexual or emotional abuse. All aspects of development are affected by the trauma and language development may give an indication of the time of this damage. Particular words may be 'blocked' or concepts halted. One woman was helped by using the idea of particular 'ages' being separate 'boxes' where she could 'contain' her experiences. By putting the words of the emotions into these metaphorical 'boxes' – initially illustrated together with the therapist – the patient eventually was able to look at each area of a problem in safety. She identified the precursors to the violent feelings when a particular set of emotions was 'opened', thus helping the team identify areas of risk for future management.

Improving articulation, voice tone and volume can end ridicule by other patients and allow a handicapped patient better integration with his or her peers and better communication with staff. The stammering, hesitant patient may have covered up their handicap by using foul language or expletives or aggressive behaviour. By dealing with the specific skill deficit so can the therapist aid the rehabilitation process.

One other patient problem area is where there is a combination of mental illness (e.g. schizophrenia) and another disability such as brain damage through accident, trauma or drug or alcohol abuse. The patient may have high levels of anxiety due to problems in communication and may reveal this by deliberate self-harm, anorexia or violence. By enabling communication between patient and speech and language therapist the anxiety may lessen. However, the patient may require the therapist to go on to be actively involved in direct rehabilitation, for example visiting the next placement or accompanying the patient as a second escort when the nurse takes the patient to hostel or medium secure unit. This requires a flexibility of roles and attitudes on the part of therapist and nurse. Hospital management must have an understanding of the necessity to provide such a service, as must the Home Office when it is involved (two-thirds of women, three-quarters of men). Here the therapist is playing a role in risk assessment. By observing how well the patient has learned to communicate their feelings of fear, anxiety or anger, so does the team gain an understanding of the risk areas.

This is the second area where I believe speech and language therapy is particularly useful. That is in the link between the patient and the team. By enabling the patient to put feelings into words so we may facilitate the control of these emotions. One patient started with only one word to express all of his emotions: whatever situation was presented by the therapist in word, picture or diagram the only word was 'anger'. It then expanded to 'anxious' and then to 'afraid'. His repertoire was limited by his early life separations from his mother. He refused to contemplate psychodynamic psychotherapy as the silence was too overwhelming. He found cognitive behaviour therapy of limited usefulness as he did not possess the language to describe his cognitions. In speech and language therapy he is beginning to make links and to associate words and feelings, although the therapist knows it is a long uphill task. The patient himself has gained in confidence and appropriate assertiveness since beginning work.

Lastly the key skills of communication and facilitation of clear understanding are of profound importance to the team as a whole. Non-judgemental analysis of language being used during meetings, forms of communication being ignored or overused often enables the group to focus on where a particular problem arose. Disagreements may be worked on constructively. Clearly the emotions and stress aroused in therapists of any discipline when they are required to listen to horrific traumatic experiences of patients requires understanding. The therapist has to come to terms with their own anger and frustration when confronted with what the patient has actually done. The inevitable crosstransference of emotion between the patient and therapist and the therapist and other disciplines means that no therapist should be working in isolation in a secure forensic institution whether is be a medium secure unit, hospital or prison. We each need the support and understanding of fellow professionals with shared skills and common experiences. I see the speech and language therapist as an enabling fellow professional who makes a contribution across the board, facilitating our understanding of the patient's lines of communication and that of the team, helping us in risk assessment, diagnosis and therapy.

References

Bailey, J. and MacCulloch, M. (1992) Patterns of reconviction in patients discharged directly to the community from a Special Hospital: implications for aftercare. *Journal of Forensic Psychiatry 3*, 3.

Gravell, R. and France, J. (eds) (1991) *Speech and Communication Problems in Psychiatry*. London: Chapman and Hall.

CHAPTER 12

The Speech and Language Therapist as a Member of the Mental Health Multidisciplinary Team

Yvette Crompton

Working as a member of a multidisciplinary team is now implicit in the practice of the speech and language therapist. Throughout undergraduate and postgraduate training, the importance of working as part of a clinical team is emphasised both for paediatric and adult client groups. In order to receive their licence to practice, a student must demonstrate an understanding of the multidisciplinary team and the different professional disciplines that the team is comprised of (Royal College of Speech and Language Therapists 1996).

The multidisciplinary team is an organisation consisting of various disciplines, whose goal is to provide holistic client care through the planning and co-ordination of their different and shared knowledge and skills. In conjunction with the clinical members, the client himself or herself is an important member of the team. Although there are recognised difficulties related to this method of working, the multidisciplinary team is a means of providing a broad spectrum of care, based on the diversity of expertise offered by the different contributing disciplines.

The multidisciplinary team

The beginnings of multidisciplinary teams

The multidisciplinary team as a model of health care began to be used significantly in the 1970s, although Appleyard and Maden (1979) refer to its early beginnings in the late 1950s (DHSS 1959). Of particular significance in the development of multidisciplinary teams was the General Medical Council's (1977) commendation of the contribution of nurses and other specialist professions to patient care, and the St Augustine's Committee of Enquiry (South East Thames RHA 1976) recommendations for multidisciplinary ward teams. Nowadays, multi-disciplinary teams are recognised as a fundamental mechanism in the provision of health care.

Why use multidisciplinary teams in mental health?

The notion of different professions working as a co-ordinated body to provide for the needs of a client seems particularly relevant to the field of mental health when the aetiology of mental disorders is considered. The widely held belief is that mental health disorders, in particular schizophrenia, are the result of an interaction of predisposing factors, primarily biological vulnerability and psychosocial stressors (Falloon and Shanahan 1990), and in psychiatry diagnosis is almost never the outcome of a single cause (Sims and Sims 1993). It follows therefore that the rehabilitation approach will need to address these different areas through pharmacological, psychological and social interventions. In order to provide this broad base of care, a variety of professional approaches is needed to implement co-ordinated, needs-based assessment and management.

The membership of multidisciplinary teams

Membership of mental health teams can vary according to the setting and availability of resources. The core team is likely to consist of a psychiatrist, psychiatric nursing staff, a psychologist, a social worker, the client and their significant other(s). Working in conjunction with these team members may be psychotherapists, nurse therapists, occupational therapists, speech and language therapists, creative therapists, pharmacists, teachers, medical registrars, dietitians and physiotherapists. Teams will also have access to other professions, such as dentistry and chiropody, as necessary.

Although the different disciplines are bringing their own specialist skills to the team, there are core skills and knowledge which will be shared by all team members. These should include a working knowledge of psychopathology and the different models used in psychiatry, basic counselling skills, and proficient communication and observation skills.

Pros and cons of team working

As can be deduced simply by looking at the number of people that need to co-ordinate and co-operate within a multidisciplinary team, there are a number of barriers that can arise and need to be overcome in order to achieve successful team working. These have been considered extensively in the literature (Bones et al. 1997; Burrow 1994; Gravell 1991; Griffin 1989; Noon 1988; Riley 1994) but may include the absence of a clearly defined common philosophy of care, poor leadership, lack of knowledge about and respect for each other's roles, and ineffective communication systems.

As a member of a multidisciplinary team, the speech and language therapist is entering a working environment which has the potential to support and enhance his or her input, provide a broader prospective to client care through the diversity of professional backgrounds and experiences, offer opportunities for collaborative working, educate about different approaches to client need and provide a holistic approach to rehabilitation. It must be viewed as part of the role of the speech and language therapist to take shared responsibility for overcoming any obstacles that prevent productive multidisciplinary working.

The speech and language therapist

What specialist skills will be brought to the team?

As mentioned previously, life stressors play a significant part in the aetiology of mental health disorders. By providing individuals with strategies and skills to overcome these life stressors, progress is made in the rehabilitation process. As speech and language therapists are acutely aware, an inability to communicate needs, opinions and emotions is a source of considerable distress, and there is known to be a high incidence of communication problems in people with mental health disorders (France and Muir 1997a). The speech and language therapist, using his or her specialist knowledge and skills in speech, language and communication, must work in conjunction with the clinical team and the client to maximise the client's communicative abilities, environment and opportunities. A number of different methods may be used to facilitate this aim and as speech and language therapists within the field of mental health are thinly spread, all available opportunities to promote communication issues must be exploited.

Whilst it is acknowledged that many clinical team members will be involved in the broader area of communication, it is important to identify the specialist knowledge that the speech and language therapist brings to the team, which enables him or her to approach communication supported by a theoretical framework and specialist clinical skills. In their approach to the assessment and management of a client with a communication disorder the speech and language therapist may consider developmental, neurological, psychological, behavioural, cognitive, physical or environmental factors. The therapist's detailed knowledge of linguistics, semantics, pragmatics, phonetics, acoustics, the cognitive neuropsychology of language, and the anatomy and physiology of speech and hearing will provide frameworks for the analysis and management of communication disorders.

Contributions to the multidisciplinary assessment

The starting point of the rehabilitation process is a multidisciplinary needs-led assessment, ensuring that whilst ascertaining the needs of the client, their strengths are also noted so they can be implemented in the rehabilitation process.

Speech and language therapy assessment will include a detailed case history and can involve both formal and informal assessment procedures. During the assessment procedure the speech and language therapist should make full use of the information provided by other members of the multidisciplinary team. Social work reports will often include information on birth events, development, family history, and education and employment histories. Cognitive neuro-psychological measures, psychometric assessments and psychological formulations can be found in the psychology reports, and functional information on daily living can be obtained from nursing and occupational therapy reports. Medical information will also detail any medication that a client is currently taking.

The speech and language therapy assessments used should be repeatable, so that outcome measures can be taken. These outcome measures, whilst looking at changes in speech, language and communication, may also provide the team with another means of assessing variations in mental state, as these changes are often reflected in a person's communication.

Areas of involvement

The areas covered during the assessment procedure should include the client's environment and whether this provides the opportunity or need for communication (this is particularly important in hospital settings in order to counteract the limits of institutionalisation), receptive and expressive language skills, motor speech, voice, functional communication, literacy, pragmatics and where necessary eating and drinking. The client's hearing and dentition are also areas that can be initially assessed by the speech and language therapist and if further assessment is needed then the client can be referred on to the audiologist or dentist as necessary. The rationale for assessment and the processes involved have been discussed in more detail in France and Muir (1997b), Muir, Tanner and France (1991) and Muir (1996).

For the purposes of this discussion it is necessary to consider what the speech and language assessment can bring to the multidisciplinary assessment procedure. Primarily the speech and language therapy findings will provide another facet of information that may otherwise only be considered in its broadest sense or overlooked entirely.

In conjunction with the nursing and occupational therapy assessments a detailed picture of the client's daily living skills can be created, with the speech and language therapy assessment providing information regarding the opportunities given for communication, the client's need to communicate and the barriers to communication that are present. The client's inappropriate social behaviours, which may be seen as aggression or withdrawal, or described as the positive or negative symptoms of schizophrenia, may subsequent to assessment be reinterpreted as the result of difficulties communicating needs and emotions.

Medication side-effects can affect motor speech, cognitive functioning such as memory, and swallowing. The speech and language therapist is able to identify these side-effects, and through discussion with the clinical team ascertain whether any changes can be made to medication or additional medication provided to counteract these side-effects. Specific therapeutic interventions can also be offered to counteract the side-effects as far as possible. In the case of swallowing difficulties, a further referral to the dietitian can be made to ensure the client's nutritional requirements are met.

Assessment of hearing, which may include pure tone audiometry if available, can provide valuable information to the clinical team. Poor hearing levels and the subsequent mis-understandings can encourage paranoia, and tinnitus may be mistaken for, or incorporated into, auditory hallucinations. The speech and language therapist can provide information that can differentiate between hearing impairment and auditory hallucinations or paranoia. Hearing impairment will also affect a client's daily living and their functioning in therapy, particularly in group settings. By assessing the particular difficulties a client experiences, such as tinnitus or background noise, the team will be able to compensate as much as possible for these.

The use of speech and language therapy assessment as a means by which to assist diagnosis has a number of applications in the area of mental health. By analysis of expressive and receptive language and the underlying cognitions necessary for language processing, it is possible to contribute to the differential diagnosis of dysphasia, dementia and psychotic speech or thought disorder. Disordered communication patterns may also occur as part symptoms of disorders such as Asperger's syndrome and identification of these communication styles and the disorders associated with them will help to ensure that appropriate rehabilitation methods are chosen.

The speech and language therapy assessment will also provide extremely important information regarding the client's potential for engaging in talk-based therapy such as counselling or psychotherapy, in education programmes or in occupational therapy. If a client's language skills are at a low level, it is unlikely that they will be able to comprehend the abstract concepts and high level language often used in therapeutic approaches, or retain large amounts of information. Their responses may be echolalic or they may simply agree with all that is said in order to disguise their lack of understanding. In other cases they may refuse to engage in any kind of therapeutic work. The speech and language therapist is able to alert the clinical team to this possibility and recommend other approaches, such as creative therapy, which do not rely on the medium of language, or he or she may work in conjunction with the client and therapists to ensure that input is at an appropriate level and that the client is understanding what is being said.

Management approaches

There are only a small number of speech and language therapists working in the field of mental health and this can often result in a single therapist being responsible for a large catchment area or out-patient or residential population. The speech and language therapist must therefore make full use of the opportunities that the multidisciplinary team offers to maximise input and encourage the generalisation of skills.

Individual work

An initial option open to the speech and language therapist, should assessment identify a comm-unication need, would be to arrange a course of individual therapy and this is often the approach that the team would expect. Individual sessions with a client will provide opportunities for intensive and focused work on a communication difficulty but the team must be utilised to increase the exposure to rehabilitation. This is particularly important when cognitive behavioural approaches are being used as the client will need continuous support and reinforcement, and the more individuals aware of the programme the more exposure there will be.

Education and training

Through the education of other members of the team in contact with a client, awareness and understanding of the communication difficulties can be increased. This increased knowledge affords the opportunities for rehabilitation strategies to be reinforced in a wider range of environments and for other people's communication to be modified if necessary. In cases where ongoing individual sessions with a speech and language therapist are not possible or not appropriate, recommendations and rehabilitation programmes can be provided and imple-mented by staff or carers with support from the speech and language therapist.

When other members of the team are involved in a client's communication programme, it is essential that the speech and language therapist provides education and support that is sufficiently detailed and aimed at an appropriate level. This may also include written and diagrammatic information.

Education and support can also be used in the wider context of group training. An increased number of clients can be accessed, and their communication needs considered, if a larger number of disciplines have an understanding of communication and the potential areas of breakdown. A more detailed knowledge of communication disorders should also result in more appropriate team referrals to speech and language therapy services.

Group work

Group work is popular in mental health rehabilitation and the benefits of this approach are well known. Groups offer safe opportunities to experience and practise interpersonal and social functioning, thus reducing the anxiety and stress often experienced in social situations. They also provide a forum for problem solving with the support of peers. On a more practical note and with resources in mind, they also provide the speech and language therapist with an opportunity to provide input for a larger number of clients.

Groups may range from specific language or speech-based groups to the wider remit of communication skills groups. The latter are particularly popular in mental health rehabilitation as they provide opportunities for practising conversation skills, rehearsing life situations such as employment interviews, and developing assertiveness skills. A number of multidisciplinary team members, including occupational therapists and psychiatric nurses, have knowledge and experience of communication skills training and this provides opportunities for collaborative working within the team. The speech and language therapist can also provide communication-based outcome measures for other types of groups that team members are facilitating, thus adding another dimension to the group remit and another means of measuring change.

Counselling

The speech and language therapist in mental health will find that their role involves some degree of counselling. Whilst this may be true of speech and language therapists in many settings, clients who already come under the mental health bracket may be particularly vulnerable or have more complex needs. Further training in the area of supportive counselling is beneficial, but in conjunction with that, the multidisciplinary team offers opportunities for the therapist to receive supervision and training from team members with specialist knowledge in this area, and the therapist can also refer the client on to a more appropriate discipline as necessary.

Feedback of information

In order for multidisciplinary teams to function successfully, communication between the team members is of fundamental importance. The speech and language therapist must provide regular feedback to the team, through clinical team notes, attendance at team meetings and case conferences, and the provision of speech and language therapy reports. This encourages team awareness of the different inputs that a client may be taking part in, and hopefully prevents any conflict between or reduplication of methods. Regular feedback will also provide valuable information for the team on an individual's current mental state as reflected in their communication or lack of it.

Summary

Working as a member of a multidisciplinary team can be a rewarding experience for the disciplines involved. The team, whilst ensuring that holistic care is provided for the client, also provides support and education for team members and a means of maximising input.

Many different disciplines are involved in the field of mental health and although there are only a small number of speech and language therapists, this does not make their contribution any less important. Communication is a fundamental function of daily living and is not only the means through which we express our basic needs, but also how we share emotions, opinions and experiences. Therefore, by enabling people to communicate, a step is taken towards the goal of positive mental health. The multidisciplinary team must be used as a means through which the speech and language therapist can bring communication to clients, and an increased awareness of communication to all the disciplines involved in their care and rehabilitation.

Appendix

Case histories outlining multidisciplinary team management of patients referred for speech and language therapy in a Special Hospital environment

Patient 1 (P1)

P1 was referred through the multidisciplinary team and described as having difficulties initiating social contacts, and increasingly avoiding social situations. A cognitive behavioural therapy approach was used in therapy in conjunction with supportive counselling. In order to increase P1's exposure to the behavioural programme, nursing staff were incorporated into the programme to provide reinforcement and support. In particular, P1's primary nurse was given specific activities to complete with P1. The behavioural changes were included as objectives in P1's nursing care plan, ensuring that as many members of the nursing staff as possible were aware of the programme.

P1 was attending psychotherapy sessions and had attended for two years previous to the speech and language therapy referral. A significant amount of pertinent information could be obtained through feedback from these sessions. Regular meetings between the psychotherapist and the speech and language therapist encouraged the exchange of information and interesting comparisons and reflections could be made between developments in each therapy. The meetings also helped to ensure that the two different approaches did not conflict.

During the course of speech and language therapy, P1 began to attend a group on the ward, facilitated by two members of the clinical team – a nurse therapist and a dietitian. Liaison with the facilitators enabled advice to be given on P1's particular difficulties with conversational situations, and feedback to be received on P1's functioning and progress within the group.

Case conferences and treatment reviews attended by the multidisciplinary team members involved in P1's management, and by P1, provided opportunities for feedback and discussion.

Supervision for the speech and language therapist was provided by a nurse therapist specialising in cognitive behavioural therapy.

Patient 2 (P2)

P2 was referred following discussion at a weekly multidisciplinary team meeting for dysphagia assessment and recommendations following continuous patient reports of difficulties swallowing. A number of team members were unaware, prior to the team discussion, that speech and language therapists had specialist training in dysphagia.

Prior to the assessment of the patient's swallow, relevant information was gathered from medical records and nursing notes, and through extensive discussion with nursing staff involved in the patient's care.

As P2 was psychotic at the time of the initial interview a member of nursing staff who was well acquainted with P2 attended the interview to help facilitate the conversation.

Assessment found no neurological origin for the swallowing difficulties; instead, the globus sensation causing the difficulties was attributed to a psychological origin, in particular depression. Feedback to the team was provided in the form of a written report and presentation at P2's case conference. The psychotherapist was able to expand on the link between depression and swallowing difficulties and these issues were addressed in their sessions. It was subsequently revealed by the social worker that there was a family history of this type of difficulty.

Recommendations provided following assessment to aid P2's swallowing were discussed and practised with P2's primary nurse, and the dietitian informed of the difficulties in order to ensure that nutritional needs were adequately met. The pharmacist was also able to provide some medications in suspension rather than tablet form to facilitate easier swallowing.

Patient 3 (P3)

P3 was referred to the speech and language therapy department for support with hearing impairment and training in speech reading techniques. The referral was made through the multidisciplinary team following a direct request from the patient for input.

P3 had a profound, bilateral, congenital hearing loss for which hearing aids for both ears had been provided. However, only one was worn due to a malformation of the pinna of one ear which caused the aid to fall off.

Contact was made with the audiology departments previously attended by P3 and copies of past audiograms were obtained. Through liaison with audiology departments an assessment was arranged and new tubing obtained for one hearing aid which prevented it from falling off.

Nursing staff were provided with information regarding hearing loss and how it may limit functioning. They were also able to discuss difficulties that they experienced communicating with P3 and provided with strategies for overcoming these difficulties.

An area of particular difficultly for P3 was the weekly group attended on the ward, from which P3 often reported feeling isolated. Discussion with the group facilitators on the difficulties that P3 may experience, as well as encouraging P3 to discuss these difficulties with group members and facilitators, helped to overcome the majority of these.

Generalisation of the speech reading strategies worked on in individual sessions was encouraged by incorporating P3's primary nurse and members of the rehabilitation therapies into the timetable of speech reading activities.

References

Appleyard, J. and Maden, J. (1979) Multidisciplinary teams. *British Medical Journal*, 17 November. 1305–1307.

Bones, K., Heald, M., Boxer, J. and Miller, R. (1997) In the melting pot. *Nursing Times*, August 20, 93, 2–3.

Burrow, S. (1994) A source of conflict at the heart of the team – the role of the forensic multidisciplinary care team. *Psychiatric Care*, Nov/Dec, 192–196.

Department of Health and Social Security (1959) *Review of the Mental Health Act.* London: HMSO 1978.

Falloon, R. (1992) Psychotherapy of schizophrenia. *British Journal of Hospital Medicine 48*, 3/4, 164–170.

Falloon, I. and Shanahan, W. (1990) Community management of schizophrenia. *Journal of British Hospital Medicine 43*, 62–66.

France, J. and Muir, N. (1997a) Introduction. About communication and the mentally ill patient. In J. France and N. Muir (eds) *Communication and the Mentally Ill Patient.* London: Jessica Kingsley Publishers.

France, J. and Muir, N. (1997b) Speech and language therapy and the mentally ill patient. In J. France and N. Muir (eds) *Communication and the Mentally Ill Patient.* London: Jessica Kingsley Publishers.

General Medical Council (1977) *Professional Conduct and Discipline.* London: GMC.

Gravell, R. (1991) The multidisciplinary team. In R. Gravell and J. France (eds) *Speech and Communication Problems in Psychiatry.* London: Chapman and Hall.

Griffin, N.V. (1989) Multi-professional care in forensic psychiatry – realities and constraints. *Psychiatric Bulletin 13*, 613–615.

Muir, N. (1996) The role of the speech and language therapist in psychiatry. *Psychiatric Bulletin 20*, 524–526.

Muir, N., Tanner, P. and France, J. (1991) Management and treatment techniques: a practical approach. In R. Gravell and J. France (eds) *Speech and Communication Problems in Psychiatry.* London: Chapman and Hall.

Noon, M. (1988) Teams: the best option? *The Health Service Journal*, Oct, 1160–1161.

Riley, M. (1994) Pathways to collaboration – developing the role of the multidisciplinary team in psychiatry care. *Psychiatric Care*, 19–24.

Royal College of Speech and Language Therapists (1996) *Communicating Quality 2.* London: RCSLT.

Sims, A. and Sims, D. (1993) Top teams. *Health Service Journal*, June 27–29.

South East Thames Regional Health Authority (1976) Report of Committee of Enquiry St Augustine's Hospital, Chartham, Canterbury.

CHAPTER 13

Setting Up a Speech and Language Therapy Network in Mental Health

Kathleen Gilmour

Introduction

The government's White Paper and draft framework for Mental Health Services in Scotland signals the way forward for the development of services. In response to this the speech and language therapy profession is required to consolidate and develop individual departments' aims and principles of service delivery and 'facilitate optimum communication skills amongst all clients receiving psychiatric care who have an identified communication difficulty' (Royal College of Speech and Language Therapists 1996).

Speech and language therapists have a primary role in assessment, therapeutic input and in effective care programming approaches (Muir *et al.* 1990).

As more institutional discharge programmes are instigated, with specialist institutional resources and advocacy services being required for clients, individual speech and language therapists are identifying the need for increased intra-professional liaison and support, and regular update and development of skills, procedures and resources.

Background

April 1995 was both a personal and professional turning point in speech and language therapy within the field of mental health. A multiprofessional and extremely varied programme was devised by the then SIG (Special Interest Group) in Psychiatry. The resulting symposium entitled 'Communication and the Mentally Ill Patient' had delegates from throughout Britain in attendance. Speech and language therapists had, for many years, forged positive links and developments within the field and the symposium both highlighted and cemented the relationships of the work being evolved throughout Britain.

As a Royal College of Speech and Language Therapists (RCSLT) Regional Advisor in Mental Health (Psychiatry), active links were forged with the now National Special Interest Group (SIG) in Mental Health. Further to discussion with the SIG Committee it was proposed to identify the need and instigate a Speech and Language Therapy Mental Health Support Network for Scotland. The National SIG has a well established knowledge base with a long-standing and respected core team, therefore it seemed more relevant to format a support network for therapists to closely communicate with the National SIG rather than initiate a Scottish SIG which would not have the initial expertise and background.

Process

Initially, the National SIG put an entry into the *RCSLT Bulletin* asking Scottish speech and language therapists if they would be interested in becoming SIG members/attend study days.

A proforma and covering letter was devised and sent to all Speech and Language Therapy Managers in Scotland, as listed in TASLTMS (The Association of Speech and Language Therapy Managers), and known interested therapists working in the field.

Each manager was asked to nominate a therapist in their area currently with a child/adult mental health caseload and to complete the proforma indicating the therapist's attendance at the proposed initial meeting in July 1998 (Table 13.1). The proforma asked details regarding the therapists' predominant caseload:

- Adult mental illness
- Child mental illness
- Elderly mental illness
- Dual diagnosis (learning disability and mental illness).

They were also asked for their comments on agenda/discussion topics.

Table 13.1	
Number of proformas sent	30
Number of therapists attending initial meeting	11
Number of apologies	7
Departments requesting to be kept on a database	3

Suggested agenda topics were:

- Identifying level of service across Scotland
- Referral rates/patterns/needs assessment
- Establishing a network database
- Assessment/intervention
- Discussion of dual diagnosis
- Training and support issues
- Role of the speech and language therapist in mental health
- Resources/facilities
- Working in a multidisciplinary team (MacDonald 1990; Gravell and France 1991).

The initial meeting

The day-long meeting in July was extremely productive. The group day was hosted by Lanarkshire Healthcare NHS (South Sector). The eleven therapists attending came from various parts of the country, including Aberdeen, Glasgow, Stirling, Edinburgh and the Lothians.

The initial aims of the group were to gather facts, share information and discuss needs and the way forward, with the group deciding to call themselves 'Mental Health Network (Scotland)'.

An initial reading list of articles and assessment material, available from Lanarkshire, was distributed. Each group member summarised their current remit and working practices, which included forensic services, psychogeriatrics, dysphagia, and child and adult learning disabilities.

Discussion took place on formal and informal assessments, and prior to our next meeting each group member undertook to gather together:

- assessment lists
- information on therapy practices
- types of referrals

for eventual collation into a package.

Working practices were also focused upon on the day, with several models of good practice highlighted, but with the majority of services being in the early stages of development.

The way forward

It was decided that the next meeting in November 1998 should discuss further collation of packages involving:

- assessments
- resources available
- full reading list
- therapy packages
- training packages.

Long-term group aims may be to instigate prevalence studies (Emerson and Enderby 1996), with Inter Trust packages of information looking at establishing services (Gravell and France 1991). It was considered that it may also be possible to raise research and quality and clinical effectiveness issues as the support network/working partnerships developed. It was hoped that SIG Mental Health (London) Committee Members could attend the November meeting to further links and aid direction of the support network.

To promote the group, each attending member was to discuss the matter with their local manager and colleagues. The second meeting agenda, with a covering letter restating the support network aims, was to be sent to each Speech and Language Therapy Manager (Scottish Region).

Summary of November meeting

As a follow-on to the July meeting, Speech and Language Therapy Managers throughout Scotland were again contacted, but this time with a greater mailing list. Speech and language therapists originally contacted were also re-distributed with the possible agenda (Table 13.2).

Table 13.2	
Number of Speech and Language Therapy Managers contacted	38
Number of individual speech and language therapists contacted	16
Number of therapists attending the second meeting	4
Number of apologies	4
Number of therapists/managers requesting to be kept on a database and mailing list	31

As there was only minimal attendance at this meeting, discussion took place about the way forward for such a network within Scotland. It was decided that there should be three facets to the present forum:

1. A working party consisting of six speech and language therapists working within a range of mental health services, e.g. child, dual diagnosis, adult and forensic. Initial targets of work areas proposed were:

    ○ needs assessment
    ○ pattern of referrals
    ○ assessment packages
    ○ training needs
    ○ service audit.

2. An Annual Mental Health Network (Scotland) meeting.

3. A database of those wishing to be put on a mailing list with regular updates from subgroup meetings.

It is hoped that in this current climate of development in the mental health field, though with consideration of the limitations of time and resources, that all involved can fully utilise these actions.

Conclusions

Speech and language therapy interventions currently carried out in community and mental health settings involve a variety of methods, approaches and contexts. More detailed information and promotion of good practices is required with individual speech and language therapists requiring to liaise and gain support from their colleagues and receive specialised training from those experienced in the mental health field:

> ...Speech and Language Therapists need to feel informed as to the nature and potential of their role and, with training, feel empowered to undertake interventions with people with speech, language or communication needs resultant from mental health problems... (France and Muir 1997)

Through support group networking and liaison with experienced/specialist therapists currently working with this client group, it is felt our profession can further progress in our ever developing and essential role within psychiatry.

References

Emerson, J. and Enderby, P. (1996) Prevalence of speech and language disorders in a mental illness unit. *European Journal of Disorders of Communication 31*, 221–236.

France, J. and Muir, N. (1997) Development and linguistic approaches to schizophrenias. *Communication and the Mentally Ill Patient*. London: Jessica Kingsley Publishers.

Gravell, R. and France, J. (1991) Speech and communication problems in psychiatry. *Therapy in Practice 22*. London: Chapman and Hall.

MacDonald, L. (1990) Are we moving in the right direction? *Speech Therapy in Practice*, December.

Muir, N. *et al.* (1990) Psychiatry, our developing role: its challenges and rewards. *Speech and Language Therapy in Practice*. December.

Royal College of Speech and Language Therapists (1996) *Communicating Quality 2*. London: RCSLT.

CHAPTER 14

Developing a Speech and Language Therapy Service in Mental Health

Elaine Hodkinson

Speech and language therapy in mental health

Mental health has not been one of the traditional areas for which speech and language therapists were trained, even though psychiatry, psychology, linguistics and phonetics and a range of medical studies have always been part of the curriculum. A few speech and language therapists were invited to join psychiatrists' teams as early as the 1960s; some in a consultative capacity, others as part of the assessment and therapy programme, and one or two in specialist settings, such as forensic psychiatry. Nevertheless at about this time doctors, some of whom were psychiatrists, were referring patients to speech and language therapists in general clinical settings, and some of these patients had mental health problems concomitant with identifiable speech pathology.

Some enlightened, and usually research-orientated, psychiatrists became more aware, through the multidisciplinary approach, that communication required more than asking questions, receiving answers and 'chatting' with the patients. It was therefore the efforts of these doctors that helped develop posts in mental health. At the same time there developed an increasing awareness among managers that there was a large number of neglected patients with communication difficulties in mental health wards and in the community. As there was a purposive move to house many mentally ill patients in residential homes, their communicative behaviours and ability to get on with those around them became a main ingredient in planning successful transitions. The speech and language therapist's role was, and is still, seen as assisting in this educative and enabling new aspect of management. Old style mental hospital ways grew towards new positive thinking, that patients should be supported and encouraged to 'speak for themselves'.

Due to the many types of mental illnesses and the variety of problems associated with speech and language, it was necessary to revise management procedures. Services were adapted to suit various clinical settings including those of the hospital, medium secure units, hostels, group homes, day centres and other domiciliary settings. It was gradually accepted that speech and language therapists have a role, with other professionals associated with medicine, in the everyday support and management of those people with mental health and communication difficulties.

Psychiatrists' and managers' awareness of speech and language therapists' skills

As mental health is a relatively new remit for most speech and language therapy services there is only a gradually increasing awareness of the optimum way to provide this service. As previously stated, it is often in conjunction with an individual or group of psychiatrists that provision of a service is considered. The request can also come from numerous other sources, such as managers of mental health services, particularly those dealing with clients in the community where communication is seen as a vital component in re-establishing, maintaining and developing patients' (clients') confidence and competence in human relationships. (For the purposes of this chapter the term 'patient' rather than 'client' will be used in order to prevent confusion. The term 'client' is more likely to be used when patients are returned from hospital en route to the community, but either term is used in many different settings.)

It is important to clarify how the speech and language therapist's role, knowledge and skills complement the work of psychologists, nurses and other therapists. Provision of an information network is helpful to identify this range of subjects and skills, and to emphasise them in undergraduate training. It is therefore important for doctors and managers to know how therapists are equipped to engage in new studies and projects to enhance membership of the multidisciplinary team.

Aids to personal presentations, such as charts, transparencies and videos, can demonstrate to managers and others what speech and language therapists identify as voice, speech and language as well as how they identify speech pathology. Understanding of the range of normal communication is essential and knowledge of this should not be taken for granted! When the pathology of voice, speech and language has been outlined, the relevance to mental health is immediately obvious. Various methods of working can be discussed and doctors and managers can then develop agendas which include those aspects of speech and language therapy relevant to the patient's treatment plans. This clarifies and deepens understanding about the ways in which the speech and language therapy service can be employed.

Informative communication

As a profession concerned with communication it is essential to be good communicators ourselves and to demonstrate the importance of good communication, by example, in as many ways as possible.

Organising workshops and meetings is aided by providing, for example, coloured handouts to assist in the dissemination of information about the service. These might include:

- The service, our role and expertise
- The days worked and where, if locations vary
- The range of individual and group work
- How patients can be referred, the response procedure and session plans, with review strategy

- The variety of specialised skills within the department. These will vary depending on staff training and interests, and might include, for example:
  - non-verbal communication
  - social skills development
  - aromatherapy
  - communication through poetry and drama therapies
  - prosodic features of speech
  - communication problems in the elderly
  - psychodrama
  - literacy skills
  - counselling.

As communication therapists we have access to knowledge of hearing disability, learning difficulties, discourse analysis, cognitive/behavioural and other psychotherapies, which can be shared and developed.

Aspects of communication should be made known to different groups and professions, i.e. occupational therapists, psychologists and nurses, volunteer social workers, managers and other carers; as well as to families, when appropriate. Clear information sheets can help to reinforce information. As part of formal staff training, meetings can be held in the out-patient department, on the wards and with residential staff and social workers in a community venue. It is important to update and reinforce all information.

Infrastructure and resources

A sound infrastructure, including accommodation and identified resources, is the basis for a quality service. Extension of accommodation and other needs can be successfully negotiated during reviews. Funding for new ventures, including appointing new staff, small projects and continuing education and specialist equipment (e.g. audio and video tape recorders), is sometimes difficult to achieve and when successful is the result of well prepared negotiation with managers. These resources are essential in order that the department can be efficient, with up-to-date equipment, tests and professional journals and books.

Access to a variety of rooms is required for assessing and rehearsing communication strategies: small rooms for interviews or individual therapy programmes; and a larger, comfortable well lit space for larger discussion groups or for performance. Garden and park spaces offer stimulation for broader topics of conversation and relaxation. All resources and infrastructure development require regular review.

Professional contacts and networks

The National Special Interest Group in Mental Health (SIG) of the Royal College of Speech and Language Therapists (RCSLT), which was formed in the early 1980s as a response to a national survey to act as a support and education forum, continues to provide a refreshing and informative contact with immediate colleagues. There are regular meetings with specific areas of study and where research findings are discussed. As well as the academic study of particular areas of relevant work, the group has often emphasised practical forms of therapy and practised a variety of techniques. The enthusiasm and abilities of the different speech and language therapists have made the SIG a most important professional contact.

Within the hospital, clinical teams are usually headed by a psychiatrist and his or her medical and nursing team is a focal point for the ongoing management of the individual patient. The responsibility for medical, legal and therapeutic work is held within this group in association with social services. The Professions Allied with Medicine (PAM) meet in the ward rounds, or out-patient meetings, to discuss the up-to-date relevant patient management. When these teams are effective it is a rich, profitable and beneficial experience for the patient, as everyone attempts to communicate findings clearly and plan with the patient, as much as possible, the best therapeutic programme. There are a variety of professional groups with whom to share individual or group work, for instance ward or out-patient nurses often appreciate invitations to join communication groups and are able to offer invaluable information about patients they have known for perhaps months or even years.

Shared treatment programmes in appearance, posture, gesture, movement, body attitude and physical relaxation can be developed with the physiotherapist or her helper. Knowledge shared with the dietitian about plans for over- or underweight patients can have a great effect on mood as well as appearance. Specialist input by the music, art or drama therapist gives particular insight and offers patients various outlets for self-expression or containment.

The largest therapist community is usually the occupational therapy department. Occupational therapists provide a large number of skills in every area of patient assessment and therapy programmes, and they are the best known Profession Allied to Medicine used by psychiatrists in mental health. One of their areas of interest is communication, and it is common practice to share with the speech and language therapist plans to which they contribute, and support work in specific aspects of communication which they acknowledge is not their area of expertise.

Discourse analysis can be encouraged by some psychiatrists in outlining a particular patient's conversational style, language and prosody. Communication can be considered in a new way and constitutes useful information for patient management. Junior doctors often ask to attend a session when a patient is being treated for dysphonia or dysarthria, as they appreciate discussion of the neurological features. They are particularly helpful in explaining the need for medication, changes in medication and the side-effects. If a doctor is not available to explain medication side-effects, the pharmacist is often able to point out relevant physical and/or mood changes.

A team using mainly behavioural techniques can welcome the input of a speech and language therapist, where he or she would work closely with members of the psychology department. I believe more practical and academic work can be carried out between our two professions. Assessments of patients seem to dominate the work of psychologists in some settings and they therefore have less time to carry out therapeutic work in the multidisciplinary team.

Contact should be maintained with the other speech and language therapists working locally in neurology, geriatrics and audiology and they also appreciate being included in case discussions. It should also be stressed that there is a recognisable overlap between some clients with learning difficulties and mental health problems; for instance, many schizophrenic and other mentally ill patients have had poor schooling and learning difficulties as part of their psychiatric condition. Dovetailing with the learning difficulties department gives added strength to understanding and dealing with those so disadvantaged. Combined meetings and courses facilitate learning. This is especially useful with those from similar training and types of clinical expertise. The same professional language is spoken, and provides a much needed forum to educate our colleagues about our role in mental health. With some types of patients, it is helpful to discuss differential diagnosis, when neurological features are prevalent. Hearing tests are especially important in all mental health settings due to frequent lack of awareness by other professional groups.

Social workers give tremendous support and professional help to mental health patients and it is important to maintain regular contacts at every level. This contact can be especially useful when working in the community assisting with patients and their families. Many younger patients have 'communication difficulties' as a highly significant problem and require individual social skills programmes, taking into account literacy and language, preparation and support into continuing with further education. The adolescent and the family are particularly important in this shared work. Confidentiality between therapist and patient is highlighted as the young person leaves home and wishes to lead his/her own life as far as possible. Family and patient require a therapist and social worker to provide a secure and trustworthy contact.

When involved with the psychogeriatric patient contact can be welcomed by the family. They may wish to join group sessions and often want simple means of understanding and interpreting the wishes of their parents. A designated therapist should be involved with the elderly mentally ill and provide regular group sessions as well as individual assessments and therapy programmes. This gives continuity and patients know and can rely on the recognised person.

Some general practitioners welcome domiciliary visits to reassure and encourage housebound clients with dysarthria associated with depression and the families who are trying to understand the communication difficulties of a dementing elderly relative. It could be advantageous to continue a liaison with GPs.

Residential houses may invite a contribution towards helping residential staff develop communication groups. Many of the staff believe that they can work successfully and only need encouragement, example and basic source materials to help develop their techniques and confidence.

Some volunteer groups have evening sessions with families who have patients with Alzheimer's, Parkinsonism and Depression. Family and Volunteer groups appreciate any information on communication and find comfort in discussions where they can describe the non-verbal communication and the patient's difficulties with speech and language.

A patient's religious beliefs should always be respected and where possible appropriate support given.

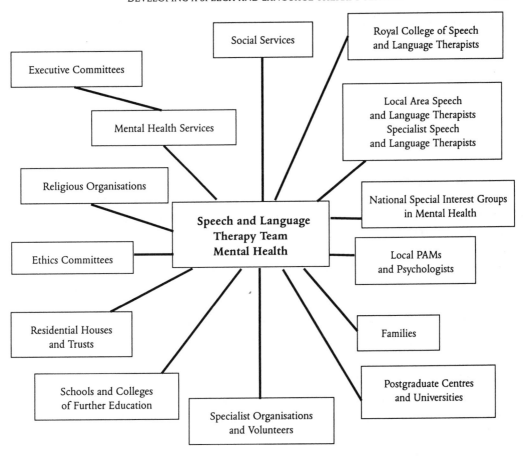

Figure 14.1 Networking

Continuing education and personal support systems

An essential part of providing an effective and informed service is to have access to a variety of opportunities for continual updating of knowledge and skills and for new learning to enrich capacity and understanding of mental health. Wisdom should be used to synthesise the processes of clinical experience with our own psychodynamic resources. Most managers of services allow time for staff to follow courses and personal study; it is in their interests to have up-to-date staff who are keen to review and improve their work rather than carry on year after year with the same uncriticised methods.

There are numerous areas of study. It is sensible to 'reinforce success' and use the interests and skills we already have and would like to have. These can include reviews of our service and identifying specialist groups, e.g. Afro-Caribbean young men, people living in mental health residential units, and the elderly in day hospitals.

Courses and lectures given in postgraduate medical centres, in hospitals, and relevant meetings in the community broaden understanding of social and political issues.

Regular internal study sessions allow for presentation of courses and meetings attended and recent publications to be presented.

New techniques are always required when working with ward patients and those in the community. Reading and writing skills, drama, poetry and literature can be part of our communicative effectiveness. These elements are part of speech therapy provision as they enhance the effectiveness of patients in spontaneous and creative communication.

Continuing education within the NHS has to be a dovetailing of what is needed to be an improved professional person and managers will understand this need within a working programme. Needless to say, reading journals, papers and courses attended are part of learning and personal department.

The undergraduate speech and language therapy training establishments usually allow therapists access to library facilities and in some cases organise specialist courses. Professions Allied to Medicine may provide new areas of shared learning in mental health management and therapy.

Support systems should be in place for all therapists in mental health work. It is common for psychotherapy departments to give time for staff to talk about their work and themselves in relation to their work. Other staff follow personal psychotherapy analysis and support. Mentally ill patients are a challenge to our thinking and behaviour; it is imperative to learn about our conscious and, when possible, our unconscious selves.

Organisation, administration and review

Organisation and administration of all departments need time and space in the daily timetable. A proper place must be found so that staff do not find themselves working hours each week outside their contracts. Time given at the beginning and end of sessions can allow for continuity in preparation, writing up, review and reorganisation. A useful device to cascade ongoing information, findings and planning is to have a typed agenda items sheet and to work to clear known and simple agendas. Staff members wanting to report new items can add them at the weekly meeting. Information is carried forward so that matters arising always promote approved new action.

Minutes from the full local speech and language therapy meetings are incorporated as part of standards in *Communicating Quality 2* (RCSLT 1996). All meetings attended by staff members should be reported and involve a planning and review service. Statistics and reports should be sent to the Area Speech and Language Services Manager as should requests for courses to attend or any change in our service.

Lists of names, telephone numbers and addresses of other speech and language therapists, and other staff in the hospital, community and social services, are essential. So too are the external organisations, e.g. Alzheimer's, Parkinson's and any special groups particularly relevant to your area, e.g. Afro-Caribbean, and residential houses for mental health clients. As there are many meetings to attend it is useful to work out those which are most important to attend and share between staff.

One of the most useful contacts is through the hospital's executive meetings, in which a profile of our work and what is offered can be presented. The Chairman of the Executive

Committees Consultative Committee or the Mental Health Services Manager is often pleased to place items on their agenda. Prepared concise information sheets identifying the organisation and staffing of the service reminds consultants, in particular, of the resources and availability.

The higher profile received from those in executive positions is well worth the additional preparation and although the speech and language therapy teams are small, the services will be appreciated and consulted by doctors and managers alike.

It is expected that information regarding the patient's time on the waiting list, when interviews take place and if and when taken on for therapy, is recorded. Flexibility in the approach to treatment is dictated by the patient's fluctuating health and this may result in programme changes.

The work of the department needs to be reviewed continually. The organisation should have inbuilt mechanisms to test and reconsider all aspects of individual staff's work and how the team, unit and mental health services in general function.

A thorough review can often change a range of tasks and programmes already in place. It also gives staff an opportunity to change direction or style of work. When it is built in to the organisational structure, discussed at meetings and minuted, it becomes part of the continuing review, which should be enabling and not threatening. Sometimes there are complete alterations in who works in which wards, out-patients and in what places in the community, and this takes into new areas that use their expertise and experience in different ways. This is an important part of staff development and gives a refreshing chance for monitoring and learning.

Research projects and teaching

Research funding is not easily found and it is important to know all the avenues through which money is granted to mental health services. It is essential to keep a research-orientated climate within any sound department. Even small projects are rewarding and give evidence of serious intentions. Research also improves the standard of work and further study. We are learning about new ways of studying and about mental health problems, better assessments and therapy strategies.

The Ethics Committee of each area served by the local health authority always provides information and guidance sheets regarding any research proposals. These allow a clearer idea of what is needed and how to go about developing an acceptable scheme, as each project has to be agreed and accepted by the Ethics Committee. If one can become a member of this type of committee a great deal of experience is gained about how a good proposal is discussed and advised.

The amount of time and money to be used has to be well thought out and several advisors may be used to help with different aspects of the research. An attachment to a University Department with supervision from an authority with experience in the proposed area is advisable.

When the department has a positive and research-orientated view it is usually lively and interested in teaching. Speech and language therapy students must be informed throughout their education of the complexities of the communication problems in mental health and this should be inspired and enlightened by clinical placements in mental health, with the advantage of being taught by mental health clinicians. No area of teaching and no information provided is too humble, whether to staff in the hospitals or residential homes of the community.

Beginning a new service to teach about what we know and can do is of prime importance and is part of the creative cycle of providing information and improving performance.

References

Royal College of Speech and Language Therapists (1996) *Communicating Quality 2*. London: RCSLT.

CHAPTER 15

General Psychiatry

Andy Hamilton

Introduction

This chapter gives an overview of the range of presenting difficulties and aspects of their care from the perspective of a clinical caseload. In doing so it is necessary to highlight the direct links between the core elements of speech and language therapy skills that are used by a therapist working in mental health and those of therapists working with other clinical groups. The aim of the speech and language therapist (SLT) in all cases remains to maximise the communication potential within the client and carer's environment.

Provision for people with mental health difficulties has shown marked change over recent years as medication used in its relief has improved and government legislation has signalled a change in philosophy. Correspondingly, much of the previous work of speech and language therapists had been done within large out-of-town institutions and is now having to adapt to providing a service over a broader geographical area, emphasising a more evidence-based holistic and multidisciplinary approach. It may be helpful to look briefly at the major legislation that has led to these changes.

Legislation

One of the major government Acts concerning the care of people with mental health difficulties is the Mental Health Act of 1983. Therapists will almost certainly meet people who are subject to its terms, particularly if they work in acute settings. However, statistics reveal that the majority of admissions to psychiatric services are voluntary (or informal). Of the 263,400 psychiatric admissions over the 1992/93 financial year only 21,356 were formal, of which 8 per cent were under court direction (Bornat *et al.* 1997).

The SLT may be called to assess and provide reports used in the court hearings for offenders and in the mental health tribunals that sit for the review of clients' status under the Act, in addition to providing therapy input to those already 'under section'. A brief list of the commonly used sections of the Mental Health Act is given in Figure 15.1.

Compulsory admissions		
Section 2	(Admission for assessment and treatment)	28 days maximum
Section 3	6 months max. renewable for further 6 months then for periods of 1 year	
Section 4	(Emergency, subject to second medical opinion)	72 hours maximum
Section 5(2)	(Doctors holding power)	As Section 4
Section 5(4)	(Nurses holding power)	6 hours maximum
Section 135	(Mentally disordered people in their homes)	72 hours, not renewable
Section 136	(Mentally disordered people in public places)	As Section 135
After care		
Section 117	(After care)	No time limit
Admission linked to court proceedings		
Section 35	(No treatment without consent)	28 days, 12 weeks max.
Section 36	(Treatment without consent)	As Section 35
Section 37	(Court admission order)	6 months maximum, renewable as Section 3
Section 38	(Admission to determine suitability of treatment)	12 week maximum, continued for 28-day periods up to max. of 6 months
Section 41	(Restrictions on discharge)	Fixed period or no limit
Section 47	(Transfer from prison to hospital)	As Section 37
Section 49	(As above but with discharge restrictions)	As Section 37

A court order is often given in the form of a combination of 37/41, which would combine the admission order with discharge criteria.

Figure 15.1 Mental Health Act 1983 – most regularly used parts of the Act and their length of detention

A second major influence on work in this area is the National Health Service and Community Care Act 1990. This Act formalised movement in policy that had been taking place over the previous decade towards community care. The four key components are:

- services to be flexible and sensitive to the needs of individuals and their carers
- minimal intervention to be used to achieve independence
- a range of options to be available for service users
- services to concentrate on those with the greatest needs (Walker 1997).

At present the government maintains an initiative which, in adherence to the final point above, concentrates services on the young mentally ill. Amongst its many aspects was the defining of the role of the statutory services and the consequent process, which continues now, of the harmonising of the work done by Health and Social Services into a 'seamless' provision of care. It is at the edge of these two services meeting that much exciting development is taking place.

At the clinical level the ramifications include joint funding initiatives for posts and improvements in Information Technology which allow freer information sharing (e.g. linked databases).

There have been a number of additional pieces of legislation since the original Act of 1990. In 1995 and again in late 1998 the government acted to increase provisions for the acutely ill, particularly those that may provide a threat to the public safety, following a number of high profile incidents. Currently, further important changes in legislation are being discussed, and the promise is that they will be implemented in the near future.

Settings for service provision

Following the shift to community care many speech and language therapists now work in community sites, in a variety of settings dependent on the structure of the employing organisation and the style of service delivery (Table 15.1).

As in other spheres of the profession, the mental health therapist himself/herself may find themselves a member of two or more teams. Often they remain part of a speech and language therapy department whilst at the same time being a member of a variety of care teams. It may be that the therapist remains an 'occasional' member of a number of teams or that they become an integral member of a small number of teams. The role of keyworker within an environment is possible, especially if working predominantly on a single site. Such teams are most likely to be multidisciplinary, led by a consultant psychiatrist. Referrals to the therapist may come from a variety of agencies, both within and outside the 'team' (Table 15.2).

Table 15.1 Sites for delivery of services
Admission/assessment ward
Extended care ward
Residential rehabilitation unit
Group home
Day centre (social/health service, voluntary agency)
Independent living housing
Hired premises in the community (e.g. church hall, community centre)

Table 15.2 Typical range of referral sources

Consultant psychiatrist

Senior house officer

Care manager

Community psychiatric nurse (elderly and acute)

Psychiatric social worker

Mental health day centre staff

General practitioner (GP)

Ward staff nurse

Community mental health team

Other Professions Allied to Medicine (PAMs) (e.g. psychology, occupational therapy, physiotherapy)

Family member

Self-referral

Service delivery

A standard range of therapy delivery can be employed. Group, individual and educative via carers are all frequently used. Joint run groups can be used as an effective means of linking communication work to all aspects of the client's life. Often the speech and language therapy resource is thinly spread, which makes indirect work attractive both with direct carers, e.g. hospital and community nursing staff.

There is a natural link between the service provision and such factors as the source of referral and site of service delivery. A referral from a GP for a client with dysphagic difficulties may require a combination of visits to such sites as the person's home, their day centre and a case conference on a hospital site. Alternatively a mental health team referral for voice work can require only out-patient type sessions at a community day service site.

Liaison has recently been more encouraged and can include a range of local and national agencies linked to the condition in question (e.g. National Schizophrenia Fellowship, Age Concern). Contact may take the form of consultation on policies or presentations to carer groups. A list of some of the organisations and their roles is given in an Appendix to this book.

An example of multidisciplinary facilitation is a group co-facilitated by a speech and language therapist and a member of the Community Mental Health. The workshops are targeted at people who have an acute illness now stable with or without medication and are already out in the community or preparing to re-enter the community after a period of in-patient treatment. A diagnosis of many of these patients is what would in the past have been labelled neuroses, and now possibly identified as social phobias. Some of the more chronic difficulties often suffered by those with psychotic problems are being addressed by the author with longer contracts of workshops.

These groups are an effective way of providing a service that takes the therapist working in a mental health team out into the community to work with those clients who have no need to attend hospital-based facilities. Such groups can take place in non-mental health sites such as church or community halls, away from a health service setting. It can be important to 'normalise' a group in this way to reinforce the person's links to the community rather than the health service. Being based in the community means that local GPs can be encouraged to make direct referrals and are encouraged to do so by the sending of workshop details to local surgeries. This could be seen as an effective means of getting a message to GPs about the work of speech and language therapy and of the mental health service in general.

A more in-depth discussion of these groups is given in Chapters 27 and 28, but here follows a brief profile of two people who have attended workshops:

Case Example 1

A client recovering from depression was able to regain contact with social contacts lost since suffering a breakdown whilst attending university. Having had the support of the group to look at the issues involved and examine them in discussion and role play he was then able to take them outside the group and 'generalise' them.

Case Example 2

A similar process to that outlined above was used by a client suffering from a post-traumatic social phobia who made use of the inherent enhanced communication environment to set goals of interaction first within the group and later outside.

This may involve adaptation of activities in the literature, such as those cited by Powell (1992). Despite the potential benefits to individual patients, group dynamics need to be considered in the selection of patients. It may be necessary to control for such factors as insight into difficulties, itself possibly linked to motivation, and the degree to which symptoms of the mental illness are currently being controlled.

Care of the elderly

SLT skills in looking holistically at a client can be of use to the care team in such areas as elderly care where the effect of sensory losses on communication style and content are apparent to the SLT and amelioration of the sensory loss can be achieved through environmental and/or electronic means. The result can be that client's presenting difficulties are better understood once the sensory component is recognised.

Case Example 3

Mr JR was admitted with a diagnosis of vascular dementia and concomitant behavioural problems together with some physical difficulties related to both aging and the physiological sequelae of the organic brain damage. Communication problems were preventing accurate assessment of these problems. Following an SLT assessment, involving the use of suitable amplification, a clearer picture of his comprehension and expression skills gave further useful information as to the nature of his behavioural difficulties and the provision of effective therapy.

Dysphagia

Eating and swallowing disorders have become an increasing part of SLT work over recent years and mental health is no exception to this trend. Many posts within this specialty are at Grade 2 level or higher and thus the clinicians have more often than not obtained their postgraduate dysphagia training thereby enabling them to deal with such referrals themselves. Referrals may be from the fields of both elderly and acute psychiatry. The range of diagnoses made is wide and covers both dysphagia resulting from a focal neurological lesion secondary to the original mental health condition and dysphagia resulting directly or indirectly from the primary mental health diagnosis. In the latter area a knowledge of the possible links between medication side-effects and dysphagic problems is helpful, a prime example of which can be the neuroleptics that can cause oral dryness. The reduced moisture leads to difficulty with bolus formation and then to deglutition problems. The therapist is able to advise on suitable food texture or possibly saliva substitutes.

Speech and language pathology

It is possible to see all varieties of speech and language pathology within this client group, either as a symptom of a primary mental health diagnosis or as a concomitant disorder.

Side-effects of medication

Neuroleptic medication, particularly anti-psychotics drugs, can produce both short-term and long-term side-effects. Short-term effects can include Parkinsonian-type symptoms and in some cases dysfluency of speech. Often a second medication (an anti-muscarinic, which has its anti-Parkinsonian effect by its action on the cholinergic system) is prescribed alongside the anti-psychotic in an attempt to reduce such side-effects (e.g. Procyclidine, Kemadrin). The cumulative effect of this medication can include tardive dyskinesia, which may be unresponsive to the anti-Parkinsonian medication. The SLT may receive a referral for such reasons as 'unclear speech', and will be interested in the client's speech production in order to make distinctions such as that between the speech that exhibits extra-pyramidal signs (Parkinsonian) and that which is of basal ganglion origins (tardive dyskinesia). The former is characterised by soft voice, poor articulation and dysrhythmic phonation, the latter by loud voice, poor articulation and involuntary oral movements.

There have been considerable advances in the medications available for the control of psychoses in recent years. Recently the traditional phenothiazine-based medications and their like, such as chlorpromazine, thioridazine and fluphenazine, have been complemented by the introduction of a group referred to as the atypical anti-psychotics, such as olanzapine and clozapine. This new generation of drugs is less likely to produce the extrapyramidal symptoms typical of their forebears and are often used when patients are 'resistant' to the traditional drugs. However, they also have their cautions, particularly clozapine which initially requires weekly blood tests to guard against falls in the white blood cell count.

Tardive dyskinesia

For those with dyskinesias, research has provided evidence that insightful clients can benefit from therapeutic intervention aimed at reducing the effects of these symptoms by bringing these involuntary movements under conscious control (Ferguson 1992). The Parkinsonian symptoms in speech can be addressed using tasks from the standard approaches used in hypokinetic dysarthria, although much attention to generalisation requires adequate liaison with those involved in the client's carer network.

Case Example 4

Mr GC, a 55-year-old, had been on long-term neuroleptic medication following a diagnosis of paranoid-delusional schizophrenia and was currently on depot injections (Flupenthixol, marketed as Depixol, by Lundbeck). Having spent some time as an in-patient in the past he was now living independently and making use of local day services. He was referred as having a 'loud voice' that was leading to interaction difficulties in his daily environment. Having first screened for hearing loss, an assessment of oral motor skills was undertaken; both were within normal limits. A discussion of the difficulty led to an awareness of the possible causes for this difficulty resulting in a decision to work on perception of stress and ways to reduce it. This in turn involved the introduction of breathing techniques together with elements of physical relaxation. Rehabilitation involved indirect work with key workers on the various day centre sites that GC attended.

Schizophrenia

As with other topics in this chapter, work in this area is covered in more detail throughout this book. Links are increasingly being made between schizophrenia and disorders of language. Work by Thomas (1997) has linked thought disorder analysis techniques and linguistics. In doing so, features of schizophrenic thought disorder can be framed in terms familiar to the speech and language therapist, such as incoherence (syntax), neologisms (phonemic or word level) and poverty of speech and speech content (pragmatics). This demonstrates the applicability of SLT involvement in the professional care team, in both the assessment and remediation process.

There are many theories as to the precise nature of the language disorder in schizophrenia. One such theory postulates that disordered discourse may be described in terms of inappropriate use of language (Frith 1996). Thus this theory, language difficulties are described in terms of pragmatics, which will be in familiar territory for the SLT. Such links have already been made by SLTs; for example, Walsh (1996) has investigated the use of informal groups as a means of looking at more complex pragmatic skills and improving self-monitoring.

Different theories are reflected in varied therapeutic approaches. This results in many simple techniques being put to effective use with both individuals and groups. These may include the use of visual prompts during individual and group work to aid with difficulties in attention and concentration, and photographic teaching material (PTM) style stimuli used to elicit discussion on inference. All these activities would come comfortably under the heading 'language work'.

One aspect that SLTs, and all other therapists, will recognise as important in therapeutic intervention is a client's insight into their difficulties, but even prior to this their basic listening skills. In the field of schizophrenia this can be a difficult aspect and when seemingly gained may be partial and transitory. As such, language/ communication work may include this aspect in its aims. As other theories are investigated, these are paralleled by innovative therapeutic approaches. The following case example may help to illustrate this.

Case Example 5

AF is a young man who was diagnosed as having a schizophrenic condition in his early twenties. His compliance with prescribed psychotropic medication has been variable since this time and over the past eight years he has struggled to come to terms with this diagnosis and has remained unable to accept that the intrusions of hallucinations and paranoia could be due to an illness. Having attended a communication skills workshop three years previously and been seen by the facilitators as very defensive and unable to participate, he was offered a place on a new workshop with some reservations on the part of the facilitators. At this time he was noted as saying that he was troubled by worries that people were not understanding him and he not understanding them. However, the supportive small group environment, consisting of people with a variety of mental health difficulties other than his own, was able to provide feedback on his discourse and general communication behaviours to the extent and in such a manner that AF was able to examine methods of improving his topic maintenance and, equally importantly, to gain positive self-regard when given sustained and positive feedback from his peer group. One of the main benefits for AF was that he was able to make links between elements of his paranoia and his communication difficulties, thus gaining insight into aspects of his mental health difficulties. It was noted that during the three-month period of the workshop AF began taking his medication on a regular basis and so it was hoped that with an increase in insight and the perceived benefits he may feel able to continue with his medication programme.

Beyond the client's communication difficulties in schizophrenia are the language and communication skills the therapist uses in interaction with the client. An aspect of an SLT's work in this area, as in all areas, is to model effective communication with our clients. Techniques such as neuro linguistic programming (Bandler and Grinder 1990) can form a basis for communication in both formal counselling sessions and in informal interactions.

Dual diagnosis (mental health and learning difficulties)

In the past the services for people with mental health difficulties and learning difficulties were regularly directly linked. More recently the services have tended to be separated. This has tied in with the move from large hospital sites to community care. However, it remains common to meet clients with a 'dual diagnosis' within either service provision. Within mental health services it is possible to meet people with learning difficulties as referrals to communication skills workshops, voice therapy and other facets of the speech and language therapy provision. In these cases liaison with colleagues in the complementary service may be indicated as often the client's education took place within that service prior to the diagnosis of mental health problems, often later in life. SLTs with their extensive background training will find themselves well placed to be able to deal with the combination of techniques and knowledge of the presenting difficulties required in these cases.

Head injury

Head injury often being of a diffuse nature can be a difficult area in which to find suitable services for a client's placement. Often physical disabilities feature highly in this decision; however, an enduring mental health issue can complicate this and thus it is possible to meet clients with these difficulties in a mental health post. The difficulties may take the form of psychosis or affective disorder together with insight and motivation problems as often seen in frontal lobe lesions. It is possible that clients will be seen on an ongoing basis to provide support in a variety of aspects of communication. It may be that a speech and language therapist will see the patients on a more long-term and/or frequent basis, and this may enable the speech and language therapist to gain valuable insight into long-term difficulties, which in turn may carry with it an element of the advocacy role. It may be in this area that we work at the environmental level and address such issues as communication opportunities and client–carer interaction as well as the area of self image.

Case Example 6

Mr MN had a motorcycle accident in the late 1980s, in which he suffered extensive head injuries. Following intensive neurological rehabilitation MN had been living in a long stay psychiatric setting until recently moving to independent living accommodation with 24–hour live-in care. Residual difficulties include disorders in the movement of all four limbs and a psychosis controlled by medication. Over the past three years the speech and language therapist had moved from work based on dysarthria to broader issues concerning the patient's communicative environment. A computer was purchased as an opportunity to broaden interests with the hope that in time an Internet correspondence would be possible. More recently using a strong interest of MN a project involving the repair of old motorcycles was commenced. Within this approach cognitive aspects such as attention, memory, planning and organisational skills were tackled, together with physical aspects such as dexterity and environmental issues of communication networks.

Outcomes of therapy

Outcomes present a challenge in an area of work where much of what is done is best measured in qualitative rather than quantitative terms. The 'Health Care Aims' system, currently being developed in the South-West Thames Region of the NHS, may provide a useful framework. This system allows the clinician to define their intended area of work (the Care Aim) in terms of Community Minimum Data Set

(CMDS) categories, which are non-diagnostic in origin. In turn the clinician will be able to set goals and outcomes under the designated Care Aim. The system allows repeated Care Aims to be set by the clinician as the client case develops and this has proven to be more flexible than many previously used systems. Its use has the potential to provide clients, clinicians and managers with clear useful information about the clinical work being done (Malcolmess, personal communication (1999)). Further ideas for the measurement of clinical intervention can be gained from the audit manual published by the Royal College of Speech and Language Therapists (1993).

Management issues

Whilst much of this chapter has dealt with clinical issues, the management of caseload and the other commitments of a post should not be forgotten. A job which can mean travelling over a number of sites in a day, let alone a week, has its ramifications in terms of time management and paperwork organisation. Frequently in the speech and language therapy profession secretarial back-up is limited. This is highlighted in the post of a 'mobile' community clinician who may need to think about formalising secretarial back-up from the various work sites when the departmental provision is insufficient. An alternative might be to develop an adequate level of information technology (IT) skills so as to make use of a laptop or personal computer (PC) provided by the employers.

At a time when statistical returns are high on the management agenda the clinician working in mental health may find it worthwhile ensuring that records are up to date and relevant. To ensure this it is necessary to delineate details such as the sites where the clinician is and the range of diagnoses of patients. A full range of therapeutic approaches should be allowed for in the original data entry. A well-informed clinician is one who can call on relevant statistics when called upon to justify a post of to design expanded posts. A combination of both diagnostic and CMDS-based information could prove valuable in such instances.

Supervision

Within this specialism supervision is of particular importance due to the nature of the client group. This can be provided in group or individual form and can be from one's own profession or from an allied discipline working in mental health. It may be preferred to obtain supervision from the latter group when a speech and language therapist from the same specialisation is not available, rather than using a non-specialised colleague. In some instances a suitable supervisor may be obtained from another district or through freelance sources or another profession. In addition to this, membership of Special Interest Groups provides a more loose but no less supportive supervisory network and is a highly useful means of furthering knowledge in the area.

Future developments

Following the recent change of government and a resulting change in political emphasis in health care provision, the next challenge for community therapists is integration into Primary Care Groups (PCG). Each PCG should be aiming to have a representative from the PAMs (MSF

1998); such a post would be open to any PAM, including ourselves. At a clinical service level some degree of marketing of a service may be required to go through the PCG in their role as commissioning agents for local services. Communication of relevant information to the PAM's representative as well as to the board in general would become important in terms of service planning and provision. Once the creation of PCGs has reached its Fourth Stage they will be established as Primary Care Trusts, with responsibility for the provision of community health services for their population. By this stage it would be important for therapy services to have established an effective means of communication with the board.

Under the current government's initiative, Health Service Trusts are being encouraged to merge; and with sequential/consequent merging of speech and language therapy departments there are the inevitable opportunities and threats for professions and the individuals within them. With the mixing of skills within a department, common ground can be found between therapists. Also it will be seen that the skills of speech and language therapists have a universal application within the varied and occasionally challenging environments present within the health care service of the present and future. There undoubtedly remains a need for a communication specialist within the area of mental health who will be prepared to deliver his or her expertise and knowledge in a variety of settings. Such variety within a clinical post in the area of mental health ensures that a high degree of satisfaction can be found from a post in this field.

References

Bandler, R. and Grinder, J. (1990) *Frogs into Princes.* Eden Grove Editions.

Bornat, J., Johnson, J., Pereira, C., Pilgrim, D. and Williams, F. (eds) (1997) *Community Care, a Reader.* London: MacMillan.

British National Formulary 36, BMA/RPSGB, September 1998.

Bryan, K. (1993) *The Right Hemisphere Battery.* Whurr.

Department of Health, HMSO (1983) *Mental Heath Act,* London.

Diagnostic and Statistical Manual of Mental Disorders (DSM IIIR) (1987) Washington DC: American Psychiatric Association.

Duboust, S. and Knight, P. (1995) *Group Activities for Personal Development.* Winslow Press.

Emerson, J. Enderby, P. *Management of Speech and Language Disorders in a Mental Illness Unit.*

European Journal of Disorders of Communication, 31, 3 (1996) Royal College of Speech and Language Therapists. France, J. and Muir, N. (eds) (1997) *Communication and the Mentally Ill Patient.* London: Jessica Kingsley Publishers.

Ferguson, A. (1992) 'Speech control in persistant tardive dyskinesia: A case study. In *EJDC 27,* 89–93.

Gravell, R. and France, J. (eds) (1991) *Speech and Communication Problems in Psychiatry.* Chapman and Hall.

Hutchings, S., Comins, J. and Offiler, J. (1991) *The Social Skills Handbook.* Winslow Press.

International Classification of Disorders (ICD 10)

Jones, R. (1996) *Mental Health Act Manual.* London: Sweet and Maxwell Ltd.

Kingdon, D.G. and Turkington, D. (1995) *Cognitive–Behavioural Therapy of Schizophrenia.* Psychology Press.

Malcomess, K. (1999) Care aims – using care aims in the care planning , service delivery and commissioning process. *Health Service Journal.*

MSF (1998) The Primary Care Fax, MSF fact sheet.

Powell, T. (1992) *Mental Health Handbook.* Winslow Press.

The Mental Health Act 1983

The Care in the Community Act 1990.

CHAPTER 16

Services for Older People in Mental Health Settings

Jane Maxim and Cathy Timothy

The service context

Provision of speech and language therapy services for older people in mental health settings is variable and, in the UK, is dependent on the contracts held by the service provider. Although there are standards and best practice guidelines, the driving force behind the development of services is usually the speech and language therapist provider and the multidisciplinary team, rather than the purchaser. Services to this population therefore vary dramatically between areas where there are well-established speech and language therapy programmes which provide input to a number of different settings and those where there is effectively no provision at all (RCSLT 1993; ADA 1996).

The RCSLT position paper on speech and language therapy and the elderly with dementia (1993) reported that the majority of speech and language therapy service providers offered services to the elderly population and, at that time, about 25 per cent offered specific services to the elderly mentally ill, usually in a hospital context. Since 1993, there is some anecdotal evidence from Specific Interest Groups that service provision has spread, particularly in the provision of speech and language therapy input to training care staff in residential care and that new posts have been established in hospital-based mental health teams (see Maxim and Bryan 1994 for a review of the role of the speech and language therapist in dementia management).

This apparent standstill in speech and language therapy mental health provision has occurred at a time of great change in health service management and in the context of increasing numbers of old elderly, defined here as 85+ years. In this age group, the prevalence of moderate or severe cognitive impairment is estimated to be 21.9 per cent, compared with 7.2 per cent in the 75–84 year age group and only 2.3 per cent between the ages of 65 and 74 years (Raleigh 1997). Psychiatric illness and cerebrovascular disease also have an increased incidence and prevalence in the post-65-year age group, as do the numbers of elderly people presenting with multiple pathologies (Melzer, Ely and Brayne 1997).

The Community Care Act 1993 focused the delivery of care on community-based local services, rather than hospital-based services. Domiciliary services have long been a feature of speech and language therapy provision, although many areas do not provide this service.

Recently, rehabilitation-at-home programmes for the elderly have begun to be implemented, adding yet another type of service to this complex picture of provision.

The focus of this chapter is to consider all aspects of the wide role of the speech and language therapist in the old age psychiatry area and in particular to:

- highlight the role of the speech and language therapist with this population who have very specialist needs regarding both communication and swallowing

- discuss the current standards set by the RCSLT and the settings in which clients receive input

- consider the types of disorders and intervention, including both assessment and speech and language therapy management.

Standards and guidelines

The main source of information on standards and guidelines for speech and language therapists can be found in *Communicating Quality 2* (RCSLT 1996). The sections encompassing 'The Elderly Population', 'Mental Health – Adults' and 'Dementia' are all relevant because, together, they summarise the objectives of service provision, from receipt of referral, through to assessment, intervention and discharge, including the importance of multidisciplinary liaison and the speech and language therapist skill mix required.

The aims and principles of service delivery to clients with a dementia are as follows:

1. To provide assessment and intervention of communication and swallowing.

2. To deliver services with and through carers within the client's environment, as well as to the client.

3. To offer advice and support to carers in the client's environment.

4. To work within a multidisciplinary framework – sharing goals of intervention, and, where appropriate, preparing joint goals with other professionals/carers.

5. To enable carers and other professionals to have a clear understanding of the communication strengths and needs of each client and provide the opportunity for the carer and other professionals to develop the appropriate skills in facilitating the client's communication.

The aims and principles of service delivery to adults with mental illness are set out in more detail than those for dementias and are broadly similar except for the following points:

- There is specific reference to facilitating optimum communication skills with clients who have an identified communication difficulty.

- The concern of the speech and language therapist is not only the communication skills but also the welfare of the individual client.

- The principles stress that communication difficulties are highly correlated with mental illness and that this feature is important for diagnosis and management.

- The speech and language therapist has a role in enabling transition into and maintenance in the community.

- Communication skills may be compromised by medication, as well as other factors.
- The speech and language therapist has a remit to provide education and training in the field of communication in mental health.

These sections are somewhat different in their emphasis. In the elderly population section there is practical detail of the type of service delivery suggested, whereas in mental health and dementia there is talk of facilitation, contribution, enabling and maximising client strengths and needs regarding communication. It is helpful to consider these sections together as all three essentially describe the service that is provided to older people in mental health settings. Although training is mentioned in mental health as part of the speech and language therapist's role, it is perhaps surprising that this facet of work does not feature in working with clients who have dementia, given the widespread use of training for care staff in this area.

Communicating Quality 2 defines services along three axes: client groupings, disorders and service settings. In the section on client groupings, it is recognised that older people with a communication deficit may have any of a wide range of underlying disorders which contribute to their difficulties. It is common to encounter more than one communication deficit in a client, especially if there is co-existing mental or physical illness. Client groupings which are pertinent here are:

- Acquired neurological disorders (cerebrovascular-vascular accident, dementia, traumatic brain injury, progressive neurological disorders)
- Elderly population
- Mental health
- Hearing/visual impairment.

Careful assessment is required to diagnose communication disorders and to try to understand the relative contributions to the presenting disorder. The most prevalent communication disorder in mental health settings for older people is the language disorder secondary to a dementia. The focus here is therefore on services to the older person with dementia but, in discussing these services, it is important to consider other diagnoses and the settings in which they are seen. Dysphagia, for example, is a common reason for referral to speech and language therapy and often co-exists with a communication disorder. Successful intervention almost always requires attention to both swallowing and communication disorder together for this client group.

Decision-making in old age psychiatry

What influences the decision-making process?

Following receipt of a referral, the speech and language therapy service offered to the client is dependent on several factors. These will include the skill of the therapist, access to support, the resources available and the setting the client is to be seen in. However, the presenting disorder and factors relating to the client as an individual will have the greatest influence on the type and level of assessment and management to be offered.

Factors relating to the client

The elderly population without mental illness can be a complex entity. Older people are more likely to present with sensory deficits associated with normal aging, such as hearing and visual impairment. There is an increased probability of illness and of more than one illness concurrently. Related to this is the medication that they may be taking at any one time, the possible toxic side-effects of these drugs and the reactions they may have to each other. Older people are more likely to present with acute confusional states associated with infection or medication (Miller 1996), and increased susceptibility to fatigue is another factor which should not be forgotten.

Socio-cultural factors in assessment and management are also important. The adage of 'respect your elders' has particular relevance here and perhaps should be changed to 'respect the dignity of your elders'. There is likely to be a large age gap between the service provider and the client, whose wealth of knowledge and experience should not be underestimated. This is despite the fact that many elderly people completed their schooling at the age of 14/15 years and their education may have been disrupted during the Second World War. In view of the possible curtailment of formal education and the consequent variable literacy skills in this population, there may be anxiety and fear of failure, especially if the client is being asked to complete or take part in what seems to them school-like tasks. An insensitive interactional approach on behalf of the therapist can result in reduced co-operation and motivation in any client which, in turn, may prevent adequate assessment of their disorder.

Factors relating to the disorder

The client is unlikely to present to the speech and language therapist with only age-related changes to their communication abilities. The presenting disorder will often be multifaceted, comprising both physical and mental aspects, exacerbated by the age-related changes. A likely scenario is the referral of an 85-year-old woman with dementia, who has a severe hearing impairment, chronic chest infections and a history of mental illness. Although she is referred for the assessment and management of related communication difficulties, the approach taken by the therapist will rely on the following:

The severity of the disorder

Any input will depend on the severity of the disorder. It may be possible to complete a full, validated verbal and written assessment and to give some formal therapeutic input with the client who has a mild dementia. This same level of input, however, will not be possible where the client has a severe dementia and is likely to have difficulties in attending to tasks, understanding instructions and giving clear verbal responses in an interaction.

The type of disorder

A client may present with any number of disorders relating to organic or psychiatric illness, in addition to the changes of the normal aging process. In relation to dementia alone, the type of dementia may result in the presentation of differing types of communication impairment and progression. There may be complications due to neurological or psychiatric disorders as well as other more peripheral sensory impairments of hearing and vision. External social factors such as the move from living independently to residential care may also have an impact on communication. Yet despite the nature and extent of the disorder or factors individual to that client, different clinical settings will often dictate the type of input that can be provided.

Factors relating to the environment in which the client is seen

Imagine the 85-year-old woman described previously. The nature of the assessment and management could depend almost entirely upon the environment in which she is being seen. In the busy acute hospital ward, formal lengthy assessment may not be possible. Acute hospital staff may lack the skills of general communication with older people or those with dementia or the time to achieve any recommendations made by the speech and language therapist. The therapist may lack the time, resources or experience to provide any detail of input. This may be in direct contrast to the acute psychiatric ward for older people, where a specialist speech and language therapist is employed. Staff working in this setting are more likely to possess the skills and knowledge for working with both dementia and the elderly. There is likely to be a greater focus and understanding of communication difficulties due to the mental health aspect of the ward, and probably more time to provide the assessment and input. As well, the all-important multidisciplinary team should be well established in this setting, providing opportunities for interdisciplinary working to facilitate optimal communication.

Factors relating to the speech and language therapist

It is the skill of the therapist that untangles all of the above factors when presented with the referral. It is the experience of awareness in a multifaceted scenario, at the centre of which is the client or individual who requires a service. It is the ability to work as part of a closely linked multidisciplinary team, to liaise as necessary and highlight the strengths and needs of the communicatively impaired client. If the therapist has limited experience with the older mentally ill, then it is the ability to allow time to 'sit back' and observe all the factors in order to enable the decision-making process. It is this awareness that determines the nature and level of the service that is provided, whether it is assessment or intervention. In summary, the role of the speech and language therapist in old age psychiatry is:

- assessment and provision of information for differential diagnosis
- making recommendations for further referrals
- provision of information regarding abilities and difficulties, strengths and needs
- provision of advice regarding the facilitation of optimal abilities and ways to overcome or compensate the difficulties
- reduction of communication stress and burden imposed on caregivers
- specific therapy and programmes, both individual and group
- monitoring and review of patients' abilities and difficulties over time and updating information as necessary (e.g. with dementia)

- contribution to multidisciplinary problem-solving and liaison (e.g. behaviour difficulties)
- teaching and training staff, clients and carers in communication related skills (and also regarding feeding and swallowing)
- providing a resource for students/staff training in these areas
- advising on setting up homes and hostels etc., to ensure an optimum environment for communication
- enhancing quality of life
- promotion of good practice which helps to prevent breakdown of communication.

Assessment of communication in old age psychiatry

Ideally, assessment should take place within the framework of a multidisciplinary team and, as *Communicating Quality 2* stresses, with the purpose of the assessment being made clear to the client (RCSLT 1996). However, clients who are unable to respond to formal testing, or for whom that process is stressful or difficult to understand, may respond better to observation of their communication skills in conversation with the speech and language therapist. The speech and language therapist working in this area has to acquire the skill of assessing flexibly, depending on the client's initial reactions on meeting. Depending on the context in which the service is offered, assessment may range from formal testing and report provision in a memory or diagnostic clinic, to extensive data collection in a number of settings and with a number of significant people in that client's life, to ensure that a broad view of the client's communication is gained.

Speech and language therapists working in this area use a number of formal assessments which are well reviewed in Armstrong (1996), some of which have been designed for the particular client group and others which are adapted. Collecting information from carers is usually of great benefit, either by questionnaire or interview. The following assessments are of particular relevance to this client population:

- Arizona Battery for Communication Disorders of Dementia (ABCD: Bayles and Tomoeda 1993; Armstrong *et al.* 1996)
- Armstrong Naming Test (Armstrong 1996)
- Functional Linguistic Communication Inventory (FLCI: Bayles and Tomoeda 1994)
- Conversation analysis profile for cognitive impairment (CAPPCI: Perkins, Whitworth and Lesser 1997)
- Severe Impairment Battery (Saxton *et al.* 1993)
- Stevens' screening test (Stevens 1992).

Any test or profile used needs to be matched up against the goals of the assessment and particular care is needed to check that chosen assessment procedures take into account the age and disorder range of this client group. Where this is not possible, clinicians need to use their knowledge of the normal range of communicative behaviour and cognition as well as making adjustments in the assessment procedure itself for the possible effects of the aging process. The following factors may need manipulation in order to assess older people accurately: increased time to adjust to the assessment process; increased time in explanation; short testing sessions to avoid fatigue; increased time for responses; repetition of instructions and test items; and enlargement of test stimuli (Armstrong 1996).

In addition to assessments which are viewed as within the usual remit of speech and language therapists, in some settings where there is no clinical psychologist, tests of cognitive function may be carried out by the speech and language therapist or other members of the multidisciplinary team. Eccles *et al.* (1998) recommend that for dementia screening health-care professionals should use the Mini Mental Status Examination (MMSE: Folstein, Folstein and McHugh 1975) in conjunction with the clock drawing test, a daily living activities measure such as CAPE (Pattie 1981) and an abbreviated mental test score such as Hodkinson (1972). An adapted form of CAPE which briefly describes both impairment and communication disability has been put forward by Maxim and Bryan (1994) and which attempts to be neutral to the underlying disorder. Where a disorder can be specified, the Therapy Outcome Measures core scales can be used to rate impairment, disability, handicap and well-being/distress (Enderby 1997).

In some multidisciplinary teams, skills sharing is practised, meaning that team members learn core assessment skills and the resulting information is then discussed amongst the team to inform overall management provision. While each member of the team remains an 'expert' in their own area, this method of working is highly suitable in situations where the client may be confused by interaction with a number of professionals or where the service is provided on a domiciliary basis; however, it requires team building, planning and mutual trust.

Deciding on the purpose of assessment is the first crucial step in choosing which methods of assessment are appropriate. A formal assessment needs to be valid (to measure what it purports to measure) but many useful assessments may fail a strict reliability test because individual clients show great variability in their communication ability or in specific language skills. Clients with certain psychiatric disorder or with a dementia due to lewy body disease, for example, may show marked variation in their communication over the course of a day. Many speech and language therapists working in this area find that formal assessments do not illuminate the communication difficulties with which their clients present, nor do they inform service provision; but there is still a need to make sure that accurate observations are made so that change over time with or without intervention, either direct or indirect, can be monitored.

Intervention

In speech and language therapy, intervention can mean a number of different approaches, depending on the aims of working with different client groups. In old age psychiatry, the full range of interventions is observed because of the disparate nature of the population that may present to the clinician at any one time. The intervention will therefore vary from assessment and advice 'packages of care' to one of intensive therapy, focusing on specific aspects of communication. Woods (1996) uses the term 'management' in working with dementia, preferring this to 'treatment' or 'therapy'. He reports that 'therapy' gives the impression of 'lasting improvement', whereas 'management' suggests 'aims of ameliorating certain aspects of the disorder, reducing disability in certain circumstances, or lowering the frequency of behavioural problems associated with the disorder, without a particular expectation of the maintenance or the generalization of the effects of the intervention' (p.310). He is implying that the 'management' will not 'cure' the disorder and will not be offered over a limited amount of time, but will be ongoing.

It is a mistake to generalise, but much of the speech and language therapy provision to old age psychiatry will follow the definition given by Woods, although intervention via specific individual or group therapy sessions is certainly not unknown. Prior to embarking on the 'management' as such, the clinician will need to determine specific aims of the input, and have clear reasons as to how or why the client will benefit. This is especially the case with clients who have a dementia, where the focus is most often upon compensation for the difficulties observed, in order to facilitate the optimal level of communication. Lubinski (1991) states that 'all demented patients have the right to maintain optimal use of their functional residual communication abilities' (p.242). This relates to a common theme in dementia care: an enhanced quality of life through successful interaction with others, where the communication difficulties and resulting stress experienced by the caregivers will be reduced. Lubinski describes eight principles of communication management in order to promote individual strengths and provide communication opportunities for the client. These principles provide an excellent and clear overview upon which to base the goals of any communication-related intervention within old age psychiatry. Following the assessment of the client and once the aims of intervention are clear to the therapist, the most appropriate approach will become evident.

Direct input

Traditional speech and language therapy has usually involved the therapist and the client working together in the one-to-one situation, with the focus on impairment-based difficulties. This approach may be relevant to the old age psychiatry client group, depending on the nature and severity of the underlying disorder. The stroke patient with a presenting dysphasia or dysarthria and a history of depression is an example here. However, it is necessary to consider and allow for the mental, as well as the physical, illness during the therapy process. Those with early multi-infarct dementia may be candidates for individual therapy (Swinburn and Maxim 1996).

A further example is the elderly schizophrenic patient who presents with a mild tardive dyskinesia and dysarthria, worsened by ill-fitting dentures. It is often the speech and language therapist who may spot this, making the appropriate referral to remedy the situation, thus improving speech intelligibility. In another client, if there is any doubt over the diagnosis of dementia where specific language disorders are evident, it is necessary to give the opportunity of a trial period of direct speech and language therapy input, in order to assess the response to such input and therefore contribute to the diagnostic process. Other disorders benefiting from direct input are specific voice or fluency disorders.

Lubinski (1991) discusses working directly with patients in the early stages of dementia, either individually or in groups. Direct patient management strategies which are 'patient-generated' are described, to help with specific difficulties in understanding, expression and the use of language. Woods (1996) includes internal and external memory techniques and reduction of the cognitive demands placed upon people, in order to facilitate more successful communication. Recently, the use of counselling has been positively reported both for people with dementia and their carers (Whitsed-Lipinska 1998). Muir (1996) states that the training and knowledge base of speech and language therapists promotes skills in adopting a supportive, counselling-type role in working with clients. If traditional counselling is restricted with people who are unable to verbalise their thoughts and feelings, the speech and language therapist may be able to work non-verbally, promoting communication strengths and enabling expression. This is the background to Validation Therapy (Feil 1993), where the emotional content of expression is recognised rather than just the verbal composition, or what the person actually says. A client who constantly follows their carer, repeating a question about when is it time to catch the bus home (when they are living in residential accommodation which is their home) may be expressing insecurities about being in that care facility or insecurities about what has been left behind in their homes prior to becoming ill. To explore this possible insecurity might result in a reduction of the repetitious behaviour (Miesen and Jones 1997).

Indirect input

The speech and language therapist may decide not to work directly with the client, but rather serve to effect a change through modifying the communication styles around them. This includes working both with carers and the environment in which they are interacting, again to facilitate optimal communication function. The decision to adopt this approach may be taken if the client is presenting with a more severe level of communication or cognitive breakdown, or if there are few generalising effects of the direct intervention. It is extremely important, at this point, for the therapist to have a sound knowledge of the communicative level of the client and how they respond in different situations and interactions, including the reasons for communication breakdown. The therapist can then pass on this knowledge in discussion with the caregiver. Once the carer has a good understanding of the different client responses, they will be better able to modify their communication style in order to encourage maximal abilities from the client.

This process of enabling the carer to understand was evident in a study by Tanner and Daniels (1990), where the increased carer awareness of communication helped to define individual strategies, resulting in consistently enhanced interaction with their relatives. Barnes (personal communication) reports that helping carers in this way might diminish potentially difficult communication situations, increase fulfilment in the caregiving process, and in turn reduce the need to depend on institutions.

Throughout this process, the communicative environment cannot be neglected. The stereotyped but often still accurate view of a nursing home, with several elderly people seated around a very noisy television screen, none of whom appear to be interested in the programme content, induces a non-communicative image. Again it should not be forgotten that these people have the right to make choices. However, they need the opportunity to make these choices and this can only be achieved through the medium of communication. Lubinski (1991) devotes a whole chapter to practical environmental considerations. The importance of defining the nature of the environment in relation to individual, physical, topographical and social issues is described, together with the need to be able to identify the 'communication-impaired environment'.

Goldsmith (1996) also writes about the effects of the environment in providing opportunities for communication. The speech and language therapist is well able to advise on practical strategies to encourage these opportunities, benefiting both the client and their caregiver. The single most important factor for the speech and language therapist in old age psychiatry is multidisciplinary team working. All those who are part of the team, including the caregiver, will communicate both with the client and with each other, in order to provide successful care of and intervention with that client. Often the speech and language therapist will have only a small amount of the time to assess and provide input, taking perhaps a consultative role. They are therefore dependent upon the whole team, including the carers, to carry out any advice given. They are also dependent on feedback from the team to assess the effectiveness of any input or the progression of the illness. This is especially important in relation to the effects of medication on communication; a role of the speech and language therapist in this situation may just be to monitor and register specific change over time, with any alteration that is being made in the medication.

Zabihi and Bryan (1996) report that the client requires a multidisciplinary team in order to allow for a multidimensional view of the presenting symptoms and breakdown which are so often evident in old age psychiatry. This relates to assessment, diagnosis and care, so that every area of need may be addressed concurrently. They describe a 'core team' comprising professionals from medicine, psychiatry, nursing, social work, physiotherapy and occupational therapy. This should also include specific carers and even the clients themselves. Those external to this core, such as the clinical psychiatrist, speech and language therapist, dietitian, audiologist and dentist, will be requested to contribute as necessary. The core may vary, however, often depending on historical involvement and profile within the team. It may be argued that, as communication is paramount to the provision of 'good care', the speech and language therapist should be regarded as a core member of the team.

Clients with severe dementia

Speech and language therapists working in settings with these clients are often faced with questions from the staff about the type of service that it is possible and effective to offer. This is especially with regard to the severe memory and attention disorders that are often present, with speech that is either unintelligible or not able to be elicited. Another issue is that these clients have, in effect, a terminal illness, which again can result in queries about the usefulness of any intervention provided.

It can easily be argued, however, that a service that helps to enhance or preserve quality of life, at any level, is a worthwhile service. Speech and language therapy is able to offer such a service, purely due to the focus of maximising communication and positive interactions. The difficulty here is demonstrating effectiveness regarding impact upon quality of life. Lubinski (1991) suggests the evaluation of client–carer interactions, overall communication situations and the effect of specific strategies given. The measure may be in terms of reduction in carer frustration, stress or load. It may be in relation to the number of meaningful exchanges of information. The questions to be asked might be: 'Is the communication management effective?'; 'For whom is it effective?'; 'When is it effective?'; 'What techniques and strategies are effective?' (p.250).

Goldsmith (1996) reflects that 'communication is possible [with this client group], although it is often a difficult and complex process.' He acknowledges the significance of non-verbal communication, although this is often not recognised by the caregivers. Armstrong and Reymbaut (1996) report that within an expressed message, 55 per cent is visual information, such as facial expression or posture, 38 per cent is vocal, such as intonation or loudness, and 7 per cent is the content of the actual words that are spoken. In total then, the amount of information conveyed by the non-verbal part of the message is 93 per cent.

Kitwood (1993) also stresses the importance of non-verbal language in people with severe dementia, suggesting that the words in their conversations are not the most important information-carrying device, but rather accompany the more important non-verbal communication. Carers often struggle to understand the words of their demented relatives, becoming frustrated at the meaningless content. If they listened, however, to the gestures, the body language, the facial expression, the tone of voice, they might just understand the message communicated. By allowing this communication and interaction, there is the expression of feelings and opinion, and an association between the two parties involved. Validation therapy and validating approaches are again relevant here (Feil 1993).

In relation to this, it is essential to focus upon the whole of the interaction, with the carer making the effort to alter their mode of communication in order to facilitate the best communicative function possible (Jones 1992). Hamilton (1994) identified this when she examined language of one elderly female Alzheimer's patient from an interactional, socio-linguistic perspective, over a period of 4.5 years. During her introduction, she criticises the professional relationship in relation to communication competency. She describes a 'power relationship' between the client and the professional which she feels will inevitably affect the quality of the interaction. This influences how the client perceives the formality of the situation and expectations regarding performance.

So-called 'challenging behaviour' may be the result of the reduced quality of such interactions, or perhaps it could be related to miscommunications or communication breakdown. Goldsmith (1996) refers to wandering or aggression as examples of such behaviours in relation to clients not making themselves heard or understood. He urges that carers (including the multidisciplinary team) give time to understanding the nature of such behaviours and examine their own reactions in difficult communication situations. Maxim and Bryan (1993) suggest some solutions to verbal abuse which also incorporate the need to identify what the person is trying to convey by such behaviour. If speech and language therapists have assessed sufficiently, through consultation with the multidisciplinary team, they will be able to provide an overview to caregivers of communication strengths and needs for individual clients, giving advice and information to reduce any communication breakdown and improve function.

When working with clients who have severe dementia, and particularly within institutional settings, the most important mode of increasing awareness of communication is by the provision of training programmes for care staff.

Training programmes for care staff

Intervention in the UK has moved into two related areas: that of extending the role of the speech and language therapist into training programmes for care staff and caregivers and in specific training for communication partners of individual clients. There is clearly a need for training of care staff in communication skills and in communicating specifically with older people who have communication difficulties (Lubinski 1995; Orange *et al.* 1995), a need which does not seem to have been met within existing schemes such as NVQ, although there is potential to do so.

Rainbow, Painter and Bryan (1996) outline a programme devised for use in both ward and nursing home settings which included: the communication environment; communication skills and opportunity; stimulation and choice; communication disorders in older people; talking about specific clients; and swallowing/feeding. Working on an intensive basis with staff for up to one month and repeating this level of input approximately every 3/4 months improved the working relationship between the staff and the speech and language therapist. This scheme used video workshops, with brief clips of care staff and clients made in each setting, to provide the basis for discussion. The speech and language therapist acted as a facilitator rather than a trainer. Some training programmes have been published, allowing the speech and language therapist to use and adapt them for different contexts (Lester *et al.* 1994; Ripich and Ziol 1996; Stevens *et al.* 1992) The Communicate programme (ADA 1995) is provided on a bought-in basis, delivered by SLTs who have been accredited by ADA. Validation therapy is also an approach which requires a training programme (Feil 1993). Handbooks for care assistants which include information on communication and communication difficulty are also available but there has been little formal evaluation of how much they are used or of how useful they might be, although Toner (1987) found that written guides for carers can be effective in providing information.

Some interventions have been targeted at communication between individual clients and their carers. Shadden (1995) used discourse analysis successfully with individual residents of a nursing home and their carers. Tanner and Daniels (1990) observed communication between people with dementia and their relatives, identifying facilitative and non-facilitative behaviours which were then used in workshops with the relatives. Bryan and Maxim (1998) describe the use of life stories and conversation analysis to increase communication between nursing home residents and their carers. Clark and Witte (1990) used applied pragmatics to promote communication and care management.

The evaluation of training programmes with speech and language therapy involvement suggest that they benefit carers and caregivers. In addition, they may have a benefit outcome for the client, although measurement of such outcomes is not always easy. After an intensive educational and support programme, people with dementia had an increased chance of remaining at home (Brodarty and Peters 1991). Using a validating approach, Clarke (1997) reports on a single case study where a client's medication for challenging behaviour was reduced after a combination of staff training and individual input (see also Bryan and Maxim 1998).

Feeding, swallowing and eating

The role of speech and language therapy in dysphagia has been questioned in a recent discussion forum. Speech and language therapists discussed the idea that it is an area for specifically trained 'swallowing therapists', leaving the rest of the profession to manage the reportedly neglected area of communication (*Bulletin*, August 1998). Whether or not the profession feels comfortable with its role in dysphagia, however, feeding and swallowing are clinical areas that speech and language therapists are now extensively involved in, with specialist skills that are readily applicable.

The prevalence of feeding and swallowing difficulties in residential or nursing home settings is significant. Steele *et al.* (1997) administered a mealtime screening tool to 349 residents in a home for the elderly. They showed that 87 per cent of the residents presented with what they described as 'mealtime difficulties' and 68 per cent with specific dysphagia. An earlier Australian study (O'Brien and Barrow 1991) observed 83 nursing home residents with an average age of 84 years, over the course of a meal. They showed that 53 per cent had swallowing difficulties relating to reduced oral, pharyngeal or laryngeal function. Poor limb function, posture, dentition and/or cognition resulted in eating difficulties with 24 per cent of the residents. Of the 22 residents with a chest infection, 90 per cent had swallowing problems. Although these studies are focused generally on elderly populations and not specifically with the cognitively impaired, the implications of such studies on the need for specialist input regarding feeding and swallowing is significant. In view of the specific knowledge held by speech and language therapists about oral, pharyngeal and laryngeal function, they are in a prime position to offer the relevant skills to feeding and swallowing disorders.

The role with elderly people, and especially those with mental health problems, differs from other impairment groups seen by speech and language therapists in relation to a number of factors. The effect of age-related changes on the swallowing process must be considered, although previous research is not in total agreement about the precise nature of these changes (Tracey *et al.* 1989; Ekberg and Feinberg 1991; Nilsson *et al.* 1996). Feinberg (1996) distinguishes between 'primary aging' (or age-related changes affecting the eating process) and secondary or external, disease-related changes; however, he advises clinicians to show more interest in 'individual aging'.

The effect of medication on eating or swallowing is prominent, especially with regard to those prescribed in mental health settings. Complaints of a dry mouth and difficulties with swallowing are commonly related to medication. Involuntary oro-muscular movements or tardive dyskinesia may often be associated with specific medication, as are extra-pyramidal side-effects. Speech and language therapists should therefore ensure that they take a full drug history and consider the effects of medication prior to giving advice.

It is necessary to differentiate between behavioural eating disorders and actual swallowing difficulties in order to establish the presence of an underlying dysphagia. Feinberg (1997) defines eating as the total voluntary process that occurs prior to the swallow reflex, stating that 'the majority of oral intake disability in the elderly is due to eating rather than swallowing impairment' (p.51). Kaatzke (1992) describes the impact on both of these through the different phases of dementia, but relates that the role of the speech and language therapist is one 'in which our opinion will be appreciated and considered but not necessarily implemented' (p.12). Again, the multidisciplinary approach is absolutely paramount, with a focus primarily on maximising remaining function.

Ethical questions will arise because of the type of assessment to be completed: for example, access to and the appropriacy of invasive procedures such as videofluoroscopy. The key issues when giving advice are: whether to treat it all, how to balance safety, quality of life and well being/distress issues (Clibbens 1996). If the very elderly person who is obviously aspirating fluids, and whose medical prognosis is poor, constantly asks for a cup of tea, should this be denied for reasons of safety or distress, or should it be given with advice to facilitate the most safe (but not risk-free) mode of swallowing? The speech and language therapist should not expect to answer these questions alone, but as a member of a team, providing useful information in order to help the decision-making process.

Summary

The government White Paper *The New NHS: Modern, Dependable* (DoH 1997) sets out an agenda for setting, delivering and monitoring quality standards which will include the provision of clinical audit, risk management and quality assurance. Clinical governance should provide an impetus to better evaluations of the role of the speech and language therapist working with older people who have mental health problems. These problems may include communication and swallowing, making it important to consider the patient holistically in any assessment or intervention offered. Multidisciplinary working is paramount; the speech and language therapist cannot work alone. Communication is common to all professionals in this area but it is the speech and language therapist's responsibility to disentangle the patient's disorder and suggest strategies to maximise strengths and meet needs. Old age psychiatry is an area in which speech and language therapists have clarified their role but that role needs a higher profile, backed up by research demonstrating evidence-based practice. RCSLT guidelines in *Communicating Quality 2* are evidence of the place of speech and language therapy in old age psychiatry and there are also two active specific interest groups in the United Kingdom (North of England and South of England) through which speech and language therapists can receive professional support and maintain a network. Overall, it is an area of work that is sure to expand into the millennium.

References

Action for Dysphasic Adults (1995) *National Directory: Register of Language Opportunities for those with Dysphasia and their Families.* London: ADA.

Action for Dysphasic Adults (1996) *Communicate: A Practical Workshop for the Professional and Lay Carers of Communicatively Impaired People.* London: Action for Dysphasic Adults.

Armstrong, L. (1996) *Armstrong Naming Test.* London: Whurr.

Armstrong, L., Bayles, K.A., Borthwick, S. and Tomoeda, C.K. (1996) Use of the Arizona Battery for Communication Disorders of Dementia in the UK. *European Journal of Disorders of Communication 31*, 2, 171–192.

Armstrong, L. and Reymbaut, E. (1996) *Getting the Message Across: An Introduction to Interpersonal Communication for Staff Working with People who have Dementia.* Stirling: Dementia Services Development Centre.

Bayles, K.A. and Tomoeda, C. (1993) *The Arizona Battery for Communication Disorders of Dementia.* Oxford: Winslow Press.

Bayles, K.A. and Tomoeda, C. (1994) *Functional Linguistic Communication Inventory.* Tucson, AZ: Canyonlands Publishing.

Brodarty, H. and Peters, K.E. (1991) Cost effectiveness of a training program for dementia carers. *International Psychogeriatrics 3*, 11–23.

Bryan, K. and Maxim, J. (1998) Enabling care staff to relate to older communication disabled people. *International Journal of Language and Communication Disorders 33*, Supplement, 121–125.

Bulletin (1998) Dysphagia: hard for therapists to swallow. Issue 556. London: RCSLT.

Clarke, F. (1997) Korsakoff Syndrome: A Validating Approach.

MSc Thesis. London University: University College London.

Clark, L. and Witte, K. (1990) Nature and efficacy of communication management in Alzheimer's disease. In R. Lubinski (ed) *Dementia and Communication.* Philadelphia, PA: B.C. Decker.

Clibbens, R. (1996) Eating, ethics and Alzheimer's. *Nursing Times 92*, 50, 29–30.

Department of Health (1997) *The New NHS: Modern, Dependable.* Command Paper 3807.

Eccles, M., Clarke, J., Livingstone, M., Freemantle, N. and Mason, J. (1998) North of England evidence based guidelines development project: guideline for the primary care management of dementia. *British Medical Journal 317*, 19 September, 802–806.

Ekberg, O. and Feinberg, M. (1991) Altered swallowing function in elderly patients without dysphagia: radiological findings in 56 cases. *American Journal of Radiology 156*, 1181–1184.

Enderby, P. (1997) *Therapy Outcome Measures: Speech-Language Pathology.* London: Singular.

Feil, N. (1993) *The Validation Breakthrough: Simple Techniques for Communicating with People with Alzheimer's Type Dementia.* Baltimore: Health Professions Press.

Feinberg, M.J. (1996) Editorial: A perspective on age-related changes of the swallowing mechanism and their clinical significance. *Dysphagia 11*, 185–186.

Feinberg, M.J. (1997) Editorial: Swallowing versus eating impairment in nursing home residents. *Dysphagia 12*, 51.

Folstein, M.F., Folstein, S.E. and McHugh, P.R. (1975) Mini-mental state – a practical method for grading the cognitive state of patients for the clinician. *Journal of Psychiatric Research 12*, 189–198.

Goldsmith, M. (1996) *Hearing the Voice of People with Dementia.* London: Jessica Kingsley Publishers.

Hamilton, H.E. (1994) *Conversations with an Alzheimer's Patient.* Cambridge: Cambridge University Press.

Hodkinson, M. (1972) Evaluation of a mental test score for assessment of mental impairment in the elderly. *Age and Ageing 1*, 233–238.

Holden, U.P. and Woods, R.T. (eds) (1995) *Positive Approaches to Dementia Care.* Edinburgh: Churchill Livingstone.

Jones, G. (1992) A communication model for dementia. In B. Miesen and G. Jones (eds) *Care Giving in Dementia, Research and Application.* London: Tavistock/Routledge.

Kaatzke, M. (1992) Swallowing difficulties in patients with dementia. *Australian Communication Quarterly*, Spring, 9–12.

Lester, R., Boddy, M., Evans, J. and Trewhitt, P. (1994) *Care staff training. Volume 1: Communication Disability.* Sheffield: Communication Therapy/Community Health.

Lubinski, R. (1991) *Dementia and Communication.* Ontario, BC: Decker.

Lubinski, R. (1995) State of the art perspectives on communication in nursing homes. *Topics in Language Disorders 15*, 1–19.

Maxim, J. and Bryan, K. (1993) How not to give as good as you get. *Journal of Dementia Care 2*, 1, 25–27.

Maxim, J. and Bryan, K. (1994) *Language of the Elderly.* London: Whurr.

Melzer, D., Ely, M. and Brayne, C. (1997) Cognitive impairment in elderly people: population based estimate of the future in England, Scotland, and Wales. *British Medical Journal 315*, 462.

Miesen, B. and Jones, G. (eds) (1997) *Care-giving in Dementia, Research and Applications.* London: Tavistock/Routledge.

Miller, E. (1996) The assessment of dementia. In R.G. Morris (ed) *The Cognitive Neuropsychology of Alzheimer-type Dementia.* Oxford: Oxford University Press.

Muir, N. (1996) Management approaches involving carers. In K. Bryan and J. Maxim (eds) *Communication Disability and the Psychiatry of Old Age.* London: Whurr.

Nilsson, H., Ekberg, O., Olsson, R. and Hindfelt, B. (1996) Quantitative aspects of swallowing in an elderly nondysphagic population. *Dysphagia 11,* 180–184.

Norris, A. (1986) *Reminiscence with Elderly People.* Great Britain: Winslow Press.

O'Brien, P.J. and Barrow, D. (1991) Prevalence of eating problems of nursing home residents. *Australian Journal of Human Communication Disorders 19,* 1, 35–43.

Orange, J.B., Ryan, E.B., Meredith, S.D. and MacLean, M.J. (1995) Application of a communication enhancement model for long-term care residents with Alzheimer's disease. *Topics in Language Disorders 15,* 20–35.

Pattie, A.M. (1981) A survey version of the Clifton Assessment Procedures for the Elderly. *British Journal of Clinical Psychology 20,* 173–178.

Perkins, L., Whitworth, A. and Lesser, R. (1997) *Conversation Analysis Profile for People with Cognitive Impairment.* London: Whurr.

Rainbow, D., Painter, C. and Bryan, K. (1996) Working in the community – care and legislation. In K. Bryan and J. Maxim (eds) *Communication Disability and the Psychiatry of Old Age.* London: Whurr.

Raleigh, V.S. (1997) The demographic timebomb: will not explode in Britain for the foreseeable future. *British Medical Journal 315,* 442–443.

Ripich, D. and Ziol, E. (1996) A survey of service provision to the cognitively impaired in the USA. In K. Bryan and J. Maxim (eds) *Communication Disability and the Psychiatry of Old Age.* London: Whurr.

Royal College of Speech and Language Therapists (1996) *Communicating Quality 2.* London: RCSLT.

Saxton, J., McConigle, K.L., Swihart, A.A. and Boller, F. (1993) *The Severe Impairment Battery Test.* Bury St Edmunds, Suffolk: Thames Valley Test Company.

Shadden, B. (1995) The use of discourse analysis and procedures for communication programming in long-term care facilities. *Topics in Language Disorders 15,* 75–86.

Steele, C.M., Greenwood, C., Ens, I., Robertson, C. and Seidman-Carlson, R. (1997) Mealtime difficulties in a home for the aged: not just dysphagia. *Dysphagia 12,* 43–50.

Stevens, S.J. (1992) Differentiating the language disorder in dementia – the potential of a screening test. *European Journal of Disorders of Communication 27,* 275–288.

Stevens, S.J., Le May, M., Gravell, R. and Cook, K. (1992) *Working with Elderly People.* London: Whurr.

Swinburn, K. and Maxim, J. (1996) Multi-infarct dementia – a special case for treatment? In K. Bryan and J. Maxim (eds) *Communication Disability and the Psychiatry of Old Age.* London: Whurr.

Tanner, B.B. and Daniels, K.A. (1990) An observational study of communication between carers and their relatives with dementia. *Care of the Elderly 2,* 6, 247–250.

Toner, H.L. (1987) Effectiveness of a written guide for carers of dementia sufferers. *British Journal of Clinical and Social Psychology 5,* 1, 24–26.

Tracey, J.F., Logemann, J.A., Kahrilas, P.J., Jacob, P., Kobara, M. and Krugler, C. (1989) Preliminary observations of the effects of age on oropharyngeal deglutition. *Dysphagia 4,* 90–94.

Vogel, D. and Carter, J.E. (1995) *The Effects of Drugs on Communication Disorders.* San Diego: Singular Publishing Group.

Whitsed-Lipinska, D. (1998) Counselling services for people with dementia. *The Journal of Dementia Care 7,* 5, 10–11.

Woods, B. (1996) Cognitive approaches to the management of dementia. In R.G. Morris (ed) *The Cognitive Neuropsychology of Alzheimer-type Dementia.* Oxford: Oxford University Press.

Zabihi, K. and Bryan, K. (1996) The team approach to working with the elderly mentally ill. In K. Bryan and J. Maxim (eds) *Communication Disability and the Psychiatry of Old Age.* London: Whurr.

CHAPTER 17

Child Psychiatry

Alison Wintgens

This chapter stands somewhat apart in a book that is largely concerned with adult mental health issues. Consequently it will attempt to cover a wide range of aspects which could be the subject of an independent book.

In the first part there will be a brief description of the speciality of Child Psychiatry, looking at its history, structure and purpose. Then it will consider the classification, prevalence and assessment of child psychiatric disorders. It is not appropriate for this part to be lengthy. There are various good books on the subject: particularly recommendable is the excellent, practical and readable introductory book by Goodman and Scott (1997) and the comprehensive and detailed volume by Rutter, Taylor and Hersov (1994).

The second part of the chapter will briefly define communication disorders and look at their relationship to psychopathology. This will be followed by a discussion on the role of the speech and language therapist (SLT) in communication assessment, intervention and multi-disciplinary work with this population. These areas are less frequently described. A recent American book edited by Rogers-Adkinson and Griffith (1999) is to be recommended.

Throughout the chapter inevitably there will be aspects that are similar to the adult field and those that are rather different, with the opportunity to consider what we can learn from each other.

Definition, history and structure

Child and adolescent psychiatry (child psychiatry for short) is concerned with disorders of emotions, behaviour and relationships in children up to school leaving age.

Historically the speciality has gradually developed over the century. The multidisciplinary nature of the work took shape in the 1920s, with the child guidance movement which started in the USA and spread to London. Parallel specialised clinics within health services were also set up in hospitals and the term 'child psychiatry' emerged in the 1930s. However the most significant advances have been made since the Second World War.

Nowadays most health authorities have a Mental Health Trust that includes a specialist Child and Adolescent Mental Health Service (CAMHS) incorporating the various forms in which the service was previously delivered. As far as the NHS is concerned, recent guidance has been that child mental health work can be seen to operate at four different levels, or tiers:

- Tier 1 – professionals in contact with children who can influence mental health but are not primarily employed to do so (e.g. health visitors, SLTs, GPs).

- Tier 2 – professionals employed to work solo with child mental health problems in places like health clinics (e.g. clinical psychologists, clinical nurse specialists).

- Tier 3 – multidisciplinary teams based in hospitals or community settings.

- Tier 4 – highly specialised clinics, such as for children with gender identity problems or anorexia nervosa, as well as psychiatric in-patient or day-patient units.

Tiers 2–4 are the specialised parts of the service.

It follows that child mental health teams (at Tiers 3 and 4) vary in size and in the degree and nature of specialisation. Consequently the range of disciplines from which the team members are drawn varies somewhat. A list of possible team members is shown in Table 17.1.

Table 17.1: Possible members of child mental health teams	
Most usually found	**Sometimes found**
Child and adolescent psychiatrist	Occupational therapist
Clinical child psychologist	Speech and language therapist
(Psychiatric) Social worker	Community paediatrician
Child psychotherapist	Educational psychologist
Community child psychiatric nurse (Clinical nurse specialist)	Arts therapists – Music, drama, art, dance and movement
Family therapist (Often social worker or nurse)	Specialist teacher/educational therapist

Assessment, classification, prevalence and description of common child psychiatric problems and their management

Terminology in child psychiatry (or Child Mental Health) is inconsistent, both amongst providers and users of the service. To begin with, the problems of children who are seen in child psychiatry can be described in a number of terms: 'psychiatric disorder' is the common term, whereas 'mental illness' is used for severe disorders such as schizophrenia. Parents and older children and adolescents can feel that there is a stigma attached to being seen in a psychiatric or child mental health department or clinic, and having psychiatric or even psychological problems. To get round this, names such as 'child and family clinic' have been adopted, and it can be more helpful to talk about 'emotional or behavioural disorders (EBD)' although there are limitations in that term, particularly because some problems are reflected in relationships and distorted psychological development.

Assessment

When referrals are accepted and assigned to one or more team members, an assessment is carried out which involves several stages. Clinicians working with adults will note that in a CAMHS information is sought not only from the referred patient but also those around them. These are the likely steps:

- Taking a history from the parents, covering the presenting problem, the child's current functioning in social relationships and independence, the family history and the child's personal history.

- Seeing the child alone for interview and observation as appropriate.

- Observing interactions between family members or carrying out a whole family interview.

- Obtaining information from school.

- Doing a physical examination, although this may be purely observational.

- Carrying out further investigations in some circumstances, such as psychometric or speech and language assessments, or special neurological or genetic investigations.

It is then usual to reach not just a diagnosis but also a formulation of the child's problems. This gives a broader understanding of the aetiology taking into account the unique factors within and around the child, evaluating any vulnerability or protective factors and giving pointers for management and prognosis.

Classification

Classification of child psychiatric disorders is a complex issue. Traditionally there are two main classifications: the World Health Organisation's International Classification of Diseases (ICD-10), the official system in Britain, and the American Psychiatric Association's Diagnostic and Statistical Manual (DSM-IV). Although quick and relatively simple to use, and often used by adult mental health services, many children's clinicians feel these classifications are rigid and less appropriate. To choose only one diagnostic (psychiatric) code can render the information meaningless for clinical, audit, management and research purposes because child patients often have more than one diagnosis. The problem is illustrated when trying to classify a child who has both autism and mental retardation, or one who has attention deficit hyperactivity disorder (ADHD), a language disorder and a history of abuse. This is an important issue since a developmental problem associated with a psychiatric disorder in a particular child may not ordinarily be recorded as a diagnosis. It has probably led to the underdiagnosis of developmental disorders (such as language disorders) in children with psychiatric disorders.

So-called multiaxial approaches are a partial answer to this by encouraging the clinician to make a statement in each of a series of areas. For example, a special version of ICD-10 offers six axes – psychiatric, developmental, intellectual, medical, social and psychosocial disability (or adaptive functioning).

Prevalence of common problems

Most studies report that overall 10–25 per cent of children have distressing psychological symptoms or behaviour problems, and about 5 per cent have a significant level of impairment. The problems are more common in inner city areas, more common in boys than girls until puberty, and overall more common in adolescents than younger children.

The largest proportion of children and adolescents are referred to the service with antisocial or disruptive behaviour. Anxiety and depressive disorders are also common, although it has been suggested by Goodman and Scott (1997) that it is hard to estimate the frequency of these emotional disorders since their impact is less significant. Referrals of hyperkinetic disorders have increased sharply, as have those of younger children with eating disorders.

Child psychiatry treatment

The commonest treatments for a child or adolescent with mental health problems are various forms of family therapy, supportive psychotherapy and behavioural treatment. Group work may be found in some centres, as may parent training programmes, cognitive-behavioural therapy and individual psychodynamic therapy. Medication is used with relatively few children, usually as part of a multimodal treatment programme.

Classification of disorders of communication

Terminology in this field is complicated by the fact that many of the words are used to mean different things in different contexts. In a professional context it is obviously important to understand their technical meaning.

First it is important to distinguish *speech*, that is the production and effective use of meaningful sounds to form words, from *language*, which refers to the conveying of concepts and ideas through symbols, such as spoken or written words and signs. Some children just have *speech disorders*, that is difficulty pronouncing and using the sounds in words. Others may have a combination of *speech and language disorders*. *Language disorders* can be divided into *receptive language disorders*, difficulty with verbal comprehension, understanding or decoding, and *expressive disorders*, problems translating ideas into words and sentences.

There are different aspects of language: *syntax* is synonymous with grammar, *semantics* deals with the meaning of words, and *pragmatics* refers to the ability to use and decipher language appropriately for social interaction to take place effectively in different contexts.

Speech may be divided into *articulation*, the forming of the sounds, and *phonology* which refers to the use and patterns of the sounds.

There is also *prosody*, which refers to pitch (often assessed in intonation), volume, rhythm and fluency.

Relationship between child psychiatric disorders and disorders of communication

There has been an awareness of the co-existence of children's emotional/behavioural problems and various communication disorders for a long time. The reason for the connection is obvious even to a lay person. Verbal communication is important for operating effectively in society and children with language impairment are likely to be frustrated, socially isolated and at a disadvantage educationally. A range of studies carried out in the last twenty years and evaluated by Donahue, Hartas and Cole (1999) has sought evidence of the size and nature of the relationship. Yet the implications of these findings are slow to take effect in terms of awareness by health and education professionals, and availability of adequate language assessment and treatment for this client group.

Evidence of co-morbidity

The literature seeks evidence of co-morbidity in two ways, primarily by looking for speech and language disorders in the child psychiatric population (or amongst children with emotional and behavioural disorders), and also the reverse, evidence of emotional/behavioural disorders in children in speech and language clinics.

At first glance the incidence of disorders of communication in studies of child psychiatry populations seems varied and sometimes startlingly high. Around 5 per cent of the general child population have significant communication disorders whereas the literature on child psychiatry out-patients shows between 25 per cent and 65 per cent (for example, Cohen *et al.* 1993). Remarkably high figures appear in a study of 50 pre-adolescent in-patients (Giddan, Milling and Campbell 1996) where 49 of them, that is 98 per cent, had some degree of communication problems. A further study by Camarata, Hughes and Ruhl (1988) found that 97 per cent of children with behaviour disorders in special education classes had significant disorders of communication.

The diversity in the figures of the various studies inevitably stems from the different definitions of the nature and severity of the various communication disorders and the measures of psychopathology in the populations that are studied. Rutter and Mawhood (1991) outline six main methodological problems and look critically at the most significant studies. There are also difficulties in getting good assessment data from these children, which is discussed later in the chapter. Nevertheless, there is overwhelming evidence of strong co-morbidity of disorders of communication and psychiatric disorder in childhood.

Undetected communication disorders

The high incidence of *undetected* disorders of communication in children with emotional and behavioural problems is also of concern (Cohen, Davine and Meloche-Kelly 1989, Giddan *et al.* 1996). The author's experience as a speech and language therapist in a CAMHS would echo this, judging by the number of children referred for their first communication assessment. The situation is particularly significant because there is some indication of more severe psycho-pathology in children where language disorder has been unrecognised (Cohen and Lipsett 1991).

The most obvious reasons for overlooking these children's communication problems are examined by Cross (1997). She points to the understandable preoccupation with what is often challenging or difficult behaviour, and also a lack of training about speech and language disorders for professionals working in this area. Giddan, Wahl and Brogan (1995) state that communication and communication disorders are essential issues in child psychiatry training and suggest goals for a training programme. The lack of speech and language therapists in CAMHS and EBD schools also seems to be both a symptom and a cause of the problem of undetected disorders of communication.

Nature and severity of psychiatric disorders in children with disorders of communication

There have been some attempts to describe the types of emotional and behavioural disorders of children with various communication disorders. Gordon (1991) describes speech and language impairment leading to excessive temper tantrums, withdrawal aggression or bizarre behaviour. Cohen *et al.* (1993) found that children with unsuspected language disorders were more likely to show oppositional behaviour, hyperactivity and aggression.

Nature and severity of the various disorders of communication in children with psychiatric disorders

A little work has been done to analyse the nature and severity of the different communication disorders in children with psychiatric disorders. There is evidence that language disorders have more serious effects on children's behaviour than do speech disorders. Baker and Cantwell (1982) found that children with pure language disorders, followed by a second group with speech and language disorders, had both higher rates and different patterns of psychiatric disorders than those with pure speech disorders. Giddan (1991) found children with emotional/behavioural disorders most commonly had problems with semantics, pragmatics and listening skills.

Long-term psychosocial effects

In the study by Beitchman *et al.* (1996), children with receptive and extensive speech/language problems at age 5 demonstrated greater behavioural disturbance seven years later than the control group; and children without receptive language problems showed superior social adjustment.

Rutter and Mawhood (1991) found that severe receptive disorders in boys of normal non-verbal IQ led to serious social abnormalities and, in a few, psychoses in adult life: fewer lived independently, they lacked vocational training, encountered difficulties in employment and had deficits in friendships and love relationships.

How and why the two areas are linked

There are several explanations for the association between communication disorders and emotional/behavioural disorders. The most obvious thing is to consider whether one area causes the other, an important consideration although it may be over-simplistic. Viewed this way, a stronger case can probably be made for communication disorders leading to emotional/behavioural disorders. Poor verbal communication can lead to social rejection, educational failure and low self-esteem, out of which emotional and behavioural problems grow. Children with developmental language disorders are also hard to parent: they cause parents high levels of stress and may cause a parent to be over-protective or rejecting, which in turn can lead to the child having emotional or behavioural problems. A linear causation in the opposite direction is possible though less plausible: if a child has a psychiatric disorder, is perhaps hyperactive, irritable or unresponsive, the language stimulation they receive from their carers may be reduced sufficiently to cause language impairment. A third possibility is that a common cause, such as neglect, deafness or pervasive developmental disorders, gives rise to both the emotional/behavioural disorder and the disorder of communication.

In the past there has been a tendency to ask which area is primary or secondary. The author (Wintgens 1996a) explains why it is best to avoid these terms: they are again over-simplistic and for some people refer to chronology (which started first and caused the other) and to others dominance (which is the major or most evident). Moreover there is a danger of children with deficits in both areas falling between help from different services. A speech and language therapist may delay giving support, advice or treatment for a child thought to have a primary behaviour problem while the psychologist decides that work on the child's language will result in improvement to behaviour. For clinical purposes the two areas of communication disorders and emotional/behavioural disorders should be regarded as having a complex and interlinked relationship, and management of the child by either the SLT or the psychologist must take both areas into account.

Involvement of speech and language therapy

Given the evidence for the co-existence of psychiatric and communication disorders, one might expect routinely to find speech and language therapists in settings such as a CAMHS and an EBD school. Unfortunately this is not the case. Therapists have been slow to define their role with this population, and professionals in child mental health and education have been slow to see the advantages of multidisciplinary work with speech and language therapists.

Equally a greater knowledge of emotional/behavioural disorders and more confidence in their management is needed by most paediatric speech and language therapists regardless of their clinical setting. Awareness of local psychology and psychiatry services and when to refer is also crucial.

There is some indication that the situation is changing. Whereas the Royal College of Speech and Language Therapists (RCSLT) just had a special interest group in adult psychiatry in the mid-1980s, since 1994 there has also been a child and adolescent version. A paper entitled 'Emotional and behavioural problems in children – a growing awareness?' (Wintgens 1996a) was presented at the golden jubilee conference of the RCSLT. There has also been more literature written by SLTs in the 1990s (Burgess and Bransby 1990; Cross 1997; Law and Conway 1992; Wintgens 1996a, b), although more extensive publications perhaps in the form of collaborative research are desperately needed. Courses for SLTs on emotional/behavioural disorders, such as those run by the charities AFASIC and I-CAN, have become more frequent and popular.

Specialist SLT posts exist within a CAMHS in a few areas, and in some EBD schools and settings run by social services and charitable bodies for foster care. In some areas a specific SLT in a general community clinic is designated to make links with the local CAMHS. This may be a start, but ideally the SLT should be on-site and part of the multidisciplinary team in view of the complexity of many of the children and some of their families' difficulties in attending appointments.

Role of SLT on multidisciplinary teams

Gualtieri *et al.* (1983) state that 'speech and language therapists seem to be much more aware of psychiatric problems in their clients than psychiatrists and psychologists are of language disorders in theirs'. Fifteen years later there still seems to be a need for SLTs to inform team members of the importance of recognising and assessing communication disorders. In addition, psychiatric assessment and treatment is largely verbal so there may be a need to advise other team members on an individual child's language levels.

Many authors, such as Kotsopoulos and Boodoosingh (1987), suggest routine language screening of children referred to child psychiatry, particularly in view of the number of previously undiagnosed communication disorders that have emerged in the various studies. Screening itself is a major task and a controversial business, and care should be taken to ensure it is as sensitive, specific and predictive as possible. It might be appropriate for new entrants to EBD schools, but in settings such as a CAMHS with vast numbers of referrals perhaps emphasis should be on improving the skill of colleagues at recognising those who are most at risk.

Suitable additional training and skills for SLTs

As with all specialist areas of work, basic undergraduate training alone is insufficient to equip an SLT to work in child psychiatry. Some further training is necessary for three main reasons. First, there are some useful techniques and approaches to incorporate into the therapist's repertoire. A second reason is the importance of gaining further knowledge of the skills of colleagues, both to assist co-working and to indicate when to recommend a child for a particular type of management. Lastly, greater psychological awareness of oneself and others is crucial in this area of work. An informal survey of therapists working in the field and belonging to the RCSLT's special interest group in emotional/behavioural problems shows that clinicians value and draw from the following range:

- a good knowledge of the theory and use of behavioural treatment methods
- an introduction to systemic family work
- counselling skills
- some knowledge and/or experience of psychotherapy
- educational therapy and therapeutic teaching
- play therapy.

Clearly to some extent the choice depends on personal preference and the nature of one's job. Also if further training is achieved it is important to define whether one is working as an SLT who happens to have additional skills, or, for example, as a play therapist.

Communication assessment

A speech and language therapist's assessment of the communication of a child with psychiatric problems is in many ways similar to that of any child with complex special needs. However, it is worth emphasising certain points which may be particularly significant for this client group, such as how the family and child may present and be engaged, and principles about the various ways of gathering assessment data.

How the child and family may present

For many reasons the presentation of these children can be a considerable challenge to the therapist who needs to assess them. They are often emotionally vulnerable, with low self-esteem and a ready fear of failure. In some this is manifested in withdrawn behaviour or even mutism, while others may be more assertively unco-operative and disinhibited. Many have deficits in the expected levels of attention, concentration and co-operation; in addition, separation from their parents may be an issue even within the room.

Most parents are somewhat anxious when they bring their child for any assessment, but this may be heightened given the nature of the department they are visiting and if their child is exhibiting particularly worrying or stressful behaviour. The parents may be confused or suspicious about who they are visiting and why, and may have past negative experiences of mental illness in the family, mental health services or people seen to be 'in authority'. They may not understand the reason for investigating their child's communication, being absorbed by concerns about their difficult behaviour or feeling pessimistic about the value of speech and language.

How to engage with the family

Given the ways in which the child and parents may present it is particularly important that the assessment is selective but thorough. These families do not want endless appointments, involving time, money and missing school; yet the children are complex and the therapist should aim to provide a level of expertise which the family would not get in a non-specialised service.

A good rapport with both child and parents may need a little more attention than usual. A successful contract is based on good communication and clear information about what to expect, why certain procedures will take place and to what purpose. Time should be spent ensuring the child also knows why he or she has come and what they need to do. If the therapist can work in partnership with the family the prognosis for assessment and intervention will be optimal.

Standardised assessments

Standardised batteries have their place but should be used with caution. It is undeniably important to get valid and reliable objective measurements of the child's language levels, especially as this may not have been achieved before, but to put a vulnerable child through testing should only be undertaken after due consideration and not automatically.

The various assessments that a therapist may use will be familiar to speech and language therapists in other clinical settings. However, depending on the diversity of both age and intellectual level of the children and adolescents, experience in administering a wide range of tests may be required. Information about the most commonly used tests is given in Table 17.2.

Administration of standardised tests needs to be flexible while adhering to the necessary criteria for validity. The therapist should take into account the optimum timing of carrying out tests, for example waiting a while with a child who is 'slow to warm up'. Sometimes the tests need to be approached in very small stages over a number of sessions, and incentives such as stickers should be given judiciously. It may be advantageous to 'test to the limits'; in other words (perhaps with a child with ADHD) to carry out all test items rather than stop as instructed at the test ceiling, which may be four consecutive errors, in order to get the fullest picture of what the child can achieve.

Table 17.2 Commonly used assessments of language and play

Test	Age	Purpose
British Picture Vocabulary Scale II (BPVS II)	3–16 years	Assesses understanding of vocabulary by pointing to one of four pictures
Clinical Evaluation of Language Fundamentals – Revised – UK (CELF)	5–16 years	11 sub-tests to assess semantics and syntax receptively and expressively
Clinical Evaluation of Language Fundamentals – Pre-school (Pre-school CELF)	3–7 years	Measures semantic and syntactic language receptively and expressively
Pragmatics Profile of Everyday Communication Skills in Children	9 months – 10 years	Interviews parents (and teachers) to assess a child's communicative functions, response to communication, interaction and conversation
Pre-school Language Scale-3 – UK (PLS-3)	0–6 years	Measures expressive and receptive language
Pre-Verbal Communication Schedule (PVCS)	Any age	Checklist to assess communication skills of those with little or no speech
Receptive-Expressive Emergent Language Scale (REEL)	0–3 years	Checklist to evaluate expressive and receptive language
Renfrew Action Picture Test (RAPT)	3–8 years	Elicits samples of expressive language in response to 10 pictures to assess information and grammatical structures – good for screening
Renfrew Bus Story	3–8 years	Elicits continuous expressive language through retelling a story
Renfrew Word Finding Vocabulary Test	3–8 years	Tests expressive vocabulary through naming pictures
Reynell Developmental Language Scales III	15 months – 7 years	Uses toys, pictures and finger puppets to assess comprehension and expressive language
Symbolic Play Test	1–3 years	Assesses early concept formation and symbolisation
Test for Reception of Grammar (TROG)	4–12 years	Tests comprehension of grammatical structures by pointing to one of four pictures
Test of Pretend Play (TOPP)	1–6 years	Assesses symbolic play in structured and unstructured situations

Test of Word Finding (TWF)	6–12 years	Tests word finding skills – accuracy and speed of naming
Test of Adolescent/Adult Word Finding (TAWF)	12+ years	Test word finding skills – accuracy and speed of naming
Test of Word Knowledge (TWK)	5–17 years	Semantic and lexical knowledge assessed receptively and expressively

Having completed standardised assessments the interpretation of test performance and discussion of the resulting test scores are critical in order to use the data to the full. Indeed, an abnormal finding might lead to exploration of further different tests. Indications for therapy and management guidelines can be gleaned from noting how the therapist got the best out of the child, and from observations of the child's approach to the various tasks.

Informal assessment and observation

Bishop (1994) emphasises the importance of a balance between standardised assessments and clinical observation as a way of avoiding one of the pitfalls in assessment of children with speech/language disorders. From the moment of meeting in the waiting room, information can be gleaned about the whole breadth of the child's communication skills by observing him or her and their interactions with their parents. In addition it is common for an SLT to supplement formal testing with informal materials, tasks and conversation.

Information from parents and other professionals

As with a psychiatric assessment, a full assessment of a child's communication draws on a detailed history from the parents of past and present levels of communication, and related areas such as feeding skills and hearing. Detailed questions need to be asked about the child's communication in a range of situations and supplemented by relevant comments from teachers, psychologists and the like; and this should all be used alongside and in comparison with information gained from standardised tests. Some of the information may be gained by use of interview assessments such as the Pragmatics Profile.

From assessment to treatment

Assessment and advice only

A considerable amount of many SLTs' time is spent purely on assessment and giving advice on management and this is likely to be the case in this population. To some extent it is a very good use of a therapist's limited time: the diagnosis of a language disorder can alter teachers' and parents' perceptions of a 'difficult' child and therefore their expectations and way of managing them. A thorough language assessment is also important as part of a multidisciplinary assessment in the differential diagnosis of suspected conditions such as ADHD and autistic spectrum disorders.

Direct speech and language therapy treatment with children

Flexibility is perhaps the most important skill required in working with children with emotional and behavioural disorders as they are likely to be unpredictable. The therapist should discern when to be structured or to use a freer, perhaps child-centred, approach. The therapist needs to be resourceful with children who are shy or withdrawn, very active or lacking in motivation, some of whom respond to interesting or adult-like equipment, perhaps using a bull-dog clip to hold picture cards or a tally-counter to record what has been achieved. Suggestions and techniques for therapists, along with some principles for dealing with other difficult behaviours, are set out simply by the author elsewhere (Wintgens 1996b).

Social skills as well as basic language skills can be learnt effectively in groups of children and adolescents from this population. The SLT has a role in advising on the management of communication skills and planning group activities, while sharing with colleagues, such as occupational therapists, teachers and nurses, ideas on how to manage the emotional and behavioural aspects.

Joint working

In the author's experience of working as an SLT in a CAMHS, joint working, or co-working, is particularly appropriate for children and families with certain types of disorders.

Referrals of children with both speech and language disorders and conduct disorders can usefully be seen by an SLT and a colleague such as a clinical nurse specialist, clinical psychologist or child psychiatrist. Both mental health professionals might be involved in the assessment and differential diagnosis. Then there may be joint sessions with both professionals where the conduct problems are addressed in the light of the child's speech and language disorder, interspersed with blocks of speech and language therapy.

Children with selective mutism can usefully be seen by SLTs and clinical psychologists who together have the combined skills to carry out effective assessment and implement treatment techniques such as stimulus fading.

There are some children with psychiatric disorders alongside severe and long-term disorders of communication whose families have need of support, management advice or perhaps family work, separate from the child's direct speech and language therapy which may take place in a school setting. Here it is an advantage for the SLT to work jointly with a colleague such as a social worker or a psychotherapist in order for both aspects of the child's difficulties to be addressed.

References

Baker, L. and Cantwell, D.P. (1982) Psychiatric disorder in children with different types of communication disorders. *Journal of Communication Disorders 15*, 113–126.

Beitchman, J.H., Wilson, B., Brownlie, E.B., Walters, H., Inglis, A. and Lancee, W. (1996) Long-term consistency in speech/language profiles: II Behavioural, emotional and social outcomes. *Journal of the American Academy of Child and Adolescent Psychiatry 35*, 6, 815–825.

Bishop, D.V.M. (1994) Developmental disorders of speech and language. In M. Rutter, E. Taylor and L. Hersov (eds) *Child and Adolescent Psychiatry: Modern Approaches* (third edition). Oxford: Blackwell Science.

Burgess, J. and Bransby, G. (1990) An evaluation of the speech and language skills of children with emotional and behavioural problems. *College of Speech Therapy Bulletin 453*, 2–3.

Camarata, S.M., Hughes, C.A. and Ruhl, K.L. (1988) Mild/moderately behaviourally disturbed students: a population at risk for language disorders. *Language, Speech and Hearing Services 19*, 191–200.

Cohen, N.J., Davine, M., Hordezky, M.A., Lipsett, L. and Isaacson, B.A. (1993) Unsuspected language impairments in psychiatrically disturbed children: prevalence and language and behavioural characteristics. *Journal of the American Academy of Child and Adolescent Psychiatry 32*, 595–603.

Cohen, N.J., Davine, M. and Meloche-Kelly, M. (1989) Prevalence of unsuspected language disorders in a child psychiatric population. *Journal of the American Academy of Child and Adolescent Psychiatry 28*, 1, 107–111.

Cohen, N.J. and Lipsett, L. (1991) Recognised and unrecognised language impairment in psychologically disturbed children. *Canadian Journal of Behavioural Science 23*, 1, 376–389.

Cross, M. (1997) Challenging behaviour or challenged comprehension. *Royal College of Speech and Language Therapy Bulletin 545*, 11–12.

Donahue, M.L, Hartas, D. and Cole, D. (1999) *Research on Interactions amoung oral language and emotional/behavioural disorders.* In D.L. Rogers-Adkinson and P.L. Griffith (eds) *Communication Disorders and Children with Psychiatric and Behavioural Disorders.* London: Singular Publishing Group.

Giddan, J.J. (1991) School children with emotional problems and communication deficits: implications for speech language pathologists. *Language, Speech and Hearing Services in Schools 22*, 291–295.

Giddan, J.J., Milling, L. and Campbell, N.B. (1996) Unrecognised language and speech deficits in preadolescent psychiatric inpatients. *American Journal of Orthopsychiatry 66*, 1.

Giddan, J.J., Wahl, J. and Brogan, M. (1995) Importance of communication training for psychiatric residents and mental health trainees. *Child Psychiatry and Human Development 26*, 1, 19–28.

Goodman, R. and Scott, S. (1997) *Child Psychiatry.* Oxford: Blackwell Science.

Gordon, N. (1991) The relationship between language and behaviour. *Developmental Medicine and Child Neurology 33*, 86–89.

Gualtieri, C.T., Koriath, J., Van Bourgoridien, M. and Saleeby, N. (1983) Language disorders in children referred for psychiatric services. *Journal of the American Academy of Child Psychiatry 22*, 2, 165–171.

Kotsopoulos, A. and Boodoosingh, I. (1987) Language and speech disorders in children attending a day psychiatric programme. *British Journal of Disorders of Communication 22*, 227–236.

Law, J. and Conway, J. (1992) Effect of abuse and neglect on the development of children's speech and language. *Developmental Medicine and Child Neurology 34*, 943–948.

Rogers-Adkinson, D.L. and Griffith, P.L. (eds) (1999) *Communication Disorders and Children with Psychiatric and Behavioural Disorders.* London: Singular Publishing Group.

Rutter, M. and Mawhood, L. (1991) The long-term psychosocial sequelae of specific developmental disorders of speech and language. In M. Rutter and P. Casaer (eds) *Biological Risk Factors for Psychosocial Disorders.* Cambridge: Cambridge University Press.

Rutter, M., Taylor, E. and Hersov, L. (eds) (1994) *Child and Adolescent Psychiatry: Modern Approaches* (third edition). Oxford: Blackwell Scientific Publications.

Wintgens, A. (1996a) Emotional and Behavioural Problems in Children – a Growing Awareness? In *Caring to Communicate: Proceedings of the Golden Jubilee Conference, York, October 1995.* London: Royal College of Speech and Language Therapists.

Wintgens, A. (1996b) Links between emotional/behavioural problems and communication difficulties. In M. Kersner and J.A. Wright (eds) *How to Manage Communication Problems in Young Children* (second edition). London: David Fulton Publishers.

CHAPTER 18

Mental Health, Offenders
and the Criminal Justice System

Karen Bryan and Nicci Forshaw

The criminal justice system places huge demands upon the communication skills of every individual involved in it. Communication is the means through which processes such as defending a suspect, providing a witness account, giving a victim statement, interviewing a suspect or treating an offender are achieved.

We might therefore have particular concerns about three groups of communication-impaired people in relation to criminal justice:

- the mentally ill who offend
- offenders with learning disabilities
- offenders who have speech, language and communication problems which are not associated with either of the above, for example people with a stammer, pervasive articulation difficulties, lower than expected levels of language comprehension and production, literacy problems and social interaction difficulties. There will also be a small proportion of offenders with acquired communication disorders, which may be associated with conditions such as head injury, stroke, Parkinson's disease, motor neurone disease and the dementias. Such conditions may be acquired before or during a custodial sentence.

This chapter will discuss the incidence of communication problems in offenders and will then examine the involvement of speech and language therapy services within the criminal justice system.

Incidence of mental illness in offenders

It is widely accepted that significant numbers of people entering penal establishments are mentally ill (Gunn, Maden and Swinton 1991). Links between mental health and language difficulties are under-researched, but can be apparent in a number of ways. Language difficulties are often cited as an antecedent factor (among others) for the development of mental health problems. Mental health problems may lead to difficulty in communicating, e.g. in schizophrenia. Also, pervading language difficulties may interact with mental illness to give a more significant communication problem, for example a client with articulation and language comprehension difficulties originating from childhood who has great difficulty in inter-personal interaction associated with personality disorder.

Incidence of learning disability in the prison population

Hayes (1997) concludes that in many Western jurisdictions, offenders with learning disability are over-represented in the criminal justice system. Studies that attempt to identify and diagnose learning disability vary in their methodologies so that prevalence findings differ. Brown and Courtless (1971) found 9.5 per cent of 90,000 inmates in the USA had IQ scores of less than 70. Denkowski and Denkowski (1985) estimated that the prevalence of learning disability in USA prisons ranged from 1.5 per cent to 19.1 per cent. Svendsen and Werner (1977) found that 10 per cent of the prison population in Denmark had learning disabilities.

In the UK, prison inmates are not routinely assessed to establish IQ, but the prison service has recently identified the presence of a significant number of men with an IQ of less than 80 within the sex offender population. The prison service has also identified the need to offer their sex offender treatment programme in a different format to meet the cognitive and communication needs of this population (Forshaw 1997).

Murphy, Harnett and Holland (1995) screened 157 remand prisoners, asking them if they had reading or learning difficulties or had attended a special school. 33 answered positively but were not found to have a learning difficulty on assessment. They were, however, found to have a lower mean verbal IQ, full scale IQ, reading age, numeracy age and higher General Health Questionnaire scores compared with other prisoners. They were also more likely to have a recent history of mental illness or psychiatric hospital admission. These figures suggest that there are a significant number of offenders with communication difficulties that are primarily associated with cognitive or psychological difficulties despite them not being technically classified as learning disabled.

A survey of speech and language therapy services to offenders in 1997 (Bryan and Forshaw 1998) showed that 68 of the 101 offenders receiving speech and language therapy input had learning disabilities, and constituted by far the largest aetiological group identified. (Details of the survey are discussed later in the chapter.)

Incidence of communication problems in prison populations

Within the UK population as a whole there are about 2 per cent of people with communication problems (Enderby and Philipp 1986), but we do not have accurate figures on the incidence of communication problems within the prison population. We can only suggest that of those who are free of mental illness, a greater proportion than 2 per cent may have speech, language or communication problems. Any difficulty with communication will affect education, job prospects, and contact with both law enforcement and health and social care agencies.

There is evidence from the USA to suggest that a much larger proportion of the prison population have problems with communication. Wagner, Gray and Potter (1983) reported that 44 per cent of female inmates had problems with one or more of the following aspects of communication:

- hearing
- receptive language (comprehension)
- fluency (stammering)
- voice.

However, difficulties with interpersonal communication were not assessed so this is likely to be an underestimate.

Jacobson, Jacobson and Crowe (1989) reported a 28 per cent incidence of hearing difficulty in male inmates. Crowe and Jackson (1990) suggest that there may be a link between hearing loss and criminal behaviour. Hearing loss leads to social isolation which may make a child vulnerable to crime, especially if difficulty acquiring language also occurs as this may combine with the hearing problem to result in educational difficulty, school failure and a spiralling drift into crime. This may explain the high incidence of hearing problems among offenders.

4.5 million adults in England and Wales are estimated to have some degree of literacy difficulties, i.e. 16 per cent of the adult population (Gregory 1996). So we would expect at least this proportion of the offender population to have literacy difficulties.

A survey of speech and language therapy services to offenders in 1997 (Bryan and Forshaw 1998) showed that after learning disabilities, stammering and acquired neurological impairments were the most common problems within the 101 offenders actually receiving speech and language input.

Incidence of communication problems in young offenders

Concern has been raised regarding the numbers of young offenders with communication difficulties. HM Inspectorate of Prisons (1997) highlighted the number of offenders who are dyslexic and who are excluded or self-excluded from the education system where their literacy problems are a factor in their offending. Similarly, the National Association for the Care and Rehabilitation of Offenders has highlighted unaddressed specific learning difficulties as a significant contributing factor leading to criminal behaviour (Sleight 1998).

A study at Polmont in Scotland (Johnson 1994) showed that, from 1972–1992, 11 per cent of the young offenders had communication problems. All young offenders entering the institution for 3 months or longer were screened using a brief questionnaire. Problems were apparent in one or more of the following categories:

- hearing
- articulation
- voice
- fluency
- language
- memory dysfunction (sufficient to affect communication)
- pragmatic/social communication referring to a reduction in communication ability associated with difficulty in interpreting, synthesising and using verbal and non-verbal information appropriately within changing communication contexts.

The Polmont study used a questionnaire to assess the young offenders and is therefore to some extent reliant upon self-report, although the speech and language therapist had an opportunity for informal assessment during the interview in which the questionnaire was completed. A recent study of young offenders using a detailed language assessment would suggest that the Polmont study might be an underestimate of the problem. Pryor (1998) assessed a small number of successive admissions to a young offender institution. The results showed that 72 per cent (8/11 subjects) aged between 17 and 20 years, had difficulties on the CELF–R (Semel, Wiig and Secord 1987) with a mean age equivalence of 12 years, 4 months and on the BPVS with a mean age equivalence of 11 years, 1 month. In addition, 63 per cent of the subjects had significantly lower expressive language skills compared with their receptive language skills.

What both of these studies confirm is that, in the UK, large numbers of young men entering young offender institutions have speech, language and communication difficulties. For whatever reason, the problems have not been dealt with prior to detention. Johnson (1994) suggests that for many inmates, the period of detention is an opportunity for them to reflect on their lives and to work on their difficulties. This may be facilitated by the young person being free of financial, domestic, educational, and other stresses while being detained, although clearly detention brings other stresses. Johnson also highlights the difficulty of arranging (and ex-young offenders sustaining) therapy after they are released. This adds further weight to the argument for treating them while they are detained.

Incidence of communication problems within special hospitals

Another sector of the criminal justice system concerns those entering special hospitals. There are three special hospitals in the UK (Ashworth, Broadmoor and Rampton). They provide treatment and special security for people who have mental disorders and are subject to compulsory detention on account of their dangerous, violent or criminal propensities. A recent population study of the three special hospitals discusses the association between mental disorder and violence (Taylor et al. 1998).

Figures from a special hospital population of 'young' (up to age 27) offenders (personality disordered or schizophrenic) suggests that 90 per cent of this group have problems in communicating. This may be a more structural problem such as difficulty in articulation or a more general problem in interpersonal communication.

Systematic assessment of all patients entering a high security hospital over a six-month period showed that 75 per cent had speech, language and communication problems that would affect interpersonal functioning and which would need to be considered in verbally mediated interventions (Bryan 1998). The incidence of literacy problems was also high.

Current provision of speech and language therapy services for offenders

A survey of speech and language therapists working with offenders (Bryan and Forshaw 1998) shows great diversity in the provision of speech and language therapy services to offenders. There are SLT services in each of the three special hospitals, which mainly treat clients with serious mental health problems. A large proportion of these clients are offenders. Two of the hospitals have an SLT establishment of one and the other has an establishment of 1.4.

Within the prison service, six secure units and two young offender institutions have some provision and one hospital for people with learning disabilities and mental health problems extends speech and language therapy provision to offenders. The services originate from existing services to clients with learning disabilities, or from existing mental health services. There are some ad hoc referrals by prisons to local community speech and language therapy services. Two therapists had seen clients at a local health centre/hospital with the client under escort. Two prisons used SLT services brought in on an occasional sessional basis. The remaining provision involved SLT time for individual clients on an ad hoc basis.

Referral sources varied with medical officers, psychiatrists, service managers (learning disabilities), ward staff (secure units), psychologists and other therapists (non-SLT) all making referrals. The number of referrals per institution varied from 1–35 with units which had an SLT service having considerably more referrals than ad hoc services, which tended to include 1–4 referrals per year. SLT service time was primarily dependent on whether or not an SLT was employed, with provision of 0.4 to 1.4 in funded services all of which originated from clinical services for people with learning disabilities and were NHS funded.

Aetiology

101 clients were seen in 1997 from the fourteen respondents to the survey. The disorders seen were as follows:

- 68 adult learning disabilities
- 5 fluency difficulties/stammering
- 5 dysphasia following CVA
- 3 language disorder/semantic pragmatic difficulties
- 2 head injury
- 2 hearing impairment
- 2 dyspraxia/speech production difficulties
- 1 head and neck cancer
- 1 literacy difficulties
- 1 neurological impairment
- 1 mental health problems.

The results indicate that a wide range of people with communication difficulties is found within the offender population. The slightly arbitrary nature of diagnosis was evident with a number of respondents noting that clients had more than one pathology. For example, a number of clients with learning disabilities or dysfluency as their principal diagnosis also presented with hearing impairment or language and literacy difficulties. Some SLTs commented that despite the client's diagnosis, work focused on social skills and enabling clients to access other services.

Funding arrangements for SLT services were varied and unclear in some circumstances. In 1 case there was a specific contract between the Scottish prison service and a health board, in 6 cases there was co-operation between the prison service and SLT services to provide a package of care, 3 NHS trust services extended to cover offenders in secure units and in the remainder contractual arrangements were unresolved.

SLTs appeared to liaise with a variety of staff who cared for the offenders. This partly reflects the different settings in which offenders were treated. Contact with medical and psychology staff was most prevalent. Unfortunately most SLTs were not involved in the pre-release planning process, and a number noted that it was very difficult to follow-up offenders who left the prison service. Several mentioned that speech and language therapy being a condition of probation service arrangements would be helpful.

The role of speech and language therapists working with offenders

Special hospitals

As well as providing assessment and remediation programmes on an individual basis, for a whole variety of speech, language and communication disorders, speech and language therapists in special hospitals are involved in multidisciplinary team working aimed at changing patterns of forensic behaviour. Chapter 24 discusses the special hospital milieu. A specific example of such therapy integration is an integrated modular approach to therapy with victim empathy being the ultimate aim described by Quayle, France and Wilkinson (1995). Here patients may need to take part in unstructured groups such as current affairs with one of the main aims being the acquisition of the linguistic skills necessary for in-depth reflection on their past histories and being questioned and confronted by other group members and therapists. Thus, even within a specialist psychotherapeutic and cognitive behavioural treatment regime, there is a need for remediation or development of language skills so that patients can benefit from other therapies offered.

The survey showed that six secure units currently have speech and language therapy input in the UK. In addition there is some evidence to suggest that medium secure environments may be a developing area for speech and language therapy with plans to develop services in two more secure units.

Young offenders

Polmont provides a model for a low-cost effective speech and language therapy service within a young offender institution. Approximately fifty inmates per year are offered therapy. The therapy is usually offered by a contract for a limited period. Therapy usually takes place within the educational wing. Once an episode of care is negotiated and agreed, the young man is seen as an equal partner in the therapeutic process. He is encouraged and enabled to own the problem and is expected, within the limits of his own resources, to work with the therapist towards achieving the agreed goals.

Small group therapy is also carried out when a resident group of young men can benefit from a group approach. Regular reviews are undertaken of progress and steps are taken to practise and integrate newly acquired skills within the daily routine. Therapeutic goal setting is used, although goals are adapted to the time restrictions imposed by shorter sentences. Therapy is then evaluated in terms of goal achievement; examples of highly specific goals would be:

- acquiring a particular sound
- reduction of blocking (or other aspect of a stammer) to an agreed level

- maintenance of eye contact
- use of a strategy to improve intelligibility, e.g. specifically stating what the topic is.

Other goals such as increase in self-esteem or increase in self-confidence are less easy to measure objectively, although they may be important to the client and report from other members of staff may be significant.

The speech and language therapy service at Polmont functions within the multidisciplinary team and particular links are with:

- the education services by contributing to assessment and dealing with communication problems so that educational provision can be of greater benefit; also preparation for employment, job interviews, etc. as part of a job-preparation package
- the medical services where sensory or physiological problems were involved (this might involve acquired disorders in an older prison population such as communication disabilities arising from head injury, CVA, drug side-effects, etc.)
- the psychological services where problems in communicating are a contributing or resulting factor associated with emotional, behavioural and other psychological difficulties
- the social workers mostly associated with clients who have complex language problems and where release is imminent; this may lead to contact with community social workers
- the prison officers for exchange of information and advice on communication.

Bryan, France and Kramer (1996) discuss the value of communication therapy for the prison population. However, further research is needed to look at whether re-offending rates are reduced, or rates of post-release employment are increased, to set the value of speech and language therapy into the wider context of what the prison service is trying to achieve. Ideally the service offered at Polmont, which is a highly effective but low cost service, should be available in every young offender institution in the UK.

Prisons

Within the prison service itself, prison staff may need practical help and support in caring for people who have communication difficulties. Similarly, it is likely that offenders with communication difficulties are unable to benefit from other available treatments such as drug rehabilitation or anger management as these programmes are usually verbally mediated.

A person who has difficulty in communicating or in communicating effectively may lash out or use other behavioural means to show their frustration. Such people will be easier to care for if they are able to verbalise what it is that is troubling them or what it is that they want, thereby reducing frustration. Similarly, by verbalising their frustration/anger rather than using inappropriate physical means. SLT therefore has a role within the multidisciplinary team of enabling inmates to derive maximum benefit from other therapies, which are dependent upon interpersonal communication such as anger management, counselling and education and life preparation schemes. A specific example of such involvement is the work done by a speech and language therapist to modify the Sex Offender Treatment Programme to make it accessible to offenders with a low IQ (Forshaw 1997). The modified programme involves simplified language, use of total communication strategies, e.g. gesture and symbols, and additional study blocks to ensure that terminology and basic concepts used in the treatment programme are understood.

The survey indicates that speech and language therapy services are only available to offenders within limited parts of the prison system. There is also considerable variation in how these SLT services are linked to the prison system and how they are funded. Previous published reports have indicated that there is a need for services to assist communication-impaired offenders (Bryan, France and Kramer 1996; Crowe and Jackson 1990).

The prison health service inspectorate has recommended that the prison service recognise and use the expertise within the NHS for the commissioning and delivery of health care (Reed and Lyne 1997). There is clearly a need to strengthen links between NHS speech and language provision and the provision of health services to offenders within the prison system to ensure that all offenders with speech, language and communication problems have access to appropriate speech and language therapy services.

Addressing communication needs within the wider criminal justice system

There are numerous processes within the criminal justice system which place huge demands upon the communication skills of those involved, for example arrest, reading of rights, cautioning, going to court, giving a statement and being interviewed.

The treatment of suspects with learning difficulties raises management issues at all levels of the criminal justice system. For example, how can people with special communication needs be identified and managed after arrest; are they able to be interviewed; will their evidence be acceptable to a court; is an appropriate adult required to be in attendance? These questions also apply to vulnerable people who may be victims or witnesses (Clare and Gudjonnsson 1995). Similarly, these same questions and issues are applicable to people with communication difficulties due to brain injury, mental illness and the influence of drugs (Rix 1997).

There is growing evidence that many suspects arrested by the police are intellectually impaired (Gudjonnsson et al. 1993; Lyall et al. 1995). The Police and Criminal Evidence Act (PACE) (Home Office 1995) recognises that suspects with intellectual disabilities are vulnerable to making misleading statements and need special provision. However, there is consistent evidence to suggest that suspects with intellectual disabilities are often not identified by the police (Bean and Nemitz 1994). (See Chapter 20 for more information.)

Under the PACE code of practice, to try to safeguard the interests of a vulnerable person, such as people with learning disabilities or mental illness, the police are required to have an appropriate adult present. This might be a parent or guardian, a social worker or, failing that, a responsible person who is not employed by the police. The duties of an appropriate adult are to ensure that the vulnerable person understands why they have been detained and what their rights are. Then the appropriate adult is present at the police interview, and should advise the detainee, 'facilitate communication', and ensure that the interview is conducted properly and fairly. There are implications here for the quality and validity of information gained during police interviews. Blackie (1996) states that the role of the appropriate adult is to protect mentally vulnerable people who are accused of committing a crime and to ensure that they are dealt with in a way which is appropriate to their vulnerability and protects their rights. To achieve this, appropriate adults need suitable training, clear understanding of their role and respect from the police. Speech and language therapists have much to offer, for example in the training of appropriate adults, but are also ideally qualified to act as appropriate adults in certain situations. Indeed, it is possible that in a number of situations it is only through the involvement of a speech and language therapist that communication needs are recognised and adequately addressed.

Conclusion

This chapter has highlighted the significant number of offenders who have communication disabilities and the diversity of communication needs that exists within the criminal justice system as a whole. It is essential that offenders' communication needs are identified and met to enable them to derive maximum benefit from other services which are offered to offenders.

Further investigation of the speech and language therapy needs of specific groups of offenders such as those with learning disabilities and those with mental health problems is required.

There is clearly a role for speech and language therapy services within the criminal justice system, but there are a number of issues for the speech and language therapy profession to address in relation to working with offenders, including:

- the speech and language therapists' role in working with offenders
- defining models of good practice
- safety and support needs for therapists (RCSLT currently has a working party examining legal issues)
- the role of the profession in lobbying prison and possibly probation services about the communication needs of offenders.

References

Bean, P. and Nemitz, T. (1994) *Out of Depth and Out of Sight*. London: MENCAP.

Blackie, I. (1996) Appropriate Adults. *National Association for the Protection from Sexual Abuse of Adults and Children with Learning Disabilities (NAPSAC) Bulletin*, June, 3–7.

Brown, B.S. and Courtless, T.F. (1971) *The Mentally Retarded Offender*. Washington DC: US Government Printing Office, Department of Health Education and Welfare publication no. (HSM) 72–90–39.

Bryan, K. (1998) *Speech and Language Therapy Assessment. Broadmoor Hospital January–June 1998*. Lecture to Special Interest Group in Mental Health. London. November.

Bryan, K.L. and Forshaw, N. (1998) Crime and Communication. *Royal College of Speech and Language Therapist's Bulletin*, November, 7–8.

Bryan, K., France, J. and Kramer, S. (1996) Communication therapy for the prison population. In N. Squires and J. Strobl (eds) *Healthy Prisons –A Vision for The Future*. Liverpool: University of Liverpool.

Clare, I.C.H. and Gudjonnsson, G.H. (1993) Interrogative suggestibility, confabulation, and acquiescence in people with mild learning difficulties (mental handicap): implications for reliability during police investigations. *British Journal of Clinical Psychology 32*, 295–301.

Clare, I.C.H. and Gudjonnsson, G.H. (1995) The vulnerability of suspects with intellectual disabilities during police interviews: a review and experimental study of decision making. *Mental Handicap Research 8*, 110–127.

Crowe, T.A. and Jackson, P.D. (1990) Hearing loss in a Mississippi penitentiary. *Hearing instruments 40*, 2, 8–10.

Denkowski, G.C. and Denkowski, K.M. (1985) The mentally retarded offender in the state prison system: identification, prevalence, adjustment and rehabilitation. *Criminal Justice and Behaviour 12*, 53–70.

Enderby, P.M. and Philipp, R. (1986) Speech and language handicap: towards knowing the size of the problem. *British Journal of Disorders of Communication 21*, 151–165.

Forshaw, N. (1997) Working with sex offenders. *Royal College of Speech and Language Therapists Bulletin*, March, 12–13.

Gregory, W. (1996) *The Informablity Manual. Making Information more Accessiblein the Light of the Disability Discrimination Act.* London: HMSO.

Gudjonnsson, G.H., Clare, I.C.H., Rutter, S.C. and Pearce, J. (1993) *Persons at Risk During Interviews in Police Custody: The Identification of Vulnerabilities.* Royal Commission on Criminal Justice, Research Study No 12. London: HMSO.

Gunn, J., Maden, A. and Swinton, J. (1991) Treatment needs of prisoners with psychiatric disorders. *British Medical Journal 303*, 338–341.

Hayes, S. (1997) Recent research on offenders with learning disabilities. *Learning Disability Review 1*, 3, 7–15.

HM Inspectorate of Prisons. (1997) *Young Prisoners: A Thematic Review.* London: The Stationery Office.

Home Office (1995) *Police and Criminal Evidence Act.* London: HMSO.

Jacobson, C.A., Jacobson, J.T. and Crowe, T.A. (1989) Hearing loss in prison inmates. *Ear and Hearing 10*, 3, 178–183.

Johnson, S. (1994) *A Review of Communication Therapy With Young Male Offenders.* Internal Report: Scottish Prison Service.

Lyall, I., Holland, A.J., Collins, S. and Styles, P. (1995) Incidence of persons with a learning disability detained in police custody. A needs assessment for service development. *Medicine, Science and the Law 35*, 61–71.

Murphy, G.H., Harnett, H. and Holland, A.J. (1995) A survey of intellectual disabilities amongst men on remand in prison. *Mental Handicap Research 8*, 81–98.

Pryor, A. (1998) *A Systematic Assessment of the Prevalence of Communication Difficulties Within a Small Group of Young Offenders.* University of Reading: Unpublished Thesis.

Quayle, M., France, J. and Wilkinson, E. (1995) An integrated modular approach to therapy in a special hospital young men's unit. In Cordess and Cox (eds) *Forensic Focus, Forensic Psychotherapy.* London: Jessica Kingsley Publishers.

Reed, J. and Lyne, M. (1997) The quality of health care in prison: results of a year's programme of semistructured inspections. *British Medical Journal 315*, 1420–1424.

Rix, K.J.B. (1997) Fit to be interviewed by the police. *Advances in Psychiatric Treatment 3*, 33–40.

Semel, E., Wiig, E.H. and Secord, W. (1987) *Clinical Evaluation of Language Fundamentals – Revised.* Sidcup: Psychological Corporation.

Sleight (1998) *Dyslexia, Educational Failure and Young Offenders.* NACRO Briefing Paper – Draft.

Svendsen, B.B. and Werner, J. (1977) Offenders within ordinary services for the mentally retarded in Denmark. In P. Mittler (ed) *Research to Practice in Mental Retardation, Volume I, Care and Intervention.* Baltimore: University Park Press. pp.419–424.

Taylor, P.J., Leese, M., Williams, D., Butwell, M., Daly, R. and Larkin, E. (1998) Mental disorder and violence. *British Journal of Psychiatry 172*, 218–226.

Wagner, C.O., Gray, L.L. and Potter, R.E. (1983) Communicative disorders in a group of adult female offenders. *Journal of Communication Disorders 16*, 269–277.

CHAPTER 19

Forensic Psychiatry

Jenny France and Sarah Kramer

Psychiatry has developed or is developing systems for assessing and treating those who have a mental disorder and who are also offenders through: assessment and management of risk in people with mental disorder; providing courts with relevant information; research; assessment and treatment of problems created by criminal victimisation; open debate on controversial ethical issues; and providing specialist training (Taylor 1997).

The mentally disordered offender is a criminal who suffers from a mental disorder, but only a very few of all offenders suffer from such a disorder. Due to their mental health problems many of these people are not fit enough to plead in court. Difficult decisions have to be made regarding possible treatment and if so where it should be provided. A number of these people will be admitted to a special hospital under sections 35, 36, or 38 of the Mental Health Act 1983 for assessment prior to the final court decision as to their most appropriate placement. This will be determined by whether the person can be managed safely in the community; if not, then in a psychiatric hospital, medium secure unit, prison, or secure hospital.

Secure psychiatric hospitals

There are three secure psychiatric hospitals which cover England and Wales: Broadmoor, Rampton and Ashworth Hospitals. These hospitals straddle the penal system and mental health services, with a patient population in which the biases are not fully understood, but which has special needs (Taylor 1997). Rampton Hospital provides specialist services for patients with learning and hearing disabilities. Broadmoor and Ashworth have a few isolated patients with mild learning disability, and many more with hearing disabilities; these patients will have treatment packages specially designed to suit individual needs.

The hospitals consist of a secure perimeter wall and an 'air-lock' entrance system, so that all movements into and out of the hospital, as well as the patient movements within the hospital, can be monitored at all times. Facilities for daily life include working in specialised areas such as carpentry, printing, gardening, the hospital shop and the patients' library for example, where patients are closely supervised and are trained to acquire the necessary skills for their occupation.

At Broadmoor Hospital there are a number of specialist units. The admission unit is where each patient has extensive multidisciplinary assessments, support and treatment, and where they will stay for approximately six months; the women, who are many fewer, are also placed in an assessment group within a larger ward. The young men's unit houses between 25 and 30 patients where the greater proportion suffer from personality disorders and the remainder from other mental illnesses; the therapy programmes are designed equally to include any patient and so there is likely to be a mix of personality disorder and mental illness in all group work. The addictions unit provides special programmes based on the need to treat addictions such as alcohol, abusive drugs, gambling, etc.; patients are referred to this unit from other wards and units within the hospital. Parole wards, with lesser security and more freedom of movement, organise treatment and rehabilitation taking into account the patient's planned move from the hospital.

There is an extensive educational programme to provide as many opportunities as possible. Emphasis is placed on gaining literacy skills with the additional use of computers. Programmes are designed to cater for all levels of competence, i.e. from total illiteracy to taking formal national examinations in English. Other academic subjects are also available, as well as art, music and cooking, for example. Many patients go on to gain certificates at various levels of competence and some even attain an Open University degree.

Relaxation and socialisation plays an important supporting part in the patient's rehabilitation; see Chapter 24 on Milieu Therapy for further details.

Multidenominational religious needs are met through chapel services. The hospital chaplain and visiting colleagues are always available for pastoral support, and the chaplain also plays an important therapeutic role.

The hospitals are staffed by forensic psychiatrists, psychiatric nurses, medical doctors, chaplains, librarians, social workers, psychologists, occupational therapists, speech and language therapists, art, drama and music therapists, administrative and clerical staff, catering and domestic staff.

The patients

The association between mental disorder and crime is common (Taylor 1997). There is a long-standing link between violence and mental disorder, and in particular schizophrenia and offending. Research shows that acting on delusions is very common, whereas the association between hallucinations and violence is less clear.

Approximately 74 per cent of patients in secure hospitals are diagnosed as having a mental illness, most of which will be schizophrenia. The remaining 26 per cent suffer from personality disorder (psychopathy), and all of these patients are detained on a court order. Section 37 of the Mental Health Act 1983 will apply to all patients detained on a court order, and many will have a section 41, a restriction order, added. About 10 per cent of patients will be on a section 3, which is a treatment order, and about another 10 per cent will have been transferred from prison on a section 47/49 (Faulk 1988). Offences include homicide, other violent acts both towards others and self, arson, sex offences and causing criminal damage.

Patients are admitted to a secure hospital because of the risk they pose and the risk to hospital staff, in particular, is high (Taylor 1997). The patient's stay is usually for five or more years; short stays are unusual unless the individual is sent to the hospital for assessment prior to sentence and then found unfit for treatment. Some patients may have suffered long-term mental illness and institutionalisation will have occurred, either in psychiatric hospital or in prison.

Men and women are nursed in separate units, but join for education, church services and other social events. Some therapies are also planned for both sexes.

Services provided by special hospitals are extensive, but assessment, diagnosis, medical and pharmacological treatments for mental illness are similar to those in other psychiatric settings. Therapy programmes are likely to be planned over a long term and include a number and variety of approaches – psychodynamic, cognitive/behavioural, educational, for example – either separately or in combination as the clinical team prescribe.

Rehabilitation focuses on the present, that is on being able to understand and accept the mental illness and cope with daily living. Therapy is directed towards understanding the past, and the development of the mental illness; acknowledging the patient's grief for the victim(s) and self; and finally to being able to consider a future in a less secure setting. The skills gained aim to help the offender patient to eventually become an accepted member of the community.

Medium secure units

Medium secure units provide care for those patients who are too difficult or dangerous to be managed in the community or any other open setting, but who are not so disturbed as to require a secure hospital. Most regions in Britain now have either an interim unit or regional unit, and these vary according to the security provided. Patients are, whenever possible and if desirable, placed in units close to their families. Rehabilitation is planned to enable the return to the community where the patient, in progressive steps, will experience freedom to move unaccompanied outside the unit. These units are small, around 50 beds, enough for staff to manage easily, where men and women live and are treated in the same environment.

Patients from secure hospitals often move on to a medium secure unit for the final part of their treatment and rehabilitation.

Schizophrenia is the predominating mental illness, with most other patients having a personality disorder. 25 per cent of patients are referred from National Health Service hospitals, 20 per cent from special hospitals, 40–50 per cent from courts and remand prisons, approximately 10 per cent from community services and 1–2 per cent from ordinary prisons (Faulk 1988).

The length of stay varies from unit to unit, though is mostly between six to twelve months and in some units more than two years. Restricted patients will tend to stay the longest and some chronically ill people might have their length of stay determined by the difficulty of placing them back in the community. Other patients can be admitted immediately as emergencies, either for assessment or treatment. The multidisciplinary approach and staffing levels, which are high, make it possible to organise individual programmes for each patient's needs. Treatment programmes are similar to those in other psychiatric settings and aim to continue and develop previous care plans when necessary.

Secure wards

Secure wards in psychiatric hospitals are for nursing patients who, as a result of an acute illness perhaps, are disruptive or dangerous and who cannot be nursed on an ordinary psychiatric ward. Once the acute disturbance is over the patient can be returned to their former ward. There will be a higher staff-to-patient ratio on these wards in order to give support and individual attention. The length of stay may vary from a few days to a few weeks, and in some extremely difficult cases, such as those who respond poorly to medication, for months or years. This last group is on the decline now due to the increasing effectiveness of new anti-psychotic drugs.

Mental illness in prison

Mental illness in prison is similar to that found in any population. About 3–4 per cent suffer from psychoses and stress-related disorders; 80 per cent have personality disorders; 50 per cent suffer from alcoholism; 25 per cent suffer from drug abuse; and epilepsy is 1.5 times the normal rate. Mental handicap is possibly about 14 per cent, according to Faulk (1988). Gunn (1977) reported that prisons contain large numbers of psychiatrically disturbed people and in a survey in the south-east of England he found 31 per cent of prisoners to be psychiatrically disturbed. Medical services are provided in prison and teams consist of a prison medical officer assisted by hospital officers, some qualified psychiatric nurses and visiting psychiatrists. Medication and some forms of psychotherapy can be provided.

The role of the speech and language therapist in a forensic setting

Patients in secure settings suffer from the same kinds of mental illnesses as others and so their communication problems will be similar, as will be any concomitant speech pathology. It is the offence(s), and offending histories and disruptive or dangerous behaviour, that necessitate secure placement. The speech and language therapist is likely to be a member of the admission assessment team, where formal and informal assessments will be carried out once the patient has settled on the ward. (See Chapters 7, 8 and 9.)

On long stay wards speech and language therapists will provide new assessments and reassessment, any form of individual or group therapy relating to the communicative needs of the patient, and will attend team meetings and case conferences will be a part of the service (Grounds et al. 1987). Multidisciplinary working is encouraged and joint therapy programmes benefit both patient and staff (see Chapter 27). Programmes which take into account not only the patient's mental illness, but also encompass previous difficult areas such as the offending history and present behaviour problems, will be specially designed to address specific needs. Many of the treatments will be with a psychologist and nurses as co-therapists (and other professionals when available and if able to commit time to regular sessions), as the cognitive/behavioural approach is the basis for much of this work.

Therapies, most of which rely on an ability to communicate adequately, and which during involvement in treatment communicative competence is likely to be enhanced, might include anger management, social skills, victim empathy, family awareness, self and sensory awareness, and sex education. The style of these educational groups is cognitive and behavioural in origin:

Quayle, Deu and Giblin (1998) found that sexual knowledge was significantly improved by educational programmes for sex offender and non-sex-offender patients in secure hospitals; and Quayle and Moore (1998) have evaluated the impact of structured group work with men in a secure hospital. Dynamic psychotherapy, with a psychotherapist, other professionals such as a speech and language therapist, psychologist and nurses, supports and is supported in turn by this work; there is an interesting overlap from one therapy to the other and participation in therapy additionally helps promote linguistic competence.

Due to their past traumatic histories it is important for the patient to understand and own his or her past. The opportunity and ability to be able to talk freely and fluently is essential. It is necessary to be able to talk about the past, describe the offence and events and relationships leading up to it. This is daunting and made all the more difficult if language skills are poor. Hence the need to provide opportunities for the acquisition of language-building skills; these are helped by introducing the specialised vocabularies that accompany subjects such as sex education, anger management and social skills.

The ability to talk openly and honestly during treatment leads to the next stage of rehabilitation; this is to modify and extend the use of language in order to enable the patient to fit into society, presenting acceptable codes of communicative behaviour. Being able to adapt from one social setting to another, an institutional setting to the community for example, and from one group of people to another, demands sophisticated communication skills which need to be learned or relearned as part of the rehabilitative process; this is one of the most difficult skills to acquire.

Speech problems can still be caused or exacerbated by medication, although the new drugs are producing fewer side-effects; they do, nevertheless, need careful monitoring in order to reduce the possibility of dysarthria.

The traditional role of the speech and language therapist in these settings takes into account the length of the patient's stay in the hospital or unit. If the patient is detained without limit of time, that is on a section 41, then there is the possibility that a number of years will be spent in hospital. This naturally affects the way in which treatment plans are delivered and is a unique opportunity to see these programmes through to a conclusion. Therefore long-term treatments, such as language programmes and stammering therapy, can benefit in these environments.

References

Faulk, M. (1988) *Basic Forensic Psychiatry*. Oxford: Blackwell Scientific Publications.

Grounds, A.T., Quayle, M.T., France, J. *et al.* (1987) A Unit for 'psychopathic disorder' patients in Broadmoor Hospital. *Medical Science and the Law 27*, 1, 21–31.

Gunn, J. (1977) Criminal behaviour and mental disorders. *British Journal of Psychiatry 130*, 317–329.

Quayle, M., Deu, N. and Giblin, S. (1998) Sexual knowledge and sex education in a secure hospital setting. *Criminal Behaviour and Mental Health 8*, 66–76.

Quayle, M. and Moore, E. (1998) Evaluating the impact of structured groupwork with men in a high security hospital. *Criminal Behaviour and Mental Health 8*, 77–92.

Taylor, P.J. (1997a) Forensic psychiatry. In R. Murray, P. Hill and P. McGuffin (eds) *The Essentials of Postgraduate Psychiatry* (third edition). Cambridge: Cambridge University Press. pp.563–601.

Taylor, P.J. (1997b) Damage, disease and danger. *Criminal Behaviour and Mental Health 7*, 19–48.

CHAPTER 20

People with Borderline-Mild Learning Disability

Karen Elliott and Nicci Forshaw

It was clear on beginning this chapter that it would be impossible to cover in any depth the whole field of learning disability. Even just focusing on describing communication needs in this client group would be difficult because of the diverse and complex nature of the problems and their presentation. The focus of this chapter will, therefore, be those people who present with a borderline-mild learning disability. This is a developing area of work for speech and language therapists who historically have been more involved in services for people with moderate to severe learning disabilities.

Assessment and diagnosis of learning disability

There has been and continues to be a considerable amount of debate about the precise definition of learning disabilities (mental handicap). However, it is generally viewed as a developmental disability characterised by: (i) impaired intellectual functioning; and (ii) impaired social functioning.

Intellectual functioning is usually assessed by a psychologist using a psychometric test such as the Wechsler Adult Intelligence Scale, Revised (WAIS-R) (Wechsler 1986). A full scale IQ of less than 70 is usually considered to be an indicator of learning disability with a score of 50–69 being classified as 'mild', 35–49 as 'moderate', 20–35 as 'severe' and below 20 as 'profound'. Social functioning (which may also be referred to as adaptive skills) refers to a person's ability to meet the demands of his or her everyday life. 'Adaptive skills are difficult to classify as they relate to a large range of behaviours…they are difficult to measure accurately as they occur in many situations, with some behaviours being very specific to particular situations' (Nunkoosing 1995).

Assessment of social functioning/adaptive skills usually involves collecting information from people who know the person (e.g. parents, carers, teachers), as well as direct observation and questioning of the person. The quality of the information gained from interviews is, therefore, only as good as the people and processes involved, and often a higher level of expertise is required due to the complex communication problems within this client group. A comprehensive measure such as the Vineland Scales of Adaptive Behaviour (Sparrow, Balla and

Cichetti 1984) may be used for this assessment. It is important to realise that as Clare (1993) points out, among people with mild learning disabilities, '…there can be great variation between the pattern of skills of individuals with the same level of intellectual ability.' Gravell and France (1991) point out that 'approximately three-quarters of all those diagnosed as mentally handicapped fall into the mild group.' They go on to stress that, '…there is a continuum with normal intelligence and the boundaries are impossible to define solely on numerical criteria, as associated factors may mean two individuals with similar IQ levels function very differently.'

Finally, Berger (1997) says that, 'a cardinal principle in the use of test information is that it should never on its own be taken as some absolute truth, rather, test information is part of the totality of clinical information and needs to make sense in that context. Inconsistencies should be checked through various other investigations.'

Service provision

Assessment of intellectual and social functioning is central to the process of actually diagnosing learning disabilities, and the information gained is vital in planning services. Only by carefully tailoring support and services to individuals' needs will their autonomy, independence and development be assured.

Spencer (1997) explores the concept of learning disability in terms of factors that are:

1. Constant:

    - its occurrence
    - its nature
    - the everyday needs and rights of people with learning disabilities
    - the presence of people with learning disabilities who have high dependency, behavioural disorders or mental illness.

2. Variable:

    - society's reactions, attitudes and responses to learning disability
    - terminology
    - knowledge
    - treatment and prevention of conditions associated with learning disabilities
    - the way that people with learning disabilities' needs are met
    - the availability of therapies and the expertise of professionals and specialised services.

He goes on to say 'As these variables change and develop we are likely to continue to see changes in how learning disability is defined and measured and how services are set up to meet clients' needs.' It is the responsibility of those services and professionals within them to maintain an open and exploratory approach to developing their understanding of learning disabilities and the needs of people with learning disabilities. It is currently not uncommon for people with borderline-mild learning disabilities to fall between mainstream and learning disability services with neither understanding their needs. For example, someone with borderline learning disabilities may be excluded from a learning disability service that would meet their needs because they have an IQ score of 75. Equally the reverse may occur with someone assessed to have an IQ of 65 being inappropriately placed in a service for people with learning disability.

Perhaps it is a symptom of the above issues about diagnosis that people with borderline-mild learning disability are found in a very wide variety of services, including:

- Local Learning Disability Services (Health and Social Services)
- The community (living independently or with support)
- High Security Hospitals
- Regional or Medium Secure Units
- Prison Service.

While their presence in a variety of settings is not in itself a problem, inappropriate placement is likely to have a detrimental impact on a number of different areas:

- choice
- dignity and respect
- community presence
- relationships
- opportunities to fulfil potential.

This is caused by difficulties accessing appropriate treatment, education programmes, social and leisure activities and work placements.

Characteristics of people with learning disabilities

There are a number of problems that people with mild learning disabilities are more likely to experience than the general population:

1. Physical

    (a) sensory impairments

    (b) epilepsy.

2. Cognitive

    (a) memory and retrieval

    (b) attention

    (c) sequencing

    (d) generalisation

    (e) problem-solving and coping strategies

    (f) abstract reasoning.

3.   Social/communication

  (a) interpreting and responding to social situations (e.g. Asperger's syndrome)

  (b) reading and writing

  (c) understanding complex language and concepts

  (d) difficulties with verbal and non-verbal expression

  (e) low self-esteem and poor assertion skills

  (f) poor awareness of the needs of others

  (g) poor impulse control

  (h) behavioural problems

  (i) limited and/or negative past social experiences.

These can all contribute to the communication difficulties of an individual and it should always be borne in mind that all the above factors may be present at different levels and interacting in different ways for each person and in different situations.

Communication skills

Several studies have demonstrated the link between learning disability and communication impairment and there is a general agreement that the more severe the learning disability, the more severe and complex the communication impairment is likely to be. However, people with borderline-mild learning disability present with subtle communication problems which often go unrecognised for much of the person's life. In general social situations people may appear to be able to cope adequately as they do not tell others about their difficulties and needs and actually become skilled at concealing them. This is driven by a need, which we all have, to appear 'normal' and to belong. The possibility that revealing problems may lead to rejection means that many people with learning disability become over-compliant. There is a significant amount of literature describing the communication skills of people with mild–moderate learning disabilities, much of it focusing on suggestibility, acquiescence and confabulation within police interviews. The following definitions are from Gudjonsson and Clare (1986):

Suggestibility

Interrogative suggestibility is 'the extent to which, within a closed social interaction, people come to accept messages communicated during formal questioning, as the result of which their behavioural response is affected.' This comprises two components: 'yielding to leading questions' and 'shifting' initial response to negative feedback.

Acquiescence

This is a person's tendency to respond to questions affirmatively whether or not they agree with the content.

Confabulation

This is when people replace gaps in their memory with imaginary experiences which they believe to be true.

Clare and Gudjonsson (1993) explored the relationship between these factors and the presence of mild learning disabilities. They concluded that people with mild learning disabilities were more likely to yield to leading questions, be acquiescent and to confabulate compared with people with 'average intellectual ability'.

Although the research focused on police interviews, these findings clearly have great significance for anyone interacting with people with mild learning disabilities in any situation. They are all factors that may be present but be extremely difficult to spot. We would suggest that suggestibility and acquiescence are broader issues than the previous definitions perhaps imply. People may yield to leading questions or acquiesce for a number of reasons, for example:

1.   Problems with comprehension may mean that the person appreciates the structure of a question and therefore knows that a yes/no response is needed. In most social situations the expected response would be 'yes'. The person can appear to respond appropriately without fully understanding the content.

2.   Compliance, i.e. an eagerness to please, to keep others happy.

3.   Susceptibility to non-verbal cues, e.g. a slight nod of the questioner's head.

Any one or all of these may be operating at any one time. This will vary for an individual depending on the situation, topic, mood and communicative partner. All of these reasons for acquiescence are driven by a basic need to belong and to maintain social interactions. However, it must be stressed that they are often not even recognised and therefore the reasons for them are not explored. These issues must be addressed if we are to meet clients' needs.

There are numerous other areas of potential communication breakdown; these include:

1.   Understanding and using complex verbal and written language

    (a) vocabulary/word finding

    (b) abstract concepts, e.g. time, feelings

    (c) semantics

    (d) grammar, e.g. tense markers, plurals

    (e) syntax, e.g. passives

    (f) articulation

    (g) sentence length

    (h) figurative language

    (i) ambiguity and inference

    (j) humour.

2. Understanding and using para-linguistic features

    (a) volume

    (b) intonation

    (c) pitch

    (d) rate

    (e) fluency

    (f) nasality

    (g) vocal quality.

3. Understanding and using non-verbal communication

    (a) posture

    (b) facial expression

    (c) eye contact

    (d) gesture

    (e) touch

    (f) proximity

    (g) sounds, e.g. groans, sighs, tuts

    (h) pictures/symbols/objects.

4. Pragmatics/social communication

Pragmatics is about how we use our communication skills with various people and in different situations. It involves the way communication is used to dictate how, when and with whom to talk, and for what purpose. Problems with pragmatics and social communication can affect the following areas:

    (a) initiation

    (b) turn-taking

    (c) perspective-taking

    (d) topic selection and maintenance

    (e) clarification and repair

    (f) closure

    (g) compromise, negotiation

    (h) accepting and giving criticism

    (i) appropriate style.

The effect of impairment in just one of these areas cannot be overestimated. The lack of recognition of problems potentially leads to misinterpretation of communication in all situations. An example of this is:

A client who has literal understanding of spoken language comes back from the pub and is asked if his friend is still there. His indignant response of 'I don't know' is interpreted as him being difficult and unhelpful. In actual fact, he feels that he cannot possibly know as he is no longer there. He thinks this is an impossible question to answer and is confused about why he is expected to know. Someone without literal understanding would have a shared expectation with the questioner that any information given would be a 'best guess', e.g. 'I think so, he was there when I left.'

We have tried to demonstrate the range, complexity and subtlety of the communication needs of people with borderline-mild learning disability. The interaction between communication and cognitive difficulties is highlighted by Walker (1997) who also stresses the importance of addressing communication needs:

> Learning disability has a reciprocal relationship with communication: poor communicative ability exacerbates poor cognitive function, which in turn slows or prevents improvement in communication skills. However, it is at the communication skills level that this negative cycle can be broken most easily, and the degree of handicap from the underlying disability reduced.

Learning disability and mental health

It is clear from research that all forms of psychiatric illness that occur within the general population are also seen in those with learning disabilities. This results in an added dimension of possible problems and needs which once again must be carefully assessed in order to ensure appropriate access to services. As has already been discussed, even a mild learning disability can result in a wide range of difficulties that have a huge impact on the individual's potential level of functioning in many different areas. The difficulties associated with the learning disability are not simply due to the underlying problems:

> Not only is the individual deprived of the ability to think, read, write, discuss at the same level as their non-disabled peers, but also...has to experience the loneliness of being different in a way that people would not choose to be. (Sinason 1997)

For those with borderline-mild learning disabilities, describing their thoughts, feelings and ideas can be an area of huge difficulty which from an early age often contributes to problems with social functioning and behaviour. As Gravell and France (1991) state, '...satisfactory social relationships go hand in hand with effective communication', and it is therefore highly likely that a breakdown in the latter will reduce the possibility of the former. Alongside this is the knowledge that social isolation and poor social effectiveness can be a factor in precipitating mental health problems. If, as previously stated, there are pervasive and subtle communication breakdowns in those with borderline-mild learning disability, as well as the more widely recognised problems in the moderate to severe learning disability groups, it is not surprising that studies show that psychiatric morbidity and learning disability often co-exist. The possible reasons for this co-existence may be that:

1. The learning disability is causing the mental health problem.

2. The mental health problem is resulting in an apparent learning disability.

3. Both the mental health problem and the learning disability have a common cause.

4. The learning disability and the mental health problems co-exist but have different causes.

It is likely that aetiology will vary with each individual.

Diagnosis of mental health problems is fraught with difficulties within the general population and debate between practitioners about one person's diagnosis can be great with individuals receiving different diagnoses on different occasions. This is because the facility to use physiological tests, often used in diagnosis in general medicine, is rarely available in psychiatry, e.g. blood tests may reveal diabetes but there are no tests to confirm a diagnosis of schizophrenia. Diagnosis in psychiatry relies heavily on the patient's verbal report of symptoms and observation of their verbal and non-verbal behaviour. It is therefore not surprising that the diagnosis of mental health problems within the learning disability population becomes even more complex.

Many verbal and non-verbal behaviours which may have little or no psychiatric significance in people with a learning disability are seen as highly relevant in the general population, e.g. echolalia may be indicative of language impairment in a person with learning disability, but may be considered indicative of a mental health problem in someone without a learning disability. Conversely it is important not simply to dismiss symptoms because they are often seen in people with learning disability; it may be that in some individuals they are a possible indication of mental health problems. It is essential that any diagnosis takes into account all the information available, including past functioning and behaviours. Moss *et al.* (1996) looked at the differences in the nature and frequency of psychiatric symptoms reported by patients with learning disability and key informants. Results showed that informants were more likely to report autonomic and psychotic symptoms whilst patients reported anxiety and depressive symptoms. Overall only 40.7 per cent of cases were reported by both interviewees. This clearly shows the importance of good information-gathering before any diagnosis is made.

Although diagnosis of mental health problems is difficult in people with learning disability, it is essential that any problems are identified and treated effectively. This client group may already have many difficulties and these can only be compounded by the presence of psychiatric illness. The presentation of these problems may also be modified or altered by the presence in the individual of a learning disability, as is discussed later within the individual descriptions of each illness.

Depression

Much of the research into depression in learning disability has been directed towards children rather than adults. It suggests that many of the problems experienced in the area of communication and social skills result in a higher likelihood that these people will develop a depressive illness at some point in their lives and, as in the general population, this likelihood actually increases with age (Cooper 1997). Wright-Strawderman and Watson (1992) found that 38.85 per cent of the children with learning disability in their study scored in the depressed range on the Children's Depression Inventory, and Stanley, Dai and Nolan (1997) stated that both learning disabled and behaviour disordered students reported a higher level of mild depression than their 'normal' counterparts. However, although many of the findings suggest a higher rate of incidence, there have also been studies which have not confirmed this, e.g. Maag and Reid (1994) who found no difference in the incidence of depression in children with a learning disability and those without, both levels being found to be 10 per cent.

Overall, the weight of evidence would tend to suggest increased likelihood of depression and also increased risk of suicide in this group (Huntingdon and Bender 1993). It is clear that this does not always reflect in rates of diagnosis and treatment, with many cases of depression simply assumed to be part of the learning disability. This may be because many of the verbal and non-verbal indicators of depression, e.g. reduced use of pitch, intonation and volume and reduction in the complexity of language, are features which are common in people with a learning disability. The assumption that these symptoms are part of the learning disability can have wide-ranging repercussions. The recognition of a depressive illness is essential if the individual is to be enabled to fulfil their full potential.

Psychotic disorders (including schizophrenia)

One of the main difficulties with the diagnosis of psychotic illnesses in individuals with learning disabilities is the reliance as previously stated on verbal ability in order to report symptoms, e.g. it is difficult to assess whether or not someone is hearing voices without them being able to give a full description and without them having a full understanding of what psychiatry means by 'hearing voices'. Once again the problems of suggestibility, acquiescence and compliance come to the fore and very careful interviewing is essential if the true nature of the individual's symptoms are to be understood. Alongside this is the suggestion that for some people with a learning disability the symptoms may be qualitatively different. Gelder *et al.* (1986) suggest that delusions and hallucinations may be less elaborate in this population. As suggested previously, it is possible that some of the idiosyncratic behaviours that the person with a learning disability may demonstrate could be misinterpreted as a psychotic symptom or that a psychotic symptom may be assumed to be part of the learning disability.

Diagnosis of these disorders within the learning disability population is essential if effective interventions are to be established. There have been great improvements in both the pharmacological and psycho-social treatment of schizophrenia in recent years and good diagnosis can allow the person with learning disability access to them. However, there does appear to be increased likelihood of side-effects from medication occurring within this population and so careful monitoring of this must be established, as once again the individual may find it difficult to describe the symptoms, e.g. extra-pyramidal side-effects, which may in themselves also affect communication.

There have been and continue to be problems with differential diagnosis between schizophrenia and autistic spectrum disorders. The Autistic Society has shown great concern about the numbers of people who are drawn into the psychiatric services at many different levels with a mis-diagnosis of a psychotic illness. In particular they have recently undertaken some research into the number of people with autistic spectrum disorders who are cared for within the high security hospitals. This mis-diagnosis, if it occurs, means that the patient's real difficulties are not recognised and therefore not addressed, alongside which is the possibility they may receive antipsychotic medication which could be unnecessary and may exacerbate problems.

Dementia

There is a wealth of research evidence to support the link between brain pathology and learning disability, but this does not preclude the presence of progressive brain conditions in this group of people, the most obvious of these being dementia. As the life expectancy of those with learning disability has increased, so has the incidence of dementia. This creates yet more challenges for the carers and services, e.g. initial problems with memory, communication and social skills are compounded. Once again early and accurate diagnosis is essential if interventions to help maintain functional abilities are to be successful. It would be very easy, given the difficulties that are already present, for the initial signs of deterioration to be missed or dismissed as due to the learning disability. This is particularly true if the person is living a relatively independent life in the community. Within institutional settings where staff are aware of the stresses caused by the environment, e.g. staff changes, they may assume these to be the cause of any deterioration.

Personality disorder

A recent study carried out by Khan, Cowan and Roy (1997) looked at the prevalence of personality disorders in a group of community-based people with varied levels of learning disability. The researchers used the Standardised Assessment of Personality and the results showed that 31 per cent had a level of impairment in social and occupational domains and personal distress that would lead to a diagnosis of personality disorder. Overall 50 per cent of the sample had some degree of personality abnormality.

It may be that these personality problems and the difficult and challenging behaviours which may result actually become more of a problem to the individual's effectiveness than the learning disability. In these cases it is important to ensure that diagnosis and treatment recognises this and are appropriate. There are drugs which may be helpful in treating behaviour problems, e.g. sedatives, antilibidinal. Also, new psychological treatments are being developed for those diagnosed with a personality disorder which may be useful, with adaptations, to those who also have a learning disability, e.g. Dialectual Behaviour Therapy.

The role of the speech and language therapist

Speech and language therapists aim to make it possible for people to communicate effectively, which may mean developing new skills for either the client and/or all those coming into contact with them. The increase in the number of speech and language therapists working within services for people with learning disabilities and mental health problems reflects the growing understanding of how communication is central to the assessment, diagnosis and treatment within this client group.

Assessment

As previously stated, within mental health assessment there is much reliance on the patient's ability to understand and respond to questions about thoughts, feelings and emotions. The possibility of misunderstanding and misinterpretation when this is being pursued with patients who have a learning disability is significant. Walker (1997) points out that 'Despite some excellent attempts to adapt the mental state examination to make it more applicable in learning disability, inherent problems remain.' The speech and language therapist has specialist knowledge of communication and, therefore, is ideally placed to contribute to the multi-disciplinary assessment process.

It is essential that the psychiatrist and the rest of the multidisciplinary team have an awareness of the possible communication needs and to ensure this the speech and language therapist needs to be involved in:

1. Assessment of the communication strengths and needs.

2. Ensuring that this information is available to and understood by the multidisciplinary team. Also that information from the team is taken into account during the communication assessment.

3. Contributing to the multidisciplinary discussion relating to diagnosis.

4. Working jointly with other professionals to enable the clients to access their assessments and ensure that the results are interpreted in light of the communication issues.

5. Involvement in the assessment of the client's capacity to make decisions, e.g. consent, fitness for interview, fitness to plead, resettlement, relationships.

Speech and language therapists can provide an assessment of a client's understanding of specific information. It would be good practice to take such an assessment into account when deciding the aforementioned issues.

The specific assessment of communication should include all possible areas of breakdown which have been described earlier in the chapter. It should also include:

1. Accessing past history and case notes.

2. Factors such as general health and sensory impairment.

3. The nature of all the physical environments accessed.

4. The nature of the communication used by others in contact with the person.

5. The effectiveness of the client's communication across all settings.

6. Past and present mental health issues.

Formal and informal assessment methods should be used and it is vital that assessment is seen as an ongoing process and not as a 'one-off'. This is particularly important because the communication variations which are seen in every individual are particularly significant in those who have a learning disability and mental health problems, e.g. variations due to mental state, communicative partners, topic. There is a lack, at this time, of formal assessments designed to identify breakdown in communication as found in adults with borderline-mild learning disability and/or mental health problems. Therapists working in the field have already begun to adapt existing assessments and develop new ones. It is important that this work is shared and researched if these assessments are to be useful and generally available.

Intervention

Intervention is aimed, as it is with all client groups, at maximising the person's communicative effectiveness. This will involve working with the client and/or those coming into contact with him or her. It is unlikely that any intervention will be successful if it does not include work with carers and other professionals coming into contact with the person.

The forms of intervention fall into three areas:

1. Working directly with clients to develop skills.

2. Adapting the environment to meet the client's needs. This may involve:

    a) Formal training for staff/professionals. The importance of this is being increasingly recognised; e.g. Thomas (1997) highlights this when he states, '…at present, theoretical linguistics, and practical assessments of human communication based in this, plays no part in the education and training of psychiatrists. Speech and language therapists have an important role to play in the future education of psychiatrists.'

    b) Joint working alongside staff/professionals.

    c) Contributing to the multidisciplinary team.

    d) Influencing and developing service provision for this client group, e.g. philosophies of care.

    e) Raising awareness of clients' needs in all settings, e.g. Mental Health Review Tribunals, police, dentists, health centres, leisure facilities.

    f) Adapting assessments, education packages, treatment programmes, information, etc. in order to take into account possible communication problems.

3. Facilitating the client's communication. This is necessary in specific situations when the communicative partner is unable to meet the client's communication needs fully. This may involve:

    a) Enabling the communicative partner to identify breakdowns in communication.

    b) Enabling them to be aware of the needs of the client.

    c) Enabling them to adapt their communication, e.g. utilising total communication. This may involve developing and providing specific resources.

    d) Modelling effective communication strategies.

As France and Muir (1997) state:

> …it may be that the profession will have to look to a different model of care delivery… This may initially mean a move away from…predominantly face-to-face contacts with patients and necessitate assessment and advice which will enrich the ongoing care

planning, as well as general and specific packages of training for staff and carers on aspects of language and communication and direct management strategies.

There is increasing evidence that input is most effective when the communication environment is addressed.

Factors influencing speech and language therapy effectiveness

As both borderline-mild learning disabilities and mental health are relatively new fields for speech and language therapists, there are many implications for undergraduate and postgraduate training. At the moment clinical work is fostering new skills with therapists learning 'on the hoof', but these issues need to be addressed by specific training.

As well as needing a good understanding of the communication needs of people with borderline-mild learning disability and/or mental health problems, therapists also need a knowledge of the systems in which services are provided, e.g. Mental Health Act, criminal justice system, social services legislation and provision, and medication. Training must also enable therapists to work effectively with and influence care staff and other professionals. It is important that the needs of individual therapists working within this area, which can be stressful and frustrating, are also recognised and met, e.g. through clinical supervision, performance review and goal-setting, and counselling.

Multidisciplinary team working, comprehensive care planning and care teams open to reflection and change are essential in order for speech and language therapists to deliver an effective service. It is essential that speech and language therapy service delivery is jointly planned with the managers of the services receiving the input in order to ensure:

1.   Shared understanding of what therapists are trying to achieve; and

2.   Shared responsibility for effective service planning and delivery.

Conclusion

This is a developing and exciting area of work for therapists and the validity and usefulness of the role of the speech and language therapist is increasingly being recognised. With the emphasis in all services on the need for evidence-based practice it is vital that therapists commit themselves to research and audit. Only through this can speech and language therapists demonstrate what all those already working in the field know, that they are clinically effective and essential to the well-being of the client.

References

Berger, M. (1997) IQ, Intelligence and Assessment. In S.G. Read (ed) *Psychiatry in Learning Disability*. London: Saunders.

Clare, C. (1993) Issues in the assessment and treatment of male sex offenders with mild learning disability. *Sexual and Marital Therapy* 8, 2, 167–180.

Clare, I. and Gudjonsson G.H. (1993) Interrogative suggestibility, confabulation and acquiescence in people with mild learning disabilities (mental handicap); implications for reliability during police interviews. *British Journal of Clinical Psychology 32*, 295–301.

Cooper, S. (1997) Epidemiology of psychiatric disorders in elderly compared with younger adults with learning disabilities. *British Journal of Psychiatry 170*, 4, 375–380.

France, J. and Muir, N. (1997) Conclusion, the way forward. In J. France and N. Muir (eds) *Communication and the Mentally Ill Patient.* London: Jessica Kingsley Publishers.

Gelder, M., Gath, D. and Mayou, R. (1986) *Oxford Textbook of Psychiatry.* Oxford: Oxford University Press.

Gravell, R. and France, J. (eds) (1991) *Speech and Communication Problems in Psychiatry.* London: Chapman and Hall.

Gudjonsson, G.H. and Clare, I. (1986) Suggestibility in police interrogation: a social psychology model. *Social Behaviour 1*, 83–104.

Huntingdon, D. and Bender, W. (1993) Adolescents with learning disabilities at risk? Emotional well-being, depression, suicide. *Journal of Learning Disabilities 26*, 3, 159–166.

Khan, A., Cowan, C. And Roy, A. (1997) Personality disorders in people with learning disabilities: a community survey. *Journal of Intellectual Disability Research 41*, 4, 324–330.

Maag, J. And Reid, R. (1994) The phenomenology of depression among students with and without learning disabilities: more similar than different. *Learning Disabilities Research & Practice 9*, 2, 91–103.

Moss, S., Prosser, H., Ibbotson, B. and Goldberg, D. (1996) Respondent and informant accounts of psychiatric symptoms in a sample of patients with learning disability. *Journal of Intellectual Disability Research 40*, 5, 457–465.

Nunkoosing, K. (1995) Learning Disability: psychology's contribution to diagnosis, assessment and treatment. In R. Bull And D. Carson (eds) *Handbook of Psychology in Legal Contexts.*

Sinason, V. (1997) The learning disabled (mentally handicapped) offender. In E. Welldon and C. Van Velson (eds) *A Practical Guide to Forensic Psychotherapy.* London: Jessica Kingsley Publishers.

Sparrow, S.S., Balla, D.A. and Cichetti, D.V. (1984) *Vineland Adaptive Behaviour Scales. Interview Edition – Survey Form.* Pines, MN: American Guidance Association.

Spencer, D.A. (1997) Concept of learning disability. In S.G. Read (ed) *Psychiatry in Learning Disability.* London: W.B. Saunders.

Stanley, P., Dai, Y. and Nolan, R. (1997) Differences in depression and self-esteem reported by learning disabled and behaviour disordered middle school students. *Journal of Adolescence 20*, 2, 219–222.

Thomas, P. (1997) What can linguistics tell us about thought disorder? In J. France and N. Muir (eds) *Communication and the Mentally Ill Patient.* London: Jessica Kingsley Publishers.

Walker, M. (1997) Communication and learning disability. In S.G. Read *Psychiatry in Learning Disability.* London: W.B. Saunders.

Wechsler, D. (1986) *Wechsler Adult Intelligence Scale – Revised (WAIS-R).* Sidcup: Psychological Corporation.

Wong, J. (1997) Assessment of capacity to make treatment decisions in adults with learning disabilities. *Tizard Learning Disability Preview 2*, 3, 35–39.

Wright-Strawderman, C. and Watson, B. (1992) The prevalence of depressive symptoms in children with learning disabilities. *Journal of Learning Disabilities 25*, 4, 258–264.

CHAPTER 21

What Can We Learn From the Deaf Patient?

Alice Thacker

B was assessed for the first time by a specialist psychiatric team at age 52. She had been an in-patient in a standard (hearing) psychiatric hospital for 24 years with a diagnosis of schizophrenia. B was profoundly prelingually deaf and without speech or written English. There is no record of an interpreter or signer ever having been employed in her previous institution. She presented as highly agitated, frequently clutching her abdomen, and screaming when in the toilet. She had had abdominal surgery and a diagnosis of Crohn's Disease in her previous placement as a result of these behaviours. B refused to participate in activities off the ward.

Her keyworker on the specialist service was the speech and language therapist, who like all staff is able to use British Sign Language. Communication was established with B, who disclosed that much of her distress was linked to a rape (which occurred on an outing and was not reported by hospital staff), resultant pregnancy and termination, the latter performed without her informed consent, as it was not administered in sign. She had subsequently discovered foetal body parts in the toilet.

Counselling was begun soon after the disclosure, and distress abated markedly. The speech and language therapist was able to determine that B produced some psychotic signing and was able to monitor the effects of treatment on her functioning. B was discharged to a sheltered community setting, where she is thriving.

Another patient, L, was diagnosed as schizophrenic on the basis of delusional ideas, a first-rank symptom. She frequently told her therapist, with great conviction, that she was 'pregnant', although she had had a complete hysterectomy years before.

As the therapist began to learn about deaf culture and experience, he realised that L's problem was not delusions, but incomplete and overly concrete information. She had been told as a girl that 'sex' equalled 'pregnant'; thus, whenever she reported 'I'm pregnant', she was in fact simply disclosing a recent sexual encounter (B. Karlin, personal correspondence).

Introduction

Deaf people form a small but significant minority in every country. This chapter will deal primarily with those who are profoundly prelingually deaf; that is, who have little useful hearing from a very early age, even with amplification, and who are unable to use spoken language as a primary means of communication. This linguistic and cultural community of 25,000 in Britain (Sign 1998) clearly has distinct needs in terms of mental health provision. This chapter will describe the special considerations which have been identified by clinicians and researchers in the assessment and treatment of deaf clients and qualitative research findings on phenomenology, much of which has implications for the nature of psychosis itself. It will provide a brief overview of how services currently available in Britain are meeting needs.

General considerations in diagnosis

It is likely that there are cultural differences in the expression of mental illness, especially due to communication differences. It is equally likely that *normality* is expressed differently from hearing people. There is evidence that the deaf community itself may apply a different concept of 'mental health problems' to that held by the hearing majority. Griggs (1998) found that mental health was equated with 'coping' by her deaf informants, whereas hearing people tended to use more positive descriptors, e.g. 'happy, fulfilled, good marriage'. 'When a community experiences [educational deprivation and social exclusion] en masse, its members' concept of wellness may shift' (Sign 1998, p.45).

Mis-diagnosis and over- and under-diagnosis commonly occurs with this patient group for a variety of reasons.

Specialist mental health workers for deaf people cannot assume that the information given on referral is accurate or has been elicited appropriately. Mis-diagnoses have been common. Mental illness can be missed because abnormal behaviour is attributed to the patient's deafness (Denmark and Eldridge 1969). Alternatively a deaf patient's frustration in communication released as an 'explosive reaction' can be mistaken for evidence of mental illness (Denmark 1966). It is important for mental health workers for deaf people to report facts elicited and direct observations made in a detailed and objective fashion. Conclusions based on the facts and observations should be made and recorded entirely separately. *Non-specialist* mental health workers are not likely to be able to elicit facts nor observe communication for themselves owing to their own limited communication.

The mental health worker for deaf people, though usually seen as a super-specialist, actually needs to be a broad generalist as the services of other specialists are generally not available to the patient because of communication differences. Non-specialists in deafness might be able to take an accurate history from the patient through an interpreter, but will be handicapped in taking a mental state as the majority of this assessment relies on direct observation of the patient's behaviour, attitudes and emotions associated with the context and content of the interview (Hindley *et al.* 1994). Deaf patients' attitudes and emotional responses are easily misunderstood. The assessor needs to distinguish the patient's emotional expression and assumed attitudes that are merely part of storytelling from the genuine, immediate emotional responses and attitudes of the patient. Attention to this degree of subtlety is important for mental illness diagnoses.

The disease or trauma that causes prelingual deafness in some cases gives rise to an additional organic brain deficit, the phenomena of which must be distinguished from those of functional psychoses (Vernon and Rothstein 1968).

Physical examinations and investigations are particularly important in deaf patients to detect progressive disorders, which have significance for mental function. Significant visual impairment and blindness is commonly associated with deafness. This additional sensory deprivation can have a crucial impact on communication development. A congenitally blind child has greater difficulty in learning the rules of communication with mother through eye contact and responsive smiling. The concept of self can develop late, so that the 'I-you' distinction is delayed…in fact the individual might be labelled 'autistic' wrongly. In addition, representational play, which in many respects is the basis for symbolic language, develops much later than normal.

As a result, congenitally blind adults may have depersonalised relationships; they may seem unmotivated and 'schizoid'. Professionals are likely to underestimate mood, intelligence and personality in patients with reduced expressive behaviour. In Usher's syndrome, or retinitis pigmentosa, a genetic, usually recessive, disorder of early childhood deafness associated with later onset progressive blindness is associated with a five-fold increase in the likelihood of schizophrenia-like psychosis. Halgren (1958) described this syndrome of deafness, retinitis pigmentosa, ataxia and psychosis.

It is not uncommon for progressive visual impairment to be first detected while the deaf adolescent or young adult is a client of special psychiatric services. Counselling and practical help in regard to encroaching blindness can improve the client's ability to cope and bring about improvements in behaviour and mood.

Sensorineural deafness is the most common complication of maternal rubella, and rubella is associated with the eventual development of many other disorders. As many researchers have found perceptual problems to be linked to schizophrenia in hearing people, it is important to distinguish those symptoms from the central auditory imperception that is experienced by up to 50 per cent of people with congenital rubella. This syndrome consists of the inability to respond to sound on a cortical level, regardless of hearing threshold. It results in deficits in: localisation of sound; figure/ground discrimination; and interpretation of sound. (The same problems, in fact, that are routinely experienced by hearing aid users.) Again, this disorder often has a role in the inappropriate diagnosis of autism in adults and children.

Sever, South, and Shaver (1985), in a thorough review, report the prevalence of diabetes to be as high as 20 per cent and the prevalence of thyroid disease, mostly in the form of reduced function, to be 5 per cent in congenital rubella. Hypothyroidism can mimic depressive illness with slowness of all bodily and mental functions; if not appropriately treated it can lead to dementia. Hyperthyroidism can mimic anxiety, mania or schizophrenia. Up to 10 per cent of those with congenital rubella may suffer late onset eye damage. New behaviour disorders or epileptic phenomena can present late in congenital rubella. In addition to the common physical disorders associated with the key causes of deafness there are a multitude of minor disorders associated with genetic syndromes and traumatic causes of deafness, which will have a direct or indirect psychological effect on mental states. The assessors need to be aware of all the possibilities.

The effect of language use on diagnosis

Speech and language are the prime tools for diagnosing schizophrenia in hearing people. Deaf clients can be severely disadvantaged in this context. One in five patients seen by an NHS psychiatric unit (in-patient, out-patient and community services) had grossly inadequate *developmental* communication skills (Sign 1998). The language of deaf people should not be equated to English. Word for sign translations of sign language and the writings of many language-deprived but healthy deaf people have been found to suggest thought disorder, the communications showing a fragmented, confused quality (Altshuler, Baroff and Rainer 1963). Written samples must *never* be used in the assessment of deaf people. Communication might suggest chronic schizophrenia or organic disorder because language-deprived deaf people tend to talk in concrete terms (Basilier 1964). A potential cause of confusion is that many normal prelingually deaf people do not signal topic changes in a way that is clear to hearing people, and the ongoing lack of feedback that results from this can lead to frustration and disrupted expression. Many deaf people are said to perseverate abnormally when in fact they are using a strategy of rapidly repeating signs because they think their conversational partner has not understood them. Studies of American Sign Language have shown that repetition is also used routinely to distinguish nouns from verbs and for other grammatical and semantic functions. It is probable that BSL incorporates similar devices. On the level of discourse, the author has noted in her own practice and in interactions with colleagues that confirmation of known facts and long-held opinions through the use of repetition is much more highly valued by the deaf community than by hearing peers. This repetition of themes might appear suspect to a hearing clinician unfamiliar with deaf usage.

A client's very insistence on communicating with the hearing professional can earn them an undeserved label of 'thought-disordered'. Intrusions from *spoken* language might appear to be inappropriate or rhyming word choice, when in fact it may represent choice based on cultural usage and the demands of the situation (Thacker 1994, 1998).

Talking past the point, which can also be confused with thought disorder, is a common defence by patients against poor comprehension (Kitson and Fry 1990). A client, particularly one with poor receptive skills, might repeat another's questions or remarks slavishly, thus giving the impression of echolalia. This behaviour is in some cases a simple strategy for keeping the interchange going while the client tries to decipher what was said and formulate an appropriate response (Thacker 1998).

Idiomatic signs (those specific to individuals or small groups) can be misinterpreted as the neologistic inventions of people suffering from schizophrenia (Misiaszek et al. 1985). Regional signs can be similarly misinterpreted (Thacker 1998).

The development of a modified version (Thacker 1994, 1998) of the Present State Examination (Wing, Cooper and Sartorius 1974) brought to light the necessity of customising interview schedules for each subject to which they are administered. Modifications are required for individuals on the grounds of:

(1) **Age**. Older patients tend to use more fingerspelling and different vocabularies from those of younger people. For example, SCHOOL is shown as a bundle (of books) carried at waist level by an elderly person, rather than the gesture of passing a book before the face which is much more commonly produced by younger generations.

(2) **Education**. A subject who has been educated orally might have a limited grasp of sign vocabulary and grammatical features. That person would therefore be more dependent on English lip patterns, both receptively and expressively. Adults who have received highly didactic, prescriptive teaching are more likely to answer in the affirmative (or indeed to echo questions) when questioned by a hearing person in order to appear agreeable, though their responses are inaccurate.

(3) **Conceptual expression**. Individuals who have been exposed to an accessible language only later in childhood and, particularly, whose schooling has not been in sign might have relatively concrete concepts and possess little ability to generalise examples to a superordinate concept. An example of the latter would be a person who cannot generalise HEART POUND to a more comprehensive NERVOUS or ANXIOUS. In some cases such individuals might be expected to produce false negative answers in response to queries about perceptual symptoms. In addition, many prelingually deaf people have difficulty with formal interrogatives such as WHEN?, HOW? and WHY? Thus a multiple choice format might be required, with the attendant dangers of leading or limiting the subject.

Diagnosis and recommendations for management are based, in the first instance, on the performance of the patient in the interview. Because the life experiences of deaf people differ so widely, it is difficult to draw valid conclusions from any difficulties they have in giving an account of themselves. They might, for example, have serious difficulty in expressing time concepts. This might lead either to a lack of usable information, or to a distortion of events; e.g. the patient may try to link the onset of symptoms to a major, memorable event, thus giving the false impression that they attribute causality to it. Particularly for remote events, the patient's inability to codify in language can have a profound impact on recall, leading to greater dependence on hearing informants. These informants are often family members who, because they cannot sign, place a greater emphasis on perceived behaviour problems than on the deaf person's own feelings and cognitions.

Deaf people who have had inadequate communication models at home and school can suffer in interviews in several ways. Adults of normal intellect and mental status may, in the author's experience, have difficulty with formal questions such as 'how?' and 'why?', even in sign language. This might be because they are accustomed to being *told* rather than asked. Impoverished or rigid vocabulary and concepts can masquerade as poverty of content, tangentiality, derailment, poor insight, and social withdrawal.

Assessment of cognitive level must be approached thoughtfully. An example of problematic assumptions would be the following: sequencing tasks presuppose that a subject will organise elements from left to right. This is an invalid expectation for many deaf clients, who do badly on paper tasks but organise quite complex practical sequences very well, or who do well in activities requiring a high level of temporal or spatial organisation but which are not dependent on this particular ordering. This effect might be due to the poor level of literacy achieved by many deaf people, for whom reading and writing are not included in the central linguistic and cognitive constructs of the world.

Mental illness in prelingually deaf people

Having examined some of the factors which lead to over-diagnosis of mental disorder in deaf people, we turn now to a number of studies which describe the prevalence (Table 21.1) and expression of mental illness in prelingually deaf people.

Table 21.1 Incidence of psychiatric disorder in the prelingually deaf population	
Attention deficit disorders	Overall higher prevalence (Vernon and Andrews 1990) due to CNS and endocrine sequelae in rubella, meningitis, etc.
Personality disorder	Any increased suspiciousness is reality-based. True paranoid disorder more common in hard of hearing and acquired deafness (Vernon and Andrews 1990). Borderline Personality Disorder 'not seen' in deaf client group (Grinker, Werble and Drye 1977). Schizoid personality 'somewhat more frequent' in rubella and low-birthweight cases (Vernon and Andrews 1990).
Autism	5 of 8 congenital rubella patients (Hindley et al. 1994). Prevalence rate of 7.4% in rubella population vs. 0.7% in the general population (Chess 1977).
Depression	No difference qualitatively or quantitatively (Robinson 1978). Possibly less in deaf school-age children, though social phobia increased (Hindley et al. 1994). Linguistic and cultural differences between clinician and client can mask affective symptoms (Hindley, Hill and Bond 1993).
Schizophrenia	'Essentially the same illness in deaf and hearing people' (Vernon and Andrews 1990), though more chronicity through lack of treatment. Stress of deafness not schizogenic. Five-fold increase in schizophrenia among Usher's syndrome sufferers (Halgren 1958).
Bipolar disorder	Rarely reported in literature (Markowitz and Nininger 1984; Kitson and Thacker, 2000). No evidence of increased incidence.
Mental handicap	34% of rubella victims have IQ below 90 (Vernon and Andrews 1990). Deafness itself does not affect intelligence. Genetic deaf higher than average IQ. Some aetiologies associated with mental retardation due to concomitant brain damage (Vernon and Andrews 1990).

Forty to fifty per cent of deaf children, as compared with 25 per cent of hearing children, have emotional, behavioural, and adjustment problems.

Studies of phenomenology

Formal communication disorder

Analysis of the British Sign Language of a cohort of deaf adults with clinical DSM-III diagnoses of schizophrenia revealed that the following errors of *form* of language occurred, and distinguished this group from healthy deaf controls (Thacker 1994, 1998):

1. **Incoherence**. This category was scored when a sequence of apparently unrelated signs was produced: NOT MY MOTHER SHAPE WALL SHAPE GOOD.

2. **Topic derailment**. Switching of topic in mid discourse.

    Interviewer: ALL POLICE WORLD DISAPPEAR…WHAT HAPPEN?

    Subject: WHEN WORLD c.e.l.l. c.e.l.l. GROW SPREAD SPREAD LATER YOU KNOW d.o.n.o.s.a.u.r. WALK SIDEWAYS MONKEY RISE UP SLOW… [probably a derailment onto the film 'King Kong vs. Godzilla'].

3. **Topic/thematic perseveration**. Inappropriate insertion of signs related to a common, preferred theme rather than to the immediate context of the discourse or task. Lecours and Vanier-Clement (1976) describe this behaviour as the use of 'predilection words'.

    Interviewer: YOU FAMILY COMMUNICATE HOW?

    Subject: (predilection terms are underscored) MYSELF CLEVER MOUTH CLEVER SPEAK SIGN SPEAK MOUTH TEA FOOD h.e.l.e.n. SOME NURSE FOOD THERE BAD EAT HERE SAW c.h.e.s.t.n.u.t. NO DIFFERENT ME SAY NO BAD BOY SAY DIFFERENT w.a.l.n.u.t.

4. **Visuospatial anomalies**

    (a) Misuse of signing space. An acutely ill young woman inadvertently brushed her breast with her right hand in the midst of an interview. Her sign abruptly became unintelligible. It became apparent that she was taking two roles in a dialogue in an anomalous way. Her part of the dialogue was expressed with her left hand; her right hand took the part of her brother. Immediately after this interview she disclosed for the first time sexual abuse by her brother.

    (b) Utilisation of a non-linguistic element within an utterance in place of a sign, e.g. grabbing one's own hair to signify 'thatched roof'.

5. **Stereotypy**. The recurrent production of a specific sign or gesture in inappropriate contexts. This error is linked to borderline performance IQ.

6. **Illogicality**. Conclusions are reached that do not follow logically from previous material. There may be a discrepancy in statements:

Subject: POLICE DISAPPEAR TERRIBLE MAYBE FIRE BURN UP RAINFOREST

or a conflict arises between a signed picture description and the picture upon which it is based.

7. **Derailment based on articulatory feature / 'clang'** (Andreason 1979). Selection of sign is based on the shape of previous signs rather than their meanings. The following sign substitutions were made on the basis of similar articulatory features.

    One subject took her school sign for SENTENCE (a narrow horizontal rectangle traced in the air) and tied it around her waist. This was in the context of an established writing task. Another schizophrenic subject persisted in using the sign for BREAD to designate a male nurse. It transpired that his actual name sign (signed nickname) was BEARD. This substitution represents a cross-linguistic clang on the written English words.

8. **Sign perseveration**. This category was scored when a sign or sequence of signs was repeated more than three times in immediate succession with no discernible syntactic, semantic or pragmatic function for the repetition.

9. **Phonemic paraphasia**. The subject produces a gesture that is not a recognised sign, although the target sign may be discernible. If challenged, he or she defends the gestural choice. This descriptive category includes unusual, stereotyped handshapes for otherwise recognisable signs and phenomena not directly comparable with a spoken language.

    One acutely schizophrenic woman routinely made signs in the wrong location: e.g. she traced a circle around her face rather than over her palm to describe a JAR.

The authors of a recent and influential survey of mental health status and needs among deaf people in Britain (Sign 1998) seem to equate 'severe mental illness' with an inability to communicate well enough to take part in a BSL interview. They report that people in the deaf community themselves identify changes in communication as significant indicators of mental illness (p.51).

Assessment of 'auditory' hallucinations

One of the most salient questions in the assessment of psychosis involves the presence and nature of 'auditory' hallucinations. This is a difficult area in diagnosing profoundly, pre-lingually deaf people who have never heard intelligible speech. Yet there are a number of reports in the clinical literature which indicate that some deaf people do experience what can perhaps be described as 'verbal' (as opposed to spoken) or 'message' hallucinations (Monteiro and Critchley 1994; Kitson and Thacker, 2000).

It is important to give subjects the latitude to describe their perceptions of communication in any modality, that is, whether the content of the hallucination was conveyed through spoken language, sign, or other means. Thus, one of the author's patients was able to describe HEARING CHILDREN SHOUTING FINGERSPELLING IN MY HEAD. Another person reported her sister TALKING (generic sign) in her abdomen, which was the part of the body where she did in reality perceive the vibrations of loud sounds.

Many of the qualities of 'auditory' hallucinations described by hearing patients do not seem to accord with the perceptions of deaf people. The author's hallucinating subjects were often not able to identify whether the 'voice' was that of a male or female, even when they could supply the identity of the speaker ('it's Dr X'). Interestingly, this was frequently true even when the percept had a visual component. It would appear that perceptual parameters that are not salient in reality are not salient within hallucinations (Thacker 1997).

In this realm of phenomenology, too, great care must be taken to avoid overdiagnosing the deaf client. Kitson and Fry (1990) noted that normal mumbling in sign (Hurst 1988) can be misinterpreted as hallucinosis and that apparently abnormal explanations or beliefs may be explainable by lack of vicarious learning or naivety and not fit the criteria of a delusion. An example of this is the deaf patient who understood a science fiction programme to be factual. He was not deluded, merely naive, yet initially this was thought to be a symptom of mental illness. Often a close exploration of such phenomena is required, necessitating very accurate and detailed communication.

Much epidemiological research remains to be done by investigators who have fluent communication with this linguistically heterogeneous population.

Present provision in Britain

Although there is compelling evidence of the need for specialist services for the deaf community, present provision is in most respects inadequate. Much of the following material is drawn from a major survey on behalf of the British Society on Mental Health and Deafness on emotional and mental health needs in the deaf community. This report was commissioned by the British Society on Mental Health and Deafness (Sign 1998).

There are three psychiatric units offering in-patient, out-patient and community care in England: at Preston, London and Birmingham. Each has 20 to 25 beds. Only one of these units serves children and adolescents, and that only in an out-patient capacity at present, despite the finding (Sign 1998) that 'A conservative estimate of between 650–3,200 deaf children and adolescents a year could potentially need specialist [mental] health services' (Sign 1998, p.11). Further mental health care is provided by clinic-centred community services in Scotland and Northern Ireland.

The Sign survey found that many of the clients in residential services who were identified by staff as having mental health problems had never had a psychiatric assessment. There is no doubt that deaf people are seen with exacerbated problems in in-patient psychiatric units because lower-level services (such as marriage) are rarely accessible (Kitson and Thacker, 2000). The majority of referrals continue to be instigated by social workers. However, a recent report (Sign 1998) has found that many authorities have no provision for deaf people *per se*, and that only 18 per cent of social workers for the deaf can demonstrate the minimum requirements for fluent BSL.

Thus it seems that, even when services are *said* to be provided, they often fall short.

There is cause for optimism, however, in the specialist courses now being offered in a number of departments of Psychiatry (St. George's Hospital Medical School, University of London), Psychology (e.g. University of Manchester), Speech and Language Therapy (e.g. University College, London and City University) and Deaf Studies (e.g. Bristol University).

Conclusions

This chapter has given a brief overview of special considerations in the management of prelingually deaf people who are referred for psychiatric help, some findings of psychotic phenomena as expressed by deaf signing patients, and the evidence that, while needs have been identified and are being partially addressed in Britain, much remains to be done in terms of adequate and equitable mental health provision.

It is hoped that, as the knowledge of new generations of psychiatric workers grows, such provision will become a reality.

References

Altshuler, K., Baroff, G. Rainer, J. (1963) Operational description of a pilot clinic. In J. Rainer, M. Altshuler, F. Kallmann, and E. Deming (eds) *Family and Mental Health Problems in a Deaf Population*. Columbia: Department of Medical Genetics, New York State Psychiatric Institute, Columbia University.

Andreason, N.C. (1979) Thought, language, and communication disorders, I and II. *Archives of General Psychiatry 36*, 1315–1330.

Basilier, T. (1964) Surdophrenia: the psychic consequences of congenital or early acquired deafness. *Acta Psychiatrica Scandinavica 40*, 180, 362–372.

Chess, S. (1977) Follow-up report on autism in congenital rubella. *Journal of Autism and Childhood Schizophrenia 7*, 69–81.

Denmark, J. (1966) Mental illness and early profound deafness. *British Journal of Medical Psychology 39*, 117–124.

Denmark, J.C. and Eldridge, R.W. (1969) Psychiatric services for the deaf. *Lancet 11*, 259–262.

Griggs, M. (1998) Deafness and mental health: perceptions. First World Conference on Mental Health and Deafness, Washington DC, October 22–24.

Grinker, R.R. Sr., Werble, B. and Drye, R. (1977) *The Borderline Syndrome*. New York: Basic Books.

Halgren, B. (1958) Retinitis pigmentosa in combination with congenital deafness and vestibulocerebellar ataxia; with psychiatric abnormality in some cases. *Acta Genetica 8*, 97–104.

Hindley, P., Hill, P. and Bond, D. (1993) Interviewing deaf children, the interviewer effect: a research note. *Journal of Child Psychology and Psychiatry 14*, 8, 1461–1467.

Hindley, P., Hill, P.D., McGuigan, S. and Kitson, N. (1994) Psychiatric disorder in deaf and hearing impaired young people: a prevalence study. *Journal of Child Psychology and Psychiatry 35*, 5, 917–934.

Hurst, J. (1988) Metaphors of communication in the dreams of deaf people. *The Psychiatric Journal of the University of Ottawa 13*, 2, 75–78.

Kitson, N. and Fry, R. (1990) Prelingual deafness and psychiatry. *British Journal of Hospital Medicine 44*, 353–356.

Kitson, N. and Thacker, A. (2000). Assessment. In P. Hindley and N. Kitson (eds) *Mental Health and Deafness*. London: Whurr.

Lecours, A. and Vanier-Clement, M. (1976) Schizophasia and jargonaphasia. *Brain and Language 3*, 516–565.

Markowitz, J.C. and Nininger, J. E. (1984) A case report of mania and congenital deafness. *American Journal of Psychiatry 141*, 894–895.

Misiaszek, J., Dooling, J., Gieseke, A., Melman, H., Misiaszek, J.G. and Jorgensen, K. (1985) Diagnostic considerations in deaf patients. *Comprehensive Psychiatry 26*, 6, 513–521.

Monteiro, B. and Critchley, E.M.R. (1994) Deafness and communication. In E.M.R. Critchley (ed) *The Neurological Boundaries of Reality*. London: Farrand Publications.

Ridgeway, S. and Checinski, K. (1991) Mental health research methodology with deaf people. European society for mental health and deafness. Proceedings, Utrecht. pp.87–91.

Robinson, L.D. (1978) Sound minds in a soundless world. Washington DC: DHEW publication No. ADM 77–560. US Government Printing Office.

Sever, J.L., South, M.A. and Shaver, K.A. (1985) Delayed manifestations of congenital rubella. *Reviews of Infectious Diseases 7*, Suppl. 1, S164–169.

Sign (1998) *Mental Health Services for Deaf People: Are They Appropriate?* London: Department of Health.

Thacker, A. (1994) Formal communication disorder: sign language in deaf people with schizophrenia. *British Journal of Psychiatry 165*, 818–823.

Thacker, A. (1997) Linguistic phenomena in non-speakers: signs of schizophrenia. *Proceedings of the Winter Meeting of the Royal College of Psychiatrists*, Cardiff.

Thacker, A. (1998) The Manifestation of Schizophrenic Formal Communication Disorder in Sign Language. Doctoral dissertation, Department of Psychiatry, St. George's Hospital Medical School, University of London.

Vernon, McC. and Andrews, J.F. (1990) *The Psychology of Deafness.* London: Longmans.

Vernon, McC. and Rothstein, D.A. (1968) Prelingual deafness: an experiment of nature. *Archives of General Psychiatry 19*, 361–369.

Wing, J.K., Cooper, J.E. and Sartorius, N. (1974) *The Measurement and Classification of Psychiatric Symptoms.* Cambridge: Cambridge University Press.

CHAPTER 22

Communication and Mental Health in People with Autism and Asperger's Syndrome

Jane Shields and Dougal Hare

Autistic spectrum disorder

Autistic spectrum disorder is a complex developmental disorder which affects social and communication skills and can be accompanied by learning disabilities. This disorder is diagnosed by identifying behaviours which reflect the underlying 'triad' of difficulties: in the areas of social interaction, social communication, and imagination. As autism occurs in varying degrees of severity the term 'spectrum' is used to describe the whole range, including Asperger's Syndrome. This often misunderstood disability touches the lives of many thousands of children and adults in the UK and is found amongst all races, nationalities and social backgrounds. Classic autism affects four times as many males as females and Asperger's Syndrome affects nine times as many males as females.

Social communication: a key deficit of autistic spectrum disorder

Many people with autistic spectrum disorder develop only a limited use of spoken language and some (especially those with accompanying severe learning disability) will remain non-verbal. Within the autistic spectrum, however, can be found many individuals who present with spoken language which appears to be superficially normal. Such verbal individuals may have a diagnosis of high-functioning autism, or of Asperger's Syndrome. Despite their grasp of the form of language they still show the deficits in social communication – the use of language in social context – which form one-third of the defining triad of autism. Their communication deficits appear to result from an underlying deficit which is socio-cognitive, rather than primarily linguistic, and which shows itself principally in the area of pragmatics. Both verbal and non-verbal communication are affected, as are the understanding and use of spoken language in social context.

Communication in Asperger's Syndrome

The diagnostic label of Asperger's Syndrome remains somewhat controversial, with continuing debate as to its existence as a separate diagnosis from that of high-functioning autism. DSM-IV and ICD-10 introduced Asperger's Syndrome as a separate category for the first time. They specify the need for the presence of qualitative impairments in social interaction and of restricted repetitive behaviour and stereotyped patterns of behaviour, interests and activities – as for autism. In contrast, however, their criteria for Asperger's Syndrome require there to have been no clinically significant delay in spoken or receptive language or in cognitive development.

Although they may have developed language in childhood, individuals with Asperger's Syndrome do show abnormalities of communication, affecting both their understanding and expressive use of language in conversation. Some of these difficulties can be linked with their difficulties in making sense of other people: of mindreading (Baron-Cohen 1995). Others may relate to right hemisphere pathology (Ozonoff and Miller 1996). All show themselves as pragmatic deficits and interfere with social discourse.

The comprehension of individuals with Asperger's Syndrome is likely to be over-literal and to show poor awareness of the listener's point of view or communicative intent. There will be little allowance for context (social or linguistic) and difficulties in understanding humour, sarcasm, metaphors or polite requests. They may appear unaware of or confused by non-verbal, paralinguistic aspects of communication such as intonation, facial expression and body language. When anxious or stressed, their level of understanding is likely to fall and it may be helpful to reinforce (or replace) the spoken word by visual forms of communication such as writing or pictures.

Individuals with Asperger's Syndrome often present with odd intonation and a paucity of facial expression, their intonation and body language seeming inappropriate to the social and linguistic context. Their conversation may be one-sided and pay little attention to the listener's reaction. They may show verbosity, talking incessantly about their special interest and ignoring attempts to interrupt or change topic. This egocentric conversational style reflects their restricted awareness of another person's point of view, but may be confused with a lack of coherence resulting from other causes, including schizophrenia. Training in social skills by speech and language therapists can be helpful in developing more appropriate social communication in people with Asperger's Syndrome (Howlin 1997; Van Berckelaer-Onnes 1994).

Communication and mental health in people with autism

An important question is what role autism-related communication problems play in the aetiology of mental health problems in people with autism. Baker and Cantwell (1987) in a study of the correlates of psychiatric disorder in children found that speech and language dysfunction was the most important factor that would distinguish the psychiatrically well from the psychiatrically unwell. Moreover, language dysfunction was more likely than speech dysfunction. It has been proposed that as alternative explanations of this relationship, specifically the possibility of a third factor antecedent to both psychiatric and language dysfunction, have little empirical support (Cantwell, Baker and Mattison 1979), language problems themselves appear to be directly implicated in the onset and course of psychological disorders and may well be risk factors in such. How does this bear out with regard to people with autistic spectrum disorder in which communication dysfunction is a core feature? Szatmari et al. (1989) in a follow up study of children with high-functioning autism (i.e.

non-learning disabled) found over-anxiety, paranoid and magical thinking and obsessional-compulsive symptomatology; other studies have found similar outcomes (e.g. Rumsey, Rapoport and Sceery 1985).

A more specific understanding of why communication dysfunction seems to result in psychological disturbance in people with autistic spectrum disorder appears when one considers the results of them being cut off from important sources of information about both themselves and other people as a result of their 'mind-blindness' (Baron-Cohen 1995). The major effect of this is on the person's ability to make predictions about the world around them. Anxiety can be conceptualised as resulting from the failure of perceived events to match the predictions made about those events by a person (Kelley 1955). Such a *social-cognitive* model of anxiety in people with autistic spectrum disorder has been advanced by Rimland (1964) and Baron-Cohen (1989), who have proposed that the repetitive actions, including verbal rituals and restricted conversational topics, engaged in by people with autism are a means of coping with an otherwise incomprehensible *social* environment due to their impaired ability to understand other people or the reasons for their actions.

Psychiatric conditions in people with autism and the possibility of mis-diagnosis

The danger of 'false positives' must be considered when assessing the mental health of people with autistic spectrum disorder: we can not necessarily assume a shared phenomenology/cognitive experience between people with and without autism. For example, research (Blackshaw 1998) has indicated that people with Asperger's Syndrome are very paranoid, but for different, non-psychotic reasons when compared with non-autistic people. Similarly, Baron-Cohen (1989) proposes that the repetitive speech and actions of people with autism are different from those with obsessional-compulsive disorders. It is important to consider whether we should talk about mental health problems in the absence of the person being able to report on their own experiences.

Some presenting characteristics of Asperger's Syndrome in adulthood can be confused with the negative signs of schizophrenia. Many people with autistic spectrum disorder have unusual sensory and perceptual experiences (O'Neill and Jones 1997). The unusual and idiosyncratic language use of Asperger individuals may be incorrectly diagnosed as thought disorder. Wing (1986) cautions that an inappropriate diagnosis of psychotic illness may be given because of the way in which individuals with Asperger's Syndrome respond to questions about their mental state. For instance, auditory hyperacuity together with a literal interpretation of the diagnostic question 'Do you ever hear voices when no-one is in the room?' may produce a positive response which suggests auditory hallucinosis. A further complication in separating the developmental Asperger's Syndrome from mental illness is the difficulty in communicating feelings or emotions which is associated with autistic spectrum disorder. Howlin (1997) describes this as a major problem for clinicians since the diagnosis and treatment of affective disorders relies heavily on the individual's ability to describe feelings. She points out that the diagnostic process may also be complicated by the fact that stress and depression can manifest themselves as aggressive or even paranoid behaviours. Problems can also occur if 'challenging behaviour' is assumed to be an indicator of underlying mental health problems in people with severe language dysfunction and learning disabilities (Tsiouris and Adelman 1997). Again, a knowledge of the form and content of autism-specific actions is essential when working with this group of people, as what appears at first to represent an underlying pathology may well be autism-specific (Hare and Leadbeater 1998).

Psychiatric disorders do occur in individuals with Asperger's Syndrome, most commonly those related to anxiety or depression (Lainhart and Folstein 1994; Rutter 1970). Having acknowledged the difficulties in recognising such mental health problems, it is necessary to look at helping people with autistic spectrum disorder to communicate their psychological distress. In order to get access to important mental events (primarily thoughts and feelings), careful assessment is paramount and the use of non-verbal approaches may be most appropriate, even for people with Asperger's Syndrome. Those working in the field of mental health need to be aware of the unusual qualities of communication in Asperger's Syndrome, and of the underlying socio-cognitive deficits which these pragmatic deficits reflect, in order to use diagnostic interviews. It may be necessary to enlist the help of a relative to act as 'interpreter' when taking a psychiatric history. Questionnaires, analogue rating scales and visual questionnaires, together with the self-descriptive analogies (e.g. self as machine, emotions as a sine-wave, etc.) which may be used by some people with Asperger's Syndrome, are all valuable in this process, especially as there is some evidence that the internal world of people with autism (regardless of their language ability) is primarily non-verbal (Hurlbert, Happé and Frith 1994). In some instances, more formal assessment approaches such as repertory grids may be the most appropriate assessment technique (Hare, Jones and Paine 1999). A 'pre-assessment' assessment of language comprehension and pragmatic aspects of language, together with understanding of social language, by a speech and language therapist may also be appropriate. The danger in this instance is of a 'false negative' result, i.e. extant mental health problems may be missed in this group of people because of their communication problems and thus go untreated. With regard to treatment, some forms of symptomatic relief may be recommended (Howlin 1997), whilst appropriate counselling and cognitive forms of psychotherapy appear to be promising for people with Asperger's Syndrome (Hare 1997).

The underlying socio-cognitive deficits of the triad of behaviours found in people with autistic spectrum disorder affect many aspects of social interaction and communication. People whose difficulties lie in the able, verbal part of the autistic spectrum may be at risk of either under- or over-identification of problems relating to their mental health. The role of speech and language therapists may be of paramount importance in both assisting the person with an autistic spectrum disorder to communicate their psychological distress and also in differentiating autism-specific communication and thinking dysfunction from apparently similar psychiatric symptoms. Moreover, it can be very useful to consider the possibility of an autistic spectrum disorder, especially Asperger's Syndrome, in some instances of life-long chronic mental problems occurring in the absence of other social and psychological factors (Ryan 1992).

References

Baker, L. and Cantwell, D.P. (1987) Factors associated with the development of psychiatric illness in children with early speech/language problems. *Journal of Autism and Developmental Disorders 17*, 4, 499–510.

Baron-Cohen, S. (1989) Do autistic children have obsessions and compulsions? *British Journal of Clinical Psychology 28*, 193–200.

Baron-Cohen, S. (1995) *Mindblindness: An Essay on Autism and Theory of Mind.* Cambridge, Mass. and London: The MIT Press.

Blackshaw, A. (1998) An Investigation into the Relationships Between Theory of Mind, Paranoia, Causal Attributions and Asperger's Syndrome. Unpublished BSc(Hons) dissertation, Department of Psychology, University of Manchester.

Cantwell, D.P., Baker, L. and Mattison, R. (1979) The prevalence of psychiatric disorder in children with speech and language disorder: An epidemiological study. *Journal of the American Academy of Child Psychiatry 18*, 450–461.

Hare, D.J. (1997) The use of cognitive-behavioural therapy with people with Asperger's syndrome: a case study. *Autism: International Journal of Theory and Practice 2*, 1, 215–225.

Hare, D.J., Jones, J. and Paine, C. (1999) Approaching Reality: The use of Personal Construct techniques in working with people with Asperger's Syndrome. *Autism 3*, 2, 165–176.

Hare, D.J. and Leadbeater, C. (1998) Specific factors in assessing and intervening in cases of self-injury by people with autistic conditions. *Journal of Learning Disabilities for Nursing, Health and Social Care 2*, 2, 60–65.

Howlin, P. (1997) *Autism: Preparing for Adulthood.* London and New York: Routledge.

Hurlbert, R.T., Happé, F. and Frith, U. (1994) Sampling the form of inner experience in three adults with Asperger's Syndrome. *Psychological Medicine 24*, 385–395.

Kelley, G. (1955) *The Psychology of Personal Constructs.* New York: Norton.

Lainhart, J.E. and Folstein, S. E. (1994) Affective disorders in people with autism: a review of published cases. *Journal of Autism and Developmental Disorders 24*, 587–601.

O'Neill, M. and Jones, R.S.P. (1997) Sensory-perceptual abnormalities in autism: a case for more research? *Journal of Autism and Developmental Disorders 27*, 3, 279–289.

Ozonoff, S. and Miller, J.N. (1996) An exploration of right-hemisphere contributions to the pragmatic impairments of autism. *Brain and Language 52*, 3, 411–434.

Rimland, B. (1964) *Infantile Autism.* New York: Appleton Century Crofts.

Rumsey, J.M., Rapoport, J.L. and Sceery, W.R. (1985) Autistic children as adults: psychiatric, social and behavioural outcomes. *Journal of American Academy of Child Psychiatry 24*, 465–473.

Rutter, M. (1970) Autistic children: infancy to adulthood. *Seminars in Psychiatry 2*, 435–450.

Ryan, R.M. (1992) Treatment resistant chronic mental illness: is it Asperger's syndrome? *Hospital and Community Psychiatry 43*, 8, 807–811.

Szatmari, P., Bartolucci, G., Bremner, R., Bond, S. and Rich, S. (1989) A follow-up study of high functioning autistic children. *Journal of Autism and Developmental Disorders 19*, 213–225.

Tsiouris, J.A. and Adelman, S.A. (1997) *Guidelines and General Information on the Use of Psychotropic and Antiepileptic Drugs for Individuals with Developmental Disabilities.* Staten Island NY: New York State Office of Mental Retardation and Developmental Disabilities.

Van Berckelaer-Onnes, I. (1994). Adult Programmes. Paper presented at National Autistic Society International Conference: 'Autism on the Agenda'. Leeds, 8–10 April 1994.

Wing, L. (1986) Clarification on Asperger's syndrome. Letter to the Editor. *Journal of Autism and Developmental Disorders 16*, 513–515.

CHAPTER 23

Gender Identity Disorders

Judith Chaloner and Lesley Cavalli

Transsexualism and a differential diagnosis

The concepts of gender dysphoria and cross-gender behaviour have existed for centuries although not until the publication of the third edition of the *Diagnostic and Statistical Manual* (DSM-III) of the American Psychiatric Association in 1980 was formal classification of such conditions attempted. Subsequent revisions to this classification have attempted to categorise gender dysphoria into subtypes that deal with issues such as timing of symptom-onset, sexual orientation and type and extent of belief systems. Transsexualism features as a subclassification of this framework and will be the focus of this chapter.

A transsexual is an individual who is biologically and unambiguously a member of one sex but who has a conviction, in the absence of psychosis, that they are a member of the opposite sex. As Pauly and Edgerton (1986) state, 'These individuals attempt to deny and reverse their original biological gender and pass into and maintain the opposite gender-role identification.' Such individuals may desire to be surgically reassigned. It is the male-to-female transsexual who will receive primary reference throughout this chapter, more frequently requiring the direction of a speech and language therapist than the female-to-male transsexual who with the aid of hormones achieves an easier transition to their desired gender role. Before a firm diagnosis of transsexualism can be made, schizophrenia, transvestism and homosexuality must be excluded. Temporal lobe epilepsy has also been associated with transsexualism. Differential diagnosis can be complicated by the fact that the general clinical theme of transsexualism is now well reported and easily accessible to many seeking the help of the psychiatrist for their symptoms of gender dysphoria.

Transsexuals may be classified as either primary (true) or secondary. Primary transsexuals are rare and considered to be those where cross-gendered behaviour in childhood is proven, not simply reported, who have always been sexually attracted to their own sex and not had sexual relations with the opposite sex more than once. Secondary transsexuals are varied in their presentations and sexual orientation and have been previously described in psycho-analytical terms as dual role transvestites, fetishistic transvestites or effeminate homosexuals (Dolan 1987).

The general clinical theme of transsexualism is illustrated through the case studies towards the end of this chapter, but it should be noted that presenting histories can be very varied with no single developmental pathway. A typical history is one where the baby is born unremarkably with normal chromosomal make-up and corresponding sexual anatomy. A close relationship with a mother-figure and a distant, cold father frequently feature in the family history. Cross-dressing and doubt about their sex role may be expressed around the age of 6 years, with reports of fear and confusion about how to deal with such a major conflict. Male transsexuals report a preference for girls' toys and girls' games. They may be accepted without question by their female peers or be treated as 'different'. As they grow older, social isolation increases. The development of secondary sexual characteristics is unwelcome and members of the opposite sex offer no sexual attraction. In early adulthood, male transsexuals' attempts to masculinise themselves may manifest through their choice of partner, occupation or leisure pursuits. Cross-dressing, however, becomes more elaborate and frequent. Whilst many transsexuals' pursuit of femininity is unwavering, some will live out a period of 'normality', marrying and having children. Secrecy, guilt, deceit and anxiety are commonly expressed and episodes of psychiatric illness not uncommon. In her book *Conundrum* (1974) Jan Morris, formerly the distinguished travel writer James Morris, gives a vivid account of the psychological distress he suffered and inflicted on his wife and children as he struggled for years to deny his transsexualism. At that time transsexualism was not a subject much known to the general public. The credibility of the author and the articulate way in which the condition was described did much to lift the prejudice surrounding the subject.

Inevitably there is confusion between transsexuals and transvestites. Both cross-dress, but the latter do this for the satisfaction and pleasure engineered by the play-acting which often results in sexual arousal or as Dolan (1987) further elaborates, 'a fantasy they have when wearing the clothing'. The difference is that the transvestite does not actually want to be a woman. Although most transvestites and transsexuals deny this, there is often considerable overlap between the two conditions. It is not unusual for a transvestite to decide that he feels more fulfilled in the female role and to decide that he has mis-diagnosed his original condition. The effeminate homosexual may also cross-dress, adopt feminine mannerisms and use an affected voice, often referred to as 'camp'. In these cases there is no sense of sexual arousal obtained from their wearing of female clothes. As with the transvestite population some of these effeminate individuals decide that they would be happier as women but although some eventually go forward for the operation and often pass quite well physically as females they do not actually qualify for the label of a true transsexual.

It is also the case that many individuals with what might be termed antisocial sexual practices are extremely disturbed by their own behaviour, whether it be homosexuality, transvestism, bisexuality or forms of fetishism. In some cases to be able to give themselves the label of transsexual gives a degree of respectability to their behaviour and lifts some of the guilt feelings. There is often the question as to whether there is a homosexual quality in the transsexual's desire to change sex. Most transsexuals deny this although in the same breath some may express the desire for a male partner after the operation. In an interesting study by Blanchard *et al.* (1987), there seems to be an indication that the homosexual transsexual clients have fewer regrets post-operatively than their heterosexual counterparts. It has also been suggested that one major factor lying behind many transsexuals' unhappiness in the male role is the fact that they may desire a male relationship even if not a physically homosexual one.

There are also many transsexuals who claim to have no interest in the sexual side of any relationship. As with other aspects of this complex situation there are many permutations and one should not be judgemental. The fact is clear, however, that the search for sexual identity has led many of these individuals to seek fulfilment of their sexual needs by indulging in a variety of sexual experimentation.

Causes of transsexualism

A single cause for transsexualism is unlikely. Instead, biological, family, psychological and social variables seem likely to play a part to differing degrees in individual cases. Biological explanations have so far excluded a genetic explanation, although we should be aware that only recently research has suggested a candidate gene for male homosexuality (Hamer *et al.* 1993). Hormonal influences have also been excluded aside from very unusual cases of endocrine defects or hormone administration. Recent anatomical evidence, however, suggests that transsexual patients have different sized bed nuclei of the stria terminalis, the brain area essential for sexual behaviour, from non-transsexual males and homosexuals (Zhou *et al.* 1995).

The fact that a large number of individuals who present for gender reassignment surgery may be able to give up their request for surgery and come to terms with their gender dysphoria supports the view that psychodynamic considerations in many cases may determine the request for surgery (Ross 1986). Psychoanalytical theories of male-to-female transsexualism proposed by Stoller (1975) suggest that transsexual conflict arises from a number of psychodynamic processes including excessive identification with the mother and failure from the mother to permit separation. Other additional processes have been suggested and include taking a female identity as a way of controlling anger and destructive drives and attempting to reunite with an object of separation by taking on some of its qualities. In secondary transsexualism, the timing of these precipitating separation factors may occur much later in life with a history of only mild childhood gender dysphoria. Interactionist theories of psychosexual development may represent reality but such theories highlight how little is known about the programming of 'normal' psychosexual differentiation, and less still of its deviations. As Money and Ehrhardt (1972) comment, 'the programming of psychosexual differentiation is…a function of biographical history.' They add most significantly in the present context that 'there is a close parallel here with the programming of language development.' It is no accident that coping with the linguistic aspects of a transsexual's presentation is in its way quite as important as reassignment surgery, in developing a survival strategy for the individual. The analogy made between gender identity and language is extended by Money and Ehrhardt, to the interesting comparison between being bilingual from early exposure to two languages and the 'learning' of sexual identity, although some feel that this is not a valid comparison. Early exposure to conflicting language signals may occasionally result in a poor version of both languages; problems with gender identity may have similar causality. Further lessons relevant to transsexualism may yet be learnt from this significant parallel between language and gender imprinting.

The role of the psychiatrist and gender identity team

The complex presentation exemplifies the need for very detailed and careful collection and analysis of data relating to the patient and their physical, psychological and psychosexual development, as well as environmental influences, psychosocial situation and psychiatric status (personality, sexual attitudes and cognitive performance). Whilst aiming to differentiate the true transsexual from the secondary transsexual, the treatment programme must also manage the picture of gender dysphoria in conjunction with the patient's overall psychosociosexual well-being. Bockting and Coleman (1992) outline five treatment tasks within their comp-rehensive treatment model which include assessment, management of co-morbid psychiatric disorders, facilitation of identity formation, sexual identity management and aftercare. Managing co-morbid psychopathology, albeit usually not formal mental illness, is an essential precursor to fostering identity development with hormonal and surgical treatments, when the dramatic and irreversible effects of the latter are self-explanatory.

The process of reassignment falls broadly into three stages and is based essentially on standards of care promulgated by the Harry Benjamin International Gender Dysphoria Association Inc. (Walker and Berger 1985). The structured interviews and counselling referred to above encompass the first stage and aim to encourage the patient to decide if the best way to manage their gender disorder is to change gender. Choosing to commence the process of social gender change may involve tremendous upheaval and also requires a statutory declaration of name change. The second stage of treatment is known as hormonal reassignment and is usually dependent upon the agreement of two independent psychiatrists. The hormone therapy in the male-to-female transsexual can incorporate both antiandrogenic treatment, as well as femin-ising oestrogens and generally has the effect of creating some breast development, the degree of which is largely dependent on genetic factors, softening body hair and altering body fat distribution (Asscheman and Gooren 1992). Some clients report feeling greater emotional lability. Hormonal treatments produce no measurable change in voice function. For the female-to-male transsexual, antioestrogens and androgens effect virilisation across a 2–4 year period with desirable voice change. Frequent medical monitoring of side-effects such as thrombosis and breast cancer is necessary for both patient groups.

The third stage is surgical and proceeds if two specialists can confirm that the patient has completed a 'real-life test' of two years living full time in the chosen gender role. Surgical risks are also a necessary consideration. The demanding 'real-life test' requires the patient to show that they are accepted in society in their chosen gender role and that occupation, paid or voluntary, for at least one year is feasible. During the process of social gender change patients refer to their ability to 'pass' or to convince others in their new gender role. Speech and language therapy assists this process. It is true that many pre-operative transsexuals have an unrealistic view of their ability to organise their lives during the period leading up to the actual sex-change operation. They may also have difficulty envisioning what their lives will be like post-operatively. This is not, of course, an indication of mental illness. Also the fact that many transsexuals have what is considered to be a high level of neurosis does not in itself mean that they are more ill than many individuals without gender problems. It just means that in these cases their particular obsession about gender identity is the principal cause of their high degree of anxiety or depression, and often guilt. It is these issues, rather than the desire to change their ideas about their sexuality, that sometimes push transsexuals to seek the help of a counsellor, psychiatrist, or even to embark on psychoanalysis. A significant reduction of neurosis following surgical reassignment has been reported (Mate-Kole, Freshi and Robin 1986) and is used by some psychiatrists as argument for justifying use of public money for a seemingly non-medical problem. As well as reshaping the genital anatomy (see Edgerton 1974) patients may also undergo other cosmetic procedures that include breast augmentation, rhinoplasty, thyroid cartilage reduction and blepheroplasty. Ability to pay for such surgery should never be a factor if a patient is able to satisfy a psychiatric panel that he is an appropriate candidate for surgery, but all things being equal private funding may be the only way these clients can have this surgery without a long wait of several years due to lack of hospital surgical time. The ongoing commitment of electrolysis across several years is both mentally and financially draining for the transsexual. The total expenditure for the transsexual can thus be enormous when one also considers legal fees if there is a divorce, as often happens, and possible child support.

Few transsexuals regret going through the sex-change operation, largely because of the rigorous 'real life test', but there can be no doubt that for many, new and possibly unanticipated problems are created and in some cases these negative effects dilute the pleasure of the new life once the initial euphoria has abated. Some individuals, although appearing stable, have never been emotionally organised enough to cope with what is undoubtedly an enormous psychological adjustment. Dolan (1987) discusses this issue, and remarks, '...whereas sexual reassignment does relieve gender dysphoria, it does so without necessarily improving psychosocial adjustment and it does not have much effect on coincidental psycho-psychology.' For these patients, ongoing support from the psychiatrist may be necessary.

The role of the speech and language therapist

Not every speech and language therapist wants to work with transsexual clients. This is a very individual decision and should be respected. The whole subject of treatment is a very controversial one, whether the funding is private or public. Ethical considerations that fuel this controversy relate to a number of areas. Some believe that gender reassignment operates against the 'natural law' by interfering with normal bodily functioning and encourages a life that is unwholesome and abnormal. In addition many feel that it is morally wrong to surgically remove healthy organs, with the sin compounded by those receiving NHS treatment joining already lengthy waiting lists both for surgery and other treatments such as speech and language therapy. It is an ethical dilemma without an answer but one which is clearly outlined by Walters (1986).

Most clients will be referred to speech and language therapy after they have commenced the process of social gender change. Management of social skills, non-verbal communication and voice are essential for the majority of secondary transsexuals and some primary transsexual clients, if they are to achieve acceptable social adjustment or to 'pass' in society. Without professional direction, transsexuals may resort to self-teaching, possibly referring to some of the dubious audiotaped packages available or to Website material. Unskilful behaviour may give rise to hyperfunction and the perception of the 'hammed-up' voice of the pantomime dame. Many primary transsexuals, on the other hand, require little or no professional input, self-achieving a successful feminine image.

Helping the transsexual to achieve an adequately acceptable voice and style of communication may be a significant influencing factor when the psychiatrist assesses referral for surgery. The reality, however, is that success in speech and language therapy does not necessarily mean that the client is a suitable candidate for this irreversible surgery, but simply that the voice work has been successful.

It is as well to be aware that this is a very vulnerable client group, often emotional and usually initially with completely unrealistic expectations of the therapy. One should explain the limitations and that while a passable voice is generally achievable one must couple it with a reasonable image. Therapy contracts, as with all patients, should be clearly defined and offer sufficient opportunity for ready review of aims, objectives and therapeutic strategies. Group therapy can augment individual therapy sessions by providing opportunity to experiment with newly acquired communication skills in a sympathetic environment, learn survival techniques and establish new social contacts. Long-term reliance on the group environment is not indicated, however, as it can take on the auspice of a mutual admiration society and produce false standards for use in normal society. In large cities all over the world there are support groups for sexual minorities. Here all is tolerated and while to the outside world the whole idea may seem decadent and bizarre it is in reality simply sophisticated dressing up and completely harmless (Chaloner 1991).

Assessment

Initial consultation will follow medical referral, from which the clinician should be acquainted with the transsexual's specific diagnosis and cognitive and psychological status. Information regarding their progress within the reassignment programme is essential to ensuring therapy aims are realistic. The case history will closely mirror that appropriate for any client presenting for voice therapy with questions relating to vocal health, voice demands and use, as well as client attitudes and expectations. In addition, active observation and analysis of communication skills and behaviour begins as the client enters the room and may be video recorded. Audio recording is essential both for assessment as well as increasing the client's own awareness of those specific aspects of voice and communication requiring focus. 'Parametric listening' and charting of voice quality, resonance, pitch, volume, pitch range and variability will assist the therapist's decision as to those most salient features appropriate for modification. In some cases hyperfunctional voicing patterns require attention before development of those skills that demand higher levels of vocal flexibility. Assessment is most valid when it encompasses meaningful communicative contexts and this can be achieved through role-play and telephone conversation as well as specific testing of loud vocalisation, conversational voice, singing voice and vegetative behaviours, e.g. coughing and laughing.

Voice skills

Patients will frequently have little or no concept of what aspects of their voice and communication require change other than that of vocal pitch. Intuitively they recognise that one of the primary markers between female and male voicing is the difference in fundamental frequency (Wolfe *et al.* 1990; Raines, Hechtman and Rosenthal 1990). Although pitch remains a salient cue for gender identification and has become stereotypical, the interaction of other characteristics interferes with this perceptual judgement and can override it (Wiltshire 1995). Therefore, whilst pitch modification may be a focus of therapy, change of other vocal parameters may precede work on this area. It is also interesting to note that even if little emphasis is given to it, the client's voice pitch often becomes higher naturally during voice therapy. This is explained by Bryan-Smith (1986) as 'the client's ear becomes more acutely tuned to speech and voice patterns.'

Vocal tract resonance can greatly influence our perceptions of pitch and is dependent on variations in vocal tract size, overall physical stature and laryngeal height. Modification of resonance is often the primary focus of treatment having the acoustic effect of increasing formant frequencies through work on tongue, lip and jaw patterns and slight adjustment of laryngeal height. Further speech markers for gender identification include pitch inflection, vocal loudness and voice quality (Yanagihara, Koike and Von Leden 1966; Kramer 1975). Some clients also benefit from using 'light' articulation methods. As with most voice work, good results depend on good breath support, achieved after mastering relaxation exercises (Greene 1975). Likewise, change is dependent on structured development of motor, auditory, kinaesthetic and proprioceptive skills. Biofeedback tools can augment this skill development and all patients should be engaged in home rehearsal of voice skills together with ongoing structured observation of female versus male communication. Specific voice therapy strategies and comprehensive therapy programmes are outlined by a number of clinicians experienced in this area of work (Bryan-Smith 1986; Clark 1996; Chaloner 1986; Oates and Dacakis 1983; Andews and Schmidt 1997; Chaloner, in press).

The overtly effeminate voice and manner should be eliminated completely! The therapist should be prepared to address this problem openly and directly, pointing out that no woman ever presents voice or manner in this way. Gunzburger (1989) emphasizes this point by saying that care should be taken 'to prevent adoption of an effeminate male quality resorted to by some transsexuals instead of the female quality that is desired.'

Research into the effectiveness of voice therapy with transsexuals has focused on measures of fundamental frequency. Evidence, primarily demonstrated through single case studies, suggests that patients achieve raised fundamental frequency levels and increased formant frequencies through therapy training and manage to maintain these at least in part when therapy discontinues (Kalra 1976; Bralley *et al.* 1978; Mount and Salmon 1988; Kaye, Bortz and Tuomi 1993; Dacakis 1996). A study by Spencer (1988) examining the voices of transsexual speakers found that the most successful speakers had received speech and language therapy.

Social skills training and non-verbal communication

Part of the general assessment of the client should include 'the social skills and competence as a communicator' (Elias 1986). The teaching of these techniques is an important part of the therapy programme, but one difficult to describe because each individual will present with different needs and abilities. There is no blanket formula to follow. This is a delicate area because it infringes on the right of the individual to, as so many of them say, 'be myself' and to criticise often offends core sensitivities. To talk through the rationale behind the need to perfect the total presentation is the first step. One is not necessarily trying to create a female stereotype as much as a convincing image within the framework of the client's personality and ability. A paper by Knight (1992) cited by Wiltshire (1995) discusses the concept of gender interference in discourse, from the biological gender to the adopted one. Male discourse strategies and an authoritative style are discrepant to the desired female style of communication in some transsexuals where other behaviours and features are also unfavourably weighted, e.g. the tall, muscularised and ungainly transsexual patient. Attention should also be made both to overtly masculine language and those physical postures that call attention to themselves adversely. Whilst it is generally accepted that the boundaries between male and female language use have blurred since the feminist movement (Haas 1979; de Klerk 1992), once again the aim is not to invite opportunity for that second glance that can prevent an easy passage in society. Relaxation and eye contact exercises to help suggest a confident manner are very important. The ability to project an air of assured confidence will in a great many circumstances convince the listeners that, in spite of various possibly suspect masculine qualities, the speaker should be accepted as female with perhaps a rather idiosyncratic voice containing some masculine elements.

The transsexual can be a very self-absorbed and egocentric individual who makes little effort to relate in any but the most superficial way to other people, and has failed to develop many social conversational skills. It is quite usual for a transsexual client to look and sound very convincing as a female, but fail to continue to project this image during his conversation. In these cases it may be useful to suggest exercises where the client has to find out about other people's lives and interests and also develop some of his own not directly related to his gender identity problem. Role-play is a helpful method for doing this type of project, probably using a video so that there is a means of self-monitoring as well as having a record of progress.

Coping strategies

Attention to personal management strategies, possibly suggested by the therapist (Butcher, Elias and Raven 1993), can assist the transsexual's ability to cope with critical scrutiny about appearance or voice. It must be accepted that it is not possible for every male transsexual to pass completely convincingly as a woman, and these limits – which can be physical, emotional or intellectual – have to be acknowledged by the individual concerned. If one had to make the choice between the importance of voice and appearance in judging a client's chance of passing well as a woman, appearance would undoubtedly be the more important aspect. To accept some unchangeable situations realistically as they are, and not as the patient wishes they were, will determine the success of his eventual adjustment to the new gender role.

Counselling

People without experience of a gender identity problem can scarcely understand the distress of this group. 'Few if any surgical procedures attract as much fear, misunderstanding and plain loathing as a sex change' (Hodgkinson 1988). Nevertheless, it is a fact that allowing some of these extremely unhappy and emotionally frustrated people to have help to masquerade as convincingly as possible as the opposite sex does in a great many cases create enough stability for them to become very much more effective, organised members of society than would otherwise have been possible.

As with any other client group, one is dealing with a whole communicating individual, not just the 'faulty element', and in the case of the transsexual the needs can be very complex. The psychological needs may in fact be far too complex for the therapist to deal with except on a level that any experienced therapist is trained to handle. The speech and language therapy consultation provides some transsexuals with the first safe, accepting and relaxed setting to 'be themselves'. There is therefore the danger of an overly dependent relationship developing, as with any other similarly vulnerable patient group (Cavalli and Morris 1998). Even those with training in counselling should remember that these are clients referred by the psychiatrist for voice training and work on communication skills. Within the context of speech and language therapy, issues involving anger that they have been born as they are, guilt and remorse about the impact on their parents, wives, children, employers and friends and frustration with the process of reassignment may be manifested or overtly expressed. Many transsexuals have a history of depression and some have attempted suicide. The clinician should thus remain in close liaison with the patient's psychiatrist and be aware of their personal limitations in this area.

Surgical voice modification

A number of different techniques have been described for effecting a rise in fundamental frequency in the male-to-female transsexual patient. Early techniques aimed to shorten the vibrating length of the vocal fold through laser or knife surgery, inducing scarring. More recent techniques have involved cricothyroid approximation, closing the cricothyroid visor as much as possible and securing the two cartilages with sutures, thereby stretching and tensing the vocal folds. Early reports (Mahieu, Norbart and Wong Chung 1997; Scheduikat *et al.*, in press) indicate that there is a significant increase in fundamental frequency, albeit some increase in vocal fold irregularity. Research is in its early stages but all patients considering this procedure must understand that it has the potential to benefit just one aspect of the communication picture and is thus a solution in itself to only a few patients.

Prognostic factors

This can be a very rewarding client group to work with. As previously discussed, efficacy data is limited but does suggest a positive treatment outcome and motivation is generally very high in this client group. However, it is wise to remember that there are a considerable number of variables that can influence the success of speech and language therapy treatment. Oates and Dacakis (1986) identify a number of negative factors that include comparatively large vocal tract and laryngeal size, a wide discrepancy between the presenting and target communication characteristics, poor auditory and observation skills and hyperfunctional voicing behaviours. Psychological well-being and unrealistic demands on speech and language therapy also have a negative influence. It is important that attendance at speech and language therapy is negotiated around other ongoing and sometimes stressful commitments such as regular electrolysis appointments. If other matters take priority it is wise to consider deferring treatment.

Acknowledgements

The authors would like to thank Dr James Barrett, Consultant Psychiatrist, Charing Cross Hospital, for his advice in the writing of this paper.

Appendix

Case Study 1

It is often difficult to predict who will succeed in overcoming the monumental challenges of coping with a reversal of gender roles. Having the advantage of monitoring a large number of transsexuals who have gone through this process has the merit of being able to select some 'success stories'. So much depends on a single-minded conviction that this is the only course possible to maintain mental stability. It also depends on the ability to live with the emotional and social turmoil often left for family and others closely involved.

Giles was anyone's idea of a man who led a charmed life, running his own highly successful business, happily married with three young children. He also appeared very physically male, tall and dark with a prominent nose, deep voice and a dynamic outgoing and forceful manner. He was often away on long business trips and it was on return from one of these that he told his wife he had been living a complicated double life for years, had always felt he was a woman in a male body and at age 38 felt he had to seek gender reassignment if he was to survive emotionally. The wife's shock was total, as was the reaction of his parents and in-laws. His wife's initial reaction was to threaten to move abroad with the children, denying him access. She demanded a divorce on the grounds on wanting a normal relationship and sex life.

Giles tackled the practical details of his physical appearance with the same efficiency he had used to build up his business. He had plastic surgery to his nose and lips and a face lift. He had voice therapy, which was remarkably successful, and his warm confident manner worked to advantage in communication. He had electrolysis and dressed appropriately as a business-woman in an international company, and possibly because he did not demand approval or understanding about his new role from business associates, after the initial bombshell the altered persona was accepted. Giles always said that the fact that he had been a success in business as a man was the reason this transition, when he became Paula, was tolerated so well.

The family eventually stayed together although the children found it very difficult in the beginning to understand where Daddy had gone and what had happened. Remaining in the same area and in the same schools subjected the children to many problems; however they are now doing well in their studies for their chosen careers. The suffering of the wife was immense and ten years later she continues to have counselling, but the family unit has been sustained, if on a very difficult level.

This case study illustrates success insofar as Paula is concerned. She passes very well as a woman, has an excellent business record and feels fulfilled in the female role. She realises the problems created, but seems able to rationalise this as 'not being her problem', and this lack of guilt is possibly one feature that has made this complicated situation feasible.

Case Study 2

Adam is an only child, born when his parents were both in their forties after years of unsuccessfully trying for a baby. Their total devotion to him and wish to satisfy his every need formed the pattern of his early life. He was a clever, self-sufficient and self-absorbed child. As far back as he remembers he felt he should have been a girl and used to cross-dress whenever he had the opportunity, hating his developing male body. Physically he was below average height, slim and fine featured, and presented well in the female role.

He was clever and ambitious, entered a prestigious merchant bank from university and as he climbed up the career ladder he began to plan a gender reassignment, feeling he could cope with the inevitable problems he would meet. It was only at this time that he told his parents how he felt. He had not anticipated such a severe and totally negative reaction. Nothing prepared him for this, and their grief and shock upset him more than he would have imagined. Both his parents said the idea of seeing him dressed as a woman was impossible to contemplate, much as they loved him. Adam was at this time 28, was having psychiatric monitoring privately and had started on hormone therapy. He spent increasing amounts of time at clubs catering for transsexuals and transvestites and for the first time in his life felt socially at ease. At this time he went to the director of his firm and explained his position and that he wished to continue in the female role. He was a very productive member of the company and he expected a favourable outcome. However, the reaction was that there was absolutely no possibility of his remaining in that job if he appeared as a woman. The director was sympathetic to the situation and accepted that what he did in private would not affect his job, but there was no question of tolerating anything public.

In spite of his outward independence, Adam had not been able to sever the bonds with his now elderly parents, and there now seems to be the unspoken feeling that he had a passing brainstorm and all is back to normal. They speak of his marrying and their having grandchildren. Equally, Adam is unable to risk losing his very well-paid job, and facing a complete change of lifestyle. He feels trapped and frustrated, as do many transsexuals for many years, but he is not at the moment able to find the courage to break away from his present existence.

References

Andrews, M. and Schmidt, C. (1997) Gender presentation: perceptual and acoustical analyses of voice. *Journal of Voice* 11, 3, 307–313.

Asscheman, H. and Gooren, L. (1992) Hormone treatment in transsexuals. *Journal of Psychology and Human Sexuality. Special issue: Gender dysphoria: Interdisciplinary approaches in clinical management* 5, 4, 39–54.

Blanchard, R., Steiner, B.W., Clemmensen, L.H. and Dickey, R. (1987) Prediction of regrets in postoperative transsexuals. *Canadian Journal of Psychiatry 34*, 43–45.

Bockting, W. and Coleman, E. (1992) A comprehensive approach to the treatment of gender dysphoria. *Journal of Psychology and Human Sexuality. Special issue: Gender dysphoria: Interdisciplinary approaches in clinical management* 5, 4, 131–153.

Bralley, R., Bull, G., Gore, C. and Edgerton, M. (1978) Evaluation of vocal pitch in male transsexuals. *Journal of Communication Disorders 11*, 443–449.

Bryan-Smith, P. (1986) More than a matter of pitch. *Speech Therapy in Practice 2*, (3c), 28–29.

Butcher, P., Elias, A. and Raven, R. (1993) *Psychogenic Voice Disorders and Cognitive Behaviour Therapy*. London: Whurr.

Cavalli, L. and Morris, M. (1998) Working with transgender patients. *RCSLT Bulletin*, October, 11–13.

Chaloner, J. (1986) The voice and the transsexual. In M. Fawcus (ed) *Voice Disorders and Their Management*. London: Croom Helm.

Chaloner, J. (1991) Gender identity problems. In R. Gravell and J. France (eds) *Speech and Communication Problems in Psychiatry*. London: Chapman and Hall.

Chaloner, J. (in press)

Clark, S. (1996) The person beneath the skin. *Human Communication*, Nov/Dec, 4–6.

Dacakis, G. (1996) Maintenance of pitch characteristics following therapy for male to female transsexuals. Paper presented at the inaugural conference of the New Zealand Speech Language Therapists and The Australian Association of Speech and Hearing. Auckland. New Zealand.

De Klerk, V. (1992) How taboo are taboo words for girls? *Language Soc. Cambridge University Press 21*, 277–289.

Dolan, J.D. (1987) Transsexualism: syndrome or symptom? *Canadian Journal of Psychiatry 32*, 666–673.

Edgerton, M. (1974) The surgical treatment of male transsexuals. *Clinical Plastic Surgery 1*, 285–323.

Elias, A. (1986) Does the speech therapist have a role in the assessment and treatment of the male transsexual? (Abs.) International Conference on Gender Identity, London.

Greene, M. (1975) *The Voice and its Disorders*. London: Pitman Medical.

Gunzburger, D. (1989) Voice adaptations by transsexuals. *Clinical Linguistics and Phonetics 3*, 2, 163–172.

Haas, A. (1979) Male and female spoken language differences: stereotypes and evidence. *American Psychological Bulletin 86*, 3, 616–626.

Hamer, H., Hu, S., Magnuson, V., Hu, N. and Pattatucci, A. (1993) A linkage between DNA markers on the X chromosome and male sexual orientation. *Science 261/5119*, 321–327.

Hodgkinson, L. (1988) Our money or their lives? *The Times*, London.

Kalra, M. (1976) Voice therapy with a transsexual. In R. Gemme and C. Wheeler (eds) *Progress in sexology. Proceedings of International Congress of Sexology*. New York: Plenum Press. pp.77–84.

Kaye, J. Bortz, M. and Tuomi, S. (1993) Evaluation of the effectiveness of voice therapy with a male to female transsexual subject. *Scandanavian Journal of Logopaedics Phonetics 18*, 105–109.

Knight, M. (1992) Gender interference in transsexuals' speech. *Proceedings of the second Berkeley Women and Language Conference*. Berkley, CA: University of California Press.

Kramer, C. (1997) Perceptions of female and male speech. *Language and Speech 20*, 2, 151–161.

Mahieu, H., Norbart, T. and Wong Chung, R. (1997) Laryngeal framework surgery. *Advances in Laryngology in Europe*, 426–432.

Mate-Kole, Freshi and Robin (1986) A controlled study of the effects of gender reassignment surgery on psychiatric symptoms (abstract) *International Conference on Gender Identity*.

Money, J. and Erhardt, A. (1972) *Man and Woman – Boy and Girl*. Baltimore: Johns Hopkins University Press.

Morris, J. (1974) *Conundrum*. London: Faber.

Mount, K. and Salmon, S. (1988) Changing the vocal characteristics of a postoperative transsexual patient: a longitudinal study. *Journal of Communication Disorders 21*, 229–238.

Oates, J.M. and Dacakis, G. (1983) Speech pathology considerations in the management of transsexualism – a review. *British Journal of Disorders of Communication 18*, 3, 39–51.

Oates, J.M. and Dacakis, G. (1986) Voice speech and language. Considerations in the management of male to female transsexualism. In W. Walters and M. Ross (eds) *Transsexualism and Sex Reassignment*. Oxford: Oxford University Press.

Pauly, I.B. and Edgerton, M.T. (1986) The gender identity movement: a growing surgical–-psychiatric liaison. *Archives of Sexual Behaviour 15*, 4, 315–329.

Raines, R., Hechtman, S. and Rosenthal, R. (1990) Physical attractiveness of face and voice: effects of positivity, dominance and sex. *Journal of Applied Social Psychology 21*, 1558–1578.

Ross, M. (1986) Gender identity: male, female or a third gender. In W. Walters and M. Ross (eds) *Transsexualism and Sex Reassignment*. Oxford: Oxford University Press.

Scheduikat, M., Perry, A., Cheesman, A. and Pring, T. (in press) Pitch change in male to female transsexuals: has phonosurgery a role to play? *International Journal of Disorders of Communication*.

Spencer, L. (1988) Speech characteristics of male to female transsexuals: a perceptual and acoustic study. *Folia Phoniatrica 40*, 31–42.

Stoller, R. (1975) *Sex and Gender. Vol II: The Transsexual Experiment*. New York: Jason Aronson.

Walker, P. and Berger, J. (1985) Standards of care: the hormonal and surgical sex re-assignment of gender dysphoric persons. (Harry Benjamin International Dysphoria Association Inc.) *Archives of Sexual Behaviour 14*, 79–90.

Walters, W. (1986) Ethical aspects: is gender reassignment morally acceptable? In W. Walters and M. Ross (eds) *Transsexualism and Sex Reassignment*. Oxford: Oxford University Press.

Wiltshire, A. (1995) Not by pitch alone: a view of transsexual vocal rehabilitation. *National Student Speech Language Hearing Association Journal 22*, 53–57.

Wolfe, V., Ratusnik, D., Smith, F. and Northrop, G. (1990) Intonation and fundamental frequency in male and female transsexuals. *Journal of Speech and Hearing Disorders 55*, 43–50.

Yanagihara, N., Koike, Y. and Von Leden, H. (1966) Phonation and respiration: function study in normal subjects. *Folia Phoniatrica 18*, 323–340.

Zhou, B., Hofman, M., Gooren, G. and Swaab, D. (1995) A sex difference in the human brain and its relation to transsexuality. *Nature*, 2, Nov. 378 (6552), 68–70.

CHAPTER 24

Milieu Therapy

Tim Brett and Eric Wilkinson

Great difficulty has been experienced in attempting to discover literature relating to milieu therapy. The subject is referred to in numerous psychiatric textbooks, but little space is devoted to the subject in any detail, particularly in comparison with other aspects of rehabilitation. Nevertheless, mentally ill patients continue to require hospital care, many as in-patients. This is due to the severity of their illnesses and the resulting unpredictable behaviour which causes vulnerability and the possibility of putting themselves and others at risk.

Origins

It is thought that milieu therapy was based on the premise that, for example, only a total transformation of a child's environment over an extended period of time can lead to lasting changes in the personality of child psychopaths. McCord (1982) states that the origin of that work can be traced back to Austria in 1907 with the nation's attempt to establish military schools for all maladjusted boys where, it was thought, large doses of kindness would lead the youths to be able to form lasting relationships. McCord also reports that research has also indicated that milieu therapy has appeared useful in early manhood.

McCord (1982) continues that many have argued that the only possible cure for the adult psychopath is to lodge him or her in a non-punitive, consistent environment that totally changes the circumstances of their life. This would allow them to identify with non-criminal people, replacing mistrust with trust and rewarding them consistently for socially acceptable behaviour. McCord adds that milieu therapy with adult psychopaths appears to reduce their recidivism rate, and in the future an extended use of milieu therapy for adult psychopaths may register resounding successes.

Wolberg (1977) grouped psychotherapy into three areas: the reconstructive psychotherapies, which aim to dismantle and rebuild new personality; the re-educational psychotherapies, which attempt to teach new patterns of behaviour and social functioning; and the supportive psychotherapies, which provide support, guidance, advice and reassurance. Milieu therapy comes into the last group together with occupational therapy, music therapy, reassurance and ventilation.

Kaplan and Saddock (1985) inform us that milieu therapy has been regarded as inconclusively researched as to its effectiveness, but with the use of modern psychotropic drugs it can often deepen insight or provide new social patterns, particularly for patients in hospital care. They go on describe milieu therapy as being the therapeutic effects from the environment in which the patient is living, and this may be added to by group meetings aiming to increase self-reliance, to share responsibility for treatment, and to help other patients. Milieu therapy can also include a wide range of rehabilitation programmes to help domestic and social skills towards living a more independent life.

A treatment milieu can be a structured and safe environment for personality disordered patients, if appropriately supervised. It prevents the patient from running away from his or her problems and provides support in the patient working them through. The environment can be designed, as far as possible, to meet the patient's needs, extending from, for example, intensive care, and rehabilitation in the broadest sense. This might provide such opportunities as formal education, organised socialisation, various work/occupational activities, etc. During the course of the patient's stay he or she will be encouraged to engage and disengage (appropriately) with staff and the environment, with the aim of using the positive features of the environment and avoiding the negative features.

The milieu of the hospital

To achieve success within milieu therapy a hospital, for example, must resemble and reflect current life in society as closely as possible. All staff play an important part in this normalisation process. Multidisciplinary specialist skills are required in all areas in order that beneficial relationships evolve, enabling the therapeutic process to begin and develop.

The hospital as a whole, rather than a single ward, can provide a complete setting for those people with mental disorders who need long-term assessment and rehabilitation. Apart from access to all the forms of psychotherapy and the development and maintenance of living skills, the milieu of the hospital allows some extended freedom to gain new skills and relationships. With support the patient will be able to begin to trust and take risks, at a pace that is acceptable and where the feeling of continuous ward-based scrutiny is greatly reduced, thus leading to normality. A Broadmoor patient was once heard to remark that 'the whole of Broadmoor is therapy...', meaning that this included the ward on which he lived, his occupation or work area, attendance of formal education programmes, and social events such as discos, family visits, church services, Christmas parties and sporting activities; to which all forms of therapy can be added.

The newly acquired skills, initially gained in a ward setting, help the patient to develop insight, self-esteem and self-awareness and learn the advantages of being a good team member. These skills are constantly being added to in other hospital areas. For instance, in the occupational therapy setting, new skills are taught which are of a practical nature and in the process of learning these skills the patient will form a relationship with the occupational therapist (who might also be the key worker). A professional from another discipline might bring a fresh approach and different views, thus extending the patient's experience and so assisting progress through the hospital towards a less dependent future. Qualifications gained whilst in hospital will be tangible evidence to any future employer of the patient's ability to make progress in spite of their history of mental health problems. Educational opportunities fill past educational deficits. Many patients are innumerate, illiterate, or both, or have difficulties in these areas; with increasing educational progress, particularly if accompanied by certificates to demonstrate their progress, self-esteem is boosted and the overall quality of life is improved.

Many patients have problems interacting well with others, and the hospital provides important opportunities to meet patients from other wards, and in particular members of the opposite sex (who in the past might have been seen as a threat, or easy to abuse in one of many ways), in circumstances where support and safety are always priorities, and where social and communication skills can be put into practice. The variety of professional disciplines involved in the process of rehabilitation can help reduce the possibility of dependency and institution-alisation.

Milieu therapy on the ward

The pressures of ward life can be quite distressing to some severely mentally disturbed patients. It is important to recognise this facet, and take into account the extra pressures endured by these patients. With the aid of skilled nurses, what appear to be difficulties can then be turned to the patient's advantage.

Psychiatric nursing

The major aim of the psychiatric nurse is to gain the confidence of the patient as soon as possible after admittance. Many of the patients have been through traumatic experiences and their routes to hospital might be from children's homes, other forms of care, prison and living rough on the streets. Here neglect and exposure to many forms of abusive treatment, drugs and physical violence might have played a significant part in their lives. As a result they have taken little responsibility for anything and others have provided solutions to their problems, usually unacceptable solutions which in many cases affected their freedom and resulted in the inability to trust others. Therefore an important part of psychiatric nursing is to help the patient accept responsibility for himself or herself and their behaviours, rather than expect others to do so. When there is a problem nurses will help the patient to face it, understand its origins and share working through it towards a successful conclusion – thus breaking the habit of running away, or blaming others, and beginning to establish a new pattern of competent behaviour. Learning to share difficulties and accept help and support is a new experience for many and is the beginning of developing a therapeutic relationship and trust, upon which a future is based.

Once in hospital, other problems, previously hidden behind the illness or personality disorder, may come to light and so assist in the selection of appropriate treatment(s). This is made possible by the developing communication between nurse and patient. The fostering of this new skill will carry over and assist in other areas of treatment and hospital/ward life.

One of the primary rewards of nursing in a hospital setting, and in particular a special hospital, is the more creative side of treatment. Due to the special relationship that can eventually develop between nurse and patient there is the opportunity to discover latent skills and talents, which when used add to the patient's well-being, self-confidence and increasing self-esteem. The nurse is in an ideal position to encourage, support, co-operate, cajole, and praise efforts and progress. One of the many difficult areas is that of staff change, due perhaps to promotion, a move of location to another ward, or perhaps the nurse's decision to move out of the hospital. Great care is needed to ensure the patient feels as little disruption as possible and so minimise the repeat of past experiences of loss and rejection.

Adding to the everyday life skills and expanding social interactions at many diverse levels is another important part of the milieu therapy. This often goes hand-in-hand with therapy such as, for example, social skills training; one helps the other.

Due to the special relationship between the nurse and the patient, it is more likely that the nurse will learn about family, friends and past problem relationships. With the patient's consent, the nurse is able to bring information to other therapeutic settings, such as anger management training, sex education, psychodynamic psychotherapy and other modules of treatment working on self and sensory awareness, family awareness and interpersonal relationships – thus providing the opportunity to work through, understand, and come to terms with past difficulties and failures.

Once communication is established with the patient's primary nurse, close observation is kept as to the expansion of these skills. Forming relationships with other nurses, noting the quality of communication present, whether the relationship is trusting, and how it fluctuates, or survives, or how it all came to grief is all useful additional material in therapy. In this way the patient is encouraged to adapt to different people in different ways. This is not only a test of nurse–patient relationship but also of the nurses' relationships with each other and their ability to share this responsibility both with the patient and (relevant aspects of this information) with the clinical team.

Nurse–patient communication can develop positively in parallel with other forms of treatment by supporting current treatments, assisting during difficult times, and helping the patient survive. Supporting the patient and helping him or her to come to terms with current beliefs and attitudes is important as there is often a reluctance to accept any responsibility for the current status. All problems can be attributed to others/society and the nurse in conjunction with other members of the team assists in helping the patient learn to accept responsibility for themselves and their behaviours. Facing up to problems, discovering their origins and learning to share difficulties is the stepping stone to developing therapeutic relationships within treatment, and so become more accessible to the benefits of milieu therapy.

The types of problems are likely to determine the selection of suitable therapies. The nurse can support discussion, argument, challenge, agreement and the ability to disagree; help develop insight, test judgements and rigidly held views, applaud change, support the emergence of softer qualities, such as empathy, expressions of sadness, guilt (the qualities perceived by some patients as weakness). These tasks cannot be left to formal treatments alone. If change is to occur and be sustained, then daily, ongoing, regular input and support is essential. The nurse is in the very best position to deliver this service and is greatly assisted in this work by the support of an involved clinical team. This heightens the reward of extending the nurse–patient relationship to include family members and professionals outside the hospital, thus paving the way towards a future back in the community.

References

Kaplan, H. and Saddock B. (1985) *Modern Synopsis and Comprehensive Textbook of Psychiatry* (fourth edition). Baltimore: Williams and Wilkins.

McCord, W.M. (1982) *The Psychopath and Milieu Therapy: A Longitudinal Study.* New York: Academic Press.

Wolberg, L.R. (1977) *The Techniques of Psychotherapy.* New York: Grune and Stratton.

CHAPTER 25

Personal Construct Psychology

Carmel Hayes and Louise Collins

Introduction

Communicative competence is essential to successful social functioning and necessary to fulfil many human needs. Reusch (1987) documented the effect of mental illness on communication, and the ability to communicate, or lack of it, is seen frequently as diagnostically significant. Mental health problems can affect all aspects of speech and language, non-verbal communication and pragmatics. Institutionalisation can compound the effects of the original condition. As a result, many people with mental health problems have difficulty establishing and sustaining relationships with others. Instead, they experience failure, low self-esteem, anxiety, reduced confidence and often social isolation.

There has been much recent interest in communication dysfunction as a possible precursor to, and marker for, psychotic illness. Muir (1997) argues that much of what we currently know about schizophrenia suggests that it may result from 'unresolved developmental communication delay, compounded by personal psychosocial circumstance' (p.120). At the very least, she argues, this may be a predisposing factor for the illness.

While pragmatic difficulties may characterise schizophrenic communication and perhaps underlie the illness, for many clients it is their experience of their problem that is important, as is the implication for them of greater communicative competence. Communication skills work which has its sole emphasis on the acquisition of behavioural skills has often limited or short-lived benefits. Equally, it is often impossible to begin to discuss with people their communication difficulty without first attempting to understand the world from their point of view. For many people, behavioural changes cannot be accomplished and maintained without concomitant changes in self-perception. Therapy, therefore, needs to be carried out within a framework that acknowledges the person as a whole.

In this chapter we present personal construct psychology (PCP) as a framework that allows the therapist to both directly focus on communication skills, and address psychological issues such as: self-esteem; the meanings the person attaches to the problem, themselves, others, social situations; and change. It is an approach that focuses less on the problem and more on the person and the effect of the communication difficulty on his or her life. Rather than give a full account of PCP, we hope to give the reader a brief overview of the theory and outline the PCP perspective on psychological disorder. We also consider how the speech and language therapist in clinical practice may apply such an approach.

The theory

Kelly first proposed his theory of personality in *The Psychology of Personal Constructs* in 1955. He did not intend it to be a theory of counselling but a way of describing how human beings try to make sense of their world. Three main features are important to highlight: the philosophy behind the theory; the 'person-the-scientist' metaphor; and anticipation and construing.

Philosophy

Central to the theory is Kelly's philosophy, which he defined as 'constructive alternativism'. In simple terms this means that each individual forms their personal view of the world in which they exist. There are many alternatives available and therefore this view can change as the individual experiences the world. Kelly wrote:

> We take the stand that there are always some alternative constructions available to choose among in dealing with the world. No one needs to paint himself into a corner; no one needs to be completely hemmed in by circumstances; no one needs to be the victim of his biography. We call this philosophical position constructive alternativism. (p.15)

This notion is critical in terms of introducing the possibility of change through therapy.

Person-the-scientist

Kelly uses the metaphor 'person-the-scientist' to describe how we as individuals construct our view of the world. Scientists form hypotheses from their theories. To test these theories, they carry out experiments to decide whether they are correct. Likewise, we form theories about the world. From these theories we make predictions and behave in particular ways to test out these predictions. Thus, our behaviour becomes the experiment.

For example, Tom had always believed that camping was a miserable and uncomfortable experience so he avoided going away for camping weekends with his friends. He is persuaded to go one weekend and, to his surprise, discovers that he enjoys it. From this experience, Tom may reconstrue his ideas about camping.

However, we may or may not be good at choosing appropriate experiments. If, in the above example, Tom went camping with no sleeping bag or tent then his hypothesis may have been proven correct.

Understanding that the 'person-the-scientist' metaphor applies to everyone is important. We all use this process, even if in individual ways. This is what Kelly called 'reflexivity'. Thus, he gave us a simple way of understanding how we all operate psychologically, how this process could break down and how it could be remedied.

Anticipating and construing

Kelly states that 'a person anticipates events by construing their replications.' This statement emphasises the idea that it is anticipation that motivates the individual's psychological processes. It also emphasises the idea of being in motion; that is, we anticipate the future by construing our previous experiences of similar events. In this way, we are predicting what might happen should we behave in a particular way.

Construing means 'to place an interpretation on'. To make sense of an event, we place our own meaning on it. It is something that we do all the time, using all our senses, and is frequently something of which we are unaware. For example, we anticipate that a cake from the oven is hot and therefore protect our hands when lifting it out. We do not have to think this through – it is something we do automatically.

A construct is the name given to the interpretation we make. Constructs have a number of inherent features. They are always bipolar, that is, they have two poles, and these are in contrast to each other, providing discrimination. For example, when we think of 'tidy', some may contrast it with 'messy' but others may contrast it with 'disorganised'. Within this is the idea that we cannot have an understanding of one pole if we do not have an understanding of its contrast. It is important to note that the contrast will not necessarily be the same as the semantic opposite. Constructs are organised hierarchically and are interrelated. Those constructs at the top of the hierarchy are abstract in nature, while those at the bottom are more concrete, for example, 'happy' and 'talks to people', respectively. Moreover, constructs are unique to the individual, being a product of their experience of the world. We therefore cannot assume that we all operate using the same constructs.

Subsuming

To identify and deal with a client's particular difficulty, it is essential to see the world through their eyes, that is, subsume their system of constructs. Subsuming means that the therapist listens credulously, that is, with belief, and must avoid making judgements and assumptions, being prejudiced or disempowering the client. This process of checking out the validity of our perceptions about the client occurs regularly.

Suspension of our construct systems

Our constructs form our personality and permeate everything we do. In the interests of therapeutic interaction, however, we must perform the difficult task of suspending our construct system. We may achieve this by developing awareness of how our own system operates. This in turn enables us to find ways of keeping our constructs out of the professional context. Moreover, developing awareness of the assumptions we make about others is important. Assuming that the client will behave or respond in a particular way could prevent us from understanding the true nature of their difficulty.

Construing mental illness

As personal construct psychology attempts to explain all human experience, it therefore includes definitions of 'disorders' and 'symptoms'. Kelly (1955) viewed the medical model as a hindrance to our understanding of and ability to help people. Instead, he suggested that applying the notion of 'functioning' to people would be more useful. A fully functioning person can construe the world so that, usually, their predictions are validated. If their predictions are invalidated then they reconstrue the event.

Kelly defined a disorder 'as any personal construction used repeatedly in spite of consistent invalidation' (p.831). Symptoms and disorders are therefore not simply the consequence of biology or experience. Instead, they are the result of the person's attempt to make sense of their experiences. As Winter (1992) states: 'rather than disorders and optimal functioning being viewed as a dichotomy, they may, therefore, be considered to represent the extremes of a continuum concerning the extent to which a construction accomplishes or fails to accomplish its purpose' (p.15). From this perspective, a disorder is a strategy that a person employs as a way of coping with invalidation and avoiding uncertainty.

Viewing psychological disorder in this way 'is in itself essentially a construction', and 'like all constructs is useful only to the extent that it aids anticipation' (Button 1985, p.15). Using constructs of disorders as 'ways of viewing certain behaviour and experience' requires that we recognise that this is not necessarily the only way of so doing, and that we do not all have to agree.

Winter (1992) distinguishes between disorders of the structure of the construct system and disorders of the content of construing. Using this classification we concentrate here on schizophrenia and depression, as it is clients with these disorders that are most often referred to speech and language therapy.

Disorders of structure

Disorders of structure 'may be considered to be associated with consistent invalidation of construing' (Winter 1992, p.106). Van den Bergh, de Boeck and Claeys (1985) cite a number of pioneering studies carried out by Bannister in the 1960s who proposed that schizophrenic thought disorder reflects loose construing. Bannister reported that the cause of loose construing in schizophrenia is serial invalidation, i.e. constant disconfirmation of the person's views of themselves and their world. Loose construing leads to a person's predictions becoming inconsistent and variable and ultimately to the person being both confused and confusing to others. Van den Bergh *et al.* (1985) report their own studies which show that thought disordered schizophrenics loosen by 'taking into account only one or a few construct aspects on a random-like basis' (p.67), leading to a simplified construct system, and utterances that are incoherent and fragmented. Non-thought-disordered schizophrenics loosen by 'focusing systematically on only one or a few, but always the same construct aspect' (p.67), for example, they may describe hospital as a concentration camp on the basis that they are not allowed to do as they like. Many situations could be construed in this way and so the prediction is easily confirmed. These authors also noted that thought-disordered schizophrenics seem to have weak psychological construct relations. The loosening of psychological constructs seems specific to the construing of people. For example, the person may discuss politics coherently, but be unable to respond when the subject of family is introduced. In brief, schizophrenics adopt a strategy of loose or 'incomplete construing' in an attempt to avoid inconsistencies and invalidation and to ward off anxiety. Moreover, a study by Lorenzini, Sassaroli and Rocchi (1989) showed that schizophrenia follows invalidation of a construct that is central to what little hierarchical structure there is in the system.

Research findings show that depressed people adopt the opposite strategy of tight construing, leading to a rigid view of life. Kelly (1955) viewed depression as 'withdrawal tendencies on all fronts' (p.1116) as a result of which 'spontaneous elaboration [is] sharply curtailed [in an effort] to cut his field to a manageable size' (p.845). The person reduces the risk of further invalidation of their construct system by eliminating incompatibilities and constricting their world. Thus, 'the person may continue to feel vulnerable and self critical, but refuse to experiment with new behaviours or self-constructions that might lead to the development of a more satisfying identity or way of life' (Neimeyer 1985, pp.84–85).

A consistent finding that emerges from the PCP research on depression is that the construing of depressed people is characterised by being polarised, tight and logically consistent. Depressives tend to construe themselves under the more negative poles of their constructs (Neimeyer et al. 1983). Neimeyer (1985) cites a study by Dingemans, Space and Cromwell (1983) showing that as depression deepens, depressed people seem to record, store and encode negative rather than positive information about the self and others.

Disorders of content

Other researchers have focused on how clients presenting with psychological disorder construe themselves and others. Studies of depressed people have shown that their self-esteem is particularly low and that they view their ideal self negatively and unfavourably. Not only do depressed people evaluate themselves negatively, they also construe themselves in dichotomous terms, for example as either 'good' or 'bad' with no in-between (Neimeyer 1985; Neimeyer et al. 1983). This is additionally reflected in a tendency to view themselves as different from others. Rowe (1978) found that depressives operate from constructs that emphasise their separateness from relatives and potential friends.

A tendency to construe the self as different from others is associated with difficulty anticipating the constructions of others and lack of validation of the person's own construing by others. Tight construing is associated with poor social skills and social prediction and with inaccuracies in construing other people (Winter 1988). Research with non-depressed subjects suggests that such construing may lead to interpersonal difficulties. Perceived self-isolation may lead to actual isolation as the person becomes increasingly distant from others. As Epting and Amerikaner (1980) note, the ability to construe the constructions of others is an essential characteristic of an optimally functioning person.

Gara, Rosenberg and Mueller (1989) found that schizophrenics have poorly elaborated views of themselves compared with their views of other people. In their study, schizophrenics were found to construe feelings and emotions, in themselves and others, in a relatively unelaborated way.

Difficulties in predicting the construing of others seem central to all psychological disorders, including depression and schizophrenia (Button 1983). We might therefore consider social withdrawal to be a strategy adopted by people who have difficulty anticipating others to reduce the anxiety that they would otherwise experience. Low self-esteem and lack of confidence may underlie, result from and compound the original difficulty. Such findings have major implications for the speech and language therapist concerned with assessing and developing the client's communicative potential.

Implications for personal change

Having considered the theory of PCP and its application to psychological disorders, specific-ally schizophrenia and depression, we now consider how the speech and language therapist might apply PCP in clinical practice. Kelly (1955) viewed therapy as 'a psychological process which changes one's outlook on some aspect of life' (p.186). Therapy therefore, is essentially a process of reconstruction and self-elaboration.

The aim of the speech and language therapist is to help the client develop a more elaborated view of himself or herself as a socially competent person. The emphasis is on the person exploring new theories about themselves and others and the focus is always on communication and alternative ways of behaving. As stated earlier, the therapist adopts a credulous listening approach and attempts to subsume the person's construing at all times, conveying an attitude of respect and acceptance.

Experimentation and change can be anxiety-provoking, especially if involving funda-mental changes in construing the self. Preparing the person thoroughly and together selecting appropriate experiments are essential for a successful outcome. The therapist must also consider the meaning of greater communicative competence and confidence for the client. For many clients, increased competence, particularly in the direction of assertiveness, has negative connotations (Winter 1988). Similarly, the therapist needs to be aware of the possible perceived benefit, to the client, of the symptom.

PCP offers us an alternative way of understanding what is commonly described as 'resistance' in clients. Kelly (1955) emphasised that if a person seems to be resistant then it is 'likely that his construct system does not subsume what the therapist thinks it should' (p.1101). 'Resistance' may result from an attempt to avoid the anxiety associated with change, or because the person is simply choosing the best available way of anticipating events from their perspective. The therapist must therefore check that they have fully subsumed the client and his or her constructions. As resistance is seen as rational and meaningful from the client's point of view, we must be careful therefore not to push the client in a direction that is not meaningful to him or her. Therapy must be a partnership, the aim of which is to discover what is most meaningful and acceptable to the client. In encouraging someone to behave differently, we must always do so from an understanding of the perceived implications of change for the client's constructions of themselves, others and social situations.

Assessment

The starting point in therapy is always the person's current construction of themselves, including the problem, and their world. PCP offers the therapist a range of formal assessment procedures, for example self-characterisation, repertory grids, laddering and pyramiding. We briefly describe a number of assessment procedures as comprehensive accounts can be found in many texts, for example Winter (1992). The therapist can modify these procedures to suit the particular needs and presentation of the client. They can be used both for assessment and to monitor any change during therapy. Although usually described as assessment tools, these procedures often have therapeutic benefit in helping people increase their self-knowledge and providing clues to further areas requiring elaboration and exploration. Assessment may also include observation of the client in social situations, descriptions by others and other formal procedures to determine the level of the client's functional and receptive and expressive language abilities. The therapist may decide to postpone the administration of formal assessment procedures until later in the therapeutic process, based on their initial evaluation of the client.

Repertory grids provide valuable information regarding the structure of the person's construct system, the interrelationships between constructs and the content of the client's construing of the self, others and situations. Laddering allows the therapist and client to explore the abstract personal meanings of the client's constructs, while pyramiding requires the client to clarify his or her meanings in a more concrete way. Tschudi's ABC procedure and Implications Grids help the therapist and client understand both the origins of the problem and the positive and negative implications of constructs. Self-characterisations provide valuable clues about the themes that are important to the person and, being less structured, facilitate self-disclosure. The use of PCP is not restricted to verbally competent clients. Writing, drawing and objects can all be used to explore construing with clients who are lacking in confidence, withdrawn, or who have language impairments. Non-verbal methods can take the pressure off spoken communication and sometimes even facilitate verbal expression. Depending on what is appropriate for the client, elaboration of constructs can take place at either a concrete or an abstract level.

Therapy

On the basis of the assessment the therapist chooses an appropriate treatment method, whilst acknowledging that this method may need to be modified as therapy progresses. The therapist is free to be eclectic in their choice of therapeutic method, being restricted only by the preferences and abilities of the client.

Depending on the communicative competence of the client the therapist may play a more or less active role. In early sessions, particularly with clients who are withdrawn and greatly lacking in communicative skill or confidence, the therapist may take more of a leading role in facilitating and encouraging communication. The therapist acknowledges the client's world view, establishes rapport and enables the client to feel understood and supported. Attempting to understand a client's meanings also involves being prepared to take everything they say seriously, although this in no way implies collusion with, for example, delusions. For many, this may be their first experience of being listened to and accepted by another person. As the therapist adopts a credulous approach, communication can take place on common ground as the client's reality is acknowledged.

Although PCP is not prescriptive in terms of therapeutic approach, it does offer a number of methods that the therapist may find useful in helping their client reconstrue. Some specific techniques are described below.

The aim of therapy for the client who construes loosely is to make them both less confused and confusing to others and to develop hierarchical construct organisation. Therapy may initially be about engaging with the person and behaving in a way that is predictable to them. Van den Bergh et al. (1985) suggest that 'offering an environment that allows for stable relationships between elements and constructs to be formed on a comprehensive basis, is more advisable than to start with strengthening whatever construct relation the client has already' (p.79).

Tightening is attempted later to avoid causing anxiety and threat early in the relationship. To assist with tightening, the therapist can ask the client to explain their constructs explicitly and to summarise what is discussed in therapy. Participation in groups, answering questions requiring specific information, self-monitoring, developing new skills and completing grids all assist in the process of tightening constructs.

Tight construers, too, need support and a relatively structured approach. They require a simpler, more predictable environment than the threatening, unpredictable one that they currently experience. To reduce anxiety, loosening may initially focus on a few constructs only. For severely depressed people, Kelly (1955) suggested encouraging them to engage in occupational, recreational or social activities. He emphasised exploring the similarities and differences between what the client finds himself or herself normally doing and thinking with what happens while, for example, playing dominoes. In this way the client is encouraged to both widen their range of experiences and to construe himself or herself and their activities in ways that allow for alternatives to be considered. The therapist can facilitate loosening by adopting an attitude of uncritical acceptance, encouraging the client to relax, asking open-ended questions, using metaphor, drawing, writing, photographs and pictures, dreams, humour and chain association.

PCP interventions may also include asking the client to imagine themselves in detail in a more positive role, so that they can experience alternatives to their current constructions and develop a more optimistic outlook. The client may first be asked to predict all the possible consequences, both positive and negative, of alternative ways of behaving. Imagining the outcome of an action and its contrast enhances the client's cognitive awareness of their constructs and the tightening of construing. The client may then be encouraged to behave on the basis of these new constructs, either challenging or validating their predictions.

As the speech and language therapist is concerned with clients' interpersonal difficulties, groups are often the chosen method of therapy. Groups facilitate experimentation, provide opportunities for validation, anticipating others and carrying out social experiments. In groups, the stereotyped construing of schizophrenic clients can be more easily challenged. As some people find pairs easier than groups, discussions in twos on specific topics that facilitate cohesion, self-disclosure and participation can be used. The therapist can ask questions later of the whole group that explore sociality and commonality (Neimeyer 1988). The therapist encourages clients to appreciate that their constructs and those of others may share both similarities and differences, to see the world through the eyes of others and to consider other viewpoints. Group therapy has been found to help increase the depressive's identification with others (Space and Cromwell 1980) and widen their field of social experience (Sheehan 1981). Clients can learn to evaluate themselves, others and situations in ways that allow them to adopt different and more appropriate social roles and behaviours. They can elaborate different ways of construing social situations, in addition to exploring the similarities and differences between their experiences. Those clients who initially present as very withdrawn or institutionalised often need to first engage in activities which facilitate participation and elaboration of construing, perhaps only later being asked to elaborate verbally. The therapist may also give feedback to clients on their behaviour and how the therapist construes it. The timing of such interventions will, however, depend on the clients' needs and abilities.

As schizophrenics frequently elaborate themselves poorly and incompletely the therapist will therefore address the need for the client to develop a more comprehensive sense of self. Clients are encouraged not to define themselves solely in terms of their diagnosis or difficulties with communication and relationships. They are encouraged to view themselves as people who have interests, skills and opinions. Elaboration of a more 'rounded' self is central to a client's self-esteem and ability to present themselves in a positive way in social situations. The therapist may choose from an infinite variety of activities and games with which to help the person elaborate their construing of themselves.

Within a PCP framework, therefore, the emphasis is less on teaching isolated social or communication skills. It is more on helping the person adopt strategies with which to approach social situations differently, think about and appreciate the constructions of others. Information giving and skills training are not precluded, and indeed are often necessary to facilitate progress. The following case example illustrates the application of a PCP approach in practice.

Case example

Joanne, who had a diagnosis of schizophrenia and depression, was described on referral as socially isolated and having difficulties with relationships at work. She attended therapy for a period of eighteen months, initially at approximately two-weekly intervals, later at three-monthly intervals. She initially presented as lacking in confidence, her responses were minimal, she avoided eye-contact, initiated infrequently, and appeared habitually tense and anxious. She described her problem as 'difficulty getting the words out and keeping the conversation going' and her aim was 'to be better at communicating'.

In early sessions, the therapist played an active role in encouraging and supporting Joanne to speak about herself and her problem with communication. The initial focus was on finding out more about how Joanne construed herself and what she thought others thought of her. Using Ravenette's 'Who are you?' technique, discussed in Dalton (1994), she described herself as a quiet, shy and caring person, the contrast being someone who is selfish, outgoing and forward. The abstract implications for Joanne of being either 'quiet' or 'outgoing' were explored by laddering these constructs. Tschudi's ABC procedure provided valuable insights into Joanne's dilemmas regarding change. She construed greater communicative competence at enabling others to get to know her and also implying a risk of rejection and vulnerability to hurt. Staying the same implied safety and protection on the one hand and loneliness on the other.

Before any attempts at reconstruction had taken place Joanne reported that she had spontaneously started to experiment with different ways of relating to people at work. She began to approach people she usually avoided and to initiate conversations, with both successes and some disappointments. In sessions she was noticeably more relaxed, spontaneous and could self-disclose more easily. It seemed the assessment process itself had enabled her to see alternative ways of being.

In later sessions we began to focus on how she thought her communication might affect others, both as it was and should she become a more confident person. We explored both her current constructs and alternative constructions of other people's non-verbal communication. Pyramiding was used to help clarify her constructions of how 'friendly' people behave and communicate. After a few months Joanne reported that her colleagues had given her very positive feedback regarding her communication. She no longer avoided all situations involving speaking with colleagues or others, although was still relatively isolated. In therapy, she began to initiate discussion and the focus moved to more assertive ways of communicating. Increasing awareness of the role of non-verbal communication and ways of initiating conversation meant that she was able to be more open and welcoming towards others who, in turn, began to initiate interaction with her. Importantly, Joanne began to report that she was developing an awareness of how her thinking style affected her interactions and an ability to see 'both sides' of a situation. She began to construe others differently, that is, in terms other than 'unapproachable' or 'perfect' and to construe herself as more like other people.

By the time therapy was completed Joanne had made many changes in her life. She was able to go to the cinema and shopping alone and had booked a holiday. This contrasted with her belief at the beginning of therapy that she neither could nor should go out. She began to communicate more effectively in a range of situations, take responsibility at work and socialise with colleagues. Her self-esteem had increased – she now described herself as 'someone of value' – and she left therapy feeling that she knew herself better. She had developed problem solving skills that she could apply to a variety of situations and felt more confident and self-assured.

Summary

With its emphasis on the person, personal construct psychology provides an alternative and humane perspective on psychological 'disorders'. PCP accepts the person's constructs, however ineffective, as the most meaningful 'way of being' currently available to them. Schizophrenia and depression are therefore not irrational or 'mad' ways of being. Rather, they are strategies that the person has adopted, as a result of invalidation, to make anticipation and prediction possible and to keep anxiety at bay.

PCP provides us with professional constructs and a range of assessment procedures. It allows us to be eclectic in our choice of therapy techniques and encourages us to look at ourselves as therapists, i.e. be reflexive. PCP highlights the need to revise our understanding of clients when they seem to be resistant or 'stuck', viewing lack of movement as an under-standable reaction to the anxiety associated with change.

As a therapeutic approach, PCP is empowering, allowing people to take responsibility for themselves rather than 'being cured' by the therapist. With its emphasis on the importance of partnership in the therapeutic relationship, PCP ensures that the therapist takes the client seriously, involves the client from the outset, and uses their meanings as the starting point in therapy. The client is the expert on themselves and their problem and the therapist uses his or her knowledge of PCP to help engender change. Although a highly elaborated and cognitive theory, PCP can be used with both verbal and non-verbal clients, as it does not require that they be burdened with references to the theory or philosophy in order for change to be facilitated.

Adopting a PCP approach does not mean that we must reject other approaches to mental illness or psychological disorder. With its emphasis on both action and construing, PCP is compatible with both cognitive and behavioural approaches. Being a non-prescriptive, invitational and collaborative therapeutic approach, PCP offers the speech and language therapist an excellent framework from which to address communication and pragmatic skills with clients in a mental health setting.

References

Bannister, D. (1977) (ed) *New Perspectives in Personal Construct Theory.* New York: Academic Press.

Button, E. (1983) Personal construct theory and psychological well-being. *British Journal of Medical Psychology 56,* 313–322.

Button, E. (1985) Personal construct theory: the concepts. In E. Button (ed) *Personal Construct Theory and Mental Health.* London: Croom Helm.

Dalton, P. (1994) *Counselling People with Communication Problems.* London: Sage.

Epting, F. and Amerikaner, M. (1980) Optimal functioning: a personal construct approach. In A.W. Landfield and L.M. Leitner (eds) *Personal Construct Psychology: Psychotherapy and Personality.* New York: Wiley.

Gara, M., Rosenberg, S. and Mueller, D. (1989) Perception of self and other in schizophrenia. *International Journal of Personal Construct Psychology 2,* 3, 253–270.

Kelly, G.A. (1955) *The Psychology of Personal Constructs,* Vols 1 and 2. New York: Norton.

Lorenzini, R., Sassaroli, S. and Rocchi, M. (1989) Schizophrenia and paranoia as solutions to predictive failure. *International Journal of Personal Construct Psychology 2,* 4, 417–432.

Muir, N. (1997) Semantic pragmatic disorder and the role of the speech and language therapist. In J. France and N. Muir (eds) *Psychiatry in Communication and the Mentally Ill Patient – Developmental Linguistic Approaches to Schizophrenia.* London: Jessica Kingsley Publishers.

Neimeyer, R. (1985) Personal constructs in depression: research and clinical implications. In E. Button (ed) *Personal Construct Theory and Mental Health.* London: Croom Helm.

Neimeyer, R.A. (1988) Clinical guidelines for conducting interpersonal transaction groups. *International Journal of Personal Construct Psychology 1,* 181–190.

Neimeyer, R.A., Klein, M.H., Gurman, A.S. and Gruest, J.H. (1983) Cognitive structure and depressive symptomatology. *British Journal of Cognitive Psychotherapy 1,* 65–73.

Ravenette, A.T. (1989) 'Who are you? A structure for exploring the sense of self'. Unpublished occasional paper.

Reusch, J. (1987) Values, communication and culture. In J. Reusch and G. Bateson (eds) *Communication in the Social Matrix of Society.* London: Norton.

Rowe, D. (1978) *The Experience of Depression.* London: Wiley.

Sheehan, M.J. (1981) Constructs and 'Conflict' in depression. *British Journal of Psychology 72,* 197–209.

Space, L.G. and Cromwell, R.L. (1980) Personal constructs among depressed patients. *Journal of Nervous and Mental Disease 168*, 150–158.

Tschudi, F. (1977) Loaded and honest questions. In D. Bannister (ed) *New Perspectives in Personal Construct Theory*. New York: Academic Press.

Van den Bergh, O., De Boeck, P. and Claeys, W. (1985) Research findings on the nature of constructs in schizophrenics. In E. Button (ed) *Personal Construct Theory and Mental Health*. London: Croom Helm.

Winter, D.A. (1988) Constructions in social skills training. In F. Fransella and L. Thomas (eds) *Experimenting with Personal Construct Psychology*. London: Routledge Kegan Paul.

Winter, D.A. (1992) *Personal Construct Psychology in Clinical Practice: theory, Research and Applications*. London: Routledge.

CHAPTER 26

Neurolinguistic Programming in Mental Health

Laurie Macdonald

Therapeutic approaches to mental health rehabilitation continue to evolve in neurological, psychological and linguistic terms as the understanding of these processes in mental illness are recognised (France and Muir 1997). From a rehabilitative or psychotherapeutic point of view the advances in understanding psycholinguistic models of mental ill-health offer practical approaches to psychosocial rehabilitation. Medication provides an invaluable treatment for the positive symptoms of mental illness (hallucinations, paranoia, etc.) but does not generally offer much treatment for the negative symptoms such as semantic pragmatic disorder or disorders of mind (Macdonald 1990; Liberman *et al.* 1986). Liberman also indicated that a multi-disciplinary approach to mental health rehabilitation was most effective.

Neurolinguistic programming (NLP) is the study of subjective experience and is one of a very small family of therapies known as experiential constructivist psychotherapy. NLP complements the skills of a speech and language therapist working in the field of mental health rehabilitation. It is also a brief outcome-orientated therapy. Figure 26.1 demonstrates the areas of therapeutic intervention from the theoretical models of a speech and language therapist and neurolinguistic programming. NLP is about using a deep level of rapport, communication and specific language as a medium for therapeutic interventions. This philosophy complements the background of the speech and language therapist so well.

I became introduced to NLP through the work of Milton H. Erickson (Haley 1973). I had taken a course in Ericksonian Hypnotherapy and psychotherapy that I intended using with a group of patients attending a course in relaxation techniques at one of the day hospitals in Newham. However, I came away with a much clearer idea of how I was going to work with my schizophrenic patients as well. My understanding of semantic pragmatic disorder had been greatly influenced by 'Hello. What next? Social skills and language impaired children', a booklet (now out of print) for teachers produced by teachers and speech and language therapists on an ILEA working party. This clear and concise description of the childhood disorder seemed to be reflected in the adult schizophrenic patients that I was working with and gave me a theoretical framework for therapeutic interventions. However, first I had to get the patients to want to work with me. The understanding of deep level rapport, what motivates people and how language can be used in helping a person change their belief systems seemed to hold the answers to engaging the patients in therapy.

NLP began in the early 1970s when Richard Bandler, a psychology student, and John Grinder, assistant professor of linguistics at the University of California, Santa Cruz, began work together on the communication strategies of innovative and successful psychotherapists (Bandler and Grinder 1975, 1976). They studied Fritz Perls, the originator of the school of therapy known as Gestalt, Virginia Satir, a highly successful family therapist, and Milton Erickson, the psychiatrist who developed Ericksonian hypnotherapy and brought hypnosis into the modern medical field. Another influence in the early days of NLP was Gregory Bateson, the anthropologist who also wrote on many different topics such as cybernetics and communications theory. From these early beginnings NLP has gone on to develop into a structured, outcome-orientated, brief form of psychotherapy.

The 'neuro' part of NLP relates to the fundamental idea that the way a person behaves is based on their neurological processing of past and present experiences. An experience is processed from the information gained through the five senses (visual, auditory, kinaesthetic, olfactory, gustatory). As we experience the world through our senses we make 'sense' of all this information and then act upon it. This encompasses both 'thought processes' and cognition and our physiological reactions to events. Body and mind form one experiential unit as a human being reacts to its environment. The 'linguistic' part of the name relates to how language is used in ordering thought, behaviour and communication. The 'programming' relates to the way our thoughts and cognitive processing are translated into behaviour and action and how often this seems to follow a 'pattern' or programme.

The fields	Area of exploration	Therapeutic approach
Spiritual	Who or what else? Mission in life?	Psychotherapy
Identity	Who am I?	Psychotherapy
Beliefs	Why?	Psychotherapy
Capabilities	How?	Speech and Language Therapy
Behaviour	What?	Speech and Language Therapy
Environment	With whom? Where?	Speech and Language Therapy

Source: Laurie Macdonald 1996

Figure 13.1 Adaptation from Dilts – Unified Field Theory

Figure 26.1

NLP belongs to the group of psychotherapies known as experiential constructivism. With personal construct psychology, NLP forms the Experiential Constructivist section of the UK Council for Psychotherapy. It operates from the basic premise that we are the sum total of all our past experiences, and that the 'construct' is formed from our perception and interpretation of these past experiences. In NLP terms, constructs are known as maps or models that relate to the world the client lives in and to how they see themselves. It is also a presupposition of NLP that there is no one correct model, only models that prove useful or limiting in that individual's life.

As adults we like to think that we respond directly to situations and events as they occur in our lives, but this does not seem to be the case. The model that NLP proposes is that we do not have the time to cognitively process all the sensory information that occurs in an experience as it happens, and so in constructivism an alternative theory is proposed. A construct is our unconscious understanding of the sensory information of an experience, which is formed into beliefs about the world, how it operates, about our selves and how we operate. Some may call it instinct, intuition, or even knee-jerk reactions; in NLP terms we think of patterns of behaviour or programmes. The majority of constructs are formed early in life when most 'first experiences' occur, although a traumatic experience in adult life may cause a considerable rearrangement or even collapse of previously held constructs (e.g. post-traumatic stress disorder). When an experience occurs, unconsciously we tap into the closest already held construct relating to that event and it is from this construct that our interpretation and beliefs and consequently our behaviour and reactions are formed and then acted upon. In the majority of situations, for most of us, the system works well and we come up with appropriate reactions, emotions and behaviours for the experience we are in. If, however, mis-perceptions or mis-understandings occurred at the time of forming an initial construct then an inappropriate construct may be formed and consequently may produce inappropriate emotions and behaviour later in life. For many of us our 'limiting constructs' were formed in childhood when we had a first experience and came to our first understanding of our own and other people's emotions, the different roles people play and the relationships people form.

For some people, if there are enough misunderstandings or they are given enough misinformation (e.g. overly negative environments, overly competitive environments or punitive environments), then they can form negative or limiting beliefs about themselves, which in turn may be a contributing factor to a future depressive or psychotic-type illness. In the psychotic patient whose perception of the world is distorted by their illness, one would expect to find distorted constructs operating too. Whether or not the psychotic patient's constructs were formed because of a negative early environment, or because of the distortion of their perception of the social environment due to their pathology, is an ongoing debate within the field of mental health care. Whichever it is, or if it is a combination of the two processes, the rehabilitative approach would be similar. This basic understanding of constructs allows the therapist to work with a model that is relevant to people with wide-ranging mental health problems.

One of the other important presuppositions of NLP is that 'the map is not the territory'. This idea relates to the concept that there is no such thing as a universal reality, only subjective reality; and so there is no one 'right' map – just some that prove to be more useful than others.

Working from this model allows the therapist to respect the patient's map of the world in a sincere manner without colluding with it or the patient's inappropriate cognitions or behaviour. This is a valuable tool in maintaining rapport with patients who have a different reality to the therapist's own. Building and maintaining rapport with the patient is the most important element of any form of therapy, whatever its philosophy or orientation, and through NLP rapport can be investigated at many different levels (O'Connor and Seymour 1990):

1. Non-verbally, e.g. body language, facial expressions, posture, proximity.

2. Language and communication styles, e.g. reflective listening, matching submodalities such as visual, auditory or kinaesthetic language patterns, matching and challenging meta model patterns.

3. Meta programs (habitual and systemic filters through which we perceive our experiences), e.g. motivation strategies, problem solving strategies, working style preferences.

This approach can allow the therapist to gain rapport with even the most non-communicative or paranoid client (Haley 1973). From a relationship based on deep rapport the therapist can begin to 'pace and lead' the patient towards having more enabling beliefs about themselves and the world.

Pacing and leading is another demonstration of rapport. Observing people interacting in relaxed social environments will show this clearly. When two or more people are in deep rapport there will often be a matching of body postures, facial expressions, volume and tone of voice, to name but a few non-verbal observations. If this is at a deep enough level, when one partner makes a change in one of these parameters then the other will soon follow. If they do not, then the rapport may not have been sufficiently deep enough for that change, and to some degree was lost. These physical observations are mirrored at the psychological level as well. In this way a person can be influenced to move towards behaviours and beliefs that are more appropriate or enabling.

Could this be considered somewhat manipulative? Yes it is, but all therapy is about manipulation of one sort or another. The safeguard for the client is that one of the quickest ways to break rapport and so lose influence is to violate, disregard or in some way be disrespectful of that patient's deeply held beliefs. This means that a person cannot be influenced into a model of the world that is not right for them or is in opposition to their core beliefs (whatever the stage hypnotherapist would have us believe). It is, therefore, vital that the therapist is fully aware of their patient's belief systems and what the patient wants for himself or herself before beginning any change work.

Therapy breaks down, in simplistic terms, to three main stages. First, exploring the presently held belief systems of the patient. The enabling beliefs can become very useful therapeutic tools and the limiting ones can become the areas of focus for change. Not all limiting beliefs are necessarily unhelpful; they may serve a protective or security role and it is important not to 'throw the baby out with the bath water', e.g. a belief that dark alleyways are unsafe places at night.

The next area of exploration is the outcome for therapy or what the patient wants to be different in their life. This may seem to be an easy area to explore but it is surprising how many of us do not really know what we want in life. Or we have half thought through ideas, not anticipating their full impact on life; like King Midas who wanted everything to turn to gold, until his wife and children turned to gold, as did his food, etc. – and it seemed such a good idea at the time! In my experience, when a patient, even one with schizophrenia, explores carefully what they want in life and the consequences of getting it, or not getting it, they can come up with appropriate aims for therapy.

The final stage in therapy is to look at the limiting beliefs that the patient has that are stopping them from reaching their goals. This may be to do with beliefs about themselves and whether or not they deserve what they want. It may also be about creating goals within goals so that a goal is always within reach and expectation does not extend too far beyond present performance. If there is too great a gap between present performance and desired goal, then motivation can be lost. The thousand-mile journey begins with one step. If the patient can see that just one step is success, then nothing breeds success like success.

One aspect of NLP that many patients find beneficial is that it provides a very structured framework for making the psychological explorations mentioned above. In some other forms of therapy, the patient is required to have some existing degree of insight as well as a desire to talk openly about emotional issues. I remember a psychotherapy student, not from an NLP background, asking for potential clients to work with. His list of exclusions was so long that I felt that none of the clients I was working with at the time could be considered. His potential client needed to be articulate, preferably of university education or equivalent, prepared to commit to weekly therapy for a minimum of a year, and not on any medication. Fortunately with NLP one does not have to be so restricted: one can start with a therapeutic 'presence' when sitting in silence with relaxed rapport. This may be considered a 'success' with some of the clients I have worked with in the past.

NLP is a brief outcome-focused therapy and because of this it has been suggested that it is not a therapy of choice for long-term work with chronically ill patients. This does not take into account the flexibility of this way of working. With some of the patients that I used to work with in the NHS I saw them on a regular weekly basis for many years, but each session was not necessarily about making deep psychological changes. As mentioned already, the most important aspect of any therapy is the therapeutic relationship and so initial sessions would be spent developing this. The therapy may then enter into a period of change and insight, after which the patient may then enter into a period of being relatively well and stable. At this time they need a period of integration or 'trying on' this new way of being in their life. In this phase the therapist's role may become one of coach, encourager, rewarder and listening friend – all of which goes to reinforce the deep levels of rapport with the patient and so constitutes part of the therapeutic process. This can be very helpful if the patient relapses, as so many do. If a deep level of rapport has existed between the patient and therapist for some time, then it often remains to some degree in the relapsed patient and therapy can be resumed more quickly.

Some monitors of psychotherapy would question the validity of the therapy if there is a relapse, but that would presuppose that the therapy in question was attempting a cure. From an NLP perspective cure is not a concept that is often used as it implies that there is a pathology that must change, whereas NLP is looking for changes in cognition and behaviour. The NLP approach to relapse is that this is another opportunity to find out more about how the patient specifically 'does' their form of limiting cognitions or beliefs and what they need to do to 'manage' them differently next time so that they can eventually prevent a relapse. The concept of 'there is no such thing as failure, only feedback' is central to NLP; and this is what makes it such a close relative of cognitive behavioural therapy. It is vital that the patient has realistic outcomes for therapy and does not see being 'happy' as the only acceptable state and anything less as failure. Living in the real world means that the state of happiness is transitory for most of us, most of the time. Without this awareness a relapse could become doubly depressing. This learning and self-management model will help the patient to move away from a sense of helplessness in their illness towards a sense of taking responsibility. They will then be able to ask themselves what it was that they were doing or thinking that led them to be in their present situation and what they need to do to make things different. This may also include reviewing their compliance with medication. When this is coupled with a clear goal that is judged by the client to be both desirable and achievable, a sustainable change in behaviour is possible.

NLP can bring about rapid change for some people, but no-one would expect it to be used in that way with psychotic patients or those with a diagnosis of personality disorder. What it has to offer these patients is a structured way of working with very abstract issues which is invaluable to the psychologically naive patient and which also allows them to understand relationship issues in a more psychodynamic way (Burton 1998). As a patient gains insight into their identity, how they operate, how they respond to the world, and into the antecedents for their mental state, they are far more likely to be compliant to medication and psychosocial rehabilitation. When they have achieved a degree of stability and perceived control in their life they also improve their chances of preventing relapse. This kind of structured therapy cannot work in isolation with severely mentally ill patients. A multidisciplinary approach is vital for both the patient and the therapist. The patient requires a full range of medical and nursing support as well as a range of psychoeducational and occupational support. They will also need housing support and social workers; it is not a 'cheap' option for the care of these patients – facts that at last seem to be acknowledged by the present government. The therapist also needs to be working within a team of supportive professionals if he or she is going to prevent burnout while working with this very challenging but rewarding group of patients.

References

Bandler, R. and Grinder, J. (1975) *The Structure of Magic.* Vol I. Palo Alto, CA: Science and Behaviour Books.

Bandler, R. and Grinder, J. (1976) *The Structure of Magic.* Vol.II. Palo Alto, CA: Science and Behaviour Books.

Burton, M. (1998) *Psychotherapy, Counselling and Primary Mental Health Care.* Chichester: John Wiley.

France, J. and Muir, N. (1997) *Communication and the Mentally Ill Patient.* London: Jessica Kingsley Publishers.

Haley, J.(1973) *Uncommon Therapy: The Psychiatric Techniques of Milton H. Erickson, M.D.* London: Norton.

Liberman, R.P., Mueser, K.T., Wallace, C.J., Jacobs, H.E., Eckman, T. and Massel, K. (1986) Training skills in the psychiatrically disabled: learning and coping competence. *Schizophrenia Bulletin 12,* 4, 631–647.

Macdonald, L. (1990) Are we moving in the right direction? *Speech Therapy in Practice 6,* 6.

O'Connor, J. and Seymour, J. (1990) *Introducing Neurolinguistic Programing.* London: The Aquarian Press.

CHAPTER 27

A Multidisciplinary Therapeutic Alliance
Group Work Developed Through Cognitive Behavioural Principles

Marie Quayle

The therapeutic relationship

The relationship between client/patient and therapist has been given a position of central importance and viewed as one of the major factors associated with the success or failure of therapy. Freud (1912) saw the transference relationship between analyst and client as crucial, but also stressed the working alliance, defined as the rational, non-neurotic rapport that the client has with the therapist (Greenson 1967). Rogers (1957) described his person-centred concept of positive relationship; Prochaska (1979) referred to the existential ideal of authentic relationship; and cognitive behavioural therapy has been described as a 'collaborative empiricism' between client and therapist which allows the client to operate as a 'personal scientist' (Beck *et al.* 1979; Meichenbaum 1985).

Relationships in group work

The group therapy analogue of this client–therapist relationship is cohesiveness (Yalom 1975), a factor specific to group work, involving the client's relationship not only with the therapist but all other group members. Group therapy is seen as unique among therapies since the group, if it functions fully, provides a multilayered, dense tapestry of interpersonal action and reaction which is impossible to achieve in one-to-one therapy (Lynn and Frauman 1985). A number of therapeutic factors specific to groups, as opposed to dyads, have been identified, including the capacity of groups to develop cohesiveness or a sense of belonging; to be a microcosm of society, rewarding or punishing behaviour; to define reality for its members; to induce and release powerful feelings; and to provide a context for social comparison and feedback (Lieberman 1980). Observing others having a critical or significant emotional experience can benefit even relatively quiet group members, and groups provide an opportunity not only for self-change but also genuine altruistic facilitation of change in others.

In group work therefore, it is the group, rather than the leader alone, that is the primary agent of change. However, the role of the group leader is critical in creating a climate in which numerous meaningful relationships can thrive and enabling the group to realise its potential as a powerful force for change. The group is a complex social system, addressing personally relevant issues and normally expecting significant self-disclosure by participants. Thus group therapy not only has unique properties for change but also unique difficulties which reduce the power of change strategies found to be successful in individual therapy. Group members may not necessarily reinforce behaviours, such as expression of emotion, which the group leader wishes to encourage and may indeed allow behaviours, such as withdrawal or flight from the task, which the group leader would challenge. Group norms are not necessarily or primarily a function of leader behaviour or leader desires (Lieberman 1980) and thus the power and influence of the therapist are considerably more diffuse in this multiperson context than they are within individual therapy. The group leader may be seen as the leader of an orchestra rather than an individual soloist, or accompanist to a soloist. Rewards, if the orchestra coheres and blends in a joint enterprise, are great but the whole can be threatened by one member playing a different tune or rhythm.

Co-facilitation

It is unsurprising therefore that, whilst therapists operated singly as leader of the group when group therapy was first introduced, subsequently the majority of therapists preferred to conduct group therapy with co-facilitators (Rabin 1967; Rosenbaum 1971). Co-facilitation was seen to have a number of advantages for group members: leader attention to all members is increased and the chance of leader bias towards certain individuals or subgroups is minimised; important group dynamics or individual behaviours, verbal or non-verbal, are less likely to be missed; and members can be both confronted and supported at the same time. Co-facilitators also benefit from the sharing of roles and reinforcement of their feedback within the group, as well as peer support or challenge, and shared perceptions of group interactions following group sessions.

Lieberman, Yalom and Miles (1973), observing 16 group leaders of differing theoretical orientations, identified four fundamental functions of group leaders: emotional stimulation; support; meaning attribution; and executive functions. These functions may well be more easily fulfilled if they are shared amongst co-facilitators, who are able to change roles to complement each other, rather than held by one leader who is expected to provide all of them as required at any given moment. This may be particularly true in groups with a cognitive behavioural orientation, in which therapists are likely to play a very active, directive part, and thus it is useful to have person-orientated facilitators, as well as the task-orientated leader at any time. Moreover, since the well functioning group is an effective elicitor of psychopathology (Lieberman 1980), it may be argued that it is crucial within a forensic context, such as a high security psychiatric hospital, to have more than one group facilitator able to observe and interpret the behaviour of group members in the light of their past history and offences.

Just as group therapy has many advantages but also difficulties, so co-facilitation can benefit members and leaders but also have problems. Just as the relationship between individual client and therapist or between group members is central to the effectiveness of therapy, so the relationship between co-facilitators of a group must be viewed as a factor of crucial importance. Competitiveness between leaders (Heilfron 1969; MacLennan 1965), or support of group members in complaints about the co-facilitator, can reproduce the splitting and rivalry which occur in family situations. Disagreement about behaviours to be valued or discouraged in the group can weaken the effect of leader reinforcement and reproduce confusion about acceptable and unacceptable behaviour, which may have been experienced in earlier life. On the other hand witnessing leaders interacting between themselves and able to address and resolve disagreements can have potent positive effects on group members (Harari and Harari 1971) and may be a corrective recapitulation of early family life.

Shapiro (1978) opined that co-therapists should respect each other's abilities yet diverge in their approach. Complementarity, rather than identity, can be seen as the ideal, since this adds another element to the group over and above the working relationship between co-facilitators with similar characteristics. Difference of gender in co-facilitators has been seen as an advantage (Hulse *et al.* 1956); is this also the case for difference of theoretical background and approach when members of different disciplines co-facilitate groups?

Multidisciplinary working

Much has been written about multidisciplinary team work, viewed by the Royal College of Psychiatrists as a valuable instrument in modern psychiatric practice, although results indicate that in reality it is restricted and variable, with only doctors and nurses being almost invariably present in meetings of the team (Cowan 1991). Perceived benefits include broader perspectives in care provision and case management (Ambelas 1991) and an efficient division of labour, which utilises specialist skills and acknowledges the importance of a holistic approach to client needs (Noon 1988). Each discipline is seen to contribute its particular expertise to decision-making, as well as at different points within the total process of treatment and rehabilitation (Kane 1975).

Multidisciplinary working has been viewed mainly in terms of differing contributions to the process of management and therapy. Less has been written about co-working: the particular therapeutic alliance which is formed when members of different disciplines work together, for instance as co-facilitators of a group.

The therapeutic alliance

One such therapeutic alliance was formed when the author joined one of the editors on the multidisciplinary team working in the Young Men's Unit in Broadmoor Hospital: a female clinical psychologist and a female speech and language therapist working with young male mentally ill and psychopathically disordered patients in a ward staffed at that time exclusively by male nurses. The ward has been described in a number of papers (Grounds *et al.* 1987; Brett 1992; Quayle, France and Wilkinson 1996). Drawn together by initial links of gender and an age range which was parental in relation to the average age of patients, the female clinicians readily provided a support structure for each other and mutually benefited from a shared knowledge of the patients and ward as well as the different perspectives of their respective disciplines.

At the time the alliance was formed, in the early 1980s, there were three unstructured, slow open, interpretive groups on the Young Men's Unit, and two structured programmes of social skills and sex education, accepted on the ward as valuable for these young men who often lacked or failed to benefit from the usual learning and socialising influences. Anger management training had been introduced previously by a team from the psychology department, but was viewed negatively on the ward, being seen as psychologists 'deliberately winding up patients' in order to address anger and then leaving the nurses to deal with inevitable aggressive outbursts afterwards.

Initially the two female therapists worked separately within the existing group structure on the ward, with male nurse co-facilitators who varied from week to week, depending on duty shifts. It soon became clear that any extension of the group work offered on the ward, in particular the introduction of further structured programmes, would be more easily facilitated by two therapists working together, in addition to the varying nurse facilitator. This would provide the consistency and detailed knowledge of each patient's performance within and across groups, which would enable patient needs to be identified and the introduction of further group programmes to meet those needs.

Thus the therapeutic alliance was formed and its continuation over several years enabled the structured group programmes to be extended and established as an integral part of the therapeutic structure on the ward. Anger management training was successfully reintroduced, following a nurse training day to tackle the abiding reservations about this therapy at that time. Assertiveness training and further modules addressing issues of sexuality and relationships were added, thus extending and integrating the original programmes of sex education and

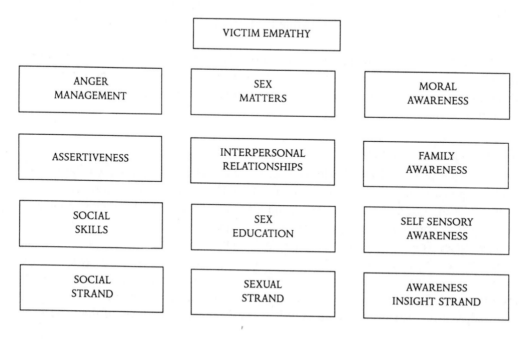

Figure 27.1. Structured Group Modules

social skills. Each change was discussed in detail with the nurse co-facilitators and training and planning days were arranged before each group module began.

When modules ended, multidisciplinary meetings were called to consider the therapeutic needs of patients and identify the most appropriate next module to meet those needs. During one of these meetings one of the nurses suggested that a different, less verbal kind of group was needed in order to 'get behind' the defences displayed by so many of the psychopathically disordered patients. The result was the 'actualisation group': a title based on the self-realisation stage of Maslow's (1954) hierarchy of needs, but in effect allowing the inclusion of several different approaches, as the group evolved initially over more than a year. Following this the programme was split into four separate modules: self and sensory awareness, family awareness, moral reasoning and victim empathy. The structured group modules regularly available on the ward at the time of writing are shown in Figure 27.1 and have been described in a previous article (Quayle et al. 1996).

These group modules, sometimes augmented by others, have become a valued part of the therapeutic programme on the ward and the 'different, non-verbal' approaches used are available in a more specialist way in the hospital, following the appointment of art, music and drama therapists. At the time the actualisation group was introduced, however, trust and blindfold exercises, sculpting, empty chair therapy and similar approaches were not usual in the hospital. Thus, before they were introduced with patients, lengthy multidisciplinary discussion was necessary, including not only potential benefits but possible pitfalls. Which trust exercises might make a patient vulnerable to a dangerous, violent impulse by another patient? Could *any* facilitators participate in exercises which required them to be blindfolded – or simply close their eyes? Was it possible to agree to the patients' request to carry out the empty chair exercise in a room with dim lighting, since they felt it would be more possible in this setting to hold a 'conversation' with a significant other person not present? What might be the effect on patients of allowing them to undertake a role reversal conversation in which they spoke both as themselves and as their victim, albeit in some cases dead? And what unpredictable emotions and responses might be evoked if group members sculpted significant people in another patient's life or answered in the role of another patient's victim? Exercises which might be taken for granted with other clients had to be considered with care in this high security psychiatric setting, in which the majority of patients had seriously offended in a violent physical or sexual way. No risk was taken without due deliberation, but the willingness of the multidisciplinary team to take calculated risks, to enable greater therapeutic gain, was endorsed many times by the response of patients during sessions or feedback following the programme on exercises they had found most difficult but most helpful.

This expansion of the structured group programme was undoubtedly facilitated by the presence of two consistent therapists working together over a number of years with the support of a number of nurses committed to the value of group work. The fact that the two therapists were female and the nurse co-facilitator in any group session was male added another element. The presence of men and women facilitated the reproduction of the family unit, identified as a benefit by Hulse et al. (1956). Additionally, the presence of two women in this otherwise all-male group provided an opportunity not only for mutual support rather than isolation, but also for patients to observe an interaction on issues which are specifically feminine or where male and female views may be predicted to differ.

Multidisciplinary working in the therapeutic alliance

A further dimension was added to the alliance by the fact that the three therapists in any group session were of different disciplines: a psychiatric nurse, a speech and language therapist, and a clinical psychologist. Did each discipline bring a unique contribution, an added extra, to the overall task of group facilitation, not possible if all were from one discipline?

No doubt the speech and language therapist and the psychiatric nurse could identify in more detail their specific contributions to the group. As the clinical psychologist of the trio I can only acknowledge what I valued and came to rely on. The nurse comes to the group with a detailed and personal knowledge of the patients, only possible for those who spend all of their working hours accompanying patients in their journey through the hospital. This 'complex relationship' between patients and nurses (Macphail and Cox 1975) allows the nurse facilitator, both within and outside the group, to support patients who are experiencing the difficulty and pain of group therapy; to act as a stimulus to those who seek to deny, avoid, or find an easy way out; and to provide a touchstone of reality which encourages openness in patients and reduces the temptation to paint a 'rosier than real' picture for other facilitators less informed of the details of ward life. The specific skills of the speech and language therapist are invaluable when patients have linguistic or hearing deficits, or problems with articulation or literacy. Beyond this, however, is the heightened sensitivity of the speech and language therapist to the patterns of communication within the group; the non-verbal, vocal and verbal aspects of that communication; the telltale body movement, word emphasis, changed tone, or difficulty with articulation which may signal the presence of strong emotions, perhaps suppressed.

Assessment and evaluation

One likely answer to a query about the unique contribution of clinical psychologists to group facilitation is psychologists' use of standardised assessments. Patient self-report questionnaires and staff rating forms were indeed regularly used in the Young Men's Unit, to assist in selecting patients for groups, evaluate individual progress, and provide an important component of the reports following each group programme. Whilst these assessments allow investigation of overall group mean change (Reiss et al. 1998; Quayle, Deu and Giblin 1998), the interpretation of ideosyncratic change within that group mean is important in evaluating individual progress (Quayle and Moore 1998). A patient whose post-group scores fall in the non-desired direction may be judged to have failed to benefit from the group, or alternatively to have gained a greater awareness and acknowledgement of difficulties, a necessary stage for change to occur. A patient who sees himself as having benefited from the group when nurses see no change or deterioration in his behaviour on the ward may have an unrealistic view of his progress, or alternatively may be exhibiting the lag which can occur between inner and outer change, especially in settings where behavioural patterns can become stereotyped and self-fulfilling prophecies. The shared yet differing knowledge of patients held by multidisciplinary facilitators is invaluable to the clinical psychologist in seeking correctly to interpret the meaning of individual change on assessment measures, a clinically vital task in evaluating progress of patients on their journey through the hospital.

Evaluation of the effectiveness of different therapies with various groups of clients is a major component of psychological research, a scientific basis on which clinical psychologists rely. Thus Losel (1998), reviewing research on the treatment and management of psychopaths, concludes that a relatively consistent picture emerges: structured, cognitive behavioural, skills-orientated therapies, based on social learning theories, have better effects on antisocial behaviour than other modes of treatment; and treatment programmes which focus on what is known of the causes of antisocial behaviour and recidivism are more indicated than interventions based solely on specific schools of psychotherapy. This integrated, eclectic, needs-led approach is the core of the therapeutic structure on the Young Men's Unit (Quayle *et al.* 1996). The structured group modules, such as interpersonal skills, anger management or victim empathy, run in parallel with unstructured, interpretive groups, within the context of individual therapies: interpretive; systemic; cognitive-behavioural; or counselling. The identified need of these young personality disordered patients for further socialisation, improved interpersonal skills and greater empathic awareness of others, leading to acceptance of responsibility for offences, was the driving force in the extension of the structured group programmes to the present time. From this basis, group modules may be changed or added as needs are assessed at any stage in the future.

Structured group work

Many professionals of different disciplines are now trained in cognitive behavioural approaches and facilitate structured, cognitive-behavioural, skills-orientated groups. Despite Eysenck's (1949) view that the role of therapist is something 'essentially alien' to clinical psychology, present-day training courses for clinical psychologists normally have cognitive behavioural therapy as a central component. Additionally, however, these courses are generic and usually involve familiarity with several therapeutic approaches. Thus it has been claimed that, unlike other disciplines, clinical psychologists use and integrate a 'variety of theoretical models', in order to tailor their therapy to the individual client (Manpower Advisory Service 1989). Moreover, the cognitive behavioural approach is *itself* a model of psychopathology and theory of behaviour change which was designed to integrate diverse approaches, emphasising not just one factor, such as irrational beliefs and cognitive distortions (Ellis 1977), or external environmental events (Skinner 1974), but the interdependence of multiple processes involving the individual's thoughts, feelings, physiological reactions, behaviours and environmental consequences (Meichenbaum 1985).

Thus psychologists, and other professionals trained in cognitive behavioural approaches facilitate structured groups based primarily on social learning principles (Bandura 1969), such as social skills training (Argyle 1975; Trower, Bryant and Argyle 1978) or anger management (Novaco 1975, 1997). In addition it may be argued that clinical psychologists' training prompts them to use a variety of approaches to meet the needs of patients, and in which other members of the multidisciplinary alliance may have more specialist skills. Thus the clinical psychologist is likely to appreciate the advantages of multidisciplinary working, in which different disciplines contribute similar or complementary skills, to the task of co-facilitation of structured groups.

Jones (1998a, b) observes that, unlike surveyors who do not teach clients how to value a house or set a homework task to report on the state of a neighbour's roof, clinical psychologists have an essentially psycho-educational role. They aim to give clients more understanding of their own psychological functioning, so that they may become personal scientists, significantly changing, if they choose, the way they behave or construe their world. However, in order successfully to pass on these 'usable chunks of psychological knowledge' they need to be expressed in language which does not psychologise everyday experience to the point where it confuses rather than clarifies; yet is not so simplified and simplistic that it adds nothing of value to the client's understanding. A tricky task and one in which psychologists by no means always succeed, judging by the typical round of jokes about the profession. The experience of the multidisciplinary therapeutic alliance described in this chapter, however, suggests that different disciplines contribute their specialist skills to the attainment of this goal. Chunks of psychological knowledge provided by the clinical psychologist were re-expressed in clear, understandable language by the speech and language therapist, and relevantly applied to the everyday lives of the patients by the psychiatric nurse.

Other therapeutic alliances may share and divide roles in other ways, contribute similar or complementary skills. However that may be, the multidisciplinary alliance of co-facilitators, who bring the unique contribution of their own professional background, in addition to skills they share in common from training and experience, is a potentially powerful therapeutic tool within the 'multilayered, dense tapestry' which is the group.

Acknowledgements

The author would like to thank speech and language therapist Jennifer France, the other consistent partner in the therapeutic alliance, and all the nurses who participated in the endeavour throughout the years.

References

Ambelas, A. (1991) The task of treatment and the multidisciplinary team. *Psychiatric Bulletin 15*, 77–79.

Argyle, M. (1975) *Bodily Communication*. London: Methuen.

Bandura, A. (1969) *Principles of Behaviour Modification*. New York: Holt, Rinehart and Winston.

Beck, A., Rush, A., Hollon, S. and Shaw, B. (1979) *Cognitive Therapy of Depression*. New York: Guilford Press.

Brett, T. (1992) The Woodstock approach. *Criminal Behaviour and Mental Health 2*, 152–158.

Cowan, C. (1991) Audit in practice: multidisciplinary involvement in hospital discharge. *Psychiatric Bulletin 15*, 415–416.

Ellis, A. (1977). The basic clinical theory of rational-emotive therapy. In A. Ellis and R. Grieger (eds) *Handbook of Rational Emotive Therapy*. New York: Springer.

Eysenck, H.J. (1949) Training in clinical psychology: An English point of view. *American Psychologist 4*, 173–176.

Freud, S. (1957, originally published 1912) *Recommendations for Physicians on the Psycho-analytic Method for Treatment*. Standard edition, 12, 109–120. London: Hogarth.

Greenson, R.R. (1967) *The Technique and Practice of Psychoanalysis* (Vol. 1). New York: International Universities Press.

Grounds, A.T., Quayle, M., France, J., Brett, T., Cox, M. and Hamilton, J.R. (1987) A Unit for 'psychopathic disorder' patients in Broadmoor Hospital. *Medicine, Science and Law 27*, 1, 21–31.

Harari, C. and Harari, C. (1971) The co-therapist encounter: a catalyst for growth. In L. Blank, G.B. Gottsegen and M.G. Gottsegen (eds) *Confrontation*. New York: Macmillan.

Heilfron, M. (1969) Co-therapy: the relationship between therapists. *International Journal of Group Psychotherapy 19*, 366–381.

Hulse, W.C., Ludlow, W.V., Rindsberg, B.K. and Epstein, N.B. (1956) Transference relations in a group of female patients to male and female co-leaders. *International Journal of Group Psychotherapy 6*, 430–435.

Jones, A. (1998a) 'What's the bloody point?': more thoughts on fraudulent identity. *Clinical Psychology Forum 112*, 3–9.

Jones, A. (1998b) Fraudulent Identity. *Clinical Psychology Forum 117*, 3.

Kane, R.A. (1975) Interprofessional Teamwork. Manpower Monograph No. 8. Syracuse University School of Social Work.

Lieberman, M.A. (1980 second edition) Group methods. In F.H. Kanfer and A.P. Goldstein (eds) *Helping People Change: A Textbook of Methods*. New York: Pergamon.

Lieberman, M.A., Yalom, I. and Miles, M. (1973) *Encounter Groups: First Facts*. New York: Basic Books.

Losel, F. (1998) Treatment and management of psychopaths. In D.J. Cooke *et al.* (eds) *Psychopathy: Theory, Research and Implications for Society*. Netherlands: Kluwer Academic Publishers.

Lynn, S.J. and Frauman, D. (1985) Group psychotherapy. In S.J. Lynn and J.P. Garske (eds) *Contemporary Psychotherapies: Models and Methods*. Ohio: Charles E. Merrill Publishing Co.

MacLennan, B.W. (1965) Co-therapy. *International Journal of Group Psychotherapy 15*, 154.

Macphail, D. and Cox, M. (1975) Dynamic psychotherapy with dangerous patients. *Psychotherapy and Psychosomatics 25*, 13–19.

Manpower Advisory Service (1989) *Review of Clinical Psychology Services*. London: Department of Health.

Maslow, A.H. (1954) *Motivation and Personality*. London: Harper and Row.

Meichenbaum, D. (1985) Cognitive-behavioural therapies. In S.J. Lynn and J.P. Garske (eds) *Contemporary Psychotherapies: Models and Methods*. Ohio: Charles E. Merrill Publishing Co.

Noon, M. (1988) Teams: the best option? *The Health Service Journal*, October, 1160–1166.

Novaco, R.W. (1975) *Anger Control: The Development and Evaluation of an Experimental Treatment*. Lexington, Mass.: D.C. Heath, Lexington Books.

Novaco, R.W. (1997) Remediating anger and aggression in violent offenders. *Legal and Criminological Psychology 2*, 77–88.

Prochaska, J.O. (1979) *Systems of Psychotherapy: A Transtheoretical Analysis*. Homewood, Il: Dorsey.

Quayle, M., Deu, N. and Giblin, S. (1998) Sexual knowledge and sex education in a secure hospital setting. *Criminal Behaviour and Mental Health 8*, 66–76.

Quayle, M., France, J. and Wilkinson, E. (1996) An integrated modular approach to therapy in a Special Hospital Young Men's Unit. In C. Cordess and M. Cox (eds) *Forensic Psychotherapy, Volume II: Mainly Practice*. London: Jessica Kingsley Publishers.

Quayle, M. and Moore, E. (1998) Evaluating the Impact of Structured Groupwork with Men in a High Security Hospital. *Criminal Behaviour and Mental Health 8*, 77–92.

Rabin, H. (1967) How does co-therapy compare with regular group therapy? *American Journal of Psychotherapy 21*, 244–255.

Reiss, D., Quayle, M., Brett, T. and Meux, C. (1998) Dramatherapy for mentally disordered offenders: changes in levels of anger. *Criminal Behaviour and Mental Health 8*, 139–153.

Rogers, C.R. (1957) The necessary and sufficient conditions of therapeutic personality change. *Journal of Consulting Psychology 21*, 95–103.

Rosenbaum, M. (1971) Co-therapy. In H.I. Kaplan and D.J. Saddock (eds) *Comprehensive Group Psychotherapy*. Baltimore: Williams and Wilkins.

Shapiro, J.L. (1978) *Methods of Group Psychotherapy and Encounter*. Itasca, Il: Peacock.

Skinner, B.F. (1974) *About Behaviourism*. New York: Knopf.

Trower, P., Bryant, B. and Argyle, M. (1978) *Social Skills and Mental Health*. London: Methuen.

Yalom, I.D. (1975) *The Theory and Practice of Group Psychotherapy*. New York: Basic Books.

CHAPTER 28

Interpersonal Skills as Part of Social Skill Training for Patients with Schizophrenia

Rachael Henton, Ruth Sinclair and Vasiliki Sideras

'Social functioning is ... so much a part of schizophrenia that it is virtually impossible to discuss this disorder without reference to its social implications.' (Shepherd 1986, p.13)

Introduction: The broad spectrum of social skills

One consistent finding of studies on patients with mental illness is that they have poor social skills, which persist even when the illness is pharmacologically controlled (Mueser *et al.* 1991; Trower 1987; van Dam-Baggen and Kraaimaat 1986). The potential effectiveness of cognitive behavioural therapy (Tarrier *et al.* 1998) and social skills training for mentally ill patients, particularly those with schizophrenia, is well documented (Benton and Schroeder 1990; Dobson *et al.* 1995; Kopelowicz *et al.* 1997; Liberman *et al.* 1998; Marder *et al.* 1996; Mueser *et al.* 1990; Mueser and Bellack 1998; Musker 1992; Penn and Mueser 1996). Further, Dobson *et al.* (1995) note a reduction in medication dosage as such training continues.

The term *social skills* however is an umbrella term, encompassing a number of social activities such as activities of daily living, family factors, communicative behaviours, psycho-pathology, motivational and situational factors, and cognitive deficits. Social skills training is widely used throughout rehabilitation programmes by the multi-disciplinary team, including nursing and medical staff, occupational therapists, psychologists, creative therapists and speech and language therapists.

This chapter will focus on one social skill, namely *interpersonal skills*, an area to which the expertise of speech and language therapists has been applied. The purpose of this chapter is not to instruct how to teach interpersonal skills as there are many excellent texts already in publication (Hutchings, Comins and Offiler 1991; Rustin and Kuhr 1989; Spence 1995; Wallace 1982), but to give an overview of interpersonal skills and how such training is used within the field of speech and language therapy in mental health.

Interpersonal skills

In our day-to-day lives we encounter a great number of interpersonal experiences and communications, whether it be formal job interviews or conversations with friends. Interpersonal skills can be seen as the foundation of social competence. Social competence can be defined as an individual's ability to interact appropriately within a given social context. Interpersonal skills are acquired gradually from infancy as a child learns through imitation of parents, siblings, peers and teachers etc. The skills will also be determined by the culture and social group in which a child is brought up. A child may additionally be instructed how to behave in a given context, and will gradually begin to learn how to behave and interact appropriately and make his own decisions about different situations. Feedback from the people with whom the child is interacting will confirm and reinforce these social decisions. The process is ongoing and continues throughout adulthood. See Dimitracopoulou (1990) for a detailed discussion of conversational competence and social development.

Interpersonal skills involve both verbal and non-verbal communication and are used to express our feelings and emotions. Amongst other functions they are the means by which we start, maintain and end conversation. They can be classified at two different levels: *micro-level* and *macro-level*. Micro-level interpersonal skills are the simple elements of social behaviour, such as eye contact, facial expression, tone and volume of voice etc. Macro-level skills refer to more complex response levels in which micro-level skills are integrated into an overall strategy in order to, for example, give a greeting, receive a compliment, maintain conversation, or negotiate with others. See Hartley (1993) and Spence (1995) for more in-depth discussion.

One of the fundamental components of successful communication and relationships is interactional-intent or goal. Some goals may be explicitly defined, such as being interviewed or asking for directions. The rewards for these goals will be extrinsic, such as getting the job or successfully finding the way. Other goals may be more implicit and less formally defined, such as greeting a friend or chatting with colleagues over lunch. For these goals the rewards will likewise be intrinsic and might include satisfaction, interest and relaxation. How successful a person is at achieving these goals will influence his actions in similar situations in the future. In addition to goals, the interaction will be formed by the individual's personality, previous experiences, and expectations of the situation.

There are a number of vital elements for successful social interaction which form the basis of one of the early models (Trower, Bryant and Argyle 1978): motivation, perception, translation, response, and feedback.

(1) *Motivation:* People interact with other people for a variety of reasons and in each situation the goals or motives will be different. Goals provide for basic needs of affiliation and achievement such as making friends, persuasion, extracting information, etc.; or more intrinsically, being happy and relaxed in the company of another person.

(2) *Perception:* An individual's perception is dependent upon their plan and motive, including how well they know the other person, their assessment of the situation, their beliefs about motives and plans of others and social stereotyping. Misperception is common, particularly in unfamiliar situations and misreading cues can lead to a breakdown in communication.

(3) *Translation:* Perception is translated into performances.

(4) *Responses:* Skilled behavioural motor responses are required so that translation stages can be implemented. They include discrete elements such as gaze, facial expression etc. and high level elements such as warmth, assertiveness, social routines and basic conversation etc.

(5) *Feedback:* is received during the ongoing activity, signalling corrective action and maintenance. Social intervention involves a number of co-existing components, including verbal behaviour, non-verbal behaviour and conversational skils.

Non-verbal behaviour

Non-verbal communication can be defined as all parts of human communication except for the purely verbal message. This includes aspects of paralanguage such as pitch, tone, volume, clarity of speech, speed of speech and fluency (Figure 28.1) and body language such as facial expression, gaze, gesture, movement, personal appearance, posture, proximity and touch (Figure 28.2). Non-verbal communication serves a number of purposes: it can totally replace speech; it can complement the verbal message; it can be used to regulate and control the flow of communication; it can provide feedback. Non-verbal behaviour helps to define relationships between communicative partners and provides guidelines for appropriate social behaviour (Wilkinson and Canter 1982; Hargie and McCartan 1986).

Figure 28.1: Aspects of paralanguage

Pitch	Can change to indicate different emotions such as anxiety, excitement, anger, intimacy etc.
Tone	Conveys underlying intention e.g. reprimanding, comforting etc.
Volume	Is used for emphasis e.g. shouting or intimacy e.g whispering.
Clarity	Adds definition or emphasis. Can portray formality, or hierarchy e.g. the kind of speech used when teaching or explaining.
Speed	Indicates different emotional states e.g. people tend to talk quicker when excited or angry.
Fluency	Portrays underlying emotion e.g. people tend to become more dysfluent if they are nervous, angry etc.

Verbal behaviour

Verbal communication is the physical act of giving a spoken message. Speech is used for a variety of purposes, from describing feelings to reasoning and arguing. The words used will depend on who the person is talking to, the context in which they are talking to them, the relationship between them, and the topic they are discussing.

Figure 28.2: Aspects of body language

Facial expression	Indicates the way we are feeling. Our faces respond instantaneously and are therefore the most effective and immediate way to give feedback to others.
Gaze	Indicates attention to our communicative partner. It is also used to open, maintain and close conversation.
Gesture	Reinforce the verbal message or can stand alone.
Movement	Gross representation of underlying emotional state e.g. fidgeting, pacing etc.
Personal appearance	Affects our own image and the way others view and relate to us.
Posture	Portrays our feelings about ourself, our relationship with others and how we feel in that particular environment.
Proximity	Indicates personal space. Differs according to situation.
Touch	Integral part of some social routines e.g. greetings. Differs according to situation and culture. A means of portraying feelings.

Conversation

The main domain of interpersonal exchanges is conversation which is the continuous two-way process of giving, receiving and interpreting messages. Conversation involves verbal and non-verbal skills and can be broken down into a number of processes. One model identifies three core skills: *receiving skills* – attending to and perceiving cues and contextual information of the interpersonal situation; *processing skills* – generating response alternatives, weighing the consequences of each and selecting the optimal response; and *sending skills* – using the selected option in response, integrating verbal and non-verbal skills (Liberman *et al.* 1985; Wallace *et al.* 1980).

Interpersonal skills and schizophrenia

Theories

The acquisition of interpersonal skills may be impaired for a variety of reasons such as lack of instruction or poor role models, physical illness, disability, emotional or learning difficulties. Skills that have been acquired might be impaired as a result of emotional disturbance or illness. Impaired interpersonal skills are often found with mental illnesses such as depression, anxiety and psychosis.

There appear to be two schools of thought when examining why patients with schizophrenia have poor interpersonal skills. The older theory suggests that the mental illness has *developed* as a result of poor social and communicative functioning (Brown *et al.* 1972). Communication deviance in parents is thought to predict the onset of schizophrenia type symptoms in their children and there is a well documented correlation with pre-morbid social adjustment and the course of schizophrenic illness (Liberman *et al.* 1982; Musker 1992).

It has been suggested that patients may have a predisposition to developing schizophrenia (Clegg *et al.* 1999; Liberman *et al.* 1985; Shepherd 1986). This more recent theory suggests that poor social functioning is just one of the many facets of impairment *caused* by the mental illness.   Looking at organic rather than social factors, this theory arises from recent advances in medical research into schizophrenia.

In normally functioning adults one hemisphere of the brain (usually the left) develops dominance and is found to be larger than the other. In patients with schizophrenia this is not the case. The two hemispheres have been found to be symmetrical, thus suggesting a lack of brain specialisation (Crow 1997; Crow, Done and Sacker 1996; Crow and Done 1997). The right hemisphere is now thought to be dominant in skills such as face recognition, recognition of emotions, and the interpretation of complex high-level communication (Bryan 1988; Bryan 1993) vital for interpersonal interaction.

Both theories are debated, but as one provides a social model and one an organic model, the authors believe that there is a probable inter-linking relationship between the two.

> The symptomatic and social status of a person with the biological vulnerability for schizophrenia depends on the way in which he and his social support network are able to modulate the impact of interpersonal, financial and biological stressors. (Shepherd 1986, p396)

Presentation

It is well documented that patients suffering from mental illness, specifically schizophrenia, either have poor interpersonal skills or are poor at applying these skills appropriately. They have difficulty expressing their feelings and interpreting how other people feel (Kavanagh 1992; Mueser *et al.* 1996), two aspects vital to interpersonal communication.

In many cases, patients with schizophrenia appear to have no social goals, their social behaviour and interactions often being described as irrational or meaningless (Liberman *et al.* 1985). Skills in initiating conversations correlate with the amount of time a patient spends interacting with others and the quality of the interaction (Halford and Hayes 1995). These interpersonal relationships, whilst the most important reinforcer for interpersonal skills, can heighten a patient's feelings of anxiety. The resulting social withdrawal and emotional dullness leads to a cycle of increasing social isolation and increased negative symptoms in schizophrenia (Liberman *et al.* 1982; Brady 1984). If social adjustment were maximised it would have considerable benefits for patients (Shepherd 1986). So the importance of interpersonal skills training in rehabilitation for patients with schizophrenia becomes clear.

Interpersonal skill training

Assessment

Before beginning assessment of interpersonal skills, therapists must ascertain the stability of the patient's mental state. Precursors to successful intervention must include the pharmacological control of psychotic symptoms and a willingness to engage in therapy.

Assessment of interpersonal skills is vital as the intervention offered will be based on its findings. Generally, the method of identifying patients in need of interpersonal skill training will differ depending upon the organisational structure. Background information will give important insights into the pattern and presentation of the social deficits, and the initial assessment offers the therapist an opportunity to observe the patient's behaviour.

The content of the assessment will be mainly universal. A variety of assessment procedures can be used for interpersonal skills, some of which attempt to examine all aspects of social skills. See for example *The Social Use of Language Programme* questionnaire (Rinaldi 1992) in which the patient is required to rate their use of social behaviours, the social context they use them in and the difficulties they experience. There are also a number of informal assessment techniques that can be used, which take the format of observation checklists and rating scales. See for example Hutchings, Comins and Offiler (1991), Rustin and Kuhr (1989). Many texts on social and interpersonal skills include sections on assessment (Bellack *et al.* 1997; Hargie and McCartan 1986).

It is well documented that many patients with schizophrenia have a lack of insight into their difficulties. They may under-report or deny any problems. Therefore it is advisable to use both patient and therapist ratings for assessment purposes. It is believed that this will give a more accurate impression of the patient's existing skills, against which change can be measured. However, therapists must be clear about whether they are measuring change to insight or to function when reporting the outcomes of training.

Training

Social and interpersonal skills training has its origins in behavioural and social psychology. The first comprehensive model of social skills was introduced in the 1960s (Argyle and Kendon 1967; Trower *et al.* 1978) and has recently been utilised by speech and language therapists in training for interpersonal skills. Learning in everyday life is often by trial and error and this can be an unreliable form of training (Argyle 1981). Skills training needs to be highly directional, using behavioural techniques as a means of compensating for the difficulties experienced by the patients, due to attention and information processing deficits (Bellack *et al.* 1997; Shepherd 1986). Such training focuses on changing social behaviour only, although generalisation may occur (Benton and Schroeder 1990; Dobson 1996; Dobson *et al.* 1995; Liberman *et al.* 1998).

Interpersonal skills training examines a patient's social competence. Social competence is measurable against a patient's interactional intent only. For example, the goal of the statement '*it's hot in here*' may be a comment on the temperature; or an indication that the window should be opened. Social competence can only be judged on the basis of whether the speaker is able to indicate his intention to his conversational partner. Equally a patient needs to be able to infer his conversational partner's intention. This has great implication in schizophrenia as patients often see intentions that are not there (delusions of reference). Patients may believe that people are deliberately hiding their intentions, or that people are conspiring against them (paranoid delusions) (Frith 1997). This ability to infer what another person is intending or thinking is referred to as 'Theory of Mind' (Frith 1989; Frith 1991). Some authors have suggested that this ability is lacking in patients with schizophrenia. See France and Muir (1997), and Frith (1992) for more in-depth discussion.

Therapists need to be wary about making assumptions about what a patient's intention might be, and avoid making sweeping conclusions about their social competence or lack of it. Such competence is best judged by whether the patient indicates that his goal has been met or misunderstood. It needs to be judged individually for the person, rather than introducing a set of stereotypical responses.

Interpersonal skills training is not about conformity to patterns of social behaviour. It is intended to increase awareness of what interpersonal skills are and how and why they are used. Also it may include more complex issues such as assertion training, anger management, work with family members, and maintenance groups (Dobson 1996). Daniels and Roll (1998) also discuss the efficacy of psychodrama techniques.

Training methods

Many interpersonal skills training sessions are held as groups and therapists need to be aware of factors affecting group dynamics (Muir 1992; Wright 1989). Equally, training can be completed on an individual basis. The key components to the training are the same in both.

Instruction

Each session will have been designed around a theme which may be a verbal or non-verbal behaviour. The therapist draws the group together to explore and discuss the behaviour, and with the group's involvement, explains why it is important.

Modelling

According to a behaviourist model of training, the therapist then goes on to model the behaviour appropriately, for the group members to watch. Prepared videos or photographs may be used at this stage and are a useful resource.

Role-play

The importance of role-play or behavioural rehearsal is stressed by a number of authors and is an integral part of the training (Bellack *et al.* 1997; Mueser *et al.* 1990). The behaviour is broken down into its verbal and non-verbal parts. It is demonstrated and practised, then both positive and constructive feedback are encouraged. The use of video-cameras to observe role-plays is useful but can be intimidating and could create anxiety in group members. Therapists need to be aware of difficulties individual members may be experiencing, and where possible, reinforce the importance of role-playing and practising situations within the safe boundaries of the group.

Problem-solving

Emphasis is also placed on problem-solving as a group (Bellack *et al.* 1997; Kennard 1987), where self reliance is encouraged rather than direction from the therapist.

Reinforcement

Once the patient has learned about a skill, seen it modelled and rehearsed it, the skill is shaped through reinforcement. This is generally done with praise from the therapist and positive feedback from fellow group members or peers. The social reward of interacting effectively acts as a positive reinforcement and, the more a patient can be encouraged to use new skills outside of the group environment, the more proficient he will become. Group members are encouraged to practise skills in every-day situations and may be given homework tasks to complete prior to the next session (Bellack *et al.* 1997; Trower 1987). The involvement of the multi-professional team is very important at this stage. Other team members can encourage the patient to practise and use the skills acquired in training sessions, and provide support and continuity.

Conclusion

In the short term, interpersonal skills training has been found to be beneficial. Successful training is maximised by the patient's acute symptoms being well controlled and by the patient having sufficient insight into their illness to participate voluntarily (Liberman and Foy 1983). Its effectiveness in patients with chronic schizophrenia has also been demonstrated (Mojabai *et al.* 1998). Patients may be better adjusted for living in the community; the illness may stabilise (Hartley 1993); and relations with family may improve (Leff 1994). The long-term effects of training are less clear (Bellack and Mueser 1992). It is possible that some changes may be as a result of attendance at other co-occurring clinical facilities (van Dam-Baggen and Kraaimaat 1986) and increased therapeutic contact (Curtis 1999). The authors conclude that interpersonal skills training does seem to be beneficial to patients when there is ongoing support and maintenance work in conjunction with a controlled drug regime.

References

Argyle, M. (1981) Methods of social skills training. In M. Argyle (ed) *Social Skills and Health*. London: Methuen.

Argyle, M. and Kendon, A. (1967) The experimental analysis of social performance. In L. Berkowitz (ed) *Advances in Experimental Social Psychology. 3.* New York: Academic Press.

Bellack, A.S., Mueser, K.T., Gingerich, S., Agresta, J. (1997) *Social Skills Training for Schizophrenia: A Step-by Step Guide.* New York: Guildford Press.

Bellack, A.S. and Mueser, K.T. (1992) Social skills training for schizophrenia? *Archive of General Psychiatry 49*, 76–77.

Benton, M.K. and Schroeder, H.E. (1990) Social skills training with schizophrenics: A meta-analytic evaluation. *Journal of Consulting and Clinical Psychology 58*, 6, 741–747.

Brady, J.P. (1984) Social skills training for psychiatric patients, I: Concepts, methods and clinical results. *American Journal of Psychiatry 141*, 3, 333–340.

Brown, G.W., Birley, J.L.T. and Wing, J.K. (1972) Influence of family life on the course of schizophrenic disorders; a replication. *British Journal of Psychiatry 121*, 241–258

Bryan, K.L. (1993) *The Right Hemisphere Language Battery.* London: Whurr.

Bryan, K.L. (1988) Assessment of language disorders after right hemisphere damage. *British Journal of Disorders of Communication 23*, 2, 111–125.

Clegg, J., Hollis, C. and Rutter, M. (1999) Life sentence. *Royal College of Speech and Language Therapists Bulletin,* November.

Crow, T.J. (1997) Schizophrenia as failure of hemispheric dominance for language. *Trends in Neurosciences 20*, 8, 339–343.

Crow, T.J. and Done, D.J. (1997) Schizophrenia as a disorder of the human capacity for language: the trajectory to hemispheric indecision. In J. France, N. Muir (eds). *Communication and the Mentally Ill Patient.* London: Jessica Kingsley Publishers.

Crow, T.J., Done, D.J. and Sacker, A. (1996) Cerebral lateralization is delayed in children who later develop schizophrenia. *Schizophrenia Research 22*, 3, 181–185.

Curtis, D. (1999) Cognitive therapy is no better than supportive counselling in schizophrenia. *British Medical Journal 319*, 643.

Daniels, L. and Roll, D. (1998) Group treatment of social impairment in people with mental illness. *Psychiatric Rehabilitation Journal 21*, 3, 273–278.

Dobson, D. (1996) Long-term support and social skills training for patients with schizophrenia. *Psychiatric Services 47*, 11, 1195–1196.

Dobson, D.J.D., McDougall, G., Busheikin, J. and Aldous, J. (1995) Effects of social skills training and social milieu treatment on symptoms of schizophrenia. *Psychiatric Services 46*, 4, 376–380.

Dimitracopoulou, I. (1990) *Conversational Competence and Social Development.* Cambridge: Cambridge University Press.

France, J. and Muir, N. (1997) *Communication and the Mentally Ill Patient.* London: Jessica Kingsley Publishers.

Frith, C. (1997) Language and communication in schizophrenia. In J. France and N. Muir (eds) *Communication and the Mentally Ill Patient.* London: Jessica Kingsley Publishers.

Frith, C.D. (1992) *The Cognitive Neuropsychology of Schizophrenia.* Hove: Lawrence Erlbaum.

Frith, U. (1991) *Autism and Asperger Syndrome.* Cambridge: Cambridge University Press.

Frith, U. (1989) *Autism.* Oxford: Blackwell.

Halford, W.K. and Hayes, R.L. (1995) Social skills in schizophrenia: assessing the relationship between social skills, psychopathology and community functioning. *Society of Psychiatric Epidemiology 30*, 14–19.

Hargie, O. and McCartan, P. (1986) *Social Skills Training and Psychiatric Nursing.* London: Croom Helm.

Hartley, P. (1993) *Interpersonal Communication.* London: Routledge.

Hutchings, S., Comins, J. and Offiler, J. (1991) *The Social Skills Handbook: Practical Activities for Social Communication.* Biscester: Winslow Press.

Kavanagh, D. (1992) Recent developments in expressed emotion and schizophrenia. *British Journal of Psychiatry 160*, 601–620.

Kennard, J. (1987) Social skills training: A problem to be solved. *Psychiatric Nursing 23*, 7–8.

Kopelowicz, A., Liberman, R.P., Mintz, J. and Zarate, R. (1997) Comparison of efficacy of social skills training for deficit and non-deficit symptoms in schizophrenia. *American Journal of Psychiatry 154*, 3, 424–425.

Leff, J. (1994) Working with the families of schizophrenic patients. *British Journal of Psychiatry 164*, 23, 71–76.

Liberman, R.P., Wallace C.J., Blackwell G., Kopelowicz, A., Vaccaro, J.V. and Mintz, J. (1998) Skills training versus psychosocial occupational therapy for persons with persistent schizophrenia. *American Journal of Psychiatry 155*, 8, 1087–1091.

Liberman, R.P., Massel, H.K., Mosk, M.D. and Wong, S.E. (1985) Social skills training for chronic mental patients. *Hospital and Community Psychiatry 36*, 4, 396–403.

Liberman, R.P. and Foy, D.W. (1983) Psychiatric rehabilitation for chronic mental patients. *Psychiatric Annals 13*, 7, 539–545.

Liberman, R.P., Nuechterlein, K.H. and Wallace, C.J. (1982) Social skills training and the nature of schizophrenia. In J.P. Curran and P.M. Monti (eds) *Social Skills Training: A Practical Handbook for Assessment and Treatment.* New York: The Guildford Press.

Marder, S.R., Wirshing, W.C., Mintz, J., McKenzie, J., Johnston, K., Eckman, T.A., Labell, M., Zimmerman, K. and Liberman, R.P. (1996) Two-year outcome of social skills training and group psychotherapy for outpatients with schizophrenia. *American Journal of Psychiatry 153*, 1585–1592.

Mojabai, R., Nicholson, R.A. and Carpenter, B.N. (1998) Role of psychosocial treatments in management of schizophrenia: a meta-analytic review of controlled outcome studies. *Schizophrenia Bulletin 24*, 569–87.

Mueser, K. and Bellack, A. (1998) Social skills and social functioning. In K. Mueser and N. Tarrier (eds) *Handbook of Social Functioning in Schizophrenia.* Boston: Allen and Bacon.

Mueser, K.T., Bellack, A.S., Douglas, M.S. and Morrison, R.L. (1991) Prevalence and stability of social skill deficits in schizophrenia. *Schizophrenia Research 5*, 167–176.

Mueser, K.T., Donna, R., Penn, D.L., Blanchard, J.J., Bellack, A.S., Nishith, P. and de Leon, J. (1996) Emotion recognition and social competence in chronic schizophrenia. *Journal of Abnormal Psychology 105*, 271–275.

Mueser, K.T., Levine, S., Bellack, A.S., Douglas, M.S. and Brady, E.U. (1990) Social skills training for acute psychiatric inpatients. *Hospital and Community Psychiatry 41*, 11, 1249–1251.

Muir, M. (1992) Group therapy in psychiatry. In M. Fawcus (ed) *Group Encounters in Speech and Language Therapy.* Leicester: Far Communications.

Musker, M. (1992) Making Contact. *Nursing Times 88*, 47, 31–33.

Penn, D.L. and Mueser, K.T. (1996) Research update on the psychosocial treatment of schizophrenia. *American Journal of Psychiatry 153*, 5, 607–617.

Rinaldi, W. (1992) *The Social Use of Language Programme: Enhancing the Social Communication of Children and Teenagers with Special Educational Needs.* (Manual.) NFER-NELSON.

Rustin, L. and Kuhr, A. (1989) *Social skills and the Speech Impaired.* London: Taylor Francis.

Shepherd, G. (1986) Social skills training and schizophrenia. In C.R. Hollin , P. Trower (eds) *Handbook of Social Skills Training: Clinical Applications and New Directions. Volume 2.* Pergamon Press.

Spence, S.H. (1995) *Social Skills Training: Enhancing Social Competence with Children and Adolescents.* NFER-NELSON.

Tarrier, N., Yusupoff, L., Kinney, C., McCarthy, E., Gledhill, A., Haddock, G. and Morris, J. (1998) Randomised controlled trials of intensive cognitive behaviour therapy for patients with chronic schizophrenia. *British Medical Journal 317*, 303–307.

Trower, P. (1987) Social skills training. *British Medical Journal 294*, 663–664.

Trower, P. Bryant, B. and Argyle, M. (1978) *Social Skills and Mental Health.* London: Methuen.

van Dam-Baggen, R. and Kraaimaat, F. (1986) A group social skills training program with psychiatric patients: outcome, drop-out rate and prediction. *Behavioural Research Therapies 24*, 2, 161–169.

Wallace, C.J. (1982) The social skills training project of the mental health clinical research centre for the study of schizophrenia. In J.P. Curran and P.M. Monti (eds) *Social Skills Training: A Practical Handbook for Assessment and Treatment.* New York: The Guildford Press.

Wilkinson, J. and Canter, S. (1982) *Social Skills Training Manual: Assessment, Programme Design, and Management of Training.* Chichester: John Wiley & sons.

Wright, H. (1989) *Groupwork: Perspectives and Practice.* London: Scutari Press.

PART III

The Way Forward

CHAPTER 29

Human Communication, Language and Mental Health

Some General Challenges for Research in this Field

Pamela J. Taylor

E S A R I N T U L O M D P C F B V H G J Q Z Y X K W

...More than an alphabet, it is a hit parade in which each letter is placed according to the frequency of its use in the French language. (Bauby 1997)

For Jean-Dominique Bauby, communication and language behaviour had become a problem after a massive stroke. Communication remained, however, remarkably effective and, given an appropriately skilled recipient, he could thus adapt sufficiently to convey a first person account of his disorder. This was a neurological syndrome – the so-called locked-in syndrome – that, almost by definition, had previously evaded such description. Part of what he conveyed is the inescapability of language as dialogue, in which both parties have to be effective. He lists some of the variance:

> Nervous visitors come most quickly to grief... Reticent people are much more difficult. If I ask them, 'How are you?' they answer 'Fine', immediately putting the ball back in my court... Meticulous people never go wrong: they scrupulously note down each letter and never seek to pierce the mystery of a sentence before it is complete. Nor would they dare dream of finishing a single word for you. Unwilling to chance the smallest error, they will never take it upon themselves to provide the 'room' that follows 'mush', the 'ic' that follows 'atom', or the 'nable' without which neither 'intermi' nor 'abomi' can exist. Such scrupulousness makes for laborious progress, but...

Human language is the phenomenon in which the symbolic representation of objects or ideas by words is linked through grammar, a set of rules for combining words, to convey information between people. It has been argued that the algorithms limiting words and grammar are characteristics which are both innate to humans *and* their distinguishing feature. It is not that other social animals cannot communicate, but that this system, which allows more-or-less infinite creativity in the absence of much conscious understanding of these rules, is unique.

This creativity depends, however, on something beyond such 'mechanistic' rules. A capacity to appreciate context, including perhaps most importantly the mental state of others, is likely to be another crucial factor (e.g. Frith 1998). This Bauby had amply retained, on the evidence of his book. People who have much greater facility with speech – with production of words and grammar – than was left to him, may ultimately be more impaired in their communications. Children normally develop between the ages of 3 and 4 a capacity for recognising the independence of mental state between self and others, and to predict and interpret the behaviour of others, including deception, in word or deed. Some never do (Baron-Cohen, Leslie and Frith 1985), or do so to varying degrees (e.g. Happé 1993). Non-verbal communication may also be impaired for this group.

If language is uniquely human, does disorder of language necessarily imply disorder of person, or disorder of mind? Well, perhaps, but Bauby's problems illustrate a point that is fundamental to study in this area – that language behaviour, or the outward manifestation of language, is not necessarily the same thing as language and the primary capacity for self-expression. Bauby had retained his language competence while showing a deficit in language performance (or pragmatics), this limited strictly by the peripheral tools of expression. By the same token people with receptor problems – such as those with deafness – are generally better construed as having language performance deficits, although in the absence of a route to symbolic representation of ideas that is not dependent on hearing, people who are deaf from birth could develop impairments in competence. Then, too, Bauby's problems are among those illustrative of a further fundamental issue – that communication ought not to be assessed with exclusive reference to the person presenting with the primary problem. The language competence/language performance distinction is widely acknowledged, and indeed many of the authors in this book are at pains to emphasise it. The latter is perhaps less generally and generously acknowledged, and there is a dearth of protocols for evaluating and assisting 'listeners', whether these be professional clinicians or the family, friends and acquaintances of those with the primary problem.

While there may be a relationship between mental disorder and language disorder, it is not invariable, and any direction in the relationship is in most cases yet to be established rather than inferred. In relation to psychotic illnesses, particularly schizophrenia, the term 'thought disorder' would appear to be describing a cognitive difficulty, although it is usually used to describe language performance which results in confusion for the listener. This is not to rule out the probability of impaired language competence on the part of such a speaker, but to stress that in clinical practice the judgement is almost invariably based on the listener's response. Within specialist speech and language services and research, there is an increased appreciation of this, reflected, for example, in the increased use of conversational analysis. This may include examination of the dialogue between two individuals or comparison of the listening skills and judgements of communication variously by professional clinicians or by partners of stroke patients. Protocols exist for evaluating such listeners to individuals with motor speech disorders, Frenchay Dysarthria Assessment (C Enderby 1998). Still, the risks of miscommunication where mental disorder is the presenting problem are perhaps less well acknowledged than where there is gross neurological disorder, and certainly extend beyond psychosis. Malcolm (1982), a journalist, graphically illustrates some of the dyadic communication defects that would perhaps benefit from *bilateral* analysis:

He [the psychoanalyst] must invent the patient as well as investigate him; he must invest him with the magic of myth and romance as well as reduce him to the pitiful bits and pieces of science and psychopathology. Only thus can the analyst sustain his obsessive interest in another...

Malcolm (1990), this time of journalists, but it might have been written of the health care dyad too:

Even as [the writer] is worriedly striving to keep the subject talking, the subject is worriedly trying to keep the writer *listening*... He lives in fear of being found uninteresting, and many of the strange things that subjects say to writers – things of almost suicidal rashness – they say out of their desperate need to keep the writer's attention riveted.

Watts and Morgan (1994) identify a problem which holds even more potential danger – 'malignant alienation'. They describe the meeting of professional and lay therapists and carers who may be unrealistic in their expectations and aspirations for care giving, with a patient who has disordered communication. They argue that the health care professional is particularly vulnerable, because the person of the therapist is perceived as, and to an extent is, the tool in the relevant, psychological therapies. Some patients are psychotically withdrawn and experienced as difficult, perhaps too difficult, because they are relatively inaccessible. Others, whether consciously or not, are unable to contain their hate for a needed person. Watts and Morgan suggest that they communicate this by projection, feeling better in the notional exchange of shared responsibilities ('I hate him and he hates me') and reduction of anxiety ('You hate me so my hate for you is justified'). How much more difficult such exchanges become if they are not recognised and explicitly articulated. Even the person with extensive brain damage begins to seem easy.

Mental disorder

The quasi-scientific terminology of health and its deficits presents language problems of its own. The title of this book implies focus on mental illness, but the contents cover a broader field. The concept of illness is commonly taken to imply a break with previous health, or at least significant disruption of previous stability. While the International Classification of Diseases (ICD-10, WHO, 1992) and its companion, The American Diagnostic and Statistical Manual (DSM-IV, American Psychiatric Association 1994) may still amount to little more than a collection of operational definitions of manner of presentation, the core concept of disorder is useful:

'Disorder' is not an exact term, but it is used here to imply the existence of a clinically recognisable set of symptoms or behaviour associated in most cases with distress and with interference with personal functions. Social deviance or conflict alone, without personal dysfunction, should not be included in mental disorder as defined here. (ICD-10 1992)

The classifiers specify that thus they have sought to avoid the 'greater problems' inherent in the use of terms such as 'disease' and 'illness', without being explicit about what those greater problems would be. I think they have to do with the implications for the term disease of the necessity of understanding causation, prognosis and relevance of specific interventions, and for the term illness that the person affected will accept the 'sick role' (Parsons 1951). For many, if not most, mental disorders there is at best partial understanding of cause and life course, and, as Watts and Morgan indicated, the sick role may not be embraced.

Study of communication and language disorders may, then, be fundamental to the elucidation of both the nature of mental disorder and the resolution of barriers to treatment. Definition and measurement of abnormalities in communication which lead to improvement in their recognition, may, in turn, lead to improvement of recognition and definition of some of the mental disorders which present the greatest challenges to clinicians. Initial interventions to ease or resolve communication difficulties, whether in the designated patient, carers or both, may be necessary to enable satisfactory assessment or specific treatment of the presenting disorder. Further, covert disorders of communication may be fundamental to the presenting pathology, whether in indicating a common cause, being themselves directly or indirectly causative, or in maintaining mental disorder through the mechanism of evoking, even at an early age, hostile and reinforcing communications from others. An almost wholly unexplored possibility, of particular relevance to my title, invoking mental *health* rather than disorder, is that well developed communication skills/language behaviours may be a key protective factor in some situations, for example in the development of people who have been subject to a deprived or abusive childhood. Widom (1991), for example, showed over a 20 year prospective follow-up of nearly 800 children who had been subjected to serious and verified abuse that half of them developed serious personal problems, including criminal offending and early death, but half did not. It is relatively easy to see that abuse not uncommonly occurs within a matrix of disadvantageous social circumstances, and Mullen *et al.* (1993) could not differentiate distinctive effects for abuse. Identification of factors which increase risk is important, but it is arguable that finding factors which increase the chance of healthy survival is even more important. Could children who later functioned well in spite of abuse have had better capacity for communication within themselves and with others, about the abuse and its effects? This is largely unexplored.

Communication and schizophrenia

Much of the research information in this book is derived from people with schizophrenia. There is good reason for that. People with schizophrenia suffer with perhaps the most reliably diagnosed mental disorder. A presenting feature for many sufferers lies in the form of speech, and this may appear to have much in common with disorders associated with discrete cerebral damage, or generalised brain damage which includes the speech areas. At its most severe, disorder of expressive language in schizophrenia affects both word production and grammar and can be reliably recognised in routine clinical examinations. For many patients, however, any deficits appear more equivocal and create the 'is it him, is it me?' kind of doubt. Failures quite to connect with the patient's narrative register on the observer, but more objective and replicable definition is needed to generate the full information base for diagnosis on the one hand and more effective management strategy on the other. Tests validated in part in neurological populations and in part among those with the most severe disorders in the form of expression of thoughts (formal thought disorder) may assist in clarifying the deficits of the less obviously disabled. Then, too, language research among people with schizophrenia has potential importance for people with other psychiatric disorders in this generation of reliable and valid tests of dysfunction.

From language work too, explanatory models both of individual symptoms and of the whole disorder may be generated. Crow (1998a,b) is particularly ambitious in his developmental hypothesis to account for schizophrenia, incorporating evidence of language disorder and impaired pre-morbid social competence, particularly among male sufferers. Here he is inferring language disorder in a core sense, rather than observed language behaviour. He suggests disordered recognition or, more probably, processing of 'indexical' symbols – the 'I', 'you', 'they' – which in turn he links with failures in cerebral hemispheric dominance, and uses to account for the emergence over time of first rank symptoms. His ideas are not unchallenged, although neither challengers nor he have yet formulated this synthesis in a way that would render it readily scientifically testable. Its importance as yet lies particularly in the demonstration that it may be possible to use linguistic theory as well as observation of communication and language behaviours to generate explanation of disorder. Such an approach may perhaps bring us closer to diagnoses, in the sense of improving identification of truly discrete disorders of more predictable courses and responsiveness to more specific treatments. In an independent effort, Frith and Frith (1991) observed likely common ground in deficits associated with early childhood autism and schizophrenia, suggesting specific models and methods for testing them. Frith (1992) sets out what may be seen as the three key components: an inability to generate spontaneous acts and expressions of various kinds, inclusive of speech; a disorder of self-monitoring of thoughts and subvocal speech; and a disorder of monitoring the intentions of others.

Language in developmental disorders

Aitchison (1996) considers the development of language itself. She associates it as much with social development as with the physical structures underpinning voice production in the human. Crucial to society are capacities to bond with and influence others. The former depends on grooming activities – in linguistic terms greetings and responses and the capacity to take turns – while the latter depends on being able to imagine events from another's point of view, to possess a so-called 'theory of mind'. Other primate species have this to some extent, and, with it, the ability to deceive intentionally. Healthy, successful humans tend to be good at giving and receiving cues from each other in both verbal and non-verbal communication, and also good deceivers, sympathisers and persuaders. Either or both sets of abilities may be impaired in developmental disorders.

Autism, and its probable subcategory Asperger's Syndrome, is a neurologically based disorder of development which has been much studied, not least because it shows clearly that human communication is much more than the sum of lexicological and grammatical exercises. Although about 20 per cent of those with autism fail to acquire useful verbal, spoken language at all, and many develop speech late, even children and adult sufferers with high tested IQ and extensive vocabularies misunderstand or fail to make themselves understood in everyday social exchanges. Commonly, communication deficits are apparent before much spoken language could have developed, for example an inability at eighteen months to track the eye gaze of an adult, or to share attention (Baron-Cohen, Allen and Gillberg 1992).

Grooming, sharing, turn-taking abilities are impaired. Later, even high achievers will tend to concrete and pedantic conversation lacking in affective interest and often in tonal inflection. They will also show inabilities to appreciate humour, irony and figurative language. Happé (1995) is among those who have studied autism and demonstrated deficits in theory of mind. She makes a distinction between first and second order mind blindness (deficits on theory of mind tests). The most able people with autism may be able to pass first order false belief tests – recognising when a deception has occurred – but not second order tests, which require appreciation or communication of intention, 'a thought about a thought'. The tests developed in elucidating this process, and distinguishing autistic deficits from healthy communication, can be and are now being applied to elucidate presenting problems in other disorders, for example established schizophrenia (Murphy 1998).

There is a view that schizophrenia is a neurodevelopmental disorder (e.g. Weinberger 1987; Murray and Lewis 1987). Notwithstanding the delay between a notional primary cerebral process, perhaps partly genetic and partly birth injury, and manifestation of the illness, a number of studies have suggested that children who subsequently develop the illness can be distinguished from those who do not, albeit generally retrospectively. Given the wealth of interest in the communication and language of adults with the illness, it seems surprising that work with implications for prediction has rarely applied linguistic evaluation. Such an approach might open opportunities for prevention or damage limitation strategies. Jones *et al.* (1994) did specify that the 30 children, of 4746 in a birth cohort from a week in 1946, who went on to develop schizophrenia were especially likely to have shown language difficulties as children.

A rounded picture of the developmental process must include work on the communication disorders of aging (Bryan and Maxim 1996) – a few, to be sure, further modified presentations of established disorders, as in the survivors of autism or schizophrenia; some, perhaps, a feature of natural aging, but most coming to clinical attention after neurological traumas of one sort or another. Major affective disorders, which may for their duration limit communication at any age, may be disproportionately disruptive in older people.

In this brief introduction to research in the field I have not attempted to be comprehensive, and it will be apparent that I am a layman in the matter of speech, language and communication science, but I hope I have represented myself as an excited layman, particularly in contemplation of 'where next?' Inevitably the pathways that I would like to see opened emerge from my clinical practice and from where research in which I am involved has generated more questions. Personality disorders are the neglected disorders in psychiatry; they pose challenges to reliable definition and diagnosis, still not wholly met, and most present challenge to the person of the therapist – much as Watts and Morgan (1994) have described.

Most attempts to classify and characterise personality disorders invoke concepts of long-standing communication disabilities – and yet where is the body of speech and language research in relation to personality disorder? Violence, to which people with personality disorder and even schizophrenia disproportionately contribute, albeit a small part of the total violence of any community, might generally be construed as perhaps the ultimate breakdown in communication. What does speech and language research have to offer to violence reduction within populations designated as also having mental disorder – or even perhaps also among the notionally mentally healthy?

Personality disorders: the next frontier for speech and language research?

ICD-10 definitions of personality disorder and its subtypes seem to incorporate concepts of language deficits in both performance and competence (my italics in the following examples):

- **Paranoid personality disorder:** a pervasive tendency to *distort experience* by misconstruing the neutral or friendly actions of others as hostile or contemptuous.

- **Schizoid personality disorder:** *limited capacity to express* either warm, tender feelings or anger towards others.

- **Emotionally unstable personality disorder:** *the ability to plan ahead* [a variant of mind blindness?] may be minimal, and outbursts of intense anger may often lead to violence...precipitated when impulsive acts are criticised by others. (My bracketed query.)

Such elements could be invoked from almost any of the acknowledged categories. Perhaps of even more importance, Westen (1997) demonstrated that practising clinicians, whether psychiatrists or psychologists, and of whatever school from the 'biological' to the psycho-dynamic, found research interview schedules, based on question and answer approaches, minimally helpful in assessing patients and preferred evaluation of narrative speech and other behaviours, which they took to include patient–therapist interaction. His solution (Westen and Stedler 1999) is to adopt a linguistic approach of a kind, presenting clinicians with 200 descriptors which they are required to rate and sort. Examples of the 'standard vocabulary' they provide to allow clinicians to provide qualitative psychological descriptions include:

Is unable to describe important others in a way that conveys a sense of who they are as people; descriptions lack fullness and colour.

Tends to blame others for own failures or shortcomings; tends to believe his/her problems are caused by external factors.

Is the first an attempt for practising clinicians at application of some aspect of theory of mind tests?

Would speech and language researchers be able to offer anything more objective or precise? If so, would this be of direct advantage in clinical practice?

Contribution to clinical assessment, definition and problem assessment once personality disorder is established seems one important role. Designation of personality disorder, with reason, as a disorder of development, raises questions of language research for elucidating aetiology. Remarkably, the key longitudinal cohort studies, rich in environmental and temperamental detail (see Farrington 1993; Caspi 1996), make little specific reference to evaluation of communication skills either in the subjects or the significant others in their environments. One is left with a distinct impression that for these children who go on to develop antisocial or behavioural problems in adult life, who were in large families under harsh or inconsistent discipline and related environmental hardships, effective communication, whether as a model for development or a means of control, was rarely within their experience. There are tantalising hints too that the vulnerable children may have their own communication problems. In his overview of pertinent research one conclusion that Caspi (1996) draws from one study (Eysenck 1977) is: 'verbally impaired children thus experience more frequent punishment events than verbally adept children, but with proportionately less result in curbing their problem behaviours.' He also cites the comments of Borkenau and Liebler (1995) on the impact on people in the subjects' environment of individual differences expressed in verbal as well as non-verbal behaviours. Reading disorder is fairly consistently noted as a correlate of conduct disorder (Hill 1997), the latter an acknowledged if not invariable precursor of adult personality disorder, although alone reading problems might be taken as likely to be consequential as causative. Happé and Frith (1996) applied theory of mind tests to children with conduct disorder, in essence finding the conduct disorder children to show, as a group, an intermediate position between healthy children and those with autism, although the conduct disorder group invariably succeeding in first order false belief tests. What they could not do in this study, and appears not to have been done in longitudinal studies, is to use the approach as a possible discriminator between those children with conduct disorder who go on to manifest adult personality disorder and those who do not. Even further discrimination might be possible between those who resort with regularity to violence or deviant aggression in some form, as a problem solving mechanism, and those who do not.

Violence as a language substitute?

In the absence of much, if any, direct evidence, speculation may provide a rich seam for communication and language research. Among people without recognised mental disorder it is generally acknowledged that girls and women are less likely to act violently than boys or men; earlier language, or at least language behaviour, development is attributed to women, and the disorders of childhood which include linguistic failures, such as autism, are very much more common in boys than girls (e.g. Hill 1997). Setting aside for a moment personality disorder, which in relation to violence and other antisocial behaviour is often confounded by circular definitions, the adult mental disorder associated with the most profound and fundamental language disorders – schizophrenia – is the one also most consistently associated with violence, sometimes very serious violence, and in the latter case almost invariably driven by the positive symptoms – delusions (Taylor 1985; Taylor et al. 1998). As already noted Crow (1998a,b) and Frith (1992) have linked delusions to core language deficits and misrepresentations. Whatever the mechanisms by which delusions may arise in the first place, there is evidence that verbal exchanges about the delusion, in particular challenge to the delusion and the effect of challenge on shaping that belief, may increase the likelihood of action on the belief, albeit not necessarily violent action (Buchanan et al. 1993). Taking a more longitudinal view of people with schizophrenia who have committed very serious violence, there are indicators that the nature of their communication difficulties may influence whether or not they have a social network. In a high security hospital setting, people with expressive thought disorder and, it is arguable, the more complete disruption of interpersonal communication, were both less likely to have a social network and more likely to manifest interpersonal violence within a specialist setting than those with a predominantly delusional presentation. The latter not uncommonly described their relationships in hospital as 'upsetting', but perhaps the mere fact that they could communicate this enabled appropriate support or other intervention by trained personnel to prevent violent responses. From the same group, however, those who had been delusional in the community were more likely to have committed extreme, directly personal violence within their family, resulting in the admission (Heads *et al.* submitted). Had miscommunications about the patients' most important beliefs contributed to such actions?

So, there are indicators that application of speech and language assessments and techniques might not only add to understanding of pathways to violence among people with and without independently diagnosed mental disorder alike, but also might offer opportunities for disrupting those pathways and increasing safety. I have not touched on discourse analysis, featured elsewhere in this volume in its usual place, tightening definition of anomalies in schizophrenic communication, but could that specifically be applied to accounts of a key violent episode – whether inflicted on self or others – to improve understanding of how it came about. Could it be used to recognise patterns in communication that might indicate increasing risk of repetition of harm to self or others?

Conclusions

One indicator of the success of established communication and linguistics research is that it is so attractive and important to speculate on applications outside what have come to seem its established fields in schizophrenia, a limited range of developmental disorders and neuro-logical disorders. More work should and will follow in these established areas, but I have sought to raise some questions with enough foundation to provoke extension of such work into newer territories.

References

Aitchison, J. (1996) *The Language Web*. The 1996 Reith Lectures. London: BBC.

American Psychiatric Association (1994) *Diagnostic and Statistical Manual of Mental Disorders (fourth edition) (DSM-IV)*. Washington, DC: American Psychiatric Association.

Buchanan, A., Reed, A., Wessely, S., Garety, P., Taylor, P.J., Grubin, D. and Dunn, G. (1993) Acting on Delusions 2: The phenomenological correlates of acting on delusions. *British Journal of Psychiatry 163*, 77–82.

Baron-Cohen, S., Leslie, A.M. and Frith, U. (1985) Does the autistic child have a 'theory of mind'? *Cognition 21*, 37–46.

Baron-Cohen, S., Allen J. and Gillberg, C. (1992) Can autism be detected at 18 months? The needle, the haystack, and the chat. *British Journal of Psychiatry 161*, 839–843.

Bauby, J.-D. (1997) *The Diving-Bell and the Butterfly*. London: Fourth Estate.

Borkenau, P. and Liebler, A. (1995) Observable attributes as manifestations and cues of personality and intelligence. *Journal of Personality 63*, 1–25.

Bryan, K.L. and Maxim J. (eds) (1996) *Communication Disability and the Psychiatry of Old Age*. London: Whurr.

Caspi, A. (1996) Personality development across the life course. In W. Damion and N. Eisenberg (eds) *Handbook of Child Psychology* (fifth edition). New York: Wiley. pp.311–372.

Crow T.J. (1998a) Precursors of psychosis as pointers to the *homo sapiens* – specific mate recognition system of language. *British Journal of Psychiatry 173*, 289–290.

Crow, T.J. (1998b) Nuclear schizophrenia symptoms as a window on the relationship between thought and speech. *British Journal of Psychiatry 173*, 303–309.

Enderby, P.M. (1988) *Frenchay Dysarthria Assessment* (British edition). NFER – Nelson.

Eysenck, H.J. (1977) *Crime and Personality.* London: Routledge and Kegan Paul.

Farrington, D.P. (1993) The psychosocial milieu of the offender. In J. Gunn and P.J. Taylor (eds) *Forensic Psychiatry. Clinical, Legal and Ethical Issues.* Oxford: Butterworth-Heinemann. pp.252–285.

Frith, C.D. (1992) *The Cognitive Neuropsychology of Schizophrenia.* Hove: Lawrence Erlbaum Associates.

Frith, C.D. and Frith, U. (1991) Elective affinities in schizophrenia and childhood autism. In P. Bebbington (ed) *Social Psychiatry. Theory, Methodology and Practice.* New Brunswick, NJ: Transactions Press. pp.65–88.

Frith, U. (1998) What autism teaches us about communication. *Log. Phon. Cocol. 23*, 51–58.

Happé, F. (1995) Understanding minds and metaphors: insights from the study of figurative language in autism. *Metaphor and Symbolic Activity 10*, 275–295.

Happé, F.G.E. (1993) Communication competence and theory of mind in autism: a test of relevance theory. *Cognition 48*, 101–119.

Happé, F. and Frith, U. (1996) Theory of mind and social impairment in children with conduct disorder. *British Journal of Developmental Psychology 14*, 3895–3398.

Heads, T., Leese, M., Taylor, P.J. and Phillips, S. (1999) Schizophrenia and serious violence: an exploration of interaction between social context, symptoms and violence. Submitted for publication.

Hill, P. (1997) Child and adolescent psychiatry. In R. Murray, P. Hill and P. McGuffin (eds) *The Essentials of Postgraduate Psychiatry* (third edition). Cambridge: Cambridge University Press. pp.97–144.

Jones, P.B., Rodgers, B., Murray, R.M. and Marmot, M. (1994) Child developmental risk factors for adult schizophrenia in the British 1946 birth cohort. *Lancet 344*, 1398–1402.

Malcolm, J. (1982) *Psychoanalysis: The Impossible Profession.* London: Maresfield Library/Karnac Books.

Malcolm, J. (1990) *The Journalist and the Murderer.* New York: Knopf.

Mullen, P.E., Martin, J.L., Anderson, S.E. *et al.* (1993) Childhood sexual abuse and mental health in adult life. *British Journal of Psychiatry 163*, 721–732.

Murphy, D. (1998) Theory of mind in a sample of men with schizophrenia detained in a special hospital: its relationship to symptom problems and neurological tests. *Criminal Behaviour and Mental Health 8*, (Suppl.). 13–26.

Murray, R.M. and Lewis, S.W. (1987) Is schizophrenia a neurodevelopmental disorder? *British Medical Journal 295*, 681–682.

Parsons, T. (1951) *The Social System.* Glencoe, New York: Free Press.

Taylor, P.J. (1985) Motives for offending among violent and psychotic men. *British Journal of Psychiatry 147*, 491–498.

Taylor, P.J., Leese, M., Williams, D., Butwell, M., Daly, R. and Larkin, E. (1998) Mental disorder and violence: a special hospital (high security) study. *British Journal of Psychiatry 172*, 218–226.

Watts, D. and Morgan G. (1994) Malignant alienation. *British Journal of Psychiatry 164*, 11–15.

Weinberger, D.R. (1987) Implications of normal brain development for the pathogenesis of schizophrenia. *Archives of General Psychiatry 44*, 660–669.

Westen, D. (1997) Divergences between clinical and research methods for assessing personality disorders: implications for research and the evolution of Axis II. *American Journal of Psychiatry 155*, 1767–1771.

Westen, D. and Stedler, J. (1999) Revising and assessing Axis II, Part I: Developing a clinically and empirically valid assessment method; Part II: Toward an empirically based and clinically useful classification of personality disorders. *American Journal of Psychiatry 156*, 258–272; 273–285.

Widom, C.S. (1991) Avoidance of criminality in abused and neglected children. *Psychiatry 54*, 162–174.

World Health Organization (1992) *The ICD-10 Classification of Mental and Behavioural Disorders.* Geneva: World Health Organization.

CHAPTER 30

Communication and Formal Thought Disorder in Schizophrenia

David Newby

There can be striking oddities about the way some schizophrenic patients speak. Consider the following example from the manual for the Present State Examination (Wing, Cooper and Sartorius 1974):

> I did suggest to you, that intrinsic or congenital sentiment or refinement of disposition would be so miracle-willed through God's 'tarn-harn' as to assume quite the opposite.

Or this example (from data collected for Newby 1998):

> ... an argument with me mother of a carpet, the burning of a carpet that they seem to think so weirdly that they recommend in a weirdo kind of way go back on a, on a reversal after every three sentences.

The salience and 'tangibility' of this disorder has led many authorities to suggest that formal thought disorder (as it is conventionally termed) is somehow central to the psychopathology of schizophrenia. Kraepelin (1919) and Bleuler (1950), who together are credited with first delineating the condition, both laid great stress on the importance of this phenomenon. Kraepelin set out many descriptive principles, but did not attempt to provide an explanatory hypothesis to link these principles together. Bleuler, however, went further, attempting to unify the heterogeneous psychopathology of the condition by suggesting that the disorder of thought or 'breaking of associative threads' underlay and gave rise to the other symptomatology such as delusional thinking and hallucinatory experiences. He viewed the abnormal speech of schizophrenics as representing a loss of *goal-directedness* in discourse (knowing what you want to say and organising propositions along the way to arrive at a specified end) which in turn arose from the intrusion of inappropriate associations between concepts or propositions. This notion of loosening of associations has influenced many approaches to the problem and can still be discerned in some contemporary formulations referred to later.

Given the wealth of research effort expended in this area in the last hundred years, this review cannot hope to be exhaustive or necessarily provide detailed criticism of all the evidence cited, but it is hoped that it will provide a feel for the diverse and sometimes ingenious techniques which have been used to investigate the problem, and also offer some 'signposts' around the new literature emerging. Before further discussion, however, consideration must be given to two problems of definition which bedevil attempts to make sense of much of this research. These concern the definition of schizophrenia itself and the concept of formal thought disorder (or 'FTD').

The concept of schizophrenia

Those new to reading the research in this area will soon encounter a plethora of studies using this term as if it represents a self-contained, singular disease process which can be reliably and robustly diagnosed in all situations. Unfortunately, this is not the case. In essence the problem lies in the fact that – at present anyway – there is no biological marker that can confirm a clinician's diagnosis of schizophrenia. This stands in contrast to many (but not all) of the conditions encountered in physical medicine. Take 'gout' for example. Here a doctor may be alerted to the diagnosis by a particular pattern of symptoms and the tell-tale 'sign' of a red, warm and tender swelling affecting the big toe. To confirm this, in the vast majority of cases they will be able to do so by syringing a sample of fluid from the affected joint which under the microscope reveals characteristic needle-shaped crystals (formed from the chemical which accumulates to cause the condition). For schizophrenia and the other functional psychoses, no such confirmatory test currently exists. (Indeed, the term 'functional' in essence means having no identifiable pathology.) As a result schizophrenia can only be a syndromal diagnosis – that is, one based on the clinician's recognition of a particular pattern of symptoms, signs and clinical course in an individual patient. This makes the boundaries of the condition harder to define.

Such are the difficulties here that some commentators (e.g. Crow 1986) have suggested that there is no categorical distinction between schizophrenia and the affective psychoses such as mania – that is, that schizophrenia is part of a spectrum of disorders all characterised by some loss of touch with reality. On the other hand, other commentators have pointed out that there may be subdivisions of schizophrenia with potentially different underlying causes. Indeed, it is notable that Eugen Bleuler (1950), who first coined the term in 1910, actually referred to '... the group of schizophrenias'. That throwaway pluralisation may be vital in understanding research into the condition. If schizophrenia is part of something greater, or alternately subdividable into different entities, it is hardly surprising if results from research are confusing when different investigators mean different things by the term.

Struck by these difficulties some authors (e.g. Bentall, Jackson and Pilgrim 1988) have argued that the term schizophrenia should be abandoned altogether. This appears to risk throwing the baby out with the bathwater. Recent classificatory systems (such as DSM-IV and ICD-10) when used together with structured interviews (such as the PSE – see Wing 1974) have greatly improved the reliability of diagnostic entities including schizophrenia. Providing the above questions are kept in mind, it seems worth retaining the terminology to help make sense out of the manifold presentations of severe mental disorder. A fuller discussion of these issues is available for instance in Frith (1992), Clare (1980) and McKenna (1994). As the vast majority of studies of communication disorder in psychosis have focused on schizophrenia, that term will be retained for this review, but the reader is always asked to keep the above in mind when considering the evidence presented, and be aware that the reported deficits may not be entirely specific to schizophrenia.

The concept of formal thought disorder

The second problem of definition concerns frequently repeated misunderstandings about the relationship between *thought, language* and *speech*. Many authors (e.g. Schwarz 1982; Rochester and Martin 1979; Maher 1972) have pointed to the tautology that arises when thought and speech are confused, leading to such arguments as: 'thought disorder is when talk is incoherent and talk is incoherent when thought is disordered'. Too often researchers have blindly assumed that thought and speech are one and the same thing, thus believing that if speech output is abnormal, it can be assumed that thought is abnormal. This is a dangerous assumption, as exemplified in an apt analogy from Maher (1972). In this he likens the relationship between language and thought to a situation in which a typist copies from a written script. The final output, the copy (equivalent to speech) may be distorted by three mechanisms. First the original script itself (equivalent to thought) may be distorted and that distortion is merely carried over by the typist. Second, however, the situation may arise where the original script is perfect but the typist adds errors in the transcription. Finally, an already disordered script may be made worse by the typist adding further errors. Most investigators in schizophrenia have assumed that the patient is correctly reporting a set of disordered thoughts – a good typist with a bad script – but it should be recognised that this is really a matter of conjecture. Chaika (1982) and Thomas (1995) discuss this issue in some detail. Chaika demonstrates how speech and thought are not always identical. In everyday terms, one may think one thing and say quite another. Furthermore, it seems clear that thought is possible without a linguistic infrastructure. Furth (1961), for example, studying deaf and normal children in a concept learning task found that children could learn concepts without knowing a word for the specific concept. Finally it is true to say that not all speech conveys thought – Malinowski (1972) referred to so-called 'phatic communication': the verbal element of social niceties – idle chit-chat and routine greetings which convey little or no specific thought. 'Lovely weather for the time of year ...' for example may be uttered when the bored speaker at the cocktail party has given no thought to the issue at all. Chaika concludes that 'speech disordered' and 'non-speech disordered' are more rational terms than their equivalents invoking thought disorder. Once again, the term FTD will be retained here as it remains in widespread use, but care should be taken to remember the possible pitfalls in this terminology. These two conceptual issues should form a backdrop to the following discussion of approaches to the study of thought and language disorders.

Formal thought disorder and its similarity to the aphasias

The distinct language abnormalities witnessed in schizophrenic patients can appear strikingly similar to those seen in patients with aphasia. Various authors, including Andreasen (1982), have therefore suggested that research comparing the two disorders may shed light on common underlying pathologies. First, though, it must be demonstrated that the similarities are real. There appear to be common features between some of the utterances of schizophrenic patients and those particularly of 'jargon', fluent or posterior aphasics. Specific studies have differed, however, on the question of how close those similarities are. Faber and Reichstein (1981) concluded that there is a specific subgroup of schizophrenic patients who show close similarities to Wernicke's aphasia in terms of fluent paraphasic speech and comprehension, repetition and word-finding disturbances. Gerson, Benson and Frazier (1977) on the other hand stressed six major characteristics that served to differentiate schizophrenics from posterior aphasics in their study. These are summarised in Table 30.1. It is worth noting that Gerson *et al.* describe one difference between schizophrenics and aphasics that has often been highlighted in clinical observations – namely that whilst the aphasic is usually exquisitely aware and will struggle with the problem the schizophrenic *tends to be apparently unaware and unruffled by their communicational disturbance.* This lack of awareness must be incorporated in any explanatory model of FTD. Overall there are tantalising similarities between aphasic output and that of schizophrenic patients which raises the possibility that there may be similarities in underlying brain pathology to account for this. At present, however, this remains conjectural.

Table 30.1 Comparison of speech in schizophrenia and posterior aphasia (taken from Gerson *et al.* 1977)

		Schizophrenia	*Posterior aphasia*
1	Length of response (open-ended questions)	Longer	Shorter
2	Awareness of communication problem	Minimal	Prominent
3	Efforts made to enlist examiner's aid (non-verbal cues and pauses)	Few	Frequent
4	Paraphasias (substitutions)	Rare	Common
5	Vagueness of response	Present ? attentional deficit	Present ? word-finding difficulty
6	Content	Bizarre reiteration of themes (or perseveration)	Normal little reiteration

Other approaches to study

Bearing in mind the fundamental dichotomy between thought and language discussed above, studies in schizophrenic 'thought disorder' can be divided into those that have attempted to tap into the presumed underlying cognitive disturbance and those that have instead taken as their object the language performance of patients. The former line of studies is well reviewed in Schwartz (1982), Neale and Oltmanns (1980) and Maher (1972) and can only be outlined here. Recent developments have been stimulated by models of human information-processing mechanisms, stemming largely from Broadbent's work (Broadbent 1958). Essentially this posits that cognitive processing involves a *limited capacity channel* which handles a continuous flood of competing information and which is protected from overloading by a notional *filter.* Deficits in the filter mechanism and in selective attention have been suggested in schizophrenic patients, and it is of interest that Cameron's (1944) notion of *overinclusion* and Goldstein's (1944) loss of abstract attitude (*concreteness*) have been reinterpreted by some authors in terms of defective filtering and poor selective attention (e.g. Payne, Matussek and George 1959). A number of studies dealing with semantic memory rightly fit into this section, and tend to demonstrate that there are deficits or idiosyncrasies in the way that schizophrenic patients access meaning in language production. Space does not permit a full discussion, but excellent reviews are to be found in Mortimer *et al.* (1995) and Chen, McKenna and Wilkins (1995).

More recent attempts to provide a 'cognitive neuropsychology' which can model the deficits in psychosis are exemplified by the work of Frith (1992). He has suggested that many schizophrenic symptoms may be understood as arising from a failure or deficit of 'self-monitoring', that is the presumed cognitive mechanism which enables the individual to register, supervise and if necessary edit ongoing mental processes in line with the demands of the task in hand. In his monograph of 1992 he goes on to invoke a theory involving 'metarepresentation' which is the process by which we reflect on how we represent the world and our own thoughts. For instance, 'typing on my laptop' is a representation of a fact about the world, something that is going on at this moment in time. If I stop to think about this, however (as I am doing now), I become conscious of the thought: 'This is me *typing on a laptop*'. This amounts to a representation of a representation and it is suggested that similar meta-representations are essential for a variety of higher order cognitive processes such as knowing our own goals, knowing our own intentions and crucially inferring the intentions of others. Frith outlines how such a deficit can lead to symptoms like hallucinations and delusions, but also to difficulties in communication when patients are unable to understand the position (knowledge or intentions) of the listener. The appeal of such work is that ultimately it may integrate basic explanatory models of cognition with the observations of communicative deficit in patients.

Studies of verbal productions

Turning to the line of studies which have focused on language parameters *per se* opens a vital line of investigation, not least because this, really, is the central riddle that begs explanation – what is it that makes 'crazy talk' (Rochester and Martin 1979) sound so crazy? Returning to the distinction between language and thought referred to earlier, it is not *necessarily* the case that crazy talk reflects crazy thinking. Overall it is likely that there *is* a relationship; but the two dimensions of study should be seen as separate, if complementary.

Just as models of information processing have influenced recent investigations of under-lying cognitive processes in schizophrenics, so the study of the verbal productions of these patients has been influenced by theoretical developments in the field of psycholinguistics. Accounts may be found in Slobin (1979), Brown (1984) and Atkinson, Kilby and Roca (1982). A comprehensive outline in Newby (1995) describes how linguistic developments have shaped research, taking into account levels of language organisation, i.e. phonology, syntax, semantics and the important domain of pragmatics, which may be particularly important in psychotic speech.

Studies of word association

These arose as a test of Bleuler's notion of an associative disturbance in schizophrenia. Kent and Rosanoff's early study (1910) was encouraging. This found that for a standard set of 100 prompt words, schizophrenic patients gave 34 per cent idiosyncratic responses (defined as any response for a particular word not given by any of the normal subjects) as compared with about 7 per cent idiosyncratic responses given by the controls. Subsequent studies have yielded contradictory results, however, and the finding is now questioned (Schwartz 1982). In any case, several authors (e.g. Chapman and Chapman 1973, p.117) have pointed out that word association tests are 'artificial' in that they remove words from their context within a goal-directed sequence of ideas. There is a distinct difference between responding to a word embedded in a continuous stream of discourse, and the response given if that word is taken in isolation. As such, then, word association tasks do not really form a test of Bleuler's principle.

Response biases

The idea of rare word associations is also contradicted in a sense by the work of Chapman, Chapman and Miller (1964). This study looked at patients' responses on a multiple choice meaning task that used items such as the following:

When the farmer bought a herd of cattle he needed a new pen.

This means:

A He needed a new writing implement.

B He needed a new fence enclosure.

C He needed a new pick-up truck.

It can be seen that, within the given context, the most appropriate response would be B. Taken in isolation, however, the most common associate to the word pen would be 'writing implement'. What the Chapmans found was that the schizophrenic patients erred in favour of this common associate significantly more frequently than normal controls. This they referred to as 'accentuation of normal response biases'. In other words, the schizophrenics opted for the common associates of words even when context should have dictated choice of a less frequent associate. Attractive though this finding is, the methodology has been questioned, and again the criticism can be levelled that this task takes words out of continuous discourse.

Verbal redundancy measures

If there are problems in focusing on single words out of context, the principle of 'cloze analysis' may be seen to have some advantage. Introduced originally as a test of the readability of journalistic prose (Taylor 1953) this technique involves 'mutilating' a sample of text (either written or transcribed from recorded speech) by deleting every, say, fourth or fifth word and then asking raters to fill in the gaps by intelligent guesswork. The idea derives from Information Theory, an outline of which is given in Maher (1972). This incorporates the notion that natural languages carry *redundancy* – that is parts of a given message may be lost but still predicted by the listener or reader using examination of remaining context. It is suggested that this in-built redundancy provides a safety margin enabling communication under difficult circumstances where the signal-to-noise ratio is low – a noisy cocktail party, for instance.

The cloze score in the standard form of this technique is simply the percentage or proportion of correct guesses, taken as a mean from a panel of raters. Most studies in the area, e.g. Salzinger, Portnoy and Feldman (1964), Silverman (1972) and Rutter *et al.* (1975, 1977, 1978), have investigated the cloze scores for transcripts of schizophrenic speech as judged by normal raters. Results have varied, but mostly confirm a reduced cloze score and therefore less predictability in the speech of schizophrenia patients. Ragin and Oltmanns (1983) demonstrated significant loss of predictability in schizophrenic speech, particularly when a clinical rating of presence of thought disorder was taken into account. Newby (1998) replicated the earlier findings using clearly defined and matched patient groups and has also demonstrated that schizophrenic patients appear to have a 'mirror-image' deficit in decoding mutilated text using the so-called *reverse-cloze* procedure.

The problem lies in interpreting these findings. Maher (1972) likens the cloze score to a reading of body temperature – it may indicate that something is wrong but not necessarily shed light on the underlying mechanism. As intimated above, however, the cloze score could be taken as an index of associative deviance in a continuous language sample – the task of the rater is essentially to guess what association the original speaker made when a particular gap occurs in the text. If the gap contained an unusual association, the probability of a correct guess will be lowered and hence a reduced cloze score will result. It can be seen that this may represent a more naturalistic test of Bleuler's associative disruption than word association tests.

A different line of investigation employing the notion of verbal redundancy involves 'statistical approximations to English' as first described by Miller and Selfridge (1950). This involves constructing samples of text that vary systematically in their level of approximation to normal English – from random word strings (zero order approximation) to continuous text. Second order approximations are obtained by presenting normal subjects with *one* word from which they are asked to construct a sentence. The word used directly after the given one is then noted and presented to a second subject who is in turn asked to produce a sentence from the given word. This process is repeated until strings of the desired length are obtained. Thus each word in the second order approximation is determined solely by the immediately preceding word of context. Higher levels of approximation are obtained by giving subjects progressively longer sequences of words to act as the prompts. (The first order approximation was a random sampling of words from the higher order samples – thus reflecting expected relative frequencies of words in the English text, but *not* contextual linkages between adjacent words.)

Miller and Selfridge used these samples in a recall task, and showed that for normal subjects percentage recall of words systematically improved as the test samples approximated closer to English – it is much harder to recall 'gibberish' than it is to remember meaningful material. Anyone who has tried to give verbatim records of the speech of a thought-disordered patient will recognise this phenomenon – the more disordered the speech, the harder it is to write down afterwards exactly what the patient said. Lawson, McGhie and Chapman (1964) used this procedure to compare schizophrenics and normals. They demonstrated that at low orders of approximation there is little difference between the groups, but as contextual constraints increase and the samples approximate closer to English, the control group increase their recall, but schizophrenics do not – they are unable to take advantage of increasing organisation of the material. Williams (1966) in effect turned this procedure on its head by obtaining speech samples from schizophrenic patients with varying degrees of contextual constraint – that is, by giving them varying lengths of prompts. This material was then subject to cloze analysis. The cloze scores did not improve significantly as the length of the prompt passage increased, suggesting that the patients pay little attention to contextual clues in the production of speech.

Studies of linguistic rule awareness

The evidence cited in the preceding discussion suggests that schizophrenic patients are unaware of organising principles in language at least at the level of degrees of redundancy. Does this also apply to linguistic organisation, and do these patients have inherent difficulties with syntactic organisation of discourse? Rochester (1978) points out that until the 1960s the answer given would probably have been an unreserved 'yes'. After all, the epitome or end-point of thought disorder is so called 'word-salad', a random jumbling of words without obvious syntactic structure. Kleist (1914) described 'agrammatism' and 'paragrammatism' as elements of the speech disorder in schizophrenia. Rochester, however, reviews evidence suggesting that mostly the acute schizophrenic speaker/listener is an adequate user of language. For instance, Gerver (1967) presented schizophrenics and controls with three different types of sentence to recall:

1. Normal sentences
    e.g. The washing dried out on the line.

2. Syntactically adequate but semantically anomalous sentences
    e.g. Furious washing dried the line around.

3. Random strings
    e.g. Dry line washing out on the.

It was found that although schizophrenic performance was uniformly inferior to that of controls, there was still a marked differential with normal sentences being recalled best and syntactically adequate sentences being recalled better than random strings. This finding has been supported by further studies, and Rochester (1978) cites evidence that most schizo-phrenic speakers show little in the way of disruptive clauses when compared with normals. Nevertheless, the problem remains of explaining those (albeit rare) instances of speech which do appear highly disorganised.

An approach developed by Morice and Ingram (1982) used a complex linguistic analysis applied to transcribed speech samples. After establishing sentence boundaries using pre-established linguistic rules, the investigators carried out a manual grammatical analysis on each analysable sentence using successive scans to detect different types of error and then finally constructed a syntax tree diagram for each sentence. This data was processed to yield a number of variables representing measures within four broad areas – complexity, variety, integrity and fluency of language use. Such were the differences between the three study groups – schizophrenics, manics and non-psychotics – that 95 per cent accuracy in classification by discriminant function analysis was achieved. Fraser et al. (1986) replicated this finding using a larger and dialectically different population (Scots rather than Australian). Thus it seems that there *are* discernible linguistic anomalies in the speech of psychotic patients.

Pragmatic deficits

Problem in referential speaking

Pragmatics can be viewed as the highest level of linguistic functioning, covering as it does the rules and mechanisms that govern the use of language in its overall goal – interpersonal communication. Rochester and colleagues (e.g. Rochester 1978) have put forward an essentially pragmatic hypothesis to account for schizophrenic language problems – that the schizophrenic speaker fails to accommodate the listener's immediate need in discourse. Evidence cited by Rochester includes the studies of cohesion analysis referred to in the next section. Other work pointing to a pragmatic problem is exemplified by Cohen and colleagues' studies of referential speaking. Cohen and Camhi (1967) gave subjects a series of closely related words (e.g. CAR and AUTOMOBILE) and asked them to provide single 'passwords' which would enable a listener to pick out one of the words (underlined for the speaker only of course!). The number of correct identifications by the listener thus represents an index of the communicative ability of the speaker. The results showed that when acting as listener, the schizophrenics were no different to controls, but when acting as speakers, performance was significantly impaired. Another experiment (Cohen, Nachmani and Ronsenberg 1974) involved the use of coloured discs varying in similarity of hue and intensity of colour. The subject had to guide the listener to a particular choice of referent disc. Where there was a distinct difference in hue, the patients' performance was similar to controls, but the closer the discs came in hue and intensity, the less successful were the patients in providing discriminating clues. So it seems that referential speaking presents particular difficulties for schizophrenic speakers when they are required to edit their responses taking into account the listener's needs.

Cohesion analysis

This method was developed by Halliday and Hassan (1976) and in essence looks at 'the means whereby elements that are structurally unrelated in the text are linked together' (p.27). In other words, it examines the devices which are used to link clauses and sentences together in a coherent or 'cohesive' way to ease the task of the listener. Rochester and Martin (1979) give a description of the recognised cohesive strategies, which fall into the categories of Reference, Substitution, Ellipsis, Conjunction and Lexical Cohesion. They revealed a number of significant differences between thought disordered schizophrenics, non-thought disordered schizophrenics and controls, particularly with regard to noun phrases with unclear, ambiguous or missing referents. These results have been challenged (e.g. Chaika 1995) but Wykes and Leff (1982) using a similar approach to compare schizophrenics and manics found that manics used significantly more cohesive ties, and in another study (Wykes 1981) it was shown that clinicians were able to make use of a rudimentary form of the analysis to enhance their differentiation of manic and schizophrenic speech.

Discourse analysis

This approach derives largely from the studies of Deese (e.g. 1978). He argued that 'an extended, multisentence text will be experienced as coherent by a listener if he or she can organise the propositions expressed by the text into a hierarchical form' (Hoffman, Stopek and Andreasen 1986). The listener's task is to examine the various propositions in a text and assign subordinate or superordinate relationships between them. If the speech segment or text can be organised by the listener into a single, well-formed hierarchy, that segment will be perceived as coherent. If not, if it cannot be organised into this sort of discourse 'tree', it will be seen as incoherent or 'loose'. Hoffman *et al.* (1982) using this technique were able to discriminate between schizophrenic and non-schizophrenic patients with 80 per cent accuracy. Furthermore, a numerical index quantifying the degree of deviance from hierarchical form was found to be highly correlated with independent thought disorder ratings made by clinicians. A recent study (Hoffman *et al.* 1986) has extended this work to examine the differences between schizophrenics and manics. It was hypothesised that the incoherence of manic speech is due to shifts from one coherent discourse structure to another, whilst that for schizophrenic speech is due to failure to construct any discourse structure at all. This was broadly supported by the results of the discourse analysis.

Mapping language deficits onto brain dysfunction

The 'Holy Grail' of research in this area would be achieved if researchers were able to demonstrate a specific language dysfunction in psychosis that could be linked to a specific neuroanatomical or pathological lesion. Although specifying the former remains elusive, studies have emerged recently which show promise in beginning to highlight areas of brain dysfunction which might account for communication problems. Such studies of brain dysfunction have been greatly stimulated by rapid technological advances in the 'imaging' techniques available to investigate workings of the brain in life. These include MRI (magnetic resonance imaging) and methods such as PET (positron emission tomography) which allow examination of dynamic brain functioning. Together with more sophisticated post-mortem studies, these techniques make it almost incontrovertible now that at least a majority of patients with schizophrenia have recognisable structural abnormalities of the brain. Frith (1992) provides a useful overview of this evidence. Notably, there is a convergence of findings from these studies pointing to lesions in the temporal lobes (especially in the dominant hemisphere) and the prefrontal cortex (see for instance Crow 1990; Brown *et al.* 1986). These areas may of course be particularly related to language functioning. Given these findings, several workers have looked at specific aspects of language in relation to structural changes.

Using MRI, Vita *et al.* (1995) studied 19 schizophrenic patients and related the structural findings to various language parameters. They found that prefrontal cortex volume was inversely correlated with total scores on the Thought, Language and Communication (TLC) scale described in Andreasen (1979). Left superior temporal gyrus (STG) volume was positively correlated with verbal fluency performance, and overall they found that the more severe were the thought and language disorders, the smaller was the left STG compared with its counterpart on the right. Nestor and colleagues (1998) again used MRI, this time looking for correlations with the Thought Disorder Index (TDI) and a battery of neuropsychological tests including some for verbal memory, abstraction and executive function. Although there were several strong correlations between the thought disorder rating and several of the neuro-psychological measures, the only structural correlation was between between working memory and frontal and basal ganglia measures.

Methodological problems

As indicated at the outset, this review has only been able to sample a fraction of the literature on thought and language disorders. Nevertheless, amongst the studies that have been mentioned, potentially contradictory findings are common. In some instances this may be an issue of interpretation, but in many others the problem is likely to lie in methodological difficulties. A brief enumeration of some of these is in order:

1 *Failure to recognise the episodic nature of FTD*

   Not *every* schizophrenic patient displays formal thought disorder, and amongst those who do, thought disorder is not necessarily present all the time. Rather it seems the case that gross thought disorder is a fleeting phenomenon, varying from day to day and almost from minute to minute. It should be recognised that potentially some indices of thought disorder will only give abnormal values for a small part of the time.

2 *Poor clinical criteria for FTD*

   Some of the descriptive criteria for this phenomenon have been as disorganised as the speech of patients themselves. Andreasen (1979) has gone a long way to addressing this problem by establishing a reliable scale for rating thought disorder. As well as avoiding undue theoretical presuppositions in its items, it recognises that thought disorder is probably a heterogeneous phenomenon and allows separate aspects of it to be studied. Table 30.2 lists the items rated in the scale.

3 *Use of 'loose' diagnostic criteria*

   This has been a feature of many studies, and a good deal of the contradictory findings that exist may be due to inappropriate comparison of quite different patient groups.

4 *Failure to recognise potential subgroups*

   This is a similar problem to the previous one. It may be that some genuine differences in patients are 'cancelled out' if inappropriate subgroups are lumped together.

5 *Failure to recognise subtypes of FTD*

   FTD itself, like schizophrenia, may not be a unitary phenomenon. In particular there may be crucial differences between FTD associated with positive symptoms such as hallucinations and delusions, and for instance the poverty of content seen with negative symptoms. Use of scales like the TLC may help clarify these distinctions.

6 *Failure to account for confounding variables*

   Language is a highly complex phenomenon, therefore a whole range of variables may profoundly affect it. Salient amongst these are age, sex, social class, region of origin (i.e.

dialect), ethnic origin and drug intake. Many older studies have failed to control for these variables.

7   *Poor experimental protocols*

Chapman and Chapman (1973, p.77ff.) and Neale and Oltmanns (1980, p.22ff.) discuss this issue. In particular the former highlight the importance of 'matched task' design for demonstrating differential cognitive deficits. This takes into account the fact that patients with schizophrenia may have generalised impairment in test performance arising from diverse factors such as poor concentration, lack of motivation, and distraction by active psychotic symptoms. Deficits found on a particular test, therefore, may not indicate a specific impairment of performance in the area under investigation. The matched task design incorporates a task of equivalent difficulty – if there is a differential deficit in this compared with the test under scrutiny, there can be greater certainty that a particular dysfunction has been demonstrated. This design merits wider use.

Table 30.2 Items from the Thought, Language and Communication Scale (Andreasen 1979)

1   Poverty of speech
2   Poverty of content of speech
3   Pressure of speech
4   Distractible speech
5   Tangentiality
6   Derailment
7   Incoherence
8   Illogicality
9   Clanging
10   Neologisms
11   Word approximations
12   Circumstantiality
13   Loss of goal
14   Perseveration
15   Echolalia
16   Blocking
17   Stilted speech
18   Self-reference
19   Phonemic paraphasia
20   Semantic paraphasia

(Full definitions and instructional guidelines for applying the scale are in the reference.)

Conclusions

Allowing for the methodological problems outlined above, it may be that some of the inconsistencies in results between different studies are less damaging to underlying theoretical frameworks than they might at first appear. The possibility is emerging that a synthesis may be found between the insights gained into information processing and those relating to language competence and performance. Ultimately these could be related in turn to specific abnormalities of brain structure or function, though as indicated above, this work is still in its infancy. Some eminent commentators surveying the field of research into FTD have been left pessimistic about the chances of such a synthesis. Maher (1991) for instance was moved to comment that relevant hypotheses '... appear from many different sources, cause a brief stir as they are tested, and then sink from sight as permanently as pebbles thrown into a pond'. The difficulty in integrating previous findings and explanatory models may have a lot to do, however, with the methodological and definitional problems outlined above and taking these into account may allow some sense to be discerned in the wealth of data.

In the understanding of schizophrenia itself, there is increasing recognition that the cause of the condition is likely to be multifactorial – different causative factors may be implicated in different cases and in different combinations. In the same way, FTD may best be explained as the result of different pathological processes, perhaps combining in their effects in particular instances. Given the complexity of language function, the most uniquely human attribute, this would hardly seem surprising. It is entirely possible that some of the models described in earlier literature may complement each other in providing a comprehensive model of the phenomenon of schizophrenic language.

Two themes that do seem quite robust in the literature are those to do, first, with associative deviance; and, second, with the observations suggesting that the schizophrenic speaker has particular difficulty taking the listener's needs into account. As regards the first, Rochester (1978) integrates a number of findings in a hypothesis linking language deficits with attentional/short-term memory dysfunction. Maher (1972) has also offered a model linking associative intrusions in the language of schizophrenics with a basic attentional deficit. The mechanisms of selective attention are seen to be deficient, allowing the intrusion of irrelevant material to break up a train of thought or a plan of discourse. It can be seen in turn that this notion can incorporate Payne's *overinclusiveness*, which is one of the most robustly demonstrated findings in the research into this area. Neale and Oltmanns (1980, p.160) point out that, in a way, ideas have come full circle and that this idea amounts to a restatement of Bleuler's insight: 'The failure of selective attention, the subsequent break down of control processes, and the eventual disturbance of cohesion and reference in speech are modern translations for Bleuler's loosening of associations.' This then remains a potentially powerful explanatory model which can accommodate diverse findings.

Interestingly, the second theme could also be regarded as a restatement of Bleuler's original description of the disposition of 'autism' seen in schizophrenia. By this he meant the tendency for social withdrawal and apparent retreat into inner mental life often seen in these patients. Such was the importance he attached to this that he classed it as one of his four fundamental symptoms of the condition. It is easy to see how this disposition could lead to difficulties in interpersonal communication if the patient is either indifferent about or unable to understand the position of the listener, and thus take their needs into account. This would account also for the observation that as compared with those with aphasia, schizophrenic patients often appear unaware of their communicative deficit. What requires elucidation is the underlying mechanism that could explain this deficit, and it is here that hypothetical explanatory models such as that of Frith's referred to above may be fruitful in directing future research.

On the basis of current understanding, therefore, it appears likely that the striking abnormalities of language production seen in schizophrenia will be found to entail disruption in several different facets of language competence and performance. The end product, however, amounts to a fundamental breach in the pragmatic use of language, and to this end it is worth emphasising that the vast majority of the studies to date have examined language function in non-naturalistic or laboratory settings. Language performance is exquisitely sensitive to just such influences, and it is likely that if the encouraging findings demonstrating pragmatic deficits in schizophrenics are to be extended, then more naturalistic language samples will have to be studied, such as those from normal conversational interactions, rather than structured interviews. That the phenomenon of formal thought disorder continues to excite a great deal of research interest despite apparently confusing findings reflects its central importance, and the view (e.g. Crow 1998) that understanding the language disruption may unlock a fundamental understanding of the condition of schizophrenia itself.

References

Andreasen, N.C. (1979) Thought, language and communication disorders. *Archives of General Psychiatry 36*, 1315–1330.

Andreasen, N.C. (1982) In F. Henn and H. Nasrallah (eds) *Dopamine and Psychosis in Schizophrenia as a Brain Disease*. New York: Oxford University Press.

Atkinson, M., Kilby, D. and Roca, I. (1982) *Foundations of General Linguistics*. London: Allen and Unwin.

Bentall, R.P., Jackson, H.F. and Pilgrim, D. (1988) Abandoning the concept of schizophrenia: some implications of validity arguments for psychological research into psychotic phenomena. *British Journal of Clinical Psychology 27*, 303–324.

Bleuler, E. (1950) *Dementia Praecox or the Group of Schizophrenias* (trans. by Zinkin, J.). New York: University Press.

Broadbent, D.E. (1958) *Perception and Communication*. Oxford: Pergamon Press.

Brown, K. (1984) *Linguistics Today*. London: Fontana.

Brown, R., Colter, N., Corsellis, J.A.N., *et al.* (1986) Post-mortem evidence of structural brain changes in schizophrenia. *Archives of General Psychiatry 43*, 36–42.

Cameron, N. (1944) In J.S. Kasanin (ed) *Language and Thought in Schizophrenia*. New York: Norton.

Chaika, E. (1982) Thought disorder or speech disorder in schizophrenia? *Schizophrenia Bulletin 8*, 587.

Chaika, E. (1995) On analysing schizophrenic speech: what model should we use? In A.C.P. Sims (ed) *Speech and Language Disorders in Psychiatry*. London: Gaskell Publications.

Chapman, L.J. and Chapman, J.P. (1973) *Disordered Thought in Schizophrenia*. Prentice Hall: New Jersey.

Chapman, L.J., Chapman, J.P. and Miller, G.A. (1964) In B.A. Maher (ed) *Progress in Experimental Personality Research*. Vol. 1. New York: Academic Press.

Chen, E., McKenna, P. and Wilkins, A. (1995) Semantic processing and categorisation in schizophrenia. In A.C.P. Sims (ed) *Speech and Language Disorders in Psychiatry*. London: Gaskell Publications.

Clare, A. (1980) *Psychiatry in Dissent* (second edition). London: Tavistock.

Cohen, B.D. and Camhi, J. (1967) Schizophrenic performance in a word-communication task. *Journal of Abnormal Psychology 72*, 240–246.

Cohen, B.D., Nachmani, G. and Rosenberg, S. (1974) Schizophrenic performance in a word-communication task. *Journal of Abnormal Psychology 83*, 1–13.

Crow, T.J. (1980) Molecular pathology of schizophrenia: more than one disease process? *British Medical Journal 280*, 66.

Crow, T.J. (1986) The continuum of psychosis and its implication for the structure of the gene. *British Journal of Psychiatry 149*, 419–429.

Crow, T.J. (1998) Nuclear schizophrenic symptoms as a window on the relationship between thought and speech. *British Journal of Psychiatry 173*, 303–309.

Crow, T.J. (1990) Temporal lobe asymmetries as the key to the etiology of schizophrenia. *Schizophrenia Bulletin 16*, 433–443.

Deese, J. (1978) Thought into speech. *American Scientist, 66*, 314.

Faber, R. and Reichstein, M.B. (1981) Language dysfunction in schizophrenia. *British Journal of Psychiatry 139*, 519–522.

Fraser, W.I., King, K.M., Thomas, P. and Kendell, R.E. (1986) The diagnosis of schizophrenia by language analysis. *British Journal of Psychiatry 148*, 275.

Frith, C.D. (1992) *The Cognitive Neuropsychology of Schizophrenia.* Hove: Lawrence Erlbaum Associates.

Furth, H.G. (1961) The influence of language on the development of concept formation in deaf children. *Journal of Abnormal and Social Psychology 63*, 386–389.

Gerson, S.N., Benson, D.F. and Frazier, S.H. (1977) Diagnosis: schizophrenia versus posterior aphasia. *American Journal of Psychiatry 134*, 966.

Gerver, D. (1967) Linguistic rules and the perception and recall of speech by schizophrenic patients. *British Journal of Social and Clinical Psychology 6*, 204–211.

Goldstein, K. (1944) In J.S. Kasanin (ed) *Language and Thought in Schizophrenia.* New York: Norton.

Halliday, M.A.K. and Hassan, R. (1976) *Cohesion in English.* London: Longman.

Hoffman, R., Kirstein, L., Stopek, S. and Cicchetti, D. (1982) Apprehending schizophrenic discourse: a structural analysis of the listener's task. *Brain and Language 15*, 207–233.

Hoffman, R.E., Stopek, S. and Andreasen, N.C. (1986) A comparative study of manic versus schizophrenic speech disorganization. *Archives of General Psychiatry 43*, 831.

Kent, H. and Rosanoff, A.J. (1910) A study of association in insanity. *American Journal of Insanity 67*, 326.

Kleist, K. (1914) Quoted in M. Hamilton (1984) (ed) *Fish's Schizophrenia.* London: Wright.

Kraepelin, E. (1919) *Dementia Praecox and Paraphrenia* (trans. Barclay, R.M.). Edinburgh: Livingstone.

Lawson, J.S., McGhie, A. and Chapman, J. (1964) Perception of speech in schizophrenia. *British Journal of Psychiatry 110*, 375.

Maher, B. (1972) The language of schizophrenia. *British Journal of Psychiatry 120*, 3–17.

Maher, B. (1991) Language and schizophrenia. In *Handbook of Schizophrenia: Vol.5. Neuropsychology, Psychophysiology and Information Processing.* Amsterdam; Elsevier. pp.437–464.

Malinowski, B. (1972) In J. Laver and S. Hutcheson (eds) *Communication in Face to Face Interaction.* Baltimore: Penguin.

McKenna, P.J. (1994) *Schizophrenia and Related Syndromes.* Oxford: Oxford University Press.

Miller, G. and Selfridge, J. (1950) Verbal context and the recall of meaningful material. *American Journal of Psychology 63*, 176–185.

Morice, R.D. and Ingram, J.C.L. (1982) Language analysis in schizophrenia: diagnostic implications. *Australian and New Zealand Journal of Psychiatry 16*, 11–21.

Mortimer, A., Corridan, B., Rudge, S., Kho, K., Kelly, F., Bristow, M. and Hodges, J. (1995) Thought speech and language disorder and semantic memory in schizophrenia. In A.C.P. Sims (ed) *Speech and Language Disorders in Psychiatry.* London: Gaskell Publications.

Neale, J.M. and Oltmanns, T.F. (1980) *Schizophrenia.* New York: John Wiley.

Nestor, P.G., Shenton, M.E., Wible, C. *et al.* (1998) A neuropsychological analysis of schizophrenic thought disorder. *Schizophrenia Research 29*, 217–225.

Newby, D.A. (1995) Analysis of language: terminology and techniques. In A.C.P. Sims (ed) *Speech and Language Disorders in Psychiatry.* London: Gaskell Publications.

Newby, D.A. (1998) Cloze procedure refined and modified. 'Modified Cloze', 'reverse Cloze' and the use of predictability as a measure of communication problems in psychosis. *British Journal of Psychiatry 172*, 136–141.

Payne, R.W., Matussek, P. and George, E.I. (1959) An experimental study of schizophrenic thought disorder. *Journal of Mental Science 105*, 627–652.

Ragin, A.B. and Oltmanns, T.F. (1983) Predictability as an index of impaired verbal communication in schizophrenic and affective disorders. *British Journal of Psychiatry 143*, 578.

Rochester, S.R. (1978) Are language disorders in acute schizophrenia actually information-processing problems? *Journal of Psychiatric Research 14*, 275.

Rochester, S.R. and Martin, J.R. (1979) *Crazy Talk: A Study of the Discourse of Schizophrenic Speakers.* New York: Plenum Press.

Rutter, D.R., Draffan, J. and Davies, J. (1977) Thought disorder and the predictability of schizophrenic speech. *British Journal of Psychiatry 131*, 67–68.

Rutter, D.R., Wishner, J. and Callaghan, B.A. (1975) The prediction and predictability of speech in schizophrenic patients. *British Journal of Psychiatry 126*, 571–576.

Rutter, D.R., Wishner, J., Koptynska, H. and Button, M. (1978) The predictability of speech in schizophrenic patients. *British Journal of Psychiatry 132*, 228–232.

Salzinger, K., Portnoy, S. and Feldman, R.S. (1964) Verbal behaviour of schizophrenic and normal subjects. *Annals of the New York Academy of Sciences 105*, 845–860.

Schwarz, S. (1982) Is there a schizophrenic language? *The Behavioural and Brain Sciences 5*, 579–626.

Silverman, G. (1972) Psycholinguistics of schizophrenic language. *Psychological Medicine 2*, 254–259.

Slobin, D.I. (1979) *Psycholinguistics.* Illinois: Scott, Foreman.

Taylor, W.L. (1953) Cloze procedure: a new tool for measuring readability. *Journalism Quarterly 30*, 415–433.

Thomas, P. (1995) Thought disorder or communication disorder. Linguistic science provides a new approach. *British Journal of Psychiatry 16*, 287–290.

Vita, A., Massimiliano, D., Giobbio, G.M., *et al.* (1995) Language and thought disorder in schizophrenia: brain morphological correlates. *Schizophrenia Research 15*, 243–251.

Williams, M. (1966) The effect of context on schizophrenic speech. *British Journal of Social and Clinical Psychology 5*, 161–171.

Wing, J.K., Cooper, J.E. and Sartorius, N. (1974) *The Measurement and Classification of Psychiatric Symptoms.* Cambridge: Cambridge University Press.

Wykes, T. (1981) Can the psychiatrist learn from the psycholinguist? Detecting coherence in the disordered speech of manics and schizophrenics. *Psychological Medicine 11*, 641–642.

Wykes, T. and Leff, J. (1982) Disordered speech: differences between manics and schizophrenics. *Brain and Language 15*, 117–124.

CHAPTER 31

Language and Communication in Schizophrenia
A Communication Processing Model

Irene P. Walsh

Introduction

Schizophrenia is a complex psychiatric disorder which has a communication disturbance as one of its possible features. Ever since Kraepelin (1896) first described schizophrenia, language difficulties, considered a result of thought disorder, have been referred to as part of the disorder's presentation. Traditionally, characteristics of thought disorder have included a general lack of coherence, poverty of speech, frequent changes of topic, tangentiality (e.g. oblique or irrelevant replies), illogicality (i.e. use of utterances that clearly do not make sense), perseverations and a preponderance of self-referential statements. Such characteristics of thought disorder result in communication difficulties, where the individual with schizophrenia has difficulty taking the listener's needs into account during the communication exchange and in communicating the appropriate context or intent.

France and Muir (1997) state that linguistic and communication breakdown is central to mental illness, both in terms of diagnosis and pathology. Mental health professionals rely on what patients tell them of their history, feelings, complaints, present thoughts, hopes and fears through their verbal and non-verbal communication (Gravell and France 1991). Thus language and communication skills can serve as a barometer to gauge the current mental health of the patient. However, if the language and communication skills of people with mental illness have not been fully described or investigated, diagnosis is difficult and understanding of the illness process may be confounded. Thus it behoves speech and language therapists, as key members of mental health teams, to be instrumental in drawing up such descriptions of the communication of people with schizophrenia.

It is becoming increasingly apparent from the literature that language disturbances in schizophrenia may be described in a number of ways which open up new avenues for exploration and discussion. In the traditional sense, language difficulties in schizophrenia may be considered the consequence of a primary thought disorder, while others view such language disturbances as being the result of a central language disorder (Murray 1994). In addition,

Thomas (1997) and others welcome the use of the term *communication disorder* as applied to schizophrenia.

This chapter proposes the use of a model of communication processing (adapted from Frith 1992, 1997) as a descriptive tool, to investigate and interpret the language and communication skills of people with chronic schizophrenia. In order to demonstrate the usefulness of the model, the results of a battery of language tests, administered to a small number of people with chronic schizophrenia, are evaluated according to the processes proposed within the model. The model then facilitates a comprehensive description of the strengths and weaknesses across and within the group assessed. Variables considered include the nature of the task (e.g. comprehension/expression), the number of processing levels primarily activated for any given task, the demand on short-term and working memory, and the type of response required (e.g. specified or unspecified). Assessment results are interpreted within the context of the model, suggesting *potential communication breakdown points* in schizophrenia and as discussed in the literature. The chapter concludes with a discussion of the usefulness of such a model for the interpretation of language assessments which in turn may serve to enhance descriptions of the communication difficulties in schizophrenia.

In order to set the scene, the model, which examines the stages involved in comprehending and responding to a spoken message, is first outlined. This is followed by a brief description of the language difficulties of people with schizophrenia as they are reported in the literature.

Communication and schizophrenia: from input to output

There are many approaches to understanding language and communication systems. A linguistic model, for example, sees language as a system of interrelationships between the subsystems of phonology (speech sounds), morphology (word formation), semantics (meaning), syntax (grammar) and pragmatics (language usage). Using such a linguistic approach, Thomas (1997) applies the framework to the language and communication of people with schizophrenia and draws parallels between features of Andreason's (1979) Thought, Language and Communication (TLC) scale and areas within linguistics (see Thomas 1997). Other approaches, using psycholinguistic and cognitive neuropsychological models, have been used in understanding what is involved in cognitive and linguistic processing. Traditionally the domain of cognitive psychologists, such models allow for the mapping of mental processes or operations which are activated in response to certain stimuli presented. These approaches, initially used to understand normal language processing, have also been extensively applied to disordered language in children and adults (Chiat, Law and Marshall 1997). Lesser and Milroy (1993), for example, present an extensive review of input-output models for the processing of single words and sentences in aphasia. Cognitive neuropsychological models have also been popular in research studies of schizophrenic language and communication (for example see Barr *et al.* 1989; Frith 1992; David and Cutting 1994; McKenna 1994; Rossell and David 1997).

Because of the complicated relationship between language and cognition, an understanding of the mental processes involved in information processing is difficult to achieve. However, psycholinguistic and cognitive neuropsychological models at least provide us with tools which facilitate investigation of this relationship. Using such models to aid interpretation of responses often provokes more questions than answers about an individual's processing capacity. Only by questioning the operations involved can we begin to piece together a holistic interpretation of an individual's processing ability. Some knowledge of what is involved in normal communication processing must, however, pre-empt a discussion of impaired or compromised processing.

A Model of Communication Processing

Processing takes place within a context which enhances the meaning of the message being decoded (received) or encoded (sent). Figure 31.1 shows a model of communication processing (adapted from Frith 1992, 1997), illustrating the various processes required for successful communication. The various stages of the model will be discussed according to the levels of activation outlined below.

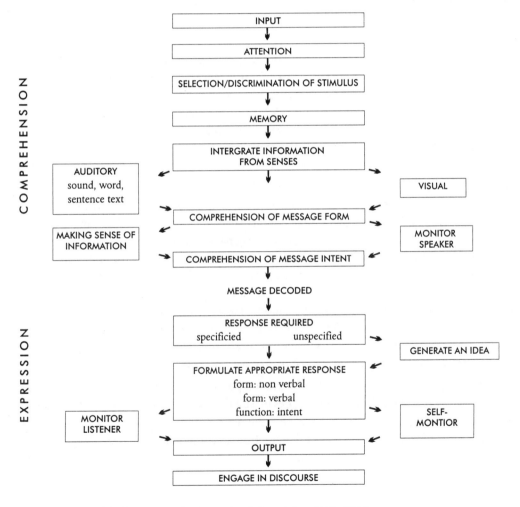

Figure 31.1 A model of communication processing (adapted from Frith 1997)

Comprehension

- *Level I.* When a speaker encodes a spoken message, the hearer attends and listens, selecting the intended stimulus from extraneous stimuli in the environment (e.g. background noise, other talk, etc.). The message is then stored in short-term and working memory (Baddeley 1986) while it is being processed. While integrating information from the senses, the message is processed at the sound, word and sentence level, which activates the subsystems of phonology, semantics and syntax respectively.

- *Level II.* When the message is processed at a linguistic level, it is then processed according to the hearer's world and social knowledge so that he or she may make sense of it. In other words, the hearer refers to past events or experiences and to the shared knowledge between the interlocutors, to help him or her interpret the current or intended meaning of the utterance and make appropriate inferences where necessary. Meanwhile the hearer continually monitors the speaker for further clues to aid message interpretation (e.g. gesture, facial expression).

Expression

- *Level III.* Once the message has been decoded, a response may be required which may be of a specified or unspecified nature. If a response is unspecified the listener will be required to generate an idea in order to respond. Consider the following: (a) *Would you like to go to the cinema or the theatre tonight?* versus (b) *Where would you like to go tonight?* In (a) the response is specified to a certain extent while in (b) the response is clearly unspecified and would require the listener to *generate* an idea in order to respond. In formulating a response the speaker may choose to respond non-verbally (e.g. a shrug of the shoulders) or verbally (e.g. *I'd like to go to the theatre*).

- *Level IV.* Constructing the speech output requires the speaker to formulate an utterance according to the phonological, syntactic and semantic constraints of his language. Using knowledge of language usage (i.e. pragmatic skills) the speaker has to respond appropriately, taking the listener's needs into account so as to give accurate, adequate and relevant information for the message to be correctly interpreted (Grice 1975). Through self-monitoring the speaker must inhibit irrelevant ideas when responding, to avoid a breakdown in the communication. Likewise the speaker must monitor the listener for signs of misunderstanding or confusion. When the response has been encoded the communicative exchange has been completed. Further exchanges between speaker and hearer result in spoken interactive discourse.

The model is presented sequentially for illustration purposes. However, it is important to keep in mind that processing at different levels goes on simultaneously, with levels being activated as required, depending on the complexity of the communication. The model may also be used to interpret the processing complexity of more formal communication tasks (e.g. language testing). Consider the following examples:

a)   *Show me 'weary'.*

   (i.e. an item from a vocabulary test, where the testee has to choose from a choice of four
   pictures the picture which best illustrates that concept)

b)   *Tell me the similarities and differences between an apple and an orange.*

According to the processing model (Figure 31.1), to process the message in (a), Levels I and III
may be primarily activated with lesser involvement of Level II (i.e. I, (*II*) and III). To process the
message in (b), however, all four levels may need to be activated (i.e. I, II, III and IV). Therefore
a 'listen and do' task may require less processing (in terms of number of levels activated) than a
'listen and say' task. A computer analogy is apt – the more complex the task, the greater the
number of programmes needed or activated.

The nature of the communication impairment in schizophrenia

It is important to state at the outset that, as for any syndrome, individuals with schizophrenia
are not a homogeneous group and thus present with varied symptomatology, which in turn
leads to different communication profiles across individuals. For example, people with
predominantly negative symptoms can present with features which include poverty of speech,
poverty of content of speech and social withdrawal. Positive symptoms, which are described as
being 'abnormal by their presence', include thought insertion, delusions of control or reference
and auditory hallucinations (see Frith 1992, p.5ff.). Variations in symptomatology therefore
must be kept in mind when considering the communication styles of people with schizophrenia. (This is a point which will be returned to later in the chapter.)

   Scanning the recent literature on language and schizophrenia, numerous questions arise as
to the nature of the communication impairment, which can be discussed in terms of the model
presented. First, research suggests that, in general, the nature of the language difficulties in
schizophrenia are predominantly expressive (production) rather than receptive (comprehension) (Frith 1992). Considering this finding in terms of the model, the implication is that
the person with schizophrenia may have more difficulty processing at the expression phase,
that is at Levels III and IV.

   Linked to the above finding of difficulties predominantly occurring at the expression phase
is the notion of processing complexity. In the model of communication processing presented,
complexity may be viewed as the number of levels that have to be activated to process a
message (i.e. to understand it and to make a response). Studies show that although there are
some deficits evident when simple processing is required (i.e. when a small number of levels
need to be activated), the main difficulties for individuals with schizophrenia are more obvious
when complex processing is required (i.e. when an increased number of levels need to be
activated) (Frith and Allen 1988; Frith 1992; Braff 1993). Using language figuratively or in an
abstract sense and engaging in and constructing coherent discourse, would all be considered
communicative acts which require complex processing. These areas have been found to be
problematic for the individual with schizophrenia (Andreason, Hoffman and Grove 1985;
Frith and Allen 1988).

Looking more specifically at components within levels, it can be seen from the model that the earlier stages of processing require the ability to store the message in short-term and working memory. It has also been reported in the literature (for example Grove and Andreason 1985; Morice 1990) that short-term memory is affected in some individuals with schizophrenia and that this, coupled with a disorder of working memory (Morice 1994), prevents the simultaneous processing and storage of the information for short-term recall. Morice (1994) discusses the possibility of the language impairment in schizophrenia being attributed, at least in part, to a disorder of working memory. Fleming, Goldberg and Gold (1994) suggest that involvement of a deficit in working memory may have a pervasive effect on the execution of a variety of tasks which require the simultaneous storing and processing of information. If this is so, processing at least at Level I (with simultaneous effects on other levels) may be affected in the individual with schizophrenia.

Another possible explanation for the breakdown in communication in schizophrenia draws on Frith's (1992, 1997) notion of a 'disorder of willed intention' which helps to explain some of the symptoms of schizophrenia, in particular poverty of action in all spheres: movement, speech and affect. As Frith (1997) explains, this means that some individuals with schizophrenia 'can perform routine acts elicited by environmental stimuli but have difficulty in producing spontaneous behaviour in the absence of external cues' (p.13). As applied to communication, such an explanation predicts that unless a response is clearly specified, subjects, especially those with negative symptoms, will have great difficulty generating a response: 'patients with negative signs should perform well with tasks in which responses are largely specified by the experimenter ... they should perform badly when there is no such specification even if the actual responses required are the same' (Frith 1992, p.43). Allen, Liddle and Frith (1993) found reduced ability in subjects with negative symptoms on a verbal fluency task. When required to name members of a certain category (e.g. animals), subjects with negative symptoms tended to give up on their search prematurely whereas subjects with positive symptoms were more likely to make errors on the task. Thus processing at Level III may be compromised in schizophrenic individuals, according to the model outlined.

Finally from the above outline of just some of the factors implicated in communication breakdown in schizophrenia, it can be concluded that the communication difficulties are complex. As referred to above, the ability to engage in coherent discourse may be affected. As Frith (1997) states: 'the abnormalities of schizophrenic language appear not to lie at the level of language competence but of language use ... the problems arise when the patient has to use language to communicate with others' (p.13).

A communication processing model allows us to examine what is involved in using language to communicate with others. Therefore it can also provide a working model to examine and discuss the areas of communication breakdown as suggested by the literature on language and schizophrenia, as outlined above. In its application, the model can assist in the interpretation of individual or small group profiles in order to achieve a holistic picture of strengths and weaknesses. Thus the following questions are posed with the resulting language and communication profiles of a small number of subjects serving to illustrate the findings:

1. Will the subjects have more difficulty on tasks testing language production than with tasks testing verbal comprehension?

2. Will the subjects perform poorly on tasks which require complex processing?

3. Will the subjects' success rates decrease on tests which require processing commands of increasing length and complexity and in recalling information presented to them?

4. Will subjects perform better on tasks where the response is clearly specified by the examiner?

Method

The subjects were assessed in order to establish their individual communication profiles and in so doing to describe their communicative strengths and weaknesses, with a secondary aim of establishing a group profile.

MEASUREMENTS

Assessing the language and communication of individuals with mental illness proves a difficult task as there are no standardised formal assessments available for this population. Therefore for the assessments in question, some standardised tests were used informally, that is, in their non-standardised forms (e.g. British Picture Vocabulary Scales, Dunn *et al.* 1982) and others were devised specifically to assess certain language functions (e.g. listening to paragraphs, inference making). This obviously means that interpretations are predominantly qualitative. However, some form of quantitative measure is useful for comparison within groups. To allow for this, some standard of measurement was needed. Therefore a so-called 'control group' of approximately age-matched, non-affected adults were assessed using the same test battery (see Frith 1992 for a brief discussion on the difficulties inherent in establishing control groups in schizophrenia studies). Calculating percentage success rates for each test administered (i.e. the number of correct responses as a percentage of the total number of test items), the control group achieved scores, as expected, within the 85–100 per cent range. Because of performance variables affecting the group with schizophrenia and the fact that they are not directly comparable to the general population, it was decided to level their expected success rate at 80 per cent.

Performance variables in the schizophrenic group result from the very nature of the illness and these include factors such as chronicity of illness, present and past communication environments (e.g. effects of institutionalisation), medication, levels of co-operation and attention, level of cognitive functioning and mental health at time of testing. (These factors will be referred to again in the discussion section.)

Table 31.1 outlines the test battery used and the language levels and areas assessed. The tests chosen and devised were designed to elicit a wide variety of responses, across a number of processing levels, from a task requiring relatively simple processing (e.g. receptive vocabulary test) to one which required more complex processing (e.g. interpretation of idioms). Table 31.1 also shows the nature of the responses required (response type) and the possible number or processing levels activated for any given task; other levels involved but not primarily activated are in parentheses. Further details of tests used may be found in the Appendix to this chapter.

Table 31.1 Details of language assessments, response types
and number of processing levels activated per task

Language level	Comprehension/ expression	Assessment tool	Response type	Processing Levels activated: Total
Word	Comprehension	B.P.V.S.	Spec./Non-V	I, (II), III: 2
Sentence	Comprehension	T.R.O.G.	Spec./Non-V	I, (II), III: 2
Command	Comprehension	INF. T.	Spec./Non-V	I, (II), III: 2
Inference	Comprehension	INF. T.	Spec./V	I, II, III, (IV): 3
Paragraph	Comprehension/ Expression	INF. T.	Spec./V	I, II, III, IV: 4
Sentence	Expression	F.L.T.A.	Unspec./V	(I), II, III, IV: 3
High level	Expression	MIRBI	Unspec./V	I, II, III, IV: 4
Idiom	Expression	F.L.T.A.	Unspec./V	I, II, III, IV: 4

Assessment tools

B.P.V.S.   British Picture Vocabulary Scales (Dunn et al. 1982)
T.R.O.G.   Test for Reception Of Grammar (Bishop 1983)
INF. T.   Informal Test
F.L.T.A.   Fullerton Language Test for Adolescents (Thorum 1986)
MIRBI   Mini Inventory of Right Brain Injury (Pimental and Kingsbury 1989)

PROCEDURES

The subjects were assessed over a number of sessions. Each subject was tested individually in a quiet room seated facing the examiner. Stimulus items were repeated twice for each subject and repeated a third time if requested by the subject. All responses on language testing were recorded by the examiner. A percentage success rate was calculated for each individual on each test.

SUBJECTS

Relevant details of the subjects A, B, C and D involved in the study can be seen in Table 31.2. Subject A is female while the remainder are male. Subject A also presents with predominantly positive symptoms and achieved a score on the Mini Mental Status Examination (Folstein 1975) which is considered 'abnormal and indicative of diffuse cognitive functioning'. All other subjects scored within the normal range and present with predominantly negative symptoms.

Table 31.2 Subjects' details including results of MMS evluations

Subject	D.O.B C.A. at time of testing	Age of onset	Intellectual functioning	Chronicity	Predominant symptom type (+), (-)	Diagnosis	Medication	Mini Metal Status Exam scores
A	7.11.59 (36 yrs)	Teens	Average 2nd Level	10 years	(+)	Chronic schizophrenia (paranoid)	Anti-psychotic (high dosage)	20*
B	4.2.48 (47yrs)	Late teens	Average 2nd Level	10 years	(-)	Chronic schizophrenia (paranoid)	Anti-psychotic (high dosage)	26
C	19.3.55 (40yrs)	Early 20s	Average 2nd Level	10 years	(-)	Chronic schizophrenia (paranoid)	Anti-psychotic (medium dosage)	26
D	29.10.34 (61yrs)	Early 40s	Average 2nd Level	10 years	(-)	Chronic schizophrenia (paranoid)	Anti-psychotic (medium dosage)	25

*abnormal and indicative of diffuse cognitive functioning

Results

SUBJECTS' PERFORMANCE ON LANGUAGE TESTS

All subjects co-operated for language testing; however, attention and concentration levels varied within and across assessment sessions. Subjects were easily distracted but could be brought back to task. When the subject's performance on language tests is examined the results show that two of the subjects scored above the previously decided expected average (80%) for the group and two scored below. Figure 31.2 illustrates subjects' mean performance according to type of language task. In general it can be seen that subjects achieved below the expected average success rate on all but three of the tests namely, comprehension at word level (COMP.WORD.), comprehension at sentence level (COMP.SENT.) and expression at sentence level (EXP.SENT.). When the subjects' results are interpreted according to type of task, answers to questions posed are offered.

1. *Will the subjects have more difficulty on tasks testing language production than on tasks testing verbal comprehension?*

   Subjects performed better on tasks of comprehension (COMP.) than on expression (EXP.) with the exception of expression at sentence level (EXP.SENT.) (see Figure 31.2).

2. *Will the subjects perform poorly on tasks which require complex processing?*

   In general, the results show an inverse relationship between the success rates and processing complexity of task; as the processing complexity increased the success rates decreased. For example, tasks such as comprehension of commands (COMP.COMM.) where two levels are primarily activated had a higher success rate than the task of expressing the meaning of idioms (EXP.IDIOMS) which required activation of all four processing levels.

3. *Will the subjects' success rates decrease on tests which require processing commands of increasing length and complexity and in recalling information presented to them?*

   As the demands on working memory increased, according to type of language task, the success rates decreased. The notable success rate on expression at sentence level (EXP.SENT.) may be explained by the fact that the subject only had to remember one word which he or she was required to put into a sentence.

4. *Will subjects perform better on tasks where the response is clearly specified by the examiner?*

   As can be seen from Table 31.1 the responses required ranged from *specified/non-verbal* to *specified/verbal* to *unspecified/verbal*. The results show that performance overall was better on tasks where the responses were specified than on tasks where the responses were unspecified. For example, success rates were higher on comprehension at word and sentence levels (COMP.WORD; COMP.SENT.) where responses were clearly specified (i.e. pointing to pictures), than on tasks where the responses were unspecified as on tasks expressing higher level language functions and the meanings of idioms (EXP.HI.LANG; EXP.IDIOMS).

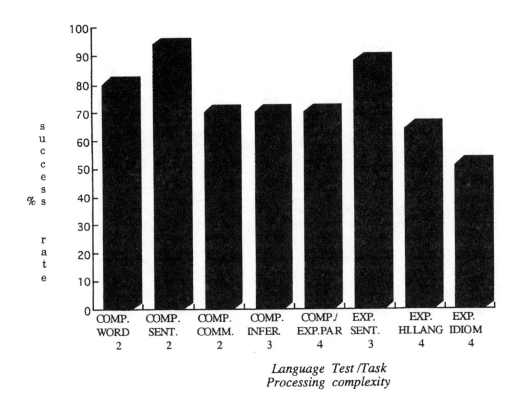

Question

1. Comprehension   Expression

2. Lower number of   ⟷   Greater number of processing levels activated
   processing levels activated ⟷

3. Less demand on working   More demand on working memory (*listen + say*)
   memory (*listen + do*)   ⟷

4. Responses specified   Responses unspecified (verbal)
   (non-verbal)   ⟷

Figure 31.2 Subjects' mean performance according to language task

When the subjects' individual language profiles are examined (Figure 31.3) it can be seen that the profiles follow similar trends across tasks and clearly reflect the mean average success rates according to type of language tasks. An interesting finding is Subject A's above expected average performance on the comprehension of inferences task (COMP.INFER.).

Figure 31.3 Subjects' Language Profiles as assessed on a series of Language Tests/Tasks

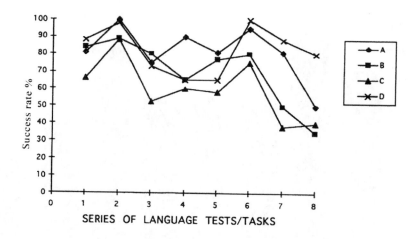

	Task type	Processes
TASK 1:	COMP.WORD	(2)
TASK 2:	COMP.SENT.	(2)
TASK 3:	COMP.COMM.	(2)
TASK 4:	COMP.INFER.	(3)
TASK 5:	COMP.EXP.PAR.	(4)
TASK 6:	EXP.SENT.	(3)
TASK 7:	EXP.HI.LANG.	(4)

Figure 31.3 Subjects' language profiles as assessed on a series of language tests/tasks

Discussion

Before discussing the above results, it is imperative to state that it would be impossible and incorrect to make generalisations about the nature of the communication difficulties from the profiles of just four individuals who were loosely compared to a 'control group' and tested according to the above parameters. That is *not* the point of this exercise. The key point is that interpreting the results of the investigations according to a model of communication processing serves to illustrate some of the communication difficulties of the person with schizophrenia, both as an individual and as part of a small group of similarly affected adults.

The shaded areas of the communication processing model in Figure 31.4 illustrate *potential communication breakdown points* experienced by the subjects and is informed by the results of the investigations and general observations during assessment.

The results of the assessments show that there may be many *potential communication breakdown points* which the person with schizophrenia will encounter in communication processing:

- *Level I.* The first potential communication breakdown point may occur when the individual is required to attend and listen to the message being sent. Bleuler (1911) was of the opinion that one of the fundamental symptoms of the condition was a disturbance of attention. More recently Chaika (1997) holds the contentious view that the manifestations of schizophrenic speech seem to be grounded in deficits of attention. Likewise, attending to the content of a conversation or any one message may prove too difficult a task; people with schizophrenia frequently complain of their inability to listen and attend for any period of time. All four of the subjects in this study had problems maintaining attention and concentration and repetition of test items were necessary. A breakdown in communication may therefore occur at this early stage of the potential exchange.

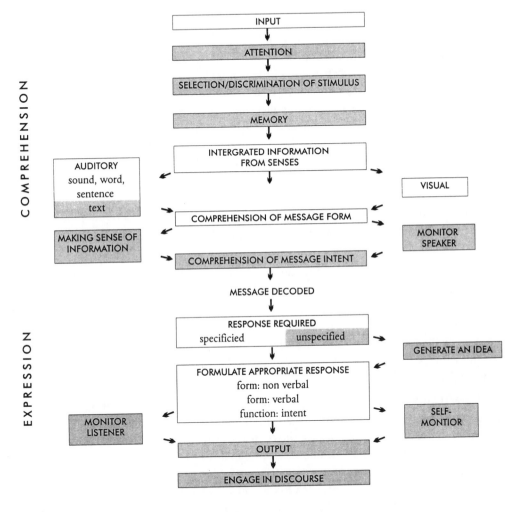

Figure 31.4 Model of communication processing with shaded areas representing potential communication break-down points for subjects studied.

As referred to earlier, it has been reported that short-term memory is affected in schizophrenia (Grove and Andreason 1985; Morice 1990) and this coupled with a disorder of working memory (Morice 1994) may negatively affect the individual's ability to process the message. The results on language testing reflect this: as the demands on working memory became greater, success rates fell and communication breakdown was more likely to occur (e.g. having to remember a paragraph as opposed to single words or short sentences proved more difficult for the subjects). Thus we may see areas of breakdown within Level I of communication processing. However, not all people with schizophrenia have memory deficits (Rossell and David 1997); chronicity of the condition and levels of medication may be important variables in this regard.

- *Level II.* Making sense of incoming messages forces us to refer to both real world and social knowledge and to the shared knowledge available to the interlocutors. It also requires the ability to make inferences where necessary. Because of reported gross semantic memory deficits, easy access to a store of knowledge about the world may be unreliable in people with schizophrenia (McKenna, Mortimer and Hodges 1994); he or she may have a distorted perception of the world and this distortion may prevent them from accurately interpreting events or utterances in the sense in which they were meant. For example when asked 'In which country are we?' (a question on the Mini Mental Status Exam), one individual responded 'I better say Ireland – I don't want to upset Germany.' All subjects with the exception of Subject A had difficulty on the comprehension of inferences (COMP.INFER.) test. Likewise poor comprehension of message intent may also help to explain the poor results overall on interpretation of idioms (EXP.IDIOM). When asked to explain the idiom 'to throw one's hat into the ring' one individual explained that it meant 'to go to Portugal for a holiday'. Thus potential communication breakdown points can be identified at Level II of the proposed model.

It is interesting to note Subject A's performance on language testing, in view of gender issues in thinking and language currently being explored in general literature (for example, Tannen 1990). As mentioned above Subject A, who is female, had little difficulty on the comprehension of inferences test (COMP.INFER.) (see Figure 31.3). Another contributing factor may be that, of the four subjects studied, Subject A was the only one who could be described as presenting with predominantly positive symptoms and thus presented with a different style of communication.

- *Level III.* At the stage of generating ideas to form a response, the person with schizophrenia (particularly with negative symptoms) may have great difficulty, unless the response is clearly specified by the context or the speaker (Frith 1992). Again this finding was reflected in the results of testing, that is success rates were lower on tests where the responses were unspecified and thus had to be generated by the speaker. From his own examples and related to the concept of a 'disorder of willed intention' referred to earlier, Frith (1997) observed that a patient answered all questions asked of him but never volunteered new information or spontaneously elaborated on answers given. Such findings, interpreted according to the communication processing model, highlight additional points of possible breakdown at Level III and point to the importance of being aware of possibly different profiles in positive and negative presentations of the disorder.

The person with schizophrenia, in the role of speaker, may be able to cope with the structural aspects of formulating a response, that is expressively they may be able to use appropriate syntax, phonology and semantics to formulate their response. This is reflected in the relatively high success rates as found on the expression of sentences test (EXP.SENT.). The syntax used may be less complex (see Thomas *et al.* 1996) and errors may be apparent; however, for the most part the message may be linguistically well formed.

- *Level IV.* Many people with schizophrenia have difficulty in monitoring their own output and suppressing or inhibiting irrelevant phrases or perseverations (Barr *et al.* 1989), which adds to the likelihood of communication breakdown. This was a feature of the subjects' test behaviour when responses given were clearly irrelevant or tangential to that which was requested. When responding, though the form was correct (i.e. a grammatically well formed utterance), the intent behind the utterance was often not clear and so the subject had difficulty expressing what he or she meant appropriately. For example, when asked to explain the incongruity/absurdity of: 'Before losing her teeth, the woman grew a new set of dentures', one individual responded with: 'She'll have two pairs of dentures when she sits in the bar for a Guinness Light.' Furthermore, engaging in meaningful discourse and using language appropriately in context (both of which require the simultaneous activation of all four processing levels) may prove troublesome and difficulties arise from a variety of sources, not least the inability of the person with schizophrenia to take the listener's perspective in an interaction (cf. Frith's (1992, 1994) application of a Theory of Mind to schizophrenia).

Finally, when the results of the group of people with schizophrenia is loosely compared to that of the non-affected 'control group', where all scores fell within the 85–100 per cent range, it is interesting to note that although the schizophrenic group's performance was markedly weaker (that is at or below the 80% mark), similar performance *trends* across test results were noted. That is, as for the schizophrenic group, tests which required increased processing were not as successfully completed as those which had a lesser processing load. In other words, the groups' profiles differed in *severity* but not in *shape*. It seems, therefore, that coping with increased demands on processing may be compromised in schizophrenia, resulting in an exacerbation of processing difficulties (see also Braff 1993), rather than a *different* processing profile. It is also interesting to consider that the language skills of some people with schizophrenia could be thought of as 'fragile' and thus more likely to break down under communicative pressure (such as a language testing situation). Performance may be better during conversational interactions where the partner in the discourse can compensate for errors and avoid possible misunderstandings by requesting clarification, thus preventing communication breakdowns.

Summary and conclusions

This chapter explored the application of a communication processing model to communication breakdown in schizophrenia. As was demonstrated, the use of such a model facilitates understanding of the complexity of the communication process and what is required of the communicator as he or she takes on the ever-changing role of speaker and listener.

From the above discussion it is not hard to see the advantages of employing a model of communication processing to aid in assessment interpretation. As Lesser and Milroy (1993) suggest, such models '... provide a framework for perception of the nature of the individual's language, which is relatively simple and easily visualised' (p.61). In doing so therefore it can highlight the numerous *potential communication breakdown points* which occur when the person with schizophrenia engages in communication. Such difficulties occur for many reasons including cognitive, social, perceptual and linguistic limitations. It is the linguistic limitations which result in communication processing failures which were focused on during testing.

A small sample, such as that used in this study, provides the opportunity for an in-depth analysis of the complex language and communication difficulties of the subjects studied; a detailed analysis is necessary if one is to understand the individual's communicative presentation and potential. When small numbers are used, however, it is only possible to comment on apparent *trends* as generalisations are not possible.

When attempting to describe and understand the complex communication skills of people with schizophrenia, the assessment of small samples, with resulting individual and group profiles, provides information which creates a forum for the discussion of ideas as to the nature of the communication processing difficulties of people with chronic schizophrenia. Individual and group profiles offer information that can prompt and guide further investigation. In this study, within-group differences may have affected the outcomes (see Allen *et al.* 1993; Braff 1993) and such differences in their own right are worthy of further investigation. For example, that three of the four subjects presented with predominantly negative symptoms may have affected the outcomes, along with the effects of differing levels of medication across subjects and the effect of same on verbal performance (see Goren, Tucker and Ginsberg 1996). With regard to the possible negative effects of institutionalisation, however, Thomas *et al.* (1990) found that poor linguistic performance could be attributed to factors within the illness process in chronic schizophrenia rather than environmental factors. Other factors to be considered include the unavailability of standardised formal assessments for the assessment of the communication abilities of this population, which results in existing tests having to be adapted and informal tests devised. With this comes the question of reliability and validity of measures used. However, because these measures were used primarily as qualitative measures, these factors may have been overcome to an extent.

Having a working knowledge of the language and communication abilities of an individual with schizophrenia has many advantages for the health care professional. The application of a processing model may provide a useful framework for health professionals in both diagnostic, therapeutic and day-to-day interactions with people with schizophrenia. Increased awareness of what is involved in communication and the potential communication breakdown points which the person with schizophrenia may encounter, leads to practical suggestions of how professionals and others may adapt their verbal input to facilitate successful communication. Practical considerations may include:

- securing the individual's attention and reducing distractors before speaking while checking attention throughout the communication, for example by mentioning the individual's name and maintaining appropriate eye contact

- reducing demands on processing by breaking down complex instructions or explanations into stages and checking comprehension before proceeding
- specifying responses required, for example using a forced alternative if appropriate rather than requiring the individual to generate a response
- using visual aids, for example diagrams or pictures, to help explain or discuss important issues with the individual
- monitoring own use of abstract or figurative language in communications as the message may be misinterpreted or misunderstood.

Being aware of the communicative abilities of the individual with mental illness can also help in daily management, as communication skills are often a useful indicator of the current state of mental health. A working knowledge of an individual's language and communication skills also may help to predict and assess suitability for inclusion in particular therapeutic approaches. For example, the precondition for successful participation in most forms of psychotherapy is adequate communication skills (France and Muir 1997). Understanding the nature of the communication difficulties in schizophrenia may prompt psychotherapists to find ways and means of making the communication more successful and avoiding communication break-down. Furthermore, the assessment of an individual's language and communication abilities renders information that is useful for planning individual and group programmes.

Likewise, because communication is so central to social interaction, knowing more about communication abilities may help workers in the field begin to understand the nature of the social difficulties encountered by people with schizophrenia. Finally, a communication processing model offers a way of looking at the communication difficulties of the person with schizophrenia which should in turn offer insights into the illness process we call schizophrenia.

Acknowledgements

I would particularly like to thank Professor Marcus Webb and Dr Phil Thomas who commented on earlier drafts of this piece of work; any subsequent errors or misinterpretations in the text are my own. Thanks are also due to my speech and language therapy colleagues, Dr Martine Smith and Clothra Ní Cholmáin, and to Noreen Coyle for her administrative assistance. Finally, I am very grateful to the individuals who participated in the study.

Appendix

Mini Mental State Examination (MMS) (Folstein 1975)

This superficially assesses several dimensions of language and cognitive functioning. Areas assessed include orientation, registration, immediate recall, concentration, naming, articulation, construction, writing and three-stage command comprehension. Maximum score is 30 points with unimpaired persons usually scoring approximately 28 points. A score of 24 points or less is considered abnormal and indicative of diffuse cognitive functioning.

Language tests and tasks

Note:

A success rate of 80 per cent was considered an appropriate expected average on language testing and tasks for reasons discussed in text.

LANGUAGE COMPREHENSION

A number of language tests and tasks were given to profile each subject's comprehension of language.

1   **Word: Comprehension (COMP.WORD)**

The British Picture Vocabulary Scales (BPVS) (Dunn et al. 1982): a test of receptive vocabulary where the individual is required to pick from a choice of 4 pictures the stimulus item named by the examiner. Items increase in difficulty from *bucket* (item 1) to *socket* (item 15) to *collision* (item 20), *talon* (item 24), *consuming* (item 27). Picture stimuli are presented, the response is clearly defined and no expressive language is required.

2.   **Sentence: Comprehension (COMP.SENT.)**

The Test for the Reception of Grammar (TROG) (Bishop 1983) formally assesses the individual's understanding of different syntactic constructions. Areas tested include passives (*the cow is pushed by the man*), post-modified subjects (*the boy chasing the horse is fat*), X but not Y (*the box but not the chair is red*), not only X but also Y (*not only the bird but also the flower is blue*), relative clauses (*the pencil is on the book that is yellow*), and embedded sentences (*the book the pencil is on is red*). The individual has to pick from a choice of four pictures the one which is described by the stimulus sentence. The test provides picture stimuli, and the response required is clearly defined with no demands on expressive language.

3.   **Command: Comprehension (COMP.COMM.)**

Test of Verbal Comprehension (INF. T.). This informal language task, which was adapted from that devised by Fujiki and Brinton (1995), required the subject to respond to commands of increasing length and complexity. Such oral directions required the subject to manipulate common objects according to instructions given. Commands consisted of both right branching (e.g. *Put the coin beside the keyring then put the comb on the matchbox*) and embedded element directions (e.g. *Put the big red pencil beside the small battery*).

4.   **Inference: Comprehension (COMP.INFER.)**

Making Inferences (INF. T.) assesses subjects' ability to draw inferences from information given. Passages were read to the subject and questions were then posed which required the subject to infer rather than simply recall details. No picture stimuli were presented. Making inferences would be considered a language function which requires complex processing.

5. **Comprehension/Expression (COMP./EXP.PAR.)**

Listening to paragraphs (INF. T.). This language task, designed for the study, required the subject to recall details from passages of increasing length which were read to the subject. No picture stimuli were presented.

EXPRESSIVE LANGUAGE

A number of expressive language subtests and tasks were presented to profile different aspects of expressive skills.

6. **Sentence: Expression (EXP.SENT.)**

Fullerton Language Test for Adolescents (F.L.T.A.) (Thorum, 1986). A subtest of this test – Morphology Competency – was used to assess the ability of the subjects to formulate sentences from a given word. Examples of stimulus words were *dishonest, faster, movement* and *untie.*

7. **High level: Expression (EXP.HI.LANG.)**

Mini Inventory of Right Brain Injury (MIRBI) (Pimental and Kingsbury 1989). Subtests of this inventory were used to assess the subjects' ability to use affective language and higher level language skills (e.g. understanding humour, explaining incongruities and absurdities and figurative language). Presentation of test items were verbal with no pictorial stimuli presented.

8. **Idiom: Expression (EXP.IDIOMS)**

Fullerton Language Test for Adolescents (FULL. M.C.) (Thorum 1986). Subtest 8 of this test entitled 'Interpretation of Idioms' was administered. This required the subject to interpret idioms read aloud (e.g. 'Pull the wool over one's eyes'; 'Barking up the wrong tree'; 'Take the wind out of someone's sails'). This test would be considered one which requires the use of complex processing skills.

References

Allen, H., Liddle, P. and Frith, C. (1993) Negative features, retrieval processes and verbal fluency in schizophrenia. *British Journal of Psychiatry 163*, 769–775.

Andreason, N. (1979) Thought, language and communication disorders: 2. Diagnostic significance. *Archives of General Psychiatry 36*, 1325–1330.

Andreason, N.C., Hoffman, R.E. and Grove, W.M. (1985) Language abnormalities in schizophrenia. In N. Menuck and V. Seeman (eds) *New Perspectives in Schizophrenia.* New York: Macmillan.

Baddeley, A. (1986) *Working Memory.* Oxford: Oxford University Press.

Barr, W., Bilder, R., Goldberg, E. and Mukherjee, S. (1989) The neuropsychology of schizophrenic speech. *Journal of Communication Disorders 22*, 327–349.

Bishop, D.V.M. (1983) *Test for the Reception of Grammar.* Manchester: University of Manchester.

Bleuler, E. (1911) Dementia praecox or the group of schizophrenia (1987 trans.). In J. Cutting and M. Shepherd (eds) *The Clinical Routes of the Schizophrenia Concept.* Cambridge: Cambridge University Press.

Braff, D.L. (1993) Information processing and attention in schizophrenia. *Schizophrenia Bulletin 19*, 233–259.

Chaika, E. (1997) Intention, attention and deviant schizophrenic speech. In J. France and N. Muir (eds) *Communication and the Mentally Ill Patient.* London: Jessica Kingsley Publishers.

Chiat, S., Law, J. and Marshall, J. (1997) *Language Disorders in Children and Adults: Psycholinguistic Approaches to Therapy.* London: Whurr.

David, A.S. and Cutting, J.C. (eds) (1994) *The Neuropsychology of Schizophrenia.* Hove: Lawrence Erlbaum.

Dunn, L.M., Dunn, L.M., Whetton. C. and Pintilie, D. (1982) *British Picture Vocabulary Scales.* Windsor: NFER-Nelson.

Fleming, K., Goldberg, T.E. and Gold, J.M. (1994) Applying working memory constructs to schizophrenic cognitive impairment. In A.S. David and J.C. Cutting (eds) *The Neuropsychology of Schizophrenia.* Hove: Lawrence Erlbaum.

Folstein, M. (1975) The Mini Mental State Examination. *Journal of Psychiatric Research 12,* 189–198.

France, J. and Muir, N. (1997) Speech and language therapy and the mentally ill patient. In J. France and N. Muir (eds) *Communication and the Mentally Ill Patient.* London: Jessica Kingsley Publishers.

Frith, C. (1992) *The Cognitive Neuropsychology of Schizophrenia.* Hove: Lawrence Erlbaum.

Frith, C. (1994) Theory of mind in schizophrenia. In A.S. David and J.C. Cutting (eds) *The Neuropsychology of Schizophrenia.* Hove: Lawrence Erlbaum.

Frith, C. (1997) Language and communication in schizophrenia. In J. France and N. Muir (eds) *Communication and the Mentally Ill Patient.* London: Jessica Kingsley Publishers.

Frith, C. and Allen, H.A. (1988) Language disorders in schizophrenia and their implications for neuropsychology. In P. Bebbington and P. McGuffin (eds) *Schizophrenia: The Major Issues.* Oxford: Heinemann.

Fujiki, M. and Brinton, B. (1995) The performance of younger and older adults with retardation on a series of language tasks. *American Journal of Speech-Language Pathology 4,* 2, 77–86.

Goren, A.R., Tucker, G. and Ginsberg, G.M. (1996) Language dysfunction in schizophrenia. *European Journal of Disorders of Communication 31,* 2, 153–170.

Gravell, R. and France, J. (1991) Mental disorders and speech therapy: an introduction. In R. Gravell and J. France (eds) *Speech and Communication Problems in Psychiatry.* London: Chapman and Hall.

Grice, H.P. (1975) Logic and conversation. In P. Cole and J. Morgan (eds) *Syntax and Semantics. Vol. 3: Speech Acts.* New York: Academic Press. pp.41–58.

Grove, W. and Andreason, N. (1985) Language and thinking in psychosis: is there an output abnormality? *Archives of General Psychiatry 42,* 26–32.

Kraepelin, E. (1896) Dementia Praecox. In J. Cutting and M. Shepherd (eds and trans.) *The Clinical Routes of the Schizophrenia Concept.* Cambridge: Cambridge University Press.

Lesser, R. and Milroy, L. (1993) *Linguistics and Aphasia: Psycholinguistics and Pragmatic Aspects of Intervention.* Harlow: Longman.

McKenna, P.J. (1994) *Schizophrenia and Related Syndromes.* New York: Oxford University Press.

McKenna, P.J., Mortimer, A.M. and Hodges, J.R. (1994) Semantic memory in schizophrenia. In A.S. David and J.C. Cutting (eds) *The Neuropsychology of Schizophrenia.* Hove: Lawrence Erlbaum.

Morice, R.D. (1990) Cognitive inflexibility and pre-frontal dysfunction in schizophrenia and mania. *British Journal of Psychiatry 157,* 50–54.

Morice, R.D. (1994) The Neuropsychology of Schizophrenic Language. Paper presented at the Royal College of Psychiatrists Annual Meeting, Cork, Ireland.

Murray, R. (1994) Sanity, Madness and the Family. Paper presented at the Royal College of Psychiatrists Annual Meeting, Cork, Ireland.

Pimental, P.A. and Kingsbury, N.A. (1989) *Mini Inventory of Right Brain Injury.* Austin TX: PRO-ED.

Rossell, S.L. and David, A.S. (1997) The neuropsychology of schizophrenia: recent trends. *Current Opinion in Psychiatry 10,* 26–29.

Tannen, D. (1990) *You Just Don't Understand: Women and Men in Conversation.* New York: William Morrow.

Thomas, P. (1997) What can linguistics tell us about thought disorder? In J. France and N. Muir (eds) *Communication and the Mentally Ill Patient.* London: Jessica Kingsley Publishers.

Thomas, P., Kearney, G. Napier, E., Ellis, E., Leudar, I. and Johnston, M. (1996) Speech and language in first onset psychosis. Differences between people with schizophrenia, mania and controls. *British Journal of Psychiatry 168,* 337–343.

Thomas, P., King, K., Fraser, W.I. and Kendell, R.E. (1990) Linguistic performance in schizophrenia: a comparison of acute and chronic schizophrenics. *British Journal of Psychiatry 156,* 204–210.

Thorum, A.R. (1986) *The Fullerton Language Test for Adolescents.* US: Consulting Psychologists Press.

CHAPTER 32

Linguistic Deviance in Schizophrenia
Preliminary Report

William H. Sledge, Ralph Hoffman, Keith Hawkins, Nancy Docherty,
Donald Quinlan and Jaak Rakfeldt

Introduction

Language, the most quintessential human capacity, mediates most human interaction and expressive behavior. It is ironic then that although most descriptions of psychopathological syndromes have contained descriptions of speech acts and language-related behaviours, language itself (and the rules governing its organisation and use) has been mostly taken for granted and treated as an invisible function by clinical investigators. With a few notable exceptions (as noted in this review) language has not been a particular focus for the study of psychopathology. This neglect of language is even more puzzling in light of the intimate relationship between language and brain function and organisation as is noted in the study of aphasia (Critchley 1964; Goodglass 1983; Lesser 1989; Rose, Whurr and Wyke 1988). With the increasing focus on brain structure and function as a paradigm for the understanding of psychopathological conditions, particularly the more severe disorders (Michels and Marzuk 1993), the study of language within diagnostic groups with probable biological underpinnings for the expression of the illness may be a fruitful avenue of investigation.

In this chapter we present a strategy of using a linguistically based method to study the neuropsychological functioning of persons with schizophrenia. We also present preliminary findings from this strategy. There is strong face validity to the strategy of using linguistically based methods in the study of psychopathology; schizophrenia is a particularly good candidate illness for our approach. The multitude of neuropsychological findings (Anand 1992; Frith and Done 1988; Goldberg, Gold and Braff 1991; Harrow and Quinlan 1985), and the clear presence of a thinking/language disorder in some patients with schizophrenia, presents an opportunity for the testing of ideas about language capacity in those with mental illness. Many people with schizophrenia speak oddly. Conventionally, this oddness has been conceptualised as a 'thought disorder' (Andreason 1979, 1982; Harrow and Quinlan 1985; Reilly, Harrow and Tucker 1973). Most scholars of this phenomenon, taking the capacity for the production of language for granted, have assumed that schizophrenic language problems derive from types of general ideational disturbances involving the co-ordination of thought. This orientation is suggested by the original writings of Bleuler (1909/1950) who noted that 'loose associations' compose the central cognitive alteration of schizophrenia. The slant of our work, on the other hand, is to conceptualise this phenomenon of talking oddly as a 'language disorder' analogous to an acquired aphasia but not based on the same types of lesions. In this regard our approach is prefigured by Kraepelin (1919).

View of the literature

Primacy of language in clinical phenomena

Regardless of the theoretical orientation, the leaders of different perspectives have emphasised the disordered language of schizophrenic or psychotic speakers.

Kraepelin (1919) and later Kleist (1960) approached psychopathology from a somatic perspective and emphasised the disordered, fragmented speech of psychotic speakers and conceptualised the problem as being one of an aphasia. Indeed, Kraepelin's terminology, with concepts such as schizophrasia and jargonaphasia, sound more like a cartography for aphasia than for schizophrenic speech.

Although Freud did not emphasise psychosis in his work, he formulated a view of psychosis that was quite linguistic in its orientation (Rosen 1977). His primary conceptualisation that addressed the language/speech problem of schizophrenia (Freud 1915) posed that the problem of schizophrenic speech is an inability to be interested in people and things outside the self so that the qualities of words superseded their socially accepted, symbolic significance and disrupted the relationship between sign and signified which non-psychotic speakers and listeners take for granted. The psychotic speaker then relates to words as things themselves rather than words as signifiers. The properties of words for sound, ambiguity or idiosyncratic meaning rather than the meaning of the word for the occasion become more important in the determination of use.

Schneider (1959) was quite descriptive and phenomenological in his approach. While he did not take a linguistic perspective *per se* in his work, he emphasised the disordered speech of the schizophrenic speaker in his clinical account of schizophrenia.

Thought and language

Language and thought are not the same. We will not attempt to justify this assertion here in any comprehensive manner – others have taken up the issue exhaustively (Chaika 1990; Rochester and Martin 1979). The matter is controversial philosophically but we do not think there is an issue clinically or descriptively other than a definitional one. Thought can occur without language and language rules apply to utterances without discernible thought. For instance there can be gibberish (with absolutely no discernible thought) that is consistent (or inconsistent) with the phonological rules of a natural language (Chaika 1990). Likewise sentences can be 'grammatical' and yet completely incomprehensible (Chomsky 1964). Not only are language and thought different constructs but there is no necessary one-to-one relationship between them. Some have asserted that language is simply a behaviour that makes thought manifest. However, the relationship is more complex since one can have thought without language; furthermore, one can have many different thoughts represented by one speech act such as in ambiguity and polysemy. And as noted one can have grammatically correct forms without discernible thought.

For our purposes here there is some need, however, to give basic definitions. Thought, then, for this chapter is a cognitive process which we infer based on specific behaviours such as test results, abstract reasoning, problem solving, discourse, etc. Many, but not all, of these behaviours are speech acts. Speech is a specific behaviour based on the rules of language. Language is the rule-governed system which employs discrete units of utterance (and their representation in writing) combined in a particular, systematic and rule-governed fashion in order to represent meaning. Language is conventionally divided into phonological (sound), semantic (word) and syntactic (grammar) domains. There are universal rules common to all languages as postulated by the transformational grammarians and others (Chomsky 1965). There are also specific rules particular to individual, natural languages.

Furthermore, when one considers deviant speech, it is important to differentiate between performance and competence. Performance refers to non-linguistic factors that may influence the production or reception of a particular speech act such as concentration, exhaustion, memory limitations, etc. Competence, on the other hand, is a measure of the individual's mastery and knowledge of his or her language. Performance, then, refers to the application of language rules in specific situations and competence refers to the individual's linguistic capacity (Chomsky 1965). Our study is an effort to explore the idea that schizophrenic speakers have an episodic failure in language capacity (i.e. competence).

Linguistic basics

As noted above, language is conventionally divided into at least three domains or levels in which the rules governing each domain are relatively independent of the rules of the other domain even though the levels are systematically linked (by rules) as well. These domains are phonological, semantic and syntactical. Phonological rules govern which basic component sounds, namely phonemes, are used in the language system and how they are put together to form words or other units of meaning (morphemes). Phonological rules also dictate which sounds can co-occur and how particular phonemes are pronounced in relationship to one another. Semantic considerations address reference (the relation of words to mental structures such as ideas, concepts, experiences, perceptions, etc.) or signifier–signified relationships and how morphemes are constructed systematically such as in the creation of plurals, possessives, tenses, etc. Syntactical considerations address the grammar or combinatorial rules that govern how words are used in relation to one another to represent a certain meaning. Transformational grammar proposes that the meaning of the surface sentence is derived from 'deep kernels' of meaning and intentionality that get progressively and hierarchically derived into surface 'strings' by rules applied to each level in deriving the subsequent level. There is substantial interpenetration between semantic and syntactical domains. Chomsky's great contribution to modern linguistics has been to put forward certain ideas about how this syntactical system is organised in his conceptualizations of a transformational-generative grammar (Lyons 1970).

Another domain involving language, but not a 'pure' linguistic consideration, is discourse analysis, in which the social and psychological contexts become major considerations in understanding deviant speech. Discourse analysis takes into consideration discourse rules dealing with interactional issues such as requests, challenges, coherence, narrative and sequencing (Labov and Fanshel 1977).

Chomsky (1964) suggested that one could judge the degree of deviance of a particular construction based on the 'abstractness' of the rule being violated. This concept prompted us to consider if there could be a clinical-neurobiological dimension to the notion of abstractness of rule violation in free speech. Indeed, many of the constructions of our psychotic patients seem to fall into Chomsky's category of semi-sentences (Chomsky 1964) so that we began to think that Chomsky's formulation concerning degree of grammaticalness might pertain to some of the pathological constructions of schizophrenic speakers. Fodor and Bever (1965) generated experimental evidence that linguistic structures had a psychological representation that heavily influenced the perception of the placement of a click inserted during the hearing of sentences. An example of the idea of abstractness of levels of the sentence is presented in Figure 32.1.

surface structure
    the shooting of the hunters was awful
phrase structure components
    the shooting was awful
    of the hunters (hunters as understood subject of shooting)
    the shooting was awful
    of the hunters (hunters as understood object of shooting)
clause structure components
    (the shooting of the hunters) (was awful)
deep structure
    intentionality and psychological representation

Language and schizophrenia-different approaches

The communication disorders of schizophrenia are among the most vexatious and debilitating components of the illness. Some investigators (Andreason 1979; Feinberg 1978; Frith and Allen 1988; Maher 1983; Reilly, Harrow and Tucker 1973; Rochester and Martin 1979) have attempted to define these difficulties as failures in the capacity to produce non-deviant speech and/or language. Such an approach has considerable theoretical appeal since the biological basis of language production is clearly established (Lenneberge 1967) and language perform-ance and acquisition depends on an interpersonal interaction at an early age.

Another rationale for a linguistic approach is the promise of a standardised means of identifying, describing and conceptualising verbal behaviour, invaluable as a tool to compare findings among investigators. If disruptions in language production can be identified and characterised, important information may be gained regarding the nature of cognitive deficits of speakers with severe mental illness such as schizophrenia. This in turn could localise dysfunction to particular parts of the brain that subtend disrupted language generation processes (Feinberg 1978; Morice 1990) and clarify aspects of the thought/language disorder of an illness such as schizophrenia (Frith and Done 1988; Spitzer, Braun and Maier 1993; Spitzer 1993). And finally, the precise identification and characterisation of a language disorder may lead to a language-oriented treatment approach (Satel and Sledge 1989).

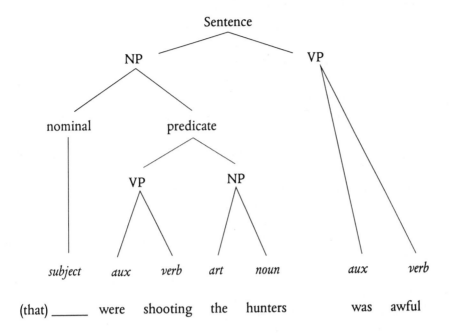

or

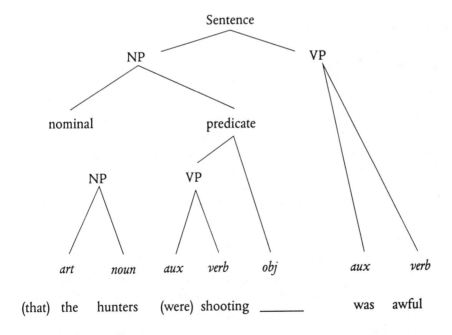

Figure 32.1 Level of abstractness of rule-governed operations in grammatical generation

Hypotheses and findings in regard to linguistic approaches to schizophrenia

A comprehensive review of the studies addressing language disorder in schizophrenia is beyond the scope of this chapter. Consequently, we will not address those studies that deal primarily with **discourse analysis** (Andreason 1979; Hoffman, Stopeck and Andreason 1986; Rochester and Martin 1979), **type token ratio** (Fairbanks 1944; Mann 1944), **cloze procedure** (Rutter, Wishner and Callaghan 1975; Salzinger, Portnoy and Feldman 1964), **content analysis** (Gottshalk and Glaser 1966; Rosenberg and Tucker 1979; Tucker and Rosenberg 1975) or **thought disorder** (Andreason 1982; Chapman, Chapman and Miller 1977; Harrow and Quinlan 1985; Maher 1983; Reilly, Harrow and Tucker 1973; Spitzer *et al.* 1993; Spitzer 1993). Instead, we will provide a selected review of the work that has addressed the grammatical capacities and performance of schizophrenic speakers. Here it is understood that grammatical will include studies that address syntax as well as the syntactical aspects of semantic studies.

Studies of the schizophrenic person's ability to understand and utilise grammar have covered a wide variety of methods and approaches with general but not unequivocal support for the presence of a specific grammatical dysfunction. What follows is a representative, selective review of this work.

Lawson, McGhie and Chapman (1964) found that schizophrenic patients remembered grammatical and ungrammatical sentences to the same extent whereas the control group of normals remembered grammatical sentences better. This finding was confirmed by Truscott (1970) but not by Levy and Maxwell (1968) and Straube (1979).

Pylyshyn (1970) developed a syntactically based method of rating the texts of psychiatric interviews and found that the measure distinguished different diagnostic groups. Morice and Ingram (1982) studied schizophrenics, manics, and controls on diagnostic and linguistic variables; they were able to achieve a 95 per cent classification rate based on a discriminate analysis using linguistic variables. They found considerable differences between schizophrenics and non-schizophrenics which was confirmed by King *et al.* (1990).

Carpenter (1976) and Andreason and Grove (1979) found no difference between normals and schizophrenics in the perception of grammatical structure as per the click test (Fodor and Bever 1965). Miller and Phelan (1980) found no difference between schizophrenics and normal controls in their ability to recognise grammatical and non-grammatical sentences.

Elaine Chaika has been one of the most active investigators in this field. As a linguist she has been particularly well qualified to utilise linguistic approaches to the psychopathology of schizophrenia. Her *Understanding Psychotic Speech: Beyond Freud and Chomsky* (1990) is a comprehensive summary of her work. She believes that schizophrenic speakers demonstrate a multitude of linguistic failures that involve pragmatic (discourse), syntactic, semantic and phonological (eventually, if allowed to deteriorate) levels. Furthermore, she hypothesises that these failures are due to 'lack of control over the selection of linguistic material combined with inappropriate preservations' (Chaika 1990, p.29). She views the language disorder(s) of schizophrenia as being similar to or analogous to aphasia in that the schizophrenic speaker with a communication disorder does not have command of the rules of language generation.

Other researchers have argued against the hypothesis that schizophrenics demonstrate an aphasic-like language deviance. These objections have been summarised in a review by

Schwartz (1982) and are essentially twofold. First, even though schizophrenics make errors in applying linguistic rules, so do normal speakers insofar as most people produce rather imperfect speech that contains a variety of errors of syntax, word choice, slips of the tongue, etc. (cf. Fromkin 1975); thus, violations of linguistic rules *per se* cannot be used as a criterion for discerning aphasic deviance that implicates neural pathology. Second, there is much evidence to suggest that schizophrenics while performing experimental tasks are able to utilise linguistic structures in the processing of language. Gerver (1967) demonstrated that schizophrenics were able to use semantic and syntactic processes to enhance their recall of word strings. Carpenter (1976) and Rochester, Harris and Seeman (1973) showed that schizophrenics, like normals, parse sentences into clause units during recall tasks.

Though the above objections highlight the need to avoid hasty conclusions regarding the nature of schizophrenic language disturbances, they do not preclude the possibility of aphasic-like disruptions for this group of speakers. As we have noted earlier (Hoffman and Sledge 1984), schizophrenic speaker errors can be distinguished from non-schizophrenic speaker speech errors on two major grounds: (1) schizophrenics at times demonstrate discrete epochs of *sustained* linguistic disruptions of certain specific types while normal speech errors are generally momentary and without repetition of linguistic structure; and (2) schizophrenic errors indicate a breakdown of linguistic structure, while normal speech errors preserve linguistic structure. Furthermore, because a major deficit is a disruption of speech *production* (this point also stressed by Andreason 1982), the previously noted psycholinguistic tests of language abilities are not definitive. None of these tests specifically addresses the capacity of schizophrenics to generate language. For instance, there is good reason to believe that detection of incorrect grammar in an artificial laboratory situation as investigated by Miller and Phelan (1980) has little relevance to the actual task of producing coherent, well-organised speech (Bresnan 1978). Furthermore, schizophrenic language difficulties are expressed only episodically; the failure of schizophrenics to demonstrate performance difficulties on the psycholinguistic tests in the studies cited above may be simply due to the fact that the testing situation did not trigger an episode of aphasic vulnerability. Finally, Hoffman and Sledge (1984) and Chaika (1990) indicate that the major source of difficulty among the deviant schizophrenic utterances under consideration involves the synthesis and generation of higher order grammatical structure. Failures of this sort could arise without there being any particular difficulty in detecting clause boundaries (Carpenter 1976; Rochester, Harris and Seeman 1973) or recalling word strings (Gerver 1967) that already have an intrinsic linguistic organisation.

The major limitation of the defect in a language production hypothesis for schizophrenia to date is that most of the supporting speech data interpreted as substantiating the hypothesis are derived from single case studies. Though this material has led to some provocative findings, results from single case studies pose generalisability constraints. What is needed at this stage of inquiry is a systematic exploration of language abnormalities among a sufficient number of schizophrenic subjects with suitable comparison groups, using reliable and accessible neurolinguistic methods. Once a reliable instrument is established, it will be possible to systematically explore the type and prevalence of a language production disorder among schizophrenic patients, exploring hypotheses of the relationship between linguistic deviance and clinical expressions of the disorder (i.e. symptoms, subtypes, course, severity, etc.), treatment (i.e. medication, psychotherapy and rehabilitation effects) and neuropsychological covariates (i.e. attention, memory and other localised as well as diffuse functional measures).

A pilot study (Hoffman and Sledge 1988) indicated that the approach of measuring linguistic deviance at the level of production of the independent clause has considerable promise as a means of differentiating schizophrenia and other psychopathological states. Audio tape recordings were made of speech produced by eleven schizophrenic and nine non-schizophrenic psychiatric patients. Speech segments were analysed for the presence of deviant grammatical structures using an earlier version of a linguistic deviance scale (LDS). Schizophrenic speakers produced grammatical deviance at a rate almost three times that of non-schizophrenic patients (.11 deviant utterances per independent clause for schizophrenic speakers versus .045 for non-schizophrenic speakers, t = 2.3, df = 18, p <.02). The rate of disordered language did not correlate with a symptom measure (BPRS). Moreover, when the severity of deviance was compared among the two groups, it was found that the most complex errors involving the organisation of multiple words into a single grammatical structure occurred much more frequently in the schizophrenic group. Six of the eleven schizophrenic speakers produced 17 Class III errors while three of the nine non-schizophrenic patients produced one Class III error each. This preliminary finding supported the hypothesis that had been proposed in the Hoffman and Sledge (1984) study, namely, that schizophrenics demonstrate a unique disruption in the ability to elaborate complex syntactic structures and that this episodic grammatical insufficiency may contribute to the incomprehensibility of some schizophrenic communication.

Study

Hypotheses

For this study we postulated that in the free speech of relatively stable schizophrenics there would be an episodic language production failure that would be characterized by more syntactical rule violations than the comparison groups, more abstract syntactical rule violations would occur in schizophrenic speakers (normal speakers would not make such errors), and these findings would be independent of defects of attention, education and cognitive/abstraction capacity.

Methods

This study utilised and further developed the Hoffman/Sledge Linguistic Deviance Scale (LDS) to measure grammar production defects at the level of the independent clause and to determine if the LDS can be reliably used by a group of trained but non-expert (in mental health and linguistics) native speakers of English.

Subjects

The subjects consisted of three groups: an out-patient, stable schizophrenic group; an out-patient, stable bipolar group; and a comparison group with no known mental illness. The schizophrenic group (n = 48) was drawn randomly from an out-patient population presently receiving active treatment and participating in a research study on the incidence of tardive dyskinesia. There was no effort to include or exclude patients with known thought disorder. The first comparison group of out-patients, many of whom also participated in the incidence study of tardive dyskinesia, had bipolar illness (n = 25) with a history of having been psychotic. The second comparison group (N = 26) was drawn from non-mentally ill volunteers who were roughly matched to the schizophrenic group by age, gender, race and education. Potential subjects with diagnoses or histories of alcoholism, drug addiction, organic brain syndrome and/or neurological disorder were excluded from participation. All subjects were required to be native speakers of English.

Measures

TEST PROCEDURE

Subjects were approached and invited to participate in the language study and offered compensation of $25 per testing session. The interview to elicit a speech sample for the language analysis lasted about 15 minutes and consisted of open-ended questions of a non-psychiatric nature (for example: 'What are your thoughts about politics?'; 'What is your family like?') as well as the response to a picture from the Thematic Apperception Test (TAT). The speech sample of the testing routine was always conducted in the middle of the testing session which took anywhere from 45 to 120 minutes with an average of 65 minutes. The sequential speech sample lasting no more than 20 and no less than 10 minutes was carefully transcribed by personnel trained to reproduce and accurately represent speech errors. These transcriptions were proofed once by the typist and once by a research assistant against the audio recorded speech sample. References (if any) to psychiatric symptoms or psychoactive medications were deleted from the final typescript. The transcriptions did not contain phonological or prosodic information other than the rough spelling of pronounced non-standard words.

LINGUISTIC DEVIANCE SCALE (LDS)

The linguistic analysis is conducted in a manner to: (1) describe the language sample reliably and accurately; and (2) rate the language along the dimensions of grammar minimising the influence of thought content and/or communicative intent.

We anticipated that an analysis of schizophrenic language was at risk of being contaminated by ideational bizarreness. A comprehensive grammar of standard English, moreover, is not available in order to decide issues of grammaticalness in every case. Consequently, a pragmatically based method for detecting grammatical deviance, the linguistic deviance scale (LDS), was designed. The procedure entailed locating deviance and rating it along a dimension of abstractness of rule violation. The application of the LDS proceeded as follows. The rater reads the transcript carefully and identifies areas that might be considered deviant. After identifying areas of possible deviance, the rater subjects the suspect phrasing to 'test-substitutions' whereby the clause or sentence containing the potential deviance is reconsidered in other imagined trial contexts. The trial contexts are unconstrained as to content, in that they may refer to any possible world no matter how unlikely or fantastical. If a context could be discovered whereby the potential deviance of the segment could be grammatically correct, then the difficulty is taken to be of a pragmatic and/or rhetorical nature and is not rated as grammatically deviant. In this way, the bizarreness of the schizophrenic's ideation and discourse failure would be less prejudicial in determining whether an aberrant text is ungrammatical or simply bizarre in context.

While pragmatically based correctability is one exclusionary criterion, a segment is not counted as deviant if the error is due to interruption by another speaker, double starts, false starts, repeated words or phrases, or corrected words or phrases. These events are collectively referred to as dysfluencies. Slang was identified as a separate category.

Non-correctable, non-dysfluent loci are classified as grammatically deviant and are further classified according to severity. An assessment of the 'severity' of deviance is accomplished by examining the alterations required by the segment in order to render it grammatically acceptable as well as plausible within the conversational context of the segment. In general, the more varied and complex the required correction, the higher the severity score.

This method is designed to isolate the level of syntax as much as possible from the other dimensions of semantics, phonology, and discourse. The context rule minimises the influence of meaning and logic and the transcription method minimises the information from phonological and prosodic considerations. This strategy is reasonable to the degree that these levels are, indeed, independent of one another. Obviously, they are not entirely independent, but in our effort to test the hypothesis of the presence of a grammar production disability in schizophrenia, we assume some considerable autonomy of domains of language structure.

The three deviance levels presented here are based on the degree of abstractness of the underlying structural rules violated to produce the deviance. However, the rating itself is highly intuitive.

- *Level I Minimally ungrammatical.* Deviance involves surface level elements and can be readily corrected by inserting, deleting or changing a single word. The great majority of corrections would be changes in a grammatical marker of a word and not the grammatical form of the word. Included but not limited to this category are disagreements of tense, number, voice and auxiliary ending. These deviant 'grammatical tags' mean the utterance is not grammatically correct but the sense of the sentence is clear and unambiguous. Rule-governed slang and non-standard English were not rated at this level. However, slang and non-standard English that are not rule governed are considered deviant speech. In order to make the rating easier and more consistent we treated tense and number disagreements of the verbs 'to be', 'to do' and 'to have', when used as auxiliary verbs, and the subjective ('would') as slang and, therefore, not deviant.

A disagreement of tense is illustrated thus:

(1)   The car <u>has came</u> for you.

This sentence could be corrected to:

(2)   The car came for you.

      or

(3)   The car has come for you.

A disagreement of voice is illustrated by:

(4)   The job was done by <u>we</u>.

This sentence can be corrected to:

(5)   The job was done by us.

A disagreement by number is seen by:

(6)   One of my sister goes to Harvard

Depending on the context possible corrections include:

(7)   One of my <u>sisters</u> goes to Harvard.

or

(8)   One of my sister's friends goes to Harvard.

or

(9)   My sister goes to Harvard.

While (7), (8) and (9) are plausible corrections for (6), only the one consistent with the context would be used.

- *Level II Moderately ungrammatical.* Disagreements are within an intermediate level of abstractness of formatives. That is to say, semantic selectional and syntactical subcategorisation rules are violated so that the phrase structure is ambiguous but it is relatively clear what the speaker intends. There may be several different phrase structure strategies that could be used to understand the sentence. Some of the errors will concern only one word (e.g. (10) a <u>grief</u> ago) and hence will involve semantic selectional rules. Some will be combinatorial and hence will involve syntactical subcategorisational rules such as:

(11)   I'd say early, late twenties or early thirties.

This sentence deletes the noun phrase that forms the subject of the clause fragment 'early, late twenties or early thirties'. A plausible noun phrase (suggested by the context) was 'she is in her' so that the corrected sentence would read:

(12)   I'd say she is in her <u>early, late twenties or early thirties</u>.

The speaker's intentions are reasonably clear but the underlying phrase structure is disrupted by the linguistically deviant deletion of the noun phrase, 'she is in her'.

The correctional strategy may mean changing more than one element or one word. There may be multiple word changes or one word may be substituted for another. Examples are lack of an object for transitive verbs, animate verbs taking inanimate objects (and vice versa), unclear deletion of noun phrases, the use of indefinite quantifiers for definite nouns, etc. It will be clear, however, what the sense of the grammatical unit (clause) is. These are semi-sentences; that is to say, the deep structure kernel(s) can be recovered and clearly stated.

An example of a semantic selectional rule violation is:

(13) I jumped out of <u>my checkbook</u>.

In this example 'jumped out of' when combined with a human subject must take an object (of the prepositional phrase 'out of') that carries a semantic marker of physical place (e.g. 'airplane') or role relationship (e.g. 'marriage').

Another example of a level II violation is the aphorism:

(14) misery loves company.

In this case 'misery' cannot take an animate object, 'company'. This violation is more than a 'grammatical tag' deviance and therefore would qualify for a level II rating. Most metaphors will be rated at level II except in the circumstance where the metaphor has become a 'dead metaphor' or cliché. These are examples of metaphorical constructions that have achieved such widespread usage so as to have lost their metaphorical meaning. An example is the phrase, (15) 'dead metaphor' where the idea of a figure of speech, 'metaphor', is linked with an adjective, 'dead', that usually modifies an animate noun or noun phrase.

- *Level III Highly ungrammatical.* The deep structure is not discernible at the level of the phrase structure (NP-VP) so that the subject, verb and object phrases are unclear. The grammatical unit thereby permits substantially different meanings and is ambiguous at a basic level. The correction then has many different strategies in which at least two have a different subject and/or verb phrase structure from one another and are plausible for the context. Neologisms are one-word examples of this occurrence.

Consider:

(16) colourless green ideas sleep furiously

and

(17) furiously sleep ideas green colour.

Number (16), while enigmatic and metaphorical, is more grammatical than (17). Number (16) would be rated as level II with the problems being at the level of semantic selectional rules ('colourless' modifying a noun with the quality of colour as a semantic marker, 'sleep' requiring an animate subject rather than an abstract noun, etc.). Number (17), on the other hand, is more profoundly unclear and the underlying sense is impossible to fathom. It would be scored as a level III.

The levels of abstractness principle is summarised in the analysis of the well known ambiguous clause, 'the shooting of the hunters was awful' as presented in Figure 32.1. Figure 32.2 depicts the analysis of abstractness by considering the deviant sentence:

(18) The shooting of the hunters were awful.

False starts and broken-off sentences are quite common in conversation and because these paragrammatisms are so common and may not represent matters of linguistic competence, we elected to characterise them separately. Failure to complete (FTC) refers to any start of a grammatical structure and the failure to carry it through to completion. However, such a failure would not be rated deviant if the structure was 'corrected' by a word or phrase correction and then completed. FTCs would be given ratings in addition to the designation 'FTC' which will closely parallel the overall rating system. These are as follows: FTC-1 is used when the sense is clear and there is only one formative or grammatical unit needed to complete the phrase; FTC-2 is used when the sense is clear and a phrase is required to complete the grammatical unit. (There is no rating for FTC-3 since it would be impossible to differentiate failure to complete from other severe grammatical deviance.)

When there is a FTC and a deviant typing present simultaneously in a tensed clause, the deviant typing has priority over the FTC.

Each transcript received a total score for each of the following: a weighted total (level I = 1, level II = 2, level III = 3) computed as the sum of the products of the number of instances of deviance by the level of deviance. The total is then divided by the number of independent clauses to give the weighted deviance score.

An example of the rating procedure is presented by the following 10–line excerpt from the transcript of one of the patients, subject #1, a 43-year-old African-American woman with schizophrenia, in response to the question from the interviewer as to why a list of occupations was chosen to talk about:

Transcript as it appears to the rater

Well I, I like/ what you ma start up with first?/ That nine to f—/OK, doctor and a lawyer, well, both for my helpin' people/ both of them make a lotta money/ me see, ah, both of them dealin' with the public and the, and the church/, ah, children, um, Sunday school's very important to me/ like everyday life is, for children/ it's very important, school/ and then you go to church on Sunday, make sure they get their right spiritual background/ and the preacher part is the people/ that like can't desert away from wall/. That's where the church comes in, right/ 'cause every, well, like you, you're – what are you, a nurse?

Deviance location (underlined sections)

Well I, I like what you ma start up with first? That nine to f—OK, doctor and a lawyer, well, both for my helpin' people, both of them make a lotta money, me see, ah, both of them dealin' with the public and the, and the church, ah, children, um, Sunday school's very important to me, like everyday life is, for children it's very important, school and then you go to church on Sunday, make sure they get their right spiritual background, and the preacher part is the people that like can't desert away from wall. That's where the church comes in, right, 'cause every, well, like you, you're – what are you, a nurse?

Corrections and ratings (deviance underlined, corrections in italics with additions in bold)

Well I, I like – (failure to complete-2)

what you ma start up with first? – *what (do) you **want me** to start up with first* level III

That nine to f – (failure to complete-2)

both for my helpin' people – *both **are** my helping people* – level II me see – *I see* ... – level I

children – (failure to complete-2)

then – *if* level I

the preacher part is the people – *the part of the preacher is important for the people* – level III

like can't desert away from wall – ? – level III

cause every – (failure to complete-2)

It should be noted that an earlier version of the LDS as applied to 20 hospitalised patients was substantially more complex than the version reported here (Hoffman and Sledge 1988).

LDS RATERS

The speech sample raters were four college undergraduates, native speakers of English, who had no prior formal linguistic or clinical experience. Raters were trained by RH and WS in the use of the Linguistic Deviance Scale (LDS) for over 30 hours in the initial version of the instrument. However, when we were not able to achieve acceptable reliability levels as measured by the intra-class R, we simplified the task by modifying the instrument and using only two of the original student raters. The undergraduates still were not able to achieve acceptable levels of agreement. Table 32.1 gives the revised undergraduate effort as well as the ratings by WS and RH who were blind to the subject's identity and diagnosis when the LDS ratings were carried out.

When levels I and II were combined for the investigators, the intraclass R was .68 and for the student raters it was .62. For the location of grammatical deviance, the kappa statistic was used to measure reliability. The kappa for the student agreement was .58 with the Yule weighted kappa for low frequency events being .73. The student ratings of the location of deviance were used by the investigators so that the senior investigators performed only the rating of level and not location of deviance. For the subsequent analyses in this report we will use the senior investigator (WS) ratings.

Table 32.1. Reliability (intraclass R) results with the LDS

Item	Student raters	Investigators
Level I	.68	.13
Level II	.52	.11
Level III	.33	.91
Weighted score	NA	.78

OTHER MEASURES

In addition to the LDS, several measures of attention, language, reasoning and educational attainment were administered. Reported here are the following: Cognitive, measured by WAIS Similarities; and Attention, measured by WAIS-R Digit Span (backward sections) and continuous performance test-auditory version (CTP-A).

Results

Statistical comparisons

DEMOGRAPHICS

The demographic characteristics of the three subject groups are presented in Table 32.2. There are no differences among the three groups along the dimensions of race, gender, age or education.

Table 32.2 Demographic characteristics by diagnostic categories						
	Schizophrenic		*Bipolar*		*Control*	
Gender	n	%	n	%	n	%
male	17	35	8	32	8	31
female	31	65	17	68	18	69
Race						
African-American	18	38	6	24	13	50
White	30	62	19	76	13	50
Age (yrs)	42.3		43.1		39.2	
Education (yrs)	11.5		16.8		13.3	

surface structure level I
  the shooting of the hunters were awful deviant
  the shooting of the hunter <u>was</u> awful corrected

phrase structure level II
  the shooting hunters was awful deviant
  the shooting <u>*of the*</u> hunters was awful corrected
or
  the shooting hunters were awful corrected

clause structure level III
  was the hunters awful of shootings deviant
  <u>the shooting of the hunters was awful</u> corrected
  <u>was the shooting of the hunters awful</u> corrected

deep structure type III
  intentionality and psychological representation (pre-linguistic)

Figure 32.2 Example of levels of abstractness of grammatical rule-governed deviations and appropriate corrections (corrections underlined)

LDS

The LDS values by diagnostic subject group are presented in Table 32.3. Not only do schizophrenic speakers have a greater total weighted LDS on average but the incidence of the most severe grammatical disturbances is higher for the schizophrenic group as well (Table 32.4).

Table 32.3 Linguistic deviance scale results by diagnostic category

| Level | Diagnostic category | | | Statistical tests |
	Schizophrenia	Bipolar	Control	F/p
1	.073 (.05)	.05 (.03)	.06 (.06)	2.18/ns
2	.013 (.018)	.015 (.019)	.009 (.015)	.8/ns
3	.01 (.017)	.003 (.009)	.004 (.01)	3.1/.05
Weighted score	.13 (.09)	.086 (.06)	.088 (.09)	4.67/.012

On the post hoc comparisons (Fisher's PLSD), schizophrenia and bipolar differed for level I (p = .04), there were no differences for level II, and schizophrenia and bipolar differed for level III (p = .03). The incidence of level III errors by patient diagnosis is presented in Table 32.4.

Table 32.4 Level III errors by diagnosis

	Schizophrenia	Bipolar	Control
None	31	22	22
One or more	17	3	4
	35%	12%	15%
chi square = 6.18, df = 2, p < .05			

Examples

In order to understand better the nature of the material that gets a rating of level III, the most disturbed level of grammatical representation, below are samples from the dataset of level III ratings. The 'a' sample is the original with the deviant section underlined and the 'b' sample is the corrected version. **Bold** type indicates added elements.

Subject #7, schizophrenic, Caucasian, 52-year-old man:

1a.　But they always made my birthday a big thing and … <u>one present</u> – and <u>they took</u> me to see Joe DiMaggio play.

1b. But they always made my birthday a big thing and … one present **that they gave me** was they took me to see Joe DiMaggio play.

Subject #38, schizophrenic, Caucasian, 38-year-old woman:

2a. … it's a big one, it's like a trumpet but it's got that round part on it, he plays, <u>he had MASH and God Bless America went uh</u>, he didn't play sports, he played music …

2b. he went to **(lessons)** and **played the theme song of** MASH and God Bless America.

Subject #45, bipolar, Caucasian, 64-year-old woman:

3a. As they say when you older, <u>you have a fall, when you're you fall.</u>

3b. As they say, when you **are** older, **and** you have a fall, you **really have a** fall.

Subject #61, schizophrenic, Caucasian, 38-year-old man:

4a. I like the interaction of the players and their – <u>they work out to their fit</u> and uh, you know, uh.

4b. I like the interaction of the players, **their hard work and their fitness**.

Subject #89, schizophrenic, African-American, 28-year-old man:

5a. I believe that … we'll have wars and rumors of wars … You know, somebody'd shed <u>some light on me</u> about …

5b. I believe that … we'll have wars and rumors of wars … You know, somebody **could** shed some light on **this war business for** me.

Subject #27, 51-year-old African-American man with two years of college and no psychiatric disorder:

6a. her <u>interest to see</u> that we <u>endeavor</u> to get the best that she was trying in any <u>way for</u> us to be special above other people's children.

6b. her interests **were** to see that we **had the opportunity** to get the best that **we could**, she was trying in any way **she could** for us to be special **and** above other people's children.

NEUROPSYCHOLOGICAL TESTS

The salient findings for this paper are summarized in Table 32.5.

LDS AND NEUROPSYCHOLOGICAL TEST INTERACTIONS

In order to determine if the differences between the diagnostic groups could be accounted for by differences in attention, education attainment and abstraction ability, we performed a series of multivariate analyses with the potentially confounding variable loaded in as a predictor variable. For measures of attention we used the WAIS-R digit span backwards scale and the CTP-A; for a measure of educational attainment we used the number of years of formal education; for a measure of abstraction capacity we used the WAIS-R similarities scale. These results are summarised in Table 32.6.

Table 32.5 Selected neuropsychological test results

| Test | Diagnostic group | | | Statistics post hoc comparison | | | |
	Schizophrenia	Bipolar	Control	F/p	svb	svc	bvc
Auditory CPT							
Omissions	2.62 (3.05)	2.00 (3.48)	.37 (.57)	5.83/ <.01		<.01	0.03
WAIS-R							
Digits backwards	4.73 (2.11)	6.04 (2.70)	6.04 (1.73)	4.43/ .01	0.02	0.02	
Similarities scale	6.60 (2.83)	7.76 (3.06)	8.73 (1.51)	5.78/ <.01		<.01	

A detailed presentation of the complete data is planned for later reports.

Table 32.6 Analysis of covariance (ANCOVA) of potentially confounding variables in the relationship between diagnosis and weighted LDS score

Variable	ANCOVA	F	df	p	adjusted R square
	model	4.42	5	0.0012	0.15
	diagnosis effect	4.24	2	0.017	
	effect	11.22	1	0.001	
	diagnosis* CPT	7.41	2	0.001	
scaled score					
	model	4.39	5	0.0012	0.15
	diagnosis	3.9	2	0.023	
	similarities	10.43	1	0.002	
	diagnosis*similarities	3.23	2	0.044	
WAIS-digit span backwards					
	model	3.82	5	0.003	0.13
	diagnosis	3.82	2	0.026	
	digit span backwards	5.05	1	0.027	
	diagnosis*digit span back	2.73	2	0.07	
Education attainment level					
	model	2.24	5	0.06	0.06
	diagnosis	2.4	2	0.1	
	education attainment	0.88	1	0.35	
	diagnosis*education	1.7	2	0.2	

In all instances except for educational attainment level a significant effect of diagnosis remains while controlling for the effect of the possible confounding variable. While the overall model does not remain significantly different in the case of education attainment (indicating that when controlling for education, the diagnosis overall only approaches significance in terms of differences among the three diagnostic groups), the post hoc pairwise comparison indicates that the schizophrenic group continues to be significantly different from the other two comparison groups (p <.04 and .03 for controls and bipolar patients, respectively, Fisher PLSD).

Discussion

Our data indicate that our schizophrenic speakers (stable, out-patients with a chronic history) differ from those who have been diagnosed as bipolar (with a history of psychosis) and a matched (for age, gender and race against the schizophrenic cohort), non-mentally ill comparison group for the production of deviant grammar and in the frequency of production of more deviant speech (type III). This deviance of the schizophrenic speakers is different from the comparison groups only at the level of the most severe disturbance. Furthermore, the disturbance is independent of measures of attention, abstraction and education.

We used a novel rating of linguistic deviance based on the 'abstractness' of the rule violation. However, we were able to achieve suitable reliability only on the most disturbed levels of language production. This finding supports our hypothesis that schizophrenic speakers make more (in both numbers and in quality) deviant utterances than do the speakers in the comparison groups. The fact that the patients are out-patients argues for an effect that is independent of acute psychosis.

However, in contradiction to our hypothesis that schizophrenic speakers would make qualitatively distinct errors we found that normal speakers also made a surprising number of level III errors. Therefore, we did not identify a language disturbance that is unique to schizophrenic speakers. Furthermore, we were not able to achieve a suitable reliability in our linguistic rating instrument for all levels of deviance. This calls into question several aspects of the study that will require further investigation. These are: (a) is our measure a true measure of linguistic disturbance? and (more particularly) abstraction of violated rule; (b) if this is a measure of linguistic disturbance, is this a true failure in linguistic capacity or a failure of linguistic performance only in which some other (as yet unspecified) functional failure interferes with language production?

While the LDS has been a useful means of measuring the language disturbance in schizophrenia, it still lacks several psychometric qualities before it can be of substantial use to others. It has not been possible to get adequate reliability performance of the measure on all levels despite sound reliability on the issue of location of grammatical deviance and the weighted score as well as excellent reliability on the most severely disturbed rating of grammatical failure. Furthermore, the measure has been difficult to teach to those with no linguistic background; therefore, it has not been possible to deploy it as an easy to administer, low cost, accessible clinical test.

Clearly more work needs to done. In subsequent reports of this data we will present the relationships between the LDS and other neuropsychological measures as well as the aphasia screens. We will also plan to develop other categorisation of the patient samples since diagnoses may not be the most salient means of differentiating patients. We have not yet developed the reliable, accessible measure of linguistic capacity that we intended. The next step will be to determine if we can improve our reliability by using raters with formal linguistic training.

In addition to our measurement problem we also need to determine if different states with the same patient are associated with these production failures. In that regard, a further phase (following the establishment of a more reliable instrument) might be a longitudinal study of patients with measures in states of acute psychosis and relative remission. We also would like to test patients who are more homogenous than the present group along symptomatic or other variables of categorising patients such as the negative versus positive symptom distinction and the presence of thought disorder.

The implications for understanding schizophrenia are substantial. If it can be shown that there is a specific language production failure in some or all forms of schizophrenia (our data are inconclusive but suggestive), this would point to the value of pursuing a language-oriented approach to conceptualising schizophrenia. If, on the other hand, we can demonstrate clearly that the language generation competence is basically intact, other approaches can be followed (Frith and Done 1988).

Not only would such data enhance our understanding of schizophrenia but it would also suggest possible new directions for the study of the neurobiology of language competence.

Conclusion

These results support the hypothesis that schizophrenic speakers have a disorder that fundamentally interferes with language-generating capacity, particularly in the realm of the production of grammatically correct sentences. However, the results are not conclusive. More research is necessary to clarify this issue. Such work might take an experimental approach which would then be able to systematically explore the linguistic capacity of schizophrenic speakers. The issues to be determined are: (1) Is there a diminished linguistic capacity in schizophrenia? (2) What are the correlates of such a diminished capacity?

Acknowledgement

Supported by NIMH award RO3–MH47023 to William H. Sledge.

References

Anand, A. (1992) Language and Thought Disorder in First Admission Psychotic Patients. Monash University. Thesis for the Master of Psychological Medicine.

Andreason, N. (1979) Thought, Language, and Communication Disorders: II. Diagnostic Significance. *Archives of General Psychiatry 136*, 1325–1330.

Andreason, N. (1982) Should the term 'thought disorder' be revised? *Comprehensive Psychiatry 23*, 291–299.

Andreason, N.C. and Grove, W. (1979) The relationship between schizophrenic language, manic language, and aphasia. In J. Gruzelier and P. Flor-Henry (eds) *Hemisphere Asymmetries of Function in Psychopathology*. Amsterdam: Elsevier/North Holland Biomedical Press. pp.373–390.

Bleuler, E. (1909/1950) *Dementia Praecox or the Group of Schizophrenias*. New York: International Universities Press.

Bresnan, J. (1978) A realistic transformational grammar. *Linguistic Theory and Psychological Reality*. Cambridge: MIT Press.

Carpenter, M. (1976) Sensitivity to syntactic structure, good vs. poor pre-morbid schizophrenics. *Journal of Abnormal Psychology 85*, 41–50.

Chaika, E. (1990) *Understanding Psychotic Speech: Beyond Freud and Chomsky*. Springfield, Illinois: Charles C Thomas.

Chapman, L., Chapman, J. and Miller, G. (1977) A theory of verbal behavior in schizophrenia. *Contributions to the Psychopathology of Schizophrenia*. New York: Academic Press. pp.135–167.

Chomsky, N. (1964) Degrees of Grammaticalness. In J. Fodor and J. Katz (eds) *The Structure of Language, Readings in the Philosophy of Language*. Englewood Cliffs, NJ: Prentice-Hall.

Chomsky, N. (1965) *Aspects of the Theory of Syntax*. Cambridge, MA: MIT Press.

Critchley, M. (1964) The neurology of psychotic speech. *British Journal of Psychiatry 110*, 353–364.

Fairbanks, H. (1944) The quantitative differentiation of samples of spoken language. *Psychological Monographs 56*, 19–38.

Feinberg, I. (1978) Efference copy and collary discharge: implications for thinking and its disorders. *Schizophrenia Bulletin 4*, 636–640.

Fodor, J.A. and Bever, T.G. (1965) The psychological reality of linguistic segments. *Journal of Verbal Learning and Verbal Behavior 4*, 414–420.

Freud, S. (ed) (1915) The Unconscious. *Standard Edition of the Complete Psychological Works of Sigmund Freud*. London: Hogarth Press.

Frith, C.D. and Allen, H.A. (1988) Language disorders in schizophrenia and their implications for neuropsychology. In P. Bebbington and P. McGuffin (eds) *Schizophrenia, The Major Issues*. Oxford: Heinemann. pp.173–186.

Frith, C.D. and Done, D.J. (1988) Towards a neuropsychology of schizophrenia. *The British Journal of Psychiatry 153*, 437–443.

Fromkin, V. (1975) A linguist looks at 'A linguist looks at "schizophrenic" language.' *Brain and Language 2*, 498–503.

Gerver, D. (1967) Linguistic rules and the perception and recall of speech by schizophrenic patients. *British Journal of Social and Clinical Psychology 6*, 204–211.

Goldberg, T., Gold, J. and Braff, D. (1991) Neuropsychological functioning and time linked information processing in schizophrenia. *Annual Review of Psychiatry*. Washington, DC: American Psychiatric Association Press.

Goodglass, H. (1983) Linguistic aspects of aphasia. *Trends in Neuroscience 9*, 241–243.

Gottshalk, L. and Glaser, G. (1966) *The Measurement of Psychological States Through The Content Analysis of Verbal Behavior*. Berkeley: University of California Press.

Harrow, M. and Quinlan, D.M. (1985) *Disordered Thinking and Schizophrenic Psychopathology*. New York: Gardner Press.

Hoffman, R. and Sledge, W. (1984) Microgenetic model of paragrammatisms produced by a schizophrenic speaker. *Brain and Language 21*, 147–173.

Hoffman, R. and Sledge, W. (1988) An analysis of grammatical deviance occurring in spontaneous schizophrenic speech. *Journal of Neurolinguistics 3*, 89–101.

Hoffman, R., Stopeck, S. and Andreason, N. (1986) A comparative study of manic vs schizophrenic speech disorganization. *Archives of General Psychiatry 43*, 831–838.

King, K., Fraser, W.I., Thomas, P. and Kendell, R.E. (1990) Re-examination of the language of psychotic subjects. *British Journal of Psychiatry 156*, 211–215.

Kleist, K. (1960) Schizophrenic symptoms and cerebral pathology. *Journal of Mental Science 106*, 246–255.

Kraepelin, E. (1919) *Dementia Praecox and Paraphrenia* (trans. by R.M. Barclay). Edinburgh: E&S Livingstone.

Labov, W. and Fanshel, D. (1977) *Therapeutic Discourse, Psychotherapy as Conversation*. New York: Academic Press.

Lawson, J., McGhie, A. and Chapman, J. (1964): Perception of speech schizophrenia. *British Journal of Psychiatry 110*, 375–380.

Lenneberge, E.H. (1967) *The Biological Foundations of Language*. New York: John Wiley.

Lesser, R. (1989) *Linguistic Investigations of Aphasia* (second edition). London: Whurr.

Levy, R. and Maxwell, A. (1968) The effect of verbal context on the recall of schizophrenics and other psychiatric patients. *British Journal of Psychiatry 114*, 311–316.

Lyons, J. (1970) *Chomsky*. London: William Collins.

Maher, B. (1983) A tentative theory of schizophrenic utterance. *Progress in Experimental Personality Research 12*, 1–50.

Mann, M. (1944) The quantitative differentiation of samples of written language. *Psychological Monographs 56*, 41–74.

Michels, R. and Marzuk, P. (1993) Progress in psychiatry (Part One). *New England Journal of Medicine 329*, 552–560.

Miller, W.K. and Phelan, J.G. (1980) Comparison of adult schizophrenics with matched normal native speakers of English as to 'acceptability' of English sentences. *Journal of Psycholinguistic Research 9*, 579–593.

Morice, R. (1990) Cognitive inflexibility and pre-frontal dysfunction in schizophrenia and mania. *British Journal of Psychiatry 157*, 50–54.

Morice, R.D. and Ingram, J.C. (1982) Language analysis in schizophrenia: diagnostic implications. *Australian and New Zealand Journal of Psychiatry 16*, 11–21.

Pylyshyn, Z.W. (1970) Clinical correlates of some syntactic features of patients' speech. *Journal of Nervous and Mental Disease 150*, 307–316.

Reilly, F., Harrow, M. and Tucker, G. (1973) Language and thought content in acute psychosis. *American Journal of Psychiatry 130*, 411–417.

Rochester, S., Harris, J. and Seeman, M. (1973) Sentence processing in schizophrenic listeners. *Journal of Abnormal Psychology 82*, 350–356.

Rochester, S. and Martin, J. (1979) *Crazy Talk, A study of the discourse of schizophrenic speakers*. New York: Plenum Press.

Rose, C., Whurr, R. and Wyke, M.A. (ed) (1988) *Aphasia*. London: Whurr.

Rosen, V. (1977) Schizophrenic language disturbance. In S. Atkin and M.F. Jucovy (eds) *Style, Character, and Language*. New York: Jason Aronson. pp.151–169.

Rosenberg, S.D. and Tucker, G.J. (1979) Verbal behavior and schizophrenia. *Archives of General Psychiatry 36*, 1331–1337.

Rutter, D., Wishner, J. and Callaghan, B.A. (1975) The prediction and predictability of speech in schizophrenia. *British Journal of Psychiatry 126*, 571–576.

Salzinger, K., Portnoy, S. and Feldman, R.S. (1964) Verbal behavior of schizophrenic and normal subjects. *Annals of the New York Academy of Sciences 105*, 845–860.

Satel, S. and Sledge, W. (1989) Audiotape playback as a technique in the treatment of schizophrenic patients. *American Journal of Psychiatry 146*, 1012–1016.

Schneider, K. (1959) *Clinical Psychopathology* (trans. by M.W. Hamilton). New York: Grune and Stratton.

Schwartz, S. (1982) Is there a schizophrenic language? *The Behavioral and Brain Sciences 5*, 579–626.

Spitzer, M. (1993) The psychopathology, neuropsychology, and neurobiology of associative and working memory in schizophrenia. Ruprecht-Karls-Universitaet Heidelberg, Psychiatrische Klinik. Technical Report 1/93.

Spitzer, M., Braun, U. and Maier, S. (1993). Associative semantic network pathology in thought disordered schizophrenic patients: direct evidence from indirect semantic priming. Ruprecht-Karls-Universitaet Heidelberg Psychiatrische Klinik. Technical Report 4/93.

Straube, E. (1979) Do schizophrenics use linguistic rules in speech recall? *British Journal of Social and Clinical Psychology 18*, 407–415.

Truscott, I.P. (1970) Contextual constraint and schizophrenic language. *Journal of Consulting and Clinical Psychology 35*, 189–194.

Tucker, G. and Rosenberg, S. (1975) Computer content analysis of schizophrenic speech: a preliminary report. *American Journal of Psychiatry 132*, 611–616.

CHAPTER 33

Discourse Analysis in Psychiatry

Ian Thompson

Introduction

People with dementia and psychosis have impaired conversations that relate to their cognitive decline and to deranged thinking. One method of investigating these conversations, which are functional and contextual communications, is discourse analysis. The examination of cohesion in discourse investigates the internal structure of text to determine how effectively topic and theme are generated and maintained. The purpose of this chapter is to discuss these issues and outline a system of analysis that has therapeutic relevance to speech and language therapists for the management of the mentally ill.

The last decade has seen the development of concepts of communication breakdown in cognitive disorders as the dementias and more recently speech and language therapists are beginning to consider their role in the diagnosis and management of psychotic disorders. Much of this interest has risen from psychiatry itself. Crow (1997) has provided a stimulating argument that since both language and schizophrenia are universal they may have a common evolutionary origin. David (1994) has used the model of cognitive neuropsychology that is the basis of the Psycholinguistic Assessment of Language Processing in Aphasia (Kay, Lesser and Coltheart 1992) to interpret hallucinatory behaviour. There is renewed interest in the concepts of inner or subvocal speech in psychosis that centres on Broca's area (McGuire, Shar and Murray 1993). Andreason (1979) has recast the concept of thought disorder into linguistic terms that are the basis of the DSM-IV. McGrath (1991, 1998) has argued that the lack of planning and monitoring of the language of thought disorder is an area that may be addressed from the techniques provided by speech therapy. The role of linguistics in psychiatry has been championed by the work of Thomas and Fraser (1994) and Thomas (1997). They have discussed the nature of communication and psychotic behaviour as a behavioural, economic and social paradigm rather than a medical-biological model. The thrust of many of these trends has been presented in *Communication and the Mentally Ill Patient* (France and Muir 1997), the product of the Leeds Psychopathology Symposium that emphasised the contribution of linguistics to psychiatry.

The challenge of psychiatry to speech and language therapists is the shift from the language of aphasia and dementia as a neurolinguistic construct to a psycholinguistic one, of the relationship of language to the mind and, as a pragmatic construct, about the effectiveness of the use of language in natural settings. Thompson and Copolov (1998) compared the psycholinguistic processing of language variables that are represented in the phonological loop in people with hallucinating and non-hallucinating schizophrenia compared to normal controls, matched for age, gender and education. Both patient groups differed from control groups on tasks that required abstract processing and reasoning and demonstrated a dissociation between knowledge and executive function. However, it was effectiveness of discourse that differentiated the two psychotic groups.

Conversations in neuropsychiatry are marred by communication disorder. While the vehicle of communication is speech and both verbal and non-verbal language, it is often pragmatics, the psychocognitive contexts beyond sentence level, that fracture communication in dementia and psychosis.

Conversations and discourse are rule-governed to a surprising complexity, from the speech act functions that include greeting, acknowledging, responding, requesting and initiating of ideas to the patterning and interplay of phonology, semantics and syntax as language. Paralinguistic variables also contribute to language acts, like proxemics, gaze, intonation and gesture that enhance and may indeed carry more information in communication than what is actually said. Pragmatically the speaker must plan conversation and be aware that the listener's knowledge of context will make discourse understandable; if it is not understood then language must be repaired so that the purpose of communication is met.

Discourse as text must exist in the context of a speaker–listener relationship, and it must exist in an environment that gives it relevance. A text 'is language that is functional. By functional we mean language that is doing some job in context. Any instance of living language that is playing some part in a context of situation, we shall call a text' (Halliday and Hassan 1980, p.8).

The maxims of Grice (1975) should be maintained in discourse. Discourse needs to conform to co-operative speaker roles, such that information should be adequate, truthful, orderly and relevant to topic. Schizophrenic and demented discourse can violate these maxims with such force that the speech of schizophrenia has been considered the product of deranged thinking.

The fathers of modern psychiatry, Kraeplin, Bleuler and Schneider, all regarded thought disorder as important to the central diagnosis of schizophrenia. Increasingly, thought disorder has been reviewed in linguistic terms. There are several reason for this. Thomas (1995) observed that, tautologically, we can only infer thought disorder from what people say, and if speech is disordered we infer that thought is disordered. Andreason (1979) has described positive symptoms in schizophrenia, including formal thought disorder. She defined formal thought disorder in terms of descriptors that are clearly linguistic. The descriptors classify communication disorder, language disorder and thought disorder (Table 33.1).

Table 33.1 The classification of thought, language and communication disorders in schizophrenia (after Andreason 1979)

DISORGANISED LANGUAGE

COMMUNICATION DISORDER

POVERTY OF CONTENTS OF SPEECH

    Speech may be of appropriate length, but vague and empty philosophising.

PRESSURE OF SPEECH

    Increased amount of rapid spontaneous speech that is difficult to interrupt.

DISTRACTIBLE SPEECH

    Topic changes midway through conversation in response to external stimulus.

TANGENTIALITY

    Answers are obliquely related to questions and not transitions of discourse.

DERAILMENT

    Loose associations, ideas slip to unrelated topics, disjointed speech.

STILTED SPEECH

    Formal quality about speech, quaintly polite, pedantic and pompous speech.

ECHOLALIA

    Echoing the speaker, often with mocking intonation.

SELF-REFERENCE

    Referring of neutral subjects back to himself or herself.

CIRCUMSTANTIALITY

    Long-winded speech, tedious in detail, parenthetical and difficult to interrupt.

LOSS OF GOAL

    Failure to follow a chain of thought to its conclusion.

PERSEVERATION

    Persistent repetition of, and returning to, words, ideas and topics.

BLOCKING

    Loss of thought in discourse, pauses and failure to recall topic.

LANGUAGE DISORDER

INCOHERENCE

    Incomprehensible speech, loss/substitution of word meaning, distorted theme.

CLANGING

    Homophones, rhyming, punning, similar sounds bring new thoughts in speech.

NEOLOGISMS

    Created words and phrases.

WORD APPROXIMATIONS

    Paraphysis and unconventional use of words.

THOUGHT DISORDER

POVERTY OF SPEECH

    Thought seems not to occur, speech reduction, monosyllabic, needs prompting.

ILLOGICALITY

    Speech does not follow, non-sequiturial.

Conversational and discourse analysis

Andreason also described negative symptoms in schizophrenia including alogia and blunting. Alogia is in part poverty of speech and speech content, the blocking of thought and increased latency of response. Blunting affects the paralinguistic behaviours that enhance speech, a loss of facial affect, a paucity of gesture, lack of vocal inflection and gaze avoidance.

Since conversation is concerned with the collaborative achievement of communication where success is a responsibility of both interlocutors, success involves initiation of topic, its management and generation of theme. Turn-taking, repair, cueing and requesting more information assist and enhance meaning, as do behaviours that open and close interactions. People with negative symptoms tend not to initiate or generate themes in their discourse in a manner not dissimilar to people with transcortical motor aphasia. Thomas *et al.* (1996) have demonstrated the reduced syntactic complexity in the speech of patients with negative symptomatology. Here is a conversation opened by a therapist with a patient with poverty of speech:

Alfred, what are you doing here?
Waiting to be put on, I forget the name of the medicine.

What is it all about?
Schizophrenia.

Tell me about it.
Suffered from it for the last three years.

What happens?
There is nothing much to tell.

Where are you from?
Austria.

How long have you been out here?
Twenty-five years.

Which part of Austria?
Vienna.

Have you ever been back?
No.

Tell me about yourself.
Nothing much to say.

Tell me about this place.
It's boring.

What happens?
Nothing, going to the swimming pool.

Where is the pool?
I don't know.

Tell me about yourself.
Nothing much to say.

Where did you live before Melbourne?
Victoria and Queensland.

How come you moved around?
My mother had a skivvying job. She never stayed in one place, she moved.

And you?
I moved with her.

What about school?
I used to wag school.

What school?
Primary School in St Kilda.

Tell me about St Kilda.
It's nothing much, just a school, I never go to school much, never liked school.

How old are you?
Twenty-eight.

What have you been doing since school?
Working and unemployed.

Tell me about your work.
I was working in restaurants. I was working as a kitchen hand, washing dishes.

What did you think of that?
Not much.

What's the food like here?
Pretty good.

What do you do on a typical day?
Play pool, watch TV, go to bed, lay down on the bed, go swimming.

Got any pals?
No, only one, don't know his name.

Is he here?
Yes.

Were you living in St Kilda before you came here?
I was living in Elwood.

Got any pals in Elwood?
Yes, one, two actually.

Do you see much of them?
Yes.

Are you going swimming this afternoon, and is the pool here, or do you go somewhere else?
Yes. Somewhere else.

While Andreasen's descriptors may define thought-disordered language, discourse analysis is able to provide it with a qualitative and quantitative index. Traditional grammatical analysis worked at the level of the sentence – discourse analysis defines the 'text' itself as a unit of information. The text is initiated, developed and concluded and needs to be contextual with what has preceded it, what may follow, and it must also have internal unity.

In psychiatric language these principles are useful, for when text fails it fails at the level of the relationship of clauses within the sentence, producing incoherence, from sentence to sentence, producing derailment, or topic maintenance, producing circumstantial conversation without apparent goal.

Internal unity derives from its structure. A major factor in coherence is cohesion, or the way the text 'hangs together'. Cohesion within text is maintained by words as devices that may be lexical or grammatical. Lexical devices include repetition, and the use of synonyms, antonyms or meronyms, the referring of parts to a whole. Grammatical devices include pronominalisation, demonstratives, comparatives, the use of articles, and the use of substitution and ellipsis.

Words relate to each other within the text to form cohesive ties. Many words are highly related to the text, but many can be peripheral to the text, and clearly the greater number of relevant words in the text the more cohesive or tightly wired it should read. A high number of peripheral words leads to verbiage and a listener's difficulty following discourse. This behaviour appears common to patients with fronto-orbital traumatic brain injury and thought disordered schizophrenia. This has led to speculation of the role of the medial frontal areas in thought disorder and the dorso-lateral areas in negative symptoms and poverty of speech and speech content (McGrath 1991).

Here is an example of the discourse of a 51-year-old male with a bilateral haematoma following a fall asked to talk about dreams and dreaming, and then describe the Cookie Theft picture from the Boston Diagnostic Examination for Aphasia (Goodglass and Kaplan 1963). The man is tangential in addressing the task, he is pressured of speech, he does not monitor topics, and his discourse contains a disproportionate number of peripheral words. The picture description is less than normally cohesive, and circumstantial.

Monologue (227 words in 90 seconds)

Dreaming is basically a subject which I don't have a lot of experience with but I have had a dream of recent times which is really related to getting out of this place and getting out of this place that really relates more than anything to the attitude of the people. I have basically had some experiences in here that have really sort of in fact bugged me the wrong way and got me to the stage where I have literally been at the stage where I have considered that I don't believe anything that I dream any more because really everything has got a purpose and for instance you can say to me that all this work is quite satisfactory and I believe you when I see the results. Now to say what I am saying is that I can basically mean what I am saying and in terms of not meaning what I say I basically would only be the one that really would know what would be the basis of what I am saying. There all of this stuff like this is all very well and good and would pay a big part in your assessment of me and would probably play a big part in my assessment of you and we might even use some of this material later on for other assessments.

Cookie theft (129 words)

Well, the girl actually is still oblivious to the scenery that's on behind her and that is the water on the floor underneath her feet. And the reason the water is underneath her feet is because she's oblivious to what's happening behind her. And that really is basically the first thing that is going to happen. The kid raided the Cookie Jar and basically uses the steps as a raiding device. He is about to fall, he is going to fall and crack his head on the bench when he gets down that jar. She's going to turn round and she's going to slip over. That's the secondary reason the thing is not right because she should really have hearing aids on or something similar because that's what she needs.

Within text, words form semantic 'chains', or clusters of words that are related to other chains in the text. This produces internal relevance, or 'cohesive harmony' and describes what is happening in the text, who is taking part in the text, and the speaker's purpose for producing the text. The cohesive harmony of the text is determined by how many, and how closely, these chains interact with each other. Again, the more referents that interact, the denser the cohesiveness of text.

Cohesive ties, then, are lexico-grammatical words that act as devices to give internal structure, harmony, and texture to a text.

Armstrong (1987) has outlined the steps in a cohesion analysis:

1.   The text is transcribed.

2.   It is then transcribed into clauses.

3.   It is then lexically rendered, or stripped to only those words (that are now called 'tokens') that have lexical and grammatical significance. The sum of these words is called the Total Tokens of the text.

4.   These tokens are then entered into chains, or groups of words that are semantically related by reference and classification. The tokens entering the chains are called Relevant Tokens, and those that do not are Peripheral Tokens.

5.   Since the purpose of the analysis is to see how these relevant tokens interact, then at least two of the words in a chain must have the same semantic relationship with at least two words in another chain lexicographically, as, for example, actor–action, actor–person/object, attribute–attruband. There must be two words per chain, otherwise every word would be responsible for coherence, with no difference of chain formation and interaction, and all words in a chain would interact with another word in another chain (Halliday and Hassan 1980; Hassan 1984).

6.   It is possible to give a score to the interaction by dividing those tokens in one chain that relate to tokens in another chain (these are called Chained Tokens) by the Total Tokens and multiplying by one hundred to turn it into a percentage. This score is called a Cohesion Harmony Index: 50 per cent is necessary for a text to be perceived as coherent (Hassan 1984; Armstrong 1997).

Discourse analysis and pychosis

The procedure has value in the examination of psychiatric discourse for three reasons. First, a normal speaker may only state half of what they want to convey – the other half is assumed by the listener's world knowledge of the topic in context. People with schizophrenia are not effective at taking the listener's perspective in conversations (Rochester, Martin and Thurston 1977). Second, logorrhea is more likely to create a proportion of irrelevant tokens that can lead to loss of cohesion. Thus the speaker needs to heed planning, editing and monitoring of discourse to meet the maxim of adequacy. People with thought disordered schizophrenia are poor at editing their discourse (McGrath 1991). Third, the fewer breaks in the picture of interaction, or the fewer aberrant linguistic descriptors as described by Andreason, the more coherent will be the text. Thus the text must conform to the maxims of orderliness and relevance.

Consider a cohesion analysis of the stimulus picture from *An Aphasia Screening Test* (Whurr 1974) below, and a cohesion analysis of it following these steps:

The text:

It's a picture of people getting ready to go on holiday. The mother is packing a suitcase inside, while outside a man is carrying suitcases to a car which has been moved out of a garage. On the way to the car he is passing a girl holding beach toys, a bucket, ball and spade, which makes me think they might be going to a beach for a holiday:

The text is rendered to clauses:

1. It's a picture
2. of people getting ready to go on holiday.
3. The mother is packing a suitcase inside
4. while outside a man is carrying suitcases to a car
5. which has been moved out of a garage.
6. On the way to the car he is passing a girl
7. holding beach toys, a bucket, ball and spade
8. which makes me think
9. they might be going to a beach for a holiday.

Lexical rendering to 32 Total Tokens (the verb 'to be' is not counted):

1. be picture
2. people (get ready to go) holiday
3. mother pack suitcase inside
4. outside man carry suitcase to car
5. car (moved out of) garage
6. (on way to) car man pass girl

7. girl hold beach toys

8. I think

9. people go beach holiday

Referential chains of 20 Relevant Tokens, leaving 15 of the Total Tokens Peripheral to the text. There are 15 Chained Tokens, in bold type, that interact:

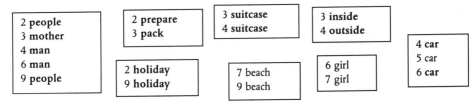

The Cohesive Harmony Index (CHI) is Chained Tokens divided by Total Tokens or 15/32 x 100 = 47%.

Here are four texts of RD, a man with a diagnosis of thought disordered schizophrenia. RD was a 38-year-old Caucasian male with a long history of schizophrenia and eleven admissions to hospital over the preceding ten years. He came from a professional Jewish family and his mother died of a stroke when RD was 16. RD held a combined degree in Arts/Commerce. Neuropsychological assessment described him as a man of above average intelligence with a Verbal IQ of 114 and Performance IQ of 82 related to high order visuospatial deficits. When the first text was taped RD had just commenced a course of the antipsychotic Clozapine at 150 mg nocte. This series of texts is an example of the use of discourse analysis in tracking the history of the disease and an objective measure of the effects of pharmacological therapy.

RD was asked to tell the therapist what was happening in the Whurr picture:

> I see her world has fallen apart, and people don't know it and they are not co-operating and they are probably about to sell the car. She's being her usual self, she wants to run away, and that's all of that, you want to have a stroke, and that's me wondering if my mother ever knew anything about the fact that I could die at her hands because she held the shovel and I held the sword.

The text is clearly thought disordered and some of the descriptors of Andreason are recognisable in this discourse. The opening is *tangential* and the following text *derailed* and the conclusion is *self-referenced*. The result is lack of coherent theme.

One month later RD was again asked to describe the picture the Clozapine dosage was 350 mg nocte. RD perceived the woman in the picture washing rather than packing (the picture is not coloured):

> It's brightly coloured today, isn't it? It seems to be brightly coloured. The woman seems to be sort of wiping up a splash, and there are brushes there. She seems to have forgotten her handbag and the envelopes, but she will notice them eventually. People don't like her very much and they are probably running away from him trying to consent to something. The car is there waiting to be used and the garage is empty. I

don't like talking about women but she seems to be trying to construct something of a happiness for herself.

Again Andreason's descriptors of disorganised speech are evident. The opening is *tangential*, 'splash' is a *paraphasia*, the text is *circumstantial* and again the last sentence is *self-referential*.

A month later, RD volunteered the following conversation after the nurses on the ward round thought he was becoming self-preoccupied. The Clozapine dosage was 450 mg nocte:

Therapist: What have you got to say to me today RD?

RD: Why aren't I forthright with my conversations? What does [the Consultant] comment on my silence? You know, people in India have not spoken for forty years.

Therapist: Is it important what the Consultant thinks of your silences?

RD: He's in charge of me. I like to relate to him, but I don't know very well why he, I don't know, he seems to see me as a comical-historical being. I don't know. I never understand his commands, he sees me as another patient. I don't know how he fits in with me fitting into any of it. As soon as I see him I go gaga. I know it. The same thing happened to me years ago. I told the psychiatrist I was sick of the whole lot of them and they didn't listen. Do you think I have a language disorder?

Again RD *derailed* the conversation, although the therapist was able to shape the conversation back to theme, and there is an element of *stiltedness* in the text. The last sentence is a reference to knowing the therapist was a speech pathologist. The text is heavily reliant on identity chains, or chains that refer to people: 22 out of 28 Relevant Tokens refer to RD or the consultant. The nursing staff interpreted this as preoccupied behaviour.

Four months after first being seen by the therapist, RD was to be discharged back into the community. The Clozapine dosage had increased 500 mg nocte (the maximum dosage of Clozapine is 900 mg daily). The therapist asked where he would go to live:

RD: It's interesting, the friends I will probably move in with eventually. I have got friends who might stay with me occasionally because things seem to be clarified. It's a question of how things relate to clarity, rather than the arrangements, I think.

Therapist: When did you last see those friends?

RD: A week ago, some, one of them, were rather terrified of the fact that I was perhaps mad, and I said 'Oh, are you?', I got good friends.

Therapist: What would you think about moving into the community?

RD: That raises the question of what I will do with myself. I think I'll travel, so I probably won't be in the community that long. I am pretty ambivalent about what sort of work I would like to do, because I think I see a lot of things very differently from how I used to imagine myself seeing things. It's actually a very difficult thing to do, it's like having a lover when you are not having a lover, you know.

Therapist: Really?

Needless to say some of the text was spoken with a wry smile on the faces of both participants, and RD also could see the humour in his interaction with friends. It was also clear that, although somewhat *stilted* at times, RD's conversation was no longer so obviously thought disordered. The text, being dyadic, could be more given to a conversational analysis.

Discourse analysis and dementia

The language of degenerative dementias, such as Alzheimer's disease, has emphasised the preservation of phonology and syntax at the expense of semantics and discourse formulation (Thompson 1987; Chenery 1990). Impairment of discourse in dementia may indicate a pre-linguistic planning capacity.

MT was a woman with a diagnosis of probable Alzheimer's disease. She was mild to moderately impaired using a standardised rating scale (Thompson 1987). Neurolinguistic abilities were reduced in a pattern concomitant to the degree of dementia with impaired comprehension, audio-verbal memory, naming, calculation and constructional praxis. The ability to complete common neuropsychological tests, the Coloured Matrices and Block Design, was also reduced. She was able to complete sentence construction tasks and there was no evidence of a phonological deficit.

MT was asked to tell the therapist what was happening in the Whurr picture:

There are suitcases there, and someone might be going away. A handbag, going shopping. Father is going to wash the car, I hope. There is a knife and envelopes. Mother is packing, the purse, a brush is there, a pin with things on, a spade and going down to the beach. There is a gate open there.

The text is difficult to parse and lexically render, the only elements of theme being 'pack', 'mother' and 'beach' but none of the words enter into a chain. Most of the relevant tokens consist of items and the peripheral tokens of irrelevancies, in the face of a preserved ability to construct sentences.

Free speech may make less of a cognitive demand than describing thematic pictures. Nevertheless, in free speech an individual must initiate, maintain relevance and continuity, conclude the topic, or hand it over to the interlocutor.

Here is the conversation of a 57-year-old woman, CR, with a probable diagnosis of Alzheimer's disease, again mild to moderately demented, and with the familiar patterns of impaired comprehension and auditory memory, but she was not dysnomic:

Therapist: Were you in the war?

CR: Yes I was.

Therapist: What did you do in the war?

CR: I was an inspectress.

Therapist: What did you have to do?

CR: Oh – just check everything that was going on there. I went through training at – em – eh – oh – oh – isn't that annoying. No, it's gone, but I've got something to think about now.

Therapist: What sort of things were you an inspectress of?

CR: Guns, small pieces and things like that, but I still had to, and when I did this, and I was quite pleased, bashing, and then I saw this, that's fine. But many a night I had to do it again because I've been too tired.

Therapist: What did you have to do again?

CR: Well this thing, you have to clean it all, that material that you're working on, even the, when you're in the living room. I keep saying living room, this keeps bugging me, this. Where was I? I got this started.

Therapist: What you were doing in the war.

CR: I know, I just, rather got lost, missed that, even the bombing and things like that. It wasn't very pleasant. Everybody was underneath the table. It's the main room. Its one of these things, you know when you've got company coming, you strip everything off, put the white cover, you know for the table cloth, for the table. I thoroughly enjoyed it, and then suddenly, this wee things coming up.

The cohesive harmony in this text is low, there is poor cohesion and poor coherence. There are pronouns without referents, incomplete clauses and the chains that are formed are weak. The result is that the text is heavily personally referenced but otherwise the chains tell you only that she was an inspector of guns and something else, but little other information. There is no thematic structure apart from 'war' at the beginning and the text is derailed by 'living room'. This is an intrusion error and not uncommon in Alzheimer Type Dementia. The therapist reintroduced the theme of war which is picked up and lost, probably with bombing and taking shelter under the table, and then CR reintroduced the living room theme. The third response from CR is an evasion used to attempt to close the conversation since she was, like many people with mild to moderate dementia, aware of her deficits but unable to repair them.

The language of Alzheimer Type Dementia and of lesions to the posterior area of the Angular Gyrus may be confused. People with Angular Gyrus Syndrome are aware of their language deficits and they make paraphasic errors in the area of the target word, while people with Alzheimer's disease are less aware of their language errors and their paraphasias are progressively less related to target words (Benson, Cummings and Tsai 1982).

This is a text from a hospitalised woman with a temporo-parietal lesion telling a therapist about a conversation with a woman in an adjacent bed. The woman strives to ensure that the therapist understands her and, at the end of text, comments that she is concerned about her dysphasia. To ensure topic her text is densely referenced on 'music' and 'family' and 'I', and most of her relevant tokens enter into chains:

She talked to me all about her. Everything I know about is her sister, who is a pianist, and knows all about music, and has music pupils. We done all that. I had a great old chat with her, now if I say I want from her, she's a music teacher, she's absolutely wonderful, knows all about that sort of thing. So he's about 14 or 15 now. That's her son you see. You see he's in the music. You see I know all that, so what am I going to do now? I really look, and this worries me.

The next text is semantic aphasia. The text was sent to a colleague who, out of context, could see no cohesion in the text at all. The text is a description of the Cookie Theft picture; the therapist was aware of many of the referents that had been communicated through deixis. When this was taken into account the text is cohesive. The point to be made is that in linguistic examination of text, meaning is a function of context, and discourse samples should, if possible, be videotaped:

> That was that girl wasn't she fell, didn't she? That girl, they helped, but the other girl was all right, though she wash, wasn't she, wash it up. But this one's broken, isn't it? The girl managed all right but she fell in that thing there. That's good because she has got to clean all that, hasn't she, it's all dirty, it's all dirty that, it's everybody, that's fixing it all up. Yes, that's coming good, that's not good, but these are good. They are washing in the centre. They are helping but they can't help that boy, they can help those boys but they can't help the other boy, but here all these, they are all good there. I don't like that there, but it's good, wasn't it? Was it good?

Finally, analysis of textual cohesion may be diagnostic. In 1995 Ronald Reagan publicly announced that he had Alzheimer's Disease. However, in 1990 he was interviewed by Clive James on the BBC and reported in the London *Sunday Observer*. The journalist, John Naughton, was aware enough to comment of Reagan's speech: 'Excuse the grammar, dear reader, but this is the way the man talks.' Cohesion analysis demonstrates the speech reveals something more sinister than an old man's ramblings – it has that same lack of pre-linguistic planning seen in the conversations of people with dementia.

James: Let me ask you about the period after the war, when you were President of the Screen Actors Guild. How serious was the threat of Communist subversion in Hollywood?

Reagan: It was very serious, and there were very few people understood or took seriously at all, and didn't realise what was happening. There were forty-three different trade unions in the motion picture industry and they infiltrated, but known as such, and believe me they did get to the very top echelons in some of these unions and then I must tell you that the FBI did interceded and I was, as you say, President of the Guild, and they called on me with some information and they kept us informed through me what was going on and the people in the industry that without anyone suspecting were actually members of the Californian Communist Party and believed in that philosophy.

Conclusions

The language of dementia and psychosis demonstrates differences from aphasia. In dementia there is a reported loss of semantic knowledge in the face of preserved phonology and syntax; however, discourse may be impaired at a pre-intentional or pre-linguistic level. In psychotic discourse there is a loosening of relationships in and between sentences and the ideas they contain, leading to a loss of cohesion and effective communication as the listener puzzles to determine the linguistic intention of the speaker.

Discourse analysis provides an instrument to describe the way that text becomes frayed and communication fails in both these disorders. It also may provide a method of measuring the severity of the disorder, its natural history and the effects of behavioural and pharmacological management.

Recent interest in communication disorders and speech therapy in psychiatry is to be welcomed (France and Muir 1997, McGrath 1998). Linguistics and imaging are providing new insights into language disorders and therapists are increasingly improving their skills at managing aphasia, now those skills could be well adapted to the diagnosis and management of mental illness.

References

Andreasen, N.C. (1979) Thought, language and communication disorders. *Archives of General Psychiatry 36*, 1315–1321.

Armstrong, E. (1987) Textual Cohesion. Paper presented to the Annual Conference of the Australian Speech and Hearing Association, Perth.

Armstrong, E. (1997) A Cohesion Analysis of Aphasic Discourse. Unpublished PhD Thesis, Macquarie University, NSW.

Benson, D.F., Cummings, J.L. and Tsai, S.Y. (1982) Angular gyrus syndrome simulating Alzheimer disease. *Archives of Neurology 39*, 616–620.

Chenery, H.J. (1990) The progressive decline of language abilities in dementia of the Alzheimer type: a description of three cases. *Australian Journal of Human Communication Disorders 18*, 99–107.

Crow, T.J. (1997) Is schizophrenia the price that *Homo sapiens* pays for language? *Schizophrenia Research 28*, 127–141.

David, A.S. (1994) The neuropsychological origin of auditory hallucinations. In A.S. David and J.C. Cutting (eds) *The Neuropsychology of Schizophrenia*. Hove: Laurence Erlbaum.

France, J. and Muir, J. (1997) Speech and language therapy and the mentally ill patient. In J. France and N. Muir (eds) *Communication and the Mentally Ill Patient*. London: Jessica Kingsley Publishers.

Goodglass, H. and Kaplan, E. (1963) *The Boston Diagnostic Examination for Aphasia*. Philadelphia, PA: Lea and Febiger.

Grice, H.P. (1975) Logic in conversation. In P. Collie and J. Morgiana (eds) *Syntax and Semantics 3: Speech Acts*. London: Academic Press.

Halliday, M.A.K. and Hassan, R. (1980) *Language, Context and Text: Aspects of Linguistics in a Social-semantic Perspective*. Geelong: Deakin University Press.

Hassan. R. (1984) Coherence and cohesive harmony. In J. Flood (ed) *Understanding Reading Comprehension*. Newark, Delaware: International Reading Association.

Kay, J., Lesser, R. and Coltheart, M. (1992) *Psycholinguistic Assessment of Language Processing in Aphasia*. Hove: Lawrence Earlbaum.

McGrath, J. (1991) Ordering thoughts on thought disorder. *British Journal of Psychiatry 158*, 307–316.

McGrath, J. (1998) The pathogenesis of thought disorder. In C. Pantelis, H.E. Nelson and R.E. Barnes (eds) *Schizophrenia: A Neuropsychological Perspective*. London: John Wiley. pp.183–204.

McGuire, P.K., Shar, G.M.S. and Murray, R.M. (1993) Increased blood flow in Broca's area during auditory hallucinations in schizophrenia. *Lancet 342*, 703–706.

Rochester, S., Martin, J.R. and Thurston, S. (1977) Thought-process disorder in schizophrenia: the listener's task. *Brain and Language 4*, 95–114.

Thomas, P. (1995) Editorial. Thought disorder or communication disorder: linguistic science provides a new approach. *British Journal of Psychiatry 166*, 287–290.

Thomas, P. (1997) *The Dialectics of Schizophrenia*. London: Free Association Books.

Thomas, P. and Fraser, W. (1994) Linguistics, human communication and psychiatry. *British Journal of Psychiatry 165*, 585–592.

Thomas, P., Leudar, I., Napier, E., Kearney, G., Ellis, E., Ring, N. and Tantum, D. (1996) Syntactic complexity and negative symptoms in first onset schizophrenia. *Cognitive Neuropsychiatry 1*, 3, 191–200.

Thompson, I.M. (1987) Language Pathology in Alzheimer Type Dementia and Associated Disorders. Unpublished PhD Thesis, Edinburgh University.

Thompson, I.M. and Copolov, D. (1998) The psycholinguistics of auditory hallucinations. *Aphasiology* (in press).

Whurr, R. (1974) *An Aphasia Screening Test*. London: Whurr.

CHAPTER 34

What is Different About the Language of Persons with Mental Illness?

Sarah Kramer

Introduction

Numerous studies describe disordered language among a substantial percentage of the population with a diagnosis of schizophrenia, as described by in Chapter 30. However, as he notes there, much of our knowledge regarding the precise disorder involves conflicting information. Possible explanations for some of the variations in findings include differences in the patients studied and/or comparative data. As again noted by Newby, it is also possible that the variations reflect methodological differences, and a large number of the studies involve relatively artificial tasks, so that it is difficult to generalise from the findings in these studies to natural language. In this chapter, after outlining the variety of research findings on language in schizophrenia, two studies involving different forms of analysis of natural language are described, studies which conform to the guidelines advocated by Thompson (Chapter 33). The analytic methods used are conversational analysis and discourse analysis respectively. It is suggested that both studies employing conversational analysis and those involving discourse analysis converge in pointing to schizophrenic difficulties in including the necessary information in a communicative encounter within an appropriate framework for effective communication.

'A schizophrenic language'?

It is widely accepted that people with mental illness, particularly with a diagnosis of schizophrenia, commonly present with a communication/language difficulty. Thus, historically, the earliest diagnostic frameworks, as established by Bleuler (1911/1950) and Kraeplin (1919), included language disorder as a key element. In a similar vein, more recent theories emphasise the presence of a language disorder. However, the precise nature of the language disorder remains largely unspecified and not understood, with the language disorder being described as involving a wide range of different comprehension and expressive difficulties either in combination or in isolation.

Varied findings as to 'the language disorder' of people with schizophrenia

Studies have varied in their findings in relation to the comprehension abilities of people with schizophrenia, possibly as a reflection of the different groups of schizophrenic subjects studied. Thus, a number of studies have reported a deficit in the processing of context, impairing comprehension. An example is provided in a study of the interpretation of lexical ambiguities by Chapman, Chapman and Miller (1964). They found that their subjects with a diagnosis of schizophrenia tended to interpret the dominant meaning of a homonym within a sentence even where context mediated the subordinate meaning. As an example, given the sentence 'The farmer needed a new pen for his cattle', the subjects with schizophrenia interpreted the word 'pen' to mean 'writing implement' more frequently than did the control subjects. They did not, however, differ from control subjects in their number of unrelated meaning responses (e.g. by choosing in this example a pick-up truck), nor in their number of errors where the dominant meaning was appropriate (e.g. where pen referred to a writing implement, they selected the meaning 'writing implement'). These findings have been replicated (Benjamin and Watt 1969; Blanley 1974; Strauss 1975). However, other studies have purported to demonstrate intact comprehension abilities. As an example, Cohen (1976) asked subjects to describe one of a set of coloured patches to enable the listener to select one patch from among similar patches. The subjects with schizophrenia provided inadequate descriptions. However, when the task was reversed, the subjects with schizophrenia were able to use explanations provided to select the chosen patch, suggesting problems with their expressive language in the face of intact comprehension.

Evidently, it is possible that these differences reflect differences in the patients studied. For example, Chapman et al. (1964) studied chronically ill schizophrenic patients, whereas Cohen (1978) described patients who were in the early stages of their first episode of schizophrenia, and therefore possibly less impaired linguistically, with intact comprehension. This would be consistent with King et al.'s (1990) findings that patients with chronic schizophrenia are more impaired linguistically, using less complex and fluent language, which is also more error-laden than that of patients in the earlier stages of schizophrenia. This finding reinforces the importance of recognising that there are subgroups of patients with schizophrenia wihch differ from other subgroups. The difficulty of obscuring genuine differences between subjects included as part of a group of schizophrenic subjects can be minimised by gathering data from individual case studies, and/or by selecting carefully patients to include only subjects who do not vary with respect to factors which are known to be significant.

It is equally possible that some of the differences in findings reflect differences in the groups of people with whom the subjects with schizophrenia are compared. Condray et al. (1995) demonstrated, within one particular study, that the majority of the subjects included in a group of people with schizophrenia performed on linguistic measures within normal limits when using the norms reported by Golden et al. (1985). These norms are based on standardisation studies that incorporated individuals with general medical conditions and individuals with known brain injury. However, when using as a standard of comparison individuals without any known history of general medical conditions and/or brain injury the group of people with schizophrenia were markedly impaired. This reinforces the importance of selecting appropriate controls, possibly including a number of different control groups, to enable for example comparisons with individuals without any known history of mental illness and individuals with illnesses other than schizophrenia.

It is likely that a large number of the differences in findings are, however, an artifact of the methodology, with a wide variety of artificial tasks being used, where these are not representative of natural discourse, and where it is not possible to extrapolate from these findings to language performance in everyday settings. As an example, there have been numerous studies using word association tasks (as described in Schwartz 1982) where subjects are asked to provide a word associated with a stimulus word, despite the artificiality of responding to a word in isolation. In contrast, discourse functioning relates closely to functional communicative abilities, and involves studying discourse samples which can be taken to portray what happens when these individuals attempt to communicate.

Discourse analysis

Discourse analysis can involve one of two main approaches, that of 'conversational analysis' and that of 'discourse analysis' with a narrower meaning of the term 'discourse analysis'. Within conversational analysis segments of text are analysed, in a bottom-up approach, with conversational interactions examined in an attempt to describe them in terms of an orderly pattern of functional categories such as question and response respectively. Discourse analysis (as an approach) enables analysis of varied types of discourse, including narrative and procedural discourse in addition to conversational discourse. It involves analysing discourse in terms of a hierarchy of linguistic units. In this chapter, some of the findings from two studies will be used to demonstrate the applicability of conversational analysis and discourse analysis respectively within analyses of the language of subjects with mental illness.

Study using conversational analysis to identify differences between psychotic speech and the discourse of a psychic

In a study by Palmer (1997), delusions with a paranormal content as recounted by subjects with a mental illness were compared with the accounts of 'psychic experiences' as described by professional psychics. This study involved the use of a comparative conversation analytic approach to determine the features of the psychotic account rendering it a reflection of psychosis as opposed to a psychic experience. This area of inquiry is a particular example of the question repeatedly asked by those studying the discourse of subjects with mental illness – what is the distinguishing factor in 'pathological language'? Delusions relating to the supernatural are, moreover, of particular difficulty for psychopathologists as it is not possible to judge whether such delusions are true or false as they involve phenomena that are not within the province of science.

In his study Palmer draws on the transcriptions of three accounts of a professional psychic's own contact with a supernatural entity and three similar accounts by an individual with delusions relating to meetings with supernatural entities in an attempt to answer the question. He notes Woofitt's (1992) and Jefferson's (1984) suggestion that an intersubjective requirement of accounts of the supernatural is that the stories are 'understandable'. This involves, first, the listener being able to understand a number of aspects of the encounter including the purpose of the paranormal entity, why it appears specifically to the person recounting the incident and, within some accounts, why this occurred at a particular point in time. Second, the professional psychic displays the ordinariness of their own reasoning by reporting an initial, incorrect response to the paranormal entity's appearance.

It is in this vein that in the paranormal stories as recounted by professional psychics, the speakers usually provide some background detail before they report encountering the paranormal encounter, as described by Wooffitt (1992). This provides a setting for the whole incident. Palmer cites an example of this, using an extract where Sue commences an account of the worst example she has had of a spirit which wants an embarrassing message delivered:

(S: Sue, and R: Researcher)

1.   S: I mean thuh-uhr the worst example of that I think
2.   Hhh wuz un I think it uh erm where was
3.   I now. I was working in a place when hhh I was
4.   Working in a hospital with a lot of other people
5.   Pause
6.   S: that were with me
7.   R: uh huh
8.   S: and um we lived in like a kind uv village you see
9.   Pause
10. S: hhh ow and I'd been into this kind of spiritualism
11.   For a few years but I wasn't really interested in it it was
12.   Just that these things kept calling on me
13. R: mm
14. S: These like spirits un hhh one day u I'm ahhh had a
15.   Bad insomnia and [perplexed] I could hear someone
16.   Playing with my typewriter...

Thus, on line 1, Sue commences her account with a story preface 'I mean the worst example of that I think', followed by background details about where she was working and her involvements with spiritualism (lines 3–14). Only then does she recount the series of events which culminated in her encounter with a spirit.

1.   S: I mean just think the eh I mean ah a simple example
2.   Which everybody's had something similar to
3.   Hhh I was living in uhm Inglan years ago
4.   Pause

5.   S: and all of a sudden I was sitting in bed one night getting

6.   Ready to go to sleep and I decided to write to a friend

7.   I hadn't seen for years in Massachusetts…

Sue then reports knowledge of an event relating to her friend of which even her friend was not aware. Wooffitt (1992) suggests that the material following a story preface may 'pre-monitor' the subsequent paranormal experience. In this example, the information in line 3 enables the listener to recognise that Sue can only be aware about events in Massachusetts through paranormal means.

Within Palmer's other accounts from the professional psychics, it is similarly noticeable that following a story preface, the subsequent material lays the groundwork for making the incident understandable. This differs from the accounts derived from the discourse of psychotic patients, where patients did not provide information to increase the understandability of the encounter that they narrated. Rather, this material was absent, and where background material was offered, this could not be related to explanations of the purpose of the paranormal entity, why it appears specifically to the person recounting the incident, nor why this occurred at a particular point in time. Thus, a comparative form of conversational analysis provided a framework to describe the pathological nature of delusions as compared with similar but nonpathological discourse. Principles of conversational analysis were also employed as part of the study described below. Details of these findings are outlined following a description of the discourse analysis undertaken on these language samples (please see page 415).

Study using discourse analysis to identify differences between the speech of people with schizophrenia in a high security hospital and a group of prison controls

In another study, using discourse analysis, measures developed to reflect the linguistic model of Frederiksen et al. (1990) were used for the analysis of discourse differences between subjects with schizophrenia, resident within a high security hospital, and subjects without any known history of mental illness, resident within a prison. Frederiksen et al.'s model assumes the existence of both conceptual frames and semantic representations, where conceptual frames are used to represent particular types of connected knowledge structures which are represented in natural-language discourse and long-term memory, and semantic representations are constructs which can usefully represent the conceptual meanings associated with language, perception and thought. A conceptual frame theory provides a bridge from the structure of meaning in memory expressed as linked conceptual frame structures to the semantic representations of natural language in the form of propositions. Thus, the model can be represented as follows: processing of conceptual frame structures, processing of propositions and processing of language units, with examples of the measures used included in Figure 34.1. This model can be applied to the various forms of discourse including narrative, procedural and conversational discourse, and can therefore record a person's communicative strengths and weaknesses within these different discourse genres (the importance of which is described by Sherratt and Penn 1990).

Discourse sample types for discourse analysis – narrative, procedural and conversational discourse

Narrative discourse involves a story based on characters or events or the relating of an event. It is commonly the mechanism for speaking about the past, and relating information and experiences (Applebee 1978). It is involved in many everyday situations involving reasoning, and can be seen as a patient's link between different environments. Narratives act as important sources of information about the world, also guiding people's expectations with regard to unfamiliar experiences. They provide a vehicle for the expression of thoughts and fantasies. They shed light on how people interact with each other (Applebee 1978), with information on society's moral codes and social customs (Stein 1982). Evidently, narratives can function as a form of entertainment. The narrative discourse samples discussed here were elicited by asking the subject to tell the story of the two characters as seen in a series of six cartoon pictures.

Procedural discourse entails a series of actions or events where the order of events is crucial to the efficiency of the message and key components of the procedure are included by all those adequately describing the procedure. This form of discourse is commonly involved in the provision of directions, but can also be involved in the reporting of a sequence of events. The procedure discussed here is that involved in making a sandwich.

processing of conceptual frame structures

frame generation	e.g. % evidence of ability to produce frames
integrative operations	e.g. % listener request for speaker to integrate of maintain topic
semantic network generation	e.g. % new information contained in propositions

processing of propositions

macrostructures inferences	e.g.% listener requests for repair on macro-level
microstructures inferences	e.g.% listener requests for repair on micro-level
semantic interpretation	e.g. % T-unit containing argument structure anomalies

processing of language units

syntactic dependency graphs	e.g. % T-unit containing anaphoric constituents
syntactic parse trees	e.g. % net words per T-unit
lexical processing	e.g. % non self correted lexical errors per gross word count

Figure 34.1 Examples of measures for discourse analysis model of Frederiksen et al. (1990)

Conversational discourse is any communicative interaction between two or more participants. Evidently, effective conversational skills are a prerequisite for acceptable participation in many everyday situations and for the development of successful relationships. It was not possible to study the conversational discourse samples obtained in the study referred to here as the researcher was not given ethical permission to obtain conversational discourse samples from the prison inmates due to the material that might have been elicited.

Adaptation of model to describe the findings using discourse analysis

Analysis of narrative and procedural discourse samples demonstrated significant differences between subjects with and without a diagnosis of schizophrenia almost exclusively at the level of frame generation, suggesting that for clinical purposes much of the discourse analysis was redundant. In contrast, the lack of detail at the level of frame generation in Frederiksen *et al.*'s (1990) model necessitated the employment of aspects of other models to further specify the analysis at this level. However, these were elements of analysis which were not time-consuming and were therefore practical for the time-pressed clinician, and are described below.

With respect to narrative discourse, narrative grammar enables the specification of the components of an episode at the frame level as setting, initiating events, response, plan, attempt, direct consequences and reaction, with one/more episode(s) constituting a narrative (refer to Figure 34.1 for a description of components of story grammar categories). It is the initiating events, attempts and direct consequences which are essential requirements for a comprehensible account of an episode, with additional components increasing the ease with which the episode can be understood and remembered (Roth and Spekman 1986).

Procedural discourse can be described, at the level of frame generation, in terms of the components of the procedure which are included as compared with those which it would be anticipated would be included on the basis of discourse samples of a 'control population', termed the 'key components'.

Although it was not possible to compare the conversational discourse samples of the subjects with schizophrenia with comparative data, it was noticeable subjectively that there were changes in the conversational style of the subjects with schizophrenia during the course of a later therapy study. Commonly, for conversational discourse, the framework which is proposed can be summarised as opening section (identification of purpose), first topic slot (introduce subject matter), topic shift (change subject matter), pre-closing section (agreement to stop the exchange) and closing section (final turn pass). Evidently, this is appropriate for the overall framework of a conversation but it does not specify details such as those which would be included in a framework for individual topics. For this purpose, the following framework of questions was adopted: who, what, where, when, why and how, to enable an analysis of the changes in the conversations of the subjects with schizophrenia during the course of the therapy study (described in Kramer, Bryan and Frith 1998).

Findings using discourse analysis as described above

Within all three discourse types, subjects with schizophrenia as a group produced fewer of the key components at the level of frame generation, whilst elaborating on frames with information which was not essential to their discourse, for example elaborating on the filling within a sandwich, whilst omitting to mention bread when describing how to make a sandwich (seven out of twelve subjects with schizophrenia omitting to mention bread as compared with none of the subjects without a history of mental illness omitting to mention bread).

Additionally, within the narrative discourse samples, where components in the narrative include among others responses (including affective responses – emotional responses such as excitement; goals – characters' desires or intentions; and cognition – statements that refer to a character's thoughts) and plans (statements which specify a character's strategy for obtaining a goal), it was noticeable that these differed between the subjects with schizophrenia and those subjects without a history of mental illness. This meant that those components which were narrated were interpreted as part of a 'different narrative' to that consistently reported by those subjects without a history of mental health difficulties, with ten subjects with schizophrenia producing a narrative which differed in its 'storyline' from that produced by all of the subjects without a history of mental health difficulties and the remaining two subjects with schizophrenia. Thus, the subjects with schizophrenia as a group produced fewer of the key components of the narrative and interpreted them differently in their 'responses' and 'plans'.

An interesting example of a response and plan that differed from other subjects was provided by the narrative of Subject 11 of the subjects with schizophrenia (in response to the cartoon pictures below):

EXAMPLE OF TASK

at the moment the little boy is around the table
and eating his banana
his father must be telling him to put his bib on

after he finishes eating the father took his plate away
a little bee must have been flying at him
and he was trying to kill a bee or something
anyway
he let the bee out the window I think
he let the bee out the window
the bee's gone after his banana skin
anyway
and the bee has jumped up on the mountain
they're they're trying to catch these bees
and the bees're after their banana
anyway they caught the bee so so far
and they didn't want the trouble

Thus, Subject 11's story involves an interpretation of the pictures which differs from that offered by other subjects, creating a different sequence of events, as described below.

Initially, the subject does not introduce the insect when introducing the other key characters and objects involved in the story. Then, despite suggesting that the discussion in the pictures is related to a bib rather than the insect, as suggested by other subjects, the story is similar, although missing out this incident also means that the irony involved in the story (in which the father initially tells the child not to swat the insect, and finally resorts to the same action) is therefore missed.

However, this same subject's later interpretation of the pictures differ even more markedly from that told by the majority of the control subjects. Whereas the control subjects note that the father is stung by the insect and he then tries to swat the insect, this subject says the following: 'they're trying to catch these bees and the bees're after their banana. Anyway they caught the bee so far and they didn't want the trouble.'

Application of principles of conversational analysis to the discourse samples

It was also considered possible that principles of conversational analysis, with their focus on how language functions to accomplish different communicative goals could provide further information on the ways in which subjects with schizophrenia accomplished their various discourse samples e.g. explaining a plan and response. For this reason, principles of conversational analysis were applied to the narrative discourse sample in which subjects were asked to speak about their life before they arrived at the special hospital or prison where they were now resident.

Findings using principles of conversational analysis

Analysing the narrative discourse sample where subjects were asked to describe their life before they arrived at the institution concerned using principles of conversational analysis reinforced the findings from discourse analysis, that the subjects with schizophrenia did not collaborate with the listener to produce a narrative in the same way as the subjects without schizophrenia, although recognising some of the criterial properties of a narrative account.

In accordance with the criterial properties of oral narratives of personal experience (Labov, 1972; Linde, 1986; Polanyi, 1989), the narrative samples of all 12 subjects with schizophrenia and the 12 subjects without schizophrenia all had well-defined boundaries and a describable internal structure. The individual subject verbally negotiated the narrative to be told, or accepted the task of telling his narrative of his life before he came to the institution, in a determination of the initial boundary of his narrative. He then recounted a structured narrative which constituted one turn, uninterrupted by the listener. The strength of this unit's boundary was demonstrated by the lack of interruptions to this unit, which was only interrupted in the case of two subjects, subject 5 with schizophrenia and subject 2 without schizophrenia (please note that subjects with schizophrenia are identified by names, in contrast to subjects without schizophrenia as an identifying factor).

Examining the content of the two narratives where the listener contributed during the narration, it is noteworthy that both narratives included a limited number of ideas, with no additional information being offered to extend the progression of the narrative, when the researcher interrupted. Thus, e.g. subject 5's narrative:

1   S: married

2   common law wife

3   wife older than me

4   a daughter who last saw now two three years ago

5   spent three years as a father

6   before being commonly law married (unclear, only deciphered later on recording)

7   mm

8   charged with GBH leading to B. (Institution where interview took place)

9   R: you said for three years a father

10   surely you're still a father

11 S: unintelligible response (possibly explaining his comment...before being commonly law married)

12   also I sung in a church choir

13 R: do you do any singing now

14 S: sometimes

15:      my father is the organist and the minister in the local church

16   all through my years I've always sung in the choir

17   it doesn't quite go with being a drug addict

18 R: I think drugs are entering into all walks of life

19 S: it was always from the chemist

20   or buying glue myself

21   so it wasn't a stark drug addict

22 R: but as you say that was at one time

23   and then you changed

24 S: no I still take them

25   (unintelligible) medication

26   (unintelligible) the same effect

27 R: I don't see)

28 S: I was addicted to) overlap

29   this was by the doctor

30   and that's about it

Thus, it can be seen that subject 5 provides a minimal narrative in which he provides a chronology of significant life events, the latter involving charged with GBH leading to B. (the institution where the interview takes place). This is followed by the researcher questioning the negative sounding comment spent three years as a father, where this is the last life event mentioned before charged with GBH leading to B., which is evidently a negative life event, and possibly a sensitive area for discussion. This is perceived by the speaker as an invitation to elaborate on the chronology to provide a narrative/a series of narratives: 'Also I sung in the choir.' This is again stated in the past tense, to which the researcher asks. 'Do you do any singing now?' The subject then provides a comment relating to the present, and described in the present tense: 'My father is the organist and the minister in the local church.' He adds, 'All through my years I've always sung in the choir.' When he continues by stating 'It doesn't quite go with being a drug addict', implying that he was a drug addict, the researcher comments 'I think drugs are entering into all walks of life', suggesting that having been a drug addict does not damn him. The subject accepts this evaluation, noting 'It was always from the chemist or buying glue myself so it wasn't a stark drug addict', accepting the evaluation that he might have used drugs whilst carrying on a more positive existence. The researcher, responding to the subject's acceptance of a more positive interpretation of his behaviour, provides yet another positive interpretation 'But as you say that was at one time and then you changed'. The subject does not accept this evaluation, insisting 'No I still take them', and he insists that prescribed medication falls into the same category as the drug taking discussed earlier, despite the researcher suggesting that these two behaviours cannot be categorised in the same way. He then states 'And thats about it' – a coda, which is discouraging further discussion.

Subject 2, in contrast, does not produce a minimal narrative, but rather produces more extensive language, without furthering the content of the macrostructure of the narrative (i.e. the plot being described). Thus, Subject 2 says:

1. S: ehm rather hectic

2.   I seem to have had a lot of problems with the police

3.   ehm gor in my younger days I used to be balmy

4.   really got me for something I done four years ago

5.   so ehm sort of grown out of criminal activities just for the hell of it

6.   it makes a lot of money

7.   doing it for that

     (2 secs)

8.   don't know

9.   probably always breaking the law in some way or another

10..   I see the stuff that I do

11.   like driving whilst disqualified

12.   and stuff like that

13.   I don't see it as a serious offence

14.   I don't see why I should come in prison for stuff like that

15.   but I I just don't get on with police

16.   and they don't get on with me

17.   they come down and trouble me with something I done four years ago

18.   I mean I'ave been out of trouble since

19.   I've spent spent a lot of time in jails since eh

20.   but I don't know

21.   about

22.   the charges that I have had were dropped

23.   and it's like

24. R: so you did it four years ago

25. S: and then suddenly four years afterwards then) overlap

26.   Yeah)

27.   then everyone come and trouble me

28.   and could have come and seen me and sorted it out a long time before then

29.   suddenly now come troubling me

30. R: when they should have sorted it out a long time ago

31.   that's why you're angry

32. S: certainly is

33. R: eh

34.   I can imagine it does

35. S: mm

36. R: are you hoping to get out soon

Thus, interruption by the researcher with subject 2 can be seen as a clarification of the factual content of the subject's narrative: 'So you did it four years ago' and 'Then suddenly four years afterwards then'. This is followed by the subject accepting the researchers understanding of this factual content, and adding emotional force to his reporting, employing the word troubling in 'Suddenly now come troubling me', and suggesting they should have sorted it out a long time ago. The researcher clarified the emotional response of the subject, 'That's why you're angry', which is accepted by the speaker 'Certainly is'. The speaker follows this with a pause filler, prompting an acknowledgement by the researcher; 'I can imagine it does'. A further filled pause by the subject suggests to the researcher that the subject is not willing/able to provide further information on this topic, with the researcher then asking an additional question relating to the narrative, but widening the scope of the content, and bringing it closer to the present with 'Are you hoping to get out soon'.

The comments contributed by the listener/researcher to both the narratives thus do not alter the topic discussed, nor the type of discourse unit prior to its completion. This is in line with Linde's (1993) description of the narrative unit as being such that a second speaker is only able to contribute questions, appreciations, side sequences…, so that the discourse unit and/or topic are not interrupted prior to the units completion. Although the speaker's narrative is temporally interrupted, the speaker does not lose his floor/his turn to listen, as described by Jefferson (1972). Rather the speaker resumes the narrative as though this was not halted – thus it can be seen that for all subjects, the narrative discourse unit has defined boundaries. The other internal property of a narrative is that it has a describable internal structure. Examining the internal structure of the narratives demonstrated some similarities and some differences between the groups of subjects with and without schizophrenia respectively. Commonly, a narrative is seen to consist of four ordered sections structurally (Labov, 1972). These include:

i.   An optional abstract;

ii.   An orientation;

iii.   Narrative clauses;

iv.   An optional coda.

The abstract, also termed the announcement (Wald, 1978), and the preface (Sacks, 1971; Goodwin, 1984) has a number of functions. It can summarize the narrative or provide an evaluation of the following narrative, where the evaluation involves introducing the listener to the nature of the narrative and/or the listeners expected response to this narrative. Goodwin (1984) notes that the placement of the abstract at the boundary of the narrative means that it contains a particularly interactive function. Thus, it can include a bid for an extended turn to include the narrative, or it can include negotiation as to whether the narrative will be told, and what constitutes relevant material.

Within the narrative samples described here, the subject was provided with the instruction 'Please could you tell me about your life before you came here', offering a preface to the narrative. Interestingly, two of the nine subjects with schizophrenia also provided their own abstract/preface to their narrative, a feature of the narratives of nine of the eleven subjects without schizophrenia.

Both subjects with schizophrenia who incorporated an abstract in their narrative, used the abstract to summarise their evaluation of their life prior to them coming to the hospital, and then to orient the listener to why this was so in a similar manner to subject 2 of the subjects without schizophrenia.

Thus, subject 2 (Michael) says:

> Well
>
> it was pretty miserable actually
>
> because you know I was in a mental hospital before that

and Subject 6 (Jimmie) says:

> my life before I came here
>
> eh eh ordinary
>
> very ordinary
>
> I mean eh ehm
>
> one of the greatest things that have ever happened to me is is discovering that there's more to life than being normal

The two subjects' abstracts can also be seen to be negotiating the content of the narrative. Subject 2's (Michael) abstract ends with a questioning intonation 'Because you know I was in a mental hospital before that?' and is followed by the listener saying:

> I don't know anything about you
>
> you tell me

inviting the speaker to provide an account of the time prior to his admission to the institution in question, including his time in a mental hospital. This is accepted by Michael, who proceeds with the chronological skeleton of the narrative, commencing with his time in a mental hospital.

In contrast, the abstract of subject 6 (Jimmie) is a statement, which is followed by the listener's acknowledgement/acceptance, demonstrated through non-verbal listening behaviour. This can be viewed as an acceptance of Jimmie's bid for the floor for the duration of his narrative and Jimmie immediately proceeds with his general account of the past six years. This then proceeds uninterrupted, with Jimmie providing some information about the past six years, which would possibly be perceived as being unusual/abnormal, but is not questioned, after

Jimmies preface that 'One of the greatest things that have ever happened to me is discovering that there's more to life than being normal'. This can be seen as an example of making the story understandable where making activities understandable can be seen as necessary with respect to activities as diverse as telling an unusual story, complaining about someone or justifying ones own behaviour. An intersubjective requirement of any story is that the story is always understandable, so that at the end of the story a recipient can understand it in terms of belief systems that the listener can accept. This requires some background detailing by the speaker, so that stories do not begin with an event/information which cannot be understood in terms of a common sense theory. Rather, the scene is set for the story, then recounted. As such, the material Jimmie initially provides 'One of the greatest things that have ever happened to me is discovering that there's more to life than being normal' pre-monitors (Wooffitt, 1992) the subsequent narrative. This is not just a frame in which the subsequent narrative occurs, but is used to make the subsequent narrative understandable.

Of the nine subjects without schizophrenia who incorporated an abstract in their narrative, six subjects questioned/confirmed the requirements of the task, examples of the negotiations including the following two examples:

Subject 3:

> before I came here
>
> mm
>
> yeah
>
> what eh
>
> immediately before I came here
>
> whatever you want to say
>
> (a about
>
> (or should I keep giving a general recount of the last sort of ten years

R: (yeah fine

R: (about

Subject 5:

> em
>
> what would you like to know

R: whatever you wish

Of the other subjects, one subject (subject 1) responded to the literal/direct meaning of the request, stating alright, and then followed by his narrative, whilst two other subjects (subjects 2 and 4) prepared the listener for their subsequent narrative.

Thus, subject 2 stated

> ehm

rather hectic

I seem to have had a lot of problems with the police

(2 secs.)

summarising the content of his subsequent chronological account of his troubles with the police,

whilst subject 4 stated

I don't know

(2 secs.)

It's just like anything else

you know

I just got on with what I gotta do to get myself sorted out

It is interesting that subject 4 is the only subject in the sample who incorporated a pause in the section which could be described as the abstract. This is accompanied by an abstract which involves a negative statement about this subject's ability to fulfil the request 'I don't know', together with a suggestion that there is nothing remarkable to tell 'It's just like anything else', where the justification for telling a narrative is that it has particular moral relevance and is relevant to be told due to it constituting an unusual experience in some way, so that it has moral implications (Polanyi, 1989). This is followed by the suggestion for a shift of responsibility to the listener 'I don't know…you know'. The speaker then provides a general statement, phrased in terms of non-specific verbs including got on, gotta do, get sorted out. This is followed by a brief narrative, involving few details and further pauses, which is concluded with a coda/ evaluation of the narrative 'That's about it really', reinforcing the speakers suggestion to the listener that there is little to recount.

After the abstract, if it is present, most narratives include orientation clauses, to establish the characters, the time, the place and the circumstances of the narrative. Orientation clauses may be included at the beginning of the narrative or interspersed with narrative clauses. Within these narrative samples the key character and circumstances of the narrative were specified in the instruction 'Please could you tell me about your life before you came here', requiring that the speaker orient the listener to the time and place of the narrative.

Schegloff (1972) discusses the methods by which co-conversationalists describe the locations of peoples and places. He notes that locations are not entirely specified in terms of their geography, but that rather the speakers relate their descriptions of locations to the location of co-conversationalists, and other factors such as the topic or activity of the interaction. This can be described as location anchoring. It is also possible for speakers to parallel location anchoring with time anchoring in which identification of times is anchored in terms of the times of relevant factors to the conversation or conversationalists.

Examining the narratives produced by both subjects with and without schizophrenia, it was possible to describe the use/lack of use of location and time anchoring by these speakers.

Four of the subjects with schizophrenia produced an appopriate account in response to the question and referred to their current location if this was relevant, but if mentioned, referred to the location by name rather than by making use of terminology such as here/there, and therefore not making reference to the location of the conversation. Three of the subjects told a narrative such that location was not a significant factor in their account, and as such the subjects narratives did not make use of time anchoring. Only subject 6 (Jimmie) and subject 8 (Bob) made use of the mechanism of anchoring, with examples used 'here' and 'the last 6 years' (subject 6), and 'and then I came to B' and 'and here I am at B'. (Subject 8).

This contrasted markedly with the subjects without schizophrenia, who, with the exception of two subjects, included anchoring to time and/or location, with particularly extensive reference to time. Examples include (subject 3):

(orientation to time)

and then about two yeah about two years ago and

in the last couple of years

(orientation to location)

doing the same course that I am doing in here

except on the outside the course got cancelled from lack of interest

In fact, the only subject including anchoring to time but not location was interestingly a subject who provided an account in present tense of his life outside of the institution where he was now resident, and who did not make any reference to his having been arrested and/or imprisoned, possibly suggesting at least at some level a denial of his current location. Notably, those subjects not describing time and location (subjects 4 and 10) were those subjects who produced minimal reports, suggesting they did not have a moral implication relevant to the interview. Minimal narratives occur infrequently. Linde (1993) notes that they generally occur when the speaker is obligated to recount a narrative which is unpleasant or painful, so that it is produced in limited format. This makes it most likely to occur in an interview situation as here the speaker may be asked a direct question where the power relationship between the interviewer and interviewee constrains the possibilities for refusing to respond with the narrative that is requested.

The main body of the narrative involves a sequence of narrative clauses. The chain of events relating to the characters and the setting, constituting the content of the narrative, can be distinguished from the method/plot via which this is communicated. It is possible for the sequence of events which occurred not to match entirely the order employed to describe the narrative. Variations include that in which the order of occurrence and the order in which events are recounted match (abc), the narrative involves a flash-back in order to describe an earlier event/occurrence (acb) and an order in medias res (bc) (Chatman, 1978).

Within the narratives described in this study, the narrative sequence for the majority of narratives followed the sequence in which the events occurred. Exceptions involving flash-backs included the narratives of one subject with schizophrenia (Subject 2 – Michael), and four of the subjects without schizophrenia (Subjects 1, 2, 3, and 9).

The narrative clauses may or may not be followed by a coda, which signals the end of the narrative. The coda, where present, can include a purely formal marker like 'that's about it really' (subject 4 without schizophrenia), or it may additionally serve another purpose such as relating the narrative account to the present, only found in this data where the coda described the subjects incarceration within the institution where the conversation took place.

Also interspersed in narratives are evaluations. These do not have a standard position in the structure of the narrative, but they are crucial in conveying to the listener the point of the story or why it is worth telling this story. Describing this in interactional terms, this is the section of the narrative which conveys to the listener the intended meaning of the narrated sequence. This is therefore the most important part of the narrative socially (Wolfson, 1982).

The evaluations within a narrative about the self can be seen to be demonstrating the speakers understanding of the listeners moral standards, and his negotiation as an acceptable member of the listeners group, so that the evaluations in a persons self narrative can be perceived as his self evaluation as an acceptable member of the group. As such, it would be expected that the content of the narratives would differ between these two groups of subjects, with the group of subjects with schizophrenia perceiving themselves as members of a group of ill patients, given their hospitalisation, whilst the group of subjects without schizophrenia would perceive themselves as members of a group of men accused of activity warranting a prison sentence, but with prison not necessarily justified, as these individuals were all on remand. Subjects with schizophrenia would see their life before they were admitted to a Special Hospital as a period in which they were demonstrating symptoms of mental illness and/or a deterioration in their lifestyle, with increasing negative thoughts and events, until their index offence. Their index offence would demonstrate them as a danger to themselves and/or others, and would mean their admission to the Special Hospital. Being perceived as dangerous would be unpleasant to contemplate, and their index offence would be seen as not entirely justified by their mental illness, and abhorrent. It would therefore be likely that the description of the index offence would not be detailed, or would be described in terms which justified the act. In contrast, subjects without schizophrenia would perceive of themselves as individuals whose activities had fallen foul of the law, but which did not justify them being in prison, which would be construed as being for bad people. It would be likely that they would suggest that either they had been falsely accused, or that their alleged offence was not of a serious nature.

These expectations were born out in the data. Narratives of the subjects with schizophrenia included a chronologue of difficulties. This was followed in the majority of these narratives (seven of a cohort of 9) by justifications for the subjects index offence (e.g. Subject 2 (Michael) in x below) and/or an allusion to the subjects index offence without further descriptions of the offence (e.g. Subject 1 (Martin) in y below).

X

Subject 2 (Michael)

I couldn't get work

and I was on the dole

and (sigh)

I was

in 1982

it was a very traumatic year for me

because me mum died

she died of pneumonia

and then my uncle a few weeks later

(additional details leading to a suicide attempt)

y

Subject 1 (Martin)

in 1986 I did some

I did something which really worried me

Interestingly, the two subjects who did not include any mention of their index offence were the two subjects within this group (subject 4 (Dennis) and subject 6 (Jimmie)) who were thought disordered at the time when this project took place. Is one interpretation of thought disorder a defense against concepts which are otherwise too difficult to contemplate? On a more practical level, this suggests the possible value of further investigations as to whether measures of thought disorder correlate with omissions of what may be considered key events within similar or more varied narratives.

Within the narratives of subjects without schizophrenia, subjects provided details relating to their life's normality. Eight of the eleven subjects followed this by a reference to their alleged offence, whereas the remaining three subjects did not make reference to this event. Where no mention was made, and the researcher asked a question which might have been perceived as a probe for further information, subjects made explicit their unwillingness to divulge certain information. As an example, subject 8 suggested:

S: there's not much about my background that is really imp really interesting because most of it is in here now most of it is in prison for the last couple of years

R: yes but you have a whole person from before you came here

S: yeah

but some of it I'd rather keep quiet

The other eight subjects of the cohort of subjects without schizophrenia all made reference to their offence and/or procedures related to their arrest. Those subjects only making reference to the latter (subjects 3 and 5) did not discuss matters relating to the arrest in any detail, rather referring to it briefly as part of a larger and more detailed narrative, thus reducing the significance of the incident to the narrative as a whole, with for example subject 5's reference consisting of

I was extradited back to England

The remainder of the narratives placed an emphasis on the person's innate goodness via one or more of a number of methods. These included justification for the action by way of difficult circumstances, e.g. Subject 3:

in the last couple of years

I've not actually been too involved in a great number of things that I used to

I didn't have access to my own children

eh

I wasn't involved with the with the narrow boat so much

because ehm

another guy that used to work on the boat with me

he used it as partly as a source of income

so he didn't lend it to the trips

over the last couple of years

and I was more of a standby

ehm it sort of financed his trips to Africa and that

and a bit later:

I was trying to get sorted at at home

and also I was trying to find a more more regular source of income workwise and that

it was a little difficult for a while

plus all the eh change in government legislation doesn't exactly make it easier for me and for a whole number of other people

minimalising the offence e.g. Subject 4

I got disqualified for speeding on a motorway;

suggesting the inappropriacy of prison e.g. Subject 2

the charges that I have had were dropped

and later:

then everyone come and trouble me

and could have come and seen me and sorted it out a long time before then

suddenly now come troubling me

when they should have sorted it out a long time ago

and an account of the alleged behaviour being a behaviour which no longer characterised the individual, but rather was something that the individual did in the past, e.g. Subject 2

in my younger days I used to be balmy

really got me for something I done four years ago

so ehm sort of grown out of criminal activities just for the hell of it

and

e.g. Subject 7:

but got over all these problems

got meself settled

These accounts can also be understood in terms of expert coherence systems and semi-expert coherence systems (Linde 1993, p.163), where the coherence system is a global cultural device for structuring experience into socially sharable narrative. The coherence system is the discursive practice representing a system of beliefs and relations between beliefs. This provides the context in which one event/statement may be considered as the cause of another event/statement. The coherence system can include both common sense beliefs which are shared or minimally understood by all persons within a culture and beliefs and relations between beliefs which are the property of a group of experts, termed an expert system. The semi-expert coherence system is a system of beliefs derived from an expert system, but used by someone with no corresponding expertise or credentials.

Jordan (1989) notes that any member of a group of experts need to learn how to tell appropriate stories, the particular story performing an information packaging function, and also identifying the speaker as having a suitable claim to membership of the particular expert group.

Consistent with this, the stories of the subjects with schizophrenia would appear to be identifying with a life in which there is a chronologue of negative events culminating in a serious incident leading to the subjects' institutionalisation, whilst the subjects without schizophrenia are seen to be leading what can be classified as a normal existence, and are then arrested, but in circumstances where their alleged offence does not justify their imprisonment.

At a social level, particular sequences of events are acceptable as constituting adequate accounts. These are seen to demonstrate appropriate causality and continuity, with the events recounted being acceptable to the listener as a sequence of events. Extra force is provided in the demonstration of adequate causality by the speaker providing multiple forms of non-contradictory evidence for the sequence of events included in the account. Thus, for example, subjects with schizophrenia provide a number of examples of events which are consistent with the negative impact of illness, whilst subjects without schizophrenia provide varied pieces of information suggesting their normality.

These accounts are dependent on the listener accepting that the sequences of events provide appropriate evidence for the evaluations made by the speaker. This requires that the speaker's account is consistent with the social systems of assumptions about the world. These are frequently semi-expert systems, derived historically from systems that are expert systems, but which have now been adopted more widely within a reduced form. An understanding of schizophrenia is considered to be the property of an expert group of psychiatrists and psychologists, whilst aspects of the illness and its impact on individuals are understood more widely, including the negative impact of the illness on people's lives, and a possibility for this being a factor in an offence. These beliefs are so pervasive as to almost constitute an invisible coherence system, which is no longer perceived as an expert or semi-expert system, but is rather perceived as a common sense set of beliefs, perceived by speakers to be known and shared by people within a Western culture, with these beliefs no longer perceived as a set of beliefs, but as a natural reflection of schizophrenic illness, and landmark events in the story of an individual with schizophrenia.

Conventionally, the life story includes certain kinds of landmark events. Moreover, the narrative's content (the items it includes and excludes) and the narratives form (the structures used to make it coherent) reflect membership of a particular culture. Aspects of the narrative form used to express the speakers interpretation of landmark events are very varied. Wolfson (1982) describes a wide range of linguistic structures and linguistic choices. These include the choice of specific words, and a switch of linguistic form from the surrounding forms, e.g. A contrast of direct and indirect discourse, paralinguistic features such as pitch or tone of voice, and nonlinguistic features such as gesture and facial expression.

Aspects of the subjects understanding of their narrative were reflected in the linguistic structure, in addition to the actual events included in the narratives, as demonstrated in the three examples from the narratives of subjects with schizophrenia, as described below:

Subject 3's (Chris) description of positive events was entirely in the past tense, whereas negative events were described in the present tense, reflecting a period in the past which he now perceives as a relatively pleasant time, prior to the onset of his illness, which he associates with unpleasant symptomatology, thus describing negative symptomatology in the present tense

e.g. Got a job as a radio controller (past tense).

And later

and now I am divorced (present tense)

Subject 5 (Conrad) included explicit use of the subject I when referring to behaviours and events which he considered to be a part of his current life as well as a feature of his life in the past,

e.g.

All through my years I've always sung in the choir

and

I was addicted to drugs

(where he explained that he perceived himself as still addicted to drugs, where this referred to predominantly prescribed drugs, but he thought of them as similar to the drugs he had previously taken for recreational purposes) whilst omitting the subject I where he perceived behaviours and/or events to relate only to his past, e.g.

Spent three years as a father before being commonly law married

charged with GBH leading to B. (location of assessment interview)

Subject 6 (Jimmie) suggested that his behaviour was the product of his illness and his youth. His account of his life prior to his admission to the institution in question was described in terms of passive utterances suggestive of events happening to him, rather than him being the orchestrator of his life, as seen below:

e.g.

One of the greatest things that have ever happened to me

and later

the last six years they have been up and down, up and down, up and down

with later

and that torment made me very unwell

This pattern of linguistic structure reflecting subjects perceptions of their life narratives was also evident in the narratives of subjects without schizophrenia. An interesting example of this is that the two subjects without schizophrenia who did not refer to their offence and the events relating to their arrest. They both spoke of events in their past in present tense, as if these related to their current activities and relationships,

e.g. Subject 6

and the only time we see Anuska (daughter) is when we pass each other on the stairs

e.g. Subject 9

play football at weekends

get down to the pub now and again

go to the odd rave

Typically, any extended narrative also includes all those issues which play a major role in a person's self definition.

Interestingly, whereas family members are mentioned within four of the narratives of subjects with schizophrenia, family is mentioned by almost all of the subjects without schizophrenia, (excluding ten of the twelve without schizophrenia, one of whom makes implicit reference to family.) The researcher was not party to subjects' interpretations of their relationship with their families, and it is possible to postulate a number of reasons for the variation between subjects with schizophrenia and those without schizophrenia as groups. It is possible that subjects with schizophrenia did not perceive their family in as integral a way as those subjects without schizophrenia due to their extended period of uninterrupted incarceration within an institution, which contrasted to the experience of those subjects without . It is also possible that subjects with schizophrenia generally experienced poorer relationships with relations than subjects without a documented history of mental illness, so that family were not perceived in as integral a way. Of course, it is equally possible to postulate other explanations for this data, which cannot be corroborated without more extensive knowledge of these subjects, which it was not possible to obtain in this study due to researcher access restrictions.

Possible explanation for discourse production in schizophrenia

It is possible that whereas discourse is generally guided by the frameworks as described in the analyses at the level of frame generation, with for example narratives being generally guided by a specific understanding of narrative grammar (which provides a requirement for categories as described in Figure I.1) and knowledge of the world in their 'responses' and 'plans', subjects with schizophrenia frequently display a decreased sensitivity to these guidelines in their language production, e.g. not mentioning the 'initiating event' in the story following an elaborate description of the setting of the narrative, or suggesting in the 'response' in the story involved in this study that the characters are trying to catch the bees, which is not consistent with a knowledge of the world.

The result of a decreased sensitivity to the requirements of a narrative and listeners' expectations based on their knowledge of the world would be apparent in the production of more irrelevant ideas and fewer core ideas. For example, in storytelling, subjects would not adhere to the structure of story grammar so that not all sections of the story would be included, with key ideas omitted, and other ideas not contributing to the structure of the narrative would be included, including possible elaboration on what is therefore irrelevant. Where key components are omitted the listener is required to make more inferences, making it more difficult for the listener to both understand and remember the story, whilst the inclusion of irrelevant material interferes with the story, decreasing its 'understandability'. Where the 'response' and/or 'plan' differ substantially from that fitting with the expectations of the listener the 'narrative'/ 'storyline' is perceived as deviating from expectations.

Implications of the studies described for clinical practice

The above findings would seem to suggest the value of a restricted form of linguistic analysis (incorporating the elements as described in this chapter) in the analysis of language of patients with mental illness, with linguistic terminology providing a non-time-consuming clinically useful form of description. The measurements can provide the clinician with a baseline and outcome measure for language therapy, as well as providing recommendations for the particular areas of language requiring attention during therapy (as described in more detail in Kramer *et al.* 1998). These benefits are particularly valuable in view of the limited implications for therapy provided at present by cognitive descriptions of the difficulties encountered by patients with schizophrenia. In contrast, the descriptions resulting from analyses as described in this chapter can be used to infer receptive difficulties as well as to describe the language production of patients with schizophrenia, and as a guide to therapy. It is hoped that this chapter will encourage more researchers and clinicians in their application and further exploration of linguistic analyses to the language of persons with mental illness.

References

Applebee, A. (1978) *The Child's Concept of Story*. Chicago: University of Chicago Press.

Benjamin, T.B. and Watt, N.F. (1969) Psychopathology and semantic interpretation of ambiguous words. *Journal of Abnormal Psychology 74*, 706–714.

Blanley, P.H. (1974) Two studies on the language behaviour of schizophrenics. *Journal of Abnormal Psychology 83*, 23–31.

Bleuler, E. (1950) *Dementia Praecox or the Group of Schizophrenias* (trans. By J. Zinkin). New York: University Press.

Chapman, L.J., Chapman, J.P. and Miller, G.A. (1964) In B.A. Maher (ed) *Progress in Experimental Personality Research*, Vol. 1. New York: Academic Press.

Chatman, S. (1978) *Story and discourse: Narrative Structure in Fiction and Film*. Cornell University Press.

Cohen, B.D. (1976) Referent communication disturbances in schizophrenia. The perseverative model. *Annals of the New York Academy of Sciences, 270*, 124–141.

Cohen, B.D. (1978) Referent communication disturbances in schizophrenia. In S. Schwartz (ed) *Language and Cognition in Schizophrenia*. New York: Erlbaum.

Condray, R. Steinhauer, S.R. and Goldstein, G. (1992) Langauage Comprehension in Schizophrenics and their Brothers. *Biological Psychiatry 32*: 790-820.

Frederiksen, C.H., Bracewell, R.J., Breuleux, A. and Renaud, A. (1990) The cognitive representation and processing of discourse: function and dysfunction. In Y. Joanette and H.H. Brownell (eds) *Discourse Ability and Brain Damage – Theoretical and Empirical Perspectives*. New York: Springer-Verlag.

Golden, C.J., Purisch, A.D. and Hammeke, T.A. (1985) *Luria-Nebraska Neuropsychological Battery* (Manual). California: Western Psyhcological Services.

Goodwin, C. (1984) Notes on Story Structure and the Organization of Participation. In *Structures of Social Action*, J. Maxwell Atkinson and John Heritage (eds) pp. 225–46. Cambridge University Press.

Jefferson, G. (1972) Side-Sequences. In D.Sudnow *Studies in Social Interaction*. pp. 294–338. Free Press.

Jordan, B. (1989) Cosmopolitical Obstetrics: Some insights from the training of traditional midwives. *Social Science and Medicine 289*: 925–37.

Jefferson (1984) *At First I Thought: A Normalising Device for Extraordinary Events*. Unpublished manuscript.

King, K., Fraser, W.I., Thomas, P. and Kendell, R.E. (1990) Re-examination of the language of psychotic subjects. *British Journal of Psychiatry 156*, 211–215.

Kraeplin, E. (1919) *Dementia Praecox and Paraphrenia* (trans. R.M. Barclay). Edinburgh: Livingstone.

Labov, W. (1972) *Sociolinguistic Patterns*. University of Pennsylvania Press.

Linde, C. (1986) *Private Stories in Public Discourse*. Poetics 15: 183–202.

Linde, C. (1993) *Life Stories*. Oxford University Press.

Kramer, S., Bryan, K.L. and Frith, C.D. (1998) A framework for assessing communication in mental illness. *International Journal of Language and Communication Disorders 33* (supplement), 164–170.

Newby, D.A. (1995) Analysis of language: terminology and techniques. In A.C.P. Sims (ed) *Speech and Language Disorders in Psychiatry*. London: Gaskell Publications.

Palmer, D. (1997) Delusions with a Paranormal Content: A Comparative Conversation Analytic Approach. Paper presented at Conference on Disorder and Order in Talk (June).

Polanyi, L. (1989) *Telling the American Story: A Structural and Cultural Analyisis of Conversational Storytelling*. MIT Press.

Roth, F. and Spekman, N. (1986) Narrative discourse: spontaneously generated stories of learning-disabled and normally achieving students. *Journal of Speech and Hearing Disorders 51*, 8–23.

Sacks, H. (1971) An analyis of the Course of a Jokes Telling in Conversation. In R. Baumann and J. Sherzer (eds) *Explorations in the Ethnography of Speaking* pp. 337–53. Cambridge: Cambridge University Press.

Schegloff, E.A. (1972). Notes on a Conversational Practice: Formulating Place. In D. Sudnow *Studies in Social Interaction*, pp. 75–119. Free Press.

Schwartz, S. (1982) Is there a schizophrenic language? *The Behavioural and Brain Sciences 5*, 579–626.

Sherratt, S.M. and Penn, C. (1990) Discourse in a right-hemisphere brain-damaged subject. *Aphasiology 4*, 539–560.

Stein, N. (1982) Whats in a story: interpreting the interpretations of story grammars. *Discourse Processes 5*, 319–335.

Strauss, M.E. (1975) Strong meaning response bias in schizophrenia. *Journal of Abnormal Psychology 84*, 293–298.

Wald, B. (1978) Zur Einheitlichkeit und Einleitung von Diskursenheiten. In U. Quasthoff (ed) *Sprachstruktur-Socialstruktur, zur Linguistischen Theorienbildung*. pp. 128–40. Scriptor.

Wolfson, N. (1982) *The Conversational Historical Present in American English Narrative*. Foris.

Wooffitt (1992) *Telling Tales of The Unexpected: The Construction of Factual Discourse*. London: Harvester Wheatsheaf.

CHAPTER 35

Language Difficulties or Emotional Difficulties – What Comes First?

Sarah Kramer

Introduction

Numerous studies confirm clinical impressions of a high co-morbidity of psychiatric difficulties and speech and language disorders, although the relationship between these two areas is unclear. A lack of recognition of the extent of the co-occurrence of these difficulties in clinical practice seems to reflect in part the paucity of information relating to speech and language therapy needs by various clinical populations accessing mental health services. This chapter summarises some of the current knowledge on this issue, and then reports on two recent small-scale studies looking at the prevalence of speech and language therapy needs in a specialist paediatric and adult setting respectively.

Co-morbidity of psychiatric difficulties and speech and language disorders in children

Children referred primarily for psychiatric disorders are frequently language-impaired, with estimates of prevalence ranging from 25 per cent to 97 per cent (Camarata, Hughes and Ruhl 1988; Cohen, Davine and Meloche-Kelly 1989; Cohen and Lipsett 1991; Gualtieri *et al.* 1983; Kotsopoulos and Boodoosingh 1987), whilst it has been suggested that children with recognised speech and language disorders may demonstrate a relatively high incidence of emotional difficulties (e.g. Cross 1998). These two strands of evidence would suggest that language-impaired children are at risk for developing a psychiatric disorder (Beitchman *et al.* 1996; Cantwell and Baker 1985) or that children with psychiatric disorders are at risk for developing speech and language problems, or that both the above are true.

Relationship between psychiatric difficulties and speech and language disorders

Most commonly, a primary speech and language disorder leads to a range of emotional and behavioural disorders, as described by Gordon (1991), with the particular manifestation reflecting the individual child's temperament. Less frequently, an emotional or behavioural difficulty would seem to result in a language difficulty such as a stammer. At times, difficulties in these two areas co-exist without any obvious relationship between them or with the varied difficulties, reflecting a common aetiology such as autism. Evidently, the relationship between problems of speech and language and emotional and behavioural disorders is also subject to fluctuations with difficulties in these two areas having a mutual influence, so that, for example, a difficulty with communicating effectively will increase social difficulties and thus the individual's sense of isolation, having a negative impact on the person's mental well-being. Equally, feelings of distress, alienation and/or confusion frequently experienced as symptoms of mental illness will reduce the opportunities for interaction, and communication with others.

Implications of the relationship between psychiatric difficulties and speech and language disorders

The high co-morbidity of psychiatric difficulties and speech and language disorders suggests the importance of a consideration of emotional difficulties in speech and language therapy provision, and a consideration of the language profile of individuals with psychiatric disorders. The importance of recognising any language impairment in children with emotional difficulties is reinforced by research findings suggesting that children with unrecognised language impairment are more emotionally disturbed than those with a recognised language impairment or normal language development (Cohen and Lipsett 1991). Baltaxe and Simmons (1988) provide evidence that even a speech and language assessment can improve carers' perceptions of emotionally and behaviourally disordered children. This suggests that even minimal intervention involving a speech and language assessment of children with emotional difficulties would provide practical benefits, reducing the impact of speech and language deficits. Conversely, communication difficulties which are not treated can exacerbate behavioural difficulties since comprehension deficits can present as non-compliance (Baker and Cantwell 1982; Cohen et al. 1993).

Additionally, it is possible that the effects of language difficulties could be perceived as symptoms of psychiatric difficulties, due to the difficulties in distinguishing these two influences when using tests which rely heavily on language (Kotsopoulos and Boodoosingh 1987). Evidently, a failure to resolve speech and language and/or psychiatric difficulties early in the child's development would also be expected to lead to an increase in the number of difficulties experienced by the individual child with maturation. This reinforces the importance of an appreciation of the emotional difficulties commonly experienced by those within speech and language therapy services, and similarly the importance of an awareness of the speech and language difficulties which are relatively common in individuals with a variety of diagnoses of mental illness. Yet, despite the extensive evidence asserting the importance of recognising the frequent co-existence of speech and language/communication difficulties and psychiatric difficulties, commonly there is little or no speech and language therapy provision within mental health services. In fact there is no speech and language therapy provision within many mental health services. This situation holds true for many children in local authority care and a large proportion of patients within a forensic mental health setting, among many other settings. Two small-scale studies, investigating the prevalence of speech and language difficulties within these settings (Cross 1998; Brotzel, Bryan and Kramer 1998), will be discussed below.

Study of the requirement for speech and language therapy in children within local authority care

In a small-scale study by Cross (1998), six children were selected at random by the Special Educational Needs Co-ordinator for speech and language therapy assessment, with an hour allocated for each assessment. The results can be summarised as follows:

LS (13 years)

Although initially appearing conversationally competent, it was apparent that LS experienced specific word-finding difficulties, with him resorting to phrases such as 'window worker man' for window cleaner, and he also demonstrated difficulties in formulating sentences. Additionally, he appeared to have a specific difficulty in producing adequate narrative discourse. His attempts were at times difficult to understand due to a disorganised narrative structure and the amount of material he included.

RS (10 years)

RS was conversationally competent, although he functioned within the low average range in his formulation of compound and complex sentences.

AB (11 years)

AB had difficulties processing language and using his language in a social context. His processing difficulties included problems with understanding pictorial representations and understanding the possibility of varied interpretations as well as difficulties with the understanding of relatively simple sentences. There were also clear indications of auditory memory difficulties, and he had difficulties with his formulation of language and in his use of language skills within social situations.

KP (15 years)

KP had difficulties in language comprehension and probable difficulties expressively with both the form and content of language. She furthermore displayed extreme underconfidence in her ability to communicate within social situations, avoiding most contact with other people.

RJ (10 years)

RJ displayed difficulties in sentence formulation, but it was not possible to determine whether this was an artifact of the particular assessment.

MT (13 years)

MT displayed some age-appropriate language skills, but also produced a number of grammatical errors and demonstrated difficulties with tasks involving metalinguistic awareness. It was also uncertain whether MT was able to use his language for thinking.

Thus, four of the six children included in the study had marked communication/speech and language difficulties despite each of these children having a statement of special educational need not identifying any communication difficulties. This would suggest the likelihood of communication difficulties in many children in local authority care where these difficulties have not been diagnosed, with the negative impact associated with undiagnosed communication/speech and language difficulties.

Study of the requirement for speech and language therapy in drug-resistant schizophrenic patients

In this project, sixteen patients were selected as subjects, with the criteria for inclusion in this study involving being a resident within the special hospital where the study took place, having a significant thought disorder score (ten or greater on the Brief Psychiatric Rating Scale; Overall and Gorham 1962), and a diagnosis of treatment-resistant schizophrenia. Of the sixteen patients initially identified, three of the patients left the hospital prior to the assessment on trial leave, and of the remaining thirteen one patient refused and another was too ill to take part. Thus, eleven patients were available for assessment. The results can be summarised as follows:

1. **Naming**

   Half of the subjects obtained a score for the Graded Naming Test (McKenna and Warrington 1983) which equates to the dull-average level of functioning. Naming abilities are generally poor with only two subjects achieving a 'superior' score.

2. **Speech**

   Gross subjective observations of intelligibility divided subjects into the following categories:

   a) Intelligible (3)
   b) Largely intelligible (4)
   c) Variable intelligibility (2)
   d) Unintelligible (2)

   This suggests that the group are diverse with respect to their clarity of speech.

3. **Expressive skills**

   Approximately four subjects could be seen to have adequate skills on tasks including various naming tasks, picture description, sentence construction, verbal reasoning and other assessments of 'expressive skills', but the remainder had marked deficits.

4. **Auditory comprehension**

   A range of abilities were apparent in auditory comprehension tasks. Using the results from the Test of Reception of Grammar (TROG; Bishop 1984), two subjects had appropriate syntactic comprehension, but the other subjects had varying degrees of difficulty.

5. **Written language**

A wide range of difficulties was demonstrated in relation to the subjects' literacy. Two subjects functioned within normal limits for reading, writing and reading comprehension. Four subjects had difficulty with reading comprehension only. Two subjects were only able to perform within normal limits for the writing exercises. One subject was only able to perform the reading tasks and two subjects experienced difficulties with all the tasks.

Thus, it can be seen that of the thirteen subjects assessed, they all had significant speech and language difficulties. This is particularly significant given that commonly assessments of psychiatric status/mental health are language mediated. Sims (1995) notes, '...It is through sounds, mostly words, that patients are able to tell us about their symptoms and reveal the signs of illness.... The speech of the patient informs both about symptoms – the nature of the complaint and the subjective experience of distress – and about signs – the evidence to an outside observer that there is psychiatric disorder, whether or not the patient is aware of it as a complaint' (p.3). For all clinicians, 'Our mastery of communication affects our efficacy as clinicians every bit as much as our technical skill and our theoretical knowledge do' (Clare 1992, p.1). The significance of verbal interaction in psychiatry is increased as laboratory procedures cannot supplant history taking and where medicine cannot effect a cure. Yet none of these subjects had been referred for a speech and language therapy assessment despite being resident within the hospital for an average of 16 years.

Implications of the findings for speech and language therapy in mental health settings

Evidence cited in the literature, together with the two more recent studies conducted by speech and language therapists and cited here, would seem to imply widespread communication/speech and language difficulties among people in contact with mental health services, with many of these difficulties unrecognised. This underlines the importance of reporting on the prevalence of these difficulties in populations served by a speech and language therapist, and of highlighting the possibility of communication/speech and language difficulties in all users of mental health services. It also underlines the importance of developing an appreciation of the importance for speech and language therapists with a paediatric caseload to develop their knowledge of mental health and to establish a mechanism for following the progress of children diagnosed as having speech and language difficulties. Information is currently being collated on these areas as part of a number of studies. It is hoped that these will form the basis for reviewing speech and language therapy services as currently available and for the publication of guidelines for clinicians and others involved with these client groups.

References

Baker, L. and Cantwell, D.P. (1982) Psychiatric disorder in children with different types of communication disorders. *Journal of Communication Disorders 15*, 113–126.

Baltaxe, C. and Simmons, J.Q. (1988) Pragmatic deficits in emotionally disturbed children and adolescents. In R. Scheeifelbusch and S. Lloyd (eds) *Language Perspectives: Acquisition, Retardation and Intervention* (second edition). Austin, TX: Pro-Ed. pp.223–253.

Beitchman, J.H., Wilson, B., Brownlie, E.B., Walters, H., Inglis, A. and Lancee, W. (1996) Long-term consistency in speech/language profiles: II Behavioural, emotional and social outcomes. *Journal of the American Academy of Child and Adolescent Psychiatry 35*, 6, 815–825.

Bishop, D.V.M. (1984) *Test for Reception of Grammar*. Manchester: University of Manchester.

Brotzel, Bryan, K. and Kramer (1998) Unpublished report.

Camarata, S.M., Hughes, C.A. and Ruhl, K.L. (1988) Mild/moderately behaviourally disturbed students: a population at risk for language disorders. *Language, Speech and Hearing Services 19*, 191–200.

Cantwell, D.P. and Baker, L. (1985) Psychiatric and learning disorders in children with speech and language disorders: a descriptive analysis. *Advances in Learning and Behavioural Disabilities 4*, 29–47.

Clare, A. (1992) The Jansson Memorial Lecture: Communication in medicine. *European Journal of Disorders of Communication 28*, 1, 1–12.

Cohen, N.J., Davine, M., Hordezky, M.A., Lipsett, L. and Isaacson, B.A. (1993) Unsuspected language impairments in psychiatrically disturbed children: prevalence and language and behavioural characteristics. *Journal of the American Academy of Child and Adolescent Psychiatry 32*, 595–603.

Cohen, N.J., Davine, M. and Meloche-Kelly, M. (1989) Prevalence of unsuspected language disorders in a child psychiatric population. *Journal of the American Academy of Child and Adolescent Psychiatry 28*, 107–111.

Cohen, N.J. and Lipsett, L. (1991) Recognised and unrecognised language impairment in psychologically disturbed children. Child symptomatology maternal depression and family dysfunction. *Canadian Journal of Behavioural Science 23*, 376–389.

Cross, M. (1998) Undetected communication problems in children with behavioural problems. *Int. J. Language and Communication Disorders 33*, supplement, 509–514.

Gordon, N. (1991) The relationship between language and behaviour. *Developmental Medicine and Child Neurology 33*, 86–89.

Gualtieri, C.T., Koriath, J., Van Bourgoridien, M. and Saleeby, N. (1983) Language disorders in children referred for psychiatric services. *Journal of the American Academy of Child and Adolescent Psychiatry 22*, 2, 165–171.

Kotsopoulos, A. and Boodoosingh, I. (1987) Language and speech disorders in children attending a day psychiatric programme. *British Journal of Disorders of Communication 22*, 227–236.

McKenna, P. and Warrington, E. (1983) *The Graded Naming Test*. Windsor: NFER-Nelson.

Overall, J.E. and Gorham, D.R. (1962) *The Brief Psychiatric Rating Scale. Psychological Reports*, Vol. 10, 799–812.

Sims, A. (ed) (1995) Speech and language disorders In psychiatry. *Proceedings of the 5th Leeds Psychopathology Symposium*. London: Gaskell.

CHAPTER 36

Communication and Mental Health
The Way Forward

Sarah Kramer

Effective communication is perceived as important for a variety of professional groups: journalists, politicians, sales staff...; whilst in other professions its significance is being increasingly recognised. Clare (1993) describes the most important feature of medical treatment as good communication. He quotes Sir Wilfred Trotter:

> ...his (the medicine man's) interest is more potent than his knowledge and skill, the latest development in science, or the utmost virtuosity in art.

> It can be seen that this is particularly important in psychiatry where the great majority of conditions are incurable. Pharmaceutical intervention facilitates an amelioration of some symptoms of mental illness but it does not effect a cure. Effective communication is necessary to understand, to advise, and to reassure. Furthermore, even pharmaceutical intervention is reliant on patient compliance (largely dependent on good communication between doctor and patient).

At the even earlier stage of diagnosis, within psychiatry there are no laboratory tests to identify a particular diagnosis. Rather, this is dependent on the combination of observable signs (many relating to the patient's language) and symptoms as reported by the patient. The significance of the patient's language within the diagnostic interview is discussed by Palmer (1999) and demonstrated in a number of studies. In an experiment by Gauron and Dickinson (1966), they divided the case histories of seven patients into 36 discrete information units. Examples of these information units were organic tests and reason for referral. Twelve psychiatrists were asked to request units of information one at a time, and then, after each presentation of an information unit, they were asked to record their diagnosis and their level of certainty of the diagnosis. Gauron and Dickinson found that '...a psychiatrist's clinical impression of a patient is his major tool in (diagnostic) decision making' (Gauron and Dickinson, 1966, p.231). The work of Simon et al. (1971) and WHO (1975) support this conclusion. Simon et al. (1971, p.435) noted that in 84.6 per cent of diagnoses, the psychiatrist did not alter the diagnosis on the basis of subsequent information from the patient's case history. The conclusion of the WHO (1975, p.141) study is: 'It is obvious that most of the psychiatrists used mainly the Present State Examination (that is, a symptom-based interview) in arriving at their diagnosis...'

These studies thus all support the fact that psychiatric diagnosis is based on the psychiatrist's careful observation of the patient's language.

It can be argued that increased awareness by psychiatrists of the relationship between different aspects of communication and diagnosis could also improve the objectivity of diagnoses, as increasingly research is demonstrating that certain language measures correlate with the symptoms and signs of mental illness. For example, 'thought disorder' is commonly used to describe confusion as a result of the patient's language usage (Rochester 1980), and is used to describe both the discourse failure and/or the deviant cognitive processes relating to discourse failure (Harvey and Neale 1983). Even where the discourse processes and cognitive processes involved are differentiated, it is found that the cognitive processes associated with thought disorder are related to language functions, e.g. response on fluency tasks where individuals are asked to name as many exemplars of a semantic or phonological category as possible in one minute.

Equally, the dependence of diagnoses of mental illness and judgements of mental health on aspects of communication by the patient suggest the key role of communication for the mentally ill patient's health and functioning. Chapters 2 to 5 outline briefly the most common mental illnesses, and describe the communication difficulties frequently experienced by individuals so diagnosed. It can be seen that although theories vary as to the causation and precise nature of the communication difficulties, there is no dispute as to their existence. In a review of the literature, Newby (1995) comments: 'That there are oddities in the language produced by many patients with psychiatric disorder seems indisputable. Indeed, particularly with regard to the psychotic disorders, peculiar speech or communication is often one of the most tangible markers that there is something wrong' (p.31). Yet, commonly, these are not explicitly involved in the care plans for mentally ill patients where mental health services do not have access to speech and language therapy (Emerson and Enderby 1996). Trevor Walt, Chaplain at Broadmoor Hospital writes, with speech and language therapy colleagues, of some of the added insight gained by carefully analysing the particular language used by patients (Chapter 6). The speech and language assessments available to screen and assess in more detail the communication of mentally ill patients are outlined by Karen Bryan and Jan Roach (Chapter 7). This provides information on how the patient communicates in the face of his or her particular medical and social history. Information gained complements that described in neurospychiatric and neuropsychological information recorded on the patient (Chapters 8 and 9).

In contrast with many other forms of information gathered on the mentally ill patient upon diagnosis and/or admission to a new unit, information about communication strengths and weaknesses can be integrated into patient management on a daily basis where the resources are available. Niki Muir describes how speech and language therapy expertise can be incorporated in patient management (Chapter 10). This is only possible when carried out by the speech and language therapist as a member of the multidisciplinary team, as described by Margaret Orr and Yvette Crompton (Chapters 11 and 12). Both these authors provide examples of good multidisciplinary working, resulting in benefits for the patients concerned. However, speech and language therapists are a relatively small profession, and as more recent members of the multidisciplinary team face the difficulties of entering in small numbers a long-established core team of professionals providing mental health services. Kathleen Gilmour describes the successes (and difficulties) of setting up a support network for the speech and language therapists in Scotland who are working within this small branch of speech and language therapy (Chapter 13), whilst Elaine Hodkinson describes what is involved in setting up a speech and language therapy service in mental health (Chapter 14).

Chapters 15 through to 23 outline the contribution made by speech and language therapy to various parts of the service. Within all the clinical areas described, it can be seen that speech and language therapists have an undisputed role to play, but with their impact limited on a national level due to lack of speech and language therapy provision for large numbers of services, and minimal provision in yet others. Where the service is provided it can be seen to encompass many different approaches and skills, some of which are described in Chapters 24 to 28. What is the way forward? How are these benefits made accessible to larger numbers of patients? France and Muir (1997) advocate a largely consultancy role for speech and language therapists and the raising of awareness by other professional groups as to the possible contribution of speech and language therapy to mental health services. The former is mostly unavoidable due to pressures on services whilst the latter is being addressed via a number of different routes.

On a management level, The Joint National Forum, as established towards the end of 1995 to forge links between the various professional groups involved in mental health, has reviewed its first three years of operation. The decision was taken to not only continue with its current biannual meetings, but to have additional meetings for joint working on various projects (a practical indicator of the success of this venture). The Sainsbury Centre for Mental Health is an organisation which attempts to influence policy and practice through a co-ordinated programme of research and evaluation, communications and development. It focuses on a wide range of issues relating to the quality of life for people with severe mental health problems. Speech and language therapy representation is included within the professional steering group of the Sainsbury Centre for Mental Health, providing another forum to increase the understanding by various professionals concerning the core skills and specialist skills of speech and language therapists. HAS 2000 (a consortium comprising the Royal College of Psychiatrists, the Royal College of Nursing, the British Geriatrics Society and the Office for Public Management, whose aim is the development of a proactive advisory and consultancy service to improve the delivery of health and social care services for mentally ill and older people) have included speech and language therapists within those to be involved in their advisory team.

Evidently, increasing the awareness of other professional groups as to the role of speech and language therapists also generates questions which the profession is not as yet equipped to answer. A survey of speech and language therapists working in mental health in Scotland was completed in 1998, followed by a survey of speech and language therapists working in mental health in England in 1999, with their findings available via the SIG Mental Health. The data is to be included within a document commissioned by the government on current and ideal levels of professional input of the different professions working in mental health (to be published in 1999).

As for practising clinicians and researchers, an increasing number of presentations and publications have been made by speech and language therapists over recent years, with attempts being made by the Special Interest Group of Speech and Language Therapists working in Mental Health to ensure that speech and language therapists are present at conferences on mental health issues where possible. This has resulted in an invitation to present papers at The Royal College of Psychiatrists Annual Conference, 1996, with papers and posters being included at conferences as diverse as 'Healthy Prisons: A Vision for the Future', 1996; ISPS Conference 'Bridging the Gap' (of The International Society for the Psychological Treatments of the Schizophrenias and Other Psychoses), 1997; and the Conference of Forensic Psychiatry, 1998.

For the individual clinician, an increasing number of affiliated SIGs (special interest groups) of speech and language therapists working in mental health are being established, with a SIG Mental Health, Scotland, and a SIG working with offenders both being registered with the Royal College of Speech and Language Therapists for the first time in 1998. These facilitate support, sharing of resources, study and supervision opportunities, and the other possibilities which are enabled within a network of enthusiastic professionals working within similar areas. They also provide a pool of more experienced members, willing to share their expertise and knowledge with presentations and the provision of written information as and where requested (or accepted).

The national initiatives cited above have been complemented by many local initiatives such as a truly multidisciplinary and international workshop at Broadmoor Hospital in October 1998 involving eminent professionals in the fields of linguistics, psychiatry, psychology and speech and language therapy with a joint focus on language in mental health and personality disorder. The enthusiasm of participants at the workshop has lent support for the development of a network enabling sharing of information and possibly data for research purposes. A further study day is planned in Autumn 1999, and participants are looking towards a two-day conference on a similar topic in the year 2000 to follow on from issues initially discussed at the workshop.

Meanwhile, an increasing number of projects are addressing research on language in mental health and personality disorder, examples of which are described in Chapters 30 to 35. Concurrently, course components on speech and language therapy in mental health are being included within an increasing number of undergraduate and postgraduate degrees leading to a qualification in speech and language therapy. This is resulting in an increasing number of student projects within the area and increasing numbers of newly qualified and more experienced speech and language therapists with a specialist interest in mental health. It is hoped that this book will assist the speech and language therapy student, the newly qualified and more experienced speech and language therapist and other professionals working in the field of mental health to achieve a better understanding of communication in mental health and ultimately a better understanding of the individuals diagnosed as mentally ill themselves.

References

Clare, A. (1993) Communication in Medicine. The 1992 Jansson Memorial Lecture. *European Journal of Disorders of Communication 28*, 1, 1–12.

Emerson, J. and Enderby, P. (1996) Management of speech and language disorders in a mental illness unit. *European Journal of Disorders of Communication 31*, 3, 237–245.

France, J. and Muir, N. (1997) Speech and Language Therapy and the Mentally Ill Patient. In J. France and N. Muir (eds) *Communication and the Mentally Ill Patient.* London: Jessica Kingsley Publishers.

Gauron, E. and Dickinson, J. (1966) Diagnostic decision making in psychiatry. I. Information usage. *Archives of General Psychiatry 14*, 225–232.

Harvey, P.D. and Neale, J. (1983) The specificity of thought disorder to schizophrenia: research methods in their historical perspective. *Progress in Experimental Personality Research 12*, 153–180.

Newby, D.A. (1995) Analysis of language: terminology and techniques. In A.C.P. Sims (ed) *Speech and Language Disorders in Psychiatry.* London: Gaskell Publications.

Palmer, D. (1999) The Methods of Madness. Unpublished PhD Study, University of York.

Rochester, S.R. (1980) Thought disorder and language in schizophrenia. In R.W. Rieber (ed) *Applied Psycholinguistics and Language 4*, 95–114.

Simon, R., Gurland, B., Fleiss, J. and Sharpe, L. (1971) Impact of history interviews on psychiatry diagnosis. *Archives of General Psychiatry 24*, 437–440.

World Health Organization (1975) *The International Pilot Study of Schizophrenia.* Geneva: World Health Organization.

Some Useful Addresses of Organisations Linked to Mental Health Work

National Council of Voluntary Organisations (NCVO)

An umbrella organisation which can provide information about local activity.

Regent's Wharf
8 All Saints Street
London N7 9RL
Tel: 020–7713 6161

Royal College of Psychiatrists

Provides a range of pamphlets on mental health issues.

17 Belgrave Square
London SW1X 8PG
Tel: 020–7235 2351

Acute mental health

National Schizophrenia Fellowship

Information and services for those suffering from schizophrenia and their relatives, friends and carers.

8 Castle Street
Kingston upon Thames
Surrey KT1 1SS
Tel: 020–8547 3937

MIND

A national organisation working for a better life for people diagnosed, labelled or treated as having mental illness. Pamphlets include a user's guide to mental health and the police.

Granta House
15–19 Broadway
Stratford
London E15 4BQ
Tel: 020–8519 2122

Headway

Headway National Head Injuries Association
4 King Edward Ct.
Nottingham
Tel: 0115-9240 800

The Manic-Depression Fellowship Society

A self-help organisation which offers a quarterly journal to members.

Castle Works
21 St. Georges Rd.
London SE1 6ES
Tel: 020-7793 2600

Older people mental health

Alzheimer's Disease Society

Gordon House
10 Greencoat Place
London SW1 1PH
Tel: 020–7306 0606

Age Concern

Astral House
1268 London Road
London SW6 4ER
Tel: 020–8679 8000

Help the Aged

St. James Walk
Clerkenwell
London EC1R 0BE
Tel: 020–7253 0253

A series of informative leaflets produced by the Department of Health are available. They cover a range of issues in acute and elderly mental health. Titles include:

- *A Guide to Mental Health in the Workplace* – designed for employers
- *Mental Health and Older People* – designed for carers and relatives
- *Mental Illness – What Can You Do About It?* – designed for service users.

A contact address is:

BAPS
Health Publications Unit, Heywood Stores
Manchester Road
Heywood
Lancashire OL10 2PZ
or telephone the Health Literature Line on 0800–555777.

The Contributors

Karen Bryan is a senior lecturer in speech and language pathology in the Department of Human Communication Science, University College London. She is currently a consultant speech and language therapist at Broadmoor Hospital.

Lesley Cavalli lectures at University College London and works at Great Ormond Street Hospital for Children.

Judith Chaloner was born in New England and graduated from the University of Vermont. She obtained her speech therapy qualification from Kingdom Ward in 1973 and from then on worked at West Middlesex University Hospital. She also ran evening classes for many years for gender dysphoric clients at Charing Cross Hospital. She has also lectured and published articles on the subject of trans-sexualism. Judith retired from West Middlesex University Hospital in March 1999 but continues to practice.

Louise Collins is a specialist speech and language therapist working in adult and elderly mental health services for Camden and Islington Community Health Services NHS Trust. She also works as the clinical co-ordinator for speech and language therapy in mental health for Haringey Healthcare.

Yvette Crompton was previously speech and language therapist in the Mental Health team of Camden and Islington Community NHS and Mental Health Trust. She is currently Speech and Language Therapist at Broadmoor Hospital, Crowthorne, Berkshire and studying for an MSc in Forensic Mental Health at St George's Hospital Medical School, Tooting.

Nancy Docherty is Associate Professor of Psychology of Kent State University and also Clinical consultant at Cleveland VA Medical Center.

Karen Elliott is a speech and language therapist at Rampton Hospital.

Nicci Forshaw is a specialist speech language therapist who works for North Warwickshire NHS Trust within services for offenders with learning disabilities. She undertakes consultancy work for the HM Prison Service providing ongoing advice and training for the Adapted Sex Offender Treatment Programme.

Jenny France developed the Speech and Language Therapy Service at Broadmoor Hospital over a period of twenty years. She set up training and research facilities at the University of London and played an active role in the Speech and Language Therapy Special Interest Group in Psychiatry, which she co-founded.

Kathleen Gilmour is a chief specialist speech and language therapist working in chief adult learning disabilities and in Mental Health Services.

Andy Hamilton works for the New Malden Community Mental Health Team, Kingston and District Community NHS Trust.

Dougal Julian Hare is a clinical psychologist, currently working at both the University of Manchester and the Manchester joint Learning Disabilities Service. He has previously worked for the National Autistic Society and continues to be involved in research and clinical work with autistic conditions.

Keith Hawkins is Associate Professor of Psychiatry of Yale School of Medicine.

Carmel Hayes is a specialist speech and language therapist working in adult and elderly mental health services for Camden and Islington Community Health Services NHS Trust.

Rachel Henton is a specialist speech and language therapist working with adults with mental illness.

Mary Hill has worked within the NHS as a clinical psychologist since 1971. Her main interest lies in neuropsychological differential diagnosis, applied within adult mental health and clinical neurology. For the last ten years she has specialized in the potential value of neuropsychological data in the understanding of some forms of criminal and anti-social behaviour, working at Broadmoor Special Hospital and teaching forensic neuropsychology to clinical psychologists in training.

Elaine Hodkinson is a speech and language therapist and a qualified teacher in higher education, and has always been involved in Education. She was instrumental in developing the four year honors degree at The Central School of Speech and Drama and was head of that department for seventeen years. Clinical work included being Head of Department at the Whittington Hospital, London and Chief Speech and Language Therapist at Mental Health, Harringey

Ralph E. Hoffman is Associate Professor of Psychiatry, Yale School of Medicine and also Medical Director of Yale Psychiatric Institute.

Sarah Kramer is a speech and language therapist. In addition to her current clinical work at Broadmoor Hospital and involvement in a number of research projects, she is chair of the Speech and Language Therapy Special Interest Group in Mental Health and lecturer at both undergraduate and post-graduate levels on language and mental health issues.

Laurie MacDonald worked for eight years in the east end of London in Newham's Mental Health Rehab Team as a community based speech and language therapist. She now works independently as a UK Council for psychotherapy registered neurolinguistic psychotherapist

(NLPt.) and a British Association for Counselling accredited counselor, offering therapy to the clients and supervision to trainee therapists in London and Kent.

Jane Maxim works in the Department of Human Communication Science, University College London. She is currently managing a research project which is evaluation a communication training package for health care workers, funded by the NHS Health of Older People programme. She has written extensively on language and communication in normal and abnormal older populations.

Niki Muir is a freelance speech and language therapist specialising in clinical work and training in all areas of mental health.

David Newby is a consultant psychiatrist and has undertaken research in communication problems in schizophrenia and related psychotic disorders, especially using measures of predictability of speech such as the 'Cloze' technique. He has also been involved in studies of first onset psychotic disorder investigating the positive/negative symptom dichotomy. Recently he has been working on developing an interview which uses 'Attributional Theory' to investigate delusional thinking.

Margaret Orr is a consultant forensic psychiatrist working at Broadmoor Hospital since 1988 and was Director of Medical Services there from 1992 to 1995. She did forensic training at the Wessex Medium Secure Unit, Fareham, Hampshire. She worked in the Prison Medical Service in the late 1980s.

Marie Quayle is a consultant clinical psychologist working at Broadmoor Hospital.

Donald Quinlan is Professor of Psychiatry and Psychology at Yale School of Medicine.

Jaak Rakfeldt is Associate Professor, Department of Social Work of Southern Connecticut State University and also Assistant Clinical Professor of Psychiatry of Yale School of Medicine.

Jan Roach qualified as a speech and language therapist in 1971. She began working at St. Andrew's Psychiatric Hospital in Northampton nine years ago, where she is now head of department. Her caseload has consisted of working with adolescents, adults and the elderly with mental health problems, some patients having learning disabilities as well. Recent work has included working with patients with Huntington's Disease.

Jane Shields manages the National Autistic Society's EarlyBird Centre. A speech and language therapist by profession, Jane has worked in a variety of settings during her career, specialising first in developmental language disorder and then pursuing research that led her into a full-time involvement with autistic spectrum disorder. Previously manager of the Speech and Language Therapy Department in an NAS school, Jane took on the development of the EarlyBird Project in 1997 at its base in South Yorkshire. She is continuing to work with families participating in the NAS EarlyBird Programme whilst developing the next phase of providing licensed training in the use of the programme and its supporting materials for other sites in the UK and overseas.

Vasiliki Sideras is a speech and language therapist currently working with children in a multi-professional diagnostic unit in Athens. She previously provided a peripatetic service for adults with mental illness in the rural Greek areas of Amfissa and Lamia. She moved to Greece in 1997 having worked three years for Surrey Oaklands NHS Trust based at West Park Hospital in Epsom.

Ruth Sinclair works for the Surrey Oaklands NHS Trust.

William Sledge is Professor of Psychiatry, Yale school of Medicine and also Assistant Chief of Psychiatry, Yale New Haven Hospital. He is Master of Calhoun College.

Alice Thacker is Senior Research Fellow and lecturer in the Department of Psychiatry of Disability, St. George's Hospital Medical School, University of London. Her interest in psychiatric and neurological phenomenology and in fair psychiatric assessment of clients who do not use conventional spoken language was reinforced by her past work as Clinical Linguistics Fellow at the NeuroPsychiatric Institute, University of California at Los Angeles, and as Specialist Speech and Language Therapist at the National Deaf Services, London. she is involved in co-operative work with speech and hearing professionals treating brain- damaged and deafened people in Kumasi, Ghana.

Ian Thompson trained as a speech pathologist in Melbourne, Australia. His PhD from the Department of Psychiatry, Medical Faculty, University of Edinburgh investigates language changes in Alzheimer's Disease. His clinical work involves dementia and neuropsychiatric disorders. He is currently a lecturer at Charles Sturt University, Australia.

Cathy Timothy is Head of Speech and Language Therapy services for the Bath and West NHS Trust and has had extensive experience of working in the field of old age psychiatry.

Irene P. Walsh is Lecturer in Speech and Language Pathology at the School of Clinical Speech and Language Studies, Trinity College, Dublin, Ireland.

Trevor Walt has worked at Broadmoor hospital since 1971 as a student psychiatric nurse, qualified nurse, Tutor/Lecturer and since 1998 as Hospital Chaplain. Currently he is the full time Church of England Chaplain and Head of Chaplaincy Services.

Pamela J. Taylor is professor of Special Hospital Psychiatry at the Institute of Psychiatry, King's College London and Honorary Consultant Forensic Psychiatrist at Broadmoor Hospital. She has published widely on the association between mental disorder and violence. She is a co-editor of the specialist journal *Criminal Behaviour and Mental Health*. Her books include *Violence in Society* (1993) *Forensic Psychiatry, Clinical, Legal and Ethical Issues* (1993, co-edited with John Gunn), and *Couples in Care and Custody* (1999, co-edited with Tom Swan).

Alison Wintgens is a specialist speech and language therapist with many years' experience in child mental health and complex communication disorders. She works on a multi-disciplinary child and adolescent mental health team seeing children who have both emotional/ behavioural disorders and disorders of communication. She writes and runs training days in this clinical area. She helped set up the Royal College of Speech and Language Therapy's SIG (Special Interest Group) in Emotional and Behavioural Disorders and was its first chair. She acts as professional adviser for AFASIC's Activity Weeks and Summer Schools.

Subject Index

abnormal personality 81, 83
abstract, in narrative 419–22
abstractness 374, 375f, 385f, 389
acquiescence 239
actualisation group 307
acute states, anxiety 29
acute stress disorder 34
adjustment disorders 33
adolescents
 anxiety disorders 29
 depressive disorders 71
 personality disorders 87
adults, mental health problems 20
affective mood disorders 65–79
age, diagnosis, deaf people 255
aggression, epilepsy 129
agnosia 139
agoraphobia 30–1
AIDS dementia 132
akinetic mutism 125
alcohol abuse
 depression 72
 neuropsychological sequelae 141–2
 personality disorders 87
alexithymia 127
alogia 396
Alzheimer's disease 130–1
amitriptyline 77
Amnesic syndrome 141
amphetamines 72
anger management training 306
Angular Gyrus Syndrome 404
anosagnosia 126–7
anterior cingulate circuit 125
anticipation, of events 286
antidepressants 77
antipsychotics 59–60, 77–8, 186
antisocial personalities 81, 82, 85–7, 88, 89, 94
anxiety
 autism 264
 epilepsy 129

multiple sclerosis 130
right hemisphere dysfunction 127
stress-related disorders 28–30
anxiety disorders 26–40
anxiety management training 39
anxiolytic drugs 39
apathy 48
aphasia 119, 337–8
Aphasia Screening Test 117
Aphasia Screening Test, An 400
Apraxia Battery for Adults 119
Area Speech and Language Services Managers 178
Arizona Battery for Communication Disorders in
 Dementia 118, 197
Armstrong Naming Test 197
articulation 211
Asperger's Syndrome
 communication 262–3
 developmental disorders 329–30
 mis-diagnosis 265
assertiveness training 97, 306
assessments
 anxiety disorders 38
 auditory hallucinations 258–9
 child psychiatry 210
 communication
  child psychiatry 216–18
  old age psychiatry 197–8
 depression and mood disorders 74–5
 gender identity disorders 272
 interpersonal skills 317
 learning disability 236–7, 246–7
 in neuropsychology 137–9
 personal construct psychology 290
 personality disorders 90–1
 psychoses 55–6
 SLTs in multidisciplinary teams 160–2
 speech and language 110–19
Aston Index 116
attention, neuropsychological assessment 138
Auditory Comprehension Test for Sentences 111
auditory discrimination 116
Auditory Discrimination and Attention Test 116
auditory hallucinations 43

assessment of 258–9
  language difficulties 112
auditory memory 116
auditory sequential memory 116
autism 54–5, 262
  communication 263–4
  developmental disorders 329–30
  management and treatment 58–9
  mental health 264–5
  social communication 262
Autistic Society 244
Autobiographical Memory Inventory 138
avoidance behaviours 35

barbiturates 72
Beck Depression Inventory (BDI) 74–5, 119
behaviour therapy
  anxiety disorders 39
  depression 73
  personality disorders 99
  psychoses 61–2
  SLT service 175
Behavioural Assessment of the Executive Syndrome 139
behavioural modelling 318
benzodiazepines 38–9
biochemistry, schizophrenia 51
biological factors
  depressive disorders 70–1
  personality disorders 88–9
bipolar disorders 43, 69–70
blind adults 253
blunting 48, 396
Boder Test of Reading and Spelling Patterns 118
body image disorders 45
body language 22, 74, 315f
boredom, resistance to treatment 96
Boston Diagnostic Aphasia Examination 111, 117
Boston Naming Test 111, 112, 117
brain damage 124–5, 126
brain dysfunction, language deficits 344–6
brain waves, personality disorders 88
British Adult Memory and Information Processing Battery 138

British Picture Vocabulary Scale (BPVS) 117, 357
Broadmoor Hospital 154–7, 231–2, 305–8
buspirone 39
butyrophenones 60

Capgras syndrome 124, 126
Care in the Community 147
caudate nucleus/striatal damage 125
Chained Tokens 399
Child and Adolescent Mental Health Service (CAMHS) 208
child mental health teams 209
child psychiatric disorders
  communication assessment 216–18
  communication disorders 211–14
child psychiatry
  assessment 210
  assessment to treatment 218–19
  classification 210
  definition, history and structure 208–9
  prevalence of common problems 211
  speech and language therapy 214–15
  terminology 209
  treatments 211
childhood disintegrative disorder 54
childhood psychoses 53–5
children
  anxiety disorders 29
  depressive disorders 67, 71, 73
  mental health problems 20
  personality disorders 87
  speech and language therapy 435–6
chlorpromazine 60, 186
classifications 21
  child psychiatry 210
  communication disorders 211
  delusional disorders 52–3
  mood disorders 66, 67
  personality disorders 83–5
  schizophrenia 48–9
  thought, language and communication disorders 395t
client-carer interactions, severe dementia 202

Clinical Evaluation of Language Fundamentals – Revised (CELF-R) 116, 117
clozapine 60
cloze analysis 340–1
CNS depressants 72
co-facilitation 304–5
co-morbidity, communication and psychiatric disorders 212, 433
cognitive behavioural approach 309
Cognitive Estimation 139
cognitive failure 139–40
cognitive functioning
    assessments 118, 137, 236
    Huntington's disease 131
    mental illness 136, 140–1
cognitive neuropsychological modelling 119, 124, 339
cognitive processing model, schizophrenia 338–9
cognitive theory, depression 73
cognitive therapy 39, 98–9
coherence system 427
cohesion, and coherence 398
cohesion analysis 343, 399, 400–3
cohesive harmony 399
Cohesive Harmony Index (CHI) 399, 401
Coloured Progressive Matrices 112
Communicating Quality 2 152, 178, 193–4, 197, 205
communication
    Asperger's Syndrome 262–3
    autism 263–4
    mental health 325–33, 439–42
    mental illness 101–9
    personality disorders 92–4
    and psychiatry 22–4
    severe dementia 202
    successful 22
    see also non verbal communication; speech and language disorders; verbal communication
Communication Assessment Profile for Adults with a Mental Handicap 118
Communication and the Mentally Ill Patient 393
communication processing model 351–69
communication skills

criminal justice system 228–9
learning disability 239–42
Community Care Act (1990) 182
Community Care Act (1993) 192
Community Minimum Data Set (CMDS) 190–1
competence
    communicative 23, 101–2, 284
    social 318
comprehension 240, 354
compulsions 33
conceptual expression, diagnosis, deaf people 255
concrete thinking 44
conduct disorder 87, 89–90, 141
confabulations 240
connections, between thoughts 44
consciousness, disorders 46
construct systems, suspension of 286
constructive alternativism 285
constructivism 299
constructs 286, 299
construing
    defined 286
    mental illness 287–93
contraceptive pill 72
conversation 315–16, 394
Conversation analysis profile for cognitive impairment 197
conversational analysis 396–9
    aphasia 119
    discourse samples 415–30
    psychotic speech 409–11
conversational discourse 413
conversion disorders 34, 39–40
coping, gender identity disorders 274
counselling
    elderly 200
    gender identity disorders 275
    multidisciplinary teams 163
criminal justice system 221–9
criminals, psychopathic 86
cross-dressing 268

deaf people 251–60
    diagnosis 252–3

effect of language on diagnosis 254–6
    mental illness in 256
    service provision 259
    studies of phenomenology 257–9
decision-making, old age psychiatry 194–7
deconate 60
defence mechanisms 46
déjà vu 45
delusional disorders 51–2
    aetiology 53
    classifications 52–3
    incidence 53
delusions 44–5, 47, 409
dementia
    AIDS 132
    discourse analysis 403–5
    learning disability 245
    Parkinson's disease 129–30
    senile 131
    SLT service 150, 192, 201–3
dementia praecox 136
demographics, linguistic deviance 385
denial 46
depersonalisation 45
Depixol 60
depression 65–6, 150
    after stroke 125–6
    assessments 74–5, 119
    classifications 67
    communication 75–6
    description of 66–7
    epilepsy 129
    learning disability 243–4
    management and treatment 76–9
    multiple sclerosis 130
    Parkinson's disease 129
    precipitating factors 72–3
    psychological theories 73
    self-perception of ability 140
    speech and language problems 113–14
    see also bipolar disorders; major depressive
        disorder
depressive episode 68–9
depressive position 73

derealisation 45
developmental disorders 329–31
diagnosis 20–1
    deaf people 252–3
    effect of language on 254–6
    learning disability 236–7, 243
    mental illness 440
    SLT assessments 161
    transsexualism 267–9
    see also dual diagnosis; mis-diagnoses
*Diagnostic and Statistical Manual of Mental Disorders –
    Fourth Edition* 18, 21
diffuse lewy body disease (DLBD) 131
direct input, old age psychiatry 199–200
discourse analysis 409
    discourse rules 373–4
    in psychiatry 175, 393–406
    schizophrenia 344, 411–31
disorder of willed intention 356
dissociative disorders 34
domiciliary services, SLT provision 192
dorso-lateral prefrontal circuit 125
drug abuse, speech and language problems 113
drug-resistant schizophrenics, SLT 436–7
drugs
    anxiety disorders 38–9
    as cause of depression 72
    neuropsychiatry 124
    personality disorders 97
    psychoses 59–60
    treatment of depression 77–8
dual diagnosis, learning difficulties 188–9
dysarthria 60, 77, 119, 130
dyslexia 138
dysphagia 119, 186, 194, 204–5
dysphasias 139
dyspraxias 119, 139

eating disorders 150, 186
education
    continuing, SLT service 177–8
    diagnosis, deaf people 255
    multidisciplinary teams 162–3
educational programmes, personality disorders 99

educational standards
  personality disorders 93
  SLTs 148
EEG research, antisocial personalities 88
elderly, SLT service
  assessment of communication 197–8
  care of 185–6
  decision-making 194–7
  direct input 199–200
  feeding, swallowing and eating 204–5
  indirect input 200–1
  interventions 198–9
  provision of 192–3
  severe dementia 201–3
  staff training programmes 203–4
  standards and guidelines 193–4
electroconvulsive therapy (ECT) 78
emotion
  after stroke 126
  disorders of 45
  right hemisphere 127
emotional/behavioural disorders 213, 214
emotionally unstable personality disorder 331
employment factors, anxiety disorders 36
environment
  assessment of elderly 196
  and communication 102
  mental health 20
  personality development 89–90
environmental stress 35
epilepsies 128–9
Ethics Committee 179
euphoria 131
evaluation
  in narrative 424
  of therapies 309
executive functions 125, 139
experiential constructivism 299
expert coherence systems 427–8
expression, communication processing 354
expressive language 105, 117, 211
Eysenck personality system 91

facial expression 74, 75

false positives 264
families
  anxiety disorders 36
  child communication assessments 216
  SLTs contact with 176
family therapy, psychoses 62
feedback
  multidisciplinary teams 163
  social interaction 314
filter mechanism, cognitive processing 338–9
flight of ideas 44, 69
flupenthixol deconate 60
fluphenazine 186
forensic psychiatry
  medium secure units 233
  prisons 234
  secure hospitals 231–3
  secure wards 234
  SLTs in 234–5
formal communication disorders 257–8
formal thought disorder 48, 335–48
Frenchay Dysarthria Assessment 119, 326
frontal lobe damage 124–5
fronto-subcortical connections 125
Fullerton Language Test for Adolescents 116, 117
Functional Linguistic Communication Inventory
  (FLCI) 197

gender
  childhood psychoses 53
  mental illness 19
gender identity disorders
  assessment 272
  case studies 276–7
  coping strategies 274
  counselling 275
  prognostic factors 275–6
  psychiatrists 270–1
  role of SLTs 271–2
  social skills training 274
  surgical voice modification 275
  transsexualism 267–9
  voice skills 273
generalised anxiety disorder 32

genetics
>anxiety disorders 29
>depressive disorders 70–1
>personality disorders 88
>schizophrenia 50

Graded Naming Test 117

grammar *see* syntax

Grid Test of Schizophrenic Thought Disorder
(GTSTD) 56

group therapy
>depression 78
>interpersonal difficulties 291–2
>in multidisciplinary teams 163
>psychoses 61
>structured 309–10
>therapeutic relationships 303–4
>*see also* co-facilitation

hallucinations 43, 44, 47, 112, 131

Halodol deconate 60

haloperidol 60, 77

Harry Benjamin International Gender Dysphoria
Association Inc 270

head injury 127–8, 189

Health Care Aims system 189

hearing
>assessment of 161
>criminal behaviour 223
>mental illness 115

heroin 72

highly ungrammatical 382–3

Hospital Anxiety and Depression Scale (HAS) 119

hospitals
>admissions, psychotic illness 43, 46
>milieu therapy 281–2

human development, interpersonal system 23

Huntington's disease 131

5–hydroxytryptamine reuptake inhibitors 77

hyperthyroidism 253

hypomania 44, 69

hypothyroidism 253

hysteria 34, 35, 39

id, and personality 89

identity, and communication 103

illness *see* mental illness

illogicality, deaf people 257

imagery, perceptions of 43–4

Images of Destruction 70

imaging techniques 56, 344–5

incoherence, deaf people 257

incomplete construing 288

indirect input, old age psychiatry 200–1

individual therapy 61, 104, 162

infantile autism 53, 54

informal assessments, child psychiatry 218

informative communication 173–4

inner voice 23

insight 46

International Classification of Diseases (ICD-10) 21

interpersonal skills 313–14
>human development 23
>schizophrenia 316–17
>training 317–19

interrogative suggestibility 239

interventions
>learning disability 247–8
>mental health problems 20
>SLT, elderly 198–9

isolation 22

jamais vu 45

Joint National Forum 441

joint working, SLT in CAMHS 219

Kemadrin 186

labelling 21

laddering 290

landmark events, in narrative 428

language
>in clinical phenomena 372
>as communication tool 22, 102
>content of 107–8
>deficits, brain dysfunction 344–6

developmental disorders 329–31
diagnosis, deaf people 254–6
domains 373–4
expressive and receptive 105
neuropsychiatry 123–32
schizophrenia, different approaches 374–5
schizophrenic 407
and thought 372–3
violence as substitute for 332–3
see also speech and language
learned helplessness 74
learning disability
assessment and diagnosis 236–7
characteristics of people with 238–9
communication skills 239–42
dual diagnosis 188–9
mental health 242–5
prison population 222
role of SLTs 150, 245–8
service provision 237–8
learning theory, anxiety disorders 30
left hemisphere dysfunction 94
legal aspects, mental health 22
legislation, mental health 181–3
Lets Talk Inventory for Adolescents 118
lexical devices 398
life experience, mental health problems 20, 51
life-long process, personality disorders 89
limbic system 88–9
limited capacity channel 338
limiting constructs 299
Linguistic Deviance Scale (LDS) 378, 379–84,
386–7
linguistic deviance, schizophrenia 371–90
literature 372–8
results 385–9
study 378–85
linguistic model 149f
linguistic rule awareness 342–3
listening skills 103–5
literacy
assessments 118, 138
skills, access to 105–7
lithium 77–8

location anchoring 422–3
locked-in-syndrome 325
loose associations 44, 48, 371–2
loose construing 287–8, 291

macro-level interpersonal skills 313
magnetic resonance imaging (MRI) 344–5
major depressive disorder 43, 68–9
Huntington's disease 131
incidence and aetiology 70–2
malignant alienation 327
mania 69
after brain injury 126
Huntington's disease 131
incidence and aetiology 70–2
manic episode 69
marriage, anxiety disorders 36
masked depression 66
maternal affection, depressive disorders 71
medial temporal lobe epilepsy 129
medical conditions, anxiety disorders 32
medication
side effects 161, 186–7
speech problems 235
medium secure units 233
memory
disorders 45
neuropsychological assessment 138
schizophrenia 356, 363–4
Memory for Designs Test 136
mental disorder 18, 327–8
mental health
autism 264–5
communication in 325–33, 439–42
criminal justice system 221–9
learning disability 242–5
legal aspects 22
neurolinguistic programming 297–302
setting up an SLT network 167–71
SLT in 172–3
Mental Health Act (1983) 18, 22, 82, 181, 182f
Mental Health Commission 22
mental illness 19–20
Asperger's Syndrome 265

cognitive functioning 136, 140–1

communication 101–9

construing 287–93

deaf people 256

offenders 221, 234

speech and language disorders 433–4

see also child psychiatric disorders; mood disorders; neuroses; psychotic disorders

methadone 72

micro-level interpersonal skills 313

Middlesex Elderly Assessment of Mental State 140

mild depressive episode 68

milieu therapy

 in hospitals 281–2

 origins 280–1

 psychiatric nursing 282–3

 psychoses 61

 ward life 282

Mini Mental State Examination 198

minimal narratives 417, 423

minimally ungrammatical 380–1

Minnesota Multiphasic Personality Inventory (MMPI) 55, 92

mis-diagnoses

 autism 264–5

 deaf people 252

moderate depressive episode 68

moderately ungrammatical 381–2

Modified Wisconsin Card Sorting Tasks 139

Modocate 60

monoamine oxidase inhibitors (MAOIs) 77

mood disorders 43, 49, 65–79

morbidity, mental health problems 19

mothers, depression 72

motivation, social interaction 313

motor speech disorders 119

motor symptoms 45

Mount Wilja High Level Language Battery 117

Mourning and Melancholia 73

multidisciplinary teams

 case histories, special hospitals 164–5

 membership 159

 need for in mental health 158–9

 in psychiatry 305

skills sharing 198

SLTs in

 areas of involvement 160–2

 Broadmoor Hospital 154–7

 child psychiatry 215

 contributions to assessment 160

 management approaches 162–4

 skills required 159–60

Multiple Errands Test 139

multiple sclerosis 130

mutism, akinetic 125

naming 117

narrative clauses 423–4

narrative discourse 412, 413, 415–19

National Adult Reading Test (NART) 118, 138

National Health Service (NHS), SLTs in 151

National Special Interest Group in Mental Health 16, 151, 152, 174–5

negative symptoms, schizophrenia 48, 355, 356

networking, SLT service 174–6, 177f

neuroleptics 59, 60, 186

neurolinguistic programming 297–302

neurological influences, personality disorders 88–9

neuropsychiatry 123–32

neuropsychology 136

 assessments 137–9

 clinical presentations 139–42

 methodological issues 142

 tests, linguistic deviance 387–8

neuroses 19, 26–40, 114

New NHS: Modern, Dependable, The 205

non-verbal communication 22

 depression 75

 gender identity disorders 274

 learning disability 243

 personality disorders 93

 severe dementia 202

 social interaction 314

normal personality 82–3

normality, deaf people 252

Nuffield Centre Dyspraxia Programme 119

obsessive compulsive disorders 32–3, 39–40, 150
offenders
        communication disorders in young 223–4
        current SLT services 224–5
        mental illness 221
        role of SLTs 225–8
organic factors, depression 72
organic pathology, anxiety disorders 36
organic psychoses 42
orientation clauses 422
overinclusion 44, 339, 347

panic disorder 30
para-linguistic features 241, 314–15f
paranoid disorder see delusional disorders
paranoid personality disorder 331
parent-child relationships
        depression 73
        personality development 89
parental loss, depressive disorders 71
parental mistreatment, language development 101
Parkinsonism 60
Parkinson's disease 129–30
passive dependent personalities 97
patients
        schizophrenia 47, 48
        in secure hospitals 232–3
perception
        abnormal 43–4
        bipolar disorders 70
        schizophrenia 49
        social interaction 313
persistent delusional disorders 51–2
person-the-scientist 285
personal change 289, 302
Personal Communication Plans 118
personal construct psychology (PCP) 284–94
        construing mental illness 287–93
        theory 285–6
personal construct psychotherapy 62, 98
personality, depressive disorders 71
Personality Assessment Schedule (PAS) 92

personality disorders 81, 83, 150
        abnormal 81, 83
        aetiology 88–90
        antisocial 81, 82, 85–7
        assessments 90–1
        classifications 83–5
        communication 92–4
        incidence 87–8
        learning disability 245
        management and treatment 94–7
        medical and case histories 91
        normal 82–3
        psychotherapy 98–9
        right hemisphere lesions 127
        schizophrenia 49
        speech and language problems 114
        speech and language research 331–2
16 Personality Factor 91
personality testing 91–2
pervasive developmental disorders 54, 116
phatic communication 337
phenothiazines 60
phobia anxiety disorders 31, 37, 39–40
phonemic paraphasia, deaf people 258
phonology 116, 211, 373
Photo Articulation Test 116
physical factors, depression 72
physical illness, anxiety disorders 36
Pick's disease 132
Pocket Guide to the Classification of Mental and
        Behavioural Disorders 18
Police and Criminal Evidence Act 228
Polmont 223, 224
positive symptoms, schizophrenia 48, 355, 356
positron emission tomography (PET) 344
possession of thought, disorders of 44
post traumatic stress disorder 33–4
posterior aphasia 338
pragmatic/functional communication 118, 211,
        343–4
Present State Examination 254, 335, 439
Primary Care Groups (PCGs) 190–1
Primary Care Trusts 191
primary transsexuals 267

prison populations
    cognitive functioning 141
    communication disorders 222–3
    discourse analysis, schizphrenic subjects
       411–31
    learning disability 222
prisons
    mental illness 234
    role of SLTs 227–8
problem-solving 319
procedural discourse 412, 413
processing skills, conversation 315
Procyclidine 186
Professions Allied with Medicine (PAMs) 175,
    190–1
progressive supranuclear palsy (PSP) 130
projection 46
pseudo-hallucinations 43
psychiatric disorders *see* mental illness
psychiatric nursing 282–3
psychiatrists
    awareness of SLT skills 16–17, 173
    gender identity teams 270–1
psychiatry
    and communication 22–4
    diagnoses 20–1
    discourse analysis 393–406
    neuropsychology in 136–42
    old age
        assessment of communication 197–8
        decision-making 194–7
    speech and language
        assessments 110–19
        therapists 15
        therapy 24, 151
    see also child psychiatry; forensic psychiatry;
       neuropsychiatry
psychic discourse, conversational analysis 409–11
psychoanalytic (dynamic) therapy 61
psychoanalytic theory
    anxiety disorders 30
    depressive disorders 71, 73
    personality disorders 89
    transsexualism 269

psychodynamic theory 71
Psycholinguistic Assessment of Language
    Processing in Aphasia 117, 393
psychological causes
    depression 71
    mental health problems 19
    personality disorders 89
psychological tests, schizophrenia 55–6
psychological theories, depression 73
Psychology of Personal Constructs, The 285
psychometric testing 137, 142, 236
psychoneurosis 28
psychopathic personalities 82, 86, 88, 94
Psychopathic States 82
psychoses *see* psychotic disorders
psychosocial development 23
psychosocial effects, child communication disorders
    213
psychosocial factors, depressive disorders 71
psychotherapy
    depressive disorders 78–9
    personality disorders 97, 98–9
    psychoses 60–1
    reconstructive and re-educational 280
    see also neurolinguistic programming; personal
       construct psychotherapy
psychotic disorders 19, 42–62
    after stroke 126
    epilepsy 129
    learning disability 244–5
    religious writing 108
    speech and language disorders 56–7, 113
    thought disorder 326
    see also childhood psychoses; schizophrenia
psychotic speech, conversational analysis 409–11
Pyramids and Palm Trees Test 117

quality of life, SLT service 201–2

rapport, NLP 300
Raven's Coloured Progressive Matrices 112
Reagan, Ronald 405
receiving skills, conversation 315

receptive language 105, 211

receptive vocabulary 117

redundancy, natural language 340–1

referential speaking, problems in 343

referral sources
    anxiety disorders 38
    speech and language therapy 147–8, 184t,
        225

regression 46

reinforcement, interpersonal skills 319

relapse, NLP 302

relationships see parent-child relationships; social
    relationships

religious language 107

Renfrew Action Picture Test 117

repertory grids 75, 290

repetitive behaviours 33, 264

repression 46

research projects, SLT service 179–80

resistance to treatment 96, 289

response biases 340

responses, social interaction 314

right hemisphere dysfunction 112, 127

right hemisphere language 118

Right Hemisphere Language Battery 118

Rivermead Behavioural Memory Test 116, 138

Robertson Dysarthria Profile 119

role-play 319

Rorschach test 55, 56, 92

rubella 253

S24 Scale 118

schizoid children 54

schizoid personality disorder 331

schizophrenia 46–7
    aetiology 50–1
    assessment 55–6
    childhood 55
    classifications 48–9
    communication processing model 351–69
    course and prognosis 51
    definition of 47–8
    discourse analysis 344, 411–31
    forensic psychiatry 232, 233

formal thought disorder 335–48
    head injury 128
    incidence 50
    interpersonal skills 316–17
    learning disability 244–5
    linguistic deviance 371–90
    neuropsychiatry 124
    SLT requirements 436–7
    SLT service 187–8
    speech and language disorders 57, 58, 112,
        328–9, 407, 408–9
    thought disorder 57–8

secondary transsexuals 267, 269

secure psychiatric hospitals 231–3

secure wards 234

self, constructions of 288

self-esteem 74, 140

self-monitoring, deficit in 339

self-theory 89

semantic disorder, antisocial personalities 94

semantics 211, 373

sending skills 315–16

senile dementia 131

sensorineural deafness 253

service provision
    deaf people 259
    learning disability 237–8
    see also SLT service provision

severe depressive episode 68

Severe Impairment Battery 140, 197

sex-change operations 271

short-term memory 356

side effects, medication 161, 186–7

sign perseveration, deaf people 258

skill impairments, neuropsychological assessment
    139

SLT service provision 16, 17, 150–2
    continuing education 177–8
    delivery 184–5
    dual diagnosis 188–9
    dyskinesis 187
    dysphagia 186
    elderly see elderly, SLT service
    future developments 190–1

head injury 189
informative communication 173–4
infrastructure and resources 174
management issues 190
in mental health 172–3
networking 174–6, 177f
offenders 222, 223, 224–5
organisation, administration and review
    178–9
outcomes of therapy 189–90
referral sources 184t
research projects and teaching 179–80
schizophrenia 187–8
settings 183
supervision 190
support systems 177–8
social class 36
social communication, autism 262
social factors
anxiety disorders 36, 37
depressive disorders 72, 73
mental illness 19, 20
personality development 89–90
schizophrenia 51
social functioning, assessment 236
social interaction 23, 313–14
social phobia 31, 37
social relationships, anxiety disorders 36
social skills
broad spectrum of 312
training, gender identity disorders 274
see also conversation; interpersonal skills; non
    verbal communication; verbal
    communication
Social Use of Language Programme, The 317
social workers, SLT contact with 176
socio-cognitive model, anxiety 264
socio-cultural factors, assessment of elderly 195
sociopathic personality disorder 81, 82
somatisation 36
somatoform disorders 35–6
South Tyneside Assessment of Phonology 116
Special Hospital Services Authority (SHSA) 154
special hospitals

communication disorders 224
multidisciplinary teams
    Broadmoor Hospital 154–7
    case histories 164–5
role of SLTs 226
Special Interest Groups 151
specific phobia 31
speech, effective communication 101–2
speech and language
assessments 110–19
pathology 186
research, personality disorders 331–2
and thought 337
speech and language disorders
anxiety disorders 37–8
bipolar disorders 69
child psychiatric disorders
    assessments 216–18
    relationship between 211–14
classification 211, 395t
depression 74, 75–6
medication 235
Parkinsonism 60
personality disorders 94
prison population 222–3, 225–6
psychiatric difficulties 433–4
psychoses 56–7
schizophrenia 58, 408–9
special hospitals 224
young offenders 223–4
speech and language therapists (SLTs)
assessment of elderly 196–7
awareness of skills 16–17, 173
forensic psychiatry 234–5
gender identity disorders 271–2
as intermediaries 17–18
learning disability 245–8
role 149–50
skills and knowledge 15–16
working with offenders 226–9
see also multidisciplinary teams
speech and language therapy
anxiety disorders 37
autism 58

child psychiatry 214–15
children, local authority care 435–6
effectiveness, learning disability 248
personality disorders 99
profession 147–8
in psychiatry 24
service *see* SLT service provision
setting up a network 167–71
special hospitals, case histories 164–5
stammering 118
Standardised Assessment of Personality 245
standardised assessments 216–18, 308
statistical approximations to English 341–2
stereotypy, deaf people 257
steroids 72
Stevens' screening test 197
streams of thought 44
stress
epilepsy 129
reaction to severe 33
schizophrenia 51
stress-related disorders
aetiology of 35–6
anxiety and 28–30
stroke, unilateral 125–7
Stroop 139
structure, disorders of 287–8
substance-related disorders 32, 42, 87
subsuming 286
suggestibility 239
super-ego, depression 73
Supervisory Attentional System 139
support systems, SLT service 177–8
supportive psychotherapy 61, 98, 280
swallowing difficulties 186, 204–5
syntax 211, 373, 376–7, 398

tardive dyskinesia 60, 187
teaching, SLT service 179–80
team working 151, 159
temporal lobe epilepsy 129, 267
terminology 20–1, 211
Test of Adolescent and Adult Word Finding 117
Test of Everyday Attention 138

Test of Language Competence 113, 118
Test for the Reception of Grammar (TROG) 116
Test of Word Finding 117
Test of Word Finding in Discourse 117
text, discourse as 394
thalamic lesions 125
Thematic Apperception Tests (TAT) 55, 56, 379
theory of mind 318
therapeutic alliance 305–8
therapeutic relationships 303–4
thioridazine 186
thioxanthenes 60
third-person hallucinations 43–4
thought, speech and language 337, 372–3
thought disorder 44–5, 57–8
bipolar disorders 69
classification 395t
psychotic disorders 326, 394
see also formal thought disorder
Thought Disorder Index (TDI) 345
Thought Language and Communication Scale 344, 346t
tight construing 288, 291
time anchoring 422, 423
Token Test 112
topic derailment 257
topic/thematic perseveration 257
training
interpersonal skills 317–19
multidisciplinary teams 162–3
SLTs, child psychiatry 215
staff, SLT service 203–4
trait approach 91
tranquilizers 97
transformational grammar 373
transsexualism 267–9
transvestites 268
trauma, to the head 127
treatment
anxiety disorders 38–40
child psychiatry 211
depression and mood disorders 76–9
PCP 290–2
personality disorders 94–7

psychoses 58–62
SLT assessment of side effects 161
tricyclic antidepressants 77

unconscious, and personality 89
Understanding Psychotic Speech: Beyond Freud and Chomsky 376
undetected communication disorders 212–13
upbringing, personality disorders 89

validation therapy 200, 202
ventral caudate nucleus 125
verbal communication 243, 314
verbal comprehension 116–17
verbal productions, studies of 339–43
verbal redundancy measures 340–2
verbal skills, personality disorders 93
Vineland Scales of Adaptive Behaviour 236–7
violence, as language substitute 332–3
Visual Retention Test 136
visuospatial anomalies, deaf people 257
vocal assessments, depression 74
vocal tract resonance 273
voice
    disorders 38
    gender identity disorders 273
    psychotic disorders 44, 57
    as reflector of emotional state 37
    surgical modification 275

wards, milieu therapy 282
Wechsler Adult Intelligence Scale (WAIS) 55, 137, 236
Wechsler Memory Scale (WMS) 138
Wernicke-Korsakoff syndrome 141
Western Aphasia Battery 112, 114
Whurr test 114–15
women
    anxiety disorders 28
    depression 72
    mental illness 19
word association, studies 340
working memory 356

young offenders
    communication disorders 112, 223–4
    psychopathic personalities 86
    role of SLTs 226–7

Author Index

Action for Dysphasic Adults 192, 203
Aitchison, J. 329
Alexander, G.E. and Crutcher, M.D. 125
Allen, H., Liddle, P. and Frith, C. 356, 366
Altshuler, K., Baroff, G. and Rainer, J. 254
Ambelas, A. 305
American Psychiatric Association 130, 327
Anand, A. 371
Andreason, N. 352, 371, 374, 376, 377
Andreason, N.C. 58, 258, 337, 344, 346, 393, 394, 395
Andreason, N.C. and Grove, W. 376
Andreason, N.C., Hoffman, R.E. and Grove, W.M. 355
Andrews, G. and Cutler, J. 118
Andrews, M. and Schmidt, C. 273
Applebee, A. 412
Appleyard, J. and Maden, J. 158
Argyle, M. 23, 309, 317
Argyle, M. and Kendon, A. 317
Argyle, M., Trower, P. and Bryant, B. 97
Arieti, S. 47, 57
Armstrong, E. 399
Armstrong, L. 118, 197, 198
Armstrong, L., Bayles, K.A., Borthwick, S. and Tomoeda, C.K. 197
Armstrong, L. and Reymbaut, E. 202
Armstrong, S. and Ainley, M. 116
Asscheman, J. and Gooren, L. 270
Atkinson, M., Kilby, D. and Roca, I. 339

Baddeley, A. 354
Bailey, J. and MacCulloch, M. 155
Baker, L. and Cantwell, D.P. 213, 263, 434
Ballard, C., Patel, A., Oyebode, F. and Wilcock, G. 131
Baltaxe, C.A.M. and Simmons, J.Q. 59, 434
Bandler, R. and Grinder, J. 188, 298
Bandura, A. 309
Bannister, D. 62
Bannister, D. and Fransella, F. 56, 62

Barley, W.D. 98
Barnes, M.P. 130
Baron-Cohen, S. 263, 264
Baron-Cohen, S., Allen, J. and Gillberg, C. 330
Baron-Cohen, S., Leslie, A.M. and Frith, U. 326
Barr, W., Bilder, R., Goldberg, E. and Mukherjee, S. 352
Basilier, T. 254
Bateman, A. 46
Bauby, J.D. 325
Bayles, K.A. and Tomoeda, C. 118, 197
Bean, P. and Nemitz, T. 228
Beatty, W.W. and Goodkin, D.E. 130
Beck, A. and Podesky, C. 98
Beck, A., Rush, A., Hollon, S. and Shaw, B. 303
Beck, A.T. 73, 119
Beck, A.T., Rush, A.J., Shaw, B.F. and Emery, G. 74
Beech, J.R., Harding, I. and Hilton-Jones, D. 119
Beitchman, J.H., Wilson, B., Brownlie, E.B., Walters, H., Inglis, A. and Lancee, W. 213, 433
Bellack, A.S. and Mueser, K.T. 319
Bellack, A.S., Mueser, K.T., Gingerich, S. and Agresta, J. 317, 318, 319
Benaish, A.A., Curtiss, S. and Tallal, P. 119
Benjamin, T.B. and Watt, N.F. 408
Benson, D.F. 123
Benson, D.F., Cummings, J.L. and Tsai, S.Y. 404
Bentall, R.P. 124, 140
Bentall, R.P., Jackson, H.F. and Pilgrim, D. 336
Benton, A.L. 136
Benton, M.K. and Schroeder, H.E. 312, 318
Berger, M. 237
Berrios, G.E. and Quemada, J.I. 130
Bishop, D.V.M. 116, 218, 358, 368, 436
Blackie, I. 228
Blackshaw, A. 264
Blair, R.J.R. 124
Blakemore, C. 46
Blanchard, R., Steiner, B.W., Clemmensen, L.H. and Dickey, R. 268
Blanley, P.H. 408
Bleuler, E. 335, 336, 340, 362, 371, 407
Block, R.I., Farnham, S., Braverman, K., Noyes, R. and Ghoneim, M.M. 113

Bockting, W. and Coleman, E. 270

Boder, E. and Jarrico, S. 118

Bogousslavsky, J., Ferrazzini, M., Regali, F., Assal, G., Tanabe, H. and Delaloye-Bishop, A. 125

Bolinger, D. 102

Bones, K., Heald, M., Boxer, J. and Miller, R. 159

Borkenau, P. and Liebler, A. 332

Bornat, J., Johnson, J., Pereira, C., Pilgrim, D. and Williams, F. 181

Brady, J.P. 317

Braff, D.L. 355, 365, 366

Bralley, R., Bull, G., Gore, C. and Edgerton, M. 273

Brandt, J. and Butters, N. 131

Bresnan, J. 377

Brewin, C.R., Wing, J.K., Mangen, S.P., Brugha, T.S. and MacCarthy, B. 111

Breznitz, A. and Sherman, T. 76

Brickner, R.M. 136

Broadbent, D.E. 338

Broadbent, D.E., Cooper, P.F., Fitzgerald, P. and Parkes, R.R. 140

Brodarty, H. and Peters, K.E. 203

Brody, M.W. 37

Brotzel, Bryan, K. and Kramer 434

Brown, B.S. and Courtless, T.F. 222

Brown, G. and Harris, T. 36, 71, 72

Brown, G.W., Birley, J.L.T. and Wing, J.K. 316

Brown, G.W. and Harris, T.O. 20

Brown, K. 339

Brown, R., Colter, N., Corsellis, J.A.N. et al. 344

Bryan, K. 113, 118, 127, 148, 224

Bryan, K., France, J. and Kramer, S. 113, 227, 228

Bryan, K. and Kent, L. 127

Bryan, K. and Maxim, J. 203

Bryan, K., Maxim, J., MacIntosh, J., McClelland, A., Wirz, S., Edmundson, A. and Snowling, M. 111

Bryan, K.L. 316

Bryan, K.L. and Forshaw, N. 222, 223, 224

Bryan, K.L. and Maxim, J. 330

Bryan-Smith, P. 273

Buchanan, A., Reed, A., Wessely, S., Garety, P., Taylor, P.J., Grubin, D. and Dunn, G. 332

Bulletin 204

Burgess, J. and Bransby, G. 214

Burgoon, M. and Ruffner, M. 22

Burns, A., Luthert, P., Levy, R., Jacoby, R. and Lantos, P. 131

Burns, M.S., Halper, A.S. and Mogil, S.I. 118

Burrow, S. 159

Burton, M. 302

Burvill, P.W., Johnson, G.A., Jamrozik, K.D. et al. 125

Butcher, P., Elias, A. and Raven, R. 274

Butters, N., Sax, D., Montgomery, K. and Tarlow, S. 131

Button, E. 62, 287, 289

Byrne, E.J. 131

Cadoret, R. 87

Camarata, S.M., Hughes, C.A. and Ruhl, K.L. 212, 433

Cameron, N. 136, 339

Cantor, S. 55

Cantwell, D.P. and Baker, L. 433

Cantwell, D.P., Baker, L. and Mattison, R. 263

Care in the Community Act 182

Carpenter, M. 376, 377

Casey 87

Caspi, A. 331, 332

Catalan, J. 70, 72

Cattell, R.B. and Butcher, H.S. 91

Cavalli, L. and Morris, M. 275

Chaika, E. 337, 343, 362, 372, 376, 377

Chaloner, J. 272, 273

Chapman, L., Chapman, L. and Miller, G. 376

Chapman, L.J. and Chapman, J.P. 340, 346

Chapman, L.J., Chapman, J.P. and Miller, G.A. 340, 408

Chatman, S. 423

Checkley, S. 71

Chen, E., McKenna, P. and Wilkins, A. 339

Chenery, H.J. 403

Chess, S. 256

Chiat, S., Law, J. and Marshall, J. 352

Chomsky, N. 372, 373, 374

Christodolou, G.N. 141

Clare, A. 336, 437, 439

Clare, C. 237

Clare, I. and Gudjonnsson, G.H. 240

Clare, I.C.H. and Gudjonnsson, G.H. 228

Clark, L. and Witte, K. 203

Clark, S. 273

Clarke, F. 203

Cleckley, H. 94

Clegg, J., Hollis, C. and Rutter, M. 316

Clibbens, R. 205

Cohen, B.D. 408

Cohen, B.D. and Camhi, J. 343

Cohen, B.D., Nachmani, G. and Rosenberg, S. 343

Cohen, N.J., Davine, M., Hordezky, M.A., Lipsett, L. and Isaacson, B.A. 212, 213, 434

Cohen, N.J., Davine, M. and Meloche-Kelly, M. 212, 433

Cohen, N.J. and Lipsett, L. 212, 433, 434

Condray, R., Steinhauer, S.R. and Goldstein, G. 408

Cooper, J.E. 18

Cooper, S. 243

Corrigan, S. 20

Coughlan, A.K. and Hollows, S.E. 138

Cowan, C. 305

Cowan, P.J. 78

Crawford, J.R., Parker, D.M. and McKinlay, W.W. 137

Critchley, M. 371

Cross, M. 212, 214, 433, 434, 435

Crow, T.J. 316, 329, 332, 336, 344, 348, 393

Crow, T.J. and Done, D.J. 316

Crow, T.J., Done, D.J. and Sacker, A. 316

Crowe, T.A. and Jackson, P.D. 223, 228

Cummings, J.L. 126, 127, 129

Cummings, J.L. and Benson, D.F. 132

Curtis, D. 319

Cutting, J. 112, 126, 148

Dabul, B.L. 119

Dacakis, G. 273

Dalton, P. 17, 37, 292

Dam-Baggen, R. van and Kraaimaat, F. 312, 319

Daniels, L. and Roll, D. 318

Davey, D. and Thompson, P.J. 129

David, A.S. 53, 124, 140, 393

David, A.S. and Busatto, G. 112

David, A.S. and Cutting, J.C. 352

De Klerk, V. 274

De Renzi, E. and Faglioni, P. 112

Deese, J. 344

Denkowski, G.C. and Denkowski, K.M. 222

Denmark, J. 252

Denmark, J.C. 115

Denmark, J.C. and Eldridge, R.W. 252

Department of Health 181, 205

Department of Health and Social Security 158

Dewart, H. and Summers, S. 118

DHSS Mental Health Statistics for England 43

Diagnostic and Statistical Manual of Mental Disorders see DSV-IV

Diamond, B. 22

Dimitracopoulou, I. 313

Dittman, A.T. 74

Dobson, D. 318

Dobson, D.J.D., McDougall, G., Busheikin, J. and Aldous, J. 312, 318

Dolan, J.D. 267, 268, 271

Donahue, M.L., Hartas, D. and Cole, D. 212

Done, D.J., Crow, T.J., Johnstone, E.C. and Sacker, A. 112, 148

Done, D.J., Leionen, E., Crow, T.J. and Sacker, A. 112, 119

Dore, J. 102

Doren, D.M. 83, 90, 96

DSM-III-R 53, 54

DSM-IV 18, 20, 21, 26, 27, 30, 31, 32, 33, 34, 35, 42, 43, 49, 50, 51, 52, 53, 65, 67, 68, 69, 70, 82, 83, 84, 85, 86, 88, 90, 147

Dunn, L.M., Dunn, L.M., Whetton, C. and Burley, E. 117

Dunn, L.M., Dunn, L.M., Whetton, C. and Pintilie, D. 357, 358, 368

Eccles, M., Clarke, J., Livingstone, M., Freemantle, N. and Mason, J. 198

Edgerton, M. 271

Effective Health Care 19

Ekberg, O. and Feinberg, M. 204

Ekman, P. and Fridlund, A.J. 74

Elias, A. 274

Elliott, F.A. 88

Ellis, A. 309

Ellis, H.D. and Leafhead, K.M. 124

Emerson, J. and Enderby, P. 111, 169, 440

Emery, O.B. 114

Enderby, P. 119, 198

Enderby, P. and Davies, P. 111

Enderby, P. and Philipp, R. 111

Enderby, P.M. 326

Enderby, P.M. and Philipp, R. 222

Epting, F. and Amerikaner, M. 288

Erber, N.P. 151

Eysenck, H.J. 309, 332

Eysenck, H.S. and Eysenck, S.B.G. 91

Faber, R., Abrams, R. and Taylor, M. 150

Faber, R. and Reichstein, M.B. 338

Fairbanks, H. 376

Falloon, I. and Shanahan, W. 159

Farrington, D.P. 331

Faulk, M. 232, 233, 234

Fearnley, J.M., Revesz, D.J. and Franckowiak, R.S.J. and Lees, A.J. 131

Feil, N. 200, 202, 203

Feinberg, I. 374

Feinberg, M.J. 204

Feinstein, A. and Ron, M.A. 126

Ferguson, A. 187

Fesenmeier, J.T., Kuzniecky, R. and Garcia, J.H. 125

Fine, J., Bartollucci, G., Ginsberg, G. and Szatmarti, P. 112

Fioretti, A., Glaccotto, L. and Melega, V. 119

Fish, D. 128

Fisher, N.J., Rourke, B.P., Bieliauskas, L.A., Giordani, B., Berent, S. and Foster, N. 140

Fleming, K., Goldberg, T.E. and Gold, J.M. 356

Fodor, J.A. and Bever, T.G. 374, 376

Folstein, M. 358, 367

Folstein, M.F., Folstein, F.E. and McHugh, P.R. 130

Folstein, M.F., Folstein, S.E. and McHugh, P.R. 198

Forshaw, N. 222, 228

Foss, D.J. and Hakes, D.T. 102

France, J. 15, 24, 37, 101, 102, 111

France, J. and Muir, N. 160, 161, 171, 247, 297, 318, 351, 367, 393, 406, 441

France, J. and Muir, N.J. 16, 17

France, R. 72

France, R. and Robson, M. 39

Fransella, F. and Bannister, D. 75

Fraser, W., Thomas, P., Joyce, J. and Duckworth, M. 150

Fraser, W.I., King, K.M., Thomas, P. and Kendell, R.E. 342

Frederiksen, C.H., Bracewell, R.J., Breuleux, A. and Renaud, A. 411, 412, 413

Freeman, C.P. 82, 83, 89, 91, 95

Freeman, C.P.L. 28, 29, 35, 36

Freeman, H. 47

Freud, A. 46

Freud, S. 30, 73, 303, 372

Frith 187

Frith, C. 352, 353, 355, 356, 357, 364, 365

Frith, C. and Allen, H.A. 355

Frith, C.D. 124, 150, 318, 329, 332, 336, 339, 344

Frith, C.D. and Allen, H.A. 374

Frith, C.D. and Done, D.J. 371, 374, 390

Frith, C.D. and Frith, U. 329

Frith, U. 318

Fromkin, V. 377

Fujiki, M. and Brinton, B. 368

Fulford, K.W.M. 44

Furth, H.G. 337

Galski, T., Thornton, K.E. and Shumsky, D. 141

Gara, M., Rosenberg, S. and Mueller, D. 288

Garratt, H., Bryan, K. and Maxim, J. 130

Gauron, E. and Dickinson, J. 439

Gelder, M., Gath, D. and Mayou, R. 45, 52, 56, 244

Gelder, M., Gath, D., Mayou, R. and Cowen, P. 29, 30, 39, 46, 56, 71, 73, 78, 81, 87, 88, 89, 92

Gelernter, C.S., Uhde, T.W., Cimbolic, P. et al. 39

General Medical Council 158

German, D.J. 117

Gerson, S.N., Benson, D.F. and Frazier, S.H. 338

Gerver, D. 342, 377

Giddan, J.J. 213

Giddan, J.J., Milling, L. and Campbell, N.B. 119, 212

Giddan, J.J., Wahl, J. and Brogan, M. 212

Gillham, R.A. 129

Goldberg, D. and Bridges, K. 36

Goldberg, D. and Huxley, P. 28

Goldberg, T., Gold, J. and Braff, D. 371

Golden, C.J., Jackson, M.L., Peterson-Rohne, A. and Gontkovsky, S.T. 141

Golden, C.J., Purisch, A.D. and Hammeke, T.A. 408

Golding, E. 140

Goldsmith, M. 201, 202

Goldstein, K. 136, 339

Goodglass, H. 371

Goodglass, H. and Kaplan, E. 111, 112, 117, 398

Goodglass, H., Kaplan, E. and Weintraub, S. 111, 112

Goodman, R. and Scott, S. 208, 211

Goodwin, C. 419

Gordon, N. 213, 433

Goren, A.R., Tucker, G. and Ginsberg, G.M. 366

Gotham, A.M., Brown, R.G. and Marsden, C.D. 129

Gottshalk, L. and Glaser, G. 376

Graham, F.K. and Kendall, B.S. 136

Graham, P. 20

Grant, I., Adams, K.M. and Reed, R. 142

Gravell, R. 159

Gravell, R. and France, J. 19, 154, 168, 169, 237, 242, 351

Green, M.C.L. 38

Green, M.C.L. and Matheson, L. 38

Green, M.F. 141

Greene, M. 273

Greenson, R.R. 303

Gregory, W. 223

Grice, H.P. 354, 394

Griffin, N.V. 159

Griggs, M. 252

Grinker, R.R. Sr., Werble, B. and Drye, R. 256

Groher, M.E. 119

Grossman, M., Carvell, S., Gollomp, S. and Hurtig, H.I. 130

Grounds, A.T., Quayle, M., France, J., Brett, T., Cox, M. and Hamilton, J.R. 305

Grounds, A.T., Quayle, M.T., France, J. *et al.* 234

Grove, W. and Andreason, N. 356, 363

Gualtieri, C.T., Koriath, J., Van Bourgoridieu, M. and Saleeby, N. 215, 433

Gudjonnsson, G.H. and Clare, I. 239

Gudjonnsson, G.H., Clare, I.C.H., Rutter, S.C. and Pearce, J. 228

Gunn, J. 234

Gunn, J., Maden, A. and Swinton, J. 113, 221

Gunzburger, D. 273

Haas, A. 274

Haley, J. 297, 300

Halford, W.K. and Hayes, R.L. 317

Halgren, B. 253, 256

Halliday, M.A.K. and Hassan, R. 343, 394, 399

Halligan, P.W. and Marshall, J.C. 124

Hamer, H., Hu, S., Magnuson, V., Hu, N. and Pattatucci, A. 269

Hamilton, H.E. 202

Happé, F. 330

Happé, F. and Frith, U. 332

Happé, F.G.E. 326

Harari, C. and Harari, C. 305

Hardy, J. 130

Hare, D.J. 265

Hare, D.J., Jones, J. and Paine, C. 265

Hare, D.J., and Leadbeater, C. 265

Hare, R.D. 88, 94

Hargie, O. and McCartan, P. 314, 317

Harrow, M. and Quinlan, D.M. 58, 371, 376

Hartley, P. 313, 319

Harvey, P.D. and Neale, J. 440

Hassan, R. 399

Hathaway, S. and McKinley, J. 56, 92

Hayes, S. 222

Heads, T., Leese, M., Taylor, P.J. and Phillips, S. 333

Heaton, R.K., Baade, L.E. and Johnson, K.L. 136

Heilbrun, K. 142

Heilfron, M. 304
Hemsley, D.R. 140
Henderson, D. 82
Herndon, R.M. 130
Hibbert, G.A. 26, 28, 30, 38, 81, 89, 90, 91, 97
Hill, G.M. 140
Hill, P. 53, 89, 332
Hindley, P., Hill, P. and Bond, D. 256
Hindley, P., Hill, P.D., McGuigan, S. and Kitson, N. 252, 256
Hitchings, A. and Spence, R. 118
HM Inspectorate of Prisons 223
Hoare, P. 29, 53
Hodges, J.R. 132
Hodgkinson, L. 275
Hodkinson, M. 198
Hoffman, R., Kirstein, L., Stopek, S. and Cicchetti, D. 344
Hoffman, R. and Sledge, W. 377, 378
Hoffman, R.E., Stopek, S. and Andreason, N. 376
Hoffman, R.E., Stopek, S. and Andreason, N.C. 344
Hoffmann, R.E. and Satel, S. 150
Holland, A.L., McBurney, D.H., Moossy, J. and Rernmirth, O.M. 132
Home Office 228
Horton, P.C. 127
Howard, D. and Patterson, K. 117
Howlin, P. 263, 264, 265
Hulse, W.C., Ludlow, W.V., Rindsberg, B.K. and Epstein, N.B. 305, 307
Hume, C. and Pullen, I. 16
Huntingdon, D. and Bender, W. 244
Hurlbert, R.T., Happé, F. and Frith, U. 265
Hurst, J. 259
Hutchings, S., Comins, J. and Offiler, J. 312, 317
Huxley, P.J., Goldberg, D.P., Maguire, P. and Kincey, V. 28
Hyland, H.H. 86

ICD-9 54
ICD-10 20, 21, 26, 27, 30, 31, 32, 33, 34, 35, 42, 43, 49, 51, 52, 66, 67, 68, 69, 82, 83, 84, 85, 86, 90, 327

Ineichen, B. 19
International Classification of Diseases see ICD-10

Jacobson, C.A., Jacobson, J.T. and Crowe, T.A. 223
Jefferson 409
Jefferson, G. 419
Johnson, S. 223, 224
Jones, A. 310
Jones, G. 202
Jones, P., Rodgers, B., Murray, R. and Marmot, M. 148
Jones, P.B., Rodgers, B., Murray, R.M. and Marmot, M. 330
Jordan, B. 427
Jorge, R.E., Robinson, R.G., Starkstein, S.E., Arndt, S.V., Forrester, A.W. and Geisler, F.H. 126

Kaatzke, M. 205
Kaczmarek, B.L.J. 112
Kalra, M. 273
Kane, R.A. 305
Kaplan, H. and Saddock, B. 50, 51, 53, 61, 280
Kaplan, H.I. and Saddock, B.J. 71, 72, 92
Kavanagh, D. 316
Kay, J., Lesser, R. and Coltheart, M. 117, 148, 393
Kaye, J., Bortz, M. and Tuomi, S. 273
Kelley, G. 264
Kelly, D. 65, 66, 77, 291
Kelly, G.A. 285, 287, 288, 289
Kendell, R.E. 21, 46, 48, 50, 57, 58, 66
Kennard, J. 319
Kent, H. and Rosanoff, A.J. 340
Kersner, M. 119
Kertesz, A. 112
Khan, A., Cowan, C. and Roy, A. 245
Khan, R.L., Zarit, S.H., Hilbert, N.M. and Niederehe, G. 140
Kielholz, P. 72
Kiernan, C. 59
King, K., Fraser, W.I., Thomas, P. and Kendell, R.E. 376, 408
Kitson, N. and Fry, R. 254, 259
Kitson, N. and Thacker, A. 256, 258

Kitwood 202

Klee, A. 125

Klein, M. 73

Kleist, K. 342, 372

Knight, M. 274

Knight, R.G. 130

Kopelman, M., Wilson, B.A. and Baddeley, A. 138

Kopelowicz, A., Liberman, R.P., Mintz, J. and Zarate, R. 312

Kotsopoulos, A. and Boodoosingh, I. 215, 433, 434

Kraepelin, E. 136, 335, 351, 372, 407

Kramer, C. 273

Kramer, S. 119

Kramer, S., Bryan, K.L. and Frith, C.D. 413, 430

Kuhl, D.E., Metter, E.J. and Reige, W.H. 130

Kupfer, J., Maser, J.D., Blehar, M.C. and Miller, R. 74

Labov, W. 416, 419

Labov, W. and Fanshel, D. 374

Lader, M.H. and Marks, I.M. 29

Lainhart, J.E. and Folstein, S.E. 265

Landre, N.A., Taylor, M.A. and Kearns, K.P. 112

Law, J. and Conway, J. 214

Lawson, J., McGhie, A. and Chapman, J. 376

Lawson, J.S., McGhie, A. and Chapman, J. 341

LeBrun, Y., Devreux, F. and Rousseau, J.J. 130

Leff, J. 319

Lenneberge, E.H. 374

Lesser, R. 371

Lesser, R. and Milroy, L. 352, 366

Lester, R., Boddy, M., Evans, J. and Trewhitt, P. 203

Levy, R. and Maxwell, A. 376

Lewis, G. and Wessely, S. 35, 36, 81, 91

Lezak, M.D. 137

Liberman, R.P. and Foy, D.W. 319

Liberman, R.P., Massel, H.K., Mosk, M.D. and Wong, S.E. 316

Liberman, R.P., Mueser, K.T., Wallace, C.J., Jacobs, H.E., Eckman, T. and Massel, K. 297

Liberman, R.P., Nuechterlein, K.H. and Wallace, C.J. 316, 317

Liberman, R.P., Wallace, C.J., Blackwell, G., Kopelowicz, A., Vaccaro, J.V. and Mintz, J. 312, 318

Liddle, P.F. 140

Lieberman, M.A. 303, 304

Lieberman, M.A., Yalom, I. and Miles, M. 304

Linde, C. 416, 419, 423, 427

Lion, J.R. 96

Lishman, W.A. 124

Logemann, J. 119

Lorenzini, R., Sassaroli, S. and Rocchi, M. 288

Losel, F. 309

Louth, S.M., Williamson, S., Alpert, M., Pouget, E.R. and Hare, R.D. 94

Lovaas, I. 59

Lubinski, R. 199, 200, 201, 202, 203

Lumsden, J., Chesterman, L.P. and Hill, G.M. 141

Lyall, I., Holland, A.J., Collins, S. and Styles, P. 228

Lynn, S.J. and Frauman, D. 303

Lyons, J. 373

Maag, J. and Reid, R. 244

McCord, M.W. 86, 89, 280

Macdonald, L. 168, 297, 298

McGrath, J. 393, 398, 400, 406

McGuire, P.K., Shar, G.M.S. and Murray, R.M. 393

McKenna, P. 140

McKenna, P. and Warrington, E. 117, 436

McKenna, P.J. 336, 352

MacLennan, B.W. 304

McMillan, T.M. and Greenwood, R.J. 128

McNamara, P., Obler, L.K., Au, R., Durso, R. and Albert, M.L. 130

Macphail, D. and Cox, M. 308

McPherson, S.E. and Cummings, J.L. 124

Maguire, T. 39, 77

Maher, B. 337, 338, 340, 341, 347, 374, 376

Maher, E.R., Smith, E.M. and Lees, A.J. 130

Mahieu, H., Norbart, T. and Wong Chung, R. 275

Malcolm, J. 326, 327

Malcomess, K. 190

Malinowski, B. 337

Mann, A.H., Jenkins, R. and Belsey, E. 28

Mann, M. 376

Manpower Advisory Service 309

Marder, S.R., Wirshing, W.C., Mintz, J., McKenzie, J., Johnston, K., Eckman, T.A., Labell, M., Zimmerman, K. and Liberman, R.P. 312

Markowitz, J.C. and Nininger, J.E. 256

Marshall, J.C. and Halligan, P.W. 123, 124

Martell, D.A. 141

Martindale, B. 131

Maslow, A.H. 307

Maxim, J. 114

Maxim, J. and Bryan, K. 129, 130, 192, 198, 202

Meichenbaum, D. 303, 309

Melzer, D., Ely, M. and Brayne, C. 192

Mental Health Act 182

Messert, B., Henke, T.K. and Langheim, W. 125

Michels, R. and Marzuk, P. 371

Miesen, B. and Jones, G. 200

Miles, C.P. 48

Miller, E. 195

Miller, G. and Selfridge, J. 341

Miller, L. 141

Miller, W.K. and Phelan, J.G. 376, 377

Misiaszek, J., Dooling, J., Gieseke, A., Melman, H., Misiaszek, J.G. and Jorgensen, K. 254

Mojabai, R., Nicholson, R.A. and Carpenter, B.N. 319

Money, J. and Erhardt, A. 269

Monteiro, B. and Critchley, E.M.R. 258

Monti, P.M. and Fingeret, A.L. 62

Morgan Barry, R. 116

Morice, R. 141, 374

Morice, R.D. 356, 363

Morice, R.D. and Ingram, J.C. 376

Morice, R.D. and Ingram, J.C.L. 58, 342

Morris, J. 268

Morris, M. 131

Mortimer, A., Corridan, B., Rudge, S., Kho, K., Kelly, F., Bristow, M. and Hodges, J. 339

Moses, P. 37

Moss, S., Prosser, H., Ibbotson, B. and Goldberg, D. 243

Mount, K. and Salmon, S. 273

MSF 190

Mueser, K. and Bellack, A. 312

Mueser, K.T, Bellack, A.S, Douglas, M.S. and Morrison, R.L. 312

Mueser, K.T., Donna, R., Penn, D.L., Blanchard, J.J., Bellack, A.S., Nishith, P. and Leon J. de 316

Mueser, K.T., Levine, S., Bellack, A.S., Douglas, M.S. and Brady, E.U. 312, 319

Muir, M. 318

Muir, N. 161, 200, 284

Muir, N. et al. 167

Muir, N., Tanner, P. and France, J. 112, 161

Mullen, P.E., Martin, J.L., Anderson, S.E. et al. 328

Murphy, D. 330

Murphy, G.H., Harnett, H. and Holland, A.J. 222

Murphy, H.B.M. 50

Murphy, H.B.M., Wittower, E.D., Fried, J. and Ellenberger, H. 50

Murray, H.A. 55

Murray, I. 95

Murray, J. 20

Murray, R. 47, 50, 62, 351

Murray, R.M. and Lewis, S.W. 330

Musker, M. 312, 316

Neale, J.M. and Oltmanns, T.F. 338, 346, 347

Neimeyer, R. 288

Neimeyer, R.A. 292

Neimeyer, R.A., Klein, M.H., Gurman, A.S. and Gruest, J.H. 288

Nelson, H.E. 118, 138, 139

Nelson, H.E., Pantelis, C., Carruthers, K., Speller, J., Baxendale, S. and Barnes, T.R.E. 140

Nestor, P.G., Shenton, M.E., Wible, C. et al. 344

Newby, D.A. 335, 339, 341, 440

Newton, J. 20

Newton, M. and Thomson, M. 116

Nilsonne, A. 76

Nilsson, H., Ekberg, O., Olsson, R. and Hindfelt, B. 204

Noon, M. 159, 305

Norman, R.M.G., Malla, A.K., Morrison-Stewart, S.L., Helmes, E., Williamson, P.C., Thomas, J. and Cortese, L. 140

Norton, K. and Hinshelwood, R.D. 87, 88, 95

Novaco, R.W. 309

Nuffield Centre for Dyspraxia Programme 119
Nunkoosing, K. 236

Oates, J.M. and Dacakis, G. 273, 275
O'Brien, P.J. and Barrow, D. 204
O'Carroll, R. 140
O'Connor, J. and Seymour, J. 300
O'Neill, M. and Jones, R.S.P. 264
Orange, J.B., Ryan, E.B., Meredith, S.D. and
    MacLean, M.J. 203
Overall, J.E. and Gorham, D.R. 436
Ozonoff, S. and Miller, J.N. 263

Palmer, D. 409, 439
Parsons, T. 328
Pattie, A.M. 198
Pauly, I.B. and Edgerton, M.T. 267
Paykel, E.S. 20
Payne, R.W., Matussek, P. and George, E.I. 339
Penn, C. 118
Penn, D.L. and Mueser, K.T. 312
Pennell, I. and Creed, F. 65, 66, 74
Pentland, B. 129
Pepin, E.P. and Pepin, A.P. 125
Perkins, L., Whitworth, A. and Lesser, R. 197
Peterson, C., Maier, S.F. and Seligman, M.E.P. 124
Phillips, G. 37
Pilowsky, I. 36
Pimental, P.A. and Kingsbury, N.A. 358
Pines, M. 95
Podoll, K., Caspari, P., Lange, H.W. and Noth, J.
    131
Polanyi, L. 416, 422
Powell, T. 185
Prendegast, K., Dickey, S., Selmar, J. and Soder, A.
    116
Prizant, B.M. and Rydell, P.J. 54
Prochaska, J.O. 303
Prutting, C.A. and Kirchner, D.M. 118
Pryor, A. 112, 224
Pylshyn, Z.W. 376

Quayle, M., Deu, N. and Giblin, S. 235, 308

Quayle, M., France, J. and Wilkinson, E. 226, 305,
    307, 309
Quayle, M. and Moore, E. 99, 235, 308

Rabin, H. 304
Ragin, A.B. and Oltmanns, T.F. 341
Rainbow, D., Painter, C. and Bryan, K. 203
Raines, R., Hechtman, S. and Rosenthal, R. 273
Raleigh, V.S. 192
Ramani, V. and Gumnit, R.S. 129
Rao, S.M. 130
Raven, J.C. 112, 137
Reed, J. and Lyne, M. 228
Reilly, F., Harrow, M. and Tucker, G. 371, 374,
    376
Reiss, D., Grubin, D. and Meux, C. 90, 95
Reiss, D., Quayle, M., Brett, T. and Meux, C. 308
Renfrew, C.E. 117
Reusch, J. 24, 284
Riley, M. 159
Rimland, B. 264
Rinaldi, W. 317
Ripich, D. and Ziol, E. 203
Rix, K.J.B. 228
Roberts, G.W., Leigh, P.N. and Weinberger, D.R.
    127
Robertson, G., Taylor, P.J. and Gunn, J. 141
Robertson, I.H, Ward, T., Ridgeway, V. and
    Nimmo-Smith, I. 138
Robertson, M. 129
Robertson, S.J. 119
Robinson, A.L., Heaton, R.K. and Lehman, R.A.W.
    125
Robinson, L.D. 256
Rochester, S., Harris, J. and Seeman, M. 377
Rochester, S. and Martin, J. 372, 374, 376
Rochester, S., Martin, J.R. and Thurston, S. 400
Rochester, S.R. 342, 343, 347, 440
Rochester, S.R. and Martin, J.R. 337, 339, 343
Rogers, C. 89
Rogers, C.R. 303
Rogers-Adkinson, D.L. and Griffith, P.L. 208
Ron, M.A. 132
Ron, M.A. and David, A.S. 123

Rorschach, H. 55, 92

Rose, C., Whurr, R. and Wyke, M.A. 371

Rose, N. 50, 51, 55, 59

Rosen, V. 372

Rosenbaum, M. 304

Rosenberg, S.D. and Tucker, G.J. 376

Ross, G.W., Cummings, J.L. and Benson, D.F. 131

Ross, M. 269

Rossell, S. and David, A.S. 140

Rossell, S.L. and David, A.S. 352, 364

Roth, F. and Spekman, N. 413

Roth, M. and Kroll, J. 19, 42, 51

Rourke, B.P. 124

Rowe, D. 288

Royal College of Speech and Language Therapists 152, 158, 167, 178, 190, 192, 193, 197, 214

Rumsey, J.M., Rapoport, J.L. and Sceery, W.R. 264

Rustin, L. and Kuhr, A. 312, 317

Rutter, D. 59

Rutter, D., Wishner, J. and Callaghan, B.A. 376

Rutter, D.R., Draffan, J. and Davies, J. 341

Rutter, D.R., Wishner, J. and Callaghan, B.A. 341

Rutter, D.R., Wishner, J., Koptynska, H. and Button, M. 341

Rutter, M. 265

Rutter, M. and Garmezy, A. 90

Rutter, M. and Giller, H. 90

Rutter, M. and Lord, C. 54, 58

Rutter, M. and Mawhood, L. 212, 213

Rutter, M., Taylor, E. and Hersov, L. 208

Rutter, M.L. 28

Ryan, R.M. 265

Sacks, H. 419

Salzinger, K., Portnoy, S. and Feldman, R.S. 341, 376

Satel, S. and Sledge, W. 374

Saxton, J., McGonigle, K.L., Swilhart, A.A. and Boller, F. 140, 197

Scheduikat, M., Perry, A., Cheesman, A. and Pring, T. 275

Schegloff, E.A. 422

Scherer, K.R. 74

Schneider, K. 372

Schoenfield, M., Myers, R.M., Cupples, A. et al. 131

Schwarz, S. 337, 338, 340, 377, 409

Seligman, M.E.P. 66

Semel, E., Wiig, E.H. and Secord, W. 112, 116, 224

Sever, J.L., South, M.A. and Shaver, K.A. 253

Seymour, P.H.K. 138

Shadden, B. 203

Shallice, T. 139

Shallice, T. and Burgess, P.W. 139

Shallice, T., Burgess, P.W. and Frith, C. 123

Shallice, T., Burgess, P.W. and Frith, C.D. 140

Shallice, T. and Evans, M.E. 139

Shapiro, J.L. 305

Sheehan, M.J. 292

Shepherd, G. 312, 316, 317, 318

Shepherd, M., Cooper, B., Brown, H.C. and Kalton, C.W. 28

Sherratt, S.M. and Penn, C. 411

Shewan, C.M. 111

Siegman, A.W. 74

Silverman, G. 341

Silverstone, T. and Turner, P. 38, 39, 56, 60, 77, 78

Simon, R., Gurland, B., Fleiss, J. and Sharpe, L. 439

Sims, A. 437

Sims, A. and Sims, D. 159

Sinason, V. 242

Skinner, B.F. 73, 309

Slobin, D.I. 339

South East Thames Regional Health Authority 158

Space, L.G. and Cromwell, R.L. 292

Sparrow, S.S., Balla, D.A. and Cichetti, D.V. 236–7

Speedie, L.J., Brake, N., Folstein, S.E., Bowers, D. and Heilman, K.M. 131

Spence, S.H. 312, 313

Spencer, D.A. 237

Spencer, L. 273

Spitzer, M. 374, 376

Spitzer, M., Braun, U. and Maier, S. 374, 376

Stanley, P., Dai, Y. and Nolan, R. 244

Starkstein, S.E., Federoff, P., Berthier, M.L. and Robinson, R.G. 126

Starkstein, S.E., Mayberg, M.S., Berthier, M.L., Federoff, P., Price, T.R., Dannals, R.F., Wagner, H.N., Leiguarda, R. and Robinson, R.G. 126

Starkstein, S.E., Robinson, R.G., Honig, M.A., Rarikh, R.M., Joselyn, J. and Price, T.R. 126

Starkstein, S.E., Robinson, R.G. and Price, T.R. 125

Starr, A. and Sporty, L.D. 123

Steele, C.M., Greenwood, C., Ens, I., Robertson, C. and Seidman-Carlson, R. 204

Stein, N. 412

Stemple, J.C. 35, 37

Stemple, J.C., Glaze, L.E. and Gerdeman, B.K. 35

Stevens, S.J. 197

Stevens, S.J., Le May, M., Gravell, R. and Cook, K. 203

Stoller, R. 269

Storr, A. 66, 74

Straube, E. 376

Strauss, M.E. 408

Sullivan, H.S. 23

Svendsen, B.B. and Werner, J. 222

Swinburn, K. and Maxim, J. 199

Szasz, T. 19

Szatmari, P., Bartolucci, G., Bremner, R., Bond, S. and Rich, S. 263

Tamlyn, D., McKenna, P.J., Mortimer, A.M. *et al.* 56

Tamlyn, D., McKenna, P.J., Mortimer, A.M., Lund, C.E., Hammond, S. and Baddeley, A.D. 140

Tanguay, P. 54, 55

Tannen, D. 364

Tanner, B.B. and Daniels, D.A. 200, 203

Tarrier, N., Yusupoff, L., Kinney, C., McCarthey, E., Gledhill, A., Haddock, G. and Morris, J. 312

Tarter, R.E., Mezzich, A.C., Hsieh, Y.C. and Parks, S. 113

Taylor, P.J. 95, 231, 232, 332

Taylor, P.J., Leese, M., Williams, D., Butwell, M., Daly, R. and Larkin, E. 224, 332

Taylor, W.L. 340

Thacker, A. 254, 257, 259

Thomas, P. 112, 119, 247, 337, 352, 393, 394

Thomas, P. and Fraser, W. 393

Thomas, P. and Fraser, W.I. 112

Thomas, P., Kearney, G., Napier, E., Ellis, E., Leudar, I. and Johnston, M. 365

Thomas, P., King, K., Fraser, W.I. and Kendell, R.E. 366

Thomas, P., Leudar, I., Napier, E., Kearney, G., Ellis, E., Ring, N. and Tantum, D. 396

Thompson, I.M. 403

Thompson, I.M. and Copolov, D. 394

Thompson, P.J. 129

Thompson, P.J. and Shorvon, S.D. 128

Thorum, A.R. 116, 358, 369

Thursfield, D. 72, 73

Tidmarsh, D. 47

Toner, H.L. 203

Tracey, J.F., Logemann, J.A., Kahrilas, P.J., Jacob, P., Kobara, M. and Krugler, C. 204

Trethowan, W. and Sims, A.C.P. 82

Trimble, M.R. 123, 129

Trower, P. 312, 319

Trower, P., Bryant, B. and Argyll, M. 19, 37, 62, 309, 313, 317.

Truscott, I.P. 376

Tsiouris, J.A. and Adelman, S.A. 265

Tucker, G. and Rosenberg, S. 376

Tyrer, P. and Alexander, J. 92

Tyrer, P. and Stein, G. 81

Van Berckelaer-Onnes, I. 263

Van den Bergh, O., De Boeck, P. and Claeys, W. 62, 287, 291

Van der Gaag, A. 118

Van Gorp, W.G., Mitrushina, M., Cummings, J.L., Satz, P. and Modesitt, J. 132

Van Lancker, D. 127

Vernon, McC. and Andrews, J.F. 256

Vernon, McC. and Rothstein, D.A. 253

Vita, A., Massimiliano, D., Giobbo, G.M. *et al.* 344

Wagner, C.O., Gray, L.L. and Potter, R.E. 222

Wald, B. 419

Walker, M. 242, 246

Walker, P. and Berger, J. 270

Wallace, C.J. 312

Wallace *et al* 316

Walters, W. 271

Ward, C.D., Dennis, N.R. and McMillan, T.M. 131

Watts, D. and Morgan, G. 327, 330

Wechsler, D. 55, 137, 138, 141, 236

Weinberger, D.R. 330

Weinstein, E.A. 126

Westen, D. 331

Westen, D. and Stedler, J. 331

Wetherby, A.M. 54, 58, 59

White, W. 136

Whitsed-Lipinska, D. 200

Whurr, R. 114, 117, 400

Widom, C.S. 328

Wigoder, D. 70

Wiig, E. 118

Wiig, E. and Secord, W. 113, 118

Wilkinson, J. and Canter, S. 314

Williams, M. 342

Wilson, B., Cockburn, J. and Baddeley, A. 116

Wilson, B.A., Alderman, N., Burgess, P., Emslie, H. and Evans, J.J. 139

Wilson, B.A., Cockburn, J. and Baddeley, A. 138

Wiltshire, A. 273, 274

Wing, J.K., Cooper, J.E. and Sartorius, N. 254, 335, 336

Wing, L. 264

Wing, L. and Gould, J. 53

Winter, D.A. 287, 288, 289, 290

Wintgens, A. 214, 219

Wirz, S.L. 110

Wolberg, L.R. 280

Wolfe, V., Ratusnik, D., Smith, F. and Northrop, G. 273

Wolff, S. 54

Wolff, S. and Cull, A. 48

Wolfson, N. 424, 428

Woods, B. 198, 200

World Health Organization 327, 439

Wright, H. 318

Wright-Strawderman, C. and Watson, B. 243

Wykes, T. 343

Wykes, T. and Leff, J. 343

Yalom, I.D. 303

Yanagihara, N., Koike, Y. and Von Leden, H. 273

Zabihi, K. and Bryan, K. 201

Zhou, B., Hofman, M., Gooren, G. and Swaab, D. 269

Zigmond, A. and Snaith, P. 119